"LEGS-ELEVEN"

Battle Honours of the 11th Battalion (City of Perth Regiment).

Lieut.-Col. J. Lyon Johnston, D.S.O., first Commanding Officer of 11th Bn.

Major J. P. O'Neil, M.C., last Commanding Officer of 11th Bn.

THE AUTHOR
CAPTAIN WALTER C. BELFORD, M.A.

"LEGS-ELEVEN"

BEING THE STORY OF THE 11th BATTALION (A.I.F.)
IN THE GREAT WAR OF 1914-1918

BY
CAPTAIN WALTER C. BELFORD,
M.A.

The Naval & Military Press Ltd

Published by
The Naval & Military Press Ltd
5 Riverside, Brambleside, Bellbrook
Industrial Estate, Uckfield, East Sussex,
TN22 1QQ England
Tel: +44 (0) 1825 749494
Fax: +44 (0) 1825 765701
www.naval-military-press.com
www.military-genealogy.com
www.militarymaproom.com

In reprinting in facsimile from the original, any imperfections are inevitably reproduced and the quality may fall short of modern type and cartographic standards.

FOREWORD

BY MAJOR-GENERAL E. G. SINCLAIR-MACLAGAN, C.B., C.M.G., D.S.O., COMMANDER 3RD INFANTRY BRIGADE (A.I.F.) 1914–1916

The 11th Battalion (Australian Imperial Force) found its personnel from Western Australia, and was physically one of the finest battalions in the A.I.F.

This battalion took its full share of all the fighting and hardships which fell to the lot of the 3rd Infantry Brigade (A.I.F.) in Gallipoli, France and Flanders, and never failed its commanders in any operation in which it took part.

The qualities of gallantry, endurance, good discipline and cheerful compliance with orders and instructions in the field, both in battle and under the often appalling conditions of trench warfare, were displayed by this battalion throughout, as they were indeed by all battalions of the brigade.

This history of a fine battalion should especially appeal to all ex-members and their families and descendants and to the families and descendants of those who made the supreme sacrifice during the Great War.

I am very proud to have had the 11th Battalion (A.I.F.) under my command for over two years.

(Sgd.) E. G. SINCLAIR-MACLAGAN,
Major-General.

COMPILER'S INTRODUCTION

After the foreword by so distinguished a soldier as General Sinclair MacLagan, no further introduction to the 11th Battalion (A.I.F.) is necessary, but I feel I must say a few words to explain how this story came to be written.

As regards the story itself, I make no apology. I have written the history of the battalion as I knew it, and from the records of the most trustworthy diarists that were available and checked everything where possible from the official diaries of the 11th Battalion and the 3rd Brigade. I have also checked all names and places from maps, as far as they have been available, and in this connection I have to thank Mr. Max. Hubbe, of Kojonup, W.A., for the loan of a collection of war maps embracing practically every locality that the 11th Battalion was connected with in France.

If the story has any merit, or brings back any proud or happy memories of the days gone by and the fine fellows we fought alongside and lived with for so long, then the thanks of the survivors of the 11th Battalion are due chiefly to Mr. Jim Kirkwood, of Dangin, for it was almost entirely due to him that the writer was first encouraged to attempt the task.

A warm meed of thanks is also due to Mr. R. W. Blair, the Secretary of the 11th Battalion Association, for his indefatigable efforts in making possible the publication of this book.

It would be impossible to name all the sources from which the story has been compiled, or to mention the names of all those who have helped, but outstanding were the diaries of Lieut. J. M. Aitken, Major Croly and Lieut. Cooke (kindly lent by Mesdames Aitken, Croly and Cook) and the diaries of Lieut. Peter Snodgrass and Captain Charlie Gostelow.

The continued encouragement of "Non-Com" (Captain Longmore) of *The Western Mail* and the help and co-operation of the 11th Battalion Association and other ex-members of the 11th Battalion and other units throughout this State and from "the other side" have made the task much lighter.

I have received much kindly assistance and advice from the Director of the Australian War Memorial, who also supplied the official diaries and many excellent photographs. Other photographs have come from many sources, and I have been reluctantly compelled to discard many excellent and interesting snaps, owing to their faded condition after so many years. I have also to thank Dr. C. E. F. Bean for help from the Official History and for permission to use maps and sketches in his volumes.

In conclusion, I would like to say that I have tried to tell the story from the Diggers' point of view. I have not tried to make an epic of it—though some phases of it are necessarily heroic—because I realise that a battalion is only as good as its personnel, and its story is the history of all its troops and not of one or two officers or men, so that I have tried to make this the record of the fine men of the first battalion from Western Australia.

Though more than twenty years have passed since all these events have happened of which I have written in this story—for it is a story rather than a history—and the desolate fields of France and Beligum are green again; and the flowers are blooming in the scarred gullies and ravines of Anzac; and the whole face of the war zone has changed save in the unchanging desert; yet still in the minds of the "boys" who suffered and fought in these places the vision of the tortured land remains; and of the "cobbers" who fought and toiled and froze, or blistered in the heat of alien lands; and for ever are the lads remembered who died in comradeship never surpassed. Though now splendid memorials have been erected all over the battlefields, there are also the silent monuments of those who sleep in the quiet cemeteries dotted up and down these lands, and in many of these lie the gallant comrades who died over there.

So, to those men of the 11th Battalion who sailed so blithely away but never returned, and to the friends and comrades who still survive, I dedicate the tale of their efforts.

Comrades all, I hope the story meets with your approval.

WALTER C. BELFORD

"Neudos,"
    Ballidu,
        Western Australia.

CONTENTS

Chapter		Page
	Foreword	vii
	Compiler's Introduction	viii
I.	Blackboy Hill Camp	1
II.	The Voyage with the Great Convoy	21
III.	Under the Great Pyramid	33
IV.	Lemnos Island	50
V.	The Landing	67
VI.	Gaba Tepe: The First Raid by the A.I.F.	91
VII.	Trench Life on Gallipoli	108
VIII.	Tasmania Post and Leane's Trench	122
IX.	The Trenches at Anzac	135
X.	Hanging on at Anzac	149
XI.	Last Weeks at Anzac	161
XII.	Winter at Lemnos Island	178
XIII.	Life on the Canal Zone; Tel-el-Kebir and Gebel Habieta	187
XIV.	Alexandria to Marseilles	210
XV.	Arrival in France	214
XVI.	First Billets in France	220
XVII.	Fleurbaix	234
XVIII.	In Supports at Fleurbaix	250
XIX.	Off to the Somme	259
XX.	The Battle of Pozieres	268
XXI.	Rest and Reorganisation at Berteaucourt	298
XXII.	Moving up to Mouquet Farm; Bonneville and Becourt	306
XXIII.	Mouquet Farm or Second Pozieres	313
XXIV.	North to Belgium: Ypres	324
XXV.	Back to the Somme	343
XXVI.	Flers	357
XXVII.	Winter 1916: Dernancourt, Flers	375
XXVIII.	Flers, 1917: Dernancourt, Bresle	385
XXIX.	Last Weeks of the 1916–1917 Winter; Bazentin Le Petit, Yarra Bank	393
XXX.	The German Retirement; Lebarque; Ligny-Thilloy	404
XXXI.	Henencourt Wood, Morchies and Lagnicourt	415
XXXII.	Noreuil and Bullecourt	442

XXXIII.	Bapaume and Ribemont	450
XXXIV.	Staple, Bayenghem; North to 2nd Army; Doulieu and Le Verrier	468
XXXV.	Third Battle of Ypres; Glencorse Wood	482
XXXVI.	Broodseinde Ridge	496
XXXVII.	Zonnebeke	508
XXXVIII.	Resting at Courset	516
XXXIX.	Messines Ridge: Neuve Eglise	523
XL.	The Hollebeke Sector	537
XLI.	Beggars' Rest Farm: the Rush to Amiens and Back Again	546
XLII.	Holding the Hun at Hazebrouck	555
XLIII.	Mont de Merris	574
XLIV.	Merris	584
XLV.	The Great Push: Lihon's Ridge and Crepy Wood	605
XLVI.	The Battle of Chuignolles	623
XLVII.	Farewell to Arms	632
XLVIII.	The Armistice	649
XLIX.	Chatelet	657
L.	The End	666

"LEGS-ELEVEN"

Chapter I

BLACKBOY HILL CAMP

"They were the boys from the Western State,
Brave Battalion Eleven;
They did not tarry, they did not wait,
When the call was given.
First to respond to their Country's need,
Nothing they feared, nor death did they heed

. . . . .

Brave Battalion Eleven!"
(Verse by S. M. Harris.)

Away out at the 105 peg on the Transcontinental Railway Line, a party of men was working. It was during the first few days of August, 1914. Occasionally tools would be dropped and an animated discussion would be held on the war that had just broken out in Europe.

Out in that desert to the east of Kalgoorlie news was scarce, and each day as the train came to the head of the line, bringing the mail and supplies, the construction gangs would eagerly grab the newspapers and devour all the information therein.

Of course the war held premier place, and when it was known that Australia was going to raise a contingent, a battalion of which was to be West Australian, there was great excitement in the camps.

The first quota to be raised in Western Australia was 1,400 men. Recruiting offices were opened in Perth and Fremantle and at various centres throughout the country including Kalgoorlie, Geraldton, Midland Junction, Northam, Bunbury, Albany and Wagin. At all these centres the offices were rushed by volunteers from all over the country, and soon trains, carrying crowds of young men, were everywhere hurrying to the city of Perth.

As soon as it was known that recruiting had started in Kalgoorlie, a number of young fellows from the construction camps of the Transcontinental downed tools and caught the first train westward bound. The date was Saturday, August 14; the party travelled all night and woke up in the Kalgoorlie station yards on Sunday morning.

After a change and breakfast, the party of fourteen reported at the drill hall, where they were examined by the Medical Officer, who told them to come back at 5 p.m. the same evening. On returning at the hour mentioned the men were lined up and the names of those who had been accepted were read out and these men told to return at the same time on the following day. Only one of the fourteen was rejected, and in view of the severity of the physical test in these early days, it speaks volumes for the fine physique of these out-back men. In this early draft were Frank Goundrey and Roy Retchford, both of whom subsequently became lieutenants in the 11th Battalion.

On reporting at the Kalgoorlie Drill Hall on Monday, August 16, they found a considerable number of other men waiting there. The whole party was marched to the station and put on a special train for Perth.

The inhabitants of Kalgoorlie gave the boys a right royal send-off. Hampers of food and bottles of the best were pushed into the compartments. It was a wonderful journey! Sergeant McLeery, of the Citizen Forces, was in charge of the troops and he had no light job. At all the stations on the journey down the train was greeted with cheers, and at every stop there were more refreshments.

It says a great deal for this draft that the men were able to tumble out of the train at Bellevue station and fall-in under Captain R. L. Leane, who marched them off to Blackboy Hill. There was no camp there at that time, and the first thing the boys had to do was to draw tents for shelters and start to pitch camp. Cooks and other details were allotted. The cooks were so only in name, and after trying their efforts nearly all the boys cleared off to Perth for a feed. At least, that was the excuse given.

Blackboy Hill Camp was officially started on August 17, 1914, and the first 11th Battalion order, Order Number 1, was issued at Blackboy Hill on this date by Lieut. J. H. Peck, the

Adjutant. Major A. H. Bridges was Acting-Commanding Officer.

After this date camp life soon started in earnest. Drafts which had been raised in much the same way as that from Kalgoorlie came from all over the State—from Albany and Bunbury, from Geraldton and Northam, and, of course, from Perth and Fremantle, so that the battalion that was to be formed was truly representative of the whole State, just as described in the verses from Winifred May:

"They come from the distant stations, bushmen bold and free,
The silent men of our silent land, knights of the saddle-tree;
They come from the rush of the goldmines, steady and strong and true—
Sons of the Southland, one and all, ready to 'see it through.'
They leave the desk in the city, they come from the survey camp;
The pearling boat on the north coast, the garden by the swamp;
From every part of the country, from every sphere of life,
Eager they come to the training camps, longing to join the strife."

As was to be expected among such a number of men from the bush and the Goldfields, there were a lot of real hard-doers, and the following amusing tales were related by the Adjutant himself. Lieut. Peck, who held that office, had been on the Permanent Staff, and besides being about the only officer dressed in complete uniform, he carried the distinguishing red tabs.

Several men had newly arrived in camp and were not very sure of their way about. Peck, noticing them, strode up and inquired if he could assist them. One of the lads getting an eyeful of the red tabs, red hat-band and general spick-and-spanness, turned to his mates and said, "Cripes! A bloody rosella!"

Another time Peck was in the orderly room, busy with lists of newcomers and company rolls, when two lately-joined men, carrying swags, ambled into the tent. They threw down their swags beside the table and one of them addressing Peck said: "I'll sling you a couple of bob if you'll look after these swags for an hour or so. We're goin' down to the pub."

It was customary, in the case of new troops, to line them up on parade and check their names from the Attestation Papers.

The names were read out in full in order to correct any mistakes that might have crept in. As each man's name was called out, he stepped one pace forward.

One day a number of names had been called out and their owners had answered to them in the proper manner to the accompaniment of a grin or two when anything out of the ordinary was read out.

When Lieut. Peck read out "John A. Archibald," "Archie" made a smart pace forward and all the boys broke into the then popular ballad, "Stop your nonsense, Archibald!" Those were the days!

The first necessity among such a mass of untrained men was to obtain non-commissioned officers with enough knowledge or personality to enable them to handle their fellows. Among these young Australians, N.C.O.'s had to be men of tact as well as possessing the natural qualities of leadership. Any men, then, with previous experience, such as those who had been in the Citizen Forces, the British Army or Territorial Forces, or who had served in the South African War, were tried out as N.C.O.'s and the following names selected at random were among those who were chosen: R.S.M. George Graves, Sergeant L. H. F. Jenkins (later went to 51st Battalion), Sergeant W. R. Hallahan (later Captain), Sergeant Phil Vowels (later Lieut.), Sergeant J. M. McLeery, C.S.M. Dave Hardy (later Lieut.), C.S.M. J. P. O'Neil (later Major, and the last Commanding Officer of the 11th Battalion).

With these and many other good men the camp at Blackboy Hill was started, and coincidental with the formation of the camp at Blackboy Hill was the birth of the 11th Battalion.

Before going on to a more detailed description of the officers and men of this new battalion, a short account of the formation of the "First Contingent," as it was generally called, and of the allocation of the various battalions and other units among the States of the Commonwealth may not be out of place.

When the Australian Commonwealth made its offer of 20,000 men to the British Government, as it did immediately after the outbreak of hostilities, this meant roughly that an infantry division and a light horse brigade were to be raised and sent overseas.

As this story deals mainly with an infantry battalion, the details of the formation of the light horse brigade are beyond its scope and it is not necessary to deal with them here.

With regard to the infantry division, it was noticeable that this division was already styled "The 1st Division," although no mention had yet been made of any further divisions. This division, following the plan of the British Army, was to consist of three brigades—the 1st, the 2nd and the 3rd Brigade. The 1st Brigade was to be raised in New South Wales, the 2nd Brigade in Victoria and the 3rd, the famous all-Australian Brigade, in Queensland, Tasmania, South Australia and Western Australia. Each brigade consisted of four battalions of infantry besides other units, and so the 1st Australian Division consisted of 12 battalions allocated as follows: 1st, 2nd, 3rd and 4th, from New South Wales; 5th, 6th, 7th and 8th, from Victoria; the 9th from Queensland, 10th from South Australia, the 11th (the subject of this history) from Western Australia, and the 12th, partly from Western Australia and partly from Tasmania.

Major-General E. G. Sinclair-MacLagan, C.B., C.M.G., D.S.O.

The 9th, 10th, 11th and 12th Battalions, then, formed the 3rd Brigade. This soon-to-be-famous brigade was placed under the command of Colonel E. G. Sinclair-MacLagan, D.S.O., who had been Director of Drill at the Royal Military College, Duntroon.

MacLagan was a soldier of considerable experience, having served in India and South Africa, and he was known to be a strict disciplinarian. He was a Scot by birth and was educated at Westward Ho! College in Devonshire, England.

MacLagan's task was rendered much more difficult than that of his fellow brigadiers of the 1st Australian Division on account of the scattered nature of his command. During the first stages of its career, the 3rd Brigade Headquarters was situated at Victoria Barracks, Melbourne, while the four battalions of his command were in the four States mentioned previously.

Colonel MacLagan paid visits to the 9th, 10th and 12th Battalions in their Australian camps, but the 11th Battalion did not come under his direct personal influence until the division landed in Egypt some months later.

The very nature of this narrative precludes any reference to the other branches of service in the division, such as the artillery, the engineers, the Army Medical Corps and other divisional troops; but frequent contact with all these services is inevitable as the story unfolds.

The position, then, soon after the outbreak of war, was that the State of Western Australia should furnish the 11th Battalion, and it has already been told how drafts from all parts of the State had been assembled at Blackboy Hill Camp, where they were formed up in eight companies. These eight companies, along with Headquarters Staff and details, formed the original 11th Battalion.

This young battalion, which was later to be so proud of its title, was thus to be known for all time as the 11th Battalion, and it may be said without fear of contradiction that no battalion ever consisted of a finer body of men. Not only was the necessary physical standard for enlistment much higher in the early days of the war than that which was accepted later, but the men themselves represented all the eager and adventurous spirits from every part of the State. There were bushmen and bank clerks, lumpers and shearers, teachers and miners, farmers and timber-getters, all being welded together into one splendid unit.

Western Australia, being a young and rapidly-expanding State, naturally had a vigorous and virile population, and it also attracted the best of the manhood from the British Isles and other countries, so that the battalion raised from these men was outstanding even amongst the very fine troops of the 1st Australian Division.

Years afterwards, when the physical standard was not nearly so high as that required for the first contingent, an American officer, referring to the 11th Battalion, said to the writer: "Say! I reckon your boys are like our Western men, all husky guys."

Not only were the men of this West Australian battalion famous for their spirit and their physique, but they had the qualities that go with the people of a young, undeveloped country; they had resource, initiative and a power for manual labour unsurpassed in the division, which qualities were often to be strikingly proved in the long and arduous years of war ahead of them.

Having thus described the manner of troops which composed this young battalion, it remains now to give a more particular account of the formation and personnel of the battalion itself.

At the start of the war, the constitution of a battalion was considerably different to that which pertained later and at the finish of the war. The Australian establishments, which always conformed very closely to those of the British Army, were in these early days organised on the pre-1915 system, and all battalions were established as eight-company battalions. This standardisation was very necessary for the free working of the immense organisation which was controlled by the British War Office.

So the 11th Battalion was established in its initial stages as an eight-company battalion, with the following officers and senior N.C.O.'s:—

HEADQUARTERS

Lieut.-Colonel J. Lyon-Johnston	Commanding Officer
Major S. R. Roberts	Second-in-Command
Lieut. J. H. Peck	Adjutant
Captain E. F. Brennan	Medical Officer
Lieut. K. McLennan	Quartermaster
Lieut. H. James	Signal Officer
Lieut. J. Peat	Machine Gun Officer
Lieut. A. H. Priestley	Transport Officer

R.S.M. G. Graves, R.Q.M.S. M. A. McGuire, Sergeants M. D. Black, A. Burgess, H. T. Shaw, P. Boyle, G.

Walker, W. R. Hallahan, Corporal Murphy, Sergeant
E. Parsonage, Corporal M. Spicer (Signal Section),
Corporal W. Wright (A.M.C. Section).

"A" COMPANY

Captain J. Millar, Lieut. W. H. Rockliff, Lieut. A. H.
McFarlane, Colour-Sergeant H. Williams.

"B" COMPANY

Major E. Drake-Brockman, Lieut. A. R. Selby, Lieut.
J. Morgan, Colour-Sergeant G. F. Charles.

"C" COMPANY

Captain C. A. Barnes, Lieut. S. H. Jackson, Lieut. F.
Stickland, Colour-Sergeant J. J. Mahon.

"D" COMPANY

Captain R. W. Everett, Lieut. A. H. Darnell, Lieut. W.
R. Annear, Lieut. J. Newman, Colour-Sergeant D.
Hardy.

"E" COMPANY

Major J. Denton, Lieut. D. H. McDonald, Lieut. A. H.
Corley, Colour-Sergeant J. J. Medley.

"F" COMPANY

Captain R. L. Leane, Lieut. M. L. Reid, Lieut. C. A.
La Nauze, Colour-Sergeant J. P. O'Neil.

"G" COMPANY

Captain A. Croly, Lieut. J. Williams, Lieut. T. H.
Mountain, Colour-Sergeant H. Ross.

"H" COMPANY

Lieut. H. Reilly, Lieut. C. Buttle, Lieut. H. W. B.
Harper, Colour-Sergeant K. Hemingway.

The foregoing list of officers and N.C.O.'s had, therefore, the task of breaking-in and training the heterogeneous mass of men that was going to form the famous 11th Battalion, and how well they performed their task the course of future events in the history of the battalion will show.

It is not always easy to realise what a difficult task this was. There was no tradition behind this battalion; there was no precedent to go by, and most of the men, especially those from the country districts and the Goldfields, had always been a law unto themselves; so that it was only their keenness and their desire to fit themselves for the job in front of them that kept them amenable to discipline. The tact and firmness of the officers and N.C.O.'s were also contributory features in the training, but even in spite of all this the task was no light one.

In these early days of camp life, when the young troops were gradually learning the routine of military training, many amusing incidents took place, of which a few are here related, which show the metal the troops were made of.

One good story is told of No. 991 Private Bill Henson. One morning, after a heavy night at poker, the troops were on early morning parade, and some of the boys were not feeling at all bright and perky.

At roll-call, the names of the men were read out, and they were required to signify their presence by calling out their regimental numbers. Sergeant George Mason, who had been one of the poker-school on the previous evening, was in charge of the group which included Henson. When the latter's name was called out, he convulsed the party by replying, "A pair of nines and a bullet." When the mirth died down, Private Henson was severely reprimanded for his levity.

Naturally, most of the lads were unused to drill of any kind, and uniformity and the necessity for strict discipline were regarded with amused tolerance, and it was a pretty hard job to convince these independent spirits that careful and exact attention to orders was necessary.

On one occasion, Captain A. Croly, who had been an officer in the Indian Army, and consequently was accustomed to excellent drilling by the troops in that country, was nearly distracted by the horrible attempts that his company was making in even the simplest exercises. However, he realised that it was all in the game and started afresh. He gave the command, "Attention!" and then followed it up with "Right dress!" On going to the flank to see if the troops had carried out the order to his satisfaction, he was so astounded at the result that he bawled out to the Adjutant, who happened to be passing, "Hey! I say, Peck! Come over here and have a look at these b——s. They're actually in a straight line!"

Captain Croly, as he then was, held a unique place among a lot of hard citizens, and his caustic tongue was famous throughout the battalion and, later, the brigade.

When the 11th Battalion was first formed in the eight companies, the men were grouped as far as possible in companies representing the major divisions of the State. Thus "A" and "B" Companies were drawn mainly from Perth, "C" and "D" Companies from Fremantle and district, "E" and "F" Companies from the Goldfields and "G" and "H" Companies from the South-West and the country generally. This classification was not only satisfactory to the men but had also the effect of creating keen rivalry among the various companies and greatly speeded up the process of welding these raw recruits

Some of the "originals" at Blackboy Hill.

into an efficient fighting machine, and it is on record that there were never any troops so keen to learn and grasp all there was to be known as these young West Australians.

It has been frequently said that discipline was sometimes a bit lax; but if it is remembered that many of these men had been their own masters from a very early age and had been accustomed to work out their own destinies, often against heavy odds, and that they rightly held themselves the equals of any man, then, the wonder of it all is, that they voluntarily submitted to a discipline and to a routine, certain aspects of which appeared absolutely ridiculous and unnecessary to most of them. Right through to the end of the war and afterwards, the Australian had always a kind of tolerant contempt for the red tape that the Army insisted on; but having become a soldier, he played the game more out of a feeling of responsibility and mateship than from any fear of the penalties imposed for non-compliance with orders.

A good illustration of this is shown by the following incident: As already mentioned, the various companies were composed as far as possible of men from the same portion of the State, and consequently mates of civilian days were often in the same tent and they generally managed to get allotted to fatigues and other duties together.

In this instance, two Goldfielders were mess orderlies together, and they thought it would be a good scheme if, instead of using cold water, as was the custom, to wash the dixies in, hot water were used instead. Accordingly, without asking previous permission, they took a bucket of cold water over to a nearby cook's fire and set it over the flames. The fireplace was a very rough and ready job, and unfortunately the bucket over-balanced and spilled the water over the fire, absolutely extinguishing it.

Then the trouble started. The four company cooks wanted to know who gave the mess orderlies permission to use their fire. The two Goldfielders were not used to being talked to in that fashion, and were just preparing to sail into the four cooks when Lieut. Peck happened to come along. The Adjutant soon settled matters by telling the boys that instead of scrapping and quarrelling, that, as soldiers in the same battalion, they should pull together. The result was that the whole six set to and rebuilt the fireplace on more stable lines, relit the fire and the two mess orderlies went off with a bucket of boiling water.

Of course they were some misfits, too. In the machine-gun section the boys used to mess by themselves and each took his turn of cooking for a week. Some of the lads were splendid cooks, and some were not so good; but Private Bettson, however good a machine-gunner he may have been, was certainly the world's worst cook. He couldn't even boil water! When his turn of cookhouse came he used to use up all his pay buying ready-cooked food for the boys. His life might have been in danger otherwise.

One of the chief drawbacks that these young soldiers had to put up with, and one that persisted for a long time afterwards at Blackboy Hill Camp, was the lack or only partial issue of uniforms. In the initial stages of the troops' service, there was doubtless great difficulty on the part of the Quartermaster in getting the necessary equipment, and what did come forward was issued piecemeal: a pair of boots one day and a set of underclothing another day; so that for a long time the men presented a most unmilitary appearance, being dressed in a mixture of civilian garb and military uniform. It is a well-known fact that uniformity of dress and pride in personal appearance are great adjuncts to *esprit de corps*, but it was a long time before the 11th Battalion had those two stimuli. Nevertheless, even under the disability of motley garb the young troops began to look smarter and more trained in a very short time.

Sir Harry Barron, then Governor of Western Australia, who always took a keen personal interest in the 11th Battalion, said that he never saw men change from civilians to soldiers so rapidly, and that statement, from an old soldier like Sir Harry, was praise indeed.

Before continuing with the development of the battalion, there is one incident that must not pass unrecorded, and that is the first battalion parade of the 11th, under Major A. H. Bridges, an officer of the Permanent Staff, who was in command of the battalion at the time pending the arrival of Lieut.-Colonel J. Lyon-Johnston from Kalgoorlie.

The following is Major J. P. O'Neil's account of the parade; Jack O'Neil was then colour-sergeant:

"The battalion was marched to Helena Vale Racecourse and halted in front of the grandstand. The Commanding Officer (who must have been a bit of an optimist) explained the movement that he wished to be executed, which in this case was to form quarter-column, and finished up by saying that when he gave the command to move he did not expect to hear any orders or commands other than those of the officers in charge of the eight companies.

"The battalion, at this stage, had only been issued with rifles, boots and puttees. The rest of the men's dress was entirely civilian and consisted of all the different varieties of garments that they had been accustomed to wear in civil life. Some of the boys had dungarees and flannel shirts, some wore stiff white collars, and many had white shirts; but if the boys' garb was varied, and their appearance far from military, the whole battalion was imbued with the one idea and that was that the intended movement was going to be a complete success.

"So, when the command 'Battalion! Form Quarter-Column!' was given, each man was straining at the leash. The Company Commanders barked their commands, and every individual made it a point that both he himself and his neighbours were in their right places. Pandemonium ensued—the boys were pushing each other into position with rifle or elbow, and the row was appalling.

"When some sort of order was restored, it was noticed that Major Bridges was a very peeved man, and he did not hesitate to tell the battalion exactly what he thought about the whole turnout."

The photographs of the 11th Battalion at this period show a very heterogeneous collections of uniforms, semi-uniforms and complete civilian outfits; but uniforms or not, there was no doubt about the amount of work the troops were made to do. The parody on the popular song, "I'd like to live in Loveland," aptly summed up the situation—

"I'd love to live in Blackboy for a week or two,
And work all day and get no pay,
And live on Irish stew."

All those troops who enlisted in Western Australia and spent some of their time at Blackboy Hill must have sung these lines at one time or another. It is not known exactly when the parody was first sung, but it was not long after the formation of the camp and it continued to be a favourite right through the war.

It is hardly necessary to give a detailed description of the various phases of training that the troops went through, but stress must be laid on the amount of marching the 11th Battalion had to do. Perhaps it may not have been very excessive compared with the amount of route-marching done by other units, but it must always be remembered that even before the advent of the motor-car the average Australian never did any walking unless he was obsolutely forced to; so that, looking back on his training the one thing that always seemed to stand out above everything else was the seemingly aimless marching up and down the roads around the camp.

An extract from a letter written by Private J. M. Aitken in the early days of camp life reads: "Am very tired; just had a busy day.. This morning went into the bush and did battalion drill, arriving back in camp at 1 p.m.; at 2 p.m. had to fall-in again and marched to Guildford and back, about eleven miles." There are many such references to these route-marches which were never popular with the troops. Sham fights, musketry practices or any constructive work were eagerly welcomed by the men, but they could never resign themselves to the seemingly endless marching.

A good tale is told by Private R. A. Batchelor on the occasion of one of these route-marches. "When in Blackboy in 1914, getting ready to go on a route-march, our company sergeant-major (Joe Mahon) noticed my cobber, George Weightman, filling his water-bottle with whisky. Being an 'old soldier,' Joe never let on, but we knew he would be along for his cut of whisky at every stop along the road, so we decided to put one over on him.

"Weightman and I swopped water-bottles so that Weightman had the water and I had the whisky.

"After we had gone about four miles we had a spell, and along came Joe with his tongue hanging out a mile. He took out Weightman's water-bottle and had a good, hearty swig —and then you should have seen his face. We could hardly control our mirth.

"Joe never said a word—just gave Weightman back his water-bottle and glared at us all. If looks could kill, we would have died on the spot."

There are very few official records available for this period of the 11th Battalion's history, but the following are from the Battalion Diary:

"On August 24, 1914, Lieut.-Colonel J. Lyon-Johnston reported for duty and was taken on the strength of the 11th Battalion, relieving Major Bridges. On the same date, Captain Leane presented a bulldog as regimental pet. This dog was christened 'Mulga,' and taken on strength."

"On August 17, the 11th Battalion regimental call was composed by Staff-Sergeant-Major Jelfs and adopted from this date. This call, that was to be heard in so many lands and in conditions that were as yet undreamt of, fitted the words, 'There's a land of sunny skies, West Australia!' "

As the battalion took shape and became accustomed to its routine the training became more intense, and few of the succeeding units were given more work than the "Original 11th Battalion." From a letter dated September 24, 1914, the following extract is taken:

"Last night we were aroused at 9:30 p.m. for roll-call, dismissed, aroused again at 11 p.m. for an alarm; had to dress, fall-in and march to the parade ground without lights or talking; were dismissed again and then aroused at 1:30 this morning for a march; each time without previous warning. We marched seven or eight miles out to where 'H' Company was bivouacing and attacked their lines at daybreak, taking them completely by surprise. They were mostly asleep and, of course, were all made prisoners. On our return, we fought an action with 'G' Company. This was a draw. When we reached home it was just 2:30 p.m."

It is proof of the fine condition the men were in and the hard training that they were undergoing that they were able to stand up to such gruelling work.

While the battalion was thus progressing in company training, the specialist sections were making good headway. These sections were the signal section, under Lieut. H. James; the machine-gun section, under Lieut. Peat; the A.M.C. section, under Captain E. F. Brennan; and the transport section, under Lieut. A. H. Priestley.

All these sections were keen and zealous and soon attained a high measure of efficiency.

The machine-gun section was equipped with two Maxim guns and had as sergeant "Wally" Hallahan, who was to become one of the most distinguished soldiers of the 11th Battalion.

The battalion transport lines were situated on the north-west corner of Blackboy Hill Camp. The equipment was complete, with the exception of horses. The late Mr. Gooch lent the 11th Battalion a number of horses for use while at Blackboy Hill.

On September 24, 1914, the 11th Battalion establishment was reported complete.

Early in October, the first reinforcement company of the 11th Battalion was formed and men who had arrived in camp too late to be included in the original battalion were drafted into this company. This 1st Reinforcement Company was the happy possessor of a piper, one Davie Howieson, who had travelled to camp from Mornington Mills bringing his pipes with him.

Davie had been a piper in the Argyle and Sutherland Highlanders and was a good exponent of his art. Needless to say, his piping was not appreciated by all the members of his company, but he managed to survive and later left with the rest of his reinforcement on the *Katoomba* for Melbourne, where they continued their training. (Howieson was killed in action on Gallipoli on May 20, 1915.)

The only other music that the battalion possessed consisted of drums and bugles. The Commanding Officer refused to have a regimental band, although the City of Perth offered to provide the instruments.

In October the troops began to hear rumours of embarkation. As they were by that time getting very tired of camp life and longing to get to the Front, those rumours were very popular and soon gained much credence. There were, of course, good grounds for these reports, as the Commonwealth was only waiting for definite intelligence regarding the whereabouts of certain vessels of the German Fleet and was making arrangements for a suitable escort before sending away the first contingent.

When, therefore, on October 7, the 11th Battalion received orders to get all kit together and everything ready for embarkation, the boys were overjoyed and all got ready in record time with sea-kit and black kit-bags packed. The roll was called and the men marched off, full of joy that the adventure had started at last.

Imagine their surprise and disappointment when they turned into the familiar Helena Vale Racecourse and found that the "troopship" was only the grandstand with its tiers of seats for decks and that the whole show was only a practice stunt. The conditions of "embarkation" were just about as unlike the real thing as possible, but that was only a foretaste of many future operations of the battalion's war service in which the actual was so vastly different from the imagined.

On October 12 commenced the famous five-day route-march which was long remembered by the boys of the original 11th. The march started on a Monday, and that day the troops were marched about 15 miles and bivouaced at Upper Swan. The next day another march of 15 miles was made, and again the troops camped in the open. Swan View was passed on the third day out, and at night the Commanding Officer took care to see that the site selected for the camp was far removed from all human habitations. It was fairly warm weather, and the troops had all their kit up and carried full packs and oil sheets, so that this march was a pretty good indication of the battalion's fitness.

Men from the Goldfields in original 11th Battalion. (Lieut.) Jim Aitken, top left. (Major) J. P. O'Neill, 3rd from right at back.

Original A.M.C. Section, 11th Battalion. Captain E. F. Brennan mounted.

At one of the mid-day halts, so writes No. 350 H. D. Russell, the machine gun section, which had somehow or other acquired a "chook," made a noble effort to cook the bird before the whistle blew for the fall-in. A hole was dug in the ground with an entrenching tool and the bird wrapped in an old bag, and it was soon cooking native fashion with the boys standing round in mortal fear that the command to fall-in should be given.

Meanwhile the bird was cooking well, and hopes ran high and mouths began to water. But alas! it was not to be. The whistle sounded and there was no way of salvaging the now red-hot bird, so the troops fell-in and had to march away, with only the appetising smell of the nicely-cooking bird to remind them of what might have been.

After two more long days of marching the boys were on the road for home, but still with a considerable journey ahead of them. The battalion transport had taken a wrong turning and was temporarily lost, and all the troops were weary. During a halt, when the boys were reclining in all sorts of tired postures, Lieut.-Colonel Lyon Johnston, riding past on his fine horse, tried to cheer up the boys by saying, "Well, my lads! It's a long way to Tipperary, but we'll get there sometime." From that date the "Old Man" was known as "Tipperary Johnston," or more familiarly "Old Tip."

The missing transport section eventually made touch with the battalion, the march was resumed, and the boys started off on the last lap for home and Blackboy Hill, and so completed the "Long Route March."

By the middle of October the battalion's training was well advanced and the raw recruits of a bare two months ago were at last looking like a disciplined battalion and the boys felt themselves quite old soldiers. As Sir Harry Barron said on the first occasion on which the 11th Battalion marched out in full dress, when the artillery and other units had turned out to give them a cheer, "Damn it all! One day you walked into this camp a mob of civilians, and practically next day you are a regiment any man would be proud to command."

But, as the days wore on, a feeling of discontent and staleness began to pervade the camp and letters from the troops during the last weeks of the 11th Battalion's sojourn at Blackboy Hill are full of impatience and annoyance at the delay in being sent over-

"F" Company, 11th Battalion, Blackboy Hill.

seas. The men felt that they had been sufficiently trained and were straining at the leash to get away. Nearly every one was of the opinion that the war would be over long before the 11th Battalion reached the scene of the struggle. Little they knew!

The 1st Reinforcement, which was, as already stated, then in training at Blackboy Hill, was not to leave Australia with the first contingent, but was sent to Melbourne and later left on the *Themistocles* with the second contingent of troopships, and to anticipate a little, this fleet arrived in Albany and lay there on Christmas Day, 1914, but none of the 11th boys were allowed on shore; and so, some of the 11th Battalion passed their last Christmas within sight and sound of their native land without being able to enjoy the seasonal festivities among their own people.

But to return to Blackboy Hill. The closing days of October found the air full of rumours and more rumours. There had been several false alarms about embarking, and the troops did not know what to believe. There had been a march through the streets of Perth, where the people of the city had given the 11th Battalion (The City of Perth Regiment) a rousing welcome, and this led the troops to believe that their departure could not be far off. Still, there had been no official intimation and the boys felt that they were being treated as children and were very disgruntled.

This was the position on October 30 when night fell, and the clear notes of the "Last Post" echoed among the hills and the gum-trees surrounding Blackboy Hill Camp.

Chapter II

THE VOYAGE WITH THE GREAT CONVOY

LONG BEFORE the customary hour of "Reveille" on the morning of October 31, the Adjutant (Lieut. J. H. Peck) sent round to all officers of the 11th Battalion warning them to report to the Commanding Officer's tent.

They paraded at 4 a.m. but paid no special significance to the order, as there had been so many false alarms about the date of departure, and they reckoned that they were merely being let in for some scheme or other to keep the men occupied pending instructions for sailing.

The Colonel bade the officers "Good morning" and then surprised everyone by informing them that embarkation orders had at last been definitely received, and that all companies were to be paraded immediately without fuss or noise, as they were to march out to Helena Vale siding, there to entrain for Fremantle

The account of the embarkation and the voyage is mainly drawn from two excellent diaries of the period, which had been kept by Major (then Captain) A. Croly and Lieut. J. H. Cooke.

When the welcome news was conveyed to the troops, there was much excitement and great rejoicing. Tents were soon struck and handed in to store and all the companies lost no time in getting their sea-kit ready and their black kit-bags ready for the voyage. The sea kit-bags were to be carried by the men and the black kit-bags were to be stored in the hold of the ship.

After breakfast the 11th Battalion moved off and made for the railway siding. The troops were soon on the train and amid great cheering were carried to Fremantle. By noon, Battalion Headquarters and all the companies except "A" and "B" Companies were aboard the transport "A11," otherwise the s.s. *Ascanius*, then lying at Fremantle Wharf. "A" and "B" Companies embarked on the s.s. *Medic* ("A7").

On board the *Ascanius* was the 10th Battalion from South Australia, commanded by Lieut.-Colonel S. P. Weir, who was appointed O.C. troops. There were 26 officers and 759 other ranks of the 11th Battalion aboard the *Ascanius* and six officers and 232 other ranks of the 11th Battalion on board the *Medic*, and there were the same number of officers and other ranks of the 12th Battalion aboard the latter ship.

Though the 11th Battalion Transport Section also embarked on the *Ascanius*, there were only three officers' chargers taken aboard, the Commanding Officer's and two others. Sergeant Alec Burgess managed to smuggle another mare board the *Medic*. The horses for the transport came from South Australia and were aboard the *Saldanha* and consisted of 54 animals. The few horses that the 11th Battalion had taken on board had been the gifts of several public-spirited people.

The *Ascanius* in particular was a very comfortable boat, and though there were about 2,000 men aboard there was no undue crowding.

There was a vast concourse of people down at the wharf to see the troops off, but no one was allowed on board. The 10th Battalion had been granted shore-leave, and though some of the South Australians had failed to report back to the vessel, the *Ascanius* left the wharf at 4 p.m. amid cheers and farewells and steamed out into Gage Roads, where she anchored some distance from the shore, there to await the *Medic*. It was learned that these two troopships were to be picked up by the rest of the convoy.

Until late in the evening all kinds of boats and launches came out from the harbour and the occupants cheered and waved to the boys. At 7 p.m. a Japanese cruiser, the *Ibuki*, steamed up and passed south.

Until November 2 an uneventful time was passed, but at 4:30 a.m. the throb of the engines awakened the troops. Soon the anchors were weighed and the vessels began to move.

Many were the eyes turned back to the gleaming lights of Fremantle and the dear shores, which hundreds of these young lads were fated never to see again. The vessels stood out to sea for some miles and then hove to. High excitement reigned, and when two British cruisers and the Japanese cruiser *Ibuki* took station near them, it was felt that things were indeed beginning to move; but the first day out passed by without any stirring incident. The sea was tranquil and the weather was glorious.

His Excellency the Governor (Sir Harry Barron) and the Acting-Premier (Mr. P. Collier) came out on one of the tugs and made farewell speeches to the troops, who were much too excited to listen.

During the morning of November 3 the troops were given physical "jerks," and another quiet day was just passing when suddenly great activity was noticed on the part of the escorting battleships, which dashed off towards a smudge of smoke on the horizon. Soon another battleship was seen coming up fast. She proved to be the scout of the main convoy. The *Ascanius* and the *Medic*, which had been moving slowly westward, now eased up and finally stopped altogether. All the troops crowded the rails and every other vantage point and gazed to the south where a haze of smoke began to show.

And now one of the most stirring sights in the whole history of the war presented itself; unforgettable by all who had the privilege of witnessing it. The whole of the convoy carrying the Australian and New Zealand troops steamed slowly into view, with the escorting warships on guard. The troopships numbered 38 and carried approximately 35,000 men.

As far as the eye could see the ocean was dotted with the ships of the convoy, and a haze of smoke stretched away for miles.

The Australian transports were in three columns or divisions and the New Zealand transports in two columns in rear. The *Ascanius* and *Medic* moved over to their places in the port division, while the *Ibuki* took station on the starboard beam.

The order of the convoy was now as follows: The cruiser *Minotaur* led, with the Australian troopships in three divisions behind and the New Zealanders astern. The *Sydney* was on the port side, while the *Melbourne* brought up the rear. The *Ibuki* was in the position as mentioned above.

The pace was set by the slowest vessel in the convoy (the *Southern*), which could only steam 10 knots, and at this pace the vast fleet moved over the Indian Ocean with its course set towards Colombo.

To regress a little, it must now be understood that the several postponements and delays in the actual embarkation of the first contingent were due to the fact that several fast modern German cruisers, notably the *Scharnhorst*, the *Gneisenau* and the *Emden*, were at large in the Pacific and adjoining oceans, and their whereabouts were often matters of mystery.

There were certain British warships detailed to search for and sink these ships, but so far the German vessels had been elusive. On one occasion the *Gneisenau* and *Scharnhorst* had visited Apia in Samoa, while the Australian Government was preparing to get the first contingent away. As Apia was only 2,500 miles from Sydney and 1,500 miles from New Zealand, it is readily understood that the Australian Government was unwilling to risk such a large number of troops on the open seas without adequate escort. Later the *Emden* was reported in the Bay of Bengal, and on October 28 this ship raided the port of Penang, in the Straits Settlements, and then disappeared.

After an anxious time wondering where the *Scharnhorst* and *Gneisenau* had got to, the authorities were relieved to learn that they were reported away over towards the South American coast. The *Emden*, however, still constituted a menace to shipping on the Fremantle-Colombo run, and though the *Hampshire* and the *Yarmouth* were hunting for that gallant raider far to the north, every precaution was taken to protect the convoy from surprise. At nights, after the first few days out, all the ships' lights were screened and the stern lights were so hooded that only a faint glow was cast on the water in rear of the ships as guides for the vessels moving in their wake. This screening of lights was so religiously carried out that even the officers' mess was put on as early as 5:30 p.m. so as to be over before dark.

Under these conditions the great convoy, possibly the greatest in the history of the world, sailed slowly north-west into the danger zone.

November 4 was a quiet day, during which the troops adjusted themselves to shipboard life with its new routine.

On the night of November 5 a mail steamer, brilliant with twinkling lights, was seen to be overhauling the convoy. She turned out to be the *Osterley* homeward bound from Fremantle. She passed close by the convoy and with her brilliantly-lit decks was a contrast to the dark troopships. As she passed on her course, she signalled "Bon voyage" and several private messages were flashed with torches.

The commander of the *Minotaur* sent a message severely censoring the captain of the *Osterley* for coming so close.

There was a good deal of conjecture among the troops as to whether the mailboat would get safely through.

On November 6, in addition to the ordinary physical drill and lectures that comprised the daily training of the troops, there was a practice alarm which the troops carried out satisfactorily. In order to keep the men fit they were exercised as much as possible; but that was not a great deal, and as all lights were extinguished at nights, time soon began to hang heavily on the men's hands and conditions were decidedly monotonous.

There were a few cases of sickness, but the health of the troops, except for the results of inoculation and vaccination, was excellent. The inoculation and vaccination which were being carried out on board generally left the troops sick and headachey, as there were so few attractions to counteract the effects of the injections.

As the convoy gradually moved nearer Cocos Islands, all precautions were more stringently enforced, and many rumours gained credence; but it came rather as a shock when, on November 7, the official news of the German victory at Coronel, near Valparaiso, in South America, was promulgated. In this battle the German cruisers *Scharnhorst* and *Gneisenau*, under Admiral von Spee, sank the British cruisers *Good Hope* and *Monmouth* (under Admiral Craddock) on October 22, 1914.

At 8 p.m. on November 7, all lights in the fleet of transports were extinguished for half an hour and the men ordered to collision-stations. All were in bare feet and they groped their way to the decks where they stood silent and motionless. Nothing could be seen but a few dim glows and the dark shapes of the nearer vessels of the convoy. It was an eery experience.

On November 8, the *Minotaur*, which had led the convoy up to this time, left her station and made off to the west, after signalling the *Melbourne* to lead. The latter vessel then moved up to the head of the convoy and the *Sydney* and the *Ibuki* still retained their stations on the port and starboard beams, so that there was now no war vessel guarding the rear of the great fleet.

The convoy was now gradually standing towards the Cocos Islands, and the intention was to pass about 50 miles to the east and so avoid any possible enemy lurking in the vicinity and also to keep clear of the main sea routes.

The even tenor of the voyage was dramatically disturbed on November 9. Early in the morning the wireless started to crackle—a short message in an unknown code was received, and almost immediately the Cocos Islands station was heard calling the *Minotaur*, but she had left for Mauritius. Then Cocos called again and sent out the S.O.S. and the message, "Strange warship approaching." After that there was complete silence.

The *Melbourne* moved over fast in the direction of the Cocos, then turned back to her proper station, first signalling the *Sydney* to proceed to the Islands. In a very short time the *Sydney* was hull down to the west and she soon disappeared from sight.

Later in the morning the *Melbourne* moved over from the head of the column to the port beam and the *Ibuki* steamed right over in front of the convoy and took station behind the *Melbourne*. This was on receipt of news that the *Sydney* was engaging an enemy vessel. Both the escorting warships were now between the Cocos Islands and the convoy.

All this movement of warships was watched by all the troops and very little attention was paid to lectures or drill that morning. All eyes were turned to the western horizon, and when the news came through that the *Sydney* was in action at 10:45 a.m., the excitement was intense. Faint and far off were heard the reverberations of the naval guns. When the great message came through, some time after 11 a.m., "Emden beached and done for," the troops went mad and cheered to the echo. "Rule Britannia" and "God Save the King" and other patriotic songs were sung, while General Bridges cancelled all parades for the day.

On the *Ascanius*, Lieut.-Colonel Lyon-Johnston was asked that all 11th Battalion prisoners in the guardroom should be released and he willingly gave his consent. He also invited all the officers of the 11th Battalion to the dining-room, where he ordered champagne, and toasts were drunk to the Navy, the Commander of the *Sydney* and a silent one to the sailors who had fallen in the action.

All the officers aboard the *Ascanius* "put in" and shouted beer for the 2,000 men on board to celebrate the event. Some of the men, however, thought that they had not pledged the Navy in full measure, so they managed to purloin a cask of beer, which they hid under a pile of hammocks in the hammock-bin. Needless to say, the beer did not last long, but it is on record that the Navy was well and truly pledged.

Although the *Emden* was reported out of action, the Commander of the *Melbourne* sent out a general signal in the evening, "Have signalled for confirmation. *Emden* known to have passed our front last night. Pending instructions, consider every precaution should be taken." This meant that the convoy was again in darkness after sunset.

On Tuesday, November 10, the *Sydney* had not returned to her station and the *Melbourne* and *Ibuki* were still out in front.

The transports were now well within the tropics, and the weather was hot. After the great excitement of the previous day reaction set in and the troops became languid. An *Emden* souvenir dinner was held by the officers aboard the *Ascanius*, but that was the only mild excitement on that date.

It was now reported that the *Konigsberg*, the only vessel of the German Cruiser Squadron that could be in the vicinity, was definitely located on the African coast. There was now no longer any need for extreme precautions, and normal ship's routine was adopted from this time. Naturally the evenings began to be more enjoyable, and the old "Crown and Anchor" boards and other means of relieving the troops of surplus cash came into their own—but not for long.

Drastic penalties followed their use, so the untiring "Pinktop" had to devise some other form of amassing money. He hit on the idea of a soup plate into which, from a prescribed distance, the boys tossed a penny. Any penny remaining in the plate was worth a shilling to the player, and "Pinktop" collected all the misses. Of course, this did not last long either, for "Pinktop" was soon stopped by an officer.

"Pinktop" lived up to his name and colour. He flared up and ended by being sent to the cells.

Though the voyage was mostly hum-drum, there were always one or two amusing incidents. While, on the whole, the meals were good and the food excellent, there were several occasions on which complaints were made by the troops. It was difficult to get redress, so the troops one day took their own method of dealing with the case.

On this occasion the meat was decidedly "off," so the troops decided to give it a decent burial with full honours. The band of the 10th Battalion was requisitioned and the meat was put into dixies and hauled in solemn procession round the decks to the tune of the "Dead March in Saul." After the full ceremony, "parson" and all, the meat was lowered into the deep.

It was noticed that the *Melbourne* had steamed ahead, and soon sailed out of sight to the north. It was learned that she had gone to Colombo to coal. The *Hampshire* (the same vessel that was later so tragically mined off the coast of the Orkney Islands with Lord Kitchener aboard) now took the lead and kept that station for the rest of the voyage of the convoy.

On November 11, 1914, the 11th Battalion had its first service casualty. Private Charlie Power, of "C" Company, who had been ill with pneumonia for a week, died, and was buried at 5 p.m. This left the troops very depressed, as a burial at sea always seems impressive and affecting.

Next day, therefore, sports were held on board the *Ascanius* in the endeavour to cheer the men up a little. The helpful effect of the sports was practically nullified by the doleful news that no shore-leave would be granted at Colombo, and that all letters for transmission from that port had to be left open.

On November 15 the *Empress of Russia* and later the *Sydney* passed the troopships. The *Sydney* was carrying the German wounded from the *Emden*, but she passed in the night and only the knowledge of her proximity was vouchsafed to the troops. The ten vessels carrying the New Zealanders passed through the convoy and made for Colombo to coal ahead of the rest of the fleet. The Australian troopships followed, steaming slowly, and arrived off Colombo about 3 p.m. There were no boats or launches allowed to come near the ship.

On this date Colonel Sinclair-MacLagan dined on board the *Ascanius*, this being his first meeting with the 11th Battalion since its formation. All the troops were impressed with his fine, soldierly appearance.

The convoy lay at Colombo during November 16 and 17. Occasionally a boat-load of Singalese divers drew near, but these were warned off by the sentries. It was a great experience for those boys who had not been out of Australia before to see the native bum-boats and catarmarangs and to hear the natives shouting, "Monee in ee waree! Monee in ee waree!" (money in the water) and to see their skill at diving for silver.

Occasionally a launch or catarmarang passed by, but there was no hope of getting ashore.

At 11:30 a.m. on November 17, the fleet was under steam again. Newspapers were distributed to the troops. This was the first news of the outside world that the boys had obtained since embarkation, and they read the papers with avidity. In the evening, about 6:30 p.m., the light cruiser *Yarmouth* attached herself to the convoy as escort.

The convoy did not leave Colombo as one fleet. The slower divisions went first, as the faster ones were intended to catch up before reaching Aden. The third division being the fastest left last, but the *Afric* was unable to make the pace set by the leader (the *Euripedes*); so on November 20, when the remainder of the convoy was caught up with, the *Ascanius* was ordered from the second division to take the place of the *Afric*, between the *Shropshire* and the *Benalla*. This was done and the voyage continued.

Early in the morning of November 21, the troops on board the *Ascanius* were awakened by feeling the ship bump into something. It caused great consternation down below. Immediately there was another bump and a grinding crash and all the troops were ordered to put on lifebelts and assemble on the troop deck. The young soldiers behaved excellently and there was no confusion or undue alarm. A full account of the happening is here given from Major Croly's diary:

"I must now describe an exciting little experience which occurred this morning, November 21, at about 4:30 o'clock. Everyone was awakened by what appeared to be a collision, and on rushing out on deck from my cabin this first impression proved to be only too true.

"Our line of ships comprised the *Euripedes*, the *Argyllshire*, *Shropshire*, *Ascanius* and *Benalla*, and for some unknown reason, though many rumours are current, our vessel ran right up to and severely bumped the *Shropshire*, about a quarter-broadside on; and in endeavouring to get out of this grave position, another bump was experienced.

"The result, I believe, meant very little to the *Shropshire*, but tore a hole in our ship about 20 feet long and 4 inches in width. Alarm bells, signals of distress and even sky-rockets could be heard and seen. It was exceedingly dark and there was a fair sea running.

"The consternation on board can be better imagined than described. The conduct of the officers and troops has been the subject of very warm compliments from all quarters. The men behaved positively heroically, put on their lifebelts and marched quietly to their allotted places, where they remained perfectly calm until an hour or more later, when it was ascertained that the damage was not of sufficient importance to cause immediate alarm.

"This aspect of the situation was not known to the men, and until they were actually dismissed they did not know at what moment they might be ordered to jump overboard to swim clear of a sinking ship and await rescue. Many terror-stricken faces were apparent, but there was not one case of outward fear or cowardice.

"The *Ascanius*, I understand, has been adjudged unfit to negotiate the Red Sea, and is to be put into Aden for repairs." (The *Ascanius* completed the trip with the rest of the convoy.— Compiler.)

Great satisfaction was expressed by the troops when they heard that a mail, which was to be uncensored, would be sent back to Australia from Aden, and all the boys made the most of their time as they had lots of news to send home.

A slow and uninteresting passage was made until Wednesday, November 25. In the early morning land appeared on the starboard and the convoy drew into Aden and anchored in the outer harbour.

Soon the bumboats were all around and a brisk trade was in progress. It is related of "Pinktop" that, as a result of fair trading, buying from the ship's stores and canteen, and reselling, he was in funds to the extent of £35, and with this money he bought up all the oranges from the bumboats and distributed them gratis to the troops.

Soon after arrival, the *Ascanius* went in to the inner harbour to coal. A Court of Inquiry was held on the *Shropshire* collision and the captain of the *Ascanius* was absolved from all blame. This must have been balm to his soul after the dressing-down he got from the Commander of one of the escorting cruisers immediately after the accident.

A carpenter and his staff were sent from the *Hampshire* to temporarily repair the damage before the *Ascanius* resumed her voyage.

On Thursday, November 26, the anchor was weighed at 5 a.m. and the transports set out for Suez. Two submarines were reported to be operating in the Arabian Gulf, and "no lights" was again the order after sunset. Dinner for the officers was finished in darkness.

Next day the escorting cruisers had a busy day intercepting and examining several vessels. One of the ships was full of pilgrims going to Mecca from Egypt. A Dutch steamer was kept from passing through the convoy till next morning. Several more vessels were seen on November 28, as the convoy was now on the line of shipping.

On this date the troops were disappointed to learn that their destination was not England but Egypt, and that their training was going to be continued near Cairo.

This great city was the subject of several lectures and exhortations, so that the troops were early primed with curiosity to see all the strange people and sights that were so carefully brought to their notice.

Before entering the Suez Canal, the troops were warned that there was some danger of marauding Arabs and sniping might be expected. Sentries were posted and every precaution taken against an attack from the eastern bank of the Canal.

When the famous Canal was entered all were on the lookout, but nothing serious occurred during the passage. Battalions of Indian troops were noticed in trenches and other defences on the right bank of the Canal and much cheering and shouting greeted the transports as they passed through.

A rather amusing hoax was perpetrated during the trip through the Suez Canal. Some wag put up a notice calling for applicants for the Royal Air Force. Quite a shower of applications were appended on the list accompanying the notice. The applicants were asked to parade at a certain time and were interviewed by the self same wag above mentioned, who was a full private dressed in borrowed Sam Browne and uniform.

None of the applicants guessed that it was not all it appeared to be, and it caused much amusement to those in the know.

By December 2 most of the fleet of transports had gathered in Port Said, and another never-to-be-forgotten sight was the mass of troopships lying side by side, with the boys hanging on to all points of vantage. Cheers and coo-ees and yells rent the air and young Australia first passed the gate that divides East from West and arrived in the great theatre of the World War.

From Port Said the transports left for Alexandria, in convenient groups, and here the troops began to disembark. The *Ascanius* lay outside the harbour awaiting her turn, and so ended the long voyage and a new phase in the life of the 11th Battalion commenced.

Though most of the 11th Battalion sailed on the *Ascanius*, it will be remembered that "A" and "B" Companies sailed on the *Medic*. This troopship carried 400 horses in addition to the 1,400 troops aboard, so that the conditions were not so pleasant as on board the *Ascanius*.

The story of the voyage is practically identical with that of the rest of the convoy; but at the end of the voyage, owing to the fact of having horses aboard, the ship was kept at sea until December 11, and the troops were not disembarked till December 13.

The *Medic* had held station immediately ahead of the *Ascanius*, up till the time when the *Ascanius* was sent over to take the place of the *Afric* on the run to Aden.

Chapter III

UNDER THE GREAT PYRAMID

FROM THE TIME of embarkation at Fremantle on October 31 until the arrival at Alexandria, the 11th Battalion had been split up in the *Ascanius* and *Medic* and mixed with troops of other units. Under such circumstances, any battalion loses its identity as a separate body of troops and becomes more a part of a ship's complement than a separate entity; and so the story of the preceding five weeks is more the tale of a voyage than the history of a battalion. Previous to this again, the 11th Battalion was merely a unit in training at Blackboy Hill, but now the 11th Battalion takes its place as a unit of the 3rd Brigade, and all its future history is bound up with that of this famous brigade, which at this time had just arrived in Alexandria Harbour and was in process of being disembarked.

Early on the morning of December 5, 1914, the *Ascanius* entered the harbour of Alexandria and tied up at the wharf. The troops were not disembarked that day, but no shore leave was granted. It was too much to expect that Australians, who had been cooped up for five weeks, would stay on board, and it is on record that not 200 men out of the 2,000 on board remained in the ship. They had all cleared off to see the sights of the town.

It can readily be imagined with what pleasure and delight the lads took to the new scenes and people about them. Everything was strange and a good deal was incomprehensible. The cheeky mendicants, with their "Halloa! Ferguson!" or "Hulloa! Mac-Gregor!"; the daylight robbers who asked fifty or a hundred piastres for a trifle, and frequently got twenty or thirty times the value from the unsuspecting soldiers, until they knew better; and the strange sights and sounds in the cafes and shops, all were wonderful to the boys just released from the transports.

But it was still more wonderful to realise that most of the boys got back to their transports and were at roll-call in the morning.

The following extracts are taken from the diary of 2nd Lieut. J. H. Cooke (later killed on Gallipoli):

December 6, 1914: "We awake to find ourselves still in Alexandria Harbour and learn that, during the night, several men had broken ship and enjoyed the night in town.

"We had dinner at 6 p.m. and by 6:30 p.m. we are ready for shore. Whilst all men are getting ready, the baggage and heavy stores are landed and taken to our train waiting on the wharf. The 11th Battalion is soon entrained and . . . We arrive in Cairo station at 1:30 a.m. and then continue until we come to a siding made for the troops. We are soon out of the train and ready to march to our camp at Mena, ten miles from Cairo, at the foot of the Great Pyramid.

"Before marching off, we are all served with hot cocoa and bread and cheese, and then informed that marching will not be necessary as trams have been requisitioned. We arrive at the tram terminus and march a mile to camp, which we find after some trouble, owing to darkness. All ranks drop asleep, and this ends our first day in Egypt."

Before continuing Lieut. Cooke's diary, the sequel to the first day in Egypt must be added.

When the troops arrived at their allotted area at Mena, there were no tents or other shelters, and the tired troops were advised to lie down and sleep just where they were. The boys were assured that it would be quite all right, because "It never rains in Egypt." Normally, and on any other occasion, this sleeping without shelter would have been a sufficiently uncomfortable experience, because out in the desert the nights are often very cold and frosty in December, which is the middle of what winter there is, in Egypt. But this night just had to be different. First a mist came down, which changed into a fine rain—which soon became a heavy shower, completely soaking the resting battalion. As morning approached, the dawn chill found the boys shivering and miserable.

It is said that there had been absolutely no rain in the vicinity for over a year; and of course it is a well-known fact that the rainfall of Cairo is practically nil, the average being only about one inch annually.

Before continuing with the account of the formation of the camp at Mena, the story of a little incident that occurred on the journey up from Alexandria may not be out of place.

11th Battalion troops in front of the "Inscrutable" Sphinx.

The mascot of the 11th Battalion was a kangaroo "joey" that had been smuggled aboard the *Ascanius* against strict orders. It had been kept concealed during the voyage, and so when the first stop was made at a station outside of Alexandria, the "joey" was taken out for an airing on the end of a chain.

The platform was crowded with "Gyppos" busily engaged in chaffering and selling, but when the "joey" appeared and gave two delighted hops along the platform there was an immediate scatter, and only one Egyptian—seemingly one of the better educated sort—remained in his place.

All that could be seen of the others were heads popping up from behind trucks and other cover with eyes sticking out like organ-stops.

"The "Casabianca" who remained came over and asked if the "joey" were a kangaroo. On being answered in the affirmative, he said he had heard of the animal but had not seen one before. He asked if it would bite and, being assured of its harmlessness, he stroked and shook hands with it.

To resume Lieut. Cooke's diary: "Monday, December 7, 1914. Rise again at 7 a.m. During the day busy bringing baggage into the camp. At night men sleep in the open, but officers in tents. An officers' mess hut is being erected by Thomas Cook and Son, and we are badly fed for 3/8 per diem.

"Tuesday, December 8. 'Reveille' at 6:15 a.m. The camp, which is to contain about 30,000 men, begins to grow. Troops from the other ships continue to pour in all day. The Egyptian authorities have been able to issue *two* tents per company. The tents are only sufficient for 12 men each. Straightening camp occupies the men all day."

The 11th Battalion, along with its sister battalions of the 3rd Brigade, was now established at Mena under the shadow of the Great Pyramid. This pyramid, "Cheops" by name, is the largest of the many pyramids in Egypt. It is composed of massive stones, some of incredible size, and an active person could climb from stone to stone and thus reach the small flat top. Cheops was the dominating feature of the landscape, but there were also two other pyramids close by of which not so much is known. Not far off was the famous Sphinx, that huge monument that in those days rose seemingly out of the sand; but even in the very short time since the 11th Battalion was camped so near, an ancient temple had been excavated below the immense front paws and no one can say what other discoveries shall be made there.

It was awe-inspiring for these young Australians to be awakened by the shrill notes of "Reveille" and to see towering above them those ancient monuments of a long-bygone powerful people, and to realise that the red sun had risen and illuminated these mighty edifices for so many thousand years.

The Citadel, Cairo.

No one can look upon the pyramids unmoved; yet it was remarkable how soon the troops became accustomed to these landmarks, surrounded as they were by the bustle and movement of many camps, and the calls of trumpet and bugle sounding out "Warning for parade" or "Come for orders, come for orders" at all hours of the days and night.

The 11th Battalion's first job was to get its camp put in order, so fatigue parties were organised to carry stones from the neighbouring rocky hills in order to mark out the camp sites for the different units.

Leave for Cairo was started on December 10. Twenty per cent. of each company and a third of the officers were allowed leave from 4 p.m. to 10 p.m., and this was made full use of.

With the exception of the pyramids and the Sphinx, which

practically every man visited within the first few hours of his arrival in camp, there was nothing in the desert to attract anyone, and there was an utter lack of any systematised camp amusements for the men, such as are usually associated with any large military camp.

This oversight on the part of the authorities drove all the men into Cairo and Heliopolis and the other suburbs of Cairo to seek amusement, and naturally there was a big rush to the tramcars when the leave hour came round. Cairo was a wonderful place to all the young soldiers, and most of them lost no time in seeing all there was to be seen. The hotels and places of amusements in the better portions of the city were more or less reserved for officers, and this had the effect of driving the men into the native quarters and the less respectable parts of the town. Many of the restaurants and other places of amusement in what was generally termed the Wazir—though the troops had all sorts of ways of spelling it—were pretty sordid.

Still, it was a great experience, and most of the troops emerged from this phase of their life but little the worse; while in many cases the events of these days were a constant theme of amusement and reminiscence in the trying times that followed.

So while the troops were in Egypt, the native quarter was thronged every night from sunset until about 9:30 p.m. and the troops had a great time. It was here that they learned their tags of Arabic, which to this day are occasionally used. All the boys knew "Saida" and "Tala hena" and "Imshi." They called each other "Walads" and referred to the gentler sex as "Bints"; and it was from these days that the word "Buckshee," from the Arabic bakshish, became an integral part of the Australian's vocabulary, signifying "anything given free."

There were a few disturbances, as was inevitable; but on the whole the boys were pretty well behaved. They went to Cairo because there was life, excitement, fun and always a crowd, and there was something elemental in the native quarter that appealed. It was just a part of life and the only recreation that was available for the troops at that time; and it can be left at that.

Up till December 13, most of the time on duty was taken up with getting the camp in order. Tons of stones were carried by the troops, and this began to grow very wearisome. December 13 was a Sunday, and was welcomed as a day of rest.

Divine service was held by brigades and it was a great sight to see brigade upon brigade massed for church parade round the mighty bulk of the pyramids.

On Monday, December 14, training started in earnest. The daily timetable was as follows (from Lieut. Cooke's diary):

Reveille, 6:15 a.m.; lecture to officers and N.C.O.'s, 6:45 to 7:30 a.m.; breakfast, 7:30 a.m.; battalion parade, 8:30 to 12 noon; lunch out in the desert, 12 to 12:30 p.m.; parade, 12:30 to 2:45 p.m.; return to camp, 2:45 p.m.; leave men go at 3 p.m.; tea, 5 p.m.; officers' mess, 6:30 p.m.; lights out, 9:45 p.m.

The battalion found the first few days of training in the desert pretty heavy, although it was winter time and the weather only moderately warm. The loose sand made walking and marching very tiresome.

From Tuesday, December 15, to Friday, December 18, training was continued on the same lines and according to the above programme.

An interesting change was in store for the 11th Battalion on December 18, for on that date King George V assumed the Protectorate over Egypt and the 11th Battalion was detailed for picket duty in case there should be any disturbance among the populace. All ranks were issued with 100 rounds of ball ammunition and all slept in their equipment and "stood to arms" one hour before reveille. There was no trouble of any kind and the battalion was relieved at 10 a.m. on December 19.

The training that the 1st Division was undergoing at this time was very severe and each brigade had a separate area allotted to it on which to train. These areas were about a mile from the camps. The constant marching back and forward, and the continual movement of wagons and transport, soon stirred up the dust so that everything about the camps was covered with a layer of fine sand. In order to counteract this menace, for such it was—seeing that the troops were consuming large quantities of this dust with their food—four large mess huts were erected per battalion and all meals were henceforward served in these shelters.

A big water scheme was under construction for reticulation to the camps and during excavations a jar of gold coins was found. They were soon disposed of.

The natural exuberance of the troops after their long confinement on board ship, and the novelty and distractions of a strange country, were beginning to have their effect on the conduct of the boys, and about this time there was a good deal of indiscipline. Much of this was only excess of spirits and was exemplified by the mad races home from Cairo after a wild night there. In their desire to get into camp in time, the troops used to commandeer all available transport, trams, gharries and taxis and oh! the wild races along the straight road to Mena! The poor gharri-drivers were urged to make their mangy steeds do their utmost and wagers were laid on the results and promises of reward were offered to the winners. Accidents were inevitable, and not a few men were hurt. Sometimes the troops forgot to pay the gharri-drivers and then there were complaints from the authorities. The native vendors of "eggs-a-cook" (boiled eggs) and "oringees! tree fora haff" (oranges, three for half a piastre) were often abused and sometimes their wares taken.

The orange-sellers used to come round with baskets, but soon found that was no good, as the fruit had a mysterious way of disappearing. Afterwards they used to carry the oranges in huge pockets sewn into the folds of their voluminous garments; but that did not help matters much either, for when they became too importunate, as frequently happened, the troops had a way of turning them upside down and all the oranges would cascade from their pockets and roll in all directions, and there was a wild scramble.

But these doings were only high spirits. Conduct of a more serious nature was taking place. Drunkenness, robbery and worse were increasing, and it was found that strong measures would have to be taken to cope with this lawlessness.

As is always the case, it was only a very few men who were responsible for the serious misconduct; but these were sufficient to bring all the Australians into disrepute, so steps were taken to deal with the worst characters.

Mention is made of this because, at that time, many people —and some who ought to have known better—were using the worst incidents to blacken the fair name of Australia, notwithstanding the well-known fact that wherever soldiers of any nationality have been camped for any length of time there have always been cases of crime, because there are all sorts of men in such a huge concourse of troops.

In the case of the Australian Imperial Force (for so the Australians were now designated), the undesirables mentioned above were deemed unfit to serve in the Australian Army and were shipped back to Australia.

It was realised, too, that the men must have some outlet for their superfluous energy, and consequently the General commanding the 1st Australian Division determined to increase the severity of the training, and it is on record that from this time on, during their stay in Egypt, that no troops ever underwent more strenuous training than did the boys of the 1st Australian Division.

During the first week or so after the arrival at Mena, the training had consisted mainly of rifle exercises and ordinary company drill, but as indicated above, the training soon began to be of a more arduous type.

Increased attention was given to smartness of turnout, the various camps and lines were improved, and most battalions had their country's badges well to the fore in some conspicuous place in their lines; and the pyramids, old as they were, saw the black swan for the first time in a rough mosaic of stone in the West Australians' lines.

All this tended to give the men a greater pride in their respective battalions, and from this time the distinctive qualities of each battalion of the 1st Division began to be manifested.

In addition to this, the 3rd Brigade was very fortunate in having a very able and energetic commander and staff.

Colonel Sinclair-MacLagan had an intense pride in his brigade, and he might well have had to command such a splendid body of men. It was his aim to make them as efficient as possible, and his efforts soon bore fruit.

His two staff officers (Major Brand and Captain Ross) had the admiration and respect of all the troops they came into contact with. The Brigade Major (Major Brand) was indefatigable in his efforts for the improvement of the 3rd Brigade, and was here, there and everywhere, and moved about at all hours of the day and night in the pursuance of his duties, often riding a small donkey which was hardly high enough to keep the Major's long legs off the ground. On account of the Major's omniscience and ubiquitousness the troops called him "The Eye of God."

The stories about him are numerous and often amusing, and the following little incident is typical both of the Major and the 11th Battalion:

Corporal "Doug" Gallagher was in charge of the quarter guard, which was liable to be turned out at any time by the Brigade Major. The Corporal was very anxious to have his guard make a good impression, so he treated his men to a bottle of whisky, and as he thought it not unlikely that he would be inspected at some unreasonable hour, he addressed his command thus: "Now, boys, the 'Eye of God' will be comin' round at any time, so I want you to be all ready and spick an' span. See that you have everything shipshape, so that the good Major will have nothin' to grouse about." And suiting the action to the word, he took the empty whisky bottle and shied it far on to the parade ground of the 12th Battalion, which lay just alongside.

About midnight, the boys heard the sentry challenge and then call, "Grand rounds! Guard, turn out!"

The boys turned out very smartly and gave the necessary salute in great style, and as far as could be seen in the faint desert light everything was as it should be; so much so that the Major was very pleased and complimented the Corporal on the smartness of his turnout and added that the guard was a credit to the 11th Battalion. After a few more appreciative remarks, and when Corporal Gallagher was just beginning to think himself some boy, the Major finished by saying: "And, Corporal, next time you have any empty bottles to dispose of, don't throw them into the neighbouring parade ground. See that they are placed in the proper receptacle. Good night, Corporal."

The "Good" Gallagher, as he was called by his mates, nearly forgot to salute. He stared after the retreating Major and his jaw dropped. It was some minutes before he recovered himself.

"Cripes!" he ejaculated. "No wonder they call the bloody man the 'Eye of God.' Just fancy him seein' that bloody bottle!"

Another story of Brand is told by Major Jack O'Neil.

One day "C" Company, of the 11th Battalion, under Captain R. L. Leane, was exercising far out in the desert beyond Tiger's Tooth. Save for the troops, the desert was one vast void. The camp and all that pertained to it seemed miles away over the rolling sandhills.

Suddenly, Jack O'Neil, who was then Company Sergeant-Major, saw a horseman materialise out of the hazy sandhills. He called his Company Commander's attention to the approaching figures.

"Good God!" said Leane. "Does the bloody man come out of the ground?" It was Major Brand!

. The 11th Battalion's first casualty in Egypt occurred when No. 194 Corporal C. R. Johnstone, of "B" Company, died in hospital. He was given a military funeral and buried in Cairo Cemetery.

During the sojourn of the 11th Battalion in Egypt, an interesting photograph was taken of the whole unit, with all the officers and men grouped on the massive stones of the Great Pyramid of Cheops.

Owing to the remarkable clarity of the desert atmosphere, a very distinct picture was obtained and most of the troops are easily recognisable.

December 20 was a Sunday and massed brigade church parades were again held behind the camp. In the afternoon, Colonel MacLagan inspected the lines. Leave was as usual, and some of the troops went to the well-appointed baths at Mena House Hotel.

Christmas Eve saw everyone that could possibly get there in Cairo. The boys were in high spirits among the light and colour of the Egyptian capital. All the places of amusement were thronged.

There were no parades except church parade on Christmas Day. Practically general leave was given. This was the first Christmas that the 11th Battalion spent on service, and the last many of the gallant lads were to enjoy. The city of Cairo was very gay and the Australians were well to the fore in the great crowd of pleasure-seekers of many nationalities.

The first Australian mail that the troops had received since leaving Fremantle was issued on Christmas Day. This was a welcome surprise to the boys, and a nice reminder of the homeland.

On December 31, 1914, Sir George Reid, K.C.M.G., arrived in Egypt from London. He visited Mena Camp in the afternoon in company with Sir John Maxwell, G.O.C. British troops in Egypt. With them were other British officers. They held an inspection of the 1st Australian Division, which was drawn up in the desert outside the camp. Here Sir George Reid delivered an inspiring speech, couched in fine language. These are his words:

"Sir John Maxwell, General Bridges, Officers and Men: I am glad to see you all. Anxious mothers have asked me to watch over you. Alas! it is impossible. We are all glad to see here the Officer Commanding all the forces in Egypt, that distinguished soldier, Sir John Maxwell. I am deeply grateful to General Bridges for the rare compliment he has offered me as the High Commissioner for Australia in London.

The camp at Mena.

"The youngest of these august pyramids was built 2,000 years before the birth of Christ. They have been silent witnesses of many strange events. Can they ever have looked down upon a more unique spectacle than this splendid array of Australian soldiers massed in their defence? Who can look upon these majestic monuments without emotion, without regret. How pathetic, how tremendous, how useless have been these gigantic efforts to preserve the bodily presence of Egyptian kings from the fate to which all mortality is doomed. Dust must return to dust. It is the souls of men's lives and the deeds that live for ever. Imperishable inspirations may spring from nameless graves on land and sea when stately sepulchres are dumb. The homes of our Imperial race are scattered far and wide, but the breed remains the same, as staunch, stalwart and loyal in the east and west and south as in our northern

Motherland. What brings your army here? Why do your tents stretch across this narrow parting of the ways, between worlds old and new? Is it a quest in search of gain, such as led your fathers to the Austral shore? Do you seek to invade and outrage weaker nationalities in a lawless raid of conquest? Thank God! your mission is as pure and noble as any soldiers undertook to rid the world of would-be tyrants. Do remember, in this bright and peaceful clime which tempts so strongly, the awful tasks so near you, the fearful risks you are approaching, the desperate battles long drawn out you have to fight and win. Do not forget Lord Kitchener's warning. Do not forget the distant homes that love you. Remember Australia's good name and unstained honour, which she has given to your keeping in a supreme sense. A few wrong ones can besmirch the fair name of a whole army. The unworthy, if such there be, must be shunned, must be thrust out. Your first and best victories are those of self-control. Hearts of solid oak, nerves of flawless steel come that way. Lord Kitchener will send you to the Front when you are fit. It is you who must get fit and keep fit. Think of the generous rivalries that await you. Think of the glorious soldiers of the British Isles, and the British Empire who long to greet you at the Front. Think of the heroes of Belgium, France, Russia, Servia and Japan. Think of the fleets watching on every sea. If any stains come on your bright new flags they must and will be stains of honour won by valour. Wide and vital as the Allied interests are, there are interests wider and more vital still. The whole world's destinies are at stake. Are the hands of fate to point backward to universal chaos or forward to a lasting peace? Backward, surely it cannot be; true culture crowned with chivalry will prove too strong once more for savage tricks and broken faith. Good luck! May God be with you each and all until we meet again."

On the conclusion of this stirring speech, the 1st Australian Division marched past the High Commissioner and the assembled officers.

On January 1, 1915, an important alteration was made to the establishment of battalions. The old eight-company organisation came to an end, and the new four-company system, in which the normal construction of brigades was by fours, came into vogue. Four sections to a platoon, four platoons to a company and so on made for greater ease of operation.

The 11th Battalion had thus now four companies, which were roughly composed as follows: "A" Company from Perth, "B" from Fremantle and district, "C" from the Goldfields and "D" from country districts. This was by no means a hard and fast allocation, but merely a general indication of the source of origin of the original companies.

As soon as the troops were sufficiently trained in the new company and platoon drill, the battalion was marched off to Tiger's Tooth, a high, rocky escarpment about five miles from camp. In this locality battalion training was carried on. It was a hard and gruelling business, but an experience which was greatly beneficial to the battalion, as it gave the troops the stamina and endurance which were to be so strikingly exemplified in later events.

The 11th Battalion used to march out each morning in full marching order with packs up and with full equipment on. The total weight was about seventy or eighty pounds. The heat at this period of the year was not great, although by mid-day the sun was sufficiently warm in the bare desert; but in spite of that, the conditions were indeed severe, as the troops were put through every possible exercise and combination of exercises.

Of Tiger's Tooth, Captain H. A. Haslam, of the 51st Battalion (but at this time a Sergeant in the 11th Battalion), writes: "We used to start out early in the mornings, take our dinner and march right out into this desert, drill all day and return home about 5 o'clock. There was a big rock a few miles out from our camp, and we used to attack it day and night and always managed to capture it. It was called 'Tiger's Tooth.' I think every soldier in that first contingent had an attack on Tiger's Tooth at some time or other. We used to capture it in the afternoon then sneak out at night and make sure it hadn't escaped." In this humorous way the writer manages to convey the fact that training at this time was very intense.

When the battalions had reached the necessary efficiency, training in brigade manœuvres was adopted. Colonel Sinclair-MacLagan had the 3rd Brigade out on several field days when the work was carried out practically on service conditions. The general procedure was that the troops were engaged in sham fighting all day, camping or entrenching in the desert at night and marching back to camp the following day.

The efficiency of the troops and their fine appearance caused many experienced British officers to express their warm admiration, and some even made the statement that a finer division had never gone to battle. Foremost in the division at that time was the famous "All-Australian Brigade," our own "3rd Brigade," which was outstanding even in that splendid company, and the 11th Battalion held no unworthy place and was, on one occasion, specially detailed to make an exhibition attack on a high position a few miles south of the camp. Numerous important personages, including Generals Maxwell, Staines, Birdwood and Bridges, were present, and the 11th Battalion went through its attack practice in front of these distinguished spectators in such a way as to excite their admiration and applause and in a manner worthy of the most seasoned troops.

So efficient and so well organised was the 3rd Brigade that after the divisional operations at the end of February, 1915, General Bridges chose the 3rd Brigade as the landing or covering force in the projected Dardanelles campaign, although the fact was not known to the troops for some time afterwards.

The men themselves were getting weary of the training, and with the impatience of youth were longing to get to the Front, wherever that was going to be. They felt that they were being left out of things.

But there was always Cairo, and nightly thousands wended their way thither. How many of all these thousands ever paused to look at the great Nile flowing under the Bulac or the Kasr-el-Nil bridges, and to think that Cleopatra and other fair women once had their barges on those star-lit waters; or that Persians, Romans, French, Turks and British all had their battles there and left their influence on the great city they were visiting?

But soldiers live in the present, and for them
"The future is hidden beneath the veil,
The past is still the past."
and it is, perhaps, just as well.

On February 28, 1915, the order was given to the 3rd Brigade to strike camp and pack all gear for an immediate move. What excitement there was, and what conjecture! Everyone was unfeignedly glad to know that they were leaving Mena and the desert where they had lived for about three months.

On the day fixed for striking camp (Sunday, February 28), a strong wind sprang up, which soon became almost a gale and then a fearful sandstorm was in progress. Sand and all kinds of camp refuse were soon blowing everywhere, and no sooner was one set of lines cleaned up than it would be deluged with all the rubbish from other parts of the camp.

The sandstorm was the one thing necessary to make a fitting climax to the sojourn of the 11th Battalion in Egypt. If the boys had begun to be sick and tired of the life at Mena and all its surroundings, the sandstorm absolutely put the finishing touches on. The troops thought they were indeed lucky to be going.

In the cool of the evening the 11th Battalion marched out of camp amid the cheers of the other brigades, who lined the roads on each side of the route.

A last look was taken at the camp and the pyramids and the inscrutable Sphinx that had seen so much of the world's history.

Little did anyone think that from the feet of these ancient monuments the 3rd Brigade was starting out to make an event in history, which not only won the admiration of the whole world but which also helped to forge the links that made the young continent of Australia one of the recognised nations of the modern world.

And down the Mena road into Cairo swung the 11th Battalion, jaunty, confident and very fit, having in a few months emerged from the raw material of Blackboy Hill into the trained and sunburnt soldiers who marched so blithely to meet whatever was in store for them.

The troops entrained at Cairo and detrained at Alexandria on March 1 in bitterly cold and rainy weather.

The 11th Battalion went aboard the s.s. *Suffolk*. On March 2 the *Suffolk* followed the *Devanha*, which was carrying the 12th Battalion, out of harbour and sailed for a destination unknown.

The 3rd Brigade was aboard the vessels *Malda, Ionian Suffolk* and *Devanha*, while the *Nizam* was the horse-boat and carried the battalion transports. Two platoons of "B" Company 11th Battalion were also on board the last-named ship.

As mentioned above, the bulk of the 11th Battalion was aboard the *Suffolk*, and this vessel was to be the home of the Battalion for a considerable time. On this voyage the troops were unescorted.

During the period the 11th Battalion was in Egypt, the Transport Section had been camped at Mena with the battalion. On the departure from Alexandria the transport wagons had been put aboard the *Suffolk*, along with a few officers' chargers, and the remainder of the horses on the *Nizam*.

CHAPTER IV

LEMNOS ISLAND

ON MARCH 2, 1915, the *Suffolk* was heading north over the blue Mediterranean with destination still unknown to the troops; but next day the vessel was reported to be making for the island of Lemnos, one of the British bases in the Mediterranean. Many islands were passed on the way and there was always something interesting to be seen.

On March 5 the *Suffolk* arrived in Mudros Harbour in Lemnos Island. The troops remained on board owing chiefly to the shortage of water on the mainland. At least that was one of the reasons given.

Lemnos is a fairly large island situated in the Aegean Sea. It lies mid-way between Macedonia and Asia Minor, almost on the 40th parallel of Latitude North. The island is just over 100 miles from the Grecian coast and about 60 miles from the Gallipoli Peninsula, and forms one of an immense archipelago famous in ancient story and legend. The inhabitants are mostly Greeks.

The 3rd Brigade was kept at Lemnos for seven weeks.

The long stay at Lemnos was a severe trial to the troops, for not only were they confined to the ship a great deal of the time, but it was a period of waiting in which delay after delay occurred; and having left Egypt with the idea that they were going into something big at last, the troops were naturally disappointed and disgusted at the enforced inaction.

One feature, however, of the time spent there was outstanding, and that was the 11th Battalion's association with the men of the British Navy. It was at Lemnos that the bonds were first forged that linked the Navy forever with the boys of the 11th Battalion who were there, and it was there that a true appreciation and understanding of that wonderful service was first gained.

The harbour of Mudros was a splendid haven, with deep water everywhere. Some of the boys reckoned that it put them in mind of Albany in Western Australia. Every day more troopships arrived until there was a mighty fleet anchored there.

Although no official notification had been issued, there was now a shrewd idea among the troops that they were going to be used to help in the attack on Constantinople, a battle which the British Navy had been engaged in for some time with little or no success.

In the meantime a great fleet was gathering in Mudros Harbour, mostly transports filled with troops, against the day when an attack should be launched against the Turk. There were also battleships of many descriptions in the harbour, from the mighty *Queen Elizabeth* (then the pride of the British Navy) to destroyers and mine-sweepers. These ships were constantly on the move and the whole scene was one of unceasing activity and animation.

The 11th Battalion lay aboard the *Suffolk* for several days, and the native vendors came round in boats selling walnuts and other commodities. The walnuts were sixpence a big hatful to start with, but the price soon stiffened.

On March 6, the 9th Battalion was sent ashore owing to the congestion on board the *Ionian* and the 11th Battalion Transport Section took their horses ashore in order that the animals might be exercised. The rations for the horses were drawn from the *Suffolk*.

After having been confined to the ship for more than a week, the troops were ordered ashore on Monday, March 8. The following account is taken from Lieut. J. M. Aitken's diary:

"The island has good roads, as we saw on Monday when we were landed for a short march to stretch our legs. We passed several villages (they are scattered about promiscuously) and I noted that the houses are all built of stone and that the Greek inhabitants are all very clean; very noticeable are the round stone buildings with windmills attached. They are very numerous and are, I think, presses for the vile wine they make. We spent all day yesterday galloping over the hills. We row ourselves ashore in the ship's boats and, needless to say, extract any amount of fun from the process.

"Rumour says that the Turks and Germans are strongly entrenched on the Dardanelles. . . . French troopships are arriving daily and are bringing Royal Marines and French troops.

Rumour again says that 25,000 French are to come, so evidently the powers that be intend making a determined attack on Turkey."

On Monday, March 15, the 11th Battalion was taken for a route-march. The troops marched for nearly fourteen miles and enjoyed the change from the life on the crowded boat. A high eminence was climbed and the coast of Turkey could be seen far over the blue Agean Sea.

On March 16, a practice disembarkation was to have been staged at 4 a.m., but, to the joy of the troops, rainy and stormy weather caused the exercise to be abandoned. On this date the troops saw a cargo-boat come into the harbour with a gaping hole right on the waterline. She immediately began transhipping cargo, as she had a big list. A battleship also came in pretty well battered about, and it was said that she had lost 30 men.

The weather was frequently very rough about this time, and on March 20 a very strong gale blew all day and the sea was extremely high. Many lifeboats were blown ashore, and about fifty were strewn along the beach, while a large barge was floating upside down alongside the *Suffolk*.

There had been a considerable movement of ships for some time and by Sunday, March 28, most of the transports had left Mudros Harbour, the *Suffolk* and the *Nizam* being two of the few remaining. The men of the 11th Battalion had been working day and night unloading cargo from the ship into one boat on one side, and loading from a boat on the other side. The cargo being loaded contained stores of all kinds, including whisky, cigarettes, jam and "tinned dog." Naturally a few cases of whisky met with bad "accidents" and some of the troops got a "bit under the weather." One man, with too much of a roll on, fell between the two vessels and was nearly jammed between them, but with the luck of the intoxicated he came to no harm save a severe wetting.

While the boys had their fun, they also had their troubles, and toothache was occasionally one of them. One of the lads in "A" Company, by name Jimmy Pettit, was a dentist in civilian life and he used to carry part of his stock-in-trade with him, namely a pair of forceps. He had also constructed a rough kind of dental chair out of three or four empty packing cases.

When any poor sufferer came along, Jimmy would pull out the offending molar. Needless to say he had no anæsthetics, so he had to get four or five big, hefty fellows to hold his patient down.

It is said that the language in this improvised dental hospital was an education in itself.

Orders had been given to practice landings and attacks among the hilly country near the beach. One company of the 11th Battalion was taken ashore daily in small boats and had practices from 8:30 a.m. till 4 p.m. Often the weather was too rough for landing, and then the troops were exercised as much as possible on board the troopship.

Practically the only means of descending to or ascending from the boats that conveyed the troops ashore was by means of rope ladders.

It was remarkable how adept the troops came to be at using these, and soon they were able to ascend or descend with full equipment up. This was a greater feat than it sounds in the telling. All this practice on the rope ladders was to be of the greatest service in the near future.

It was inevitable that, during the long stay at Lemnos, the boys of the 11th Battalion should soon become acquainted with some of the customs and most of the vintages of the island. One very poisonous "gargle" was known by the name of "Koniak," a Greek version of "Cognac" in name only.

One day, Private Read had been ashore and his condition was such that, when he arrived back to the *Suffolk*, the manipulation of the rope ladder was beyond his ability in his hilarious state. So the ship's people lowered a pig net into which he was bundled and promptly slung on board. While he was still in the net, Read became aware of Colonel "Tipperary" Johnston gazing severely at him, but that did not worry "Piggy," as he was ever afterwards called, for he smiled amiably and sang out, "Good day! Tip, old boy!"

"Piggy" had then a pretty rapid journey to the ship's cells.

On March 29 the 11th Battalion went ashore for a three-days' bivouac. Training and route-marching were carried out, and one long march was made to Thermia, famous as its name suggests, for its hot springs.

During the training both afloat and ashore there were often some very amusing incidents. The following one is related by C. S. Maloney:

"One morning, when the troops were doing landing practice, one of "A" Company's boats was trying to get away from the ship's side. The sea was choppy, and the boat got into difficulties and began to drift astern. Captain Dicky Annear was in the middle of the boat, while Lieut. McDonald was in the stern trying to steer.

"The men did not shine as oarsmen, but McDonald must have been the world's worst steersman, because he would persist in turning the tiller the wrong way. Annear kept shouting in exasperated tones, 'Mr. McDonald, I want to go out to sea! I want to go out to sea!' and all the time McDonald would turn the tiller the wrong way and the boat kept bumping into the ship, much to the amusement of the crowd that lined the taffrail.

"In the meantime, the mess-orderlies, who had been left aboard to clean up after breakfast, were tossing the slops overboard, and a most unfortunate accident occurred. Captain Annear's boat had been drifting towards the stern of the *Suffolk*, and as the party got right underneath one of the chutes a mess-orderly let fly a dixie full of slops and the poor Captain collected the lot, all over his hat and his clothes.

"He gazed aloft, and his language was awful and caused the Colonel, who had been watching from the deck, to retire hastily.

"After Captain Annear quietened down a bit, he took off his hat and gazed long and sadly at it. Then he ejaculated, 'Well! I'm b———!'

"Of course the troops above enjoyed the entertainment, and later, in 'Pinktop's' famous nomination list for the 11th Battalion Pack Handicap in the Constantinople Cup, Captain Annear's pedigree was given as 'Slops out of *Suffolk*' in allusion to the above incident."

Brigade training was now being carried out, and on April 1, 1915, 2,000 men were landed on the island. The men remaining on board the transport were engaged in re-assorting and transhipping vehicles, preparatory to the tactical (save the name) landing. There had been a bit of a mix-up with the harness and vehicles, and an attempt was being made to straighten things up. There had been a terrible muddle in loading most of the ships, and several had even to go back to Alexandria to be unloaded and the cargo re-stowed.

Friday, April 2, to Monday, April 5, was Easter time, and on Friday and Sunday church parades were held. There was also training in landing and hill-climbing, and on April 3 the Signal Section of 11th Battalion had practice ashore with men of the Royal Navy.

The gales and accompanying storms at Lemnos sprang up very suddenly. A very severe wind blew on April 5. The seas were so heavy that all training was suspended for the day.

On April 6, a redistribution of the troops of the 3rd Brigade was made, and the *Suffolk* moved with the other vessels carrying the brigade to new berths near Mudros Pier. The detention camp was stripped and the prisoners were put aboard the horse-boat, the *Nizam*. The *Suffolk* moved up alongside the jetty.

Next day the 3rd Brigade Headquarters moved into the s.s. *Malda*, and the re-embarkation of the battalions continued; but the 11th did company training ashore.

About this time it began to be generally understood that an attack was to be made by the 3rd Brigade in the very near future, somewhere on the Gallipoli Peninsula, with the idea of driving the Turks out of their forts so that the Navy could proceed past the Narrows in the endeavour to reach Constantinople; and so all speed was being made with the re-embarkation of the troops and the re-stowing and change-over of vehicles.

As the weather was fine on April 8, the ships were rationed and all horses taken aboard the transports. On this same date the remainder of the 1st Australian Division commenced to arrive at Lemnos.

A diversion was caused by the sight of a ship flying the American flag being escorted into the harbour by two destroyers. This ship was loaded with ammunition for the Turks, and had just been captured.

At 6 p.m. on April 9, the re-embarkation of the 3rd Brigade was completed and landing materials were distributed to all the transports. Maps of the objectives to be attacked were received by the 11th Battalion and the ever-welcome pay was issued. The troops were paid in ten shilling and one pound notes (the famous John Bradburys) and the notes were superscribed in Turkish, presumably so that they could be cashed in Constantinople when and if the troops got there.

The 3rd Brigade transports now moved to the north end of the bay. Several French troopships arrived carrying Souaves and Senegalese soldiers.

On April 10 the weather was too stormy for landing. The troops spent the day on board. The *Osmanieh* arrived from Alexandria with reinforcements, which were distributed to the various units of the 3rd Brigade. The 11th Battalion received four officers—Captains E. Tulloch and Hearder, and Lieuts. Mansfield and C. Gostelow—with sufficient men to bring the battalion up to war strength. These men belonged to the 2nd and 3rd Reinforcements and had left Fremantle on February 22 on the *Itonus*. On the same boat were also reinforcements for the 10th Light Horse, including Eric Throssell (later V.C.). These troops had arrived in Suez on March 17, the men being sent to Abbassia and the officers to Mena, where they underwent training for a few weeks before they joined the 11th Battalion at Lemnos, in time for the big attack.

The allocation of the 11th Battalion on troopships was now as follows: On the *Suffolk*, 32 officers and 970 other ranks, 30 horses, 3 two-wheeled vehicles and 10 four-wheeled vehicles; on the *Malda*, 1 officer and 24 other ranks, 33 horses (12 riding and 21 draught); the whole making a total of 33 officers and 994 other ranks, 63 horses and 13 vehicles.

From April 11 until April 19 the 11th Battalion was specially trained in disembarking and landing, and when the weather was unsuitable physical training was done on board. Towards the end of this period the disembarking and landing were done after nightfall in order to train the troops to descend the ladders in the darkness with all their equipment on, and anyone who has descended a swaying ladder from a tall ship to a small boat can realise just how difficult a task this was.

On the days when it was too rough for this work, it was customary for the officers to give lectures to the troops. On one occasion, Lieut. Mort Reid had finished his lecture and before dismissing his parade he put the usual query, "Now is there any man who would like to ask any questions?" There was a short silence, and the egregious "Pinktop" broke up the party by asking the still unsolved question about barmaids.

The troops had their first view of a hydroplane at this time. Naturally it caused quite a sensation skimming on the sea and then rising as gracefully as a seabird and circling overhead.

The Commanding Officers of the 3rd Brigade received the details of operations for the attack on Gallipoli on April 17, and a first idea of the magnitude of the task ahead was obtained.

On the following day all the fighting units were cleared from Mudros, and the troops were given landing practice from the battleships *Queen* and *London*. During one of these landing operations an incident occurred that well illustrated the wide-awakeness and intimate knowledge of the troops of the 3rd Brigade, possessed by Major Brand, described before as "The Eye of God."

On the occasion in question, the weather was extremely foggy, with visibility extending only a few yards and the shore somewhere ahead. All four battalions of the 3rd Brigade were making for the beach in boats and direction was pretty well lost.

In one of the 10th Battalion boats was a big sergeant-major, who rejoiced in the awful nickname of "Fishguts." As the boats drew near the shore there was some confusion, and a voice shouted, "Where the Hell do we go?" Major Brand, who was on the beach supervising the landing, called out, "Who's there?" as it was impossible to see anything at all. Immediately a voice answered out of the fog, "Fishguts!" Swift as light came the reply from the Brigade Major, "This way, 10th Battalion!"

Everything was now being speeded up for the great adventure. The base kits and the sick, and the base details, were transferred to the s.s. *Osmanieh* for shipment to Alexandria. Colour patches were issued to the brigades—the 3rd Brigade Headquarters colour patch was a rectangle or oblong of saxe-blue, and each of the battalions of that brigade had the lower half of a similarly shaped patch, coloured saxe-blue, while the upper half carried the distinguishing colour of the unit. In the case of the 11th Battalion, the patch was chocolate on top and saxe-blue underneath, so that from this time onward every 11th Battalion officer and man wore on each upper arm, just below the shoulder, a little oblong patch of chocolate and saxe-blue.

These colour patches, so casually received and fixed in position, became in a very short time the most revered symbol of the battalion, and the men of the 11th wore these patches with pride and affection.

Now that it was generally recognised that Constantinople was the goal that was being aimed at, there was a lot of speculation as to what would happen when the troops actually got there.

In the meantime, that famous wag of the 11th Battalion ("Pinktop") put up a bulletin in a conspicuous place on board the *Suffolk*. On this sheet nominations for the Constantinople Cup were shown. The conditions of the race were set forth and the candidates were the officers of the 11th Battalion who were supposed to be carrying full equipment with packs up, and odds were laid on their chances.

Captain Leane was an easy favourite. There were long odds on the Colonel under the name "Tipperary," and Captain Croly's pedigree was given as "Out of Pubs" by "Midnight." There was much hilarity and barracking over the announcement.

Some of the other nominations were as follows:—

Candidate	Rider	Pedigree
Tipperary	Puss-in-Boots	Gold Dust ex Hardwork.
Peck	Kaiser Bill	'11th Battalion ex Artillery.
Roberts	Pink Top	Daylight ex G.P.O.
Brennan (Dr.)	Dyrea	Black Draught ex Sick Parade.
Leane	Mutton	Captain ex Mistake.
Selby	Lamp Post	Leggs ex Duntroon.
Annear	Hannigan	Slops ex Suffolk.
Rockliffe	Hot Stuff	Knowledge ex Education.
Brockman	Nera	The Judge ex Perhaps.
Buttle	Oringis	Popularity ex Discretion.

The pedigrees and riders are, of course, allusions to various incidents in the careers or were peculiarities of the officers mentioned and were well appreciated by the boys on the *Suffolk* at Lemnos.

About a week previously, April 12, to be exact, the Commanding Officers of each battalion in the 3rd Brigade had been taken by warship to the Gallipoli Peninsula to have a look at the coast and to get some indication of the nature of the country to be attacked and to see the objective chosen.

Since then, whenever the weather conditions permitted, the work of preparation had gone ahead, and it was now practically up to schedule. On April 19, the complement of the *Suffolk* was increased by the addition of an engineer party and one company of the 12th Battalion. Naval ratings were also sent aboard to take charge of transport, disembarking and signal work.

Orders were now received that the troops were to cease disembarkation practice.

On April 21, detailed instructions were given to all Battalion Commanders, and the 11th Battalion's special task was made known to officers and men. The landing was to be made at a point called Gaba Tepe, and a letter from General Birdwood was issued and read to all troops, telling them of the nature of their task and exhorting them to pay strict attention to orders, and advising them on a number of details necessary for the complete success of the attack.

There was also a special order by Colonel E. G. Sinclair-MacLagan, dated April 21, 1915, which ran as follows:—

"I had hoped to have been able to see the battalions of my brigade personally and to put these few matters before you. Circumstances have prevented this, so I am asking your Commanding Officer to read you this letter.

"It is necessary that you should understand that we are about to carry out a most difficult operation, viz., 'Landing on an enemy coast in the face of opposition.' Such an operation requires complete harmony of working between the Navy and Army and unhesitating and immediate compliance with all orders and instructions.

"You have been selected by the Divisional Commander as the covering force, a high honour, which we must all do our best to justify. We must be successful at any cost. Whatever footing we get on land must be held on to and improved by pushing on to our objective—the covering position, which we must get to as rapidly as possible, and once obtained must be held at all costs and even to the last man.

"In an operation of this kind there is no going back. We shall be reinforced, as the Navy can land troops, and meantime 'Forward' is the word until on to our position, when 'Hang on' is what we have to do until sufficient troops and guns are landed to enable us to push on.

"We must be careful not to give the enemy a chance of any kind; no smoking or lights or noise from midnight onwards till after daylight. Take every chance of reorganising (under cover, if possible). Attacks must be as rapid as the ground will allow. You will probably have to drop your packs; but carry tools forward as far as you can—it may mean saving many lives later in the day. Until broad daylight the bayonet is your weapon, and when you charge do so in as good a line as possible; one or two pieces of good bayonet work now may stand us all in good stead later on.

"Every man must keep his eyes skinned and help his officers and N.C.O.'s to the utmost by reporting quickly things seen. Look out for your flanks. After taking a charger out, shut the cartridge pocket. Once ashore don't be caught without a charger in the magazine. Look after each cartridge as if it were a ten pound note.

"Good fire orders, direction, control and discipline will make the enemy respect your powers and give us all an easier task in the long run. Wild firing will only encourage the enemy. Keep your food and water very carefully; we don't know when we shall get any more.

"Don't show yourselves over the skyline and give your position away if you can avoid it.

"We must expect to be shelled when in our positions, but remember that is part of this game of war, and we must 'stick it,' no matter what the fire. One thing I want you to remember all through this campaigning work is this, and it is very important: you may get orders to do something which appears in your positions is the wrong thing to do, and perhaps a mad enterprise. Do not cavil at it, but carry it out whole-heartedly and with obsolute faith in your leaders, because we are after all only a very small piece on the board. Some pieces have often to be sacrificed to win the game, and after all it is to win the game that we are here.

"You have a very good reputation that you have built up by yourselves, and now we have a chance of making history for Australia and a name for the 3rd Brigade that will live in history. I have absolute faith in you and believe few, if any, finer brigades have ever been put to the test."

After the inspiring words of the last paragraph were read, the troops were dismissed, and they had leisure time to think upon the advice given them in the few days remaining before the actual attack.

It is necessary here to give a bare outline of the plan of attack and the country to be stormed with the objectives roughly set forth.

As mentioned previously, the British Navy had been attempting to reach Constantinople by forcing the passage of the

Dardanelles. It was rightly considered that the capture of the Turkish capital would be a severe blow to the Central Powers and would correspondingly weaken Germany.

In spite of the weight of guns and well-pressed attacks the Navy was not able to penetrate the Narrows, which divided the Gallipoli Peninsula from the Asiatic shore. (See map.) These narrows were not only guarded by well-placed guns but the waters were extensively mined.

Consequently it was decided to make a land attack, so that possession would be gained of the territory guarding the Narrows, which would then be cleared of obstructions and the Navy be enabled to sail into the Sea of Marmora.

In conjunction with other troops, both British and French, the Australians were to try to effect a landing, and the point selected for the Australian and New Zealand Corps, which was by this time known as the ANZAC Corps, was Gaba Tepe (see map), situated about mid-way between Suvla Bay and Cape Helles, the latter place being situated at the toe of the Gallipoli Peninsula.

There was a good beach at Gaba Tebe suitable for landing, and a certain amount of protection to landed troops by reason of the steep banks and hills close to the beach; but the hills themselves were almost entirely covered with dense scrub and were so steep that they would make a very difficult terrain to attack.

The objectives of the 3rd Brigade (which was now known as the covering force) were on a high ridge or rather a series of ridges running roughly about 2,000 yards from the beach and stretching from Gaba Tepe to Chunuk Bair.

This ridge, to describe it more simply, was much nearer the shore at the Gaba Tepe end, and that point was practically its southern extremity. (See map.)

The covering force was to seize this ridge and hold on while the remainder of the 1st Australian Division and the New Zealand and Australian Division were to advance and seize the high ground at Mal Tepe.

The dispositions of the covering force were as follows: 9th Battalion on the right, 10th Battalion in the centre and the 11th Battalion on the left. The 11th Battalion thus had a much more distant objective than the other battalions. The 12th Battalion was to act as support to the three other battalions.

To cover the landing of the troops, the three warships, the battleships *Majestic* and *Triumph* and the cruiser *Bacchante*, were detailed to shell the Turkish positions, and the 7th Indian Mountain Artillery Brigade was to support the attack.

The attacking waves of the 11th Battalion were organised thus: "A" and "C" Companies, under Major Roberts, were to form the first line companies and "B" and "D" Companies, with the Machine Gun Section and Engineer Demolition Party, were to form the second line.

A special feature about the attack was that rifles were not to be loaded and no shot to be fired until it was daylight.

So much for the objectives and the dispositions of the troops.

In order to land the troops, advantage was to be taken of the darkness and the men were to be landed in small boats which were to be towed close to the shore by steam pinnaces from the battleships and destroyers.

These tows were to be taken as near the beach as possible, and the troops were then to row ashore and make for land as best they could. Once on the beach they were to form up and carry on with the attack.

Before going on to the actual attack, which from the beginning could never have been anything but a forlorn hope, it is only necessary to state that the Turks must have been aware of all the preparations in Egypt and at Lemnos during the past months, so that the element of surprise which is so conducive to the success of any naval or military attack was conspicuous by its absence. Of course the enemy could not know the actual spots intended to be attacked, but as the few beaches practical for a landing were well guarded, it was almost impossible to believe that surprise could play any part in the proposed attack.

It is not intended to dwell here on the incompetence, lack of organising ability and general mal-administration of the staff controlling the whole campaign; nor to lay stress on the undue optimism, to put it mildly, that seemed to blind those who had charge of the plan.

Enough has been written by competent authorities to show that the project was mismanaged from the start, and that by the time the 3rd Brigade was ready to put its fine battalions into the attack it was simply asking the impossible of any troops.

This does not in any way detract from the great achievement which followed, but rather adds to the glory and prestige of a force which nearly accomplished what the British General Staff had long recognised as an impossible feat.

Of all those in immediate charge of the operation, Colonel Sinclair-MacLagan stands out as having a true estimate of the situation. Major-General Brand (then Brigade Major to the 3rd Brigade) states that when the officers of the staff were inspecting the position from the battleship *Queen*, Colonel Sinclair-MacLagan said: "That post is too big for a brigade," and later he again voiced his opinion in no uncertain manner. Dr. Bean says: "MacLagan was deeply impressed with the difficulties; Bridges thought him pessimistic, Birdwood rallied him. To other officers . . . the difficulties did not appear so great." And later when Bridges was saying good-bye to Mac-Lagan before the attack, the former said: "Well, MacLagan, you haven't thanked me yet." And MacLagan replied: "Yes, Sir, I do thank you for the great honour of having this job to do with my brigade. But if we find the Turks holding these ridges in any strength, I honestly don't think you'll ever see the 3rd Brigade again."

So spoke the quiet Scot, who had so ably sized up the situation.

Meanwhile preparations were going ahead fast for the great attack. Originally the first movement of troops was to have commenced on April 21 and the landing to have taken place on April 23, but one of the frequent gales sprang up on April 21 with the result that no small boats could ply in the harbour. All operations were therefore held up, and the move postponed for another 24 hours. Next day conditions were still very bad and the operation again postponed.

On this date (April 23, 1915) Colonel Lyon-Johnston ordered the 11th Battalion to be assembled in the waist of the ship while he took up a position on the top deck.

"Boys," he said, "We have been instructed along with the 9th and 10th Battalions to form the covering party for the Australian landing on the Gallipoli Peninsula. 'A' and 'C' Companies will go from here on H.M.S. *London*, 'B' and 'D' Companies on destroyers and the landing will be effected in the way that we have been lately practising. The position of honour has been assigned to us in being thus chosen as vanguard for one of the most daring enterprises in history."

The troops were silent and excitement held them tense.

"Boys," continued the C.O., "the General informs me that it will take several battleships and destroyers to carry our brigade to Gallipoli; a barge will be sufficient to take us home again!"

The lads appreciated the grim humour.

Cheers and cheers greeted the Colonel's speech and one and all of the 11th Battalion determined to do or die.

A message was then read from Sir Ian Hamilton, G.O.C. Mediterranean Expeditionary Force.

After a stormy day on April 23, the winds moderated towards evening and gradually the normal harbour activity awakened again, and by nightfall the business of transhipping the troops was once more under way. Just before the troops were transhipped, an inspection of the men was held. As Captain Croly was giving his company a look over, he spied Paddy Reid with a golf cap on his head instead of the prescribed headgear. After looking Reid up and down, Croly said: "Everything seems all right, Reid. But where's your golf bag?"

Shortly after noon on April 24, "A" and "C" Companies of the 11th Battalion, under Major Roberts, were transferred by destroyers to the battleship *London*. Five hundred men from the 9th Battalion and an equal number from the 10th Battalion went to the *Queen* and *Prince of Wales*, respectively. The remainder of the 11th Battalion, the second wave, "B" and "D" Companies, with H.Q. and Machine Gun Section, remained on the *Suffolk* and were to be transferred along with the men who were still on the *Nizam* to the destroyers *Usk* ("B" Company) and *Chelmer* ("D" Company).

When all the transhipment was completed and everything was reported ready, the great super dreadnought, *Queen Elizabeth*, led the line of battleships out of Mudros Harbour. What a glorious sight! In front was the mighty dreadnought, the then pride of the British Fleet; cleaving the waters behind were the battleships and cruisers, and astern of these were the little destroyers; while bringing up the rear were the four 3rd Brigade transports and other vessels. As the fleet cleared the harbour the cheering was deafening and to the plaudits of all the other troops—Australians, French and British—the 3rd Brigade set forth on its first entry into the Great War. It was a most impressive sight.

Outside the harbour the fleet divided, the battleships sailing round the north-west of the island of Lemnos, while the destroyers and transports headed straight for the island for Imbros, situated about a dozen miles from the Peninsula of Gallipoli.

The fleets sailed all afternoon and after dark the transports and destroyers were lying off Imbros, while the battleships were further ahead and lying between Imbros and the Peninsula.

11th Battalion troops on H.M.S. "London." Note the caps of the men.

The final preparations were now made and last instructions given. The troops on the crowded warships were advised to take as much rest as they could. The crew of the *London* treated the boys of the 11th Battalion to an issue of rum, and on the destroyers, to which the other companies had now been transferred, hot cocoa was provided by the sailors. A bond of friendship was fast being forged between the Australians and the Bluejackets, which increased in strength as the action proceeded and the sailors' efficiency made for a lasting admiration of the Navy.

While the troops were spending the final hours before the attack on board the battleships and destroyers, some of the men tried to sleep, and some spent the night yarning; while others made use of these few remaining hours to write what was in many cases their last letters home. Some of these letters give a good idea of the splendid stuff the troops were made of. The following extracts from letters of No. 412 Private J. E. Carrington, of the 11th Battalion, show the spirit that was typical of the boys:

"April 14, 1915. I think things are getting pretty close, and by the time you get this I will have had my first taste of fire. . . . I have been storeman for the company up till now, but when I found that the storeman had to stay at the base, well, I worked it, as a base job was no good to me, so they are sending another chap back . . . if I did not go on and have a bit of a scrap I would never be satisfied."

"April 24, 1915. After waiting all these months at last we have made a decided move. . . . I guess that a good many of the 11th Battalion have seen the sun rise for the last time. . . . We have a nice little load to carry with us . . . which weighs eighty pounds, so I guess we have our work cut out without fighting. Things are moving . . . so I must stop. If this should happen to be the last, which I hope not, you can take it as a good-bye letter. We are under steam! Hoo roo!"

With this letter was enclosed a shoulder patch of chocolate and saxe-blue, typifying the sender's pride in his regiment, the 11th Battalion. It is anticipating a little to state that the above was indeed the gallant lad's last farewell.

On the last phase of the voyage to the landing the troops exchanged knives and other mementos with the sailors, and some of the members of the 11th Battalion still treasure these keepsakes. The naval men were very solicitous for the welfare of the troops and did everything to make them comfortable; and later, in their actions and demeanour, showed themselves worthy descendants of those sea-dogs of whom Rudyard Kipling writes:

"We have fed the sea for a thousand years
And she calls us still unfed;
Though there's never a wave of all her waves
But marks our English dead.
We have strawed our best to the weed's unrest,
To the shark and the sheering gull;
If blood be the price of admiralty,
Lord God, we ha' paid in full!"

So, in the care of those men whose "doom and pride" it was to serve the sea, the 11th Battalion rested quietly as they drew nearer and nearer to the scene of the great attack.

Chapter V

THE LANDING

In the very early hours of the morning of April 25, 1915, the line of battleships, containing the first landing party, lay motionless on the calm seas and the destroyers came slowly up in rear. It was a moonlight night, but cloudy, and everything was favourable for the enterprise. The troops were mustered on deck and the tows got ready. With their full equipment on, the men gradually descended the swaying rope ladders and, as the boats alongside were filled with men, they slowly dropped to the rear until there were strings of tows behind each battleship. It was now about 3 a.m. and the moon was almost below the western horizon and the darkness became more intense. The destroyers with their tows now moved forward and passed the motionless battleships with the long strings of tows drawn out behind. The troops detailed for the landing had been orderly and quiet, but underneath all a fierce excitement was burning and a certain amount of strain was necessarily present: the dim shapes of the ships, the shuffle and clank of equipment, and the silent descending of the rope ladders into the dark boats, and the slow dropping back into position when the boat's complement was reached; all these had their effect on the men and when the order to move slowly forward was given and the whole flotilla crept onward in the eery darkness, the tension was so great that anything at all would have been a welcome break.

J. Lawrence Rintoul draws a vivid picture of the scene:

"In the deep of the darkling night,
By the storied Trojan seas,
The boats stole out to fight
On the crag-crowned Chersonese (i.e., Gallipoli).

"For the half-moon waned and sank
As the troopships shoreward drave,
And the young troops, rank on rank,
Gazed dumb at the cliff and the wave."

Just before the dawn, the battleships stopped and the tows were cast off and ordered ahead. The steam pinnaces then took them in charge and surged forward with the tows behind them in long strings. The battleships then moved on again very slowly, and the pinnaces raced for the shore, which could be seen only as a dim unreality in the darkness to the east. (See official map of landings from the battleships of various units of the 3rd Australian Brigade on April 25, 1915, at Ari Burnu, later called Anzac, on page 69.)

The destroyers were next ordered to move forward through the battleships and get as close to the shore as possible. Owing to the darkness and the confusion resulting, the pinnaces lost direction and made for the shore under the high ground at Ari Burnu instead of the flatter beach further south at Gaba Tepe.

By the time the pinnaces were ready to cast off the tows the dark mass of the land loomed up higher and higher and the naval men knew that the landing was going to be made about 1,000 yards too far north. However, it was too late to do anything else, so the rowboats were cast off and the troops started to pull them to the shore.

The 11th Battalion boats all made for the extreme left, to the north of Ari Burnu. As the boats strained for the shore the alarm was raised by the Turks. A challenge, and then a shot rang out; then a patter of bullets hit the water, and the battle was on.

There are several versions of how the alarm was first given to the Turk, but the most generally accepted one is that one of the pinnaces sent up a shoot of flame from its funnel and so attracted the attention of the enemy. Lieut.-Colonel Newman (then Lieutenant in "C" Company) writes of this incident: "After this, the boats were taken in tow by one of the naval pinnaces. All was quiet until we got within 100 yards of the shore, when the pinnace on my immediate left shot up a flame from its funnel which lit up the water for some distance around it; then the fun started, and from the black wall in front of us machine guns and rifles opened fire."

One of the first casualties sustained was in "B" Company on the destroyer *Chelmer*. "Darky," the company cook, was hit as he was standing by the funnel.

As soon as the centre boats, with the 10th Battalion on board, grounded, the troops hopped out and dashed through the water

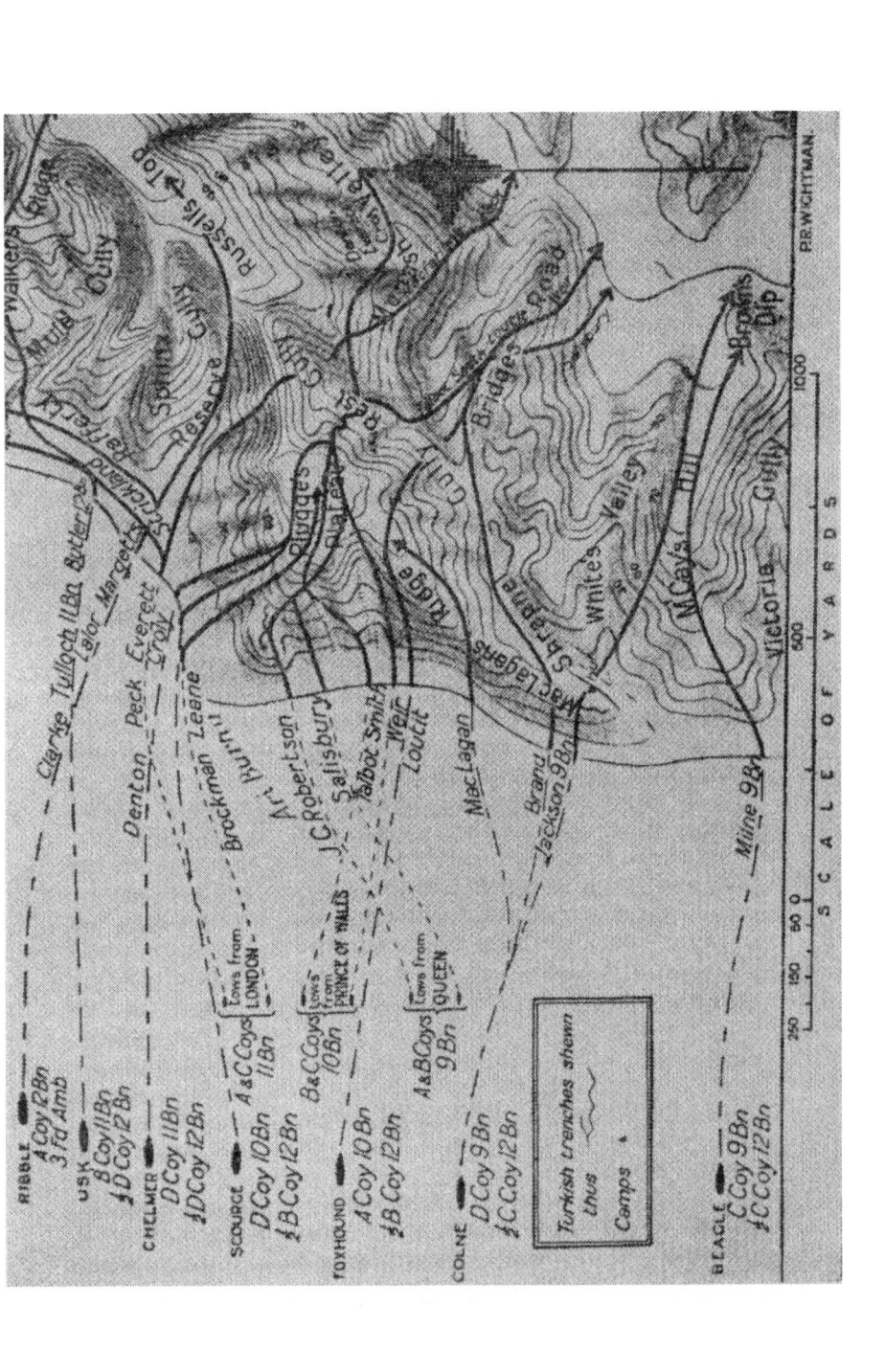

to the beach and took shelter from the storm of fire that was breaking out everywhere from the high ground in front. The 11th Battalion, however, on the left, had to get past the point of Ari Burnu, where the beach receded, and consequently had about 200 yards more to row than the other boat parties. They thus came under heavy fire while still on the water, and many casualties were inflicted before the troops reached the shelter of the land. As the bullets hissed and crackled past, "Combo" Smith said to "Snowy" Howe, and referring to the leaden messengers of death: "Hear the little birds, 'Snow'?" and there was a general laugh.

The conduct of the naval officers and ratings in charge of the tows was splendid, and the 11th Battalion will always remember the coolness and hardihood of the "middies" who had charge of the boats. When an Australian officer would have made some alteration in the navigation on one of the boats, the little "middy" immediately checked him by saying tersely, amid a flying hail of bullets: "I'm in charge of this boat, Sir!"

A little before this, when the first shot rang out from the shore, Captain Croly, sitting in one of the leading boats, immediately said: "That's a Mauser"; but the fusilade that followed drowned all argument on the subject, as the one endeavour was to reach the shelter of the shore.

The boys had the greatest difficulty in getting ashore, loaded as they were with their heavy equipment. Even those in the bows of the boats were in fairly deep water after they sprang out, and any men hopping out at the stern and thus getting totally under water had very little chance of getting ashore, and numbers must have been drowned in the dark and confusion. In some of the later boats the rowers were all shot, and they had to be pushed into the water to enable the rest of the men in the boat to get at the oars; for being packed like sardines, there was no chance of taking the place of the rowers unless this had been done, and the boats were drifting about an easy target for the enemy. If this terrible thing had not been done, not one of the men in these boats would have reached the shore alive.

After the 11th Battalion troops had splashed and scrambled ashore and gained the beach, they formed up below the cliffs. Here the men's packs were slipped, bayonets fixed and magazines loaded, but with the cut-offs closed, as no shots were to be fired before it was light enough to see clearly. Some of the men had fixed bayonets while still in the water.

Owing to the loss of direction and consequent bunching of the tows, troops of all the attacking battalions were somewhat mixed up, but there was no time for hesitation. Calling to their men, Captains Leane and Annear and Lieuts. Selby and McDonald rushed to the steep bank and clambered up, helping themselves by bushes and roots in their endeavour to reach the summit. The Turks were not in great force; but there was a trench about half-way up the first hill, in which a few of the enemy were killed and the remainder fled. After almost superhuman efforts, the men reached the top of the steep hill and the cheers of the 11th Battalion were heard as they reached a Turkish trench there. The Turks were seen fleeing for their lives back inland.

A heavy fire was now directed against the troops, exposed on the brow of the hill, and casualties began to occur. The 11th Battalion party took shelter behind the captured trench and commenced firing.

Lieut. McDonald, of "C" Company, was wounded and then Captain Annear was fatally hit in the head. He was the first Australian officer to be killed in the war. As more troops came to the Australians' assistance the enemy fire was quelled, and so with a great shout of "Come on, the B——— 11th," the boys rose and dashed off in pursuit of the Turks who could be seen running away.

Some of the men of the first wave had by this time reached a small plateau, later known as "Plugges," and were being reorganised by Major Drake-Brockman; but others had gone further north.

The second wave from the destroyers' tows were now landed and in action. They had had a particularly rough time in coming ashore, having been under fire even while with the destroyers. In Lieut. Jackson's boat, six men were hit before landing. When the second wave of the 11th Battalion reached the shore they found Lieut. Peck (the Adjutant) waiting for them under the bank. The party under Peck, Rockliff, Jackson, Everett and McFarlane started off inland about 200 yards north of Ari Burnu, and Peck reached Lieut. Newman with a party of the 11th Battalion, who were holding a small knoll. Peck was wounded here.

The tows from the destroyer *Usk* gained the shore still further north, and Captain Tulloch, with "B" Company, landed there with some of the 12th Battalion under Lieut. Butler. This party was immediately met by heavy fire, but the troops gallantly pressed on inland and drove the Turks back. They clambered up the steep escarpment and reached what was later known as "Russell's Top." The 12th Battalion had been detailed to act as brigade reserve, and so the party under Butler started to dig in on the plateau; but Tulloch, with the 11th men, remembering the instructions to push forward, maintained their advance and pushed on over the 700 Contour and down the steep slope on the far side and penetrated to the inland slope of Battleship Hill (as it came to be called).

While Tulloch and his men were dashing forward, the Brigadier had arrived at Plugges, where Brockman and the bulk of the 11th Battalion were. Colonel Sinclair-MacLagan ordered Brockman to the left towards Baby 700 (one of the main strategical points). While Brockman and Everett were organising in the deep gully below Plugges, preparatory to moving, the Turks commenced firing on the party with shrapnel from Gaba Tepe, and henceforward that ravine was known as "Shrapnel Gully." From this place these troops of the 11th Battalion again started forward on the left.

The above account is the bare tale of the Landing and nowise describes the strenuous and gallant nature of the attack; but the 11th Battalion was famous right through its history for "Deeds, not words," and the official diary of the 11th Battalion describes the above events in a few succinct lines. Here is the extract: "April 25, 1915. 11th Battalion landed under heavy musketry and machine gun fire and stormed the cliffs about 300 feet high. Pushed back the Turks and occupied the position." That is all. There is also a side note, entered probably by Brigade: "Landed 4:30 on beach mile south of Fisherman's Hut, Gallipoli Peninsula." Fisherman's Hut was a rough, stone building on the beach north of Ari Burnu.

Before going on with the development of the attack, a short general description of the 11th Battalion's heavy task may give a better perspective of the action.

When the boys reached the shore, their one desire was to get at grips with the enemy; but everything was against them from the start. They were sodden with seawater and their equipment dragged; they had landed in unknown terrain in a strange country, which rose up stark and steep in front of them. However, they clambered up hand over hand, and helped each other up the worst parts of the steep and precipitous cliffs. Meanwhile, a machine gun was enfilading them and causing many casualties, and the unfortunate wounded and killed rolled down to the beach below.

Gasping and spent, the survivors reached the brow of the ridge, to be confronted with a maze of ridges and valleys—the latter frequently deepening into ravines, with the general tendency of the country to rise higher and higher to the great central ridge. Wherever the enemy were in force they always seemed to have higher ground from which to fire, and the 11th Battalion suffered heavily in the first day's action. The nature of the country quickly disorganised any attempt at recognised formations and the 11th Battalion was quickly split into small groups intermingled with all the other units of the 3rd Brigade.

The general orders had been to press on at all costs (a command that was hardly necessary to Westralian troops), and parties were soon isolated in many of the numerous ravines or on exposed ridges. In spite of all these drawbacks, the attack had been a wonderful success and very gallantly carried out.

Mention was made above of a Turkish machine gun that was enfilading the beach during the actual landing of the troops. This machine gun, which had been firing from the direction of Fisherman's Hut, was causing numerous casualties, so a party under Lieuts. Strickland and C. Gostelow turned north, along the fringe of the coast, and dealt summarily with the machine gun crew. Some of them managed to escape, but there was no more trouble from that direction. This Turkish machine gun had caught the occupants of the northermost boat, of which four men had jumped into the water and remained on the sheltered side of the vessel; the rest of the troops in trying to gain the shore had been killed in a heap just where they landed. After the machine gun had been dislodged, the four men managed to reach the shore.

Among the notable events in the attack by the 11th Battalion was the sight of Captain Croly dashing up the hill waving a Turkish sword or bayonet and crying, "Come on, the bloody 11th!"

There was also Padre John Fahey, who, against orders, came ashore with the boys, and who was indefatiguable in succouring the wounded and helping in any way that he could.

Captain Brennan (the Medical Officer) showed himself one of the bravest and coolest of men while attending the casualties, and he won the undying admiration and respect of all the troops. During the early stages of the battle he had established an aid-post at what later came to be known as "Steele's Post," and when the stretcher-bearers brought the wounded to the slope above him, the injured men were lowered down a sandslide to the A.M.C. men below. They were then attended to and their wounds properly dressed. Captain Brennan collected all the ration bags from the wounded and stored them nearby. He also sent up food and water by any troops that might be returning to the front line. No. 398 L./Sergeant Wright did invaluable work in this post, and by his example kept his team of stretcher-bearers going at high pitch.

Everything possible was done in these advanced regimental aid-posts to facilitate the speedy removal of the casualties, and much credit must be given to all concerned for the heroic way that this was done. The stretcher-bearers' work was beyond all praise. From the aid-posts the wounded were moved to the beach as fast as circumstances would allow. When it was possible, the wounded were made to walk; but all the serious cases had to be carried by the 'bearers over the rough country between the aid-posts and the beach and, of course, the initial carrying to the top of the hill at Steele's Post had to be mostly done by the stretcher-bearers as well. When it is realised that the vast bulk of this work was done under practically incessant shrapnel fire, some realisation of the magnitude of the task will be obtained.

Every single one of the wounded that could possibly be reached was picked up by the battalion or brigade-bearers and expedited to the beach, and it was no fault of these forward-line troops that the wounded were not evacuated immediately. It is on record that the whole system of evacuation of the casualties from the beach was faulty, and it was due to the woefully bad organisation of the G.H.Q. Medical Staff that a great amount of unnecessary pain and suffering was caused to the sick and wounded troops on account of the delay and the inadequate hospital and transport facilities provided.

It would take too long to go into the details of this maladministration, and it is beyond the scope of this story; but it is necessary to show that the deaths and unnecessary suffering caused by this want of "forethought," to put it mildly, can never be attributed to the officers and men of the Medical Staffs (under Colonel Howse) that were with the front line troops. Colonel Howse himself worked like a Trojan to get the beaches cleared of wounded, but the lack of adequate transport and hospital ships hampered his efforts.

To return to the actual attacking troops. Major Brockman was still in command of the forward troops and was directing them from Shrapnel Gully. He ordered Major Denton and Captain Barnes to move along the Gully and to take up positions on the inland side. While he was preparing to lead his own and some of Captain Leane's men to Baby 700, he was relieved by Major S. Roberts, who kept Leane's company with him as a reserve, and Brockman returned to his own company in Rest Gully, where it had been reorganised, along with other details of the battalion and other units.

Here he found Captain Everett and Lieuts. Selby, Rockliff and MacFarlane, who were instructed to work up the valley and round to the high ground. With these troops on the move Lieut. Cooke came with a platoon to the reorganising point, and these troops were also sent up Shrapnel Gully towards Baby 700.

Owing to the wild nature of the country, the troops in all these advancing parties found difficulty in keeping touch, especially under the brisk and deadly rifle and machine gun fire, and often heavy shrapnel shelling, which was directed at them. Soon, therefore, these various parties were broken up into numbers of small groups, all endeavouring to maintain direction and to reach the high ground.

In spite of the difficulties encountered, a number of posts were soon established in the recesses at the head of the ravines leading up from the valleys, but the advance towards Baby 700 was not so successful, as most of the troops directed towards that point were absorbed into the fighting on the right of the valley instead of pushing on and going to the left towards the more important objective.

Lieuts. Morgan and Cooke and after them Major Brockman led their men up the valley and managed to maintain the right direction to the flank and Baby 700. While these parties were advancing, Captain Tulloch, with Captain Lalor, of the 12th Battalion, was already on Baby 700 and his two subalterns, Jackson and Buttle, were in advance of him but more towards the right. These advanced troops met with strong opposition and were driven back on Tulloch, who was then holding a position near what was known as the "Nek."

Tulloch's company and the other troops with him had advanced furthest of all the troops of the 3rd Brigade up to this time, and had reached the inland slopes of Battleship Hill and were some of the few Australians that viewed the real objective of their attack. This was the Narrows, whose blue waters were that day seen for the first and last time. They had advanced with the characteristic dash of West Australian troops and had far outstripped all other parties, even although the going was terrible and in exposed places the enemy fire was intense. At one of the frequent halts, Tulloch was joined by Lieut. Mort Reid and some more of the 11th men.

The West Australians advanced in open order until they came to the brow of the ridge. Here the firing became so intense that the troops had to advance by short rushes, and finally they had to crawl forward in the shelter of the scrub until they were held up by strong parties of the enemy with machine guns.

The conduct of these troops was a credit to the men and to their training, for though they had suffered a number of casualties, their discipline and response to orders were as efficient as if they had been on parade. But isolated as they were, they could not hope to retain this advanced position, especially as they were attracting a great deal of fire by shooting at any targets that presented themselves.

The Turks soon outflanked them on the left, and made a determined attack from that quarter. The 11th Battalion troops were surprised, for they thought that their own supporting bodies were on either side. For some time they hung on. Lieut. Mort Reid was badly wounded and retired to the rear. He was offered assistance by Sergeant George Mason, but reckoned he could make the beach unaided. He was never seen again.

In a short time Tulloch was compelled to withdraw owing to fire from nearly all around. The party withdrew by sections to Baby 700, followed by concentrated rifle and shrapnel fire. By now the fighting had become more general and the troops on Tulloch's right rear, under Captain Lalor, of the 12th Battalion, were engaged and Turkish reinforcements could be seen arriving. The party of the 11th, under Brockman, had arrived at the Nek, where Lalor was, and the battalions were soon mixed up.

This portion of the battlefield soon became one of the crucial points and the Turks made strenuous efforts to drive the invaders back, and succeeded in turning their left flank and were now threatening the rear of the 11th Battalion troops, under Denton, Everett, Croly and Selby.

Colonel MacLagan, who was anxiously watching the battle, realised the danger on the left and sent up reinforcements from the 1st Brigade to assist the troops at the Nek. Once again there was a charge forward over the summit of Baby 700 and the troops drove out the Turks and began to dig in.

By the time these reinforcements had mingled with the men of the 3rd Brigade, all units were so mixed up that it was difficult to follow the doings of any one battalion, and the 11th's story for the rest of this first day might well be the story of any of its sister battalions.

All that day the battle swayed back and forward, the Turks trying to outflank the Australians and New Zealanders, who had by this time arrived on Baby 700.

The following personal account by No. 936 Private D. B. Robinson, of the 11th Battalion, is interesting:

"Captain Tulloch at this time was near the extreme left of the line. Mr. Mort Reid decided we must keep clear of the path, so we inclined to the left where the party again grouped together in the scrub. Owing to the activity of the snipers, it was decided that a man be sent ahead to scout. Mr. Reid ordered me out with Private Gannaway, of the 11th, as a connecting link.

"After advancing some distance in this manner, I came across Captain Lalor of the 12th Battalion (affectionately known as 'Puss-in-Boots,' owing to his small stature and his habit of wearing riding boots) by himself in the scrub, and sent word back to the party to come up. Captain Lalor was under the impression that there was another party just ahead of us that required support. However, we did not see them and rushed fast on ahead with snipers continually potting at us.

"After we had advanced some distance we were held up temporarily by a party of Turks in front, and after dispersing them continued our advance. Eventually we came to open country from which the Narrows could be seen. About a thousand yards ahead of us, on the other side of the valley, we could see a large body of Turks in dark uniforms coming down the opposite ridge with 25-yard rushes. We then lay down and opened fire on them. I was lying next to Mr. Reid with Captain Tulloch towards the left of the line with about half a dozen men on our right. Mr. Reid, with glasses, was coolly directing our fire in the manner in which we had been trained. After firing on the enemy for some time, an order came that we were to entrench. This we commenced to do, alternately filling our magazines and emptying them at the enemy. Casualties were now being sustained, and it was realised that it was futile for such a small body to try and entrench and hold such an open position, as in addition another body of Turks was fighting on our right and it was considered that it would not be long before we would be cut off. Three men on our left were instructed to crawl back to the scrub and retire, then three men on the right. Mr. Reid, at this stage, was badly shot in the thigh, which commenced to swell perceptibly. Word was sent along and it was decided to hang on for a little longer to give him an opportunity to get away, and a man was sent back with him to assist him. This was the last ever seen or heard of Mr. Reid.

"We continued to hang on for a little longer, when the same method of retiring was continued with casualties still occurring, and it became evident to those in the centre that they would be left to play a lone hand; and as if by one impulse, the remainder of us all jumped up and ran back into the scrub. A few of us went back to the extreme left flank, having veered to the right under Turkish shell fire, where we got mixed up with other units, and eventually finished up with the 2nd Battalion and the New Zealanders."

There were fierce attacks from the right, but the gravest danger was always from the left. Time and again the Australians —all battalions mixed up—charged the slopes of Baby 700, but each time were driven back. Lieut. Cooke was never seen again after one of these charges. Lieut. "Jimmy" Morgan was wounded and Captain Lalor of the 12th was killed. A party of the 11th, including "Snowy" Howe, made a rush for a

U-shaped trench on the left of the high ground, but being enfiladed by a machine gun had to take shelter in the arms of the "U." This party was driven out but later attacked again under a New Zealand officer and his company. The officer was killed and the company badly cut up. From this time on the Turkish attack grew more and more determined, and later in the afternoon the tired and weary Australians were driven back and retired on the main Australian position, which had been selected by Colonel MacLagan on the second ridge.

A few men got out of touch and were left behind. Bugler Ashton, of the 11th, was taken prisoner. Howe and others of the 11th, with some New Zealand machine gunners, were the last to retire and held on till nightfall, when they dug in at the end of the Nek and hung on until they found themselves without support, when they again retired on account of being nearly cut off by the Turks. Further back they dug in again and opened fire on the enemy a short distance in front. And so the battle was waged until darkness fell.

Prominence has been given to the action on the left on this eventful day (still April 25), because it chiefly concerned the 11th Battalion; but in the centre, on what was known as the 400 Plateau, the struggle was no less fierce and if anything it was more mixed up than that on the left flank.

The bulk of the 11th Battalion under Brockman, Denton, Everett, Croly, Barnes and Selby had reached McLaurin's Ridge (as it was later named), when Peck (the Adjutant), who had been searching for the 11th Battalion, joined them. Appeals for support were received from the troops in front, a mixed party in charge of Lieut. Loutit, of the 10th. This party contained a number of the 11th Battalion, and was stated by some to have pushed forward further than any other troops on the Australian front, having reached the slopes of the third ridge just under Scrubby Knoll.

Lieuts. Peck and Newman led a party forward to support this advanced line, but this line was already being pushed back by the Turks, and Peck and Newman met the party on a low ridge opposite 400 Plateau. The retiring party was stiffened by the newcomers, but the Turks had a machine gun and subjected the troops to very heavy and accurate fire. Peck was wounded and taken to the rear. For some time the combined party held on, but were driven in again, and withdrew by the gully adjoining their position to the edge of the plateau. Here these troops dug in and formed a screen behind which other troops of the 3rd Brigade dug a line of trenches.

Not long afterwards the Turks advanced in strength, and this screen was driven back on to the defensive line. With this screen were Lieut. Newman and Wally Hallahan, machine gun sergeant of the 11th Battalion. The latter set up his gun in a position near Wire Gully, not far from where Denton, Croly, Everett and the men of the 11th Battalion were dug in on the second ridge, and this became the front line of the sector.

The battle raged all day with varying fortune, and once more the troops were ordered to advance, as the 2nd Brigade was coming in behind. The line advanced across the 400 Plateau and parties of the 2nd Brigade coming up joined in with this line, which soon became split up into little parties consisting of a mixture of all the battalions engaged.

In this last advance the troops bore over to both flanks and consequently a wide gap was left in the centre of the 400 Plateau. This gap was the scene of terrible fighting, but the 11th men were mostly to the north, and the tale of the struggle at Baby 700 and the Nek has already been related. There were still the troops in the posts in the ravines of McLaurin's Hill, whose doings are yet to be recounted.

The posts which had been formed in the early morning at the heads of the various ravines had each placed a screen of men out in front. These men lay on the forward slope of the long ridge between Baby 700 and the 400 Plateau, and this line of men dug in as best it could on the exposed slope; under heavy fire, it is true, but also in a position from which they could command the valley and some of the country beyond. Major Denton, with Selby and Everett, were in what was known later as "Courtney's Post," and Captain Barnes was close to him with Croly and some of "C" Company. Further south at Wire Gully were Rockliff and McFarlane and half of "A" Company. On the right of the 11th was the 10th Battalion.

Soon after the 11th Battalion had been established in these posts, several companies of the 3rd Battalion reinforced them. Up till then Major Brockman had been in charge of this portion of the line, then Major Bennett, of the 3rd Battalion, and later Colonel Owen took command of the mixed troops. The front posts of this line had lain all day on the forward slope of

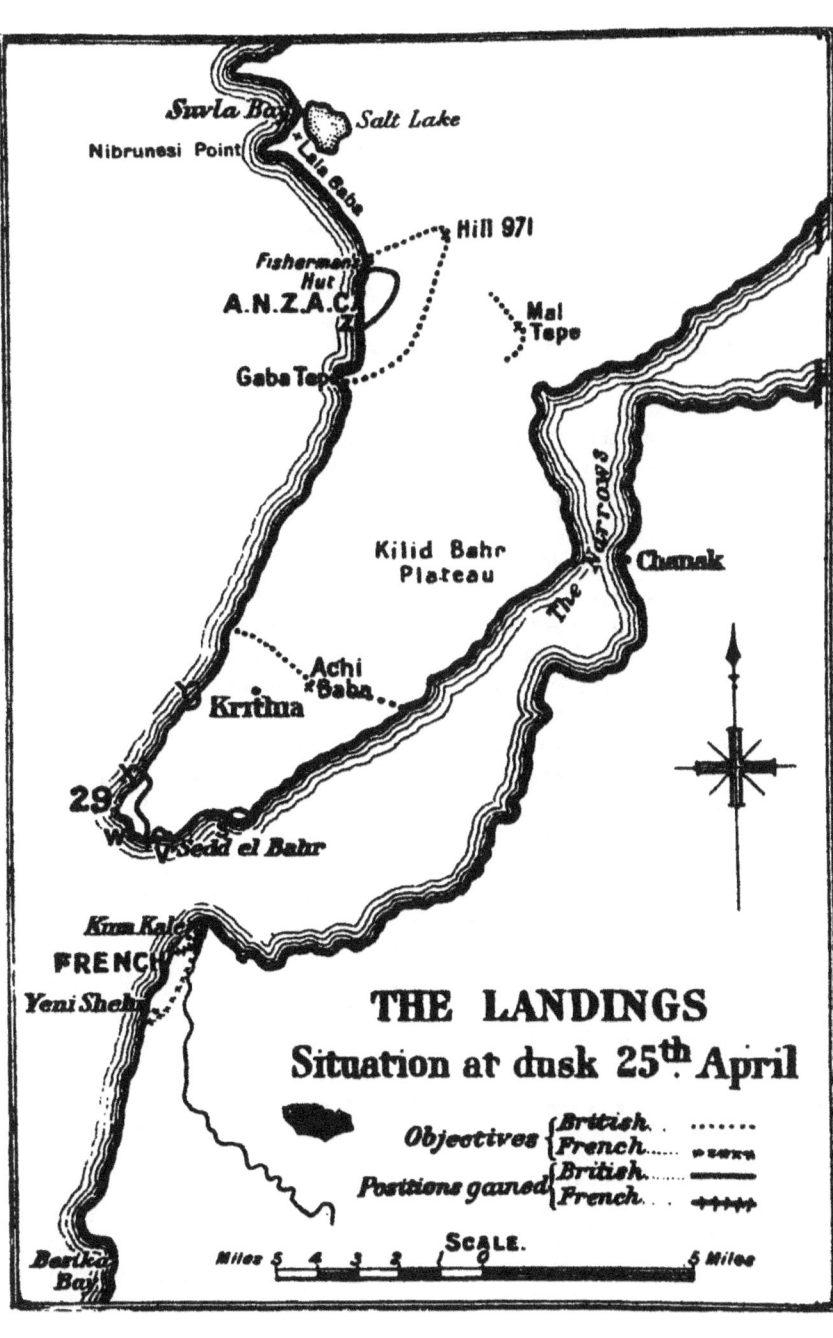

McLaurin's Hill and had suffered many casualties. The troops had dug themselves shallow rifle pits, which were fairly effective against machine gun and rifle fire, but were not much protection against the constant and heavy shrapnel fire that was maintained practically all day. Captain C. Gostelow (then Lieutenant), who lay for two days out on that exposed slope, relates the following: "Lying in rifle pits to dodge the shrapnel, I had alongside me a young Scotsman who, in quiet interludes, produced a volume that he called his 'Bible.' It was a collection of Robbie Burn's works, and the laddie regaled me with 'Robbie' quite often. . . . Whilst here, the machine gun sergeant of one of the battalions of the 3rd Brigade was with us with his Maxim. The muzzle of the machine gun was like a piece of carbon owing to excessive use."

Night was now coming on, bringing with it a certain amount of relief from the intolerable strain of the long day. The troops were now able to move about more freely, for the shellings and rifle fire greatly diminished as the light failed. Things were beginning to be decidedly better when movement was heard on the enemy's side and cries of "Don't shoot! Indian troops!" were heard, and soon large bodies of troops could be seen in front on German Officers' Ridge. The cries were perfectly clear and unmistakable, and the troops withheld their fire. Captain A. E. Croly, who had been in the Indian Army, and who had some acquaintance with Hindustani, went forward with Private Thompson. The latter went forward and interrogated the enemy and on his report was immediately sent back at the double to Major Brockman with the news that the oncomers were Turks; and Captain Croly's voice, famous throughout the 3rd Brigade, was heard shouting: "Shoot the bloody B——'s; they're Turks." Immediately the 11th Battalion opened fire and Sergeant Wally Hallahan got in some deadly work with his machine gun and the attack crumpled.

Word was received later from Colonel MacLagan that there could be no Indian troops on that part of the front.

Darkness had now fallen and with it the danger of Turkish fire was greatly reduced. The men could now move about without undue risk, and were able to strengthen their positions by digging and entrenching. This greatly encouraged the men, and when they heard their own guns beginning to retaliate it gave them a greater degree of confidence to feel that at last they were receiving artillery support.

And so the end of the first day found them tired but firmly planted on that rough enemy country; and all night long the rattle of musketry and the staccato bark of machine guns shattered the darkness; and the myriad flashes blazoned to those watching on land and sea that Australia was writing its first page of war history.

The 11th Battalion official report for the day's events is as follows: "Occupied forward ridge about three-quarters of a mile from beach and entrenched. Owing to disorganisation consequent on landing on different parts of the beach and being mixed up with other units, it was impossible to get the battalion together as the men were engaged in small parties right along the line of trenches. Captain R. W. Annear was killed on the morning of April 25 while storming the cliffs.

During Sunday and Monday trenches were dug under heavy fire from the enemy, but a line of defence was established. Casualties were very heavy, but it was impossible to ascertain the number as the mixed units were fully employed on the defensive works and could not be withdrawn."

It is always interesting to be able to look at both sides of a campaign, for, besides helping to give a more unbiassed view of the whole struggle, there is the added advantage of learning what difficulties both sides were really up against.

The following extracts are from the biography of Mustafa Kemal, the Turkish General who opposed the Australians at Gallipoli, and who by his outstanding personality became President of the new Turkish Republic and later dictator. As a soldier, Mustafa Kemal was one of the greatest military geniuses of our times, and he had the added advantage of being phenomenally lucky. The extracts are from Mr. H. C. Armstrong's "Grey Wolf":

"On Sunday, the 25th April, came the English attack. A soft mist lay over the sea. Out of it slid a great wave of steel ships—battleships, destroyers and transports. One section struck at the north of the peninsula at Bulair. It was a feint, but it deceived von Sanders. Another made to the south. The main attack came at the centre. It consisted of Australians. Its object was to land in the low ground at Gaba Tepe and drive straight across by the valley to Maidos, and then turn and take the range of hills known as the Chunuk Bair, which stood close above Mustafa Kemal's camp and which was one of the keys to the whole position.

"A strong current swept the landing ships too far to the north and the Australians landed in error at Ari Burnu, and finding themselves in the foothills made straight up the steep hills for the crest of the Chunuk Bair.

"Mustafa Kemal knew nothing of this. He had ordered his best regiment, the 57th, to parade at 5:30 a.m. to carry out an ordinary practice manœuvre up one of the slopes of Chunuk Bair. As he was moving up the hillside he saw a line of Turks, skirmishers, coming over the hilltop.

" 'What are you doing?' he shouted.

" 'The English have landed. We are the advanced pickets along the shore. We have been forced to retire.'

" 'Where have they landed?'

" 'At Ari Burnu.'

" 'Fix bayonets and turn about,' he ordered.

"A few minutes later came word from the 9th Division on his right, confirming the news and asking for a battalion to cover their left flank.

"Mustafa Kemal calculated quickly. Von Sanders, he knew, believed that the attack would be at the north end near Bulair. But Chunuk Bair was the real key to the whole position. As more news came in it was clear that a large force was landing in front of him and that Chunuk Bair was their objective. In a flash, and by instinct, he realised that he must save Chunuk Bair, and at once. He could not wait for orders; minutes counted. *Vitesse, vitesse, toujours vitesse* was a maxim of Napoleon's which he often quoted.

" 'Have we blank or ball cartridge?' he asked.

" 'Ball,' replied a staff-major.

" 'Then advance at once and as quickly as possible on to Chunuk Bair.'

"He had only a small-scale map handy. It did not even show Ari Burnu on it. With this in one hand, a compass in the other and a gendarme to guide him, he hurried ahead with 200 men. The ground was steep, covered with boulders and broken into ravines. The men could not keep up with him. When he reached the top there were only a few left. Directly below him, half-way up the last slope not four hundred yards away, he saw the head of the Australian column advancing.

"The regimental commander was some way behind him, urging his men over the rough country. Mustafa Kemal called the most senior near him.

" 'Collect all the men you can, get forward and attack the enemy,' he ordered, pointing.

"As the units of the 57th Regiment arrived, out of wind and exhausted by the climb, he reformed them himself and pushed them forward. A battery of guns arrived. He helped to wheel the first gun into position. Continually under fire, he was a raging madman of energy. On his own responsibility and without orders he called up his second regiment and threw it into the fight. He found that was not enough. He called up the third and last, and threw it in also.

"He had ignored all orders to be cautious. On his own responsibility he had thrown into direct action the whole of the army reserves; not one man remained in reserve. He was convinced that he was facing the main attack. If he was wrong and the main attack was elsewhere, his error would be disastrous. But he made no error. His instinct was right. He did not doubt his instinct.

"All that day the battle surged up and down. The Australians were two-thirds of the way up the mountain. They could get no further. The Turks were rapidly getting worn out; the 57th Regiment was decimated; the two Arab regiments were in confusion and ready to break; but the Australians were worn out, too. Five hundred men on either side would have decided the battle.

"When night fell the ridge was still in the hands of the Turks, and the Australians clinging to the hillside a little below them.

"But Mustafa Kemal did not wait. Placing his headquarters behind an outcrop of stone a few yards behind the crest, all that night and next day he worked feverishly, organising attack after attack to push the Australians back down to the sea before they could establish themselves. As each attack failed he prepared another. He was constantly in the line encouraging the men, personally arranging that they should get rest and hot food, and inspiring them with his driving energy. But though he had stopped the Australians he could not push them back down the hills into the sea.

"The crest-line of the Chunuk Bair was the key to the Dardanelles, and the Dardanelles to Constantinople. If the Dardanelles and Constantinople fell, Turkey would be cut off from Germany and forced to make peace. Greece, Roumania and Bulgaria would probably join the English. The moral effect would be world-wide. The road to Russia would be open and she would get arms and food.

"Between the attacking Australians and these tremendous possibilities was Mustafa Kemal, grey-faced, determined, and holding the tired Turks in position on the narrow crest of the Chunuk Bair by his dominating personality alone.

"Unable to force each other back, the Australians and Turks began to dig themselves in: the Australians determined to hold what they had got until they could push forward; the Turks equally determined to stop them and drive them down back into the sea."

It is clear, from the above unbiassed account of the Australians' attack on the sector of the Gallipoli Peninsula under the immediate command of Mustafa Kemal, that the Australians and New Zealanders almost won through to the Narrows; and it was no fault of the gallant fellows who made the attack, among whom the men of the 11th Battalion were pre-eminent, that their efforts just fell short of success on that first eventful day of the Gallipoli campaign.

After the strenuous efforts of the first day, April 26 found the troops mostly in a fairly deep trench, where they were moderately secure from shrapnel fire; but many of the 11th Battalion still lay in shallow rifle pits on McLaurin's Hill and the casualties continued to mount up. On this date Lieuts. MacFarlane and McDonald were wounded.

The sight of the battleships, in the open water behind the troops, was very heartening to the boys, and when the great *Queen Elizabeth* fired her mighty guns the lads took comfort in the thought that the Turks were getting a bit of their own back. The battleships had continued to fire at recognised targets from the start of the action, and were stated to have dispersed concentrations of enemy troops. The shelling of the Turkish gun positions gave temporary relief, but it could never be said that the naval shells had any real effect in subduing the enemy guns. Nevertheless, the 15-inch guns of the *Queen Elizabeth* were always a source of wonder and admiration to the troops;

the fearful rush of the shells through the air, just like the sound of a very fast train rushing through a railway station, and the tremendous explosion, which hurled dirt and debris in all directions, always seemed to the boys to be the epitome of deadly power.

There were special shrapnel shells made for these guns, with pellets about an inch in diameter, made of iron. The effect of this shrapnel on the Turkish infantry was truly terrible.

The open trenches on McLaurin's Hill were gradually connected by sapping, by which means the men were under cover while consolidating. For the 11th Battalion April 26 passed quietly, but indications were not wanting that the Turks were preparing for a counter offensive. Owing to the wild and broken nature of the country, this could hardly be undertaken except in daylight, and only a few local attacks, which were easily repulsed, were made by the enemy that night.

At daybreak on April 27, movement could be seen all along the Turkish lines. Captain Everett on the forward slope of McLaurin's Hill had a great field of view, and he was able to report a great deal of this movement, which tidings he sent back to Colonel MacLagan.

The Turks shelled the Australian position heavily, then cavalry were seen inland, and later an advance was made by these troops opposite the 11th Battalion. This attack was repulsed by rifle and machine gun fire.

In the afternoon a general attack was made by the enemy, and line after line of Turks could be seen advancing. Opposite the 11th Battalion on McLaurin's Hill a very determined attack was made, but without artillery support, so the troops in the trenches had an open go for some time and soon broke up the attack. When the Turks advanced too closely in some places, the troops rose out of their trenches and charged them; but the enemy never waited for these charges. By evening the whole Turkish attack had failed. All through the night there were rumours and alarms; there were sounds of Turkish trumpets and invocations to Allah; and as the troops expected hourly to be attacked they were on the "qui vive" all night.

When morning broke, however, it was seen that the attack was all over. This, and the fact that the troops were to be relieved that night, made things much more bearable.

The battalion entry for April 28 is as follows: "The engagement has continued without cessation, the enemy showing considerable activity on the left flank. On this afternoon Captain C. A. Barnes was killed. During the evening portions of the battalion were withdrawn from the firing line and assembled at the beach."

On the night of April 28, the Royal Marine Light Infantry moved in and relieved the troops in the line. They were mostly young, boyish-looking troops and seemed untried and inexperienced beside the big West Australians. The relief was carried out satisfactorily and the troops made back to the beach in small parties and were assembled under the cliffs.

Next day the troops were reorganised and parade states taken. The troops were rested, bathed and re-equipped as far as possible. The boys told each other their experiences and marvelled at the rapid transformation that was taking place on the beach.

The official diary for April 30 runs thus: "About 350 of the battalion assembled on the beach to-day and were marched into bivouacs in reserve."

The parade state of the 11th Battalion on April 30 was as follows: Officers, 22; other ranks, 595. Total, 617. And the casualty return was—

	Killed	Wounded	Missing	Total
Officers	2	7	—	9
Other Ranks	32	183	154	369
	34	190	154	378

The total casualties for the brigade were 1,864 all ranks.

The missing list seems great and is not a definite indication, as many of the troops were still in the line or had been evacuated without particulars having been taken of their units. There were very few prisoners lost to the Turks.

The following extract is taken from 1st Divisional Orders, dated April 28, and deals with the Landing: "The G.O.C. wishes to convey his most grateful and deep thanks to all ranks for their magnificent work during the last three days.

"It is an almost unprecedented feat for a landing to be effected on a hostile shore in the face of determined opposition, and the manner in which the covering force carried out its landing and at once advanced against a hostile force through a most difficult and jungle-covered, mountainous country is a feat of which any army might be justly proud."

The foregoing account is the bald story of the Landing and in no way describes the stress and strain of the engagement. In all these three days of the fighting, when the troops, panting and breathless, took what shelter they could—when comrade helped comrade or died for his friends; when feats of unrecorded heroism were everywhere; where stretcher-bearers and fatigue parties carrying ammunition kept on till they dropped; what words could ever adequately describe these things?

All this, too, in one of the most impossible of countries, where communications and connections were broken up almost immediately, so that the whole attack was mostly the efforts of small individual groups, led very often by one of the boys; and these small groups fought and stood by each other often till death claimed them. To quote Lieut. J. M. Aitken's (then Private) diary of Thursday, April 29, 1915: "And here I want to say emphatically that, with the exception of a few isolated examples, we were not led by our officers; the men acted on their own initiative, and by taking the whole affair in their own hands saved a very critical situation."

This is where the true discipline of the Australian troops was outstanding; not on the parade ground, nor in the streets of great cities, but where they came up against the stark and fearful realities of the terrible arena of war. Where other troops looked for the guidance of officers or other leaders, Australian troops were mostly capable of meeting emergencies as they occurred, and thus it was that in the awful disorganisation of the Landing the situation was adequately met; and though men saw their dearest cobbers shattered alongside them, and suffered the agony of being unable to help them, an agony fortunately tempered by the frightful conditions that surrounded them, still they carried on. And of the glorious dead what better epitaph could they have had than the verse of Captain James Spent, A.M.C., 3rd F.A.:

"Bury the body—it has served its ends;
Mark not the spot, but 'On Gallipoli'
Let it be said 'he died.' Oh! Hearts of Friends
If I am worth it, keep my memory."

So far mention has only been made of the storming parties and those battalions that reinforced or relieved them. There were, however, many 11th Battalion men in the beach parties which had the onerous job of landing stores, munitions and performing all the necessary work for the maintenance of the front line troops.

This work was mostly done under fire and many casualties resulted. Some of the beach parties were used to escort the Indian ammunition mules, and they had a wearisome time trudging up and down the hills from the beach and back again. When the guns were landed, the beach parties were used to cut roads up from the shore so that the guns could be man-handled into position. The following is an extract from the diary of Lieut. Peter Snodgrass (then Private), who was wounded while with a beach party: "The whole country is a succession of steep hills and gullies, and travelling is extremely difficult. We cannot go off the paths for fear of mines. An 18-pounder of the 5th Battery was landed to-day (April 25) and man-handled into position on a low part of the first range of hills. We had to cut a road slantwise up the side, but eventually got the gun into position. The stretcher-bearers are working heroically, and though nearly dropping with fatigue, go back for another load as soon as they deposit one at the dressing-station."

Thus the work behind the lines and at the beach went on, and an increasing number of ships kept coming into view with reinforcements and all the gear necessary for the conduct of the offensive.

Chapter VI

GABA TEPE: THE FIRST RAID BY THE A.I.F.

ON MAY 1, 1915, the 11th Battalion, after having had a short rest on the beach for reorganisation purposes, was sent back into the line. The strength was about 450 all ranks. During this period of rest, the troops were surprised to notice the rapidity with which the whole appearance of the beach was being altered. An immense daily transformation was taking place. To quote from Lieut. J. M. Aitken's diary: "On returning to the beach on Tuesday, I was amazed at the spectacle which confronted me: in place of the bare beach we had landed on, men, like ants, were busy in every direction with stacks of stores and ammunition; guns were being rapidly prepared for action; mules and donkeys were being hurried to the front with water and supplies; a wireless station was in full working order; a telephone station, with wires stretching to every part of the firing line; in fact the metamorphosis almost took my breath away and one could not imagine a more thrilling sight than this to realise the power of England's military authorities." Thus it was with great confidence that the 11th Battalion boys went back to the line with the knowledge that such a mighty organisation was behind them.

The Anzac Corps' position had by this time been divided into three sectors: right, centre and left sectors. Each sector had been also subdivided into sub-sectors, and the 11th Battalion was detailed to the centre of the brigade sector. with the 9th and 12th Battalions on either flank. The situation by this time was quiet, and the 11th Battalion spent its time in the line in improving the trenches and patrolling the front.

On May 2 the brigade sector was reduced by about 500 yards so that reliefs could be more frequent, various parties of the battalions being relieved every eighteen hours. Like most reliefs from the trenches, these "spells" meant more work.

The enemy shelling was very accurate and well placed; but as the troops were now in well-made trenches they soon found

Official Photo. Anzac Cove.

Official Photo. Q.M. Stores on the Beach at Anzac.

that shrapnel fire was comparatively harmless against men who were well dug in, and so the shelling that had been something to dread, while the troops were in the open or amongst the scrub, was now treated almost with indifference, and one of the terrors of the first few days of the occupation was now practically banished.

It was noticed, however, that the enemy shelling seemed particularly accurate, and it was considered that the guns were being directed from the point at Gaba Tepe, as it was reported that observers were operating there. Colonel MacLagan therefore drew up a plan of attack on Gaba Tepe with the objects of destroying the observation posts and any trenches and gun emplacements which might be found there.

Gaba Tepe was a promontory about 4,000 yards south of Ari Burnu, where the 11th Battalion had landed on the first morning. It stood well out into the sea and was strongly fortified and belts of wire could be seen running across the face of the hill and down into the sea.

The capture of this stronghold would have greatly improved the general position of the Australian and New Zealand Army Corps. Such being the case, an immediate attack was considered necessary, and it says volumes for the 11th Battalion that it was chosen for the job. Captain R. L. Leane was put in command of the operation. On May 3, 100 volunteers were called for to take part in the raid, and though the troops had barely recovered from the ordeal of the Landing, the response was magnificent. The party selected consisted of two officers and 100 men. They were taken to a bivouac on the beach and the details of the attack explained. The 11th Battalion party was to be assisted by one officer (Lieut. Rumball) and 12 men from the 10th Battalion, who were to be used to cut the wire guarding the enemy position, and there were also details of Engineers and A.M.C.

The story of the attack can best be told in the words of Captain Leane's own report of the operation.

"The force under my command consisted of Lieut. Rockliff, 98 rank and file infantry, four signallers, one officer and ten engineers, one medical officer, one A.M.C. sergeant and five stretcher-bearers.

"We bivouaced on the beach on the night May 3.

"At 3:30 a.m., on May 4, we were embarked on boats and taken out to the destroyer *Chelmer* and towed to Gaba Tepe.

"We disembarked at 4:35 a.m. The enemy held their fire until we started to disembark about 40 yards from the beach. Then they started to pour in heavy rifle fire. We rushed to the beach and took shelter under a sandy cliff about 12 feet high, which runs along the beach.

"During the landing I lost one officer, i.e., Mr. Rockliff, wounded, four men killed and 18 wounded.

"Lieut. Rockliff and about 12 men returned wounded in the boats that disembarked us. I afterwards signalled the destroyer to send off a boat for six men wounded I had ashore.

"This was done, and the enemy refrained from firing on the wounded while being embarked. It was not until they were in tow of the pinnace that the firing started.

"From my observation I decided that the position was too strongly held to attempt storming. Rows of barb wire, 3ft. 6in. high, ran all over the hill in front of their trenches. I observed from my position three machine guns and one pom-pom.

"I estimate the trenches were held by at least 150 men.

"At about 5:30 a.m., I decided to return. This I endeavoured to do by successive retirement along the beach. This I found to be impossible on account of the heavy fire that could be brought to bear.

"I therefore signalled the destoyers, asking them to send boats, at the same time pointing out the gun positions and asking them to bring a heavy fire to bear while we embarked. This was done. I lost three wounded in embarking.

"Of the men sent round the beach, two were killed. I beg to bring to notice the very brilliant way Captain Brennan carried out his duties under fire.

"(Signed) R. L. Leane, Captain."

Such is the brief account by an officer who rose to be one of the most distinguished fighting officers in the A.I.F.

In this action there were five killed and twenty wounded. Among the killed was L./Sergeant Thompson, who had only that day been promoted 2nd lieutenant, but he died unaware of the fact. During the retirement, Captain Leane was himself wounded in the hand and Sergeant McCleery was badly wounded by the pom-pom.

Of the party that was ordered to retire round by the beach, four of the lads managed to get back to Captain Leane, two were killed and four dashed round the end of the wire where it entered the sea, and these men splashed and floundered past the obstruction and three of them made the journey.

One of the men was pinned to his cover by machine gun fire (some accounts say two men, Privates Gee and O'Neil), and later rescued by a boat from the destroyer.

One of the men who ran the gauntlet round the beach was Private F. S. Goundrey (later Lieutenant). He stated that he never ran so fast in his life: the bullets were whipping up tne sand and splashing in the water all around. He was of the opinion that he must have broken all existing records for speed in his mad dash for safety, and he might well have done so.

Two of the outstanding features of this raid, if any of its features can be considered pre-eminent, were the holding of fire by the Turks while the wounded were being withdrawn to the boats, a chivalry that many Christian troops would not have observed and which immediately characterised these Moslem soldiers as clean and gallant fighters, a reputation that they worthily upheld during the whole campaign; the other incident was the exceptionally fine work of Captain "Doc" Brennan and the stretcher-bearers. Many of the boys have since stated that if any man ever deserved a Victoria Cross it was "Doc" Brennan on this occasion.

The co-operation of the Navy was also splendid, for without it and the cool judgment of Leane the attack would not only have been a failure, glorious as it was, but it would have meant that practically the whole party would have been wiped out.

Having given the official report by the officer commanding the party, it may be of interest to read the account of one of the men who was under the command of that officer. The following is from the diary of Lieut. J. M. Aitken:

"Wednesday, May 5. On Monday night we were told that an important and dangerous piece of work was to be done, for which 100 volunteers were required. Of course we all offered, and found that a fort, Gaba Tepe, on a promontory to the right had to be taken and demolished if possible. It was thought that this was used by the Turks as an observation station, and assuredly they could see all our beach operations from there;

also by some means their gun fire was being very accurately directed, so to have taken it would have meant a lot to us.

"We boarded small boats early on Tuesday morning, a destroyer took us nearly to our landing place, and then we rowed into the beach. It was Sunday (the day of the Landing) all over again, but worse. They were ready and commenced

The beach at Gaba Tepe, where 100 men of 11th Battalion made first raid in the history of the A.I.F.

firing before our boats grounded; we got out, rushed up the beach, taking cover under an overhanging wall, but got no further. There were wire entanglements everywhere and it was quite impossible to go on, so we took what shelter was possible and just waited. The Turks exploded two land mines, luckily doing no damage, but we were certainly in a very tight corner: we couldn't go forward and to venture on the open beach meant almost certain death, for they had machine guns which swept in from both land and seaward flanks of the promontory.

"It was finally decided that three gun boats and the *Bacchante* should commence a continuous fire on the fort, and under its cover we were to rush to a number of boats they were sending in and so escape. Although we were almost stunned and deafened by the proximity of the bursting shells, the smoke cloud they provided proved our salvation and we got away with about 30 casualties, but failed in our object.

"A number of men tried to run the gauntlet round the beach; a few did succeed, but the machine gun took its toll.

"I understand this was to have been our original landing place. All I can say is, that if it was so, it was indeed a providential mistake that landed us where we did."

(Compiler's note.—The intended landing place was well to the north of this wired beach.)

This raiding party which took part in the first organised raid in the history of the A.I.F. was then returned to Anzac Beach by the destroyer. It will be noted that the Australian and New Zealand Forces were already known by that combination of initials, and the name was retained by the Australians right to the end of the war.

Later in the day the destroyer returned and sent a boat ashore to pick up Privates Gee and O'Neil, who had been cut off from the rest of the party that ran round the beach.

The Gaba Tepe raid has often been referred to as "The Second Landing." The boys were not long in finding a nickname for the promontory, which also referred to the unsuccessful raid. They called it the "Gaby Glide," after a popular dance by a famous dancer of that period.

The 11th Battalion was relieved on the night of May 4, and went into reserve.

May 5, 1915. The names of the following officers and other ranks were submitted to Headquarters for recognition of special services: Captain R. L. Leane, Captain E. T. Brennan, Captain R. Everett, Lieut. A. H. Darnell, Lieut. A. R. Selby, Sergeant G. Mason, Sergeant Pugsley, Sergeant Ayling, Sergeant J. M. McCleery, Sergeant Horswell, Corporal W. Pride, Corporal A. Skuse, Private J. F. Wilson, Private F. R. M'Jannet and Private G. Smith.

The total casualties to date were: Killed, 38; wounded, 200; missing, 197. Total, 435.

The strength of the battalion was 24 officers and 742 other ranks and the brigade total was 2,825.

The brigade front was extended 500 yards northward and the 11th Battalion was ordered into the new sub-section.

On May 6, the 11th Battalion was engaged in burying Turkish dead opposite its position. A party was led by Captain Leane into the open, during the daylight, in full view of the Turks. This party was unarmed, and though observed by the enemy was not interfered with in its task of burying the dead. There were several disused trenches handy and the bodies were placed in these, a double purpose being served, namely, the disposal of the bodies and the filling up and rendering useless to the enemy of these portions of the trenches.

When these trenches were reported to headquarters, it was determined to make use of them to improve the position in front of the line and steps were immediately taken to capture them and link them up with the battalion's position and thus cut out a re-entrant south of the Pimple, a small conical rise in the 11th Battalion sector.

Major Brockman was ordered to have a redoubt established there on the night of May 7, and Captain Bage, of the Royal Australian Engineers, was ordered by General Bridges to make the preliminary survey. At 3 p.m., a party under Major Brockman, Captain Bage and Lieut. Selby, consisting of eight men of the 11th Battalion and two sappers, pushed out over the gully in front—Allah Gully—and reached the top of Silt Spur.

Selby had instructions to cover the work of the engineers. Just as Bage had fixed the line of the proposed redoubt, the Turks opened fire with machine guns. Bage was killed and Selby wounded and several men were also wounded. The party retired to their trenches and later, under cover of darkness, L./Corporal Joyce, of the 11th Battalion, went out and recovered the body of Captain Bage.

It was then realised that there was no speedy method of advancing the line and that the tedious business of sapping and tunnelling was in the end more efficacious and less likely to result in needless casualties, and so a sap was begun which ultimately reached the abandoned trenches.

The general situation was becoming daily quieter and the trenches were being continually improved and saps were driven to connect the various posts.

Sniping continued steadily from Sniper's Ridge and other points of vantage on the Turkish side, but with ordinary care casualties could be kept down to a minimum. Poor old "Pinktop" was killed early in the action through bobbing up and down in the trench, trying to get a look at what was going on. Unfortunately, he bobbed up once too often.

A number of reinforcements arrived for the battalion on May 8 and 9. In the line the shelling had been heavy, but there had been few casualties. The troops had a quiet time except for the necessary work.

The casualty report up to May 8 read: Killed, 45; wounded, 220; missing, 188. Total, 453. As before mentioned, it was extremely difficult to get an exact casualty return in the initial stages of the Anzac campaign, and the total of missing was still largely made up of men who had been evacuated without particulars having been sent to battalion headquarters. But even so, it will be noted that already half of the effective strength of the battalion had been put out of action.

On May 9, the following other ranks were promoted: To 2nd Lieutenant: Sergeant Parry, H. L., Sergeant Dunning, J. D. L./Sergeant Thompson, A. W. B. L. (since killed in action), Private Smith, G. H., vice Thompson (killed).

The following names were forwarded for recognition of special services since the Landing: Major S. R. Roberts, Major A. E. Drake-Brockman, Captain C. A. Barnes (killed), Captain J. H. Peck, Captain A. S. Croly, Lieut. W. H. Rockliff, Lieut. S. A. Jackson and No. 398 L./Sergeant W. Wright.

On the night of May 9/10, a party of the 11th Battalion moved out to the crest of Spur 400. As the men scrambled through the scrub, the noise attracted the attention of the enemy, and immediately heavy fire was met with and the party withdrew.

While in this sector the battalion was doing 24-hour shifts. During their tour in the line the men did one hour on sentry and one hour off duty alternately.. In support the men were generally working, and the periods spent on fatigues were generally very arduous, but the 24 hours spent in reserve was a welcome relief, especially at this time, as the Turk was very quiet.

The weather since the date of the Landing had been perfect, although the nights had been chilly, and so far the men had not been issued with blankets. The men were informed that an issue would be made at an early date, and almost immediately they were served out to the troops. It was fortunate that this issue arrived when it did, for on May 12 rain commenced to fall and, as in all congested areas, conditions soon became miserable. Soon the boys had a faint idea what the soldiers were suffering in France, but their own miseries claimed all their attention, though at least they now had their blankets.

As the trenches were improved and deepened, it was found that more periscopes were required for the troops, as it was now too dangerous to try to observe over the parapet on account of the accuracy of the Turkish snipers. These periscopes were gradually made available as they were procured.

On May 13, a message was received by the Corps Commander from the High Commissioner for Australia in London, commenting on the landing of the Australians in Gallipoli. "Details published to-day. All grieve for the heroic dead and wounded, and glory in the splendid valour and achievements of officers and men."

An officers' patrol was sent out from the 11th Battalion lines on the night of May 14. This patrol reported that posts 200 yards and 400 yards ahead of the line were clear of the enemy. Orders were given to the front line troops not to undercut the parapets of the trenches too much, as there was considerable danger of the trenches falling in. Also the troops were ordered to return all empty biscuit tins to the beach, as containers for water were scarce.

The 11th Battalion had taken over the trenches to the extreme left of the brigade sector, on Bolton's Ridge, and since their occupation of the sector the men had steadily improved the trenches. Naturally the amount of earth thrown out had attracted the attention of the enemy, and continual rifle fire and sniping had been kept up by the Turks but no organised attack had up to that time taken place. A considerable amount of enemy movement was noticed. This was reported and the fire of the battleships was directed on to the ridge ahead. Owing to the very flat trajectory of the naval shells, little material damage was done, although the moral effect was tremendous.

On May 15, 250 reinforcements arrived. This brought the strength of the 11th Battalion up to 23 officers and 723 other ranks. On this same date (May 15, 1915) the 1st Australian Division was unfortunate in losing the services of its Commander. Major-General Bridges had been on his way to the front lines when he was very badly wounded. He was immediately evacuated to the hospital ship *Gascon*, but the wound was mortal and he died before the ship reached Alexandria.

Divine service was held by the 3rd Brigade on Sunday, May 16. This was the first church parade by the brigade on Gallipoli, and all battalions attended.

As an indication of how artillery support was being gradually brought to the aid of the line troops, the official report also states that a fatigue party from the 11th Battalion was detailed to help emplace a six-inch howitzer in a position behind their line.

Enemy movement had been reported frequently in front of the sector, and his shelling became much heavier on May 17. The whole position was bombarded continuously. The fact that the 11th and 12th Battalions were sapping out to the ridge in front may have been the cause of the renewed activity on the part of the enemy, especially as there was always a screen out in front of the working parties, and this regular movement of troops must have been noticed. Whatever the cause, the Turkish shelling continued to be intense, and movement behind the enemy lines was reported by aeroplane. This message stated that Turkish columns were moving up.

The troops in the line were kept on the alert on the night of May 17/18. There were several warnings that the Turks were going to attack, and the boys were standing-to all night. At 3:30 in the morning the Turkish attack developed in earnest. Shouting and singing and the blowing of bugles could be heard and lastly the cries of "Allah-il-Allah! Allah Akbar!" warned the troops that "Jacko" was coming. The boys of the 11th Battalion were ready and they had a good position. To quote from the diary of Lieut. J. M. Aitken: "We had three alarms last night, and about 4 a.m. they attacked in great force. It was pitiful to see it all; the Turks kept coming on and on, numbers of them together, and our orders were to allow them to come quiet close before opening fire; they were simply mown down, and yet in spite of the terrible slaughter they still kept coming up until quite exhausted. I'm perfectly satisfied *now* that the Turk is a fanatic. From our sap trench we enfiladed them, and from our firing line we caught them head on. Numbers who escaped the early firing by hiding in the bushes are now making frantic efforts to get back to their own lines, abandoning rifles and equipment in the effort, and are being shot just like rabbits, scarcely one being successful in escaping. Wounded and dead lie in all directions.

"For a time it was a veritable inferno: Our guns, their guns, and those of the battleships, were snarling and hurling death; the spiteful spit of the bullets was everywhere and the sky was obscured with acrid shrapnel smoke; and we could not hear a spoken word. The 11th platoon (the diarist's) was in support, but do you think they could keep us out? We got up to all sorts of dodges to get in and into all sorts of positions to have a shot. I forgot to take cover. I'll admit a certain savage pleasure in firing to kill."

Lieutenant Aitken (then a private) goes on to say that, although they tried to locate the Turkish gun positions they could not see the flashes of the Turkish guns as they had hoped to; so they could not get any counter battery work on to them. The Turkish guns must have been well masked.

Another interesting version of this attack is told by Captain Charlie Gostelow. "About midnight on May 18/19, the Turk buglers raised Cain. Ever so many British calls were sounded by them. Then he came over shouting "Allah! Allah!" and he got it (not Allah) from the whole line. The attack was a failure and broke. He came on again at about 4 a.m. The Turks were driven by their officers, not led. Had they been led nothing could have hindered them from breaking our line. Jack Long and I held a sap-head, with another man loading for us at the bottom of the trench. The field of fire was not more than 25 yards. The Turks assembled in a gully and advanced on us in droves. We worked bolts with thumb and first finger, using the second finger on the trigger and keeping the rifles at the shoulder. It was straight-out slaughter, but we had to keep them out.

"During the stunt, Wally Hallahan had his machine gun along in the 1st Brigade sector and he did some deadly work (I went along afterwards and saw the results). Some of the New South Welshmen told me that Wally was like a man possessed when he found his target—massing Turks debouching from a trench into a slight depression, directly under Wally's observation. Wally, they said, was praying aloud, calling on God to keep his gun from jamming and to keep it in action. Wally, as usual, was very modest about it all."

On this occasion the whole Turkish attack was completely beaten off and hundreds of enemy dead lay in front of the 11th Battalion's position. The Turks were so demoralised that they made no further attack that day, although a fresh concentration of troops was seen behind the Turkish lines and enemy artillery was very busy on the back areas and the beach, and the Turkish aeroplanes were overhead in the afternoon.

The 11th Battalion official report of the action is as follows: "At 3:30 on the morning on May 19, the enemy made an attack on the left of the defensive line, gradually developing until the whole of the line was engaged. The enemy were in large numbers and the engagement continued without interruption for about ten hours. The enemy were repulsed at all points with heavy losses; our casualties were nine killed and eight wounded. Most of the casualties were caused by shrapnel fire. One officer and five Turkish privates surrendered. This morning one wounded Turk was brought in from the front of the trench.

"The enemy opened a heavy bombardment on our position in the course of which some damage was done to the trenches. Two men were killed by shrapnel."

The numbers of Turkish dead and wounded lying in front of the Australian position evoked feelings of pity in the breasts of the 11th Battalion, and as often happened after an engagement, any prisoners or wounded foemen falling into the hands of the boys were treated as friends and helped as much as possible. The wounded lying in between the lines were indeed pitiable sights, and the following verse expressed the feelings of many:

ABDUL

"Yes, we've seen him dying there in front—
Our own boys died there, too.
With his poor dark eyes a-rolling
Staring at the hopeless blue.
With his poor maimed arms a-stretching
To the God we both can name—
And it fairly tore our hearts out,
But it's in the beastly game."

On May 20 an incident that was not in accordance with the usual behaviour of the Turks was reported. At about 3 p.m. the 11th Battalion observers noticed numbers of Turks advancing under red crescents, seemingly for the purpose of burying their dead. These movements soon became very suspicious, as armed parties were seen behind the burial parties.

The troops were at a loss what to do, but this state of affairs did not last long, for a desultory fire broke out from both sides at different points along the line and the burial parties were recalled.

The enemy then shelled the 9th, 11th and 12th Battalions, and made a half-hearted attack which died away without achieving anything but a few more casualties for the Turks.

On May 21, some of the 11th Battalion were initiated into the mysteries of the new Japanese bomb mortar. The bombs hitherto issued—the old jam-tin bombs—were poor affairs and the Jap. bomb was looked upon as a great improvement.

A heavy thunderstorm broke over the Anzac position on May 22 and deluged the trenches. In the evening, at 10:30 p.m., a patrol was sent out to Turkey Knoll to see if it were occupied. The official account states: "A party of four officers and 160 men, Captain Everett in command, went out in front of the trenches to investigate the enemy's position on Turkey Knoll. They found only a few snipers on the Knoll but no guns, the position having been practically vacated by the enemy. Just as the search concluded, the enemy opened a heavy rifle and machine gun fire from a ridge about 300 yards distant, in an easterly direction from our trenches, which caused our party to return. We lost one man (killed)."

In Lieut. Aitken's diary, it states that a few Turks were driven from the trenches at Turkey Knoll, and these ran into their own machine gun fire, others being bayoneted by the 11th party. He also mentioned that the trench was full of dead Turks. (Lieut. Aitken was in this patrol.)

Since the Turkish attack, parties had been sent out at nights to collect the rifles and equipment of the enemy dead lying in No Man's Land. About 200 rifles were brought in on the brigade sector on May 22.

A permanent guard of one officer and 25 men was chosen from the 11th Battalion to be the personal guard of Sir Ian Hamilton, the General Officer Commanding the Mediterranean Expeditionary Force. Lieut. S. H. Jackson was appointed to command this guard and a proportion of men was drawn from each company.

A further 150 rifles were collected on the night of May 23, and next day was famous as the day of the truce. Arrangements were made with the Turkish Headquarters for a formal truce of nine hours on May 24 to commence at 7.30 a.m. A line was fixed mid-way between the two front line systems, and the Turks were to bury the dead on their side of the line and the Australians on theirs. Needless to say, it was not long before the two armies were fraternising and exchanging souvenirs. There were hundreds of Turks to bury and a few Australians.

It was a great experience and also a great relief to the troops to be able to move about in the area of danger and death without being in constant terror of their lives, even if only for a few short hours. The brief armistice was appreciated by all.

Next day, about 12 noon, all the troops were horrified to see the great battleship *Triumph* heel over from a heavy explosion. She had been torpedoed by a German submarine and sank in about 20 minutes. It was a terrible sight to watch such a fine ship slowly settle and then turn turtle. Most of the crew were saved, as there were numbers of destroyers and many smaller craft in the vicinity when the *Triumph* was struck.

Second Lieut. G. H. Smith, who had only a few days before been granted a commission, was killed in the trenches on May 26.

During the last days of May, the situation in the line was moderately quiet, and the 11th Battalion took the opportunity afforded to improve its sector in every possible way. Posts were connected up, loop-holes were constructed in the parapets and the battalion observation post was connected by telephone to brigade headquarters.

Though there was a full moon on May 27, the enemy made no active demonstration. The Turks were generally supposed to plan their offensives according to the phases of the moon, and their well-known symbol was the crescent moon. So at the full of the moon it was expected that something would be doing, but no attack eventuated.

So quiet were the Turks that headquarters thought that they might be moving divisions to another zone of operations, so efforts were ordered to be made to keep the enemy stirred up so that he would have to keep divisions in reserve in order to reinforce his line in the event of attack. These operations to harass and alarm the Turk were called "Demonstrations," of which more later in the story.

There had been a considerable amount of mining going on at a post called Quinn's, several sectors further north than the 11th Battalion's lines, and a call was made for experienced miners. The 11th Battalion, having naturally many men from the goldfields, supplied a party of 50 men who were immediately sent up to Quinn's Post.

The sinking of the *Triumph* was still a subject for discussion when a fresh disaster was reported from Helles. The battleship *Majestic* was torpedoed and sunk there. There had been a report of a German submarine working in the nearby waters for some time, and the sinking of the *Triumph* was the proof of a report that had been taken without enough seriousness by the Admiralty, though most of the larger vessels had been ordered off to Mudros and their cargoes ordered to be transhipped to smaller vessels there. The sinking of the *Majestic*, however, showed the peril all stationary ships were subject to and from that time the anchorage at Anzac, that heretofore had been busy with all kinds of shipping from which plied boats backwards and forwards, now became deserted save for a couple of destroyers and a few barges and trawlers. Any large vessels calling at Anzac would slip in under cover of darkness and be off before daylight appeared.

The effective strength of the battalion on May 31, 1915, was: Officers, 21; other ranks, 714. Total, 735.

The casualties to date were:

	Killed	Wounded	Missing	Total
Officers	4	9	1	14
Other Ranks	63	251	129	443
Total all Ranks	67	260	130	457

The total brigade casualty list since the Landing was 1,894.

It will be noticed that the number of men registered as missing was gradually decreasing, as the particulars of previously unchecked wounded were made available from hospitals or records.

"LEGS–ELEVEN"   107

Many regiments of Australian Light Horse had been on Gallipoli from about the middle of May, and the 1st and 2nd Regiments had been in the line for some time. Troops of the 2nd Light Horse Brigade were attached for experience to the 3rd Australian Infantry Brigade, and the 11th Battalion had five officers and 170 other ranks of the 5th and 7th Light Horse attached for duty.

When the light horsemen arrived on the peninsula, they were without leggings or feathers; they wore puttees and carried ruck-sacks. When the p— b— infantry first beheld the "Gentlemen" in their new rig-out, they did give them a hoy! But there was no malice in their welcome.

CHAPTER VII

TRENCH LIFE ON GALLIPOLI

By JUNE the troops had settled down to the routine of trench warfare. The weather, which had hitherto been mostly pleasant, was now becoming warm, and hosts of flies, engendered by the waste matter incidental to the presence of a large body of troops, were beginning to be a pest. Demonstrations against the Turks were now the order of the day, or rather of the nights, and on June 1 the 11th Battalion staged one of these futile shows. In these demonstrations the troops had to make a lot of noise fixing bayonets and show these over the tops of the trenches in the hope that the Turks would think there was an attack pending. Empty tins would be rattled and a few bombs thrown, and numbers of jam-tins hurled over at the Turkish lines.

A great amount of tunnelling and sap work was being done in the sector, and the 11th Battalion's position was being improved in this way. The two major activities of this period at Anzac were sapping and sniping.

On June 2, 1915, Major J. S. Denton, of "D" Company, was awarded the Distinguished Service Order, and Sergeant W. Ayling was awarded a Distinguished Conduct Medal. Sergeant Ayling belonged to "A" Company.

A large Turkish column was sighted going south on June 3, and in conformity with the policy of tying up as many Turkish reserves as possible, and thus prevent reinforcements from being sent to Helles, and also with the idea of making the opposing enemy troops as busy and jumpy as they could, the men of the 11th Battalion staged another "demonstration" that night, which was met by heavy enemy fire, but nothing serious happened.

The water supply was beginning to be a cause of anxiety. In the first few weeks there had been numerous small streams and springs, but as summer came on these dried up and the troops had to look to the supplies drawn from the beach to replenish their water-bottles. Water fatigues were now of daily occurrence and these were not popular.

In order to still further improve the 11th Battalion's position, it was determined to make a line of trenches in front of the position then held.

The engineers had laid out a plan and under their instruction the front-line companies were sapping out underground and leaving the top few inches of soil in position, so that the enemy would not discover the new system of trenches.

A party of troops was always detailed to lie out in front as a screen while this work was in progress. It was an eery job lying out on the bare slope in the darkness.

The men who were selected as the personal guard for Sir Ian Hamilton had been sent aboard the *Arcadian*, a luxury ship and truly named. These men were having the time of their lives, after the strenuous days in the trenches. Later Sir Ian Hamilton's headquarters were transferred, and the guard with them, to Imbros, on account of the danger of submarines.

While the *Arcadian* was lying off the coast of Gallipoli, a big cargo boat was laid alongside each side of the G.O.C.'s ship as a precaution against torpedoes.

Meanwhile at Anzac the routine of trench warfare continued. Considerable sniping was being carried out by both sides during the day and fatigues and demonstrations at night.

While on the subject of snipers, mention must be made of "Hitchie"—No. 443 Postal Corporal H. V. Hitch, to give him his full title. He was officially the 11th Battalion postmaster, but he was also a dead shot and a famous sniper. He lived in a little dugout behind battalion H.Q. and from there he dispensed the mail, that is, when he was at home, or when the mail arrived, which was at very infrequent intervals.

But mostly he was engaged in the more agreeable pursuit of sniping. He was truly a remarkable figure on Gallipoli, with his dark-tanned face surrounded with a great growth of beard and whiskers, dressed in shorts and carrying a captured Turkish bandolier and Mauser rifle. He was more like one of the Faithful than a son of the Golden West.

"Hitchie" used to be asked to go out and get certain Turkish snipers who had been making themselves particularly annoying, and he seldom went out in vain.

He would sometimes be away for more than a day at a time, and he was several times arrested as a spy and had to be bailed out by someone of his own battalion. "Hitchie" was distinctly annoyed to think that a good Australian like himself should be taken for a Turk.

Among other famous snipers in the 11th Battalion were Tom Rose, Ray Clarke, Harry Buswell and Dan Cocking. Each of these men accounted for many of the enemy, as they were all wonderful shots and they took up the business in a methodical and efficient manner.

The following interesting account of the sniping activities of the 11th Battalion was supplied by Lieut. R. A. Clarke (then Private):—

"The Anzacs and Turks had settled down to trench warfare and it was soon found that the Turks had a distinct advantage over the 11th Battalion, owing to the fact that their trenches occupied higher ground.

"It was found necessary to keep all loopholes blocked up, and for observation we had to resort to periscopes, dozens of which were broken by 'Jacko's' good markmanship.

"The 11th Battalion decided that this must be stopped, and when the call came for snipers, 'D' Company had in Tom Rose and Ray Clarke two former rifle club cracks who had, while in Egypt, notched first and second scores respectively against the whole of the 1st Division. Together with Harry Buswell and Dick Clarke, who acted as observers, they were relieved of all other duties and told to go ahead. Next they had to find a sniping position, and at a point where a communication trench joined the front line an ideal position was found. Some scrub was already growing on the spot to help conceal the post, and with a steel plate with a four-by-two-inch loophole, plenty of sandbags and a hard night's work, these men made a safe and concealed position. The only drawback was in gaining access to the position. It was above our front line and the snipers had to enter it at night and stay out all day, until later a shallow trench was dug so that they could wriggle flat on their stomachs to and from the 'possie.'

"At dawn on the first morning after the 'possie' was made, the sight presented to those snipers of the 11th Battalion was one they never forgot. The trenches were only 80 yards apart and every loophole in the Turkish trench was wide open with a

Turk looking through each of them. The 11th Battalion boys got their own back with a vengeance, and repaid with interest what they had to put up with during the first days of the Landing.

"It was nearly a fortnight before the sniping position was found by the enemy. One night a Turk crawled up under the parapet to within five yards of the post and waited till mid-day for a shot through the four-by-two-inch loophole. Corporal Truman, of Northam, was the victim, but within a few minutes the Turk had paid the penalty.

"The havoc which was wrought among the Turks was illustrated to us by a sergeant who deserted from the Turks and came over to our lines. He was an Armenian and could speak English.

"'Turk look through. Bang! Dead! German officer look. Bang! Dead!' and with suitable signs and the expression on his face he conveyed vividly the enemy's consternation when our snipers opened up on them. This incident was published on the Peninsula in Divisional Orders.

"From these sniping positions we commanded about 300 yards of enemy trenches. When the English troops attacked, light horsemen were sent over in a feint attack to hold Turkish troops in this part of the line, so that they would not be moved out to reinforce the defence against the main attack. Immediately the light horse attack began our snipers spotted two machine guns being moved against them and these guns were knocked out in quick time."

Mention has been made of the beard that adorned "Hitchie's" face, if the name adornment could be applied to such a growth. The story of the 11th Battalion's months at Anzac would be incomplete without some reference to the hirsute appendages of some of the "boys." The scarcity of water and the general discomfort and dislocation of the early days had made it impossible for many of the troops to indulge in their daily shave, and consequently numbers of the lads began to have a hairy-looking appearance.

After a couple of months without shaving, there was a crop of as horrible-looking beards as anyone could see outside a Nazarene settlement, and Samson himself would have been well matched in facial undergrowth by some of the West Australian boys.

There were all kinds of beards from the downy first growths of mere striplings to the wire-like appendages of some of the tough old bush-whackers from the backblocks and the goldfields.

The troops were indeed a contrast to the well-groomed and smart soldiers of a few months back; but war is war, and there were few amenities at Anzac, where life was stripped of its conventions and men had to revert in many ways almost to the primitive.

Owing to the high and mounting casualty lists, reinforcements were being rushed to Gallipoli without having completed their training. These reinforcements were trained on the beach, where they were taught drill and musketry daily. Some of these boys had very short careers as soldiers, many having been killed or wounded before their brief training was ended.

In the line the 11th Battalion was trying out the new bombs, but the range of the enemy lines was too great, and the bombs were ineffective.

On Sunday, June 6, an attempt to hold Divine service in the trenches was made. It was extremely hot and uncomfortable. At night a patrol was sent out to annoy the enemy. This party met with opposition and was fired on. Lieut. Hanly, of the 5th Light Horse (attached to 3rd Brigade) was killed.

Besides the usual trench and beach fatigues, a new road was being made in rear of the lines. This was named Artillery Road, and was a better gradient from the beach. The front was regularly patrolled at nights and the enemy kept on the alert all the time.

The Turks had made no organised attack on the Anzac sector since the disastrous attack, for them, on May 19. It afterwards transpired that the Turks had been given the same orders as General Birdwood, namely, to hold on to their then present line and not to make any major advance. As the Turks possessed an almost ideal position for defence, by even a relatively small number of troops, this policy naturally freed divisions that would otherwise have been necessary to support a more vigorous policy.

On June 9 a company of the 11th Battalion made an attack on an enemy trench over toward Turkey Knoll. A few snipers were routed out, but soon the attackers were forced to fall back before a heavy machine gun fire without accomplishing anything.

The enemy was noticed to be working close up to the 10th Battalion's position, and his snipers were very active in preventing any movement of patrols. As a counter move a demonstration was made by the 10th and 11th Battalions at night. The boys thought these "demonstrations" were good fun at first, but soon they got to loathe them.

As movement in the open was becoming more and more difficult in the 11th Battalion sector, it was resolved to tunnel out to Turkey Knoll and then consolidate a new position there. While this work was proceeding, the enemy snipers were becoming bolder and bolder and kept coming quite close up to the lines at nights. During this time the enemy shelling was very moderate, due, no doubt, to the close proximity of the Turkish posts and patrols at nights.

To counteract the enemy aggressiveness, bomb throwing was taken up in earnest about this time, and parties of ten men from each company were detailed daily to practise with dummy bombs.

On June 12, Captain Peck joined the 3rd Brigade H.Q. Staff as Staff Captain, and Lieut. John Newman was appointed Adjutant to the 11th Battalion. Immediately after Peck's appointment as Staff Captain a complaint was forwarded to the base concerning the postal services. Coming from one who had been lately in the 11th Battalion, this might seem like a reflection on the battalion postmaster, who was "mailman" only "in his spare time," but this was not so. The unsatisfactory delivery of the mails in the early days was only another example of the very poor organisation that existed in these first months of the A.N.Z.A.C. history.

The following particulars are from the Official Diary:—

"June 15, 1915, Captain J. Boyd-Aarons (late Major Julian Boyd), of the 4th Reinforcements, and 130 other ranks from 5th Reinforcements joined the battalion. Lieut. J. Williams rejoined the battalion and was promoted Captain to date from January 1, 1915. On June 16, the strength of the battalion was 18 officers, 819 other ranks. Total, 837. Wounded, 310; missing, 49."

The weather was now steadily getting warmer and the troops used to like to get down to the beach for a swim as often as they could. Sometimes when the water was crowded with swimmers, the Turk would start sending over shrapnel, and then most of the boys would dash out of the water and make a dive behind the stacks of biscuit tins or other stores with which the beach was dotted.

The swimming was a great boon to the troops in more ways than one, as besides the exercise and the bathe it also helped to keep down lice.

The extract that follows is taken from Lieut. J. M. Aitken's diary of Saturday, June 19: "A weird night was last night; dogs were barking and the Turks were making hideous noises. On the left, where the trenches are much closer, I am sure that they can see and hear much more than we do. Of course when on the lookout, the shadows make dozens of Turks and the imagination assists the delusion.

"In the south a pretty play of star-shells was going on, a little to our right a destroyer was inquisitively playing her searchlight all over the Turks' trenches, and away in the distance a moving glow indicated the position either of the position of Chanak or one of our own ships near the Narrows. We alone appeared to be in the darkness.

"Monday, June 21. Our firing line has reached the ridge we were sapping to, and now we're going still further. The Turks are also sapping towards us. They have improved their lines to a great extent, and have them protected with piles of barbed wire. We are now within range of their trench mortars and occasionally a bomb will be thrown and cause a little commotion.

"Of course our Japanese mortars are always returning the compliment."

Although the sapping and tunnelling forward was by this time the recognised method of pushing forward the line, yet the quicker method was adopted when suitable opportunity occurred.

One night, 120 men from "C" Company were ordered to assemble in full kit. They were given a pick or a shovel and marched up the sap in what was later known as Leane's Trench, and into No Man's Land. There was a covering party lying out on the forward slope of Silt Spur. This latter job was not appreciated by the troops engaged, as it was an uncanny business lying out in front in the open, seeing the flash of snipers' rifles often quite close, and being under strict injunctions not to fire or make any unnecessary movement.

The party with the tools was told to dig and to be under cover in their new trench before daylight. In full kit, this was no easy task, yet by dawn the new trench was dug. The road back to the old lines was over an exposed slope, so the party could not venture back in daylight. They remained in the new trench all day. It was well that they had dug the trench sufficiently deep, for the troops therein were sniped at through the hours of daylight.

At night the rest of the company came forward, and immediately new tunnels were started with the intention of driving forward through the Spur to its forward slope and thus gaining an improved field of fire.

On June 22, Lieut. T. A. L. Farr, Lieut. H. E. Kelly and Lieut. J. W. Franklyn reported for duty with 40 other ranks of the 5th Reinforcements and one other rank of the 2nd Reinforcements. The one O.R. was Private Peter Snodgrass (later Lieut.) who had been wounded early in the occupation of Anzac and had returned from hospital.

The battalion had received 489 reinforcements since it had arrived in Egypt.

In order to facilitate the gathering of intelligence of the enemy, each battalion was given a definite area to observe and report on, and a battalion intelligence officer was to be appointed. This is the first mention of this specialist in the battalion and also of the formation of recognised regimental observation posts.

The work on Holly Spur and Turkey Spur was pushed on during this period. A knoll in front of the 11th Battalion's position soon became known as Boulder Dump (see photograph) and a sap was driven through the crest of the hill as it was ascertained that a good field of fire would be obtained from that position.

The reinforcements were still being trained on the beach, and as a canteen had also been newly started there was an unusual amount of movement behind the lines. This was noticed by the Turks, and gun fire was brought to bear on the beach from two directions—from the Olive Grove (this was the famous "Beachy Bill") and from Anafarta. The latter battery or gun was called "Anafarta Kate."

There was an inspection of the sector by Vice-Admiral de Roebuck, who was in command of the naval operations at the Dardanelles. He was greatly struck by the amount of work that had been done and the difficulties that had been overcome. A note in Lieut. Aitken's dairy runs thus: "June 25. Just two months to-day since we landed here. There's a big differ-

Official Photo. "Boulder Dump" (named by 11th Battalion), Anzac.

ence to be seen now. A warship, shepherded by several destroyers, ventured from Lemnos this afternoon and after firing several terrific broadsides, cleared for her life. As a result, a village in the distance is aflame and probably in ruins."

Much has already been written about the tunnelling and sapping and other work that the troops on Gallipoli had to undertake. It would be safe to say that no other troops were harder worked or more constantly employed under increasingly difficult and insanitary conditions. These latter conditions were only partly due to trench conditions on the Anzac side of the line. The closeness of the Turkish lines, the numbers of still unburied dead and the increasing dryness and scarcity of water all were agents in rendering this over-inhabited section of the world insanitary and unhealthy.

It has been stated several times that the Turks had all the natural advantages of position and knowledge of terrain, and from their higher observation stations and greatly superior fields of fire they were able to successfully dominate the situation. Therefore, in order to improve their position at least cost to themselves, the Australians had to burrow forward instead of attacking over the open.

The trench system of the Anzac Corps was far from satisfactory at first and a series of positions with better fields of fire had to be obtained. This was most advantageously done by sapping out to certain points on the ridge chosen and connecting up the sap heads. (See map, page 119.) The earth from these saps and new trenches was all carried backwards and dumped in rear. This detailed a large amount of work, and of a particularly exhausting nature in the close confinement of trenches.

As this system of trench improvement and extension was largely used in all the future trench operations of the 11th Battalion, the above short description of how these new trenches came into being may serve to explain future references to the same procedure.

While the Australians were establishing themselves at Anzac, a great battle had been fought at Krithia, at the toe of the Gallipoli Peninsula, and the New Zealand Brigade and the 2nd Australian Brigade had been sent to assist. This phase of the battle was now over and these troops returned to Anzac. Hardly any improvement had been effected in the situation at Krithia.

An operation of great magnitude was now being commenced at Cape Helles and as usual General Birdwood was instructed to do all he could to prevent the withdrawal of enemy troops from opposite the Anzac front. In order to tie up as many divisions as possible and preventing reinforcements being sent to the southern armies operating against the British troops at Cape Helles, a great demonstration was arranged for June 28 along practically the whole Anzac front.

In the 3rd Brigade sector the 9th Battalion attacked Sniper's Ridge under covering fire from the 11th Battalion, parties of whose troops were lying out in the open in order to get a better field of fire. The 9th Battalion made a gallant advance but was driven back. A heavy bombardment then fell on the 11th Battalion trenches and on the troops lying out in the open.

The Official Diary states: "For the purpose of preventing the enemy from sending reinforcements from our position to the southern zone, two companies of the 9th Battalion (A.I.F.) made a demonstration against the trenches of the enemy opposite the front occupied by the 3rd Infantry Brigade.

"The 11th Battalion was detailed to assist the advance by covering fire from our front. Fire opened at 1 p.m. Owing to our forward line of trenches on Boulder Dump Ridge (now under construction) not having been completed, it was necessary that the garrison should be advanced from the support trench to the top of the ridge to obtain fire effect on the enemy's trenches in front. It was also necessary to send the men from the trenches on Turkey Knoll to the forward slopes to obtain fire effect. The enemy opened heavy shrapnel fire and the men, being extended in the open, suffered a considerable number of casualties. On the left of our sub-section the men of the left half of "D" Company, together with a machine gun, concentrated their fire on the enemy trenches at Lone Pine Ridge, thus reducing the effect of their (i.e., the enemy's) enfilade fire.

"Owing to the very heavy shrapnel fire, the men occupying the forward slope of Turkey Knoll found it necessary to retire. Those on Boulder Dump Ridge maintained their covering fire until the 9th Battalion withdrew. The engagement lasted until about 5.30 p.m., but the enemy maintained a desultory fire for a considerable time after.

"Our casualties were: Killed, officers, 3; other ranks, 18. Total 21. Wounded: officers, 1; other ranks, 41. Total, 42. Total casualties: 63.

"The officer casualties were: Killed, Captain C. A. La Nauze ('C' Company), Lieut. D. H. McDonald ('C' Company), 2nd/Lieut. H. L. Parry ('C' Company); wounded: 2nd/Lieut. H. E. Kelly ('C' Company)."

A more realistic account of the above action was recorded by Captain C. Gostelow who, as lieutenant, was in charge of one of the parties sent forward. Here is his narrative:

"At 1 p.m. on June 28, each company of the 11th Battalion sent one officer and about 40 other ranks into No Man's Land, with orders to get out as far as possible and open fire on the Turkish lines, simulating attack. The parties left the sap-heads

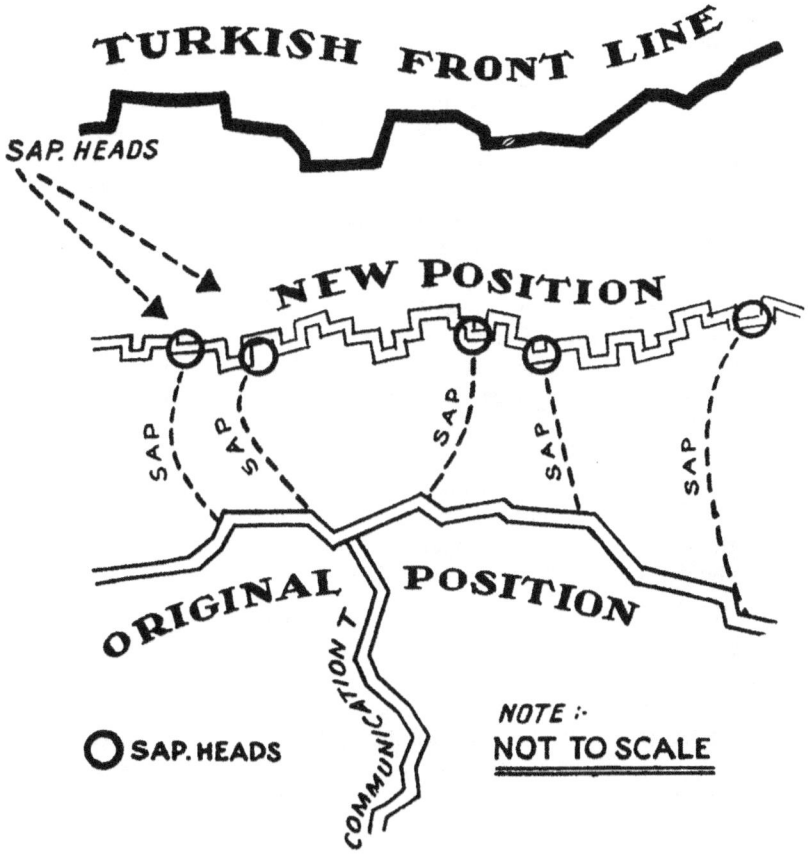

Sketch showing method of sapping out from front line to selected position nearer to the enemy.

and made across the open, where they took what cover they could, which was almost negligible; the Turk immediately opened fire with shrapnel from four guns. He gave us jip! I saw the men on our right retiring to our lines. I called them a lot of cowardly b——s. One corporal, who was quite cool, told me his officer had ordered the retirement. This conversation was yelled—not spoken. Sticking it a while longer, and seeing that many men were being hit, I sent back for instructions and also yelled but could get no response, so I took it on myself to send the men in one by one. I followed the last man in, and then met Major Denton, who told me to report to Colonel Johnston. The C.O. told me that I had done rightly in bringing in my party, as he had already lost five officers and a great number of men in the demonstration. Poor Jim Turnock, a splendid lad, was killed on Silt Spur in this stunt. On taking a tally of my men, I found that there were two missing. With Corporal Les. Truman, Ray Clarke and Tom Rose, I went to our sniper's post, and Les. thought he could see the two bodies. He volunteered to go out after dark and bring them in. We descended to make plans, and Les. went up to make further observation, and almost immediately was hit by a bullet from the flank. The wound was in his head, and though we got him to the beach as soon as possible, he died in 48 hours. He was a splendid soldier and a loyal comrade."

The great battle for Achi Baba was still proceeding in the south but it was a failure in the end, and it is questionable if the demonstrations made by the troops at Anzac would have made any difference in any case; but to the troops these demonstrations, especially when they entailed the movement of troops in the open in broad daylight in front of a prepared enemy, seemed to be the height of folly, and to show not only a lack of appreciation of the conditions that existed at the front, but also an utter disregard for the value of good men's lives.

During the last two days of the month the enemy was very agitated, and shelled the 11th Battalion position during both nights. A considerable amount of damage was done to the trenches, but this was quickly repaired, and after dark parties were sent out to recover bodies and equipment. Beyond the men repairing the trenches, there were no fatigue parties on account of the heavy shelling.

There was a box-kite flying from the 3rd Brigade area, and distributing pamphlets bearing proclamations to the enemy. A heavy rifle fire was directed at the kite by the enemy without any seeming effect.

The effective strength of the 11th Battalion on June 30 was as under:—

Officers, 17; other ranks, 912; wounded, 304; missing, 49. And the total casualties to date: Officers, killed, 7; wounded, 10; missing, 2. Other ranks: killed, 93; wounded, 362; missing, 49. Total: 523 out of a brigade total of 2,188.

Chapter VIII

TASMANIA POST AND LEANE'S TRENCH

THE FIRST DAYS of the month of July were moderately quiet at Anzac. There was the usual amount of shelling on the 11th Battalion area. "Jacko," as the boys called the enemy, was using 9.2in. shells, but these missiles were not doing much damage. These 9.2in. shells were originally 8.5in., but they had been sheathed in lead to bring them up to the larger calibre.

A terrific bombardment and interminable rifle fire had been raging for days at the southern extremity of the Peninsula, and this may have had something to do with the comparative quiet on the Anzac sector.

The report of the terrible first gas attack by the Germans at Ypres in Belgium had reached the troops, and the seriousness with which this new weapon was being regarded by the British War Office was shown by the fact that gas respirators were issued to the troops even as far away as Anzac.

These respirators were the uncomfortable old P.H.-type of helmet. There was a limited issue at first, and instructions were also issued to the troops as to procedure in case of cloud gas, which was the most dreaded form, while balls of tow were distributed, with orders to set these alight in or near the trenches if gas was liberated by the enemy, the idea being that the heat generated by the flames would disperse the gas.

The 12th Battalion was warned that enemy parties were seen by the 11th Battalion digging in front of Tasmania Post, in the former battalion's sector. On July 4 a demonstration was arranged in order to surprise the Turkish working parties. It was intended that the Turks should be allowed to come out as usual, when a harassing fire was to be put down by the 8th Battery (A.I.F.) while the 11th Battalion should co-operate with machine gun fire down the gully leading to the Turkish works. At the appointed hour this was done, and the enemy working parties were dispersed for that night.

On the same date, July 4, 1915, the following report was made by the 11th Battalion: "For a considerable time a line of forward trenches has been under construction, which necessitates the employment of a large number of men continually sapping and mining. About one half of our effective strength is thus employed. This, together with men required for ordinary fatigues (water, rations, etc.), leaves barely enough men to garrison our section of the trenches. The men being thus continually employed are undergoing a severe strain and they are more or less getting worn out. Many of them are suffering from nervous breakdown. Since landing on Gallipoli, various drafts of reinforcements have been sent us, and now over 50 per cent. of our present strength consists of these. They have not been sufficiently trained. Orders have been issued from Headquarters that these men are to be trained in order to increase their efficiency; at the same time we are told that the work of sapping must not be stopped or suspended. This, added to the fact that we are in a restricted area and subjected to continual shell fire, makes it quite impossible to carry out any degree of training with satisfactory result. Owing to casualties we have only ten company officers available for duty, and of N.C.O.'s, only about one-third remains. This shortage further increases the difficulty of training, and the strain of continuous duty on the officers is likely to lead to further casualties and sickness. For the above stated reasons it is my opinion, that the battalion is not in an efficient state, and arrangements should be made for at least one month's solid training."

Such is the official report, and it gives some slight idea of the conditions the troops were living and working under, conditions that never were quite so bad in their own way on any other front. It is to the everlasting credit of the Australians that they carried on as they did and the fact of their carrying on successfully in the face of such supreme difficulties is an indication that Australian troops had a natural discipline far transcending any discipline of barrack square or parade ground. It was the discipline based on comradeship and determination.

The mere fact that they carried on successfully and even cheerfully under such appalling conditions was the ultimate test of a disciplined army. What only a few people outside Australia have understood, is that the Australian's discipline was democratic, but it was none the less efficient on that account.

As stated in the foregoing report, the health of the troops was beginning to suffer, and from this time there was an increasing number of cases of enteric and diarrhœa.

For some days the sector was fairly quiet. There was the usual sapping, tunnelling and other fatigues, and the providing of screens to protect the working parties was undertaken by each of the companies in turn without much variation in the usual routine. There were always some casualties, but there were no outstanding happenings until July 11.

While all this sapping was going on, a special section had been detailed as tunnellers. The duty was hard and continuous. The men selected for the work were mostly experienced miners and underground workers.

Though keen on the job, some of them thought that they were doing a bit more than was reasonable, so one of these men—Alec Grant by name—suggested that he should go to see Colonel Johnston about it.

So off he went and bearded the "Old Man" in his den. He pointed out to the Colonel that, as a miner in Kalgoorlie, he used to get 26/- a shift, whereas he was only getting a miserable 6/- for working the whole 24 hours at Anzac.

When the Colonel asked him what he proposed doing about it, Grant suggested that all the tunnellers should be made corporals so that they could draw 10/- a day.

Unfortunately the Colonel did not see eye to eye with him in this matter.

On July 11, there was an interesting diversion for the troops. Lieut. Peter Snodgrass writes in his diary: "All was quiet to-day until about 3 p.m. when the cruiser H.M.S. *Lord Nelson* steamed majestically into position with escorts of torpedo-boats and bombarded Kilid Bair Hill. We could see every shot explode and the accuracy was marvellous. We could not see any target except trenches, and through glasses we could see they were badly knocked about. After about 30 shots an aeroplane went up and the H.M.S. *Bacchante* took the *Lord Nelson's* place with an observation balloon and also the aeroplane spotting for her. She put about 20 shots in quick succession on to some target, but we could not see where the shells landed."

These "strafes" by the Navy were always a source of interest to the boys, and were indeed most inspiring sights even if the material damage was often negligible. For one thing the troops had an excellent view of the whole proceedings, perched as they were on the bare ridges above the sea. There are frequent references to these naval operations, and the diarists always seem to welcome the break in the monotony when the men of the Navy came to lend a hand. And, indeed, in those months of summer, it was a thrilling sight to see those great ships, often mirrored on the calm waters of the blue Aegean, rocking to the recoil of the mighty guns, as the shells went tearing overhead, and then burst on their targets, and then the vessels would be temporarily obscured by the billowing smoke from the discharge of their guns.

In addition to the shell-fire by the Navy, the amount of artillery support at Anzac was steadily growing. A Scots' howitzer battery was placed in position behind the 3rd Brigade sector. The howitzers were much more effective against trenches than the field guns. It was wonderful how soon the boys "cobbered up" with the Scotties in the "How." Battery; there was always a great affinity between the "Aussies" and the "Jocks."

As some of the targets were beyond the reach of any of the available guns, Brigadier-General Hobbs asked for a 4.7in. gun. He was immediately told that it would be impossible to get a gun of that size up the hills to a suitable position; but Hobbs quietly told the Higher Command that they did not know what Australians were capable of when they tried. So the gun was landed and gradually hauled into position. Sometimes 100 men would get on to the job and it was all voluntary work, but in the end it was placed where it was required.

On July 15 there was a pay issued to the troops. (The illustration on page 127 shows one of the actual ten-shilling notes with Turkish superscription issued at Anzac Cove to then Private J. Murray Aitken.)

As there was by this time a canteen on the beach, there was a speedy use put to most of the money issued.

On the same date all the battalion was inoculated against cholera, which was reputed to be very prevalent in summer time in Gallipoli.

The battalion was now in reserve, and the men supposed to be resting, but there was heavy shelling of the beach and rear areas at this time and the casualties kept mounting. On July 17, nine men were hit, including Major Drake-Brockman.

As the Major was being transferred to the boat that was to take him to the hospital ship, he had with him a great pile of luggage and personal kit. One wag observing the heap cried: "Oh! cripes! He's taking his b—— dug-out with him!"

In orders it was published that the following N.C.O.'s were awarded the D.C.M. for distinguished conduct during the Landing operations: No. 697 Sergeant J. M. McCleery, No. 506 Sergeant V. Horsewell, No. 927 Sergeant G. Mason.

Something has already been mentioned about the fly pest, but daily this grew worse, and these foul insects seemed to be even more plentiful in the reserve lines than they were in the front trenches, so much so that Captain F. G. Medcalf was moved to write the following, in an article entitled "Flies on Gallipoli":—

"There is an appetising crowing of roosters over to the north-east in some Turkish farmyard. I can hear the dogs barking, too. It sounds as peaceful as a West Australian holding. Every now and then there is a screech overhead and sundry lumps of lead land somewhere they are not wanted. This gives the lie to a rural dream.

"In an hour the flies will be humming and buzzing like a flock of birds or a ton or bees, but now these birds are somnolent. I often thought that certain regions of the West (Australia) round Dalwallinu and such bucolic centres could say the final word in the matter of flies, but there is another little locality that can make an interesting speech on the subject long after the West Australian sylvan solitudes have shut down news on the subject and that place is a three-months-old trench at Gallipoli.

"The trenches are full of flies. They cluster round you in clouds, particularly at meal times. If you leave an empty jamtin on the parapet for two minutes in the heat of the day, it would be chock-full of green-backed, scaly, clustering, sticky flies. ... The flies are fearsome and warrant a page being written on them as one of the characteristically striking things of Gallipoli."

Flies are always a horrible accompaniment of war in the hot months, but on Gallipoli they were at their worst, and

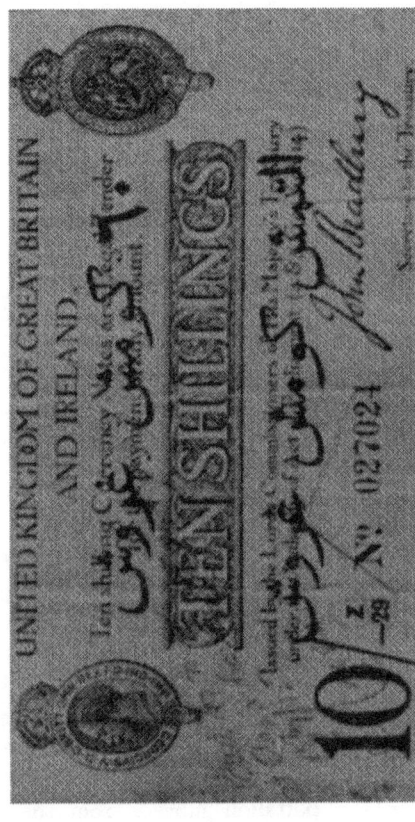

Ten-shilling note, superscribed in Turkish, issued to troops. This is the copy of an actual note issued on July 15, 1915, at Anzac.

were the cause of much of the sickness and other troubles that affected the men in the later stages of the occupation.

On July 20, 1915, the following promotions were promulgated: Lieut. W. H. Rockliff, to be temporary Captain vice Captain E. Tulloch; Lieut. S. H. Jackson, to be temporary Captain vice Captain A. E. J. Croly; No. 1048 Sergeant F. G. Medcalf, to be 2nd/Lieut.; No. 818 Corporal C. E. M. Puckle, to be 2nd/Lieut.; No. 988 Corporal G. Potter, to be 2nd/Lieut.; No. 217 Corporal C. H. Prockter, to be 2nd/Lieut. All dated July 1, 1915.

The following reinforcement officers were absorbed into the battalion: Captain J. B. Aarons, 2nd/Lieut. T. A. L. Farr; 2nd/Lieut. H. E. Kelly and 2nd/Lieut. J. W. Franklin.

Though the front was quiet, it was feared that the Turks were preparing for an attack, probably about July 23, that being an important day on their calendar; and consequently the troops were warned to be ready and they had frequent calls on them to stand-to. Nothing, however, happened except a considerable amount of shelling on both sides and the usual sniping; so after all the night of July 23 passed quietly although the 11th Battalion, which was still supposed to be having its rest in reserve, were standing-to nearly all night.

While in this rest camp the 11th Battalion had at least plenty of opportunity to bathe, and swimmers were to be seen in the water at all times. When the warning whistle blew, announcing the discharge of a shell from Beachy Bill, the troops in the water would go in up to their necks and wait till the firing stopped.

On July 26, Captain J. Williams was transferred to the 28th British Division as A.P.M., and 2nd/Lieut. T. A. L. Farr was transferred to the Engineer Corps.

On July 27, the 11th Battalion moved from the reserve lines and relieved the 12th Battalion, whose trenches the troops occupied at Tasmania Post. The men were if anything more weary after their so-called rest than they would have been if they had been in the line during the quiet fourteen days that had just passed. On some occasions there were as many as 450 men on fatigues and other duties, working for many hours at a stretch, unloading heavy cargo from the barges and performing the necessary line-carrying parties.

It was during the period the battalion was in reserve that several casks of cider escaped from the sunken *Triumph* and floated toward the beach. Needless to say the troops expedited this cargo ashore and soon broached the casks. Owing to its long immersion in the salt water, the liquor had been somewhat spoilt, but still the boys reckoned it was the "good brew" and had more than the customary eight, until one of the Brigade Staff smashed up the casks with an axe.

By July 28 the battalion had found it necessary to shorten the hours of duty, and now the companies were doing 48 hours in the line and the same amount of time in support and in reserve. The supports and reserves had, as usual, very heavy work to do.

Mines had been placed at the ends of the tunnels under the Turkish lines in Despair Gully. These lines were afterwards known as Turkish Despair. The 11th Battalion had received orders to attack this position as soon as a favourable opportunity occurred to fire the mines.

Brigadier-General R. L. Leane, C.B., C.M.G., D.S.O. (and bar), M.C., V.D. (Commanded operations at Gaba Tepe and Leane's Trench.)

July 31 was chosen for the day of the attack, and the official report is here appended from the 11th Battalion War Diary:—

"We received orders to storm and capture a line of Turkish trenches immediately in front of Tasmania Post. A party of four officers and 200 men were detailed under Captain R. L. Leane to carry out the operation.

"At moonrise, the Engineer Company exploded three mines which had been prepared in communicating tunnels towards the Turkish trenches. Immediately the storming party climbed over the parapets and charged the enemy trenches. These they occupied, bayonetting such Turks as did not run away at the approach of our troops.

"The first line of the storming party was followed by the working party close at their heels, and on getting into the trench they immediately set to work and made it defensible. The storming party was divided into four columns of 50 each, commanded by the following officers: Captain W. H. Rockliff, 2nd/Lieut. C. E. M. Puckle, 2nd/Lieut. T. W. Franklyn and Captain W. H. Jackson.

"A reserve of one officer and 50 men was placed on either flank under Lieut. A. H. Darnell and 2nd/Lieut. G. Potter.

"When the trenches had been occupied it was found that a small portion of the trench was still in the hands of the enemy, which divided our troops and prevented communication being established. An attempt from a flank having failed to dislodge the enemy, 2nd/Lieut. Potter with 25 men was instructed to make another charge on this portion of the works. This was carried out with great dash and the whole length of the trench secured to us.

"The whole operation was carried out with great dash and coolness and was led in a brilliant manner by Captain Leane. Communications were soon opened up to the craters created by the explosions of the mines and further tools and supplies were taken forward to the trench.

"The garrison, under very heavy fire, continued throughout the night the work of improving the trench, and by daylight it was fairly well protected. Our casualties during the operation were: Killed, 2nd/Lieut. C. E. M. Puckle; other ranks, 35. Wounded, Captain R. L. Leane, Captain S. H. Jackson, 2nd/Lieut. G. Potter; other ranks, 70.

"It is estimated that the enemy's casualties were 60 killed, the wounded being carried away."

This was a brilliant operation by a tired and weary battalion whose vitality and reserve of strength was at an exceedingly low ebb. The burden of the attack fell on "C" Company, but the work of consolidation and carrying was borne by the rest of the battalion, and the fact that such a feat was accomplished was a wonderful tribute to the West Australian troops.

The trench that was captured in this operation was ever afterwards known as Leane's Trench, and as it was one of the most important operations of the period and was an attack carried out by 11th Battalion alone, in which many of the troops distinguished themselves, a more detailed account of the battle is appended.

Tasmania Post, from which the operation was carried out, was a defensive system constructed by the 12th Battalion, and which that battalion always looked upon as peculiarly its own; hence the name. It was, however, badly sited, having only a short field of fire, in some places amounting only to 40 yards.

The trench faced the Valley of Despair, up which the Turks could approach to within easy bomb-throwing distance. The enemy, also, finding themselves in good cover only a short distance from the Australian trench, started digging a new trench on the edge of the slope. On the north of this position was the cultivated land known as the "Wheatfield" then covered with a fine crop of wheat and quite open to the enemy.

The 12th Battalion had wanted to attack the new line of Turkish trenches, but had been refused permission. Instead, that battalion was instructed to drive forward four new tunnels out to the edge of the gully, and later these were mined. Part of the crop in the wheatfield was cut.

The 12th Battalion was relieved by the 11th Battalion and withdrawn to reserve and, as already stated, the 11th Battalion had two tiring days in the line before the attack was launched.

Some of the details of the attack and the bare report of the operation have already been quoted, but there were a few other salient features not mentioned.

The artillery, especially the newly-emplaced Scots Howitzer Battery, was to attend to enemy batteries and known machine-gun positions, and the 3rd Field Company of Engineers was to fire the mines. The signal for the attack was to be a red flare on the parapet of the old trench.

The night of July 31 started with heavy shelling on the left of the Anzac position, but that soon died down and everything became quiet.

The 11th Battalion attacking and supporting troops were got ready, and excitement made the men forget their weariness and all were eager for the attack to commence.

When the moon rose the signal was given and the red flare glowed on the parapet. In a few seconds, one and then another of the mines exploded, but the other two in the centre hung fire. Captain Leane gave the order to advance, and the four columns dashed over the intervening ground. As they neared the objective the mine immediately in front of Lieutenant Puckle's party exploded, burying some of the men. The remainder dashed on, with dirt and debris falling all around them and drove the Turks out of portions of the trench. On the left Captain Jackson got as far as the Wheatfield and dug-in with about a dozen men while others blocked the open end of the trench, which ran into a washaway leading into the Valley of Despair (see map) and L/Corporal Taylor brought up a party of men with tools to consolidate the position.

Franklyn's party rushed the trench in front of the unexploded mine and drove out the garrison and occupied the trench; the Turks were able to get away by clearing off down a communication trench which led into this part of the line. Sergeant Louch blocked the end of this trench with sandbags.

Next to Franklyn's party, Puckle's men were having trouble. Puckle was killed while gallantly leading his men to try to cut off a party of Turks in a section of the trench. Several of the attackers were also killed at this point—but the Turks were not ejected from this portion of their lines, so a barricade was built across the trench.

Rockliff and his men reached their objective without mishap, and began at once to consolidate. They were almost immediately attacked by the returning Turks, who bombed them severely, causing a number of casualties. Rockliff had few bombs, and called for a machine gun, and Sergeant Wally Hallahan dashed up and placed his gun on the parapet. It was hardly in action before it was blown out of his hands by a bomb, which also badly wounded his hands.

The situation was desperate, but luckily a supply of bombs was found, many of which were lit by a cigarette held by Rockliff, and these were hurled at the Turks who retired at once to shelter.

All the communication trenches in the front of the captured trench leading down to the Turkish positions were now barricaded. About this time Corporal McOmish reported that there were Turks in between Puckle's party and Rockliff's party. Leane also found this out and instructed Franklyn to take a party of men and attack the Turks in rear. These men, however, in making the attack were fired on both by the Turks and their own side and fell back to their new position.

Soon after, a party under Lieut. Potter and Sergeant Ringwood led another attack against the intervening party of the enemy. Potter was wounded and Ringwood had eight of his lads wounded in the attempt to eject the Turks. Continual pressure was kept up against this stout party of Turks, who were now cut off from their own comrades, and by means of bombing and rifle fire they were eventually driven out or killed.

While the battle was in progress, the engineers had been working desperately at the tunnels to render them fit for the passage of troops, and so allow reinforcements and ammunition to be sent out to the new position.

The working parties which were to assist the advance were not able to use these tunnels, but had to cross the open. There was a considerable amount of scattered fire, but by morning the new trench had been consolidated and made defensible with a sand-bag parapet whose loopholes covered the Valley of Despair. In addition to this several small sand-bagged "possies" had been made in the wheatfield to the north of the captured trenches. The enemy shelled the captured position very heavily and also made a faint-hearted attempt to attack through the wheatfield towards morning, but this was checked by machine gun fire from the 9th and 11th Battalions.

During the battle, and while the trench was being consolidated, Lieut. H. (Jigger) James, the signalling officer, greatly distinguished himself by carrying messages and information to and from headquarters under very heavy fire.

The heavy shelling which took place about dawn was a terrible strain on the already tired troops, as the high-explosive shell that was used destroyed a good deal of the newly-erected parapet and the work had to be done all over again. There was little water for the troops, and rations were also short. The 11th Battalion had suffered a terrible ordeal in this battle and had been tried beyond its strength, for though the operation was completely successful and the spirit of the men was unimpaired, the physical effect was such that an ever-increasing number of casualties through sickness and exhaustion took place from this date.

The 11th Battalion was relieved by a company of the 12th Battalion, and this company garrisoned the captured trench, now known as Leane's Trench.

The following officers and N.C.O.'s were recommended in connection with the foregoing action:—

Major S. R. Roberts, Captain R. L. Leane, Captain W. Rockliff, Captain S. H. Jackson, 2nd/Lieut. J. W. Franklyn, 2nd/Lieut. G. E. M. Puckle and Lieut. H. James, No. 962 Corporal McOmish, No. 1046 Sergeant R. L. Richardson, No. 724 L/Corporal Taylor, No. 503 Sergeant W. R. Hallahan, No. 1310 Private G. F. Barker, No. 1336 Private W. T. Edmonds.

The battalion strength on July 31, 1915, was as follows:— Officers, 17; other ranks, 819. Total 836. Casualties since April 25: Officers killed, 7; wounded, 11; missing, 2. Other ranks: Killed, 100; wounded, 420; missing, 50. Total 590. The 3rd Brigade total was 2,263.

Chapter IX

THE TRENCHES AT ANZAC

THE 11TH BATTALION now entered upon a phase of its occupation of Anzac which may be regarded as typical of the life on the Peninsula. The most striking feature of the Australians' sector of the Gallipoli front was the excellence of the trench system, and in the 11th Battalion sector this trench digging had reached a high art. Of course it must always be remembered that many of the West Australians were miners and prospectors and it was marvellous how these men could handle pick and shovel, and some of them could take out a section of trench while others who were not accustomed to such work were wondering how to commence. It was now August, and though there were still hopes that a further advance or break-through might be made farther north, yet it was felt that the offensive had sped its bolt and the troops realised that they must settle down to trench life in earnest.

August 2 was a very quiet day after the turmoil of the previous 24 hours. At night about 30 Turkish rifles were brought in and a number of enemy dead were buried between the lines, and the corpses removed from Leane's Trench. The 6th and 7th Reinforcements of the 11th Battalion arrived at Anzac on August 4 and reported for duty. The 6th Reinforcements comprised 138 men under 2nd/Lieut. S. G. L. Hall and 2nd/Lieut. A. J. Robertson; and the 7th Reinforcements consisted of 128 men under Lieut. E. R. Pinnell and Lieut. E. W. Morris.

As will be recounted shortly, these reinforcements had one of the most terrible introductions to their unit that any troops could have had, and their behaviour under new and fearful conditions and in the face of extreme danger was beyond all praise.

On August 5, the 11th Battalion was back in the newly-captured Leane's Trench, and parties of the troops were employed in improving the position. Leane's Trench was situated on the edge of the Valley of Despair, which dropped away practically from the immediate front of the trench, so that the enemy was able to approach unseen right up to within a short distance of the 11th Battalion position.

Captain Rockliff reported that he heard enemy movement in front of his position, but could not give any details on account of the continued noise of the working parties, which were doing their usual full-time jobs.

These working parties, however, could not be stopped on account of the necessity of getting the trenches into a more defensible condition before the projected offensive, which was shortly to be made on the left of the Anzac position as part of the Suvla Bay operations. In the meantime, all portions of the line were being strengthened in order to provide for all contingencies.

At the inter-company relief, when Rockliff handed over to Captain Boyd-Aarons, he told the latter his fears that the Turks were massing under the shelter of the deep gully, but as all seemed quiet by that time the matter was allowed to drop.

In the earlier part of the evening, the Turks had opened a terrific bombardment on the 11th Battalion's lines, and Rockliff had ordered his men to be so distributed so that the boys who had come with the latest reinforcements, only a day or so back, should be mixed with the "old hands" in the trenches.

As related previously, the night had become quiet and no enemy action was reported for a considerable time. Nevertheless, the troops kept good watch, as there was a constant expectation that the Turks would attempt to recapture Leane's Trench, which was well out in front of the other Anzac positions in that sector. It was afterwards learned that the loss of the trench was treated seriously by the Turkish Command and court-martials had followed the loss of the position.

In the early morning of August 6, movement and voices were heard in the Valley of Despair and several bombs were thrown by the 11th Battalion. Immediately a very heavy rifle and machine gun fire was opened on Leane's Trench from Turkish Despair works, Pine Ridge, south of Sniper's Ridge, Sniper's Ridge and Lone Pine. Also a great volume of high explosive and shrapnel was poured on to the position. This bombardment caused many casualties, as the parapets were badly smashed.

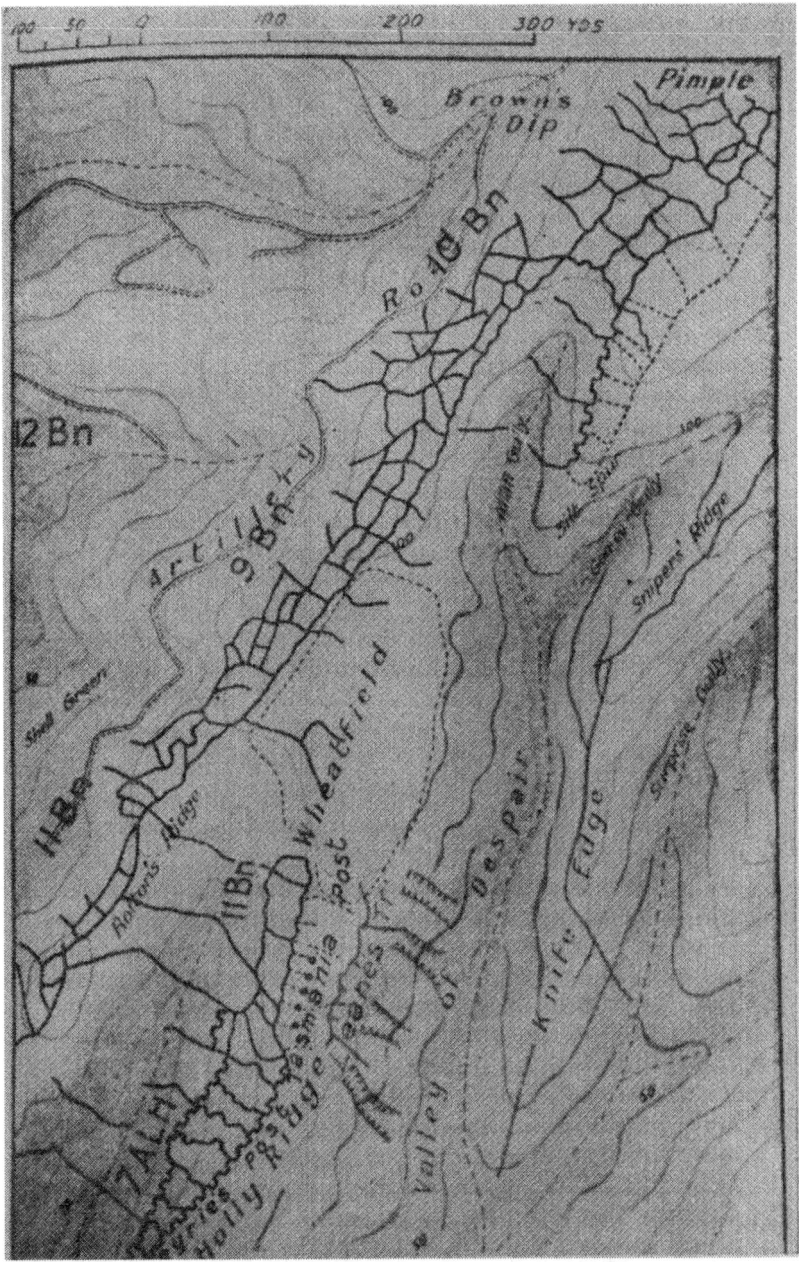

Map showing Valley of Despair, Leane's Trench, Tasmania Post, Wheatfield and 11th Battalion sector.

The official account is as follows: "About 4:30 this morning, August 6, 1915, the enemy made an attack in force on Leane's Trench, which we recently captured. They crept close up under the parapets and delivered a heavy bomb attack. So fierce was the onslaught that the enemy succeeded in getting a foothold in the right section of the trenches. Captain Aarons was in command of this section. He immediately blocked with sandbags the communication trench leading from that portion of the trench occupied by the enemy. Our men in the trench endeavoured by rifle fire and bombs from the flank to dislodge the enemy, but failed.

"A storming party was then formed of about 30 men under Lieut. Prockter to rush the enemy from Tasmania Post. This they did in a most dashing manner under heavy machine gun and rifle fire. As their casualties were considerable, I did not consider the remainder sufficiently strong to seize and hold the position, so I detailed another party of 25 men, under Lieut. Franklyn to follow on. They charged over the ground in a gallant manner and succeeded in completing the capture of the trench, shooting and bayonetting all Turks left there. It was then found that a party of Turks had retired up No. 1A Sap, where for some time they held out; but they were ultimately taken prisoners and sent off to headquarters.

"Meanwhile Turkish reinforcements had been hurried up, and they took cover close in under our parapets from where they could not be dislodged even by bombs.

"They attempted to dig in under our trenches, and as there was a danger of our trenches being blown up, I decided to launch a counter-attack from our left flank to clear out the enemy under our parapets. For this purpose 2nd/Lieut. Hall and 25 men were detailed, and they succeeded in clearing the enemy out and also arrested an attack which was developing from our left.

"The enemy attack continued for six hours, during which a heavy bombardment by many guns took place as well as incessant rifle and machine gun fire. The trenches and parapets were badly knocked about, but with the assistance of the Engineer Company they were speedily repaired. The enemy was completely repulsed with heavy losses and the whole of the trench left in our possession.

"Our casualties were heavy, especially from bomb wounds. Killed: 2nd/Lieut. Prockter, 2nd/Lieut. Robertson and 39 other ranks. Wounded: Captain J. Boyd-Aarons, 2nd/Lieut. Franklyn, 2nd/Lieut. Potter and 91 other ranks. Missing: 2nd/Lieut. S. G. L. Hall and 18 other ranks."

The total casualties for this battle were 154 all ranks.

This was another fierce and sanguinary battle fought almost entirely by the 11th Battalion, and it was chiefly notable for the gallantry and dash displayed by the late reinforcements. Of course it was to be expected that these later arrivals were fresh and unwearied, but up to date there had been the usual mild disparagement of reinforcements that is found everywhere among troops, but this action showed that the newcomers were of the same fibre as the originals and it did much to unite the old and new.

Among the many splendid incidents that happened in this battle, the appended story is told by Captain H. A. Haslam:

"Our battalion was out of the firing line, but the boys had had a very bad time. On August 1, they captured Leane's Trench from the Turks, but he got back and our unit ejected him again. But they had a bad time. They were all very proud of their cook. He was Andy Graham, a Katanning man, and if ever these pages get near him, I hope he reads these few lines at least and learns with what admiration his fellow fighters of the 11th Battalion regarded him. While the Battalion was fighting its hardest, Andy made some tea and carried it up to the fighting and distributed it to the many wounded and dying pals about—and there were many. He went back for more, and on his return a shell fell near him and buried two soldiers. He put down his tea, and worked until he nearly dropped to extricate the poor unfortunates. He did get them out, but he strained his heart in the doing of it. Undaunted, he picked up his tea and went on with his self-appointed job. Many a dying soldier drank of our good cook's tea, many a wounded one, too, and when they were satisfied he gave to the men still fighting. I believe that those who have returned to Australia, and were in that fight, will never be able to pass Andy Graham without grasping his hand—no need to say anything—I know I can't."

There were a number of names forwarded for special mention after the battle of August 6: 2nd/Lieut. G. Potter, 2nd/Lieut.

C. H. Prockter, 2nd/Lieut. J. F. Franklyn, all mentioned for extreme gallantry and devotion to duty; also No. 2044 Private Whitbread, No. 232 Private W. R. Smith, No. 398 Private T. Priestman, A.A.M.C. (attached to 11th Battalion), No. 2153 Private B. D. Johns and No. 2172 Private J. M. Morrison (both killed in action), No. 2437 Private D. Roper and Private B. J. Winzer, A.A.M.C. (attached to 11th Battalion).

It seems invidious to single out any men for distinction when all are equally gallant, but the Brigade Commander's own report is appended on the conduct of three of these men:

"Privates Johns and Morrison. On the morning of August 6, 1915, these men, together with Private Roper (mentioned below), were the only ones of 2nd/Lieut. Prockter's party not killed or wounded in the first assault on the portion of Leane's Trench captured by the enemy. I personally saw them firing rapidly and steadily at the Turks in and behind the work until after the second party successfully entered the trench, when they also disappeared into the trench.

"Each time they fired they had to stand up and expose themselves to a hail of bullets when they might have been behind the parados in comparative safety. Their action was cool and gallant to a degree. They were 6th and 7th Reinforcements and only recently joined the battalion. Both were killed.

"No. 2437 Private D. Roper, 11th Battalion, wounded on August 6, 1915. On the occasion above, was with the two men mentioned above, but remained out in the open in a kneeling position giving the reinforce signal. Seeing that all his comrades of the assaulting party were killed or wounded, he eventually ran back over the fire-swept ground to explain the situation and was severely wounded. This man was also a 7th Reinforcement.

"The coolness and gallantry of these three men under particularly trying circumstances and very accurate and heavy fire deserves special recognition.

"E. Sinclair-MacLagan, Commanding 3rd Infantry Brigade."

After the trench had been cleared of the enemy and repaired, it was found that a body of Turks was still clinging to the side of the gully underneath the trench which had been the scene of the late fighting. Whether these men were too scared to retire back to their own lines, owing to a report issued by the Turkish commander that those Turks who retreated would be shot down by their own machine guns (as a matter of fact, a copy of an order by Rushdi Bey, commanding the 16th Turkish Division, containing a clause to this effect, was captured), or whether these Turks were hanging on in order to make another attack was not known; but the fact of their nearness caused a good deal of alarm. The Turks, however, were in a pretty precarious position themselves, as they were enfiladed by the 10th Battalion from Silt Spur, and they were also exposed to artillery fire.

The 11th Battalion had been making loopholes, and Dan Cocking and Paddy Moran found positions from where they could harass the Turks and they shot down every man that they could see; and it was stated that whenever a party of Turks broke back they were mown down by machine gun fire from their own side. This, however, may have been the result of the enfilade fire from the 10th Battalion rather than the machine guns of the Turks.

The enemy who remained started to dig in, and fears of mining were entertained. The engineers were sent for, and Major Clogstoun was badly wounded while trying to find out the enemy's intentions.

Attempts were made to dislodge these Turks by throwing bombs, but these grenades merely rebounded and rolled to the foot of the gully without causing any damage to the enemy.

Colonel Sinclair-MacLagan, who had previously assumed charge of the battalion in person, and who had gone up to Leane's Trench on hearing of the impasse, ordered Captain Boyd-Aarons to use gun-cotton to dislodge the enemy. A large bomb of this powerful explosive was made and rolled over the parapet and down among the Turks, where it exploded with a deafening crash, killing a good many of those below and successfully dispersing the remainder. This was the final phase of the struggle at this point, and the 11th Battalion was left in possession of the trenches.

The next stage of the operations to help the advance on the north was to be the attack on Lone Pine, and a great amount of work was required to get Leane's Trench in a fit position to be effective in the projected attack.

The 1st Australian Brigade was detailed to make the attack on this position, while the 3rd Brigade was to give assistance by covering fire.

On August 7, the battle had started on the left, that is to the north of the 3rd Brigade position, and away up towards Suvla Bay (see map). Suvla Bay was out of the Australian sector. It was a well-protected inlet, and was faced by flat country in the immediate vicinity of the beach. The Australians perched on the higher ridges at Anzac had a fairly good view of the locality.

Now that the battle was on there were battleships and destroyers again on the coast, lending their salvoes to the attack. There were many transports also, and it was like the early days on the Peninsula to see so much shipping.

By Sunday, August 8, the boys of the 11th Battalion could see great numbers of troops and horses being landed at Suvla Bay on a new jetty that had been constructed. The noise of a heavy battle was heard on the left opposite the 1st Brigade's sector. This was the start of the famous Lone Pine battle. Further to the left a terrible conflict was also raging at the Nek, Russell's Top and towards Baby 700, where the 11th Battalion had so gallantly fought at the Landing.

Still more to the north at Chunuk Bair the 4th Australian Brigade, the 1st and 3rd Brigades of the Light Horse and the New Zealanders, under General Godley, were all involved in a tremendous battle; while for several miles beyond, on the extreme left, and right past Suvla Bay was a wide front, on which two new English divisions were floundering under such incompetent generals that three of these senior officers were recalled immediately after the battle and were removed from their commands on August 15, 1915, and three well-tried generals sent from France to take their places.

All this great front was the scene of heroic endeavour and gallant attack after gallant attack; but the stories of these places belong to the troops participating and do not much affect the history of the 11th Battalion, as contrary to its usual fortune this battalion's sector was moderately quiet during this time and the boys had an opportunity to work on their own lines and make them comfortable.

The 11th Battalion went into rest camp on August 9, and the companies were then re-organised. The Commanding Officer (Lieut.-Colonel Johnston) was sent away to hospital ship for a few weeks' complete rest.

The following names were mentioned for gallant and good work performed on the night of July 31/August 1, in addition to those already recorded: No. 594 L/Corporal F. Smith and No. 388 Private R. H. Retchford (later Lieutenant).

The undermentioned other ranks were promoted to commissioned rank as second lieutenants: No. 157 Sergeant J. A. Archibald, No. 503 Sergeant W. R. Hallahan, No. 729 Sergeant P. E. M. Vowles, No. 927 C.S.M. G. Mason, No. 1724 Private R. D. Bradshaw, No. 923 Sergeant T. S. Louch, No. 752 Corporal B. E. Bardwell, No. 329 Sergeant T. McKean, No. 1880 Sergeant H. Ringwood, No. 121 Sergeant A. Burgess, No. 494 Corporal J. F. Wilson, No. 171 Sergeant A. C. Elliot, No. 525 Sergeant F. Coombs.

The 11th Battalion was soon back in the line again, and the troops were again instructed to assist, from Leane's Trench, with rifle fire against the Turkish positions opposite Lone Pine, where the battle was still raging with unabated fury. These positions were a considerable distance away and it was not really much the troops could do except give occasional bursts of fire on any movement that might be observed, or covering fire in the event of an attack. Meanwhile, the trenches were improved and extended.

The extent of the trenches in the Leane's Trench and other 11th Battalion sectors was almost inconceivable. Visitors were aghast at the amount of work that had been done. Some idea of the works may be had from the perusal of this extract from Lieut. J. M. Aitken's diary of August 11, 1915: "Back in the firing line again to-day. I am now in charge of a section. . . . It's a hard life certainly, as is evidenced by the number of men going to hospital daily—33 to-day—with diarrhœa and dysentery mostly, and by the number put on 'no duty.' (This going to hospital is called 'Pulling out the big sugar.') . . . Little did I imagine that now I'd be living like the worms underground, and scarcely able to show my head above ground for fear of having it knocked off. I've dreamt of subterranean cities, but if this bewildering criss-cross maze of trenches were lit up, we'd have one here on the spot. What with underground and concealed firing lines and both ourselves and the Turks continuously sapping, the opposing firing lines creep, creep to one another until the position becomes untenable —made so by bombing. Then we have to take a Turk's trench or two as we did on July 31, and then the creeping begins all over again. . . . When we take up an entrenched position we don't sit down and wait, but continually dig toward the Turk so as to keep driving him back, and at the same time keep our casualties down.

"Each company may have as many as four saps out in front —where convenient the trenches and saps are open, but when secrecy is required (for concealed firing lines and observation posts) then tunnelling must be done. When saps are far enough forward they are connected up, thus bringing new firing lines into being, and consequently there are many obsolete lines which are useful for supports and other troops may avail themselves of the protection thus afforded.

"And the trenches! They are not round nor straight, nor any other shape, but just a system of short jerks and turns; not even zig-zagged, and they suggest to me what would surely happen if some thousands of miners and prospectors got madly drunk and attempted to dig their individual ways round the world, no one going in the same way as any other (see map). This seemingly extravagant digging is to minimise the danger from shrapnel fire.

"When the opposing lines come close enough then comes a race to see who gets under the opposite trench first. The first there blows the other's trench or sap up, and then follows a scrap for the crater caused by the explosion.

"If they can't be taken from underneath, a charge must be made over the top, the victors adding them to their line where possible."

The above excellent description written in the lines themselves at the very time all this was going on gives a very vivid impression of the conditions the troops were living under in their mazes of trenches, and is some indication of the immense amount of work the 11th and other battalions had to do on Gallipoli.

Around this time, there are many references to the poor health and physical condition of the Australian troops. In Lieut. Peter Snodgrass' diary of August 11, 1915, is written: "If all the Australian troops are like my own unit, they are not fit to make any attack on a large scale. For the present they are about done as a fighting unit. Nearly four months of the trials and hardships of waging war in a confined space has taken its toll of the old hands. The sick parade numbered 45 to-day, and 20 were put on 'no duty.' The Medical Officer has sent in a report that the 11th Battalion is unfit."

Another interesting extract from the same diarist, on an aerial scrap, is worthy of note in view of the later development of synchronised guns: "August 12, 1915. Last night just before dark we witnessed an aerial fight. A Taube was flying low over our trenches when it was seen by one of our airmen who at once set after it.

"He flew to cut the Taube off, and as the 'planes drew near each other we could hear *revolver shots* from each. The Taube at once started on a descent, but I don't know whether it was forced.

"It is not likely that revolvers would have much effect at the range."

In passing, it is instructive to note that the very early aeroplanes of the war were not regarded as combatants, nor were they armed with machine guns for a considerable time.

On August 13, the battalion was relieved by the 12th Battalion and went into brigade reserve. Fatigues and the usual digging went on, but the situation was very quiet. The shelling had practically ceased, and it was reported that the Turks were very short of ammunition. As is now known, the Turks had such a limited supply of ammunition that they were only able to use their issue for defence or attack. The comparative immunity that the beach- and water-front generally enjoyed was due solely to this state of affairs. Why the Turk did not concentrate his whole available supply on the beach and landings, which were under direct observation, will always remain a subject for discussion.

On August 16, the following promotions were promulgated: Captain R. L. Leane, to temporary Major; Captain Peck, to temporary Major (rejoined battalion from Brigade Staff-Captain); Lieut. A. H. MacFarlane, to be temporary Captain; Lieut. A. H. Corley, to temporary Captain; temporary Captain W. H. Rockliff to Captain.

The 11th Battalion reached the first anniversary of its formation on August 17, 1915, but that interesting fact passed unnoticed by the troops.

Next day the troops of the 3rd Australian Infantry Brigade were redistributed in the brigade sector, and the 11th Battalion was allotted a position between the 9th and 10th Battalions. The position on the right of the 11th Battalion's new location went under the impressive name of the "Black Hand." The troops moved into their new position during the day.

The number of men away sick in the 3rd Brigade now amounted to 1,150.

On August 26, a report was received by Brigade Headquarters from Mex Camp, in Egypt, where the Brigade Transport Group had been encamped since disembarking from the s.s. *Suffolk* and s.s. *Malda*. The report was satisfactory.

To revert a little; when it was found impracticable to land the various battalion transports at Anzac, at the time of the Landing, the 11th Battalion Transport, under Lieut. Priestley and Sergeant Alec Burgess, was sent to Alexandria. The *Suffolk* called in at Cape Helles and picked up some Indian troops. After landing, the Transport Section went to Mex Camp, about ten miles west of Alexandria, where it did second line transport work, unloading cargoes from ships to Army Service Corps and Ordnance depots. The troops also helped to unload cargoes for Anzac and Mesopotamia.

As may be imagined, this life was a perfect picnic as compared to the life at Anzac, but the boys of the 11th showed their independent spirit and bluntness of dealing here as elsewhere. One amusing incident illustrates this. There was always a considerable movement of troops, and one day an English transport section, which had been in lines near the 11th troops, was packing up its gear preparatory to moving out.

A young and energetic English officer was cantering up and down his lines, keeping an eye on things generally and on Australians particularly, as these latter might have seized on the opportunity of making up deficiencies in their kit from articles left lying about in the bustle and upset of shifting camp.

"Mulga" Tonkin, of the 11th Battalion, who had been grooming his horses, wandered over to the "Tommy" lines carrying his dandy-brush in his hand. As he, along with a few of his mates, was standing gazing at the busy "Tommies," the young officer already mentioned came galloping up to the party and, pointing to the brush in "Mulga's" hand, shouted, "Hi there! that man! Drop that brush!" "Mulga" took no notice at first, but when the officer came right up and repeated him command, it was too much for the lanky Australian.

Stepping quickly forward, "Mulga" thrust the dandy-brush right up under the officer's nose, and pointing with his forefinger to each letter in turn spelled out the name deeply cut into the back of the brush, "M-u-l-g-a-, b———y Mulga? Have you any b——— Mulgas in your mob?" He then stalked off in high dudgeon, leaving the poor young officer utterly dumbfounded.

This tale now jumps from the sunny, easy life in Egypt to the terrible conditions of Anzac, where the battalion was spending the few remaining days of August in doing the usual routine of front line, support, reserve and rest and working at full pressure all the time. The number of evacuations kept increasing, and all the companies were much under-manned.

Luckily, there was no severe action, and the front opposite the 3rd Brigade was mostly quiet. Several times the troops carried out a ruse in order to keep "Jacko" thinking. Sometimes whistles would be blown and rifles fired and bayonets shown over the parapets. This would usually stir up the enemy and bring down a certain amount of retaliation on the men; but the troops felt that, in view of the very heavy fighting on both sides of them, it was only fair that they should suffer some strafing if, by annoying the Turks opposite, it would lessen the task of their mates north and south of their position.

One of the chief works in the new trenches was the making of efficient loop-holes. These had to be carefully constructed both for concealment and safety, and they also had to possess a good field of fire. These loop-holes were very necessary, as there was no other way of keeping down enemy periscopes or using rifle fire without undue danger.

There was naturally a lot of sniping on both sides, but very little artillery fire on the brigade sector, although heavy bombardments had been almost unceasing on the left for the three previous weeks.

Some time previously, white patches had been ordered to be sewn on the backs of Australian tunics, and the troops had been wearing them up till August 27. On this date these patches were ordered to be removed, and that same night an enemy patrol wearing white patches attacked the 11th Battalion trench, but they were successfully dispersed by bombing.

On Sunday, August 29, divine service was held under very uncomfortable conditions. Later on in the same day the front line was improved by cutting down scrub in front of the position and the trenches were recessed.

On the last day of the month enemy aeroplanes were extremely active, but the brigade front was quiet all over.

The 11th Battalion state on August 31, 1915, was as follows: Officers, 15; other ranks, 507. Total: 522.

The casualties since April 25, 1915, were as under:—

Officers killed, 9; wounded, 19; missing, 3. Total 31. Other ranks: Killed, 159; wounded, 617; missing, 72. Total, 848. Totals: Killed, 168; wounded 636; missing 75. Total 879.

The 3rd Brigade total comprised 3,015 all ranks of which the 9th Battalion had 749 casualties, the 10th 611, and the 12th Battalion had 763 casualties and others 13. It will be noticed that the 11th Battalion had well over one-quarter of the brigade casualties at this time, and exceeded considerably all the other battalions of its own brigade.

Chapter X

HANGING ON AT ANZAC

"Life was no joke in those hard days, yet jokes would always come
When everything was upside down, and everyone was glum.
In most unlikely spots they grew, from most unlikely ground
They sprung, not wholly free from dirt, and sent the grins around.
And never shall we quite forget the jokes that came along
And helped to make things bearable when everything went wrong."
—Oscar Walters.

IT WAS now September, and the 11th Battalion was so worn out by privations and sickness that the remaining men were not fit to carry out any strenuous work, though that did not prevent the Higher Command from insisting that the usual amount of work was carried through. The medical authorities were constantly urging that the men who had been several months on the Peninsula could not be classed as fit troops, and advocated a long rest away from the sight and sound of the battle area. Of the battalions of the 3rd Brigade, the 11th had suffered most casualties and its effective strength was the lowest in the Brigade. Nevertheless, the battalion was called upon to do its part equally with the other units of the brigade.

September 1 and 2, 1915, were extremely quiet days, hardly a movement had occurred in the brigade sector; so, when suddenly a terrific rifle fire burst from the Turkish lines all the troops thought that something was doing. "B" Company was in the front trenches and all the boys immediately "stood to." But the demonstration, or whatever it was, soon ended and it was thought that it had been arranged to cover some digging or other work.

Sniping was practically the only activity most of the time, while it was light enough to see. The tours of duty were now

48 hours in the line, and the same time in support and reserve. This was found to work better than the shorter tour, as it gave the troops some chance to sleep. Owing to the flies, it was almost impossible to sleep in the daytime, and when the troops had been engaged on night work there was no way of making up sleep, unless there was at least one clear night's rest.

About this time were heard the first rumours that the battalion was going to be sent back to Egypt, or more likely Lemnos, for a spell. The troops had been glad to get out of the sand not so long before, but the thought of getting back to the old familiar places caused a glow of anticipation and satisfaction all round.

Due to the troops living in what were practically catacombs, the danger of casualties from artillery fire was now almost negligible, and the number of killed and wounded from this source, right to the end of the occupation, hardly amounted to more than an unfortunate accident here and there.

The 11th Battalion had moved to a sector of the brigade front where there was a better defensive position. This was on the right of Leane's Trench. These new trenches were on the edge of what was practically a cliff, and they were difficult of assault even by a determined enemy.

On September 2, word was received that the s.s. *Southland*, an Australian transport travelling between Alexandria and Lemnos had been torpedoed and that there had been some loss of life. Owing to the steadfastness of the troops, the boats were mostly got away in safety and the Hospital Ship *Neuralia* came to the rescue when the great majority of the troops were taken aboard that vessel and several others that quickly arrived on the scene. The *Southland*, though deep in the water and with only one bulkhead holding, was navigated to harbour at Lemnos by a volunteer crew, many of whom were Australian soldiers of the 6th Brigade—a very fine piece of work. This incident is mentioned as the *Southland* was the first Australian transport to be torpedoed and the story created quite a stir on Gallipoli at the time.

From intelligence received, it was expected that a Turkish attack would be made during the next few days, and consequently all troops were warned on September 3. It was noticed that considerable preparations were made by the enemy, such as cutting scrub in front of their trenches, putting up barbed wire entanglements and other defences and digging was heard every night. Patrols were sent out to investigate on the night of September 5, one from the 9th Battalion on the right front and one from "C" Company, 11th Battalion, on the right, which also acted as a screen to a wiring party. No warning had been given to "B" Company and the screen just missed being fired on by "B" Company.

But in spite of the rumours of attack, the area still remained very quiet and no attack was made by either side.

In a letter dated September 4, 1915, Major R. A. Leane acknowledged comforts from the Kalgoorlie Working Bee and mentioned that the following men had received parcels and were duly grateful for them. The names are interesting, as they represent practically all those remaining of over 200 Goldfielders who landed with the original 11th Battalion. Here are the names: Sergeant-Major D. Hardy, C.Q.M.S. J. M. Aitken (the diarist whose records have been so valuable), Private O. H. Peterson, Sergeant W. Coates, Sergeant L. F. J. Jenkins, Corporal R. Finlason, Corporal W. K. Thirloway, L/Corporal J. B. Northcott, Private J. Cooper, Private A. V. Samson, Sergeant L. M. Delbridge, Corporal L. B. Taylor, L/Corporal W. Johnston, Private A. F. Hall, Private H. J. Turner, Private M. Cleary, Private G. Rowley, Private J. Cropper, L/Corporal A. Boyd, Private W. H. Hurrell, Private T. J. Smith, Private W. W. Deering, Private H. J. Cash, Private A. E. Stinson, Private J. Thompson, Private W. E. Beard, L/Corporal C. Smith; 27 names in all.

About this time the 2nd Australian Division had begun to arrive on Gallipoli, and there was a little bitterness between the 1st and 2nd Divisions for some time. The Australian newspapers had been praising up the men of the newer division, stating that the men who joined up later did so, well knowing the conditions that were before them, unlike the men of the 1st Division, who joined up more for the sake of adventure. Hence the new division was known as the "Dinkum" Division, or more generally satirically described as the "Dinkums." This little estrangement was never carried too far, nor did it last long; but for many months the 2nd Division was known by the name given to it when it first arrived in the region of hostilities.

While occupying a sniper's "possie" in the line, the following incident is recorded by Lieut. P. Snodgrass: "September 7, 1915.

Some howitzers put a few 5-inch lyddite shells into the trench opposite us. One shell blew a Turk clean out of his trench on to our side of his parapet. How he lived at all beats me, but he was alive all right. He scrambled to his hands and knees, had a good look all round No Man's Land and crawled back into his trench. He stood up in the trench and gazed our way for a few seconds and then disappeared. Not a shot was fired at him, although he must have been seen by many others besides myself."

For a day or two there was practically a lull in the trench warfare on the 3rd Brigade sector. An interesting change was provided when a French monitor, carrying a 14-inch gun, hove in sight and started to bombard some Turkish position which, however, was not visible to the troops. The Turks replied in kind, and shells dropped all round the monitor, without seeming to do any material damage.

After this little episode, nothing serious disturbed the even tenor of trench life for some days. Both sides seemed to realise that it was practically useless to shell deep trenches, unless with high explosive, and there was not too much of that class of shell available on either side at this time.

If conditions were a little more favourable as regards actual warfare, the troops had sufficient worries of their own to counteract this enemy quietude. One constant trouble, among a multitude of others, was the lack of sufficient water. There had been a few soaks and wells in the early part of the occupation from which a constant, if limited, supply was drawn; but these had petered out during the summer months and what small supplies were still available were greatly contaminated by the presence of so many troops.

The main supply had to be brought to Anzac by barges and pumped into tanks ashore, and from these water-fatigue parties had to draw their battalion's allowance and hump it up the steep slopes to their units. Naturally the men in the trenches only received sufficient to keep body and soul together, without any hope of receiving any water for ablutions.

When the troops were in reserve or rest, there was always the opportunity of a bathe in the sea, and though the boys risked the chance of being sniped at with shrapnel by "Beachy Bill," these bathes were really the salvation of the troops.

Occasionally in the line there was a cool spell, and a man might have saved enough water from his daily ration to collect a pint or two in order to get a shave or the substitute for a wash.

One day when General Birdwood was going round the lines, he noticed a big fellow doing his best to have a wash with the limited amount of water that he had at his disposal. With his usual genial habit of talking to the men, "Birdie" inquired pleasantly, "Well, my man. Are you having a bath?"

Imagine the General's surprise when "Big Bill" turned round and, thrusting out a small tin of water, sarcastically inquired: "What the hell do you take me for? A bloody canary?"

The 1st and 2nd Australian Brigades had now been relieved and were resting at Mudros, in the Island of Lemnos, and naturally the one topic of conversation in the 3rd Brigade was the expected relief. As the days dragged on, however, it seemed as if the 3rd Brigade had been forgotten, and the boys began to think that the reports of relief were only "furphies." (The Australian troops' word for idle rumours.)

It had been hoped that the 28th Battalion would have relieved the 11th, but that battalion was put in on the left of the Anzac position.

After all the talk about a rest, the hopes of the 11th Battalion were definitely shattered when the Acting Brigadier told the troops that they would not be relieved for a month. The Acting Brigadier at this time was Colonel Lyon-Johnston, who had been temporarily appointed to the command of the 3rd Australian Brigade on September 11. Major R. Leane took over the command of the 11th Battalion temporarily.

Major Leane was an officer who had gained the confidence of all the troops, and his appointment as temporary commander of the unit was received with general satisfaction. He had all the gifts of a great soldier and his name was always honoured in the 11th Battalion.

In pursuance of an inquiry into the health of the troops on Gallipoli, Colonel Purvis-Stewart, A.M.S., inspected a percentage of men of all battalions for the purpose of ascertaining their fitness for continued service. The report on the 11th Battalion dated September 12, stated that 25 per cent. of the men were not fit to be on duty at all, 50 per cent. were able for average work and would last for a short time longer, and that there was little probability of the remainder standing a winter campaign.

It may be thought, from some of the foregoing references to the condition of the troops, that the 11th Battalion was now a dispirited and melancholy unit. Such was far from being the case, because however bad the fortunes of war, or the conditions of trench life, the 11th Battalion boys always met life with a jest, and even at this time this spirit is shown by the various nicknames some of the "hard-doers" of the battalion went under. Among others, the old hands of the battalion will remember "Achi Baba Harry," "Bivouac Bill," "Anzac George," "Maidos George," "Anafarta Bill," and "Gallipoli Jack," the last being that doughty old warrior, Jack Cropper, of "C" Company.

About this time there was a special effort, following the medical recommendations, to increase the amount of canteen stores so that the troops could buy little luxuries to supplement the scanty and often unpalatable food that was issued as rations. The prices of even ordinary goods were very much inflated, but as anything at all was welcomed as a change, the troops did not object to pay the prices asked.

Some of the prices were as follows: Eggs, 3/- to 5/- a dozen; tinned pineapples and apricots, 3/- a tin; tomatoes, 3/6 a tin; milk, 1/9 a tin, and sometimes double that price; while butter was retailed at 45/- for a 14lb. tin.

The troops were paid on September 15, and soon got rid of their cash in buying from the canteens at the prices quoted.

It was now the middle of September, and already the first signs of winter were noticeable. There was some rain which was welcome at first, as it laid the dust and freshened up everything, but with the rain the weather grew chillier and the nights became cold.

A great number of new troops had been landed on the beach. There were some cavalry units both British and Indian, and many of these troops had not had a tour in the line at this date. The beach was crowded with troops and huts of all descriptions, and a tram line ran the whole length of the shore. What with the bustle and noise the place was more like a great city, but without houses or shops; and when on September 16 there was a heavy fall of rain, the unceasing traffic made all tracks and roads muddy and uncomfortable to walk on after the long period of dry and dusty ground conditions to which the troops had become accustomed.

On the same date, a "ruse" was carried out at night by the 11th Battalion. This was done to keep the Turks from having too small a garrison in the front lines, or in the vernacular of the boys "to keep old 'Jacko' thinking."

The method employed on this occasion was that strong rifle fire was opened on the Turkish trenches, and burnt jam-tins filled with stones were hurled against the enemy line. This demonstration drew very heavy retaliation from "Abdul" and he kept up his fire till 11:30 p.m., but he was not able to do any damage. Next day, while in the lines, Captain A. R. H. Corley was killed by a sniper. He was shot through the heart when he was in Sniper's Post on Silt Spur.

An interesting note on the above sniping "possie" is from (then) Sergeant H. A. Haslam. He writes: "The post on the high side of the valley nearest the Turks was called Sniper's Post, and from there lots of us used to do quite a lot of shooting. The post was fitted up with five or six loop-holes through which we shot. . . . As time went on, "Jacko" found this post and would fire at us quite as much as we fired at him. Unfortunately for us he had telescopic sights—which we didn't have, and with his glasses found the hole through which we observed. With great accuracy he fixed a rifle and trained it on this spot. One morning while I was in this particular post, a young chap named Cambden named each of these loop-holes in turn, 'England,' 'Egypt,' 'Lemnos Beach,' 'Australia,' meaning that if we opened the loop-hole so named we would get wounded, slightly or severely, according to the plate we moved. He chose 'England,' opened the loop-hole and looked through. Sure enough a bullet came through and struck his eyebrow, breaking the bone. He went to hospital in England. Though he was badly wounded, we all thought him lucky in leaving Gallipoli, as conditions there were terrible. Some weeks after the above incident, Captain Corley, of our unit, looked through the same loop-hole and was shot through the heart and was killed."

On September 18, the Turks evidently thought that they would get a bit of their own back, as the troops would say. At 4:45 p.m. they suddenly opened a very heavy fire along the front held by the 11th Battalion. Though a large number of shells fell on the position, there were no casualties. The fire died down towards 5:10 p.m. The enemy's trenches on Lone Pine and Sniper's Ridge seemed to be full of troops, who had bayonets fixed and gave the impression that they were going to attack. No attack followed. Possibly they were only copying the tactics of the 11th Battalion of a few nights before.

The Turks had been doing a considerable amount of work in improving their positions on Weir Ridge, and they had made an attack in strength on the left; but the troops had been expecting this and the attempt was easily repulsed, although two strong waves of the enemy had advanced.

A Turk who had previously given himself up gave warning of this proposed attack, so it had not much hope of success.

At this time the enemy seemed nervous of attack, largely due to the fact that the sentries in the 3rd Brigade sector had been ordered to fire at least ten shots during their tour of duty. Most of them fired considerably more, mostly for the purpose of keeping themselves awake rather than in the hope of hitting anything, for the only targets were the flashes of "Abdul's" rifles.

The official diary entry for September 20, 1915, gives a striking picture of the low strength of the 11th Battalion and the poor condition of the troops. This is the report:—

"Anzac, Northern No. 1. Two companies of 11th Battalion were relieved for 48 hours by 150 men from the 12th Battalion. My men are in a very poor state of health. The total strength of the battalion is 13 officers, 349 other ranks."

An entry in a private diary of the same date states: "We had roast beef for tea—rather tough, but nevertheless very enjoyable."

It is from little entries like the above that a true idea of the terrible conditions existing on Anzac is obtained. When an issue of tough beef was looked upon as something of a treat it does not take much imagination to visualise the drabness of the food ordinarily served.

A number of Turks, who had been captured, were in the bivouac area where the relieved troops were sent. These prisoners seemed very pleased when they knew that they were to be sent off to a concentration camp at Lemnos. The above diarist notes: "Two of them were enormous men, but I don't think that there were more than two or three pure Turks, the rest being Syrians, Armenians and Greeks."

The Turks had been concentrating on some building work on Sniper's Ridge, and it was noticed on September 21 that they were building some kind of platform with heavy beams of timber. When this building was reported, a number of observers were detailed to keep a strict watch on the works and to report any developments. It was soon discovered that trench mortars and machine guns were emplaced here by the enemy.

Next day a mountain gun of the Indian Mountain Battery was run up and placed in a recess in Ledge Trench for the purpose of opening fire on the platform on Sniper's Ridge, as well as a covered trench that had been located nearby.

The mountain gun was well laid because it only took eight rounds to demolish both positions. Lieut. P. Snodgrass recorded the following in his diary in reference to this shooting: "The Indians only fired six shots (Official Diary states eight) and "Jacko" did not get a return shell in until the Indians had been gone 20 minutes and were safely back on the beach. These mountain guns are carried in pieces on mules, and the gunners are well trained and quick. I saw the first gun landed from a barge, already loaded on the pack-mules (on April 25, 1915).

"The men led the mules on to the beach, unloaded them to test them, assembled the gun to test it, reloaded the mules and had their gun in action over the first hill, half a mile distant, in about 20 minutes. It took these gunners not more than about ten minutes to assemble their gun, fire six shots and repack the mules and get away."

Truly as Kipling says—
"And never a man forgets
That it's only the pick o' the army
That handles the dear little pets."

After the above nice piece of work, the Turk was very much annoyed and returned a heavy fire which did much damage to the parapets of the 11th Battalion lines and to the 3rd Brigade observing station; but there were no casualties.

The night of September 23 was a brilliant moonlit one, and the shattered platform in the Turkish lines was quite discernible during most of the night. Machine guns sprayed the position at intervals; but in spite of this, as soon as it was daylight it was noticed that the Turks had managed to fill up the gaps in the trenches, though the timber of the platform was still pointing all ways and had evidently not been touched.

The 11th Battalion official report for September 24 is quoted here:—

"Anzac, 11:15 a.m. Northern No. 1.

"Enemy opened heavy artillery fire from Gun Ridge, Olive Grove and the rear of Gaba Tepe. Several shells fell near Ledge Trench and a number in our support lines. We suffered three casualties, none of them serious cases.

"1:15 p.m. General Birdwood and Admiral Weymss inspected the battalion trenches.

"9 p.m. A demonstration took place to-night and was fairly successful in drawing the enemy's fire, particularly artillery from 7:45 p.m. until 8:10 p.m. Our artillery opened a heavy fire on Turkish trenches. Complete silence was maintained in the trenches. 8:10 p.m. a burst of machine gun and rifle fire opened along our whole front; this continued until about 8:30 p.m. when the enemy's fire died away. No casualties."

It is obvious from the above report that the Turks had got wise to "demonstrations" and were not to be stampeded by them, even although as on this occasion a red flare was burned in the centre of the 11th Battalion lines as if for a signal for an attack. As both sides were so well dug in, both artillery and rifle fire were practically useless.

The hectic days of early Gallipoli had gone, and the troops were now fighting out a wearisome battle of positions. This was a severe nervous strain if kept up for long, but a form of fighting that was not liable to show a high casualty list.

A few venturesome snipers who took a risk in order to obtain a better field of fire offered practically the only chances to each side. Some of the Turks were very cleverly concealed, but a chance shell sometimes dislodged them. One Turkish sniper was blown out of his position and was seen to be clad in sand-bags, while another who was forced out was shot at and lay as though dead for about an hour. When he thought things had eased up a bit he sprang to his feet and rushed into his trench.

The 11th Battalion was still operating on the 48-hour reliefs and the system was working smoothly and satisfactorily, as far as that was possible under the conditions. The Anzac front was quiet, but on September 26 a great bombardment was heard at Cape Helles and also over towards the Narrows.

On September 27, the following entry is recorded in the 11th Battalion Official Diary: " 'C' and 'D' Companies of the 11th Battalion were relieved at 10 a.m. by a detail from the

12th Battalion for 48 hours' rest. This relief is a fine concession to the men. At present, on account of the small number available for duty, it comes very hard on both officers and men.

"The food being issued is fairly satisfactory, except that we do not get enough fresh vegetables.

"Platoon cooking is working well, except that wood is rather short.

"Now that the winter is approaching, it would be well if a sufficient supply could be available for heating purposes.

"There seems to be something wrong with the hospital system, quite mild cases have gone to England; and though this has been going on for some months now, none seem to return. . . . It makes it very hard for the few who remain. As a civilian, one could not afford such a loss of time. I think it is a matter that requires more supervision, otherwise those lacking in sense of duty may be tempted to take of advantage of it."

There was certainly something very far wrong with the evacuation and treatment of the sick and wounded at this time. Unfortunately the whole position of the Australian Imperial Force was so complicated and so mixed up with the Imperial Army that a great deal of mismanagement and consequent abuse could not but occur.

The relations between the two medical services were not too happy, some cases of sick and wounded coming under the British authorities and some under the Australian, with the result that many of the men who were evacuated were lost sight of, and it was difficult to find out exactly where they were and who was responsible for them.

It is beyond the range of this history to go into further details, but sufficient may be gathered from the official report to understand that the system at that time was far from satisfactory; and when the exceedingly low strength of the 11th Battalion on September 30 is taken into account, it will be granted that the complaint of the commander of the battalion was justified. The strength on this date was 11 officers and 319 other ranks, or a good deal less than one-third of the normal strength of a battalion.

On the last day of September, the Colonel of the 5th Norfolks visited the 11th Battalion lines and he was very much impressed by the amount of work done, and he was especially struck with the cleanliness of the trenches. This latter was a feature of the 11th Battalion's occupation of trenches or other quarters right through to the end of the war.

A number of Maltese labours had been brought to Anzac as a labour unit. These men were greatly scared of aeroplanes, irrespective of nationality. As soon as the drone of a 'plane was heard, these men cleared for their lives and hid in any handy place until the "bus" had gone, in spite of the shouts and commands of the N.C.O.'s in charge.

Names were called for by brigade headquarters of any men men who were able and willing to play in a band. This was looked upon as "the good oil" for an early move to a more salubrious climate; but anything at all at this stage was looked upon by the boys as a "sign."

The 3rd Brigade strength on September 30 was only 2,060 men, composed as follows: 9th Battalion, 550 men; 10th Battalion, 650 men; 11th Battalion, 330 men; 12th Battalion, 530 men.

A comparison of the figures shows how very weak the 11th Battalion was, numerically, in relation to the other battalions. In a previous chapter it was pointed out that the 11th Battalion had been overstrained in the Leane's Trench fighting, and the above monthly strength statement is ample proof of the number of evacuations since that date.

Chapter XI

LAST WEEKS AT ANZAC

WHETHER the 3rd Brigade consisted of an exceptionally tough lot of men, or whether its commanders recognised it as the "willing horse" and worked it accordingly, will always be a subject that will bear a good deal of discussion; yet the fact remains that this brigade, now reduced to less than half its normal strength, and having been the first to land on Gallipoli, was still employed as front-line troops, while its sister brigades had by this time been out on rest at Lemnos for a considerable time. It was not as if this brigade had had an easy time. The exploits of the 11th Battalion alone, and the amount of work that had been done in the 3rd Brigade sector were ample proofs to the contrary. In the diaries and letters of this time, when such are available, there is no word of complaint or suggestion that the battalion was being treated unfairly, but the dominant question was always, "When are we going to be relieved?"

The routine of duty which had now been in force for a considerable time was still 48 hours in the front line system, and 48 hours in the support lines. The duties were carried out with the lethargy that was the result of over-tiredness and nerve strain. The promised rest seemed to be as far off as ever, and most of the troops now regarded it merely as a device to keep up their spirits.

It was remarkably quiet in the Anzac lines, though a persistent heavy bombardment could be heard away to the south; and on October 1, a monitor sailed into the bay and fired several 16-inch shells on Gaba Tepe, as it was believed that some kind of a depot or other work had been installed there. Though there had been more or less constant shelling of that point, no apparent damage had been done so far.

It was obvious that winter was now fast approaching. On the morning of October 2, there was such a heavy fog that everything was obscured. The trenches were damp and clammy and visibility was restricted to a few yards until after 10 o'clock, when the mists began to dissipate.

On October 3 a big Australian mail was distributed among the troops. There were also parcels distributed from the Comforts Fund and other societies in Perth and Kalgoorlie that did a lot to provide little extras for the boys from Western Australia. These parcels were always greatly appreciated.

When a roll call was taken on October 4 of all the men who had been with the 11th Battalion at the Landing, and who were still serving on Gallipoli, it was found that there were only 69 who had never left the Peninsula. When it is remembered that nearly a thousand men landed only a short five months previously, it will be realised what a terrible toll had been taken of the 11th Battalion, and that the many references to the terrible conditions of the troops were founded on facts that were irrefutable. It is now almost inconceivable that troops should have been asked to carry on for such a length of time without relief, because the men were *always* under the sound of guns and shell fire.

The so-called rest bivouacs were only a quarter of a mile or so from the front line and afforded little or no relief. The best that can be said for them is that they offered a change, and the chance of a bathe.

At 10:30 a.m. the 12th Battalion took over the trenches for 48 hours, and "B" Company of the 11th Battalion relieved "A" Company while that company went back for a rest.

For the next two or three days there was very little to report; but on October 7, a train of camels was observed moving along a road near some demolished buildings known as "The Ruins." Information was at once sent to the 3rd Artillery Brigade, which immediately commenced firing, but without any visible success.

A mountain gun detachment reported to the 11th Battalion at 8:30 a.m. and set up its gun in Ledge Trench. The gun commenced firing about 3:45 p.m. and soon got on to its targets, demolishing the parapets of the trenches on Pine Ridge and also an observation station that was situated there. The mountain gunners might well quote Rudyard Kipling when he makes them say—

"For we fancies ourselves at two thousand,
With the guns that are built in two bits."

On the evening of the same day, the 11th Battalion was instructed to carry out a demonstration for the benefit of "Jacko." At the appointed hour numerous rockets and star-shells were fired into the air, and jam-tins containing stones were thrown over the parapet and rifles were fired. The enemy must have thought that an attack was going to be made in earnest after all this preliminary, for he replied with nearly everything he possessed. While the demonstration was in progress, a pair of destroyers shone their searchlights over the valley in rear of Gaba Tepe, and they fired round after round as fast as they could load the guns for nearly half an hour. Although a furious fusilade was returned by the Turk there were no casualties reported.

Next morning the sentries who were on duty noticed that the Turks had completely repaired the damage done by the artillery fire of the previous day.

A detail of the 12th Battalion relieved two companies of the 11th Battalion for 48 hours. These temporary reliefs were about the only concession the troops were allowed, and they were appreciated to the full.

With the onset of winter the weather grew rougher, and even stormy on occasion. When the wind was in the west or south-west, the waves came pounding in on the open beach at Anzac. On October 8, the first serious storm that the troops had experienced since their arrival at Anzac burst with great fury on the beach. In a very short time there was an entire disorganisation of traffic, and a woeful destruction of material and jetties and other structures for the convenience of discharging cargo and troops. The pumping plant was seriously damaged, thus causing a shortage of water which affected the troops for several days.

Like most of the storms in the Mediterranean and its branches, the disturbance did not last long; but it was long enough to have serious consequences. Of this storm Lieut. P. Snodgrass writes in his diary: "The beach presents a rather sorry spectacle after the storm—all the jetties except one are badly broken and damaged, barges are stranded half up the beach, cases of food broken up, including a few cases of rum. Altogether the beach looks tattered and torn. The landing stages were no doubt broken by the iron barges being tossed against them by the heavy seas. The rum, I have just heard, is a serious affair as far as the front-line troops are concerned—about 114 cases or 250 gallons were stolen—and the front line will go short in consequence."

It was a remarkable thing that, right to the very end of the war, whatever casualties might be inflicted on other stores the good old rum always held pride of place.

The storm brought home to the staff the conditions that the troops would be likely to exist under in the winter time, and all battalions were urged to make all the necessary precautions for the severe weather that might be expected from this time onward.

On Sunday, October 10, the 11th Battalion relieved the 12th Battalion in the front line. The trench conditions were becoming quieter and quieter, and often for hours there would hardly be a shot fired. Regarding this, the above diarist writes: "There are sometimes hours and hours when no one would dream that there was a war being waged, because not even a shot is heard. As a rule the only shooting during the day is at periscopes or at a loop-hole. We hardly ever see a Turk, except by accident and at a great distance. One we see every morning and evening; he is evidently a cook or a cook's assistant, and if he isn't deaf he is a brave man. He walks about a hundred yards to a well carrying a brace of buckets, and he is about 900 or 1,000 yards away—perhaps a little less. Someone always has a pot at him, and though our shots throw up a spurt of dust quite close to him, he has never been seen to alter his pace or to take any notice whatever."

It was reported from Lemnos that scarlet fever had broken out among the troops on the island. This meant that neither of the other brigades of the 1st Division would be able to relieve the 3rd Brigade, and so the 11th Battalion was forced to realise that the chances of a rest were still as far off as ever.

A change in the weather took place on Monday, October 11. The sky became overcast and some rain fell, and for some time the troops expected another storm to blow up; but though it looked very black overhead, only a moderate shower was the result.

It was indicative of the quietness of the front at this period that names were asked for of any men desirous of being "confirmed." Needless to say, the list was not a large one, as besides other reasons, the troops invariably looked askance at any requests for names as they reckoned there was always a catch somewhere even in the most harmless looking shows.

On the above date, Major Leane was promoted to the rank of Lieut.-Colonel, in place of Colonel Johnston, who had been evacuated sick and since seconded.

For a long time the 11th Battalion had been taking turns of duty with the 12th Battalion in the usual 48-hour tours; one tour in the line and one tour in rest. During the time the

All that were left out of "D" Company, 11th Battalion, after six months on Anzac.

troops were in the line, when the men were not actually on duty, they would try to get a little sleep in the tunnels. These tunnels had been good retreats while the weather remained mild, but as soon as winter conditions set in these tunnels became extremely draughty and cold, and the troops used to lie shivering and generally spend a miserable time.

When in reserve or rest the conditions were considerably better, but nevertheless the approach of winter was being felt very keenly by the greatly weakened troops.

Since the medical report on the exhausted condition of the men, the rations issued had been a good deal better, and fresh bread and meat had been sent to the troops. Of course the colder weather had a lot to do with the better conditions of these rations.

The remnants of the companies that were with the 11th Battalion at the Landing were photographed on October 14.

They were pitiably small groups compared to the splendid companies that had so gallantly stormed the cliffs on the historic April 25, and their meagre numbers were tragic records of what the 11th Battalion had gone through.

For some time past the mails had been fairly regular and comforts and other parcels had been coming forward with the mails. The letters of the period indicate how much these little comforts were appreciated by the troops, living as they did in the isolation of that small bit of Turkish soil that was Anzac.

Lieut.-General Sir J. Talbot Hobbs, K.C.B., K.C.M.G., V.D., temporary in command 12th Australian Division at Anzac, October, 1915.

There was, just around this date, a considerable change - over among "the heads." General H. B. Walker, who had commanded the 1st Australian Division since Major-General Bridges had been mortally wounded on May 15, was himself wounded in the arm and was evacuated. Brigadier-General Talbot Hobbs was appointed to command the 1st Division temporarily.

General Sir Ian Hamilton, the general officer commanding the Mediterranean Expeditionary Force, was recalled to England on October 16, so that a quite unbiassed opinion on the question of the evacuation of the Gallipoli Peninsula could be obtained before the winter months set in in earnest. On the following day, General Birdwood became temporary Commander-in-Chief and Sir Ian Hamilton left

Imbros, where his headquarters had been for some time, and proceeded to England.

Hamilton's successor was Sir Charles Monro, an officer whose opinions inclined in the direction of one main offensive in the principal theatre of war which, of course, was in Western Europe, so it was not difficult to anticipate what his decision would be on the question of evacuation. Monro arrived at Gallipoli at the end of the month of October.

The usual "furphies" concerning relief and "spells" were going their rounds with greater vigour than ever, and had the troops but known, this time with a much surer foundation. But the troops were so disappointed with the frequent false alarms and delays that they began to look on all rumours of relief as mere creations of the imagination of their war-weary comrades. So much so that one of the diarists who has been so often quoted, in referring to a fresh rumour, breaks out into the following low verse:—

"You can't chisel me, oh! no, you can't chisel me,
He cleared off with my old dear;
I went back and drank his beer,
For you can't chisel me."

From now on active warfare was almost at a standstill. Occasionally there would be a demonstration, and occasionally when some new target was reported there would be a burst of shelling; sometimes the 11th Battalion would be made to "stand-to" all night, when some particular operation was carried out, or when it was known that one of the Turkish festivals was about to be celebrated, and consequently an attack by the enemy was quite likely to happen. But nothing of the sort did happen and taken as a whole there was not, at this late stage of the occupation of Anzac, much variation from day to day.

The only serious fighting on the Peninsula at this time was over at Suvla Bay, where frequent heavy bombardments were heard, and to the south the boys could often see the smoke and dust flying on the slopes of Achi Baba. The warships, too, were constantly finding targets, and that at least created an interest if it did nothing else.

A fine sight was frequently witnessed when the weather was clear. A large airship used to take off from Imbros and make for the direction of the Asiatic coast. Though the troops often saw this airship pass over, yet it was never seen on its return journey.

The official battalion records are extremely meagre around this period, and the chief sources of information about the battalion's doings are from the diaries of Lieuts. Aitken and Snodgrass.

On the afternoon of October 20, Colonel Collett and a party of officers from the 28th Battalion visited the 11th Bat-

Capt. C. Gostelow (11th Battalion). Photo. taken as sergeant 86th Infantry, A.M.F.

Tommy Stokes' (11th Battalion) grave in Shell Green.

talion sector. These officers from Western Australia were all very much impressed with the amount of work done in trench construction and other defensive works, and they spent an instructive few hours in the sector of their sister battalion.

At this time, sniping was being regularly carried out by two posts in each company frontage. It was considered that this activity was of great use in that it not only harrassed the enemy, but was also instrumental in destroying many of the Turkish sniping "possies."

On October 22, a recommendation was made by the 11th Battalion headquarters that gum-boots, sheepskin vests and water-proof coats should be issued to the troops for the winter.

As it had been raining during the whole of that day, the recommendation might have been expected to carry some weight. Second Lieut. Wilson reported back from hospital on this same date.

Lieut. A. H. Darnell was evacuated sick on October 23. The 11th Battalion was relieved by the 12th Battalion and went into reserve, where the troops occupied the position vacated by the 12th above Shell Green.

The 8th Reinforcements of the 11th Battalion, consisting of two officers and 135 other ranks, arrived at Anzac on October 24, and they were instructed to remain at the reinforcement camp until further orders.

On this date, also, definite information was sent to all battalions of the 3rd Brigade that, as it was not convenient to relieve the brigade for some time, the 3rd Brigade would remain on the Peninsula pending orders. And so a few more dreams of peace and rest were rudely shattered.

To celebrate the occasion of having been six months on Gallipoli, and to compensate for the disappointment of the cancellation of their expected relief, the troops were granted a special issue of rum on October 25. The good old S.R.D. may not have been dedicated to the toast of "The Landing," but it was none the less appreciated for all that.

No comforts or special issues of rations or other concessions were ever the same to the troops as an issue of rum. In spite of all that has been said on the subject, the rum issue created more happiness and did more good both physically and mentally than anything else the troops received during their period of active service.

A party of three officers and 43 other ranks returned to duty with the 11th Battalion on the last-mentioned date.

Now that conditions on the Anzac front had settled into a groove, with all the regularity and routine of fixed trench warfare, men from the various units made it a practice to visit friends in other parts of the line. When friends who had not seen each other since they left Australia met for the first time, many and wonderful were the tales that were told of their experiences.

On one occasion, "C" Company had just come out from its 48 hours tour of duty in the line, and the usual yarns were circulating. After most of the boys had fallen silent, one man said: "I was talking to a Turk over the parapet last night, and had quite a long yap, too." Immediately there was a yell of derision, "Get out, you stupid cow! You can't wongi 'Jacko' lingo!"

"I tell you I was," insisted the first speaker, in quite an injured manner. Then he added more quietly, and drawling it out: "But I think he must have been dead, for he didn't answer me back."

Meanwhile, events had been moving quickly in high places. On October 27 General Sir Charles Monro arrived from England and took over the command of the Mediterranean Expeditionary Force from General Birdwood. He immediately went into all the details of the Gallipoli operations and visited the various areas of activity. On October 30 he came ashore at Anzac, where he made an inspection, and he also visited Suvla Bay on the same date.

Next day, October 31, 1915, he sent his recommendation to Lord Kitchener, stating that in his opinion the Gallipoli Peninsula should be evacuated without delay. His telegram concluded with the following trenchant words: "On purely military grounds, therefore, I recommend the evacuation of the Peninsula."

Of course this recommendation and its effects were not known to the troops until several weeks later.

A very fine description of Anzac and neighbouring sector at the time of Sir Charles Monro's visit is given by Lieut. J. M. Aitken in his diary, dated October 27, 1915. He describes a visit to a unit at the extreme north of the Australian sector.

"For a long way we went along the beach, and it's just as busy as a bee-hive for over five miles; and what I saw on my first return to the beach away back in April is nothing to its appearance now.

"There are several large depots for stores and ammunition, besides stables for the mules and donkeys used in their transportation; also tramways run along the beach, thus facilitating the handling of heavy goods. Then there are numerous working parties, as well as a corps of Maltese which does the permanent work here. I also noticed a lot of big machinery, boring and drilling plants, with engines and boilers, so I expect they will be looking for artesian water before long.

"From the beach to the positions to the left there are two roads; one sunken for use during the day, as a great deal of shelling goes on; the other, of course, is perfectly safe at night; naturally we followed the sunken road, and it twists and turns all ways. As the Turks have command of all the high positions in this vicinity, and can snipe down into the road, it is banked up and screened wherever dangerous.

"After a deal of climbing, we found the 28th Battalion on Cheshire Ridge, in rear of the Apex, so called because it is a wedge-shaped position running right out from our general line of trench.

"I had a good view from here and could see many positions of interest. Away on the left were the 'Chocolate Hills,' 'W' Hill (it has an almost perfect naturally formed 'W' on its slopes), Hills '60' and '70,' and beyond them the ruined village of Anafarta. Immediately in front was Chunuk Bair and Hill '971,' while behind us to the left was Suvla Bay. All these places were in our possession at one time and that of Chunuk Bair for 48 hours, but owing to mismanagement and the Turks, of course, we have now these places to get; the pity of it all is that many of the Tommies' bodies are now lying between the lines, and I could plainly see biscuit and water-tins, where they had bivouaced during their short tenure. . . .

"I was struck by the peculiar run of the trenches here; they writhe in and out like a live snake, in parts almost touching, while they were 750 yards apart in others. Cheshire Ridge connects with Chunuk Bair forming an enormous 'V,' and although the Turks are on the summit, our apex is within 25 yards of them. Then the trenches gradually follow the contour and fall farther apart.

"'971' is the highest point in this region, and it is rear of Chunuk Bair; it is a commanding position and I'm afraid the Turk is going to take a bit of shifting. In the far distance the trenches go up hill and down dale until they contort themselves out of sight.

"On our way back we saw a canteen, and lined up quite prepared to pay two shillings for a morsel of sod-cake; we waited for an hour and then found out that they had sold out. Damn!"

The above letter is instructive, not only from its excellent description of the positions and trenches, but more so from the

11th Battalion's point of view, for though the War Office was even then considering the question of evacuation, this letter shows that the troops, however weary they were, still had the idea that they were to press forward when the time came, and they regarded the future undismayed.

On the last day of October the battalion lost the services of Captain John Fahey, the Chaplain, and a man if ever there was one. He had done continuous fine work since the Landing and had gained the respect of all ranks. He was evacuated sick. On this date also, Lieut. J. Newman returned to duty from hospital.

The month of November started with fine and mild weather, which was welcome after the taste of winter that the troops had experienced. The battalion routine remained the same as in the previous weeks.

On November 3, a large number of troops was landed, including the 1st, 2nd and 4th Brigades, which had been resting on Lemnos. The 1st Brigade relieved the 9th, 10th and 12th Battalions, but the 11th Battalion still had to carry on in the line.

Available records do not state why the 3rd Brigade was so long in being relieved compared to its sister brigades, nor do they state why the 11th Battalion alone of the 3rd Brigade was still unrelieved on the above date after having fought continuously for over six months at Anzac. As long as no other reason is forthcoming, it can only be deduced that the 11th Battalion was without equal in stamina and endurance, as well as in military qualities in its own brigade, and that the 3rd Brigade held an equally proud place in the 1st Division.

On the same date as above, General Sir Charles Monro was transferred to the command of the Salonika Force, and Birdwood was appointed Commander-in-Chief of the Mediterranean Expeditionary Force.

On the following day, although the troops did not know it at the time, General Birdwood was asked by Lord Kitchener to draw up plans for the evacuation of the Gallipoli Peninsula.

Though, as mentioned in a previous chapter, most of the shipping had for a long time ceased to anchor off Anzac, yet there were usually three hospital ships in the bay. These had never been interfered with in any way by the Turks since first they were stationed there. Besides the hospital ships there was now generally a number of small craft, trawlers, supply-ships and the like dotted all over the bay; three cruisers were usually stationed in Suvla Bay, and since the landing at the former place, a cruiser was on duty in Anzac Cove. Several monitors were always moving about, while further out there were three or four screens of destroyers, which kept up an incessant patrol. They dashed from point to point, with the water foaming behind them, and all over the surface of the blue seas were lacy traceries of foam where they had passed and repassed.

Occasionally some of these destroyers would stand in and assist in the shelling of land targets. Besides these ships in the immediate vicinity, numerous other vessels were to be seen with smudges or trails of smoke right over as far as the horizon. The ships and shipping were always of great interest to the troops, marooned as they were far from all the social amenities. Their coming and going and their manœuvres were practically the only novelties in the lives of the boys; the boats were the only links that bound them to the outside world.

There was hardly any hostile action at Anzac in November, but on the right, half-way towards Gaba Tepe, the light horsemen were having a small local battle for the position between their own lines and the Turks. On November 5, the light horse, having tunnelled forward, were apprehensive of attack, and 200 men of the 11th Battalion were detailed to act as reserve. The 11th men moved into position at 5:30 p.m. expecting to have a stirring evening, but nothing of importance occurred and the following day the 11th Battalion troops were withdrawn.

Much has already been written about the promised relief of the 11th Battalion, and though the subject does not want to be laboured, it was too much the burden of all the records and diaries of the period and was so much in the daily thoughts of the men that this record would not be a faithful account of the last days of the occupation if due mention was not made of this subject. Though the disappointment at not being relieved was very keen, the troops could always make a joke about it, and the following tale, first told by the cheery Captain "Doc" Brennan at a concert held on the slope at the back of Ledge Trench, met with a good reception.

Here is the tale: "One day, long after the war was over, a party of American tourists was visiting the historic battlefields of Anzac. They wandered from point to point in the now abandoned trenches, commenting on the various positions until they came to the 3rd Brigade sector, where they were amazed to see two queer-looking old birds, with rifles and a pile of bombs alongside. One was sitting down while the other was gazing through a battered periscope. These old men looked infinitely weary and emaciated, and they were very much surprised to see the party.

"One of the tourists inquired: 'Say! Who are you guys?' The old chap who was sitting down replied: 'Oh! We belong to the 11th Battalion, and we're just waiting to be relieved!' "

One of the brigade reports about this time states that when an enemy machine gun was located at Pine Ridge, although the range was only 1800 yards, the supporting guns were unable to shell the position owing to the worn condition of the barrels.

On the night of November 10, a detachment of 100 men was sent from "C" and "D" Companies of the 11th Battalion to assist the 5th Regiment of Light Horse at Chatham's Post. These latter troops had still a bit of straightening to do before they could consider their position satisfactory. The light horsemen were successful in bombing the enemy out of his advanced positions without any trouble. Two men of the 11th Battalion were wounded, but there was no serious fighting, and next morning the party of the 11th was relieved.

Owing to increased enemy activity in strengthening his positions and putting out new wire entanglements, besides making redoubts and other strong points, there was an apprehension that the Turk was preparing for an attack on a big scale. Added to this was the fear of a gas attack, especially as the Turk had been using some incendiary bombs that gave off a lot of smoke, and others that lay hissing after they were thrown. In view of this danger, Lieut.-Colonel Leane ordered a surprise gas attack on the night of November 12. The lads refused to take the matter seriously, and the usual larking and tomfoolery went on. Through some hitch, one of the companies was not warned, and when a report was required as to how the men had prepared for the supposed danger, the C.O. was annoyed to hear that the men were still all asleep and remarked that if such were the case the men must have all been suffocated. Old Jack Cropper, who was standing near, asked very innocently, "How many died, sir?"

The same wag, who had been for some time employed doing odd jobs round the quartermaster's store, had been excused all official parades and had become a bit casual about his uniform and equipment.

One day a muster parade was held and old Jack appeared on parade without a rifle. Naturally, he was soon asked, in no polite terms, why he was on parade without a rifle. "Hell!" he exclaimed. "Have I got to have a rifle? I thought I was neutral now-a-days!"

As a result of all the discussion and criticism that had taken place on the Dardanelles operations, Lord Kitchener himself determined to visit the Gallipoli Peninsula. After a conference with the various responsible officers, he visited Anzac on November 13.

He was soon recognised by some of the troops, although he came without any ostentation or fuss. The boys gave him a cheer, and then Kitchener spoke a few words to the troops and conveyed to them the King's message of appreciation.

His own words, "You have done better than I ever thought you would," seem to leave a hint of disappointment; but as he was a man of few words and not given to lengthy orations, he may have implied a great deal more than he said.

As a result of his investigations, he was fully seized with the necessity for a speedy evacuation, as immediate events showed.

At 2 p.m. on the same day, the long awaited and welcome news came to 11th Battalion headquarters that the 9th and 11th Battalions would leave for Lemnos on the night of November 14, and an advance party was immediately detailed to leave for that island early on the following morning.

This party, under Company Quarter-Master Sergeant J. M. Aitken, embarked on Sunday, November 14, in a launch and went aboard the *Princess Ena,* which at once started for Lemnos. On board the boys renewed their acquaintance with some nicely buttered bread. This unaccustomed treat caused Jim Aitken to burst out into this panegyric:—

"Oh! butter, thou art the essence of joy.
By jings! thou saved this hungry boy!"

It can be better imagined than described with what joy the troops received the news that the long service on Gallipoli was at last going to be recognised, and that relief was only to be a matter of hours. Seven months was a considerable period to have been away from all the amenities of modern life, and it was only natural that the thought of seeing even the island of Lemnos again put new life into tired troops.

When the next two days came in stormy, and great seas prevented the embarkation of the troops, the boys felt that fate was indeed unkind; and though the 11th Battalion was ready to move at 15 minutes' notice, yet it now seemed as if the warning to move would never come.

It rained all day long on November 15, and on November 16 the weather was still so rough that it was considered impossible that the men could be evacuated that night.

However, in a remarkably short space of time, the weather improved and the sea became calm, and the air so clear and still that the mountains of Samothrace, situated on an island 25 miles away, could be seen perfectly distinctly, clearly defined by the setting sun. The welcome order to get ready for embarkation came along that night, and about 9 p.m. the 11th Battalion went aboard the s.s. *Abbassieh,* in company with the 9th with cries of "Inta magnoon. Abbassia bukra!" (Egyptian for "You're mad! Abbassia to-morrow," and a common tag among the boys that served in Egypt-Abbassia or Abbassieh being a military detention camp near Cairo).

The *Abbasseih* set off for Mudros at 9:30 p.m., and as the vessel left the shore the Turks sent a few messages of farewell, in the form of spent bullets, which would occasionally hit the ship or drop harmlessly into the water alongside. There were no casualties during the embarkation.

And in this wise the 11th Battalion said "Farewell to Gallipoli" and the long weary days and nights in the trenches which had cost the men so many hours of unremitting labour. Though the boys did not realise it at the time, they were taking their last look at that dim and fast-receding shore, whose gloomy heights contained the graves of so many of Australia's best, and those their own dear mates of only a short time previously; and as the lights of Anzac twinkled and gradually faded into nothingness, the thoughts of many must have turned to those heroic days of the Landing, when they so nearly succeeded in achieving the impossible.

And, irony of ironies, the very name that was by a mere chance given to those few acres where they had fought and suffered and fallen, the name "Anzac" is a word that, in the Turkish language, means "Almost."

"LEGS–ELEVEN" 177

As the *Abbassieh* pushed into the more open seas, conditions became rough, and soon the troops were feeling the effects of the vessel's rolling, and most of them were unfeignedly glad to see the old familiar windmills above Mudros harbour once again. The *Abbassieh* berthed at 8 a.m. on November 17, 1915.

So ended the 11th Battalion's active service on the Gallipoli Peninsula. The troops left the battle front at Anzac with feelings of thankfulness and joy, but had they known they were relinquishing their dearly-bought gain for all time, their mood would have been inexpressibly resentful and bitter.

The 8th Reinforcement of the 11th Battalion, under Lieuts. G. Campbell and Owen, which had landed at Anzac about a month previously but had remained at the reinforcement camp without joining up with its unit, had been left at Gallipoli, where it had been continuously employed on heavy work, as the men were fresh and unwearied compared to those who had been continuously serving on Anzac.

Chapter XII

WINTER AT LEMNOS ISLAND

ON ARRIVAL at Mudros, the 11th Battalion immediately marched to Sarpi Camp. This was part of a huge camping area, and instead of being allocated to tents the men were housed in small marquees, each holding 40 men. The weather was very bleak and extremely cold, and the men, in their exhausted condition, had little power of resistance to the elements and they suffered accordingly. The troops were given the day to themselves and spent the time in trying to make themselves comfortable and to gain a little warmth where they could.

Next day, November 18, the weather conditions were no better. In fact they were so bad that nothing could be done in the way of the much-needed reorganisation, and the bugle played that most popular of airs, "No parade to-day."

Lemnos was now one vast camp, with thousands of troops everywhere, and white tents made the prevailing colour in the landscape round the great harbour. There was bustle and activity everywhere and a constant coming and going of troops. The harbour was full of shipping, among which was the mighty *Aquitania*, and transports and freighters were constantly on the move.

During the next two or three weeks, after the necessary organisation had been affected, the companies of the 11th Battalion were drilled when the weather was suitable—which was not often—and organised games were encouraged. The parades were mainly devoted to short route marches and physical jerks, and any exercises that would help to keep the men warm. The official diary has very few entries for this period, but there is one for November 25 which reads:—

"The weather has been extremely bad ever since we arrived. Very little training can be done. Mudros seems a very unsuitable place to send troops for a rest, and I am much afraid if the weather we are getting continues a great number of the men will get ill."

Members of "C" Company, 11th Battalion, at Mudros, Lemnos Island. All that were left of those who landed in April, 1915, at Anzac.

The s.s. *Olympic* arrived in Lemnos Harbour on November 24, and many of the men of the 11th Battalion had the privilege of seeing over this gigantic vessel. The weather was mostly stormy, but occasionally there was a fine day and a most wonderful scene would present itself. There was the magnificent harbour filled with all kinds of shipping; the hills on the island crowned with the funny old windmills; and the white tents in rows and squares dotted about everywhere. When night fell, it was a sight never to be forgotten.

The whole harbour was ablaze with lights, every ship lending its quota; and on a calm evening these lights and their reflections cast a dim radiance over the waters; while on the land the twinkling of myriads of camp fires gave that cheerful and comforting look to the night that no other form of illumination can quite equal. Sometimes a searchlight would play its beams over the sea and sky, shining (as one poetical diarist described it), "like a great brilliant in a setting of gems."

On November 28, Corporal Ritchie, who had been sent to hospital, was found to be suffering from diptheria, so the whole 3rd Brigade area was put under quarantine, thus restricting the liberty of the troops to a very great extent.

The official diary entry for November 30 is as follows:—

"The weather has been simply awful. Very little training is possible. The men have so far been unable to get a warm issue (of clothing) and consequently are not able to withstand the cold. We had a sick parade of 64 this morning, which is very large considering our small strength. Major Lorenzo, of the 10th Battalion, assumed temporary command of the 11th Battalion vice Major (temporary Lieut.-Colonel) Leane to hospital, ill."

A double cordon of piquets was placed round the 3rd Brigade lines to prevent the men from breaking quarantine. This kept those men in who wished to stay in, and as the weather had improved in the last day or two, the confinement to camp was not so unbearable as it had hitherto been.

In the meantime, the reorganisation of the 11th Battalion continued. The specialist sections were brought up to strength and exercised in their various functions, while the companies were instructed in platoon and section drill.

On December 4, Major S. R. Roberts assumed command of the 11th Battalion, on his return from hospital, and Major Lorenzo returned to the 10th Battalion.

Another case of diptheria was reported on December 5, and there were many men reporting sick with sore throats; but the health of the troops was, on the whole, improving, and advantage was taken of the fine weather to play cricket and football. This was in itself an indication that the men were getting back to normal.

The sick report on December 10 gave some cause for anxiety, for No. 1953 Private H. Heyes was reported to be suffering from meningitis, and all in his tent were immediately removed and isolated, while Heyes was sent to hospital. There was also another case of diptheria.

Lieut.-Colonel S. Roberts, D.S.O.

The isolation camp was fairly strictly guarded, but the quarantining of the 3rd Brigade was only a farce, for men could get out without very much trouble, and it can hardly be imagined that Australians, who had just been relieved from months of warfare, sickness and frightful living conditions were going to worry about the dissemination of a few disease germs.

The 8th Reinforcements of the 11th Battalion, which had been left at Anzac under Lieuts. Campbell and Owen, joined up with the battalion on December 12. When these reinforcements had arrived on Gallipoli, about seven weeks prior to this date, they numbered 155 other ranks; but when they were absorbed by the 11th Battalion, their numbers had fallen as low as 73 men.

The company parades, which up to this time had only been of short duration, were increased to three-hour periods, as the physical condition of the men had improved very considerably.

The following promotions were read out in orders: Lieut. MarFarlane to be captain; 2nd/Lieuts. Potter, Burgess, Mason, Bardwell, Combs, Bradshaw, O'Neil, Miller, Boddington, Hemingway and Walther to be lieutenants.

Colonel G. J. Johnston, C.B., V.D., commanding 3rd Brigade, left for Egypt, and Lieut.-Colonel Robertson, of the 9th Battalion, assumed temporary command on December 13.

There was very little of interest during this period. The battalion was only doing routine work, and was gradually getting back to its old health and vigour. A few more cases of diptheria broke out, and another case of meningitis. Private Heyes, of the 11th Battalion, died of the latter disease on December 17.

The contacts of this dread disease were still isolated in their marquee, and were quarantined about 500 yards away from the rest of the battalion, and there were sentries posted to keep the boys in the area. Lieut. Peter Snodgrass (then Corporal) who was one of the "contacts" relates this story of the isolation camp:

"As the time hung heavily on their hands, some of the wilder spirits began to get restless, and one night a party, led by a gigantic fellow named Mort Hair, determined to make a trip out to the warships to see if they could purchase any liquor. A muster was made and seven of the boys set out. There was only one boat in sight, and that one a Greek's. The sentry who tried to stop them from leaving the quarantine ground was brushed aside, and the party made for the boat. It was fastened to a stout post by a strong chain. As the chain defied their united efforts to break it, the bad lads pulled up the post and tossed it and the chain into the boat and sailed off.

"After a bit of trouble they managed to purchase half a case of whisky from one of the warships. On the return journey, Mort Hair wanted to broach a bottle, but the rest of the boys would not let him. There was a fight and Hair was pushed overboard into the chilly water. He immediately set out for the shore and reached it as soon as the boat did.

"Half a case of whisky was only an appetiser for 40 men, and the wilder spirits determined to procure some more. They could not go out in daylight, so they had to wait till nightfall.

When darkness fell, Mort Hair, who had not changed his wet clothes of the preceding night, led his six bandits out in search of more 'neck oil.' They reached a nighbouring Greek village, and after hunting around they spied a huge bottle like those displayed in a chemist's window; this was filled with a brownish liquid. It was 'wet,' so the men offered to buy it. The Greek shook his head, so Hair strode in and came out again with his arms wrapped round the huge bottle, and in spite of protests bore it off to the isolation tent.

"The raiders returned about 11 p.m. and the boys sat drinking the stuff, which had a most delectable flavour, until 9 a.m. next morning. Then they fell asleep. But not for long. One after another they awoke with raging thirsts and called for water. The more water they drank the drunker they became, and it was not till the day following that they reverted to normal. The liquor proved to be moastique, a very potent Greek drink tasting of aniseed."

Meantime, troops had been arriving daily, chiefly from Gallipoli, and rumours of the intending evacuation were becoming rife. These, however, were treated as "furphies," as the boys could not bring themselves to believe that the British War Office would give up that which had taken so much blood and other expenditure to capture and hold.

Rumour, alas! though mostly a "lying jade" was this time discovered to be a true prophet, and on December 20, 1915, it was definitely known that Anzac had been evacuated, with only a few casualties. The news of the evacuation was intensely dispiriting to the men, and was like to have made a very miserable Christmas for all. When the boys remembered all the defensive lines of trenches and tunnels and galleries that had taken so much time and effort to make, the hardship and perils so lately undergone, and all their dead mates, whose sacrifice had now been rendered futile, it was only natural that they should be depressed.

Added to this was the feeling of lost prestige. When a division has the proud motto of the 1st Australian Division, "What we have, we hold," it was a bitter pill for the men of that division to swallow when they heard that Anzac had been evacuated; and it was only when they heard of the details of the evacuation itself and of how the last troops had got away without casualties and without the Turks being aware of the retreat, that their despondency was in some way mitigated.

As the 11th Battalion was not concerned in the actual evacuation, the story of that great withdrawal is out of range of this story; and all the devices and strategems to deceive the Turk and to allay his suspicions that a retreat was in progress have been well described elsewhere; and the wonderful luck in withdrawing so many troops with so few casualties from such vulnerable beaches is well known. Whether the success of the operations was due to brilliant strategy on the part of those in command, or whether it was due in a large measure to pure luck will always be open to comment, but there never can be any doubt about the skill and ability of the troops who carried out the measures necessary for the complete success of the operation, known afterwards as "The Evacuation."

The total Australian loss on Gallipoli was 26,094 men, and that of the New Zealanders, 7,571. The Australian killed numbered 7,594 and the New Zealanders 2,431. These losses were only a fraction of the total of the whole campaign. To mention only one British division, the splendid 29th Division, which was often associated with the 1st Australian Division in the later years of the war, the casualties of this single division amounted to the staggering total of 34,011 all ranks, or a replacement of the fighting personnel four and a half times. Thus, though the enormous sacrifice made by the Australians seems to have been far from justified by the results of the ill-advised expedition, their case was hardly so bad as many of the British divisions.

The foregoing paragraph is inserted to prevent a distorted view of the Australians' part on Gallipoli being held. While no troops could ever have done more or behaved with greater gallantry than the Anzac boys, it is only fair to remember that other divisions played their honourable part in that unfortunate undertaking.

While the troops were discussing the unforseen and disappointing ending to the Gallipoli adventure, and recalling all the incidents of their first venture into the arena of war, the days were drawing nearer to Christmas and preparations were made by those in command to make the season as gay as circumstances would allow. Sports were held and cricket and football matches were played between the battalions.

In the midst of all these preparations for Christmas, the order came through, "All leave stopped. Be ready to move at five minutes' notice." Though there were plenty of rumours afloat as to the next move, the boys were not at all certain as to their destination, though the general opinion was that it would be Egypt.

On the same day, December 22, the 3rd Brigade quarantine was lifted, and next morning the Christmas billies were distributed. These were full of good things, and helped to make life a little brighter; the only complaint, and that a not unreasonable one on the part of the 11th Battalion, was that the billies came from Victoria, when it was quite generally known that their own dear folks in Western Australia had sent more than ample for every West Australian on active service.

Christmas Eve passed quietly, and next dawn ushered in the second Christmas Day that many of the 11th Battalion had spent away from their homeland. It was not a wonderful festival on Lemnos Island. There was the usual divine service in the morning and the rest of the day was a holiday for the troops. In addition to the billies already distributed, the boys received plum puddings which were also the gifts of the good people of Australia, who were always very generous to the troops. In the evening Christmas carols were sung by some of the boys in the Y.M.C.A. marquee, and there were also many other kinds of carols sung in the tents of the troops.

It was now definitely known that the 11th Battalion was to be sent to Egypt along with the rest of the 3rd Brigade, and the remaining days of December were spent in pleasurable anticipation of the return to the land of "Saeeda" and "eggs-a-cook."

On December 26 the 3rd Brigade Headquarters and the 10th Battalion left Mudros Harbour for Alexandria on the s.s. *Seang Bee*. The remainder of the brigade came under the command of Lieut.-Colonel Gellibrand pending its departure.

For the last few days of 1915, the 11th Battalion went through the usual routine of camp life; there were parades daily and route marches and battalion drill were carried out. On the last day of the year it was learned that the 11th Battalion would embark on January 1, 1916, for Alexandria. "A" and "B" Companies on the s.s. *Lake Michigan* and "C" and "D" Companies on the s.s. *Empress of Britain*.

There were the customary celebrations on New Year's Eve, especially by those members of the battalion who laid claim to Scottish blood, and all the ships in the harbour added to the clamour of bringing in the New Year of 1916 by a great hooting and blowing of sirens. But on the whole the day and night passed quietly, and so ended the wonderful and terrible year of 1915.

CHAPTER XIII

LIFE ON THE CANAL ZONE
TEL-EL-KEBIR AND GEBEL HABIETA

As MENTIONED in the previous chapter the 11th Battalion had received embarkation orders, as after the many representations made by responsible officers it had at length been considered that Mudros was not a suitable place for the wintering of Australian troops, especially those who had spent a long time on Gallipoli, and had been so weakened physically that they were in no state to stand the rigours of a severe winter. Therefore, the 1st Australian Division had been ordered to proceed to a camp in Egypt, where the drier air and more healthy surroundings would be a factor in building up the troops. The 11th Battalion received its movement order on January 1, 1916, and the troops went aboard the two ships already named, the *Lake Michigan* and the *Empress of Britain*.

The troops were quartered aboard for several days before the vessels sailed. The good fare that the ships provided was greatly appreciated after the montonous food that had been issued to the troops for so long, and meal-times were eagerly looked forward to.

A number of horses had to be loaded on to the *Lake Michigan* from barges. This had to be postponed on account of the rough seas preventing the barges from lying alongside the transport. On this account sailing was delayed for several days.

Enemy submarines had been fairly active, and all possible precautions had been taken against them. The ships had small guns mounted and a torpedo net was stretched across the harbour mouth. Beyond the entrance was a screen of trawlers with a covering fleet of destroyers further out.

Early on the morning of January 4, 1916, the two ships sailed. All the troops were wearing lifebelts and submarine lookouts were posted. There was an escorting cruiser for a part of the voyage. Once on the open seas the usual tales of submarines seen and torpedoes dodged were passed among the troops. The vessels zig-zagged across the waters of the Levant, leaving curiously shaped trails of foam on the sparkling seas.

When some distance from Mudros, the cruiser was relieved by a destroyer which now assumed the duties of escort. A vessel was seen ahead, which was soon overhauled. The destroyer stopped and boarded her, but evidently found everything satisfactory as she was allowed to proceed on her voyage. She was a Greek vessel.

Nothing exciting happened during the remainder of the voyage, and on January 6 the two vessels containing the 11th Battalion were off Alexandria. The seas, however, were too rough for the pilot to come aboard, so the ships anchored in the roads where the vessels rolled heavily and strained at their anchors. This unusual motion caused many of the men to be sick.

Later in the day the vessels moved in alongside the wharf, and when the order for disembarkation came the troops were marched straight on to the waiting trains, which moved off almost immediately into the darkness. The troops travelled in iron trucks which soon cooled with the motion of the train, leaving the men shivering and miserable. No idea of the route they were taking was possible to the boys owing to the darkness, but the town of Zagazig which was known to be close to the great wireless station was passed about midnight, and soon after the train pulled up at Tel-el-Kebir, where the cramped and frozen troops dragged their shivering limbs out of the trucks.

As there were no tents, the troops had to camp out in the open desert with no other protection other than their greatcoats and oil-sheets. All ranks were unfeignedly glad when morning broke and a hot breakfast soon changed the complexion of things. There was never anything quite so good as steaming hot tea from the company kitchens when troops were chilled to the bone, unless it was a judicious issue of rum.

The battalion transport section, consisting of one officer (Lieut. Alec Burgess) and 36 men, which had been detached for over eight months, had already arrived from Mex Camp; and from this time, except for a short period on the Suez Canal and a day or two here and there when circumstances of rail or sea transport interfered, it was never again completely separated from the 11th Battalion.

When the boys learned that they were only a short distance away from the site of the historic battlefield of Tel-el-Kebir, where Arabi Pasha had been defeated by the British under Sir Garnet Wolseley in 1882, there was an immediate rush to visit the old Egyptain trenches. These extended for about three miles on the north side of the camp, and though the battle had been fought so long ago, there were still some souvenirs to be picked up.

There was a vast system of sidings at the railway station. This was taken as an indication that a mighty camp was going to be formed at Tel-el-Kebir, and immediately reinforcements and other troops began to pour in.

On the day of the 11th Battalion's arrival, 367 officers and men of the 9th, 10th and 11th Reinforcements, as well as a big draft of returned sick and wounded and other details arrived for the battalion from Cairo. The following officers reported for duty: Captain J. T. Milner (9th/11th), 2nd/Lieuts. Williams and Le Nay (10th/11th) and 2nd/Lieuts. J. S. D. Walker, Cook and W. Kruger (11th/11th) Reinforcements.

Brigadier-General E. Sinclair-MacLagan had again assumed command of the 3rd Brigade before the 11th Battalion had arrived at Tel-el-Kebir.

Before proceeding further with the story of the 11th Battalion, a little digression is necessary to explain the reason for the formation of a large military camp so far away from all the conveniences of organised transport and other amenities.

In the first place, a large and conveniently close base was necessary for a concentration of troops to defend the Suez Canal and adjacent territory. This area was generally known as "The Canal Zone," and it was regarded as one of the vulnerable points at this stage of the Great War, and more especially after the failure of the British thrust against Constantinople.

The second reason was that, owing to the withdrawal of such a vast number of troops from Gallipoli and Lemnos, there was a great congestion at all the already existing camps in Egypt, especially so as reinforcements were coming forward in ever greater numbers from Australia, as the people of that country were realising the increasing necessity of supporting "The Old Country."

There were several other reasons that had also a great deal to do with the selection of this camp at Tel-el-Kebir, not the least of which was the Australian Government's objection to its troops being camped too near to the great cities of Cairo or Alexandria, with their multitude of temptations, and the Egyptian Government's fears that there might be a repetition of the disturbances that took place on Christmas Eve in Cairo, if all these troops from the front lines with considerable accumulations of back pay were quartered near either of the two large cities. Besides it was known that the troops would be much more easy to handle out in the desert than near the distractions of a city.

Mention has been made of the disturbance on Christmas Eve in Cairo. This had taken place only two weeks previously, and it certainly was a wild night and was always referred to by the boys as "The Second Battle of the Wazir," the "First Battle" having taken place about a year previously. As there were about 600 reinforcements for the 11th Battalion camped at Abassia (between Cairo and Heliopolis) at this time, it was only to be expected that many of these troops were present at the "battle," so a short account of the disturbance is appended.

As this affair was outside the actual history of the 11th Battalion, it is only necessary to say that a feeling of resentment had been growing against a section of the populace, and that the authorities were aware of this and thought that the troops would be more tractable if there was no liquor sold. So, on December 24, all the restaurants and shops were liquor was procurable were closed.

The troops resented this very strongly, and led by a few of the wilder spirits they descended upon the native and loose quarters of the city and started looting and burning. Most of the boys regarded the affair only as a wild rag, but there were some that went too far, and certain very objectionable elements crept in and there was a considerable amount of damage done, some estimates being £20,000.

The affair looked serious for a while, but the troops were mostly persuaded to leave the city before midnight; and Christmas Day dawned quietly, and there were no more disturbances.

But the result was that the Egyptian authorities were so startled that they at once took steps to try to prevent a repetition. One of the direct consequences was that a camp was formed

70 miles away from Cairo, and orders were issued that there should only be a very limited amount of leave for the troops.

Thus, then, the 1st and 2nd Australian Divisions were sent to Tel-el-Kebir, while the Australian and New Zealand Division was sent to Moascar, near Ismalia.

On January 8, 1916, the 11th Battalion was reorganised and the new reinforcements and details absorbed into the four companies. The men were still sleeping out in the open, and unfortunately the weather had been wet and cloudy so that the boys were unable to dry their blankets and consequently they spent several miserable nights.

Troop trains kept continually arriving and the camp kept increasing until a great extent of ground was covered with men bivouacing. Headquarters and quartermasters' staffs worked at high pressure to cope with this great influx. The mail alone was a serious item, for it had been held up for two months and was now arriving in huge quantities. Some of the boys received fifty or sixty letters at one time; but then mail was generally a feast or a famine.

Leave was granted to two per cent. of the men and five per cent. of officers. It is hardly necessary to add that Cairo was the "Mecca" of these pilgrims.

It was not until January 10 that tents began to arrive for the men, and after erecting the lines of tents and making the camp ship-shape, training started in earnest. The battalion was put through the exercises in the Infantry Training Manual from the beginning, including the hated "saluting by numbers," as many of the men required a brush up, especially those who had been a long time in hospital or on detached duty such as mining on Anzac and the like. Some battalion drill was given on January 14 as a preparation for a review on the following day by the General Officer Commanding the Mediterranean Expeditionary Force, who at this time was Sir Archibald Murray.

The 1st Australian Division was reviewed as a complete unit on Saturday, January 15. The twelve battalions of the division took just one hour to pass the saluting-base, marching past in column of platoons, and they presented a magnificent spectacle, so much so, that the G.O.C., an officer who was extremely punctilious in the matter of ceremonial, expressed warm approval of the men's bearing and appearance.

For some time Sir Archibald Murray had been rather shocked at the casual and what he considered undisciplined conduct of the Australian troops, which was a sore trial to a soldier of the old "spit-and-polish" school as he was; and the sight of the splendid manhood of Australia in such a disciplined display must have come as an agreeable surprise.

There was not very much of outstanding interest during this period of the battalion's life, and after the village of Tel-el-Kebir and the surrounding country along the banks of the Sweetwater Canal had been explored and their possibilities exhausted, there was very little for the troops to do; so naturally the great national game of "two-up" came into its own, especially as the troops had plenty of money and little to spend it on. Big "schools" used to be formed behind the lines after parades were over, and there were often some well-sustained efforts at "headin' 'em." On one occasion, Alec Bonney, of "C" Company, cleaned up the school, and finished with £175, or to be more correct, its equivalent in piastres.

Though very little leave was granted, and that only for 28 hours, a good many officers and N.C.O.'s were sent to the various specialist schools at Zeitoun, near Cairo, and this was a welcome break for those who were selected, as there was plenty of opportunity to visit Cairo for those who so desired. Selected officers and men from the reinforcements of the 11th Battalion were also sent to the same schools from the nearby camp at the aerodrome, Heliopolis, and these men had the opportunity of meeting many of their future comrades-in-arms and hearing something of the great deeds and other happenings on Gallipoli.

Meantime, the training of the 11th Battalion continued at Tel-el-Kebir, and daily the men became more fit under the influence of the healthy desert climate and the system of physical training and drill included in the prescribed routine of the troops.

On January 22, musketry practice was held at the 25-yard rifle range behind the station of Tel-el-Kebir, and on their return the troops were greeted with the fateful words, "All leave stopped." The boys wondered what was going to be the next move, for the above order was generally the harbinger of a speedy change of scene.

The change was not long in eventuating, for next day the 11th Battalion received instructions to proceed to the Canal front. Tents were struck and returned to Ordnance, and the battalion moved off to Tel-el-Kebir siding and entrained for Serapeum, which was reached on January 24. Serapeum was one of the bridgeheads on the Suez Canal. These bridgeheads were several in number and consisted of movable pontoon bridges thrown across the Suez Canal at suitable points to enable troops to be quickly transferred from one bank to the other in case of need or to carry the necessary supplies to the defensive zone. These pontoon bridges were operated by the engineers and were moved to the side of the canal when any shipping required to pass.

The battalion had left Tel-el-Kebir in two parties, "A" and "B" Companies under Major Peck, arriving several hours later than the first party. The detraining point was on the western bank of the Canal, close to one of the pontoon bridges. The troops had been able to have a good look at the country traversed on this occasion as it was daylight and they had been transported in open trucks.

On arrival at Serapeum, the troops were marched down the slope to the pontoon, a long swaying bridge on great red iron floats. This was crossed, and the battalion marched into the staging camp on the eastern bank of the Canal. There was an insufficient supply of water at this time and not enough water-carts to bring an adequate allowance. Drinking water only was issued to the troops.

The initial stages for the Canal defence scheme were well forward by this time, and great stores of all kinds had been accumulated at the staging camp for the furtherance of the project. Roughly stated, this defensive scheme was to consist of a line of trenches about ten miles east of the Canal, with lines of communication, water pipes, roads and light railways based on the bridgeheads.

No serious attempt at constructing trenches had yet been made, but there were mounted patrols operating all along the front and the 8th Australian Brigade had an outpost on the high ground at Gebel Habieta, eight or nine miles due east of Serapeum. A Decauville railway was being constructed and the railhead was already over two miles inland. All along the banks of the Canal were native dhows laden with stone for the roads and landings, waiting their turn to be unloaded at the small pier near the pontoon bridge.

It has hardly ever been realised just how important this barren part of the earth was at this period of the Great War. The Turks, flushed with the success of having foiled the British at Gallipoli, had only to capture the Suez Canal to render the already difficult campaign in Mesopotamia almost impossible of continuance. Many other complications would also have arisen; and though, as will be shown, a fearful expenditure of material was made on the Canal defences, who shall say that the results did not justify the measures taken?

The 11th Battalion lay at Serapeum for some days till, on January 31, the order came to march to Gebel Habieta, with full equipment up. It is no light job to walk in deep, loose sand at any time, and the battalion's task that day can only be imagined. Luckily it was winter time—though the days are often hot enough in the desert—and the men were in good fettle. The route led ever upward through the loose sand, and switch-backed through wadis and over hummocks of harder ground, with only very few sparse and miserable tussocks of wiry vegetation here and there. The occasional halts were more than welcome, and it was with feelings of great thankfulness that the outpost on the high hog-backed ridge was reached; and outpost was the right name for it, unless "Ultima Thule" be substituted, for it was indeed the last and uttermost fringe of the world. No habitation, save the tents and bivouacs of the troops could be seen at all; there was no vegetation and no sign that man had ever been there before; there was nothing except an interminable waste of sandhills.

In a hollow between two hummocks the battalion bivouaced for the night. Outposts were provided by "A" Company.

On February 1, the 11th Battalion erected tents for a camp and next day started on the work of digging the defensive line on numbers 7 and 8 posts. The strength of the battalion was now 28 officers and 943 other ranks, making a total of 971. This was nearly full strength.

Outposts of two platoons were sent out to selected positions at nights, but through the day only posts for defence and observation were stationed. As for the trenches, the digging was easy enough, but the loose sand kept running back all the time into the excavations, and the sides of the trenches as well as the parapets and parados had to be revetted with sand-bags and later with "A" frames and stamped metal sheets. In spite of this, the work progressed quickly, and in a fortnight the 1st Division had constructed 12 miles of trenches and outposts.

There were often very strong winds, and the sandstorms were a great annoyance; for besides making the meals a nightmare, these winds kept filling up the newly-constructed trenches, and these had to be kept continually clear of sand. Even after a relatively quiet night it was nothing to see a foot and a half of sand on the bottom of the trenches, and the top sand-bags would be half emptied by the continuous action of the wind making the sand trickle through the hessian, of which the bags were constructed.

Every night piquets were sent out and there were patrols between post and post and between the neighbouring units. One of the hardest jobs at night was to find direction, for the wind quickly obliterated all tracks. These piquets were under the charge of an officer, and all ranks used to camp in rough shelters made by throwing up a mound of sand on the windward side. These certainly kept the icy winds off, but the constant showers of sand made the shelter of doubtful value. On taking over for the night, the piquets used to make a large arrow-head in the sand, pointing to the next post, and it was the duty of the sentries to keep this mark distinct all night, so that the patrols going from one position to the other would at least get a start in the right direction.

There was an occasional rumour of enemy camel patrols, and scouting aeroplanes several times reported at no great distance the presence of small wandering tribes of Arabs with herds of camels and other stock. The 11th Battalion scouting patrol, under Lieut. W. Kruger, captured one ragged individual, who was reckoned to be quite harmless, and he was sent on his way rejoicing after a good feed. It is quite possible that his stupidity and ignorance were assumed.

The 11th Battalion transport section, which had left Tel-el-Kebir with the rest of the troops, was not taken to Habieta with the battalion on account of the difficulty of transporting forage and water, though a few officers' chargers were taken to the outposts for the convenience of the senior officers.

The desert was quite impracticable for wheeled traffic, so that the transport was left at Brigdehead, where it was used mainly to cart the iron pipes for the desert water scheme. Lieut. A. Burgess was transport officer at this time.

General Godley and staff visited the defence works on February 9. After his visit, orders came through that all work should be suspended until further orders. The reason was that the siting of the trenches was now regarded as unsuitable to the class of warfare that might be expected in the desert, as the Turks had little or no hope of dragging big guns across the desert. The work was not resumed till February 24. Owing to the fact that the old works had not a sufficient field of fire, new works were started in front of the old, and the latter retained as support lines.

The battalion scouts found a man of the 5th Ghurkas about one and a half miles east of Number 8 Post in a famished condition. This man stated that he had been for seven days without food and water. He was sent back to headquarters.

The following decorations appeared in orders on February 14, 1916: Military Cross, Major R. L. Leane and Lieut. H. James; D.C.M., No. 1186 Sergeant A. J. Wallish.

Owing to the fact that the battalion transport was unable to make use of its vehicles in the heavy sand, all rations and supplies were brought out to the defensive line by camel train. All the water had to be brought out in little tanks, two of which made a fair load for a camel. It followed that water was a very scarce commodity. The troops were supposed to be allowed a gallon per day, but of course the cooks received a good portion of this for making tea and washing up, so that the men only received one water-bottle full every day. Naturally there was very little for bathing purposes, and the men used to club together and share what little they could spare and do a communal wash. Occasionally there would be a dewy night, and oil-sheets would be spread to catch the moisture. It was wonderful how much could sometimes be caught in this manner.

The one event of the day was the arrival of the camel train. At about the expected time of arrival, generally pretty well on in the afternoon, all eyes would be turned to the skyline to the west, while small groups would congregate to wait for the welcome shout of one of the boys who had gone to some point of vantage. When the call of "Here they come!" was heard, there would be a rush of troops from all directions to the unloading point.

The long, undulating column seemed to take a good while to arrive, but at last the grinning camel-boys would bring charges to a halt, amid yells of "Saeeda walad!", "Ooshta!" and "Estanna!" and other tags of Arabic and semi-Arabic, and the N.C.O. in charge would slide off his mount and try to answer the thousand and one questions that were hurled at him by all and sundry.

Though the camels were generally laden to capacity, and carried not only rations and water but bundles of sand-bags, stamped metal sheets, frames for the trenches, fodder for the horses, ammunition and timber, yet space was sometimes found for a load of "comforts" or a bag or two of mail would arrive, and the boys would then realise that they were not entirely cut off from the world. Nowhere were the little amenities of civilisation so appreciation as in circumstances like these.

While the troops were thus engaged in the desert of Sinai, events of great importance were happening in the history of the A.I.F.; events that were of vital importance to the early-formed battalions of the first four Australian infantry brigades in particular.

R.Q.M.S. J. Murray Aitken at Gebel Habieta.

It has already been mentioned that reinforcements were coming forward in increasing numbers, and by the end of 1915 there were already something over 30,000 Australian reinforcements in Egypt waiting to be absorbed into their respective units.

After some deliberation, it was determined to create three new Australian divisions. But the serious drawback to this was that there were not sufficient numbers of trained officers and N.C.O.'s to run these new divisions. However, a way was found out of the difficulty by taking half of each of the existing battalions of the first four infantry brigades of the Australian Imperial Force, with the officers and N.C.O.'s attached thereto, and making these halves the nuclei of sixteen new battalions. Thus it was arranged that each new battalion of the four brigades to be formed in this manner would have half its personnel consisting of tried and experienced troops, and the remainder of reinforcements.

When this decision became known, and the order was promulgated among the battalions, there was much heart-burning among the boys, and many long and animated discussions over the projected split of the battalion. Until the actual date of severance, the 3rd Brigade was to be split into two wings, called the right and left wings. The right wing was to consist of the halves of the 9th, 10th, 11th and 12th Battalions, and the left wing was to consist of the other halves which were to go to form the 49th, 50th, 51st and 52nd Battalions, in that order.

It will therefore be seen that the left half of the 11th Battalion would form the new 51st Battalion.

Of course no one wanted to leave the "Old Battalion" and all the mates he had lived with for so long; but the decree had gone forth and the troops had to bow to authority and take what fortune sent.

The method of division into wings varied in different battalions. In the case of the 11th Battalion, the split was made by forming the right wing (the 11th Battalion) of the odd sections, 1, 3, 5, and so on; and the left wing (the new 51st Battalion) of the even sections, 2, 4, 6, up to 16. In this way an impartial division was made and the new battalion started its career with exactly the same quality of personnel as the older battalion, only the traditions of the older unit were lacking. The new battalion soon, however, made traditions of its own. The formal division was made immediately after the receipt of the order authorising the formation into wings, but the troops were treated as one unit until the end of February.

On February 24, Captain Reilly and Lieut. Kelly reported for duty from England.

An unrehearsed incident occurred one day, owing to the fact that a "furphy" originated somewhere in Egypt concerning some indisposition of the Emperor of Germany. It was not long before the message was being flashed from station to station, and by the time the "news" reached the desert outpost, the signallers were passing on the message that Kaiser Wilhelm was dead. On receipt of this intelligence, the troops on parade were notified and a photograph taken of the companies cheering like mad and waving their hats on the tops of their fixed bayonets. Of course the old gentleman is still well and hearty even at the time of writing this (over twenty years later), but the whole incident showed how unofficial reports soon became magnified and how really unimportant incidents lost their true perspective out in the desert.

On February 28, 1916, the 11th Battalion lost a good soldier when Major R. L. Leane left to assume command of the 48th Battalion. The troops were pre-occupied with the impending split, and it was a hard wrench for those comrades who had been through so much together when at last the order came for the left wing to move out. Those who were to go silently made their preparations, or made some derogatory remark about the battalion they were going to leave, anything at all to hide their real feelings, and their mates watched the preparations with poker faces.

The boys of the 51st Battalion paraded for the last time on the old ground, and then with the cheers and good wishes of all who remained they marched out of Gebel Habieta and down the long sandhills towards the Suez Canal.

After resting at the railhead, these troops passed through the staging camp on March 1, and crossed the pontoon bridge at Serapeum. As they marched to entrain they passed the reinforcements of the 11th Battalion who were to take their places, and who were that day, March 1, 1916, setting out for the battalion at Gebel Habieta.

At this point in the story, these men of the "Old 11th" pass to another division, but their subsequent history is well told in "The 51st Over There," the story of their exploits in the Great War by A. V. Barber, a member of the newer unit.

The reinforcements for the 11th Battalion consisted of three officers (Lieut. F. G. Griffin, 2nd/Lieut. W. C. Belford and 2nd/Lieut. J. Miller) and 482 other ranks. During a short halt alongside the outgoing troops, many greetings were passed between old friends, and then the troops for the 11th crossed the pontoon and set out for the staging camp and from there marched to the railhead, which was reached about dark. Here they were met by Captain "Packy" MacFarlane, who instructed the troops to camp for the night.

Early next morning they set off for Gebel Habieta and the 11th Battalion. It was a gruelling march, but this was a fine body of men in good condition and they arrived at battalion headquarters before mid-day and rested there in the sand awaiting distribution to the four companies.

These boys had reached the goal to which all reinforcements eagerly looked forward to, which was their adoption into their regiment. As reinforcements, they were really nobody's children and they might be allotted to any battalion; but once they were allocated to a unit the boys felt that they had at last got a home, and home it was in a very real sense to all these lads that served with the 11th Battalion.

Just as these reinforcements arrived at Gebel Habieta, a small mounted party was seen approaching. This party was seen to consist of two naval officers with some mounted guides and about 25 naval ratings. The officers were found to be "middies." These were later introduced to the officers of "B" Company, who invited them into company headquarters, which was also mess. The middies were noticed to be rather woebegone, and on inquiry admitted to saddle-soreness, as they had not been astride horses for months.

Lunch was just about to be served and the middies were invited to partake of the rough fare. Seating accommodation was at a premium, and very Spartan at that, and the midshipmen looked askance at the hard forms and begged for something soft to sit on. What a vain hope in the desert! However, with a few sandbags they were made as comfortable as conditions permitted, and they did justice to the meagre fare, showing that whatever their physical condition their constitutions were still sound.

On being asked why they chose to spend their leave in toiling over the desert, they became worked up and said it wasn't their idea of a pleasant Saturday afternoon at all, but that their skipper, who was a whale on efficiency, had arranged the little party for their benefit in order that they might have some idea of the conditions the Australian troops were working under. Their subsequent remarks on skippers in particular and horses in general were anything but polite.

The middies were splendid fellows, and like the majority of naval men, were quite at home among the Australians, there being a mutual respect and understanding between them. The boys were sorry to see them go and wished them the best of luck and an easy passage back to their ship, which could be seen far off in the Bitter Lakes.

On March 3, the newly-reinforced companies paraded and the daily routine of the battalion was carried out with full complements. The reinforcements were almost, without exception, from Western Australia, and naturally had many friends among the "old hands," and they were soon completely absorbed in the unit and became an integral part of the 11th Battalion, sharing its honours and its fame, and they were to play their part splendidly in the stern days that were to come.

A number of men who had done consistently good work with the 11th Battalion were promoted to commissioned rank to take the places of the officers who had gone with the left wing. Among these were 2nd/Lieuts. Aitken, Clarke, Nicol, Brodie, Brook, Rogerson, Hastings, Forbes and Walters.

The weather was now getting gradually warmer, and during the day the troops used to get company drill for an hour or so in the early morning and the rest of the day was spent in trench construction. The troops worked one hour and rested the next, while a relief carried on with the work. The men who were resting used to strip to the waist and spend the time carefully examining the seams of their shirts in the strong sunlight in search of unwelcome pests.

Before commencing work, the troops used to fix bayonets and, instead of piling arms as was generally the custom, they would drive their bayonets deep into the sand and leave their rifles sticking up in the air well out of the sand and grit. The rifles were also easily available if wanted.

All the spare gear and the tunics would be hung on these rifles, and the boys were disposed on both sides of them busily engaged "chatting." It was a picture always associated with Gebel Habieta.

The life on this high, windy ridge was uneventful but pleasant. Though the nights were cold, the days were perfect and the air like champagne, pure and invigorating; and the troops were in better health and condition that at any time afterwards. Big and bronzed and full of the joy of life, these

West Australians made a picture of young manhood that could nowhere be surpassed.

Sometimes the even tenor of life would be enlivened by some amusing incident, as when the second-in-command forgot the password when on a tour of inspection one night and was held up by the sentry at one of the posts. This is the story:

One night while a shivering sentry was wondering when his relief would be coming along, he heard a mounted party floundering about in the sand some distance ahead, and from the conversation, which carried for miles in that clear desert atmosphere, it was obvious that the party was lost, and the major, whom the sentry easily recognised by his voice, was distinctly annoyed and was expressing his feelings in no uncertain manner.

At length the guide found his bearings, and led the party up towards the invisible sentry. Suddenly, the unmistakable sound of a rifle-bolt was heard pushing a cartridge into the chamber of the rifle, and a voice cried, "Halt! Who goes there?" "Friends," was the answer. "Advance one, and give the password," rasped the voice. But no one knew the password, and the party hung back.

Meanwhile the sergeant of the sentry-group had come up, and was enjoying the major's discomfiture. "Advance one, or I fire," said the sentry. "Dammit, man! Don't you know me?" cried the major, "Is that rifle pointing at me?" "Too right," said the sentry. But the sergeant thought it was time to chip in, and he advanced with another man and identified the major, who was now doubly furious.

Ignoring the grinning sentry, the major turned to the sergeant and remarked that efficiency was all right up to a point, but there was no need for the damned sentry to have kept him covered with a loaded rifle all the damned time. The major may not have enjoyed the experience, but the troops relished the tale.

The halcyon days quickly passed, and many of the troops looked back in after years to that quiet time as one of the pleasantest that the 11th Battalion experienced in its overseas career.

About the end of the first week in March, the officers of "C" Company, finding that they were eating an undue amount of sand with their meals, determined to wangle some timber and hessian and to get one of the pioneers to build a little mess hut.

A rather striking-looking kiosk was the result. It was octagonal in shape, and when a table and rough forms were put inside it, there was just enough room for the six officers of that company to sit. Still, it was a great comfort, and a source of admiration and envy to the other messes. Reg. Hemingway, or Jack O'Neil, who had been in hospital in England, named the kiosk the "Trocadero," after that famous London restaurant, and a name was painted over the door. The sequel was the forerunner of many such experiences right through the long years ahead. As soon as the troops made a tidy or comfortable billet they immediately received the order to move one.

The day after the completion of the kiosk, the 11th Battalion received orders to proceed to the staging camp at Serapeum, and on March 8 everything was packed up and the battalion set off for Serapeum, and the little "Trocadero" was left out in the wilderness.

The battalion had not proceeded far on its way when it passed the 10th Light Horse Regiment (a Westralian unit), which had come out from Serapeum to take over the Canal defence line. The troopers were to be used as mounted patrols, and the idea of the continuous line was abandoned.

There was a short halt, during the handing over, and many friends had an opportunity of greeting one another before the two units went their different ways.

By order of division, the site of the abandoned trenches was marked with long stakes, as it was expected that the sand would soon obliterate all trace of them if they were not kept continually cleared; and it was later reported by the light horse that this is exactly what happened, and all the efforts and labour of the troops and all the wealth of material used passed into the limbo of forgotten things.

When the battalion set out on its return journey to the staging camp at Serapeum, it was resolved to march straight across the desert instead of first marching to railhead, which was by this time considerably advanced. This made the journey considerably shorter. In place of the usual marching in column of route, the battalion was extended over the desert in echelon of platoons, and the different companies took it in turn to set the pace. This mitigated the dust to a wonderful degree and proved much more comfortable travelling.

With well-regulated halts and steady progress, the battalion reached the staging camp towards nightfall. There was a long wearisome wait while the C.O. and adjutant were finding out the battalion's lines. As the boys were leaning on their rifles, or resting in the most comfortable position they could assume, the camel baggage trains begain to arrive. Some of the "shrewd heads" who had dodged the long desert march had managed to wangle a ride on a "humming-bird" (i.e., a camel) and these lads jeered at the tired troops as they undulated past.

The camel trains also came to a halt, and opposite "C" Company was one big brute with three batmen—Syd. Hollands, Frank Sims and "Curly" Knight—who belonged to the same company, comfortably seated on various portions of his anatomy. These boys had wide grins on, and were making all kinds of disparaging remarks about their less fortunate comrades. This was too much for the troops, who immediately started to make those horrible noises that the camel-boys utter when they want their chargers to kneel down.

Everyone knows the see-saw or switchback motions that a camel makes when it decides to kneel. This camel was an exaggerated edition of its species, and it evidently thought that a rest was about due. So it suddenly depressed its rear end and Sims, who was nearest the tail, slid ungracefully to the ground; the other two looked round and started laughing at their comrade in distress, and were caught unawares by the forward throw of the camel, which shot "Curly" Knight over the beast's neck and sprawled him on to the ground. Hollands was still clawing wildly in mid-air and was not prepared for the second backward flop of the camel, and he went head over heels on top of his disgruntled mate just as he was picking himself out of the sand. What a roar of laughter burst from the troops. Tired as they were, this little incident helped them to forget their weariness and in a few minutes they marched to their new camp in good heart. As they arrived the welcome sound of "Cookhouse" was received with cheers, and their cares for another day were over.

The 11th Battalion was camped close to the Suez Canal, and about a mile and a half from the scene of the battle with the Turks a year previously. There was a graveyard of Turkish dead not far off, and one of the graves was that of a German major named Von Der Hagen.

The country round Serapeum was, in places, much harder than out at Gebel Habieta, and in certain areas it was even gravelly, so that training was more easily carried out.

A refresher course was started, and every morning company and battalion drill was carried out and much attention was given to smartening up the men. In the afternoons bathing parades were held, when the spectacle of two whole Australian divisions could be seen lining the banks of the great canal in all stages of undress and thousands of men were always diving into the water or swimming in the warm current which flowed steadily southward. These bathing parades were a source of continual joy, and they compensated for the dustiness and discomfort of the staging camp.

There was a steady stream of traffic going through the canal, and the pontoons were frequently open for long periods. When this happened, a large punt was used to transport the troops and stores across the canal. Fatigue parties, facetiously called by the boys "chain gangs," from the various battalions used to pull this ferry over the canal, and the troops used to chant the ditties of the "Gyppos" as they hauled on the big, heavy chain.

Sometimes a native working party was transported from one bank to the other, and the boys would utilise their services to haul on the heavy punt chains; then one or more of the "Gyppos" would chant a plaintive melody and all the rest, and often the troops, too, would join in the refrain. The refrain was generally the well known

"Kam lelo, kam youm,
Yahabibty salaman."

of which the English translation is, "How many nights and how many days before I see my darling?" The troops used to laugh at the "Gyppos" and their plaintive melody, but little any one of them realised the meaning of the words of the chantey, or the long years that were to be the answer to the song.

Lieut.-Colonel S. Roberts was now in command of the 11th Battalion with Major J. S. Denton as second-in-command, and Lieut. R. Hemingway as adjutant. The company commanders were "A," Captain MacFarlane; "B," Captain Mansfield; "C," Captain J. Newman and "D," Major J. T. Milner.

On March 13 General Birdwood paid a surprise visit to the 11th Battalion at its training ground, which was situated about two miles from camp. There was a serious discussion going on at headquarters at this time as to the fitness of the Australian divisions for service in France, and numerous visits were paid to the troops to see how they were progressing.

It shows how little the high command really knew of the Australian character when, at this time, the implied opinion was that the troops were too wild and undisciplined to take to France. If this opinion is compared with the actual happenings in that country and the conduct of the troops there, and above all the opinion of the French people with whom they came in contact, all of which will be related in this story in due course, it will be seen that a great error of judgment was being made at this time.

It was also stated that some of the Australian divisions were not sufficiently trained to be sent. In the case of the 1st Division, it was not stated that the division had been reduced to practically a nucleus only a fortnight before this, and it was not so much want of training that should have been criticised, but rather that credit should have been given that the division was so well forward in its new organisation.

It was now being rumoured that the next more was to be to France, but there were also those who had heard that Salonika was to be the destination.

On March 15, General Chauvel, who had been in command of the 1st Australian Division after General Walker had been evacuated wounded at Anzac, made a farewell speech to the 3rd Brigade. After the usual compliments to the troops, General Chauvel spoke strongly of the respect due to the Turkish graves in the vicinity, and urged the troops to do all they could to keep them inviolate. The constant shifting of the sands tended to uncover the remains, so that the cemetery was placed out of bounds.

General Chauvel was transferred to the command of the Anzac Mounted Division, and General Walker reassumed command of the 1st Australian Division.

The 11th Battalion was inoculated against typhoid fever on March 16 and 17, and the customary 24 hours' "no duty" was given to the troops.

A brigade church parade was held on March 19. The Prince of Wales (the present Duke of Windsor) was present, and after the service there was a march-past the Prince and the General

Officer Commanding and their staffs. There was one of the greatest displays of brass hats and red tabs on record, and the troops were nearly dazzled by the sight. All the troops were greatly interested in the Prince, for he was the first member of the British Royal family that most of them had seen. The Prince did look boyish and shy in the presence of so many big, bronzed Australians, who regarded him with frank curiosity and with little of that deference to which he was accustomed.

A number of seats had been obtained from some place or other, and these had been arranged for the convenience of the Royal party; and before the march-past, General Birdwood had come forward with the Prince and had addressed the brigade thus: "Boys! The Prince of Wales has honoured us with his presence this morning. He takes this opportunity of wishing good luck to you, who are on the eve of making history in France." During the march-past, the Prince took the salute.

General Birdwood also conveyed on behalf of the Prince the thanks of His Majesty the King (George V) to members of the A.I.F. for their work on Gallipoli.

When the parade was completed, and H.R.H. was attempting to withdraw, he tripped over a form and measured his length on the sand. This tickled the fancy of the troops, and some of their grins were audible, much to the consternation and horror of authority.

"Teddy," however, arose and grinned back at the boys, thus saving what might easily have been an awkward kind of a situation.

After Birdwood's speech, it was now definitely known that the Australian divisions were destined for France, and lecturettes were frequently given on the subject of behaviour in an allied country. Talks on gas and gas-masks and other information likely to be helpful to the troops were incorporated in the daily training.

The 2nd Australian Division, whose battalions had not been split up like those of the 1st Division, and which had practically all its units complete, was already preparing to leave for France, and it was understood that the 1st Division was to be the next to leave.

Muster parades of the 11th Battalion were held on March 22, when a complete overhaul of clothing and equipment was made and deficiencies made up. Next day, the battalion was marched by companies to the west bank of the canal, and all the troops had to strip while their clothes were sterilized in the trucks of a Hunter's train. The sterilizing was for the purpose of destroying typhus germs, but the boys called the train a "delousing plant" and they were very much disgusted to get back their clothes in a very much worse condition, as regards lice, at least, than before. The troops reckoned that the steam merely hatched the eggs.

Next day all spare kit was sent to the railway siding and all rifles were handed in and new ones issued to take Mark VII ammunition, as this was the type then being used in all theatres of war.

On Sunday, March 26, 2nd/Lieut. J. M. Aitken was detailed to take his platoon and patrol the bank of the Suez Canal for two miles, in order to prevent any bathing by the troops. General Birdwood had given instructions that he was bringing a party of ladies down the canal in a launch, and as the boys never bathed in anything but their birthday suits, the General's kindly forethought saved them considerable embarrassment.

There were many new establishments being created at this time to bring the A.I.F. into line with British Army establishments. Among these were additional artillery units, Pioneer battalions, machine gun companies and trench mortar batteries. The infantry battalions were issued with four Lewis guns in place of the two Maxim or Vickers' guns previously used, and the heavier guns were issued to the newly-formed machine gun companies. The Lewis gunners were trained at a school in Ismalia. Lieut. L. L. Le Nay was the battalion's first Lewis gun officer.

The battalion was expecting every day to receive the order to move off. A number of men being surplus to strength were detailed to remain behind, and Captain J. P. O'Neil and Lieut. J. Miller were appointed to remain in charge of this party. There were not any wilder men in the whole Australian force than these two when they learned that they were to be left behind. They both paraded to Colonel Roberts and asked him to reconsider the matter, but to no purpose. Captain O'Neil rejoined the battalion, later on, in France; but Lieut. J. Miller went to the 49th Battalion, so that he could be sure of getting to France in as short a time as possible.

The 3rd Australian Infantry Brigade Headquarters moved out of Serapeum and entrained for Alexandria on the night of March 26/27. The 9th Battalion, 10th Battalion and brigade headquarters left from No. 2 siding, and the 11th Battalion, 12th Battalion and Machine Gun Company remained at Serapeum under the command of Lieut.-Colonel S. Roberts while awaiting departure.

CHAPTER XIV

ALEXANDRIA TO MARSEILLES

THE FINAL STAGES of the 11th Battalion's sojourn in the desert were now at hand, and the troops were ready to say "Good-bye" to these barren wastes for the last time. In its overseas career so far, the 11th Battalion had spent twelve out of the seventeen months' service away from all the comforts of modern life, and of the rest more than three months had been spent aboard ship and the remainder in a bleak camp at Mudros in the island of Lemnos; so it was with feelings of joyful anticipation that the troops, especially the older hands, were looking forward to their service in France.

On March 27, 1916, the 11th Battalion Transport Section marched out and entrained for Alexandria. Vehicles were left behind in Egypt, and troops and horses embarked on the s.s. *Maryland* en route for France. Next day the 11th Battalion entrained at Serapeum west for Alexandria. The journey was made in open trucks along the pleasant western bank of the Suez Canal, so different from its eastern counterpart. Alexandria was reached about 4 a.m. and later in the morning the troops went aboard the s.s. *Corsican*, in company with the 12th Battalion and the 3rd Brigade Machine Gun Company. There were also the pay section and other details to make up the ship's complement. The *Corsican* was one of the Allan line of steamers and a very good sea boat.

Lieut.-Colonel Roberts was O.C. troops and Captain R. Hemingway was ship's adjutant.

Alexandria was left behind on March 30, and though there were still considerable numbers of reinforcements and other details of the battalion in the camps and hospitals of Egypt, this was the 11th Battalion's farewell to the land of the Pharaohs, though for a long time afterwards tags of Egyptian and Arabic formed a considerable part of the vocabulary of the troops.

The battalion's strength on leaving Egypt was 28 officers and 942 other ranks.

The s.s. *Transylvania*, with the corps commander and staff and many other officers and details on board, left Alexandria at the same time as the *Corsican*, but the former was a very much faster boat and she soon left the latter troopship well astern. As soon as the vessels got away from the shelter of the harbour, they immediately started to zig-zag, leaving fanciful wakes in the blue waters. There was a good deal of apprehension on account of submarines, the more so because the transport *Minneapolis* had been sunk only a week previously as she was returning empty on her return journey from Marseilles, where she had only recently landed troops.

The s.s. *Corsican* was too crowded for any drill to be carried out to any extent, but rifle exercises and boat-drill were done when circumstances allowed. All the troops had to wear life-belts continually and crews were constantly in charge of the two machine guns on either side of the ship. There was also a 4.7 naval gun in the stern.

On the whole, the troops had an easy and pleasant time during the voyage. Not so the ship's captain. He never left his bridge from the time the ship left Alexandria until she arrived in Marseilles. On the second day out, April 1, the look-out spotted a submarine on the port bow. The *Corsican* made a great sweep round and turned her stern to the enemy and was soon zig-zagging away at the best pace she could make, leaving a creamy wake that indicated the erratic course she was taking. After the excitement died down, one of the lads said: "The old scow made an April fool of that submarine."

A good deal of shipping was seen, including mine-sweepers, destroyers and an occasional cruiser. Sometimes a destroyer would accompany the troopship for several miles, but for long periods the *Corsican* travelled by herself, as the *Transylvania* had disappeared over the western horizon on the first day out.

On Sunday, April 2, there was church parade in the morning, and of course the padre took advantage of the occasion to impress on the troops the need for good behaviour when in France. The troops were generally a good deal disgusted at being lectured and spoken to as if they had the mentality of little children, but they accepted these homilies woodenly and kept their remarks for afterwards.

In the afternoon the *Corsican* had reached Malta, but the vessel only lay off while the skipper received orders. The troops were not able to get much idea of the capital, or of the harbour, but it could be seen that the harbour was heavily defended and that there were huge stone forts in many commanding positions. The spires and steeples of Valetta could be seen rising behind the forts, and in rear all the lovely soft green of the terraced gardens and vineyards rose high in the air, a refreshing sight to eyes long used to the tawny sands of the desert. Rumour quickly spread that a ship had been sunk by torpedo only two hours ahead of the *Corsican,* but there was no official confirmation.

Malta was left behind and the voyage continued without escort. On April 3 some wreckage was passed and during the previous night three ships had been passed that were reported to be standing by a vessel that had been torpedoed. But there were no alarms on board the *Corsican.*

During these quiet days, the officers of the 11th Battalion were instructed to give lecturettes to their men on the billeting and other innovations that were likely to take place in France. Imagination came greatly into play on these occasions, but no doubt the lectures served their purpose by keeping the troops occupied and giving them something to think about. A more serious note was introduced when gas-masks were issued to all the boys on April 4. These were the old P.H. type, and were never very satisfactory.

Several entertainments were arranged for the men, among which were a boxing tournament and a concert. Both these were well appreciated, for any kind of a break was welcome. Of course the troops had a lot of popular little games of their own, and officers coming suddenly into the mess-deck would hear the old familiar "If you don't speculate, you won't accumulate"; "What's the old Crown done?"; and there would be a hasty folding up of a Crown and Anchor board, as the boys pretended to discuss the latest war news.

The fact that the ship had to travel at nights without any lights necessarily limited the chances of the boys' amusement; but all agreed that the voyage could not have been more comfortable when everything was considered. Naturally fun and high spirits prevailed everywhere, and Captain George Campbell used to create a bit of amusement at the expense of a certain officer who hailed originally from Scotland. Whenever this officer addressed George, that worthy used to solemnly shake his head and feign ignorance of the language he was addressed in, and after a few apparently vain attempts to understand, he would bawl out for an interpreter. Up would dash one of the other boys, and he would explain to the now grinning George Campbell that the "foreigner" was only asking when he was going to be allowed to wear his kilt, or something equally ludicrous.

In the afternoon of April 4, the *Corsican* passed the coasts of Sardinia and Corsica, and then turned north and reached Marseilles in the mists of the early morning of April 5. At first all that could be seen was the beam of the lighthouse, winking through the gloom, then gradually the outline of the shore became more distinct and the great rocky mass of the Ile D'If with the famous chateau, immortalised by Dumas, could be seen materialising out of the mists; and soon the great harbour with its guns frowning from all sides and the extensive wharves crowded with shipping lay before the wondering gaze of the troops. All hands crowded the rails and occupied every point of vantage. All were eager to see the land that had been in the forefront of their minds since the day of enlisting. It seemed incredible that at last the battalion had reached this country of high endeavour and perilous adventure; but ahead lay the smoky haze of a vast city, with its multitude of spires and chimneys, stretching over a wide valley. It was the great city of Marseilles! The 11th Battalion was in France!

CHAPTER XV

ARRIVAL IN FRANCE

FRANCE! La Belle France! From the very commencement of the Great War the main idea of most Australian troops had been to get to France and to come to grips with the German Army. A great reason for this was undoubtedly due to the propaganda of German atrocities in the early days of the war, and the bitter feeling that had been engendered against Germany as the aggressor and as the spoiler of Belgium. But chiefly was it felt that the Western Front was the most important theatre of war, where the most decisive blows of the war would be struck at the German power, and it was natural to most Australians to desire to pit themselves against the best troops that the enemy possessed and to be in at the death, so to speak; so that the arrival of these young and eager troops in Marseilles was looked upon by them as the first step in this great and glorious adventure. Fortunate it was indeed that none were able to visualise the terrible road the troops had to follow before the end of the adventure was reached.

The *Corsican* pulled in alongside the wharf, and berthed close to the s.s. *Braemar Castle*. There were some Australian nurses on board the latter vessel, and it was not long before some of their friends managed to renew acquaintance with them. There was not much chance of seeing much of the city for most of the troops, as the quay was closely guarded; but it would have been very strange if some of the lads had not managed to elude the sentries. Lieut. Rex Hall, of the 11th Battalion, who had made the journey from Alexandria on the *Translvania*, came over to the *Corsican* and expressed his delight at finding the battalion safe and sound, for it had been reported that the *Corsican* had been torpedoed and sunk, and a great loss of life had been feared.

The troops remained aboard nearly all day, and then the order came to march to the entraining point. The troop train was only a short half-mile distant, but the journey lay over cobbled roads, only too prophetic of the long, weary marches to come over the "pave" roads of northern France and Belgium. The streets were thronged with wildly enthusiastic French people, all cheering and shouting, "Vive l'Australie! Vivent les Australiens!"

Old gentlemen with silk hats, and lovely young girls mostly wearing black, and matrons with eyes streaming with tears, all lent their voices to the general welcome with that whole-hearted abandon which the Gallic peoples make so peculiarly their own.

This acclamation from a cultured people was a thing that the troops never forgot, more especially as they had just come from the desert and from Egypt, where most of the boys had been long removed from the influences of civilisation and the society of people of their own kind.

The troop train was soon reached and the boys piled in. They stowed their kits as best they could and prepared for the long journey north. A train guard was detailed to prevent the boys from straying at the many stops that were to be expected during the journey. What a hope! Rations were carried on the train in a truck reserved as a quartermaster's store.

When at length the train pulled out of the town, no words could ever adequately describe the excitement and high spirits of the men. The 11th Battalion was again at a peak of efficiency and virility, and literally bursting with the joy of life and the desire to do something to prove itself; and now that they were actually on the train that was to bear them to the actual battle zone, nothing could have added to the pleasure and satisfaction of the boys.

The story of the wonderful journey northwards, from Marseilles to Godewaersvelde, has been told by nearly every diarist and historian in the Australian forces which served in France, and, in the most glowing language, and any one of these descriptions could fittingly be applied to the 11th Battalion's trip north; but it was such a vivid memory to most of the men who survived the war and an experience that made a lasting impression on so many of the troops that a brief account of this wonderful trip must be given here.

It was nearly nightfall when the train steamed out of Marseilles. The impression gained was mostly of bridges and viaducts, and more bridges and low hills embowered in trees, and then lights twinkling as darkness deepened. The small compartments on the train were faily comfortable as long as daylight lasted, and the men were sitting or standing about; but when the troops tried to settle down for the night, it was found that the amount of space was too limited. A readjustment of kits was made, but did not help much, and on the whole the boys passed a sleepless night. When the train pulled into the small town of Orange there was a halt, and for the first time the call of "There's a land of sunny skies, West Australia!" was sounded in France, followed by the ever popular "Come to the cookhouse door, boys!" The boys gladly tumbled out of their cramped compartments and relished the meal and drink of hot tea that was provided. At about 2:30 a.m. the train moved forward again, the train guards having seen that all the troops were aboard.

Next morning the boys were astir betimes and hanging out of the windows and doors long before dawn. The little villages showed through the mists of early morning and the lovely scents of early springtime rose from' the moist earth and from the hundreds of orchards in bloom.

The River Rhone, alongside of which the railway ran for over 200 miles, gleamed palely under its well-wooded banks as the obscuring mists unrolled and lifted.

When dawn came and the sun dispelled the vapours, the most entrancing scene unfolded itself to the long-starved eyes of the troops. For many months previously their gaze had been accustomed to dwell on unlimited miles of sand, barren of all vegetation; and so, when this vision of surpassing greenness met their eyes, it seemed as if this must be surely the most lovely country in all the world. Add to this the old-world buildings nestling among flowering orchards and pale-green vineyards, with the beautiful Rhone winding in and out along the valley that the train was ascending, with bridges spanning here and there, and mountains and hills and often snow-clad peaks in the distance, and an unforgettable picture was left on the mind of every man in the 11th Battalion.

It was strange, too, to pass towns whose names were famous in history, and to see chateaux perched at the top of high hills at whose feet nestled villages, recalling some mediæval tyrant or perhaps that of some national hero.

And the people! It is enough to say that the boys took them to their hearts in one great spontaneous wave of liking and respect, and kept them there right through the long years they lived in France, and the kindly remembrance of whom is kept undimmed to this day.

It was gradually noticed as the train progressed through the country that while there were plenty of women and girls and children, and a sprinkling of old men, there were no able-bodied men to be seen in the villages or working in the fields. Even the operatives on the railway, at the level crossings and on the stations were mostly women. The great drain on the manhood of France was making itself felt, and all the men and youths of military age had been called to the colours. In the fields were seen women holding the ploughs or driving the cultivators, and girls and little boys were doing the work about the houses and farms. The troops were very interested in the method of driving the horses by means of one rein only, and one Digger (for it was just about this time that the famous word became generally applied to all Australian troops) was heard to say, "Well, boys! I'm goin' to learn how to drive a horse with one rein, and then I'll go an' marry a French tabby."

One of the features of this old-established country that was specially noticed by the troops was that all the village churches had tall, thin spires, and the weather-cock perched on top quite took their fancies. All the long day as the train steamed northward the troops cheered and waved and threw kisses to the women and children seen near the railway. The French girls and children kept up a continual cry for souvenirs, and Egyptian coins, badges, buttons, money of all sorts and other articles rained from the carriages as long as the supply lasted.

The journey lay through the fine city of Lyons, but the train did not stop there, and no really long halt made until Macon was reached, where a meal was served about 11 a.m. As soon as the boys knew there was to be a halt of any duration, there was an immediate rush out of the station or into the country on either side of the train. Sometimes some ventured too far, and the bugle had to recall them at the double; but though occasionally the boys had to run to catch the train, none got left behind. Chalons was passed, and the next stop was made at Avillon. A good meal was given to the troops here, and a number of the Diggers visited the town and returned with more rations, mostly liquid. It was simply marvellous how the boys found their way about in the dark in a strange country.

At Dijon, the troop train was besieged with lots of pretty girls who were charming and shy, but curious and evidently full of admiration for the big Australians. But trains must ever onward. So the boys were borne off to Jurisy and the dark eyes at Dijon were forgotten. As the troops were being carried north to St. Germains, there was a hope that they might be lucky enough to see the wonderful French capital; but a glimpse of the far-off Eiffel Tower was the only thing seen of the city of Paris, though the great Palace of Versailles, situated among superb gardens, was seen not far from the railway, and was an indication of the splendour that was associated with the great city.

After passing Versailles, the general direction of the journey was changed, and a more north-westerly direction was maintained. Also on account of the much greater amount of traffic, mostly of a military nature, the pace of the train grew gradually slower and long stops were much more numerous. At one of these halts, some of the boys were desirous of making a hot drink from a tin of cocoa and milk. Some houses were near and a few of the boys took their mess-tins and tried to explain to the occupant of one of the houses that they would like some hot water. But the good lady understood neither their language nor their signs. They were giving up in despair when an officer, who had some knowledge of the French language, came along, and the needs of the lads were explained. Instantly madame was all smiles. "Mais, oui! Certainement! Tout a l'heure." (Yes, certainly; in a minute), and she went in and came out with a steaming kettle of water and filled up the mess-tins. There was no French needed to show the troops' gratitude and appreciation, but the lady only repeated the phrase, which was soon to become an integral part of their daily conversation, "Ca ne fait rien." (In Digger language, "Sanafarian," meaning "That's no trouble," or "no matter.")

The country was now flatter and less picturesque. Vineyards had disappeared and cereal and root farming seemed to occupy most of the land. Industrial centres were closer together, and even the cries of the children had changed. Instead of the shrill shouts of "Souvenir! Souvenir!" the clamouring had changed to "Bullee beef! Bullee beef! Biskit! Biskit!" and sometimes some of the poor little nippers would be hurt in trying to catch the tins that the troops threw to them.

Amiens was the next large city passed, and then the troops recognised that they were indeed in the war zone. Troop trains became more common. Guns, ammunition and other stores were seen on the passing trucks. The general feeling was that the battalion was getting near to the real thing at last.

At Abbeville, close to the mouth of the Somme, most of the transport section detrained, as the drivers had to pick up vehicles to replace those that were left in Egypt. "Cookhouse" brought the usual cheer from the men, and a halt of about an hour was allowed at this town. Some comforts were distributed by ladies on the station.

Then the most wearisome part of the journey commenced, for not only were the boys by this time tired by the long trip, but from this point the rate of progress was spasmodic and apparently uncertain. The train would start and run for a few miles, then be held up by an adverse signal; then start again with a jerk that sent kit and equipment flying to the accompaniment of bad language and curses. A few more kilometres would be travelled and something else would hold up the train. This style of progress was endured all through the night.

During this last stage of the journey the 11th Battalion passed through many towns whose names were to be almost in daily use by the Diggers, among which were Etaples, Calais, St. Omer and Hazebrouck.

At Calais the route turned to the south-east, and the train lumbered on through the night, while the now thoroughly exhausted troops slept by fits and snatches, and a feeling of irritation and annoyance had taken the place of the boisterous spirits with which they had commenced their long journey; and in this wise, a quiet and subdued battalion slowly drew near to Godewaersvelde.

CHAPTER XVI

FIRST BILLETS IN FRANCE

EARLY on the morning of April 8, 1916, the troops were awakened by the cessation of motion. It was quite dark and there was no special bustle to indicate that anything out of the way had happened. No one took much notice of the fact that the train had stopped, and beyond a bit of grousing and here and there a weary adjustment of limbs or kit, the troops merely turned over and endeavoured to get a little more sleep before daylight put an end to all chances of repose. The four platoon officers of "C" Company were in one compartment, and one sat up suddenly and said: "Listen! you fellows! I can hear artillery fire!" "Aw! got to sleep!" said the others. The grumbling of the guns grew louder and all listened intently for a few minutes. "Too right! We've arrived at the war," said Wally Hallahan, and then all dropped off to sleep again.

Meantime, the train had pulled into Godewaersvelde, which lay only a few hundred yards ahead. The troops received the order to detrain and form up in companies ready to move off. Unfortunately the four officers of "C" Company had been overlooked, as their compartment was at the extreme end of the troop train.

It was Captain George Campbell's voice heavily loaded with sarcasm that fell on the ears of the sleeping platoon commanders, asking them in no bedside manner if they thought that they had bought the train with the idea of making a permanent home in it, that awoke these young men to realities.

And wasn't there a rush to get equipment on and puttees rolled and all gear collected before dashing on to parade. Then four very shame-faced young men were lined up to the company commander to receive a good dressing-down.

The battalion which had been waiting for "C" Company to report "all correct" now moved off and, after several halts in wet, drizzly weather, in order to find out the direction of its billets, it was guided to the villages of Fletre and Rouge Croix and the troops were billeted in houses and farm buildings.

The boys took to the country like ducks to water and soon made friends of the people; and though they used more "Gyppo" words than French ones, calling the girls "bints" and the boys "wallads" and telling the estaminet owners to "iggeri" when they wanted more beer, they had no difficulty in making their wants understood. The Diggers tried the wines of the country and reckoned them, at any rate, cheap; and the beer was beer and that's all that could be said about it. If any remark was passed to madame about the quality of the brew, she would simply shrug, and raising her hands would utter the usual formula, "C'est la guerre!" This was a specific for any or all contingencies. But the "omelettes" and the "cafe et Cognac" and the "Pommes de terre frites" soon found a host of eager consumers, and the troops settled down contentedly to their new life.

The boys were at first rather shocked at the look of the rough billets that were allotted to them, and when one company was shown a large, bare shed, which was to be the temporary home of the troops, the faces of the boys registered first astonishment and then dismay. As the first of the disillusioned troops began to file in, some wag, thinking no doubt of the shearingsheds in far-off Western Australia, started to bleat like a sheep, and soon there was the most wonderful chorus of "maa-ing" and "baa-ing" that ever afflicted the eardrums. The noise and clamour that they made soon restored the troops' good humour, but what madame thought of the mentality of the troops on that occasion has never been divulged.

The barns and outhouses where most of the boys lived and slept were certainly rather rough, but they were generally well built and weatherproof in this part of France and voted an improvement to sleeping in a crowded train; while the farms and villages were something entirely new in the boys' experience and were a great source of interest and amusement. It was not long before big Diggers from Western Australia could be seen turning the handle of the mangold-wurzel cutter for madame (all the French men having gone off to the war) or helping Jeanette with the cows or pigs. Of course Jeanette and her kind had been used to the attentions of all kinds of soldiers for the previous eighteen months, and were long past the stage of being flattered by the attentions of handsome soldiers; but the big, free and easy men from the other end of the world were something new, and they won a place in the hearts of the French in Flanders and later in Picardie that endured to the end of the war, and is still kept green after more than 20 years.

The 11th Battalion was early instructed in measures to be adopted against gas, for on Sunday, April 9, the troops were marched to a gas demonstration school, where all the boys were put through chlorine and tear-gas in their new P.H. helmets in order to give them some degree of confidence if cloud-gas should be realised by the Germans opposite to their sector. Gas was, at this time, the bug-bear of the General Staff.

Training started on April 10, but very little could be accomplished on account of the wet weather. Instruction in the use and care of gas helmets was specially emphasised, and all the troops were made familiar with the instructions issued with each helmet. When it was not too wet, parades and route marches were held in the narrow lanes and sometimes in an empty field. The land in this particular area was so valuable and so intensively cultivated that there were not many fields available for training, and those that were allotted were generally so small as to be practically useless for any open order work.

An amusing incident happened one day on one of "C" Company's parades. The day had dawned wet, and as the hours passed conditions grew worse, so parades were cancelled. The troops made the most of their opportunity, and as both "plink plonk" (vin blanc) and "vin rouge" were plentiful in the billets, it was not long before the boys were having quite a nice time.

An officer visited the billet in the morning while the rain was teeming down, and was asked by C.S.M. Gallagher if he thought the rain was going to stop. The answer was in the negative, so the boys proceeded to enjoy their little party.

The unexpected happened, and it ceased raining suddenly. A company parade was ordered for immediately after dinner, and "C" Company fell-in, along a little narrow lane with high hedges and deep ditches on either side. The "Good Gallagher" (he was always styled the "Good Gall") was carrying considerably more than the issue, and was just able to perform his duties, but he had a slight wobble.

The company was drawn up in line and there was hardly any room for any movement, the platoon officers having to step back into the line of men behind if anyone wished to pass.

When the "Good Gall" handed over the company parade state, "All present and correct, sir," he made a noble job of it, and all would have been well; but after he saluted, he took a smart pace to the rear, overbalanced and disappeared into the

Some "originals" including C.S.M. Gallagher (the "Good Gall.").

deep ditch running alongside the road. He was dragged out, with mud and water streaming from his hair and pouring off his groundsheet, which was worn cape-fashion. He was the picture of utter demoralisation and woe. And, of course, the "Good Gall" went up before the good captain and got the good wigging he deserved.

On April 11, the 11th Battalion Transport Section, under Lieut. Alec Burgess and Sergeant A. Wells, arrived from Abbeville where the section had detrained with the horses, in order to pick up new vehicles. The transport went into lines at Rouge Croix, and from this time until the end of the war they fulfilled their function as first line transport.

One of the features that intrigued the troops on their first arrival in the area was the number of small fields with great poles and spars sticking up from the ground. There were many conjectures as to their purpose, and one bright lad reckoned that they were for the purpose of keeping hostile aeroplanes from landing. Later the men learned that these spars were hop poles, and it was not many months before the hop plants grew to that beauty that was such a feature of this locality in summer and early autumn.

During the next week training was carried out as well as possible in the limited space at the disposal of the battalion. In the evenings far to the east could be seen the aeroplanes circling high in the air over the Mont de Cats, one of a range of little hills in the neighbourhood. Often, too, the dull rumbling of the guns could be heard, and when this swelled into a roar the boys would wonder when their turn would come to face the shelling.

It did not take the troops long to find out all there was to be known of the area and its surroundings, and many of them learned a lot that was to be of great value in later years when the battalion was in action over the same ground.

It took the boys some time to get used to the idea of seeing dogs utilised as beasts of burden. Not only were they attached to small carts, which conveyed milk or other commodities, but they were used to drive great wheels, which in their turn drove separators or churns. Sometimes also they were chained under handcarts which they helped to pull, while a man or woman held the shafts.

While the troops were taking note of all these strange customs, things were moving at headquarters, and already officers and N.C.O.'s had been sent to bayonet and physical training schools in the Armentieres area, and these men came back with tales of the forward area, where the 2nd Australian Division had already gone.

It therefore came as no surprise when, on April 19, the 11th Battalion received orders to proceed to Sailly sur la Lys, a straggling town on the River Lys and also on the main Armentieres-Hazelbrouck road. The 11th Battalion was at first billeted along the road leading from Sailly, south to the railway crossing near Rouge du Bout. The 3rd Brigade was acting as divisional reserve and the 11th Battalion was now in the war zone.

Strict injunctions were given about not moving about in large parties and not making any unnecessary movement by day;

but the troops, being new to the game, did not take much notice of the orders.

Parades were held in the courtyards of the farms, out of sight of any German observers from across the line. The famous Aubers Ridge, which was in enemy hands, and which gave them such a wide view of all the country to the north-west, was almost opposite the sector the 3rd Brigade was billeted in, and all movement was easily picked up by the Germans, who were not slow to act, with generally tragic consequences.

There was always a cobbled footwalk round a big midden inside the general run of farm buildings in this part of the country, and it was on this footwalk that the troops were drawn up for instruction when required. They were sheltered from observation by the buildings of the farm, but often when the troops were so drawn up, "Fritz" would start shelling, and it was not easy to get the troops to focus their attention on lectures or training when the shells started to scream and whine overhead, even if these missiles were not actually falling near the billets. Naturally all ears would be strained to hear the report of the guns, mostly howitzers, and then all would wait for the rush of the shells overhead and listen for the detonations.

On the day of the battalion's arrival a billet, occupied by the 9th Battalion, which battalion was temporarily attached to the 1st Brigade, was shelled, and though not many shots were fired, the 9th Battalion suffered over 70 casualties, one officer and 24 other ranks being killed. There had been a Taube flying overhead and possibly more than ordinary movement had been observed, although all the "Archies" in the neighbourhood had been firing at him. ("Archies" were anti-aircraft guns.) Not far from this billet, the writer happened to meet the famous "Fighting Mac," one of the famous padres of the Australian forces. The good padre was very anxious to procure the nose-cap of an anti-aircraft shell, and was hunting around where the pieces were falling. The nose-caps were regarded as interesting souvenirs when first the troops landed in France, but it was not long before their only interest lay in the distance the troops could get away from them.

As a result of the shelling of these billets, and because training was so restricted, the 11th Battalion was withdrawn to billets in the village of Sailly itself, and these proved to be much more comfortable in every way and the facilities for training were very much improved.

The area in which the troops were operating was known generally as the Armentieres Sector, named after the town of Armentieres on the River Lys. This town was about 55 miles from the sea at Boulogne and was of moderate size. It was only a couple of miles or so from the front line, yet at this time it was practically untouched, though it lay mid-way between the towns of Ypres and Loos, both of which towns had been the centres of the most sanguinary fighting on the front up to this time. The great city of Lille, which was the centre of one of the most densely populated parts of France, lay not far away, but on the German side of the line; and as this city provided an extensive billeting area, the German High Command was careful to not start anything that would have made the city and surrounding district dangerous or even impossible as a rest area for German troops.

Armentieres will always be chiefly associated in the Diggers' memories as the sector in which they gained their first experience of warfare in France, and even more so on account of that sweet but entirely mythical young lady, "Mademoiselle from Armentieres," who figured so prominently in so many of the Diggers' songs. Some of these are printable, but most are not. They were mostly sung to a then popular French tune entitled "Sous le Pont de Paris." One example is given:

> Apres le guerre finit,
> Australia will always do me,
> Mademoiselle from Armentieres.
> Two piccaninny, two souvenirs,
> Apres la guerre, fini.

and of course the still popular song, "Mademoiselle from Armentieres, parlez-vous," is still sung at all reunions of the troops, though the air of this song has probably been sung for hundreds of years by soldiers of British regiments that had fought in continental wars.

During the time the 11th Battalion was at Sailly sur la Lys, great attention was paid to gas drill and instruction in the proper use of gas-masks. Bayonet fighting was also much practised, and daily instruction in the then new Mill's grenade was given to all the troops. The area was dotted with gas schools, bayonet and physical drill schools and bombing schools, and officers and

N.C.O.'s were continually being detailed to attend these centres of instruction.

An occasional route march with full packs up was part of the programme, but no formation greater than a company was permitted to march in daylight on any road within ordinary shell fire of the enemy's line.

While at Sailly, companies of the 11th Battalion were on night fatigue digging a trench intended to hold an underground cable, and the engineers allotted a certain portion to each man per night. The amount to be taken out was three yards in length and five feet deep, or until water was struck. It was on jobs like these than the good "banjo" men shone. Some of the prospectors or miners, or well-sinkers like old Bill Beck, would have their portion out in no time, and then would spend the rest of their time yarning or smoking in the trench that they had dug, for it was an order that no lights were to be shown, as the cable trench was not very far from the line.

In addition to the ordinary training, parties were occasionally issued with steel helmets and sent up to the front line to get an idea of the conditions existing. The steel helmets were very heavy at first and caused headaches; but it was surprising how soon the troops got used to them, and how uncomfortable they felt in the line without them. When the boys came back from the trenches and told their mates all the wonderful things that happened, it whetted the appetites of the rest to have a look for themselves.

On the anniversary of the landing at Anzac, an inspection was held by the Army Commander, General Sir Herbert Plumer, accompanied by General Walker and Brigadier-General Sinclair-MacLagan. General Plumer inspected each battalion of the brigade on its own. This was regarded as a compliment, but may have been due to other reasons. The parade went off well and Lieut.-Colonel Roberts expressed himself satisfied with the turnout.

Anzac Day, which then had not the significance that it has since acquired, passed off quietly. An issue of beer and some extra rations and a brigade concert in the evening were the only celebrations.

More important to the boys was the fact that leave to England was to start on April 26, and one officer, one N.C.O. and seven other ranks were to be nominated every day from the 3rd

Brigade for eight days' leave. The older hands were especially bucked about this concession, and soon had their approximate dates worked out. Arrangements for finance were hastily made, and the lucky ones waited patiently for the day that would send them flying to catch the leave train.

Sailly was always looked back to with pleasure by all the boys who had lived there, for here the battalion had a fairly long stay in an area little devastated by the war. There were plenty of shops and estaminets in the village and in the neighbourhood. Excursions were made to Estaires and even to Merville and Bailleul. The people were friendly and took a real interest in the Diggers, and the troops returned the compliment by helping madame wherever possible, even to sitting up at night round the old stove waiting for a cow to calve and drinking the coffee that madame always had hot on the stove. Instead of using sugar to sweeten the coffee, a small lollie was placed in the mouth and the coffee then drunk. The boys used to be tickled with the idea of the lollies.

By this time the 11th Battalion had been about a month in France and the troops had fallen into the new conditions of life as if they had always been used to them. The Digger picked up a little French and knew how to ask madame for "oeufs" and "Pommes de terre," and at nights they could be seen round the tables of the estaminets, what time Marthe and Lucille brought round the big jugs of light beer, and madame sat at the receipt of custom, or in some corner where she could keep an eye on the room. The boys gave no trouble, and they made many friends among the civilian population.

While the battalion was billeted at Sailly sur la Lys, there were a great many rumours about spies in the village, and certainly the immunity that the village enjoyed, in common with all the thickly populated district from Armentieres right along to Estaires, would seem to have been sufficient evidence that there were friends of Germany quartered in the area. On the other hand, the fact that Lille and Tourcoigne and Roubaix were all within easy range of the British artillery may have kept the Hun quiet, as these great centres provided him with excellent billets for his troops and were, besides, valuable for their factories and other wealth.

Some said that two young and attractive ladies that lived in a nice house not far from the Mairie were none other than agents for the enemy, but nothing was ever proved, though they certainly could have given enough information to have kept the German Intelligence Department working overtime. There were also lights that showed and disappeared at some of the higher windows late at nights. These were frequently reported, but no notice seemed to be taken by the authorities of the reports. These high windows would have been quite visible to the Germans, who were only a few kilometres away.

Lieut. Le Nay, the 11th Battalion machine gun officer, was one day poking about just outside the battalion area, and much to his indignation was arrested as a spy and hauled before headquarters to prove his identity.

Then, of course, there was the famous white horse—there may have been several—whose owner used to plough in a curious fashion and who, according to the patterns he used to make, was reputed to give warning to the Germans of any important happening, such as reliefs that might be taking place. He was supposed to have a code that was easily picked up by the Germans.

There may have been a great deal of foundation for these reports, but the writer can testify that one day, the poor farmer, if he was a spy, got more than he bargained for. On this occasion the writer had to pass near this farmer, who was ploughing with a brown and white horse (the brown and the white were supposed to have something to do with the code). The horses in that part of France were always driven by only one rein. On this occasion, the farmer seemed to have some difficulty in getting his horses to go just where he wanted them. His performance certainly looked suspicious.

Suddenly out of the blue came a shell and dropped in the small field where the man was working. The rest of the salvo followed immediately; the brown horse reared and plunged and kicked himself clear of his harness and galloped off for his life, and the "Froggie" was left with the white horse galloping in circles round him, held by only the single rein, while the plough swung dangerously close to him every time the horse gave a fresh plunge. It was with difficulty that he eventually managed to get the animal unharnessed, and he made pretty good time home to the steading. He looked as scared as a rabbit, and with good cause, too, for the last shell had landed too close to be pleasant.

During the time spent at Sailly sur la Lys, the Intelligence Platoon, under Lieut. W. Kruger, was brought to a very high state of efficiency and proved itself of value to the battalion during the forthcoming tour of the line. When names such as Dan Cocking, "Pard" Riches, Drummond and others of like calibre were found on its roll, the section could not but be efficient.

A bombing platoon, under Lieut. Ray Clarke, was also formed. This was a very enthusiastic unit and performed prodigies of work. Clarke was as keen as mustard, and soon had a battery of miniature bomb-throwers ready for action. The personnel of this platoon was famous throughout the battalion for its camaraderie and its fine spirit, and not only were the men outstanding in efficiency, as will be duly narrated, but they were a body of troops that conferred an honour on whoever commanded them.

The Signal Section, under Lieut. A. Brodie, and the Lewis gunners, under Lieut. Le Nay, during this time also, laid the foundations of efficient specialist sections that were to prove their worth in the hard times that lay ahead.

On Thursday, April 27, General Sir Douglas Haig, Commander-in-Chief of the British Army in France, inspected the 3rd Brigade in two sections. The 11th and 12th Battalions were paraded together. General Haig was not a main given to many words, but it was understood that he was satisfied with his inspection.

That same night, when all the troops were comfortably in billets, a great clamour suddenly burst out; whistles, bells, sirens, Klaxon horns and rattled shell-cases all lending their din to the general alarm. It was the dreaded gas warning, and soon everyone had his gas-mask on, civilians as well, and all the chinks and crevices of the doors and windows were hastily filled up with paper and rags and the next move waited for.

It was not long before the "all clear" signal was given. The guns could still be heard pounding away, and out of doors the faint, sweet, sickly smell of chlorine could be just felt. There were no casualties in the 11th Battalion, but next day some of the fields of beans near by that had been so beautifully green had turned quite yellow by the gas.

As the Australian troops came more under the Great British organisation in France, and conformed to the general routine, it gradually became apparent that a tremendous amount of administration was necessary to keep the various units fit and ready for the trenches. Not only were there great ordnance and supply stores, stacks of coal, forage, timber, wire, iron and every conceivable thing necessary for the prosecution of the war, but there were also huge divisional baths, where changes of clothing were issued to the men. There were, as previously mentioned, schools of instruction for bombers, Stokes mortar, Lewis gunners and gas instructors, just to name a few, besides which there was the control of civilian activities, such as the sale of liquor and the safeguarding of lights. While the 11th Battalion was in Sailly, the estaminets were only open between the hours of 11 a.m. and 1 p.m., and 8 p.m. to 10 p.m., so that during the short time these places were available they were crowded with troops who used to look on them as clubs where they could foregather and have a pot or two of light "biere" or of "plink plonk," as they had already learned to call the common brand of "vin blanc."

These estaminets, which must have multiplied exceedingly since the commencement of the war, had often quaint names, much in the style of the old English inns. There was "Au Moisson d'Or" (to the Golden Harvest) and "A l'Epi de Ble" (to the Ear of Corn) and "Au Coq d'Or" (to the Golden Rooster), round whose hospitable tables the lads used to gather in the long spring evenings, and where many a pleasant hour was spent. Doubtless the estaminets still flaunt their gaudy signs; but many of the gay, careless boys had gone forever before the spring came round again.

However pleasant the leisure was at Sailly, the round of training and fatigues was not in any way relaxed. Since the weather had become warmer and the roads a bit drier, route marches were the order of the day, and these were gradually made longer and more exacting. At nights there were inlying piquets, and there were large parties detailed to unload barges on the River Lys and to assist on the ration dumps at Bac St. Maur and other localities.

Amid all this training and regimental work, the troops were not always good parade ground soldiers. Sometimes they came up against authority, and authority must frequently have thought that the Australians were pretty casual birds.

On one occasion, "Scotty" Mearns, of the 11th Battalion Transport, thought he would like to visit a friend billeted in Laventie, a village a few miles distant. The "cobber" was duly met and the meeting well and truly celebrated, with the result that "Scotty" finished up the night in a Tommy cooler. His mates of the transport heard about it, and put their heads together, with the result that old Bill Ayre, "Scotty's" bosom pal, borrowed a tunic and a general pass belonging to the 3rd Brigade veterinary sergeant, "Jock" Vernon, who was practically an 11th Battalion man. Armed with these, and an "escort," Bill set out for the Tommy guardroom. On arrival there "Sergeant" Ayre produced on order for "Scotty's" release. The latter was duly handed over and a receipt signed, and the prisoner was marced back to his rejoicing friends in the battalion transport lines at Bac St. Maur.

The time was rapidly approaching when the battalion was due for its first tour of duty in the trenches, and officers and N.C.O.'s were sent forward to inspect the sector that the battalion would occupy. Some of the older hands, men who had been on Gallipoli, were not impressed with what they saw, but a quiet day on the front may have led them to be too sanguine. Here is an extract from a letter dated May 7, 1916:

"And they call these trenches! In reality there are no trenches—not as we knew them at Anzac, anyhow—but simply sandbag breastworks. We entered a communication trench, and after many twists and contortions came out in the front line to see men roaming around quite happily, and apparently perfectly safe. There is only the front breastwork, no back to it, and you can wander away from the shelter quite unwittingly and be sniped. . . . Dug-outs are non-existent; their place is taken by sandbag erections in which are forms, tables, chairs, etc.; altogether they seem to have a regal time compared with Gallipoli."

The above lines were written by an officer who was right through the whole of the Anzac campaign, from the Landing to November, 1915, and it will be interesting to compare this letter with an extract by the same officer, only a few weeks later, which shall be given in its proper place.

During the last portion of the battalion's stay at Sailly sur la Lys there was an increasing amount of night work. Not only were there digging parties on the cable-laying, or rather cable-burying, but various parties were sent to such places as Twelve-

Tree Farm or some other topically named spot on one kind of fatigue or another. As nearly all the men were occupied at nights there were few parades during the day.

On May 19, word was received that the 11th Battalion would proceed to the trenches on the following day, so all the necessary preparations were made and hurried forward.

There was an air of excitement and expectancy about the troops. The untried men were wondering in their hearts how they would acquit themselves, and each might say with Captain J. E. Stewart (Border Regiment)—
"I was afraid of fear,
Not of the foe."
and yearn for the opportunity to test himself.

CHAPTER XVII

FLEURBAIX

AT LAST the order to move up to the line was given, and on the evening of May 20, 1916, the troops moved off in companies. As the leading platoons fell into their swing, some of the boys started to sing with great feeling

"When this bloody war is over,
Oh! how happy I shall be.
When I get my civvy suit on,
No more soldiering for me."

The song was truly appropriate to the occasion and as platoon after platoon disappeared into the murk of the May evening, loaded up to the teeth with all equipment, helmets, gasmasks, periscopes, bombs and all the paraphenalia of the modern soldier, the plaintive melody could be heard rising and falling.

The official entry is the following: "Sailly sur la Lys, France. May 20, 1916, 11th Battalion.—The battalion, less transport, moved into the firing line with 27 officers and 929 other ranks and occupied the left sector of the brigade frontage, in the Petillon area."

Regimental staff: Commanding, Lieut.-Colonel S. R. Roberts; second-in-command, Major J. S. Denton, D.S.O.; adjutant, Captain R. Hemingway; quartermaster, Lieut. G. R. Egg; commanding "A" Company, Captain A. F. MacFarlane; commanding "B" Company, Captain F. G. Medcalf; commanding "C" Company, Captain J. Newman; commanding "D" Company, Major J. T. Milner.

It was the first time in the line, unless the experience in the desert counted, for most of the boys; and it was with mixed feelings, but chiefly curiosity and a desire to get to the real thing, that the platoons filed up the long communication trench, known as Cellar Farm Avenue. An occasional shell passed overhead, and the hiss of machine gun bullets high up could occasionally be heard; but the relief of the 4th Battalion was carried out without mishap and the 11th Battalion was in the line for the first time in France.

The whole area in this part of the line was called "The Nursery," as it had the reputation of being a quiet sector, and here new troops were introduced to the firing line before being sent off to more dangerous sectors. The actual sector was a frontage of about 1,000 yards between Cordonnerie Farm and the ancient abbey of Chartreux; but the name by which the boys of the 11th Battalion always referred to the sector was "Fleurbaix," after a village to the left rear.

A study of the map of this part of France reveals the fact that all the country south of the Lys River, between Estaires and Armentieres, was a mass of streams, ditches and water channels. The Petillon sector, over the then German line towards Aubers and Fromelles, was perhaps the worst bit of the whole area, as far as ditches and streams were concerned, and it is safe to say that every field was surrounded by a ditch full of water and that the water level was never more than a foot or two below the surface of a very large part of the country. This was probably the chief reason that there was not much movement of front lines in this sector. The country was naturally extremely flat, except where the ground rose to a slight elevation at the famous Aubers Ridge.

Captain R. Hemingway, M.C. (11th Battalion)

The waterlogged condition of the country had little bearing on the 1st Australian Division's or the 11th Battalion's history in the line at Fleurbaix, but had things been ordered otherwise these swampy conditions might have had the same dire results as happened to the 5th Australian Division in this area.

This short description will give some idea of the ground conditions under which the 11th Battalion found itself during its first tour of the line in France.

The actual disposition of the troops was "D" Company on the left, "C" Company in the centre and "B" Company on the right, with "A" Company in support. Three platoons of each line company were in the front line trenches, and one platoon of each in the second line of defence. Colonel Roberts and staff had battalion headquarters in a shelter just off the main communication trench, Cellar Farm Avenue, near Cellar Farm itself. There were two other communication trenches named York Avenue and Dead Dog Avenue, but at this time both were so full of water as to be practically useless.

In "B" Company's sector were a number of mine shafts, leading to tunnels that had been under construction by a British tunnelling company, but which had lately been taken over by the 2nd Australian Tunnelling Company.

This, then, was the front the 11th Battalion had taken over. "The Nursery" or "Fleurbaix," though it was a dread name for some of the troops, yet on the whole for most of the Diggers that were in that sector it was one of the most pleasant times that the 11th Battalion had in the trenches. Only one incident seriously spoiled the tour of duty for some of the troops, and this will be related in due course.

It must be granted that everything was new and interesting, that only enough shell-fire and sniping occurred to make it exciting, and the patrols and wiring parties at nights lent a spice of adventure to the usual routine.

The ordinary day's proceedings were as follows: "Stand-to" for all troops at about an hour before dawn and "Stand-down" when everything was found to be quiet or normal. After that rifles were cleaned and inspected. A cheerful activity then prevailed, while the men in small groups prepared their breakfast over braziers of charcoal. The charcoal was used so that there would be no smoke, but wisps of smoke from damp wood and coal could be seen everywhere and over in Fritz' lines it was just the same.

All the time there were two sentries in each bay provided with periscopes, and these kept an eye on the trenches in front. Very often the tinkle of broken glass would be heard, indicating that some German sniper had "rung the bell."

After breakfast there was a general cleaning up of the trenches and the daily fatigues and trench duties continued all day till sundown, when "stand-to" was ordered. At nights there were patrols and wiring parties and a general activity all along the trenches.

As this was the longest tour of duty that the battalion had in the actual firing line without relief in France or Belgium, a short description of the prevailing conditions is warranted.

The trenches, a misnomer in the first place, were really built-up sandbag mounds, which had been battered out of all shape by shell fire and weather. The ground in the vicinity was low lying and just drained and no more by the Laies River and tributary ditches, so that it was practically impossible to dig dug-outs of the type used on Gallipoli or so well known later on the Somme. All the shelters were surface huts, built of filled sandbags and timber, often with galvanised iron roofs covered with a layer of sandbags, just enough to make them splinter proof. Most of the men lived—or rather slept—in burrows dug under the wide parapets. It was wet weather when the 11th Battalion took over the trenches, so all the troops were issued with rubber thigh-boots, called by the boys "gum-boots," and in these the troops used to slither up and down behind the ramparts. There was a duck-board track over the worst sections, but with the constant traffic the slats soon broke and it was often more of a trap to walk on, especially at nights, than the slippery ground itself.

There was also a firestep right along the wall of the parapet, and here the men would sit and yarn or smoke, as it was one of the few dry places, outside of the shelters at least, where the troops could sit with any comfort.

But one man evidently thought that the firestep was not high enough or dry enough. This was Lieut. Hastings, of "D" Company, who used to run up and down along the top of the sandbag parapet after dark. The boys soon had a name for him and dubbed him "The Mad Mullah."

In the days that followed the troops had their introduction to the various projectiles that "Jerry" used to hurl over from his lines. These were numerous and were distinguished by the wonderful names that had been given to them by the troops, mainly the Tommies, in the earlier days of the war. The missiles consisted of large low-velocity shells such as "Jack Johnstons" and "coal-boxes"; big trench mortars called "rum-jars," "Minnies" and "flying pigs"; high-velocity shells of small calibre, mostly 77 millimetre, referred to as "whizz-bangs"; large shrapnel shells bursting into a cloud of brownish-looking woolly smoke; the famous "woolly-bears" and small trench mortar bombs called "pineapples" and a great many more. It was not long before the boys were able to distinguish between the various missiles and to make the necessary reactions, which often meant a headlong dive for cover.

As the action of most of these missiles was generally very local, it was often a source of great amusement to onlookers —such a strange thing is war—for men to see their mates making a quick dash out of the way of some particularly obnoxious ironmongery. On one occasion, Lieut. Wally Hallahan was particularly amused at the antics of the company batmen, who were scared into unusually fast action by a bomb landing near their "possie." These lads made a dash for a nearby bay of a trench and almost collided with another bomb. This sent them hell-for-leather back to their original position, just in time to run into a third burst. How they escaped being casualties was a mystery, but Wally always reckoned that if Fritz had not considerately stopped his little bit of hate in time that the batmen must have dropped from pure dizziness, as they had kept running round and round on practically the same spot. Wally nearly hurt himself with laughing, yet he was one of the most tender-hearted of men and would have been the first to have run to the boys' aid if any of them had been hit, no matter what the danger.

Gas was the most feared weapon of the Germans at this time, and the trenches were plentifully supplied with all manner of gadgets to prevent the troops being taken by surprise. Gongs, klaxon horns and iron bars were in great evidence, as were also 18-pounder shell cases. Rattles were also used and a special S.O.S. rocket to be fired if gas were actually seen issuing from the enemy's line.

There were also numerous little wind vanes, some beautifully made to represent aeroplanes, which the troops would religiously gaze at from time to time to see that the wind was not in Jerry's favour. A few gas scares occurred, the most important being on the night of May 30, when all precautions were used and the troops wore their helmets in the ready position all night, with the result that the acid in the flannel of the old P.H. helmets burned many of the boys' foreheads and some had such bad sores that they had to be medically attended to.

It did not take the boys many days to get into the ordinary routine of trench life, and then they had to think of something to make life more interesting. In the mornings after stand-down, the Germans used to have the sun directly behind them and consequently the Australian lines stood out clearly and distinctly. At this time the enemy snipers were most active and fired at all periscopes and any movement that they could spot. There was no doubt about these fellows being marksmen. The boys of No. 11 platoon, "C" Company, used to hold up on the end of sticks emergency ration tins. These were about three inches by two. They were carefully pushed above the parapet and Fritz, taking the shiny surface for mirrors, used to fire at them. It was computed that he put two bullets out of three through these tins. The nearest point of the German lines at this point was 350 yards distant.

Brigadier-General Sinclair-MacLagan used frequently to make his rounds of the trenches in the early mornings, and he was very particular as to waste and used to make a great fuss if any empty cartridge cases were left lying about; so the troops were exhorted to collect all the empties left from the shooting that generally took place at nights. These they picked up and placed in an empty sandbag for sending back, but no doubt most of the cases were simply thrown into No Man's Land.

One morning, however, a pile was missed in the corner of one of the bays of the trench, where possibly a machine gunner had been doing his stuff the previous night. When the General saw the heap he went very sour about it, and it took more than a little skill to pacify him. These visits of the General, although the boys would have been quite satisfied if he had come less often, at least showed that he desired to see for himself what the front line conditions were like, and this was one feature about commanders that the boys appreciated more than any other.

In the afternoons when the sun was in the west, and consequently behind the Australians, the troops had their chance to retaliate in the matter of sniping, and the "possies" in the parapets, specially constructed for the purpose, were used; sometimes with good effect, but sometimes some sportsman on the other side would wave a miss with a spade or entrenching tool.

As night came on both sides used to waken up a bit and the evening hate would start, a matter of trench mortars and bombs generally; minnenwerfers and grenades from Fritz and "plum-puddings" and rifle grenades from the Australian side. ("Plum-puddings" were large circular bombs with a long shaft.)

Lieut. C. Shenton, of the Trench Mortar Battery, was often in charge of the "plum-pudding" bombs. The trench mortar crowd was not too popular, however, for though most of the boys were interested in the entertainment while it lasted, and were delighted when one of the big bombs lobbed in the enemy trenches, yet they were not so pleased to see the trench mortar sections dismantle their weapons and make off for their lives as soon as they had fired a few shots and thus leave the poor infantry to collect all the return hate. It was not long before the Trench Mortar Battery was called "The Cut-and-Run Brigade."

On one occasion when the "plum-pudding mob" had started operations, one bomb was seen to be well on the way to its mark. As the big missile sailed high up into the air, turning over and over, every head in the sector was above the parapet watching to see where the bomb would land.

A great shout of satisfaction went up when it was seen to land over the enemy's parapet, but this soon changed into groans of disappointment when the bomb failed to explode. And then the "Toc emmas" (T.M.'s) did their usual disappearing trick.

Later that night, when everything was deathly quiet and only the rising German flares lent a weird movement to the darkness, a terrific explosion was heard somewhere near where the "plum-pudding" had dropped. What really happened will never be known, but all the boys hoped that a crowd of German stickybeaks were round that dangerous toy when it went off. Such were the feelings engendered by war.

Besides the Trench Mortar Batteries there was the 11th Battalion Bombing Platoon, under Lieut. Ray Clarke. This was known as "Clarke's Light Artillery" and was the subject of much abuse by the rest of the troops. Clarke would bring his lethal weapons to various points of vantage in the lines, and from these proceed to discharge Mill's grenades at the enemy trenches. "B" Company's lines were nearest to the Germans and this position was much the most suitable place for the discharge of small bombs, and naturally that company received most of the return strafing. "B" Company realised this, but felt that as there was a war on it had just to put up with the inconvenience and danger.

Though no mention has been made of casualties so far, yet there was a constant trickle of wounded to the aid-post, which was situated in "C" Company's lines quite close to the tramway, down which stretcher cases were sent. On one occasion a stretcher-case was noticed on the trolley with a huge, satisfied smile on his face and a large notice on his breast which bore the legend, "Blighty first stop!"

After stand-to, as darkness began to deepen, the main business of the day began to be carried out by both sides. Rations were brought up to the line and stores and supplies of barbed wire and corkscrew pickets distributed to the companies. Patrols were sent out and wiring parties improved the wire or repaired any serious breaks, and scouts went forward to examine the enemy's wire. Talking and laughing could sometimes be heard in No Man's Land, but when a flare was fired it was seldom that anyone could definitely say that he saw anything, as the flickering lights made all sorts of moving shadows.

The machine guns on both sides would spray the wire and the parapets, but it was not often that there were any casualties though Private Lamerton had a bullet through his tin hat—from one side to the other—but without even scratching him.

One German machine gunner was so expert at controlling his fire that those boys who were opposite to him reckoned that he could play tunes on his machine gun.

It was not often that there was any serious shell fire at nights and most nights passed pretty peacably considering there was a war on. After stand-down in the mornings, the boys had various ways of cleaning their rifles, but the chief method was to fire a shot and then clean the barrel while it was hot.

Private Murphy, a real cantankerous old citizen, was one day noticed resting his rifle on the parapet at an angle of 45 degrees before he fired. An officer in passing asked Murphy what the bright idea was. Murphy replied: "Sorr, ye niver know but what I moight be hittin' wan av thim bastards away ahint the lines there an' him not knowin'," and he waved an arm that might have embraced all the German back area.

The battalion Lewis gunners were among the keenest of the specialists and they were very active. They were exceedingly proud of their new guns and their officer, Lieut. Le Nay, was always on the hunt for enemy targets. The sentries would pick up working parties or other movements behind the enemy's lines, and in a short time Le Nay would be along with his gunners and give these targets a burst or two of fire. The officer always used to be very sanguine about results, and frequently claimed hits. Where the enemy trenches were breached by shell fire, machine guns used to be trained on to these points at night in order to catch the parties repairing them. The Lewis gun was found to be extremely handy and convenient, but it had the disadvantage of jamming at times, and these generally when it was most needed.

On the night of May 23 a party of scouts from the 11th Battalion was out looking at the wire opposite "B" Company's front and Private Drummond was well into the enemy's wire when the enemy opened fire and Drummond was killed, his body falling on the German wire, where his body was seen next day.

It was resolved by his mates to bring in the body that night. After dark a machine gun barrage was skillfully placed round that part of the German trenches by Private W. Plunkett and others, while the scouts crawled over to the wire and Dan Cocking cut the wire and freed the body, and with the help of Les. Riches tied a rope on it and pulled it clear. Then the body was brought back to the 11th lines and buried in the cemetery close to Cellar Farm.

On May 25, Lieuts. C. G. Ross, A. C. Elliott and H. Davidson, with 66 other ranks from reinforcements, arrived from Etaples. These men were distributed among the various companies.

The days were enlivened by the sight of the aerial observers dodging among the "Archie" bursts, and one airman, known as "The Mad Major," was the admiration of everyone. He would circle low over the enemy's lines, while shells and bursts of machine gun and rifle fire followed him everywhere. He seemed to bear a charmed life.

One day an aeroplane was seen flying low heading straight for the German lines. It was greeted with intensive fire, which suddenly ceased; but the 'plane sailed straight over the German lines and disappeared in the direction of Lille, which was only a few miles to the East. At the time it was thought that some accident must have befallen the machine or the airman, but it was learned afterwards that the pilot was a German who had trained in England, and had so hoodwinked the authorities that he had been entrusted with flying one of the new 'planes.

On the first opportunity he got away and flew across the Channel, over the trenches and into German territory. It was certainly the act of a brave and enterprising man.

Thus the days passed until May 30, which was moderately quiet except for a few shells on different positions in the morning. It afterwards transpired that the enemy was registering new batteries on selected points. The afternoon was warm and peaceful and the evening so still that if the troops had been more experienced they would have known that some trouble was brewing. The troops were standing-to, chatting and laughing when, at 8.15 p.m., a single shell burst high overhead right above the centre of the 11th Battalion trenches. All eyes had turned to look up at the heavy, dark smoke from the burst when, with a terrific crash, an intensive bombardment was laid on "A" and "B" Companies' lines and the right flank of "C" Company was smothered in shrapnel fire, while Cellar Farm Avenue, the main communication trench that led into "C" Company's sector, was rendered impassable. This severe bombardment lasted about an hour and a half and absolutely flattened the parapet in many places, notably in "B" Company's sector, and killed and wounded about 120 men. During a lift in the bombardment the Germans made a raid on "B" Company's trenches and secured some prisoners.

There was practically nothing the troops could do in the shelled area, but Bill Plunkett and "Darkie" Hodge stuck to their machine guns; and although Plunkett was twice knocked over by the explosions of bombs, both men maintained their positions. The boys on the flanks were lying on the top of the parapet, peering through the murk and smoke in the hope of seeing something to shoot at.

Captains McFarlane and Medcalf had collected what troops they could find, and these were strung out in rear of the attacked portion; but being new to the game, none of the officers or men realised that it was just a local raid, terrible though it was in its intensity and effect. The raid was beyond their experience, and they did not realise the nature of the attack nor the steps necessary to counteract its effect. But the conduct of the troops was everywhere excellent, and many acts of heroism were witnessed. Captain Bradshaw, though badly wounded and unable

Top: Captain "Wac" Connell (12th Battalion), killed in action; Lieut. D. McCallum (51st Battalion, original 11th), killed in action.
Bottom: Lieut. J. F. Wilson, Captain Bradshaw (11th Battalion), severely wounded at Fleurbaix.

to move, kept cheering and rallying his men, and by his gallant conduct encouraged many of the boys. One shell landed in the shelter occupied by the scouts, killing eight out of the ten inmates; but the remaining two reported to battalion headquarters for instructions immediately the shelling slackened.

When daylight appeared on May 31, what a scene of destruction met the eye. "B" Company's lines were like a shambles, and though some of the worst breaches had already been repaired there was a terrific amount to be done before the trench was anything like in order again. One shell had carried away the end of "C" Company's officers' mess hut at the end of Cellar Farm Avenue, and the communication trench was well battered about.

One of the "old originals" who had been on Gallipoli said: "By cripes! We never had shelling like that on Anzac."

There were 118 casualties, including two officers wounded (Captain R. D. Bradshaw and Lieut. A. B. Brook), 36 other ranks killed and 69 other ranks wounded and 11 missing, some of which were taken prisoners.

Commenting on the above raid Private Harrald, of the 1st Australian Light Trench Mortar Battery, writes: "I recall that disastrous raid against the 11th Battalion on the night of May 30, 1916. It may be interesting to note that the steadiness of your men, and the methodical way officers and men set to work to repair the destroyed parapet, deeply impressed me as a young soldier of another arm, namely, the Trench Mortar Battery." He goes on to say: "Next morning I went to have a look at the scene of destruction; by that time some of the huge gaps in the front line parapet had been roughly filled in, and the men of the 11th Battalion were busy digging out the poor mangled bodies of their cobbers who had been caught in the blast and re-erecting the parapet in business-like manner, in spite of the salvos of whizz-bangs and numerous rifle grenades Fritz was sending over, well knowing that this work would be going on. While I was on the scene I saw three men wounded by a rifle grenade.

"To add to the horror, the shelling had dug up many decomposed bodies of Tommies who had been buried not far behind the parapets, and the stench was awful."

The above description, by an entirely unprejudiced observer of the 11th Battalion and its activities under fire is a just and impartial appreciation of this West Australian battalion.

To the troops without previous experience of German artillery massed for attack it seemed as if nothing could ever surpass the shelling on this occasion for intensity, and many of the young troops, especially those who had been close to the shelling, felt that they had been in a major operation; but the affair was only a thoroughly planned minor operation by a very skilful enemy.

The shelling indeed was an eye-opener to everyone. It was scarcely believable that such an intensity of fire could be concentrated on a limited area by the small number of batteries engaged. The following entry is from the diary of the old Anzac soldier, whose remarks were quoted in the previous chapter. The entry shows how quickly his opinions changed: "Wednesday, May 31, 1916. Had it pretty hot last night on our right: the Germans bombarded from 8:15 p.m. till 9:30 p.m. and blew the parapet to atoms; it was worse than any bombardment we had on Gallipoli, and I'm afraid 'A' and 'B' Companies had rather a bad time. (Later) Have just been along to have a look at the damage. My word; but it's *awful!* Gallipoli was never a patch on this; parapets and dug-outs are razed to the ground and shell-holes are everywhere . . . the wonder to me is, that so many lived through the inferno."

The total casualties in the 11th Battalion for the month of May were 47 all ranks killed and 71 all ranks wounded. There were still several missing still unaccounted for. These were later found to be prisoners captured by the Germans in the raid.

As has been already mentioned, leave to England had been instituted and some of the early-leave men were now returning to the battalion from their good time in Blighty. No. 1111 "Frosty" Campbell was complaining to all and sundry that it would be just like his luck to be "smacked" before he was due for leave. C.S.M. Gallagher had just returned from leave, and he turned to "Frosty" and told him he was the last man that should worry. "Cripes! 'Frosty'! he said, "A man with a number like yours will go right through the good war. One, one, one, one! Four bloody aces! What better deal could you expect than that?"

The "Good Gall" went on to recount some of his experiences in London, much to the amusement of the boys, for he was a real wag, and a little later was just going to his dug-out when a shell landed close and a fragment struck him and killed him.

Sergeant Wally Graham had come to take over Gallagher's duties, as he was senior sergeant, and he was railing at the sad occurrence and the strange ways of fate when a runner told him he was wanted at company H.Q. In a few minutes Wally came running back; he was out of breath and his eyes were sticking out with excitement. "Out of the way e-everyb-body!

I'm for leave! (he always stuttered when excited). L-let me get out of t-this be-f-f-fore I'm like the 'Good Gall,' " and seizing the few necessaries for his trip he rushed off down Cellar Farm Avenue and was not seen again for about a fortnight.

Few of the days in the line passed without some unusual incident. But even on the quiet days the boys used to derive a lot of fun from seeing the intelligence officer and his section going their rounds twice daily to take the depth of the water in the Laies "river."

This "river" was a drain that carried off the surplus water from the immense flat in which the trenches were situated, and which emptied itself into the River Lys near Armentieres. The boys used to call this measuring of the water "taking the tide." It seemed such a trivial thing to be have been done daily, but if the "river" had been blocked by shell-fire or otherwise the whole district would have been soon waterlogged and unfit to live in.

While on the topography of this area, it is interesting to note that right opposite the 11th Battalion sector but in the German lines was the Ferme de Mouquet (Mouquet Farm). This must not be confused with the Mouquet Farm of the Somme area, of which mention will be made later in the narrative.

The story of the 11th Battalion's tour of duty at Fleurbaix would be incomplete without an allusion to the rats of the trenches. Fleurbaix was the home of rats; they could be seen at all times, but mostly they preferred the dusk or the darkness. Great, big, ugly brutes they were. They used to scamper up and down the parapets and were everywhere in the dug-outs and shelters. The troops were often awakened at nights with the brutes running over them. They seemed to live and thrive in the worst conditions of the war. Even gas seemed to pass them over, but doubtless many were suffocated.

The boys would trap them in various ways. One popular method was to stick a bit of cheese on the end of a bayonet, fix the bayonet on a rifle and hold the loaded rifle against the parapet at a convenient height. When a rat came along he would start to nibble the cheese and the Digger would press the trigger and murmur the "Soldiers' Farewell." Occasionally some of the more expert or more lucky would do a successful lunge or "long point," but the brutes were very difficult to stick or even shoot, for they were never still for more than a moment at a time.

On June 1, the troops had a surprise when they saw a captive balloon, which up till then had been securely anchored, suddenly come sailing majestically towards them. As soon as it came near the trenches Fritz let fly with everything that might be effective and the two observers hopped out and parachuted gracefully to earth, while the huge sausage-shaped balloon, apparently escaping all the missiles fired at it, floated buoyantly away in the general direction of Germany; as one of the boys remarked, "Destination unknown!"

Towards nightfall on this same date Fritz sent over five minenwerfers, the much-hated "rum-jars" of trench parlance. These fell in "B" Company's trenches with shattering detonations and made craters of about twenty feet across by about ten or twelve feet deep. These huge bombs fairly put the "wind up" the troops, but they had one redeeming feature, if only a little one. They were not difficult to dodge if the troops kept their heads, as they could be seen coming and there was plenty of time to get out of the way; at night they left a trail of sparks as they travelled through the air. The reason of their being fired at "B" Company's sector was that this was the Cordonnerie Salient, which was not only the nearest portion of the Australian lines to the enemy but also because of the mine shafts that were located there.

After the experiences of the last few days the boys were beginning to think that someone must have made a mistake in naming the sector "The Nursery." It was felt that if "Fleurbaix" was a nursery, that part of the trenches where a real man-sized war was being waged was a place to be left well alone.

On the afternoon of June 7, there were more "rum-jars", which were again hurled at "B" Company. The flanking companies could see the great missiles thrown high in the air and could watch their descent on to the objective, while the ear waited in dread for the terrific explosion and then the debris would keep falling for quite a long time afterwards. "B" Company on this occasion had seven casualties, one man being killed.

The long tour of duty came to an end at last, and on the night of June 8 the 12th Battalion relieved the 11th Battalion, the latter unit taking up position in support.

After the battalion had come out of the trenches it was learned that Lord Kitchener had been drowned when the H.M.S. *Hampshire* struck a mine and sank off the coast of the Orkney Islands in the north of Scotland on June 5. Many of the boys recollected the cruiser that had led the great convoy of the first contingent from Colombo to Alexandria in December, 1914.

Chapter XVIII

IN SUPPORTS AT FLEURBAIX

THE 11TH BATTALION was relieved without any unusual incident and without casualties and marched back to its new position. The companies of the battalion were very much scattered, but the troops were mostly quartered round La Croix Marechal and the Rue des Lombards, two localities about a mile behind the sector of trenches that had lately been occupied. The area was divided into a number of posts, and each company was responsible for one or more. Some of the quarters in the posts were pretty fair, but some on the Rue des Lombards were very much knocked about by shell-fire. Still, there was cover and protection in most of the billets and the troops were able to relax to a certain extent.

The battalion strength was now 31 officers and 870 other ranks. The total casualties for the first tour of the line, certainly a long period compared to future service in the actual front line, were 43 killed, 115 wounded and six missing; a total of 164. This was a fairly heavy total for a quiet sector, but the 11th Battalion had been very unfortunate in having had to suffer a raid while in the line. That could only be regarded as a piece of bad luck and might have happened to any battalion holding the sector at the time.

On June 9 Lieut.-Colonel Roberts asked Captain Medcalf to take charge of and train a party of the 11th Battalion in order to make a raid on a point called "The Tadpole," opposite to the trenches held by "D" Company, while it was in the line. This was to take place in the near future. Volunteers were to be called and officers were to be selected, and the whole party to be immediately taken to a good billet in rear, where they were to be well fed and trained for the job. The next day the party was collected and marched off. There were 60 men chosen as raiders, including Lieuts. Clarke, Davidson, Hallahan, Hastings and Kruger.

During the time the battalion was in the support line nearly all the work was done at nights, as this minimised the movement during the day around the billets, and also because much of the work was done on redoubts, emergency roads to the communication trenches and other such work of a tactical nature.

All day long the troops rested or went picking strawberries, which were now ripe and plentiful round the deserted farms. There were, of course, sentries and gas guards, and it was here that the story of the Australian sentry who made the mistake of taking the general "for one of them Pioneer b———s" first went the rounds.

It was here also that old Bill Beck failed to salute one of the majors of his own battalion. The major was naturally indignant and, looking at Bill, said haughtily: "Look here, my man! Don't you know who I am?" And Bill, staring back at the major, answered: "Too right I do! You're the butcher from Northam, ain't you!" It is only fair to both men to state that old Bill had imbibed one too many.

It was now summer, and most of the days were warm and fine. There were still occasional showers and the ground in this low-lying part of Flanders was still muddy, and after the showers invariably sloppy. The previous wearing of gum-boots for long periods in the trenches and the constant wet feet of these days in support tended to soften the feet of the troops, and the effect of this was very noticeable later on when the battalion had heavy route-marching to do.

On June 12, the following officers and men reported for duty: 2nd/Lieut. J. L. Barry, 2nd/Lieut. L. J. Bickford (from reinforcements), 2nd/Lieut. P. E. M. Vowles (from hospital) and 29 other ranks from reinforcements.

There was a change-over of posts on June 13 when "C" Company, which had been nearest the line and consequently had the roughest billets, made a transfer with "D" Company.

Several gas alarms occurred while the battalion was in support, and on several occasions the troops had to stand-to until the command "All clear" came through. On June 14, the date that the "daylight saving" order came into force, in support of the decree of the French Government, there was a gas attack on the front near the 11th Battalion and the troops were on the *qui vive* all night; the effect of the gas was felt in Sailly, about three miles in rear, and it was reported that some civilians were suffering from the gas, but no one in the 11th Battalion was affected.

A great artillery battle took place on the night of June 16 and the troops in support saw the tremendous picture of a big barrage and heavy shell-fire, but luckily only from the onlookers' point of view. The scene was terribly magnificent, and everything stood out clearly outlined in the vivid light caused by the bursting shells. Then, from far and near came the sounds of bells, gongs, rattles and beaten shell-cases, indicating that another gas attack had been launched by the enemy. Again the gas was felt in the rear areas, but there were no casualties in the battalion.

Now that the weather was generally fine and clear an increased amount of aerial activity was noticed. As this form of warfare was new to most of the troops—very little having been seen on Gallipoli—it was a source of great interest, and generally all hands would stop whatever they were doing to follow the wonderful evolutions of the fighters high aloft. In fact, right to the end of the war an aerial scrap held the attention of the troops more than any other form of warfare.

Owing to this increased aerial activity on the part of the enemy, there was considerably more shelling of billets and back areas. On one occasion the Germans shelled and set fire to a billet which was situated next to an estaminet. The latter soon went on fire also. As the liquid assets of the estaminet were in serious danger of being destroyed, the troops managed to rescue them first.

On June 18, 2nd/Lieut. W. C. Belford was promoted lieutenant, dated May 29, 1916; 2nd/Lieut. Bickford was sent to the Lewis gun school at Camiers, along with one other rank (his batman).

The great Somme offensive was now being planned, and for some time the commanders of the armies in the north had been under instructions to make as many demonstrations as possible in order to retain as great a force of the enemy in the northern sectors as possible, and to prevent him transferring any divisions down to the Somme area. To this end, and also for the purpose of identifying the units opposed to them and so fixing the position of as many German divisions as possible, a great number of raids were ordered, not only by the Australian divisions, but also by British units in the northern sectors.

For one of these raids the party of the 11th Battalion, under Captain F. G. Medcalf, was training in quarters behind Sailly, not far from Doulieu. Maps and plans of "The Tadpole," for such was the name given to the portion of trenches to be attacked, were distributed to all the raiders, and these were carefully studied and a model of the plan to be adopted in the actual attack was used in the daily practice. The party had a splendid time during its period of training and was in great heart.

The first Military Medal to be gained by a member of the 11th Battalion was awarded to No. 3682 Private C. E. Williamson on June 20.

On June 21, Lieut. W. Belford was sent to a school of instruction in German words of command and phrases used in trench life. This school was at Hazebrouck. Second/Lieut. Elliot and seven other ranks were sent to the divisional bombing school for a course of instruction and two other ranks were sent to Erquinghem to a bayonet-fighting course. On June 23, Sergeant Naylor went to a school of musketry and in the course of the next few days 2nd/Lieut. Nichol went to a sniping-school at Mont des Cats and 2nd/Lieut. A. C. Brodie to a school for signallers. It will be seen from the foregoing that a constant effort was made to keep the officers and men as efficient as possible and to train them in all the latest methods of carrying out their part of the war.

Seventy-three reinforcements joined the battalion on June 23.

Word had reached the troops that the 4th Australian Division had arrived and were billeted in the neighbourhood of Sailly, and on the night of June 24/25 "B" Company was relieved by troops of the 50th Battalion, and there was some excitement over the fact that the 51st Battalion would be coming into the trenches near by. It was almost four months since the boys of the 51st had parted from their old mates in the 11th Battalion, and naturally the troops in the latter unit were anxious to see their friends. But the 51st relieved the 10th Battalion and there was no chance of old comrades meeting, as the relief took place late at night on June 28/29. The three remaining companies of the 11th Battalion were also relieved and marched back to Sailly sur la Lys, where they occupied billets on the Sailly Estaires road. Although the two sister battalions were almost within speaking distance, the fortune of war decreed that they were not to meet until the 11th Battalion had lost more than half of its men.

For the next four days there was a little company drill, but as the battalion had a considerable amount of night fatigues to perform the men were generally resting through the day, and so were able to visit their French friends in the village and surrounding country.

The 3rd Brigade was going to carry out two raids early in July, and the raiders were hard at work training for the job. There seemed to be increased activity on the Fleurbaix front, but as the various batteries had to register for the raids there was a good deal of covering fire to prevent the registering from being too obvious.

On June 28, Lieut. P. E. M. Vowles was sent to an engineering school. Captain G. F. Combs was seconded to command No. 3 Trench Mortar Battery. The following officers were promoted to lieutenant: G. S. R. Walters, E. Parsonage, E. Rogerson, A. B. Brook, J. M. Aitken, A. C. Brodie, R. A. Clarke, T. G. Nicol and S. T. Forbes.

The battalion Lewis gun establishment was increased to six guns on June 30, and reserve crews of 24 men were immediately selected and instructed in the use and care of the weapons.

The 9th Battalion made a very successful raid on the night of July 1/2, in which 21 prisoners were captured.

On the following night the 11th Battalion received a sudden order to move, and about 9 p.m. set out for Oultersteen, a small village close to Merris. On the way there that fine young officer, Lieut. Jock Millar, who had been left at Serapeum when the battalion left the Suez Canal, rode up and greeted many of his old friends. He had been in charge of the big draft of reinforcements that made up the battalion after the "split," and the 11th Battalion lost the services of a splendid lad—as later events proved—when he went to the 49th Battalion.

After a long march, which finished about midnight, the 11th Battalion arrived at its destination. There was a good deal of hunting round in the dark, but eventually the troops were settled in their billets. The officers of "C" Company were not so lucky. When they had seen to the comfort of their men they started to look for their own billet. They went to the house that had been pointed out as their temporary home, but somebody must have got in before them, for Madame cried "Pas de logement, ici" and shut the door against them, first pointing to a house on the opposite side of the street and indicating that the officers might find a billet there.

The tired warriors crossed the street and tried the door, but it was locked, so all sorts of devices were tried to attract the attention of the inmates. The use of an entrenching tool handle did not seem to have much effect, so the shuttered windows and bolted door were assailed with a particularly choice barrage of French, English and Arabic. Finally Captain George Campbell let go in the best Australian he could muster, and that was saying something. This must have done the trick, for a window was thrown open in the upper part of the building and a sleepy voice asked, "Qu'y a-t-il?"

The owner of the voice was quickly asked to open the door. He immediately withdrew, the flicker of a lighted match was seen and footsteps were heard descending the stairs, and the amazed officers were confronted by an old man in a very short nightshirt and holding a lighted candle above his head. This old fellow led them to a room upstairs, with a few rough beds in it.

It was by this time early morning, and the officers were feeling in need of a little refreshment. On being asked if he could produce anything drinkable, the old rascal winked and said: "Moi aussi, j'ai fait la guerre en soixante-et-onze" (I, too, went to war in 1871), and went off chuckling to find some wine. He came back still chuckling with a couple of bottles and helped to drink some of the very indifferent vintage.

It was late next day when the troops were awakened. There was an unholy row going on in "C" Company officers' billet. The lady of the house was accusing the old soldier of being up to some of his tricks, but the old rascal kept shaking his head and chuckling to himself. Possibly he had made a raid on the cellar to get the wine during the previous night, for the good Madame kept on saying, "Brigand! Voleur! Larron!" Truly, "old soldiers never die."

On the same morning the troops heard the result of the raid of the 11th Battalion which took place on the previous night. The actual date of the raid had been kept a secret until the day before the event. At the appointed time Medcalf led his party up to the front line. All watches had been synchronised with the artillery. At zero hour the guns opened with a crash and the shelling was well on the target. The wire in front of the enemy trenches had been smashed by trench mortars earlier in the day.

Captain Medcalf's own report of the operation is the following: "Under cover of our concentrated artillery fire, we crawled forward across No Man's Land in our formation and came to a halt within 50 yards of the German parapet. . . . Our artillery was bursting its shells right on top of the Hun's parapet, and there we lay in perfect safety only 50 yards short of it, waiting for it to lift so that we might follow along and enter the German trench. One would have thought that the boys were on the parade ground—the only difference was that they were keener and steadier and better disciplined at that moment than ever they were on parade. By and by our guns lifted and put a curtain of fire behind the Hun's trench, in order to prevent him bringing up supports.

"This was the moment we were so anxiously awaiting, so I sat up and gave the order to adopt our attacking formation and move forward. The boys doubled through the wire in silence; one or two were hooked up in the barbs, but most of the wire had been smashed previously, so it did not offer much difficulty. Through the breach in the Hun parapet we went and spread out inside the trench, seeing many dead and taking numerous identification papers, helmets and respirators. There was only one Hun left in all that amount of trench; our artillery had been so deadly. Unfortunately an over-zealous private bayoneted this man instead of taking him prisoner.

"When we had been in the trench for the specified time, I gave the order to return through the place by which we had entered and make for our own trench again. The men just walked home across No Man's Land. I was never so surprised in my life as to see our chaps walking in that particular area, where a man generally crawls gingerly on his stomach. But our artillery and machine guns were so effective in silencing the Huns that it was quite safe. Every man in our party returned safely to our trenches."

The members of the raiding party were at once checked and sent to the rear, where motor waggons picked them up and hurried them back to billets. After a few hours' rest the raiding party followed the 11th Battalion to Oultersteene.

The identifications gained by this raid proved that the trenches were then held by the 21st Bavarian Regiment of the 6th Bavarian Reserve Division.

The 3rd Brigade was now in billets about ten miles from the trenches and a programme of training was at once adopted. Physical training and route-marching were given a prominent place in the scheme in order to counteract the effects of the long period in the wet and mud of the trenches. The 11th Battalion was billeted quite near Merris and Meteren, and not far from Fletre and Caestre, where the troops had their first billets in France.

A batch of 30 reinforcements joined up with the battalion on July 3. This brought the total strength up to 32 officers and 920 other ranks.

There were daily route-marches of increasing length from July 5 to July 8, mostly in dull, drizzly weather. The country round about was so intensely cultivated and all the production so urgently required by the French nation that it was hardly possible to find sufficient ground for company or battalion drill, so the troops had to be exercised in the only way possible.

During these marches in these early days in France, numbers of young girls and boys used to accompany or follow the line of marching men. These French children used to sell chocolate and other delicacies and at the hourly halts they used to do a lucrative business.

A church parade was held on Sunday, July 9, when both the 9th and 11th Battalions attended. General Birdwood attended the service, which was long remembered by the troops for the sermon preached by the padre. It always seemed a pity that so few padres understood the mentality of the troops. On this occasion the padre told the boys that life was "a mere incident" and that its loss was nothing, and more to the same effect. As rumours had been going round that the Australian divisions were going down to the Somme, where there had been such a colossal loss of life already, the troops resented this form of address and ever afterwards referred to the padre as the "Mere Incident!" It was rather a tactless sermon to give to troops who were about to be thrown into the terrible maw of the Somme battlefield.

After the service there was a short address by General Birdwood, who then definitely informed the troops that they were going to the Somme, where the "Big Push" had recently started. Birdwood told the boys that they would have a chance of open fighting, which, he said, he was sure that the Diggers would prefer to the trench fighting that they had been engaged in up to this time in France.

The news was received with great joy by the boys, and they marched back to their billets entirely satisfied with themselves and the world generally.

Immediately after mid-day the 11th Battalion received orders to "fall-in" and it was marched off to billets about a mile and a half north-east of Meteren. Next day, July 10, orders were given to pack up and be ready to move off at a moment's notice. No move was made till 7:15 p.m., when the battalion was moved off to the north past Le Coq de Paille to Mont des Cats, where the troops bivouaced for the night. It was fine weather, and it was no hardship to sleep out among the fields and trees that beautiful summer night.

CHAPTER XIX

OFF TO THE SOMME

THE PEACEFUL NIGHT on the slopes of Mont des Cats was the ending of another phase of the life of the 11th Battalion. The original battalion had been practically wiped out on Gallipoli and a new battalion had been built up since the days of Tel-el-Kebir and Gebel Habieta; and although there was a sound sprinkling of men who had been right through from the beginning, the great bulk of the men were reinforcements of the splendid type of men who had been coming forward in 1915 and 1916. Most of these men were well trained and had now had a preliminary introduction to warfare, and they were keen to show that they were as good as the gallant fellows that they had replaced. There was a splendid esprit de corps at this time, and a comradeship between men and officers that could not possibly have been surpassed. Indiscipline was practically unknown, for though the lads were high-spirited and fun-loving, there was that co-operation among all ranks that made for smooth running. This battalion of splendid men, all unknowing of the terrible days ahead of them, was about to be plunged into what was generally admitted to be some of the heaviest fighting in the whole of the war.

Early on the morning of July 11, 1916, the bugle aroused the bivouacing troops. It was 3 a.m. and breakfast was immediately served and the troops marched off to the railway station at Godewaersvelde, where with transport and field kitchens, they entrained at 4:30 a.m.

The transport was loaded in the record time of 35 minutes. This excellent performance was a credit to Lieut. A. Burgess and his men. This was most of the troops first experience of a French troop train after their journey from Marseilles, when the boys had mostly been in carriages. Some of the trucks (Hommes, quarante-Chevaux, huit en long) which, as the legend indicated, carried either 40 men or eight horses, had obviously been used to transport the latter, for the floors were many inches deep in horse-manure. So much so that one man complained to Captain George Campbell and pointed out the state of the truck that he had been detailed to occupy.

George Campbell had a look and a sniff, and then turned to the Digger with a grin and said: "Well, my lad, what do you expect *me* to do? Charter another train?"

So the boys had to make the best of it, which they did by covering up the mess as well as possible, and then they piled into the trucks. The journey lasted about three hours, and then Doullens was reached. Here the battalion detrained, the transport taking only 32 minutes, with loaded waggons. When all were ready the troops moved off out of the town and marched for a mile and a half, when a halt was made for a meal.

It was a warm day and the troops were tired owing to the sleepless night they had undergone and the tiring and crowded train journey. The boys were carrying full packs, besides greatcoats and waterproof sheets. It was generally stated that the weight of a soldier's equipment was evenly distributed over his body; but in practice it was found that most of the weight was on the shoulders and back, and when the troops were carrying up to eighty pounds and often more it was a considerable burden to carry at the rate of three and a half miles an hour.

The battalion set out up the long hills leading to Halloy, and at the first halt the troops threw themselves down and rested in all positions. As the journey progressed there was a noticeable lagging of feet, and it was with difficulty that some of the men kept their position. It was fine to see the comradeship and help given by such men as old Bill Beck, who was to be seen carrying his mate's rifle and some of his equipment as well as his own.

At the next halt, Lieut.-Colonel Roberts addressed the men and told them that they must on no account fall out.

Then the march was resumed. The day grew hotter and still hotter, and here and there men began to drop behind. Major Milner, of "D" Company, dashed up and down the lines on his horse, endeavouring to maintain the ranks of his company intact, but to no purpose; and by the time the whistle blew for the next halt the troops were straggled out a long distance behind. In passing, it may be stated that Australian troops never took much notice of anyone mounted telling them how to march, and why they must not fall out. If the footslogging platoon officers were unable to hold their men, there was very little hope of even a mounted general getting them to keep their place in the ranks.

The route lay through Candas, Canaples and Feiffes. Eventually the battalion reached its billets in Halloy, after a very long and trying march. The relief and the rest were welcome. This was the one really bad route-march in the history of the 11th Battalion, but all the other battalion histories tell the same story of the march over the same distance and on the same route, and many of the battalions made a much worse job of it than the 11th Battalion.

It was lovely weather when the troops reached the new concentration area, and the men enjoyed the beautiful countryside to the full. The country was a change after the flat lands of Flanders. The new area was undulating and more open. The villages were fewer and farther apart, and generally in the valleys. Instead of the fat, rich, red clay lands of the country round Armentieres and Hazebrouck, the country now consisted of chalky downs, with a considerable amount of woodland. The farm buildings were much poorer and were mostly huddled together in the villages.

After resting a night at Halloy, the battalion moved forward next day to Naours. This was a shorter march than that of the previous day, and besides the troops had benefitted by the good night's rest; and the battalion that swung along the roads of Picardie that morning would have been admired in any company of troops. For now the boys knew that they were going into something big, and they rose to the occasion.

Practically all the troops had now had some experience of actual warfare, and the battalion felt sure of itself; and while physically it may not have been quite equal to the original 11th Battalion—that would have been too much to expect—yet most of the troops were men who had joined up realising the full responsibilities of the business before them, and they were willing to tackle anything that came along. Added to all this, most of these men had had their outlook on life greatly widened by travel, by their sojourn in Egypt, and in the desert and lately by their experiences in France. Many of the older men had also been to England, and though the troops were fresh and eager they had now long passed the raw, unsophisticated stage.

The battalion was at a peak of efficiency and training and war-like spirit. It is safe to say that there was no finer battalion in France than the 11th when it marched down to the Somme in those days of July, 1916.

The fine figure of Lieut.-Colonel Roberts, with his dark, saturnine face and black moustaches, riding his big, black mare, and followed by four companies and transport of tough, hardy, Westralian troops, along the white roads of Picardie, singing and jesting as they went, was a sight that can never be forgotten by those who saw them. There was a splendid feeling existing between officers and men, and most of the platoon officers loved and took an intense pride in their platoons which they had been associated with so long, mostly dating back to Gebel Habieta and the formation of the new 11th Battalion nearly six months before. Never again were officers and men to be associated with each other for such a long period in the history of the 11th Battalion.

This, then, was the battalion that marched in pride and confidence to battle.

Naours was reached early on July 13 and two or three days were spent there, during which special attention was paid to bombing, bayonet-fighting and musketry. A short route-march was also made in the morning of July 14. This march was along one of the bosky valleys leading from the high downs, and the beauty and peace of the scene always stood out clearly, possibly only by contrast with the days that were soon to follow.

There was a pay while the battalion was at Naours, and as the boys spread themselves through the surrounding country at nights the adjoining villages did good business.

Orders were received to move forward again on July 16. The battalion set out early in the morning and, after passing through Talmas, reached Rubempre, where a halt was made for the night. It had been a long march, especially as the Commanding Officer had on one or two occasions mistaken the road, and he had to halt the battalion several times while he consulted his map. After arrival at Rubempre, one of the officers who was handy with a pencil and colours drew a large-sized coloured picture on a white-washed wall of a farm building of the C.O. mounted on his big, black mare earnestly studying his map at a cross-roads, with the legend, "The blind shall lead the blind," and left "Steve" (the Old Man) to find it.

At Rubempre the troops as usual were soon in all the cottages, interested in the preparation of flax by the old hand method, helping Madame and Marie and quaffing the good wine and the "biere" wherever they were available. But their pleasures were not always so innocent.

Early on the ensuing day, July 17, a tearful Frenchman came to the rough billet where "C" Company's officers were having their frugal breakfast. He held the decapitated heads of several fowls as a kind of "exhibit 'A'," and kept murmuring, "Les pauvres poules" and something about "guillotinees."

After a little inquiry, Captain Campbell elicited that the troops must have got down on the poor man's fowls in the yard attached to the estaminet opposite, and, horror of horrors! they had executed the unfortunate birds.

The company was paraded, and the situation put before the men. "Nigger" Black stood out and admitted that the boys had taken nine fowls, but that they were quite willing to pay for them.

This was explained to the owner and he was somewhat mollified, and immediately fixed a stiff price for the slain birds; but he went off still shaking his head and moaning his password of "guillotinees."

When "Nigger" came along with the money—which was indeed an exorbitant amount—he reckoned that the feed had been worth it, but he added, "We must have been half-sozzled when we took the dam' birds, because we burned up all the feathers but we left the b—— heads lying in the yard." The boys had chopped off the fowls' heads with their bayonets.

Next day a long march was made through the towns of Herrisart, Toutencourt, Harponville and Varrennes to Forceville, where the troops bivouaced. Towards the end of this march the troops began to tire, and as the custom was after each halt, a different company took the head of the column. On this occasion, "D" Company had just taken the lead, and as soon as the march was resumed this company struck up a song, and led by "the singing six" the troops kept up cheerful music and good, tuneful singing right to the end of the long march.

This was the stuff the battalion was made of, and showed what a fine type of Digger was marching down to battle in the early days of the Somme. Those who were in that march will always remember the battalion singing "They were only playing leap-frog" to the tune of "John Brown's Body." In the words of Lawrence Binyon—

> "They went with songs to the battle, they were young,
> Straight of limb, true of eye, steady and aglow."

While the battalion was bivouaced at Forceville all preparations had been made for the coming attack. All surplus gear and equipment were collected, greatcoats and oil-sheets were to be bandoliered, steel helmets to be worn, and a pink cloth square was sewn between the shoulder blades on each tunic as a distinguishing mark for the 1st Australian Division. Officers were to go into action dressed as the rest of the troops. Necessary trench equipment, Very-light pistols, periscopes, wirecutters and flares were issued, and rifle ammunition was made up to 150 rounds. Picks and shovels were also issued.

Before proceeding further with the move forward to the line, a short account of the progress of the Battle of the Somme as far as it affected the present history is given here, along with a general idea of the task ahead of the 1st Australian Division.

The junction of the British and French armies was just north of Curlu, on the River Somme, and a big Allied thrust had been in progress on both sides of this boundary since July 1 with a small gain of territory, but at a wholly disproportionate and truly exhorbitant cost. The cream of the new British armies had been wasted in a vain effort to break through, and all available divisions were required to keep up the hammer blows that Haig was directing on this too solid front from Thiepval to Guillemont.

By the time the 1st Australian Division had reached the neighbourhood of the battlefield, the line was still badly held up at Thiepval, although the strong positions of Ovillers, La Boisselle, Contalmaison and Mametz Wood had been captured. The 1st Australian Division was detailed to attack along the right side of the road leading from Albert to Bapaume, from the direction of the south, with Pozieres as the immediate objective.

The Australians were eager for their task and considered that, under the direction of the British General Staff, the operations would be interesting, exciting and skilfully conducted. With regard to their last-named expectation, they were quickly undeceived.

The general idea of the attack on Pozieres was to push a wedge behind Thiepval, and so make that position untenable for the Germans.

The British had now a preponderance of artillery, though the troops found that hard to believe in the battle that followed; and with this weight of guns Haig was determined to hammer at the German positions and throw in division after division until the enemy's defence was broken through or the Germans so exhausted that they would be forced to retire.

The British Staff regarded Pozieres as the crucial point of the local situation, and the capture of that village and ridge meant that the artillery would be able to take up positions in Mash Valley, a long, sheltered depression that was entirely commanded by Pozieres, which had a most favourable position as regards observation and field of fire.

Several attempts to take Pozieres having failed, the 1st Australian Division was now to be given the task of taking the position.

As frequently happened throughout the war, the 3rd Brigade was chosen by the commander of the 1st Division for the most difficult operations, and so this brigade and incidentally the 11th Battalion led the Australians into the first of the Somme fighting.

On the afternoon of July 19, the 11th Battalion received orders to proceed to Albert and from there to move up to the line.

From this point onwards the enormous extent of the attack in progress became evident. Every possible thing that could be imagined that was necessary for the prosecution of a campaign was passed on the way—dumps of all kinds of stores, guns of all calibres, ordance workshops, sausage balloons, ammunition parks and strings of limbers and G.S. wagons, prisoners' cages, with newly-captured Germans, and here and there small parties of some British unit moving to a rear area with the trophies of their recent fighting.

All these things were interesting and strange to the troops, and the distance to Albert was soon covered. The appearance of the relieved troops gave the boys rather a shock: the men looked so haggard and worn and had such a vacant and dull look. Little did the stalwart fellows that looked so pityingly at these few remnants of once fine battalions foresee that the small remnant of their own splendid battalion would be even more haggard and shell-battered in the short space of seven days.

Albert, that was to be such a landmark in the battalion's life in the Somme, was passed late in the afternoon, and the troops gazed with interest at all the shattered buildings. The Virgin and Child hanging precariously from the church spire being the most impressive sight—the famous "Stooping Virgin" of Albert.

After passing through this town, the battalion rested on the slopes of "Tara Hill," where a welcome meal was provided by the cookers.

Refreshed by the meal and the spell, the battalion moved on past Becourt Wood through pads in the fields until Sausage Valley was reached. This valley was an eye-opener to all the troops. It was absolutely crowded with all the machinery of modern warfare in actual battle conditions. There were batteries of artillery so numerous that it was impossible to estimate their numbers; from heavy howitzers to light field pieces. There were rows upon rows of horse-lines and transport lines. Signal stations and headquarters of many units. Whole battalions bivouaced on the slopes of that long sausage-shaped valley which was to be the main avenue for all the essentials of war for the troops from the outside world during their tour of the line.

Instead of advancing to their position by roads or communication trenches more or less at right angles to the front, the battalions detailed for the attack had to advance on a line parallel to the position. This made the relief very slow, and later it was to be a serious disadvantage to other battalions making for the line. As the 9th Battalion was to be on the right of the 11th, that battalion led the way and the 11th followed.

The route lay through a sunken road near Gordons' Dump, and then the troops entered the communication trench known as "Black Watch Alley." It was now dark and the troops were approaching the front line; "C" Company was leading the battalion and "D" Company followed. The night was fairly quiet, but the enemy was firing gas-shells. These could be heard coming with a soft whine and they exploded with a subdued thud. "D" Company had several men gassed. As "C" Company was proceeding up the muddy and often corpse-filled "Black Watch Alley" there was a desultory sniping from the German trenches about 400 or 500 yards off. Parties of Tommies could be noticed passing wearily back as they were relieved. Occasionally a flare would go up and illuminate the weird scene, and the troops could be seen walking over the open rather than flounder up the horrible trench.

Only one company of the Durham Light Infantry could be found to take over from, so the battalion followed on after the Queenslanders.

A machine gun started to play up and down, so the troops got back into the trench. Suddenly there was a commotion and a groan and a portion of the line was held up. "What the hell is the delay for?" shouted "Nigger" Black. "The captain has been wounded," yelled someone. "Shove the old b—— on top and let's get on with the game," replied "Nigger," who had recently been on the mat. The O.C. wanted to know who the unsympathetic Digger was, but time was precious so he was put on a stretcher and sent to the rear while the company pushed on. The captain was lucky to get a wound so early in the action.

A few hundred yards further on and the 11th Battalion was in position. "C" Company on the right, with the 9th Battalion on its right flank, "D" Company was to the left of "C" and then followed "A" and "B" Companies. The 1st Brigade was on the left flank of the battalion.

The trenches were in a very poor condition, and the troops set to immediately and made them as comfortable as possible. They then dug "possies" in the front wall of the trench. The soil was very light and friable and it was easy to chop out one of these holes with the entrenching tool. In the morning men could be seen curled up in these little cubby holes, or in the case of the more energetic nothing could be seen but a pair of boots sticking out into the trench.

The 11th Battalion was in position for the famous attack on Pozieres. The officers in charge of companies were: Captain A. H. MacFarlane, "A" Company; Captain H. A. Mansfield, "B" Company; Captain G. G. Campbell, "C" Company; and Major J. T. Milner, "D" Company.

CHAPTER XX

THE BATTLE OF POZIERES

ON THE MORNING of July 20, 1916, as soon as it was light all eyes were turned on the village of Pozieres on the brow of the ridge a few hundred yards to the north. Most of the buildings were still standing, but were battered about and practically every roof gone. The church could easily be distinguished, one whole side of which was still intact or at least held up by the buttresses on the wall. The trees of the orchards and gardens still showed green and the dividing hedges round the little fields surrounding the village were easily distinguishable. In spite of the heavy shelling, the village still looked as if it might have been a prosperous centre of a farming community only a short time before. This was the appearance of the village from the south on the above date, though some accounts state that it was already flattened to the ground before this. These accounts are incorrect as this narrative will show. There was definitely a village of houses, trees and gardens when the 1st Australian Division took position for the attack on Pozieres.

It was a strange new war zone that the troops found themselves in. The boys were pleased with the freedom of movement and the fact that they could look round and over the trenches in comparative immunity. It was to be expected that the Boche would snipe if he got the chance, but the boys took the risk; and though the shelling was fairly constant, it was not at first very heavy. The first day in the trench was spent in improving the position and trying to get rid of some of the worst sections of the lines by digging loops round them.

The ration-parties used to prefer going over the top to walking in the congested and muddy trenches, and there were several casualties owing to this practice, and one man in "C" Company had his pay-book, which was in his breast pocket, cut in halves by a bullet that passed through both upper pockets. On showing the book to his platoon officer he asked what he should do about it, as his pay-book was ruined. "What you should do,

Dig., is to cheer," was the reply, "for if that bullet had been a couple of inches closer you wouldn't be worrying now."

Still, the sniping was comparatively innocuous at this stage, as most of the troops on both sides were more interested in watching the effect of the heavy shell fire, chiefly British, on the buildings and trenches, or following the manœuvres of the many aeroplanes that were circling overhead.

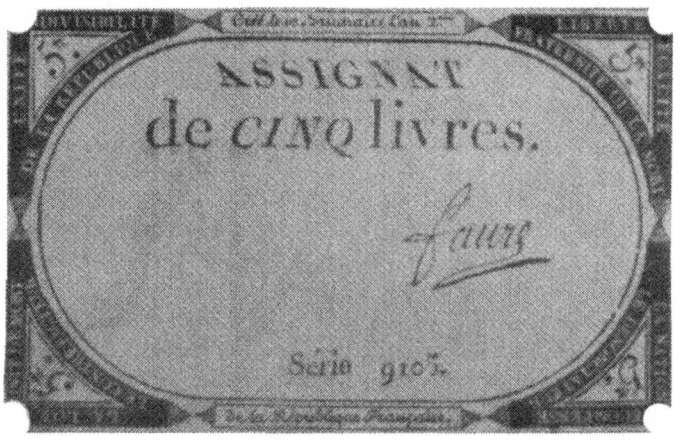

French banknote of the year 1791 found in ruins near Contalmaison at the Battle of Pozieres.

On July 21 orders were received that only 20 officers were to go into the first action. The troops were engaged the whole day in improving their lines, in carrying bombs, small arms, ammunition and water to advanced dumps in preparation for the advance.

The British heavy artillery was now concentrated on Pozieres and all day long the thunder and crash of huge shells was heard among the fast disappearing buildings, while a dust haze of a reddish colour rose from the shattered brickwork and hung over everything.

Lurid flashes showed through this red dust cloud, when a big shell burst and tongues of orange-coloured flame burst from incendiary shells. For hour after hour this bombardment was kept up until there was hardly any part of the village that had not been hit, but still a few buildings managed to escape destruction. It was astounding to see these surviving buildings after the heavies ceased firing. The church had early crumbled into dust and hardly a vestige remained, but the walls of a few cottages still managed to stand.

Occasionally there was an air scrap. One morning several German 'planes were seen chasing an Allied 'plane (later it was found to be a French aeroplane) and they shot it down. It fell close behind "C" Company's lines. This depressed the troops a little, but on the evening of the same day a British 'plane was engaged with a German monoplane, and the boys were bucked up to see matters made even by the shooting down of the German. The victor was cheered all along the line.

Some little time after the French 'plane had crashed behind the 11th Battalion's line, movement was noticed, and the pilot waved feebly. Many of the boys prepared to hop the parados and go to the airman's assistance, but Sergeant Fred Stahl, who was closest to the 'plane, sprang out and ran over and dragged the pilot out of the cockpit and clear of his machine. Some of the other lads had by this time hopped over the back of the trench, and these hoisted the injured man on to Stahl's back and, under heavy enemy fire, he was taken to the brow of the rise and then was taken up by another man who carried him back to the protection of the rear slopes of the hill. Fred Stahl then ran back to his own trench. It was later reported that the man who carried the airman back, after Stahl had rescued him, received the Victoria Cross.

Later in the day some artillerymen came to have a look at the 'plane and, while they were doing so, Fritz started sniping and all cleared off except one man. He was deeply interested in the machine and bent over to examine it more closely. The dust of a bullet was seen near him. He looked up. Another bullet zipped past him and knocked up a spurt of dust a few yards ahead. Still he lingered. The next one must have been very close indeed, for he bounded upright, gave one startled glance in the direction of Pozieres and then streaked for it, followed by a few helping bullets to judge by the spurts of dust that punctuated his going.

The attack was originally to have been made almost immediately the Australians had taken up position, but it had to be postponed for several reasons. This delay was welcome to the 1st Divisional Staff, who did not want to be rushed into such an important undertaking without first making provision for all contingencies.

The chief difficulty from a tactical point of view was that the right flank, which was held by the 9th Battalion, was 150 yards behind the line which they were supposed to have taken over, and though several attempts had been made to improve the position the line had not been carried forward. There was a strong point in the O.G. lines (old German lines) which caused the Munsters and other British troops heavy losses in trying to capture it, and the 9th Australian Battalion was equally unfortunate in its assault.

The main attack on Pozieres which was to have taken place on July 21 was again postponed, as Generals Walker and Sinclair-MacLagan were still far from satisfied.

The jumping-off trenches had not been completed and the position on the right was still of grave concern, so that this in addition to other matters concerning artillery and barrages necessitated a further delay, and plans were finally drawn up for an attack on July 23.

In the meantime the troops were watching all the preparations for the attack. A new jump-off trench was being dug in front of Pozieres Trench, and ration parties and fatigues for all kinds of work were constantly being requisitioned.

Lieuts. Nicol and Hastings, of "D" Company, were sent out on patrol to reconnoitre the ground over which the battalion would attack, and Lieut. Nicol was shot dead on the night of July 22. Captain MacFarlane, of "A" Company, was also killed by gas-shell on the same date.

In a last attempt to straighten up the position on the right, the 9th Battalion attacked along Munster Alley and after a partial success was driven back with heavy loss. One of the reasons of the Germans' superiority in trench warfare at this stage was their use of "egg" bombs, a smaller missile than the "Mills" and one which could be thrown considerably farther; certainly a big advantage in trench warfare.

As all hope was now abandoned of improving the jumping-off position on the right before the main attack, the assault on Pozieres was ordered for midnight, or rather immediately after that time on the morning of July 23.

In spite of the strain of waiting and the anxiety caused by the increasing number of casualties, due to the German shell-fire, which was becoming heavier and more constant as the enemy discovered the positions of the troops opposite to them, the unfailing humour and resource of the boys shone as brightly as ever.

While on fatigue or ration parties the boys would have to go down to Gordons' Dump (named after the famous Highland regiment), where the transports or other details would be met.

Private Oscar Bauer, of "A" Company, used to make use of the present writer's signature—all unknown to him, of course —to procure a case of whisky from the canteen. The money was subscribed by the troops interested, but an officer's signature had to be obtained before a case was allowed to be purchased. If the good "Scotch" in any way mitigated the horrors of the terrible experience which followed, the forgery was more than justified.

During the afternoon of July 22, all officers and non-commissioned officers who were to take part in the attack were given the necessary instructions regarding objectives, barrages and the preparations to be made before zero hour.

The objectives were these: The first objective was Pozieres Trench. This was a loop from the old German trenches round the south of the village of Pozieres. (See map.)

The light railway through Pozieres was the second objective, and the southern side of the main road to Bapaume was the third objective.

The 11th Battalion was to capture the first and second objectives in two attacking waves. "A" and "B" Companies for the first objective and "C" and "D" Companies for the second objective; while the 12th Battalion was to leap-frog the 11th Battalion and capture the third objective. Half an hour was to be allowed for consolidation purposes between the first and second, and half an hour between the second and third objectives. The artillery barrages were to conform to these attacks, and special instructions were given to the 11th Battalion not to over-run the second objective which was, as stated above, the light railway running through the village.

All troops were to carry 220 rounds of ammunition and at least two bombs. Picks and shovels were to be also carried by most of the troops, and bombers, machine gunners and other specialists were to be distributed among the troops.

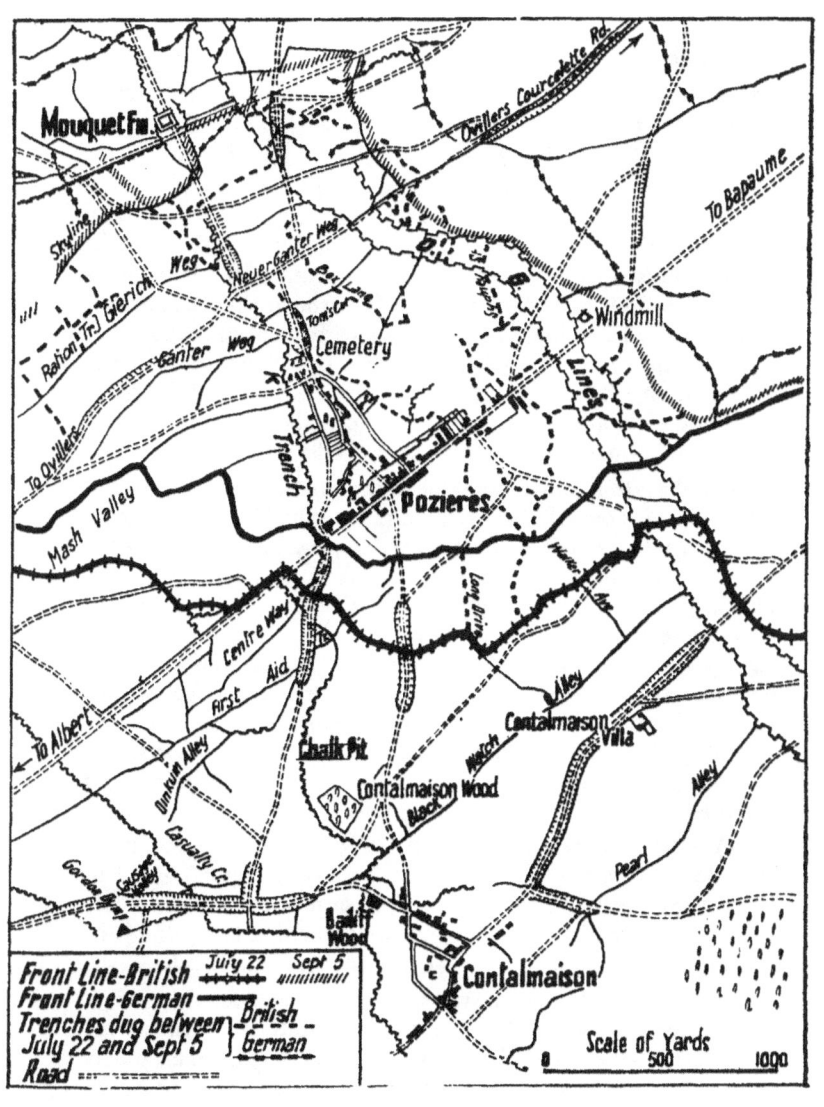

Pozieres and Mouquet Farm. (Official Map.)

Among the other instructions issued for the battle were that all tunic sleeves were to be rolled to the elbow for the purpose of identification, and that for communication purposes ground flares were to be carried and used for signalling to the contact aeroplane. For this purpose, green flares were to be lit in the leading positions at 8 a.m., 12 noon, 4 p.m. and 8 p.m.

When to all the above equipment and tools were added wire-cutters, periscopes, electric torches, maps, emergency rations and extra tins of meat, army biscuit and many other necessaries, it will be realised that the troops were carrying a load of up to a hundred pounds and often over. When the greater part of this load is carried for days on end, often without being removed at all, even the lay mind will realise that this alone, without the added strain of shell-fire and hard work, was a great factor in causing the absolute exhaustion of troops, who were subjected to battle conditions for even a few days. This is by the way.

On the afternoon before the attack in the trenches facing Pozieres, the boys of the 11th Battalion could be seen writing letters, shaving and going over their equipment and watching the effect of the shelling. One of the lads was shaving with the aid of a small periscope (little mirrors fitted to fix on the end of a bayonet were often used as periscopes) when a German shell passed close overhead and burst just behind him. "If you do that again, you b—— I'll be cutting myself and be had up for a self-inflicted wound," he said, and continued with his scraping. The shelling had caused a number of casualties, but the troops were in good heart and laughed and joked and watched the heavy shells crashing into Pozieres.

A good meal was served to the troops and there was more than an abundance of everything, because already there had been a considerable number of men evacuated, and this left their rations to be divided among the remaining troops.

And so the long summer aftternoon wore on. Aeroplanes wheeled in the sky, and nearer the earth a bewildered lark flew about disconsolately on the bare fields behind the parados. Final instructions were given to the boys and the platoon commanders went round their small commands to see that everything was just right, and laughed and jested with them as man to men. In this manner those splendid lads passed the time before what was to be the most terrible of all the battles that the 1st Australian

Division was engaged in, and in which the 11th Battalion suffered more casualties than any other battalion in the division.

After sunset the preliminary bombardment started, and some time later a heavy barrage was placed round Pozieres.

When the time arrived, the first waves of "A" and "D" Companies of the 11th Battalion crept into position, followed by the second wave at about 30 yards distance. As the troops crawled over the exposed slope, a machine gun stuttered and a few bursts were fired on the advancing troops, but the bullets mostly passed high. Lieut. Hastings, of "D" Company, was killed while trying to gain contact with the left flanking battalion, on the right of the 1st Australian Brigade. On and on the troops crawled, any noise or movement being screened by the feint bombardment which was taking place. In the flickering light of bursting shells, or the occasional light of a flare, the troops could be seen advancing in a stooping position or crawling with faint curses among a patch of thistles. In "C" Company the troops crawled so close to the enemy that they could see Pozieres Trench just in front, though most of the men were unaware that it was so near.

It seemed very still and quiet waiting for the barrage to fall. The men were all tense and eager, and nothing save utter annihilation could have stopped the West Australian troops that night.

The German flares rose hissing in the darkness and burst into white dazzling light, then fell; and as they died out, the blackness of the night seemed more intense: the artillery boomed in the distance while an occasional shell whined overhead and crashed somewhere near; and all this time the troops lay out, waiting for the seconds to tick off to the longed-for zero.

At 12:28 a.m. on the morning of July 23 the barrage of the 1st Australian Divisional Artillery fell on Pozieres Trench, just in front of the leading wave. The bursting of the shells rendered everything visible, and lines of troops with eager, intense faces could be seen lying waiting for the lift. The barrage was very accurate in front of the 11th Battalion and only a few casualties occurred through pieces of high explosive shell flying back.

At 12:30 the signal for advance was given. The troops sprang up and rushed Pozieres Trench and the second wave was soon through the first wave, which had captured the trench without much opposition. The rush carried many of the men over the second objective and through the village itself, many of the troops passing through the barrage and well beyond the third objective.

During the first advance a German machine gun had been causing many casualties. This gun was firing from Pozieres Trench. It was silenced by a bomb thrown by Captain Medcalf and the gun captured. The gun was afterwards used by the 11th Battalion.

After the first barrage had lifted it was almost impossible to judge where the other barrages were falling, as shelling seemed to be pretty general. The magnificent attack of the 11th Battalion carried the troops so far forward that it was with the greatest difficulty that they could be recalled and reorganised on the second objective, where they had been ordered to consolidate and wait for the 12th Battalion.

Many of the troops had rushed forward right into the barrage and had been much split up and disorganised by the shell-fire, and parties were coming back or dashing about looking for signs of the enemy, or somewhere definite to dig in.

One officer who was waiting just in front of the second objective looking at his watch from time to time, to note when the barrage would lift, was collecting what men he could find when a great number of men came dashing back through the shell-fire. They were quite disorganised. These were collected by sending some N.C.O.'s after them, and the position speedily explained. Though they belonged to another company, one big fellow yelled: "Right oh! sir. You say when, and wherever you lead we'll follow you." Though much exhausted by two rushes through the barrage they quickly recovered and were game for anything.

There were not many German casualties noted at this stage, but a few prisoners were captured. On the left in the copse, which still had trees in it, some guns were taken, but the 11th Battalion boys were too busy to take steps to claim them and did not mark them as prizes. Another battalion claimed them later.

C.S.M. Wally Graham, of "C" Company, and Sergeant F. H. Baggs, of "D" Company, with a good number of the troops charged forward as far as Pozieres Windmill, and even beyond, and found practically no opposition at all. Small parties of

Germans were met with everywhere, but these were all retiring and were attacked by the West Australians.

Meanwhile the troops who had reached the second objective were anxiously waiting the arrival of the companies of the 12th Battalion, who were now much behind time.

Before proceeding further, it is necessary to explain why the 12th Battalion troops had not arrived. As stated previously, the only approach to the position to be attacked was along the communication trench known as Black Watch Alley, which meant that the third wave had to march along two sides of a right-angled triangle in order to reach its position. Also, practically all the troops had to pass through the greatly constricted neck at the head of Sausage Valley. The Germans, who had only lately occupied this part of the country, were well aware of all the vulnerable points, and they used to pound this area with H.E. and drench the valley with gas, so that troops could only pass through this exit from Sausage Valley very slowly; and as the 12th Battalion had to move up to the line through this shelling, naturally there was a considerable delay, and it was some hours before the 12th Battalion reached the actual battle area.

In the meantime, the troops on the second objective had pushed on to the third objective, beyond which the officers of 11th (Le Nay, Ross, Hallahan, Rogerson and Belford) would not allow their men, at least those of the battalion that they had collected, to proceed.

A big dump of explosive, probably German howitzer charges, blew up in the copse. In the dark this sent out a great shooting yellow flame. "Flammen werfer," cried out a startled voice. Instantly there was a rush back, but only for a minute.

The men were set to dig a line of trench along the copse and to connect up some of the larger shell holes in the village. An officer of another battalion came rushing up, and cried: "We are surrounded. I suggest that we retire." It was suggested that he should go to hell, so he disappeared for a short time only to be brought back by the indignant Wally Graham, who had just returned from his excursion into German territory. "W'will s'somebody shoot this b'bastard," yelled that great warrior, who always stuttered when he was excited or angry. "He's goin' r'round puttin' the w'wind up the troops."

The officer, who was a bit hysterical, was told off a second time and asked to remove himself, or stronger methods would be adopted. This officer was afterwards awarded the M.C. on the recommendation of his battalion commander.

Wally Graham then said: "Christ! The road's open to Berlin! Let's push forward. There's nobody in front. We've been past the Windmill and over the hill."

The 12th Battalion had not yet arrived, and it was thought that no advance should be made until it was heard definitely what the 12th Battalion was going to do. It would have been sound judgement to have advanced at that time if only the movements of the other attacking troops could have been co-ordinated and the artillery advised in time Also the orders were definite that the 11th Battalion was not to go beyond the tram-line, although it had done so. The 11th Battalion, then, dug-in in Pozieres Village among the houses and trees. The troops dug with a will, and unfortunately made the trenches only too deep and the "possies" in the sides only too far in in the soft walls of the trench.

By this time most of the senior company officers had been killed or wounded. Among those who had fallen were Major Milner, Captains MacFarlane, Mansfield, Newman and Campbell; Lieuts. Griffin, Hastings, Nicol and McKean were also casualties. Captain F. G. Medcalf was placed in charge of the front-line companies, which were already short of officers. Captain Medcalf had been with the first wave which was consolidating on its objective. He now came forward and a reorganisation of the troops was made insofar as it was possible.

After what seemed a very long time, the first of the 12th Battalion troops came up; but as the 11th Battalion was now on the third objective, the 12th took up position on the right where they dug in on the same line. Touch was gained with the 3rd Battalion in the copse on the left, so that the position as far as the 11th Battalion was concerned was sent back to 3rd Brigade H.Q. as perfectly satisfactory before dawn on July 23.

With the coming of the light, all ranks were curious to have a look at the position; and parties began going forward, poking among the ruins and "souveniring."

There were scattered parties of Germans in the houses and in portions of the trenches. These began sniping at the Australians moving about in the open, and soon there were quite a lot of little scraps in progress. Prisoners began to come in in fair numbers. These Germans, who looked badly shaken in many cases, offered cigarettes and chocolate and were relieved of all their surplus gear. The boys obtained quite a number of knives, watches and other souvenirs. There were also a few automatic pistols handed over. These prisoners belonged to the 157th Infantry Regiment, and that name was on the holsters of several of the pistols taken.

The sniping began to get very severe and men were continually dropping. The stretcher-bearers, who were doing magnificent work, were now unable to keep up with the clearing of the increasing stream of casualties, and only those cases that did not look absolutely hopeless were taken to the aid-post. Many good men were hit at this stage, mainly because they did not realise the seriousness of the sniping and because, as was natural to the men, they were always willing to take a risk. The officers had to order them to keep in cover as well as possible.

There was a house which was still pretty intact from which sniping was being done. S.M. Wally Graham dashed up and threw a bomb in the door and followed up. He looked inside and, seeing no one, went further and discovered a cellar. This was full of Huns. A German officer saw him and shot at him with an automatic pistol. One bullet cut a piece of skin and flesh off Graham's head. Wally immediately pulled the pin out of another bomb and heaved it down the stairway shouting: "Share *that* among you, you bastards!" The survivors were only to glad to render themselves prisoners, and there were a lot of casualties among them when they managed to get out.

"Tiger" Lyon, of "D" Company, had been scouting round and he had already rounded up half a dozen or more prisoners. He said that he could see a lot more Germans in a covered trench just beyond the hedge to the north of the village, and he reckoned that it would be a simple matter to capture them. While discussing this possibility, a shout was heard, "Here they come," and lines of Germans could be seen approaching from the direction of Courcelette, past Pozieres Windmill. Immediately a well-directed rifle and Lewis gun fire was trained on these troops and the attack withered. Later these Germans could be seen retiring from the shell holes into which they had dropped, and they immediately came under a well-directed fire again.

It was noticed in firing at these troops that both in their advance and in their retirement they seemed to be moving very slowly and deliberately, and they seemed to offer a very easy target, and indeed many of them were hit. While it is well known that heavily-armed or heavily-burdened men must of necessity travel slowly, the apparent slowness of the enemy troops was probably due to the fact that all the faculties of the men firing on them were strained to high pitch due to the excitement of the attack, and consequently the movement seemed slower than it really was.

After the counter-attack was repulsed, and it had no hope at all of success against entrenched troops without artillery support, the 11th Battalion settled down to the better consolidation of its position. Captain F. G. Medcalf was in charge of operations and allotted the companies to various sectors. Lieut.-Colonel Roberts and Major Denton visited the lines and confirmed the dispositions.

After some discussion, it was determined to make an attack on the covered trenches in front of the 11th Battalion position. These were practically parallel to the old German lines, and therefore almost at right angles or end on to the captured position.

These German trenches came to be known as the "Artillery Dug-outs." Lieuts. Hallahan and Forbes were in charge of the operation.

The party advanced through the hedge on the north boundary of the village and made for the trench. When they got near, Forbes saw a number of the Germans throw up their hands and heard them shout "kamerad." But an officer or N.C.O. was seen to dash along the trench and beat down the upraised hands, and shots were fired at the patrol. Then Hallahan arranged that he should attack from his position while Forbes took his men round to the left, so as to attack the trench from two sides. The two parties again crept through the hedge and were making for their objective when a very heavy fire was directed on both parties. Lieut. Forbes and "Tiger" Lyon were killed and several men were wounded. Hallahan gave the order to retire, as the position was too strong to be rushed, and the troops dashed back through the hedge, Wally Hallahan being the last man to go through. His batman was immediately in front of him and got stuck half-way through the hedge, so Wally helped him through with a hefty kick on the posterior.

When the troops had been collected and sent back to their positions in their trench, the batman came up to Hallahan with his hand still holding the sore spot and complained, "Hey! Mr. Hallahan, what the hell did you boot me so hard for?" Wally grinned, "It was your behind or me, and I thought that you had better take the risk."

There seemed to be a great deal of confusion back at H.Q. as to the exact state of affairs, and numerous orders were given and then countermanded. This, of course, is almost inevitable in every big action, as there are always unexpected contingencies to be met.

But in the Battle of Pozieres a certain want of co-ordination and confusion was very noticeable. The difficult approaches to the battlefield and the intense German shelling on the rear areas had much to do with this; but in addition to this there was a great deal of confusion and poor staff work.

While only a very perfunctory criticism can be given of the conduct of the battle, the above statement is necessary in view of succeeding events.

Up to this time the German shelling had not been very heavy; but now more batteries began to register on Pozieres and the adjoining positions, and all day long on July 24 the troops were shelled with 4.2's and 5.9's. This shelling was constant and well directed, and many of these shells landed on the newly-dug trenches, making large craters and often burying many of the troops. Some of the boys managed to struggle out, others were rescued by their mates; but many who had dug themselves only too well in were completely buried by the great upheavals of earth.

There was now a constant stream of wounded to the rear, and the stretcher-bearers were doing their utmost. Many cases that under less severe conditions would have been carried were forced to walk through lack of men to do the "bearing." The fortitude of some of the severely wounded men was marvellous. Lieut. Peter Snodgrass has the following entry in his diary: "One case I noticed particularly—a man of the 4th Battalion. He walked from the aid-post, a mile or more. He had a bandage just above his left ankle and another just above each knee, a shot through the left shoulder rendering that arm useless, his jaw in a sling and his right arm was broken mid-way between the elbow and the shoulder. His broken arm was held in a light sling and he had only a small bandage round the actual wound which was bleeding profusely. When told he would have to go on a stretcher or in an ambulance, he inquired how far it was, and when told one and a half miles, he said he could walk it easily and leave room for a *more urgent case*."

A story illustrating quite a different type of Digger is told by Sergeant W. Wright, A.A.M.C. After the first attack on Pozieres a German doctor was captured and sent back through the aid-post. He volunteered to assist with the wounded, and as Captain Fisher had found that he could not carry on, he and the German M.O. arranged, using what Latin they knew, for neither could speak the other's language, that the German doctor should start on some serious cases that were waiting attention. Fisher asked the German doctor to fix up one chap who had a thigh wound and a fractured femur. The German immediately bent over the Digger to examine the wound and received a kick from the Digger's sound leg fairly in the midriff, while the latter exclaimed, "Get out, you German b——, I'd sooner die than let you fix me up." That was the end, so far as the German medical officer was concerned, and he was sent to join his comrades in the P.O.W. cage.

Such were the men that made the heroes that lived and died in this terrible battle.

To get back to the forward area in the village of Pozieres. In the initial advance and during the succeeding period, there was a considerable amount of war material captured. Besides the howitzers already mentioned there were scores of rifles and bayonets, many of the latter weapons having a saw edge. A good deal of food was also found: tinned butter and tinned meat and black bread. There was even a motor car. The troops also found quantities of stick and egg bombs, shells and ammunition. A few bicycles were also amongst the booty, if it could be called such, for in a comparatively short space of time the continuous shelling had smashed everything up. But some of the troops managed to save their trophies, and a bundle or two of letters were sent back to headquarters.

While the forward troops were digging in and trying to advance where they could, communication trenches were being dug in rear and the position linked up with the old lines. All this time the enemy continued to shell, and the village gradually lost all semblance of ever having been a cluster of human dwellings. Only an isolated gable or two and a precarious chimney balancing on the remnants of a wall showed that a village had once, and that only a short week or so before, existed. With every shell masonry would fly in all directions, limbs of trees would be shattered and flail about in whining arcs, iron rails and railings were bent and twisted into grotesque shapes, trees with their iron guards would be blasted clean out of the ground and the heavy metal guards flung far into the fields; while over all hung a pall of pinkish-gray brick dust, a great cloud that shut off the place where the village had been from the rest of the world. It was like a scene from Dante's Inferno.

The dust and shattered bricks kept continually falling, and there was a thick film over everything; and rifles and machine guns had to be kept constantly wiped to keep them in working order and to prevent jamming.

In the afternoon orders came up from brigade that the artillery dug-outs were to be occupied that night. Plans were made to rush these trenches under cover of darkness with the assistance of a light artillery barrage. As these trenches were practically at right angles to the Australian position, a flanking movement was first necessary before the troops got into position for attack.

Just before the attack Lieut. George Walters was noticed to be rather quiet, and on being rallied about it he said: "I'm going to get mine to-night. I know I won't come out of this stunt." Those around him only laughed at him, but he just shook his head and gave a wintry-sort of smile.

At the appointed time, after darkness had fallen, the attacking parties lined up and waited for the barrage. This seemed surprisingly light, and in fact only a few flashes of shells at some distance beyond the objective were noticed. There was not much shelling by either side at this time. The troops advanced on time, but there was no opposition as the Germans had abandoned their position. Artillery Dug-outs Trench was taken over. The men were instructed to connect up the new position by digging back to the trench behind the hedge or what was left of it. While standing supervising operations, an officer in "C" Company saw a shell burst some distance away and almost immediately received a hard clout on the shin from a spent piece. At the same time he noticed a man fall over not far away. Limping across in the fitful light he turned the body over and found that it was Lieut. George Walters, and that he was quite dead. His premonitions had been realised. Lieut. J. M. Aitken was knocked over and slightly wounded by the same shell.

Meantime the troops had kept digging away, but were suddenly interrupted by a burst of rifle and machine gun fire on the left front, and a strong attack developed. The 11th Battalion, being on an exposed rise with very little trench dug, was ordered to retire the short distance to the hedge already mentioned and there take up a defensive position. From this shelter a brisk and deadly fire was at once poured into the attackers, who were immediately stopped. It was just beginning to change from the murk of night to that indeterminate visibility which comes before the dawn, and the opposing forces hardly offered any target unless they moved.

Lieut. George Walters, killed at Pozieres

The 11th Battalion kept up a steady fire and Lieut. Le Nay had his Lewis guns well to the fore, ready for anything. The rifles were jamming badly with the dust, and many of the boys had two or more rifles in action, using a cool rifle when the hot weapon stuck. Entrenching tool handles were often used to knock back the bolts of the rifles, as they became too stiff to be moved by hand.

All this time the opposing forces were advancing by short rushes, and the light was getting brighter and brighter and the fire more deadly. Suddenly Le Nay, who was using his glasses, yelled: "For Christ's sake stop firing. They're our own chaps"! There was an instant's unbelieving silence and then the "Cease fire" whistles blew, and men here and there ran forward. The troops that the 11th Battalion had been firing at belonged to the 8th Battalion. The most awful feeling of horror and desolation took hold of the boys. They threw down their rifles and cursed, calling down anathema on all the responsible parties. It was reported that there were fourteen men and three officers of the 8th Battalion killed in this stunt. The feelings of the 11th Battalion troops were impossible to describe. Some of the boys were so shocked at this mistake that war, which up to this time had been a kind of game, even if a deadly one, ceased to interest them. It became merely a horrible duty, to be performed conscientiously, but without enthusiasm.

When it was definitely discovered that the 8th Battalion had been allotted the same objective as the 11th, the latter troops handed over the Artillery Dug-outs position to the 8th and retired to its former position.

In receiving orders for the attack above described, neither battalion had been instructed that the other was operating; and as the objective was attacked from different sides by the battalions detailed, it was only natural that each should take the other for the enemy in the darkness.

Unfortunately, a tragedy of this sort, entirely due to bad staff work, destroyed the confidence of the troops in those who were supposed to be responsible for the efficient organisation of all battle activities.

The 11th Battalion was now holding a line on the north of the village and in places clear of the houses and remains of other buildings. The 12th Battalion was on the right, mostly in good dug-outs which had been found in the old German positions, and portions of units of the 1st Brigade were on the left and slightly in front and clear of the village. The contact aeroplane was over several times and flew very low. Flares were lit when the 'plane sounded its Klaxon, but a number of those gave out very poor lights; and as they were lit by troops all over the place, it must have been a difficult job for the observer in the 'plane to get correct bearings of the front lines, owing to the bad visibility caused by the dust and the continual shell-fire.

The amount of movement in the early morning and the continuous small advances alarmed the German staff, who had regarded Pozieres as a key position; and after accurate registration on the village and trenches to the rear, one of the heaviest and most prolonged bombardments of the whole war was directed on the doomed area. Nothing quite so terrible was ever experienced in the whole history of the 11th Battalion. The men took what shelter they could, which was not much. Most of the 11th Battalion men were in the open, in shell holes and bits of trenches that had been left intact from the previous heavy shelling. Early in the morning Captain Medcalf was wounded and was brought to a shell-hole in which Lieuts. Hallahan and Belford had made their headquarters. Sergeant-Major Alley, of "A" Company, was there wounded, lying waiting for a stretcher, and 'bearers were also called for to carry Medcalf to the rear.

The gallant 'bearers under Sergeant Wright, than whom none worked harder or more bravely and usefully that day, had already much more work than they were capable of, and had suffered many casualties; so it was some time before any stretchers were available. While the above officers were in the shell-hole, which was a large and deep one not far from the main communication trench, they were joined by the intelligence officer (Lieut W. Kruger) and the signal officer (Lieut. A. Brodie), who had been visiting the front line on their own specialist business. The German shelling was increasing, and huge "Crumps" were bursting overhead, sending pellets everywhere, while the high explosive was making the ground tremble everywhere. None of the party had eaten since the day before and, as the rations had just managed to come through, it was suggested that some refreshment should be taken. When everything was ready—meat cut up, bread spread from a nice tin of butter that had just been opened and tea poured out, a big "woolly-bear" burst right overhead. The two poor fellows who were wounded each collected another one, and the appetising "spread" was all overturned and buried in the dust and debris.

The fresh wounds were dressed and shortly afterwards Major Denton came up with a stretcher party for Captain Medcalf. But that fine fellow insisted that Sergeant-Major Alley be placed on the stretcher while he hobbled out with the assistance of two others who were returning to headquarters.

It may not be out of place at this stage to mention something of the work of the stretcher-bearers. Most of the following details have been supplied by Sergt. W. Wright, A.A.M.C.

Before marching down to the Somme, the stretcher-bearer section consisted of 38 men, 16 being regular 'bearers, 16 reserves and the A.M.C. Section. These men were all well trained in their work and were a keen and efficient lot of fellows.

When the 11th Battalion took up position for the attack, the aid-post was established in an old German gun-pit just behind the jump-off position, as it was considered fairly central. A route for the 'bearers was chosen, but this proved to be useless as the German barrage soon obliterated all communications soon after the attack was launched; so that right from the start the 'bearers had a particularly heavy and hazardous job. Immediately the battle started the casualties poured in at such a rate that urgent requests were sent to C.C.S. for additional 'bearers.

A few hours after the "hop-over" Captain Fisher, the M.O., was incapacitated and Sergt. Wright had to carry on until relief came. Later in the day Captain Tozer arrived and immediately set to work in spite of very heavy shelling. Next morning the aid-post was blown out by a direct hit, all the wounded inside being killed. Captain Tozer was rendered unconscious through a wound on the head and Wright was wounded in the leg, and most of the medical stores were destroyed. Sergt. Wright reported to Colonel Roberts and asked that another M.O. be sent up, saying that he could carry on in the meantime. No relieving officer came and Sergt. Wright had to do as best he could until the battalion was relieved. More than 1,000 wounded passed through the 11th Battalion aid-post.

Constant appeals for new stretchers to replace those smashed by shell-fire had to be made, as well for additional medical stores.

After two gruelling days the stretcher-bearers began to be knocked up, and Colonel Roberts gave instructions for the battalion pioneers to assist. These did excellent work, but the numbers of wounded were too great to cope with and some of the poor fellows had to lie out all night. These were given a tot of rum when brought in to warm them up. This put new life in these poor fellows.

The congestion in the aid-post was exceedingly great at times, and the main stretcher route was often blocked. Fortunately a less-shelled detour was found and the walking cases all sent round that way. This relieved the congestion to a great extent.

Near the end of the battle, when the battalion stretcher-bearers, or those that were left of them, had been going for six days all out, they were very weary, but three men managed to stick it out. The other 'bearers were either casualties or shell-shocked cases.

Sergt. Wright, in spite of his wound, carried on to the very end and well deserved the great opinion the troops of the 11th Battalion always held of him.

Lieut. Wally Hallahan was now senior officer of the 11th Battalion in the forward area. The battalion must have suffered about 400 casualties by this time, and as the village was being terrifically shelled the remainder of the line-troops advanced to a shallow trench just clear of the village which had been held by posts and machine guns. Here they were just clear of the worst of the shelling.

Now commenced a period which had no equal in the history of the 11th Battalion, and perhaps was not equalled on the Western Front for intensity and duration of heavy shelling.

It was still early morning, and the bombardment had already been falling on Pozieres for some hours. When the remnants of the 11th Battalion pushed forward to the outskirts of the village, there were practically no troops left there save some of the 12th Battalion in deep dug-outs on the right; but all the positions in the village had either been obliterated by shell-fire or the troops in the remaining semblances of trenches had relinquished them for the better positions further forward. Messengers and runners sent forward from battalion H.Q. either failed to find the line-troops or were themselves "knocked," although Privates Heasman, Parmenter, West, Gennoe and Kynaston did wonderful work, passing through the curtain of fire time and again. Many others did work equally gallant, but as the village assumed more and more the appearance of a mound of rubble, it became increasingly difficult to find a way through and many reports were brought back that the 11th Battalion could not be found, only its gallant dead lying sprawled over the tortured ground. It was now freely stated that the 11th Battalion was wiped out, and messengers sent from the front line asking for artillery support rarely reached the rear, and many were so badly shaken that they were unable to give a coherent report.

Lieut. Brodie had endeavoured without any success at all to get telephonic communication through, though over seven miles of wire had been run out. It was immediately smashed to pieces and though the linesmen under Sergeant Pine did heroic work, it was impossible to keep the line intact for more than a few moments.

It is almost impossible to describe the actual conditions of that long day; but viewed from the shallow trench in which lay those of the 11th Battalion who still survived, the scene was one of death and destruction unforgettable. All day long there was a deluge of shells; and this is no mere figure of speech, for they fell out of the heavens in a continual downpour. Most of these shells fell on the village of Pozieres and on the immediate supports. It was quite possible to watch the shells falling: inconceivably swift dots of black, rushing earthwards with plumes of smoke and dust following their detonation. Some of the shells fell too near, and death and shattered limbs were the results. The boys were perfectly cool; a little dazed and weary perhaps, for those troops had had no sleep for at least three days; their eyes were fixed and glassy, but ever and again they would look over toward the enemy's lines and *hope* that he would attack.

In front of Pozieres and a little to the left of the 11th Battalion's position, troops of the 1st Australian Brigade could be seen moving about in a shallow trench, casually it appeared; and occasionally they would dig and shovel away some earth that was displaced by a shell bursting close.

There were a number of German rifles lying around and plenty of ammunition. These rifles never seemed to jam, and in order to pass the time—for there was really nothing to be done but endure the terrible shelling—the boys would take up one of these rifles and have a shot at some brick standing precariously upright on some shattered gable or chimney. So steady were the nerves or so deadened by the strain that it seemed impossible to miss these shots, and the troops were burning to have some real enemy to shoot at. The general feeling was that the barrage was due to stop at any minute, and that a strong German attack would then be made; and how the troops were longing for that attack!

In a very short space of time there were no walls at all left in the village, and the ranging of the guns seemed to be shorter and more shells began to drop in the trenches where the troops were. A burst took place and several men were killed and some terribly wounded. Lieut. E. Rogerson was knocked senseless. The wounded were dressed, Lieut. Wally Hallahan being quick and efficient at dressing, and soon all were bound up.

One young fellow, a mere boy, was frightfully injured. The hue of death soon overspread his face. Nothing could be done except make his last minutes as comfortable as possible. He knew he had not long to live and asked for a cigarette. One was lit and started and placed in his mouth. He puffed in content for a minute. On being asked if he wanted anything else, he smiled and said, "No, Mr. ——, you can't do anything more for me. I'm settled; but if you could get one or two of these bastards over there I'd die happy." Poor young lad!

Hallahan sent Brodie back to headquarters to ask for artillery support. Brodie had a fearful trip back through the welter of shelling, and if any artillery support was given it was not noticed by the troops who looked so anxiously for some abatement of the German shelling.

The conditions still remained the same in the forward area. All the boys could do was to hold on and hope for an enemy to shoot at. Lieut. Wally Hallahan was his usual smiling self, jesting with the boys, cursing fluently and funnily at the shelling, and helping the wounded in every way he could. He was not so much a leader as an inspiration and an example, and the boys would have died for or with him.

During this constant fall of heavy shells two men were noticed who must have come upon some strong spirits, perhaps some rum, for they were standing scowling at the German lines and muttering imprecations. An officer going his rounds came near. They pointed to the Hun line and said: "We'll fix those bastards! Think they can shell us all day for nothin'? We'll show 'em!" and they prepared to get over the parapet in the direction of the enemy. The officer told them not to be damned fools and dragged them back, and they subsided into the trench still cursing. A hurried call to some post a considerable distance away necessitated the officer's departure, and in the subsequent worry and stress of front-line happenings he forgot the pair of warriors. When he returned to their "possy" he found the birds missing, and all inquiries as to their whereabouts met with no success. The poor fellows were never seen again. They must have hopped the trench and advanced on Fritz through that terrible fire, and met with death almost immediately. Their passing must have been serene and unafraid.

Captain W. R. Hallahan, M.C., M.M.
(11th Battalion)

One of the batteries was now registering very consistently on the trench, which was being frequently struck. It was now late in the afternoon and if anything the shelling was heavier or at least more concentrated. A 5.9 shell was heard coming and then another, and the next one landed among a party, killing some and wounding and stunning many. Rogerson, who had been lying stunned for about an hour and a half, was jarred back to consciousness; Belford was bleeding profusely about the head, and all were pretty sick. When the party had recovered somewhat, Hallahan asked Belford to take Rogerson back and also to get his own wounds dressed. At the same time he sent a message back to headquarters strongly asking for counter-battery work, and left Belford to explain the position to Colonel Roberts.

Rogerson was still dazed but able to walk, and the two set off. Going through the inferno that was Pozieres was like wandering through the regions of the damned, inhabited only by the dead. These lay everywhere. All the time great missiles kept falling, and the ground was continually being blasted by fearful explosions. The crash of the shells, the sickening fumes, the reek of the dead and the ever-rising pall of dust that shut off the area from the rest of the world seemed to create an illusion of remoteness and isolation. No sign of troops could be seen. It was certainly the world's most frightful spot that day.

Just outside the curtain of fire the trenches were blocked by a mass of troops. Word had come through that the 1st Division was to be relieved that night, and already the relieving battalions were arriving and troops were withdrawing in expectation of the relief. There were terrible scenes there, but they do not affect this narrative. The two "C" Company officers had to keep to the top of the trenches as all communications were blocked with troops. Rogerson still managed to stagger along behind, stunned and battered, and many were the curious eyes cast upon the battle-scarred pair.

At length they reached battalion headquarters, which was full of wounded, weary and hysterical men. Lieut.-Colonel Roberts was just dictating a message to brigade, stating that the line had gone and that the 11th Battalion had been completely wiped out. He had every reason to believe this, because all reports had confirmed this; and Pozieres, and the trenches that had been first dug by the 11th battalion, had, as already stated, been evacuated by all troops except those who were sheltering in the few dugouts available. But the 11th Battalion's line was intact and the troops holding it were ready for all emergencies, but further forward than when Roberts and Denton had visited it on the previous day.

When Roberts saw the battered pair he gave them a pitying look and went on with his dictating. Then he asked how things were and if he could do anything for them. He got the shock of his life when he was asked if he could arrange, first, for some counter-battery work to help his much-shelled front-line troops, and second, if he could raise a good feed somewhere. In a minute he had arranged for his batman to bring some tea and stew, and in the meantime he was listening to the latest bulletin from his front line.

He immediately gave orders to hold back and cancel the message that was being sent, and then dictated another on the news that he had just received which, if far from being cheerful, was at least reassuring and in accordance with what he might expect from his battalion.

It was now 6 p.m. on July 25, and the shelling began to ease off. With the cessation of the barrage reaction began to set in among the troops of the 1st and 3rd Brigades, and they found themselves infinitely weary and in some cases absolutely knocked out. Relief came shortly after dark, the 5th Australian Brigade taking over the 3rd Brigade sector, and the 11th Battalion was relieved.

The battle-worn remnants of the fine battalion of a week ago dragged their slow way out past Gordons' Dump along Sausage Valley and past Becourt Wood. As the exhausted troops came out of the line and started to get out of the worst of the shelled area, they came to one of the forward canteens of the Australian Comforts Fund, about a mile from Contalmaison. Here coffee and biscuits were handed round to the boys. This was a most appreciated refreshment, and the men that ran these forward comforts stalls deserved all the praise they received. Unlike some of the other canteens, the business was run without any idea of making a profit out of the troops, and the services were given generally where they were most appreciated, often well within the shelled areas.

The little rest and the hot coffee put new life into the boys, and they started off again much heartened by the kindly and thoughtful service. After what seemed a long march in the darkness the troops reached the brickfields at Albert, and here they bivouaced for the night.

The relative quietness of the bivouacing area was like balm to the tired troops, who lay down just as they were under an ample supply of blankets and slept the sleep of utter exhaustion and freedom from fear of death or responsibility.

After what was to most of the boys the most enjoyable repose they had ever experienced, they were awakened for breakfast on the morning of July 26: the smell of breakfast was on the air, and the odour of rum and hot tea assailed the nostrils in most appetising fashion. Never did breakfast appeal so much. The rum put new life in the troops, but for all that it was a subdued meal. There seemed to be an air of quiet wonderment on the faces of most of the troops, a feeling of astonishment that they were alive and able to enjoy a meal in comparative quietness.

As for the troops themselves, no more war-worn men could be imagined. They were haggard and unshaven, with glassy, tired eyes sunken in their heads, and all their movements were infinitely weary. Most of them, however, had brought out trophies and souvenirs, and after they had been revived by the good food a wonderful display of German helmets and other equipment began to be displayed by the small band of survivors.

But when the roll was called and all the names whose owners would never again answer to them were read out, the awful blow that the 11th Battalion had suffered came to be fully realised. The casualties were 19 officers and 511 other ranks. This was the highest in the division, and was a great deal more than half the effective strength. "A" and "B" Companies came out of the line with all the officers casualties, while "C" and "D" Companies had only two officers each left, and two of these were wounded. "D" Company went into the line with 176 men and came out with 39, and "C" Company was hardly in any better plight. It was a terrible penalty to pay for the small advance made, much as it was lauded at the time.

Later in the morning General Sir William Birdwood came along and made the usual complimentary speeches, and went around among the boys. This may have appealed to some of the men, but in view of the terrible casualties sustained, most of the boys were very little impressed with the Corps Commanders' kind remarks.

And so ended the first phase of the battle that was always described as Pozieres, at least as far as the 11th Battalion was concerned; but the physical and mental results lasted many months, and in some cases were never entirely obliterated.

The battalion strength on July 26 was 17 officers and 576 other ranks. These included some newly-joined reinforcements under Lieut. R. Hall, who had reported for duty during the engagement.

Each company had lost its commander and second-in-command. Of the twenty officers that led the battalion into action only three were unwounded.

The following list of names was submitted for recognition of outstanding services, but there were scores of men whose deeds passed unnoticed in the turmoil of battle, many of whom died in circumstances that called for the greatest of gallantry. Numbers of brave comrades and true soldiers passed over to

Valhalla in this engagement and Australia is still greatly the poorer for their passing. "We shall never see their like again."

List of officers and other ranks recommended by commanding officer for the Pozieres battle, July 22/25, 1916:—

For conspicuous gallantry: 2nd/Lieut. Cyril George Ross, Captain Ferdinand George Medcalf, Lieuts. Louis Leon Le Nay, Walter Rieve Hallahan, Walter Cheyne Belford, James Murray Aitken and Edward Rogerson, L/Sergeant William Wright, A.A.M.C., No. 2132 Private William George Elias, No. 1063 Private Robert Roy Gennoe, No. 2145 Private Gilbert Arthur Heasman, No. 1971 Private Edward Harvey Kynaston, No. 3146 Private Leonard Walter West, No. 5177 Private William Henry Parmenter, No. 5139 Private Thorby Long, No. 993 Private George Edwards, No. 717 Sergeant Frederick James Francis Stahl, No. 2332 Corporal Bruce Walker, No. 1112 Private Reginald James Camden, No. 2480 Private Edwin Gardner.

For valuable services: Major James Samuel Denton, D.S.O., Captain Reginald Hemingway, Lieuts. William Kruger, Alexander Charles Brodie and Raymond Arthur Clarke, Captain Eric Hortley Fisher, No. 441 W.O. and R.S.M. David Hardy, No. 915 Sergeant Tom Lodge Hollins.

The officers killed were Captains MacFarlane and Mansfield and Lieuts. Forbes, Walters, Hastings and Nicol. The wounded were Major Milner, Captains Newman, Medcalf, Campbell, Griffin, Lieuts. Rogerson and McKean, 2nd/Lieuts. Bickford, Davidson, Vowles, Elliot and Lieuts. Aitken and Belford wounded but remaining on duty.

The casualties of the four battalions of the 3rd Brigade were: 9th, 316; 10th, 327; 11th, 531; 12th, 421.

There were many complimentary messages sent to the 1st Division after the capture of the village, and the following from the 1st British Division may be taken as typical:—

"The 1st (British) Division desire to express to the 1st Australian Division, alongside of whom they have been fighting for the last few days, their profound admiration of the magnificent feat of arms which culminated in the capture of Pozieres."

The "feat of arms" was certainly magnificent, as much as courage, dash, .endurance and disregard of death could make it so; but there seemed an utter lack of any skill behind the atack. What had been gained was due simply to the splendid spirit of the men. A fortnight previously Haig had caused the troops to be informed that the battle was more than half won, and that by steady and unrelenting effort a few more days would turn the scale in favour of the British arms. Since then the cream of the new British armies had fallen, many battalions suffering even heavier than the 11th Battalion. There had been over 100,000 casualties, and then the Australians were simply thrown into the maw of that great battlefield and thousands of men wasted in the attack. This seems a hard criticism, but when an officer of very high rank in the Australian Army, in referring to the capture of the few acres that used to be Pozieres, stated that "the Chief" was "awfully bucked" about it, and this in spite of the fact that the 1st Australian Division had lost 5,285 officers and men, then it must be obvious that there was something radically wrong somewhere.

No comprehensive criticism is possible in this narrative, but as the Australian soldier always took an intelligent interest in his campaigns, the above remarks are necessary in view of the troops' reaction after this battle.

In the meantime the troops were too stunned to worry about anything, and spent the time resting and waiting for the next move, which all ranks understood was to be a long rest for reorganisation and re-equipment purposes. The necessity of these last was only too apparent, for some of the men had come out of the line without even their rifles. This seemed to point to certain amount of demoralisation, and Lieut.-Colonel Roberts severely rated the men who had left their rifles behind; but the fact of some of the men having no rifles was due to the men having been used as stretcher-bearers and leaving their rifles with their mates, or putting them down while they were digging trenches; and though in the early part of the occupation there were hundreds of rifles lying all over the place belonging to the dead and wounded, yet the whole area was so severely shelled, and everything smashed or buried, that men were unable to find any of the weapons or equipment that they had left, even only a short time before. Consequently there was a heavy loss of equipment and gear.

Lest it may be thought by the reader that the conditions on the battlefield of Pozieres have been exaggerated, and that other battlefields were equally terrible; and though there is a recorded instance where the shelling was even more terrible, if not so long sustained, yet in all the battles that the Australians fought in Pozieres must always stand out as the worst.

There is a plain stone on the site of Pozieres Windmill that bears this inscription. It is there for all to read and runs thus:—

> "The ruins of Pozieres Windmill which lies here was the centre of the struggle in this part of the Somme Battlefield in July and August, 1916. It was captured on August 4 by Australian troops who fell more thickly on this ridge than on any other battlefield of the war."

CHAPTER XXI

REST AND REORGANISATION AT BERTEAUCOURT

ON THE afternoon of July 26, 1916, the ragged and battered remnants of the 11th Battalion were paraded and marched off to Warloy, where they camped for the night in good billets. As the troops marched along the road they were loaded with German trophies, while "pikelhaubs" (the leather helmets with steel or brass spikes which were a part of the uniform of many German regiments), bayonets, uniforms and many different kinds of souvenirs hung from the travelling kitchens. All the British regiments in the vicinity lined the roadsides and cheered to the echo. When the battalion passed Henencourt Wood, great numbers of Scotties in their khaki kilts came running up from their huts and joined in the great ovation that was given to the troops of the 1st Australian Division. There was always a great comradeship between the Diggers and the Scotties, and the latter passed over many encouraging messages and several bottles of beer were also given to the boys of the 11th. Two "Jocks," a little in rear of the others, and partly screened by some bushes, were noticed having a little argument, and as the battalion marched past one could be seen holding up a partly-emptied bottle of beer to the light, and his remark was heard: "Och, mon! A wish A hadna' drunk that beer, noo." His companion answered, "Weel, Sandy! Gi'e them what's left." But the first man shook his head and said: "It doesna' look nice," and looked regretfully at the Aussies. This was a clear case of natural generosity struggling with native delicacy. On marched the battalion, and as the last pitiful remnants of "D" Company went by a Jock rushed out and thrust a bottle among the Australian ranks and rushed away without a word. Generosity had triumphed!

After an easy march Warloy was reached, and the troops had ample time to arrange themselves for the night. It was good to be in Warloy, and the people were kind; but it was not long before every man had turned in and all were soon fast asleep in the coma of utter exhaustion.

In the morning there was a big sick parade for such a small battalion, mostly men with small wounds to dress, and such as were not so serious as to require the sufferers evacuation. Some of the men were bruised and black and blue all over, due to being hit with lumps of earth or broken bricks during shelling.

Later there was a parade, when a nominal roll was taken and particulars of such men that were known to be killed were taken. There were a great many missing that were never accounted for, and who were eventually recorded as dead. It was a mournful business calling out name after name and receiving no answer. Then perhaps the mate of the man whose name was read out would say quietly: "Killed by a sniper," or another would merely mutter, "Killed!"

The battalion parade strength was 241, but of course this did not include transport or any of the other details.

After the mid-day meal on July 27, the 11th Battalion moved off in column of route for La Vicogne. What a blessed relief it was to march along the leafy lanes, away from all the discordant noises of war. Every step took the boys further and further away; and though the ear-drums still buzzed from the ceaseless detonations of the past battle, and the roll of the guns could still be heard to the east, yet already the troops seemed to be entering a new world. When the battalion halted for tea in a green glade near Val-de-Maison, the Diggers threw themselves down on the grassy banks and the evening meal was brought along from the travelling cookers. Already the war seemed far away. The grass gave out its sweet, aromatic smell; the birds sang their evensong and the tired and still dazed Diggers drank in the peace and beauty of the spot. After a spell, the battalion marched to La Vicogne a few kilometres further and bivouaced in a large park attached to the beautiful chateau near that village. The more cheerful hum of conversation before the boys fell asleep showed that the troops were returning to normal.

Next morning, July 28, the battalion set off on a long march to Naours, where the troops dined. In the afternoon the march was resumed and the route lay through pleasant country. A most agreeable surprise awaited the troops when they reached Halloy, for here the 11th's sister battalion, the 51st, was lined along the road to greet the "Old 11th." The boys of the 51st gave their mates a great "hoy!" as they went past, and Lieut.-Colonel Roberts halted his battalion so that old comrades could have an opportunity of meeting those whom they had parted from away in Gebel Habieta, far in the Sinai Desert. It seemed as if ages had passed since those tranquil days, and many were the sore hearts at the pitifully small remnant of the fine 11th Battalion that they had remembered. Questions innumerable were asked about this and that lad, and many were the shocked faces over the big tally of those that were no more. Finally, amid cheers and good wishes all round, the battalions parted and the 11th moved off to Berteaucourt, where the small companies were settled in comfortable billets.

When the inhabitants heard that they were housing the troops that recently captured Pozieres, their enthusiasm knew no bounds. They clapped the Diggers on the back and called them all sorts of complimentary names and brought out bottles of wine with the cobwebs and dust barely disturbed. Glasses were filled and the French inhabitants and the Diggers pledged each other.

Berteaucourt was a pleasantly situated village in undulating country, quite close to Vignacourt and not far from the considerable town of St. Ouen, which was further down the same stream that ran through the first-named village. There were flax and jute spinning mills in the district, and consequently there was more bustle than was usual in the Picardie villages.

After a good night's rest the troops were informed that there would be no parades on July 29. Most of the troops managed to get down to the river for a much appreciated swim. A number of workers in the fields nearby were very interested in the temporary nudist colony.

The day was spent in reorganisation and medical inspection. There were several cases of sore feet through the men having had to wear their boots for too long a stretch, as during their tour in the line there had been no opportunity of taking off their footwear.

On Sunday, July 30, there was a church parade and an address by Brigadier-General Sinclair-MacLagan, commanding the 3rd Australian Brigade. The Brigadier, in thanking the troops for the great work that they had done at Pozieres, said that no troops could have done more. While the General was a man of few words and the last man to overpraise anyone, and though the troops realised that he was quite sincere in what he said, yet they also realised that the survivors of the terrible shambles that they had recently come out of were merely lucky, and that whatever there was of honour or praise really belonged to the dead that had so gallantly fallen at Pozieres. However, the troops were intelligent enough to realise that speeches of the sort were part of the General's job, and they left it at that.

The following quotations from diaries of this date give a good idea of the troops' feelings in the matter. The first is from Lieut. J. M. Aitken's: "Sunday, July 30, 1916. The brigade paraded this morning and was thanked by the Brigadier for the good work it had done. *A lot of jam.*"

Lieut. (then Sergeant) Peter Snodgrass writes this: "We had church parade this morning and an address by the Brigadier, in which he thanked everyone for their good work and said that others might have done as well, but no one did better than the 3rd Brigade. Of course we always get this sort of stuff after a stunt."

Though as yet no definite idea had been formulated in the minds of the troops, the first seeds of disillusionment and doubt had been sown and these were to form a growth that took many months to eradicate.

During the course of the war many weapons were tried out and some were abandoned. Among the new weapons, the Lewis gun, that had first been issued to infantry in July, 1915, had so proved its usefulness and efficiency that the establishments were being gradually increased. It was now learned that the battalion quota was to be raised to two guns per company and four guns as battalion reserve and extra crews were to be trained.

On July 31, the battalion strength was 17 officers and 576 other ranks. Next day Lieut. R. Hall and 63 reinforcements paraded before Major-General H. B. Walker, commanding 1st Division, A.I.F., in accordance with the expressed desire of the divisional commander to inspect all reinforcements arriving on or after July 25, 1916.

On August 2, the new establishment of Lewis guns came into force. There was now one detachment of two guns for each company with a personnel of one N.C.O. and 12 other ranks, and two detachments for headquarters with one officer, one N.C.O. and one other rank in addition, making a total of one officer, seven N.C.O.'s and 75 other ranks. This large establishment at this stage of the war is indicative of the growing importance of the machine gun and the necessity of having well-trained crews.

When the 11th Battalion was first formed, there were only two machine guns allotted to the unit.

A bathing parade was held in one of the factories in the village on August 4. Needless to say, the factory was idle at the time. A change of underclothing was issued to the troops. On the same date Lewis gun teams were exercised on a 30-yards range near the village, and "B," "C" and "D" Companies had musketry practice.

An issue of new clothing to replace the battle-worn garments of the troops was made on August 6. It may have been thought that too much stress has been placed on the dilapidated and ragged appearance of the troops after Pozieres, but the men's clothes and equipment had been so much cut about that new issues were authorised, and the above entry is in the official diary of the 11th Battalion.

A very pleasant twelve days was spent at Berteaucourt, during which time the reorganisation of the battalion was the chief activity. Company training was held on the slopes of a fine grassy hill, which rose at the back of the village. In between exercises the troops reclined on the short, sweet-smelling grass, redolent of thyme. It was ideal weather during this period and even the route-marches were enjoyed. The country was at its best, in the fulness of late summer, and already the crops were turning yellow; while the dark greens of root-crops and the intense blue of the fields of flax now in flower made a variegated picture. Red poppies nodded alongside the roads and in the fields. There were also many pine woods around the district and the restful nature of the whole countryside soon had a healing effect on the troops, who gradually became their usual fun-loving selves once again.

There were several amusing incidents associated with the stay at this village. As before mentioned, reorganisation was the chief activity in the battalion and new specialists were being trained in all the sections to replace the losses lately sustained.

The bombing platoon, under Lieut. Ray Clarke, usually created a good deal of interest, so much so that "Mulga" Tonkin, one of the farriers in the transport section, was so intrigued with the game that, after the bombers had finished their practice, he tried himself out at bomb-throwing. He succeeded so well that he began to give himself airs and spent all his spare time and a lot of other time as well in throwing dummy bombs. In fact he made himself so much of a nuisance that Albie Wells, the transport sergeant, had recourse to a little guile in order to bring him back to normal.

Noticing "Mulga" at his eternal bomb-throwing one day, Wells said to him: "I say, 'Mulga,' the bombing officer has been noticing what a fine thrower you are. He asked me if I thought that you would like a transfer to the bombing platoon, so I told him that I would speak to you about it. You can think it over." There was dead silence on "Mulga's" part.

It was noticed for some time after this that "Mulga" was the most conscientious farrier in the division. Bomb-throwing was decidedly off!

There is a story, too, of Lieut. Alick Burgess who, feeling energetic one morning picked up the cook's axe and chopped through a fair-sized log lying by the wayside near a cottage. Suddenly there was a shout and a torrent of abuse in vociferous French and a most indignant Froggie dashed up and threw his arms all over the place, nearly knocking "Burgie" over in his efforts to show him that he had committed a very serious crime. To the Australian mind it was inconceivable that such a fuss should be made over a mere log of wood, and Burgess was wondering what harm he had really done. He was duly enlightened later when a complaint had been lodged at battalion headquarters, and he received a bill for about 200 francs, this being the amount charged "for the destruction of valuable timber."

On Saturday, August 5, there was a birthday party given to one of the officers at his billet. When all were seated at table the ladies of the house, who happened to be the sisters of the village *cure*, brought up from the cellar half a dozen bottles of the most wonderful cider and presented them to the party with many wishes for the good fortune of all. This little incident is mentioned to show the cordial relations that existed between the French and the Australians, and the kindness with which the troops were almost invariably received.

On Sunday, August 6, church parade was held in the fields near the village. It was a beautiful warm morning, typical of the best days of the French summer. The troops lay among the sweet-scented thyme, a scent for ever associated with this rest at Berteaucourt. The padre droned on, in company with the bees that flitted from flower to flower. The troops were hardly paying any attention. It was just bliss to be lying there doing nothing. Lieut.-Colonel Roberts and Major Denton were lying down in front, with the other troops lying in a semi-circle behind them.

The faint jingle of coppers could be heard from the rear rank as some of the boys playing a sort of miniature two-up tossed the "browns." Gradually the troops began to sit up and take notice. The padre (the "Mere Incident" of pre-Pozieres fame) was raising his voice in order to attract attention. His subject was "Angels," and he told the wonderful story about the "Angel of Mons." He spoke thus: "Yes! I believe in angels. I am better educated that any of you men, and I believe in angels. Angels do exist. I'll give you an example: One night two comrades, an old and a young soldier, were in a certain town, and the elder was trying to persuade the younger to go into a house of ill-fame; and just as the younger was about to agree he felt, as it were, a hand on his shoulder. Now, what do you think that was?"

The padre paused dramatically. Instantly a tired voice from the back drawled, "The sergeant of the picket, I suppose."

Not a sound! Then a ripple of laughter that rocked the whole battalion. The Commanding Officer, the Second-in-Command and all the rest of the officers buried their faces in the grass, and then Major Denton managed to growl, "Silence in the ranks!" and the service proceeded.

On August 7 the following promotions were announced: Lieut. L. L. Le Nay to be Captain vice MacFarlane, killed in action, dated July 24, 1916; to be 2nd/lieuts., dated August 5, 1916: No. 956 Corporal Dent-Young, No. 882 Sergeant L. C. Cooke, No. 1142 C.S.M. A. J. Long, No. 868 Sergeant R. Beattie, No. 2103 C.Q.M.S. F. R. Beasley, No. 2161 L/Corporal P. W. Lyons, No. 925 Sergeant L. G. Riches, No. 1618 Corporal C. Prout.

While the 1st Australian Division was resting in the Vignacourt area, a lecture was given to selected officers by the chemical adviser to the 3rd Army Reserve on the organisation and method of use of smoke clouds in the field.

All good things come to an end, and the 11th Battalion's sojourn in Berteaucourt came to a close on August 9. It was with regret that this pleasant village was left, and it was never again visited by the battalion during its long service in France. The battalion, considerably augmented since its arrival, marched out with a great send-off from the villagers, who wept to see the boys go and sent them off with many a "bonne chance" and "bon voyage."

After marching about ten kilometres the battalion reached the village of Bonneville, where a stay of several days was made.

CHAPTER XXII

MOVING UP TO MOUQUET FARM
BONNEVILLE AND BECOURT

IT WAS NOW KNOWN that the 1st Division was again moving up to the line after its short spell. As the 3rd Brigade had been given the most onerous task on the last occasion, the other two brigades were to be sent up first and the 3rd Brigade was to follow. It might have been thought that a battalion that had suffered so many casualties as the 11th would have been allowed the maximum time for reorganisation; but such was far from the actual case, for almost immediately on arrival at Bonneville "C" and "D" Companies, six officers and 88 other ranks in all, under temporary Captains Hallahan and Belford, were sent forward to Becourt Wood to operate as burial parties under the direction of Padre Major Dexter. These troops were ordered to camp in a disused trench in the shelter of the wood, and daily parties under an officer and intended to be accompanied by a padre were sent up to Pozieres and beyond to bury the dead from the fierce battles that had raged there.

The general procedure was for the party to move up to a selected area and bury all the dead that were to be found there, first taking all the particulars available and any paybooks or personal belongings from the body. The graves were marked with light crosses with the particulars of the soldiers hung on these, so that a more or less permanent record of the place of burial was made. When all the bodies in the sector were buried the padre, if there was one, said a burial service over them collectively and then the party returned to headquarters in Becourt Wood, and all the particulars of the soldiers buried—the number of men, their units, locations of burial and any other facts of interest—were handed to Major Dexter, as officer in charge.

It was not a very pleasant job for these officers and men to be gathering and burying the dead on the dust-heap that once had been Pozieres, especially when so many of the corpses were those of their own dear mates of only a fortnight before; and to make it worse, Fritz still kept sending his devastating 5.9 shells over; not in dreadful curtain barrage it is true, but sufficiently heavily to make the job dangerous, and what was worse these shells disinterred the recenty buried bodies on several occasions. It was really a terrible time for these men, and it must be admitted that the utmost had been asked of them. Kipling's words almost fit the occasion:—

"Nor was their agony brief, or only once imposed on them,
The wounded, the war-spent, the sick received no exemption:
Being cured they returned and endured and achieved our redemption.
Hopeless themselves of relief, till Death, marvelling, closed on them.

. . . .

To be senselessly tossed and retossed in stale mutilation from crater to crater."

War has many aspects, and not many of them are glorious; but it certainly has the power of making men very callous, and so these lads were able to carry on.

Before returning to the remainder of the battalion at Bonneville a few incidents illustrative of the daily routine may be of interest. On August 14, Padre Dexter told the officer in charge of the party for the day to call at a building near the "Chalk Pit" and pick up a padre there to accompany the burial party to Pozieres, which was now a considerable way behind the line.

On reporting at the building, which was still pretty well intact, and which was next to a dressing-station, the officer halted his men and went to inquire for the padre. Instructed to ask at the mess the officer found a chaplain and asked if he were detailed to go up with the burial party that day. The padre replied: "Ah! no; that must have been Mr. ——, that is Captain ——; I don't think he's up yet. I'll go and see."

Meanwhile the medical officer in charge of the dressing-station came out and requested that the troops be moved along, as Fritz had his aeroplanes up and the party was liable to draw crabs. The C.S.M., Wally Graham, was instructed to take the troops forward into the first empty trench and wait.

Still no chaplain. At last another padre appeared in his pyjamas. He also knew nothing about going up to the line.

The 11th Battalion officer became annoyed and told the chaplains that they had better toss for it as he could not wait there all day. After a bit of argument, one of the chaplains said that he would come. There was another long wait, but at last the padre was ready. When the pair reached the waiting troops, Wally Graham said, "Cripes, sir! I thought you were stayin' for lunch."

The party shouldered picks and shovels and filed up the long communication trench. The Germans were dropping a few shells in Pozieres just ahead. The officer led the party, the chaplain followed, then came the boys and the C.S.M. brought up the rear. No one knew just when or how it happened, but suddenly it was discovered that the padre was missing. He had ducked off up a side trench, and in spite of shouts and a good deal of hunting, the party could not find him. But not all padres were like that one. There were many like John Fahey and "Fighting Mac."

While the men were busily engaged in searching for and burying the dead, the officer and S.M. had a look round. They found a deep dug-out, with only a ladder as means of ingress. They descended and found the dug-out deep and very dark. Something touched both men's legs. Out came revolvers, but nothing further happened. A droning sound was now heard which increased in volume, so a match was struck and the tension was relieved by the sight of a tiny kitten purring estatically. Then Graham saw a bayonet sticking in the wall of the dug-out. He wanted to pull it out. "Not on your life," yelled the Captain, thinking of booby traps; but Wally Graham wanted the bayonet and started to tug away at it, so the other grabbed the kitten and made a dash for the ladder. "I'll wait for you up on top, Sar.-Major," he cried, as he did two rungs at a time.

But Wally came up immediately afterwards with the bayonet. Shells continued to fall all day, but they were pretty well scattered and there were no casualties. A good look was taken at what was left of "Gibralter," a very strong reinforced concrete shelter, which was almost the only recognisable feature of the village. Some of the boys tried to locate their old positions during the battle, but the awful shelling had churned up the ground so often that nothing could be made out but the fact that a village had once stood there.

Perhaps it was just as well that all remembered places were blotted out, for Pozieres must always stand as the most disastrous engagement that the 11th Battalion ever took part in, if the number of casualties is considered, for on these few acres over 500 of the 11th Battalion were killed or wounded in less than one week's fighting and the terrible effect of the battle was to persist for a very long time.

The boys in the burial parties realised these things; but war is war, so they carried on from a sense of duty and thought about the terrible place as little as they could.

One day on returning to headquarters an officer stripped for a wash. Lieut. Rex Hall noticed that a wound on the other's back was very much inflamed, and advised an immediate visit to a dressing-station which was just handy. The officer put on a flannel shirt, similar to those issued to the troops, and wandered round to the dressing-station.

The M.O. on duty was a tall, haughty-looking officer, and he immediately subjected the seeming "troop" to a lot of questions. He asked him where and when he was wounded, when the wound was last dressed, if an anti-tetanus injection had been given, and so on. The patient replied that he came to have his wound dressed, and added that anti-tetanus injections were not necessary in the chalk districts.

This naturally upset his highness and he at once became the heavy superior officer. The patient said: "If I had known that you were going to make so much bloody fuss, I wouldn't have come to your old joint." This riled the M.O. who said to the astounded corporal, who was standing by: "Take this man's name and particulars," and he then stalked off in high dudgeon.

The following conversation then took place: "What is your number?" "Haven't got one." "What is your unit?" "Eleventh Battalion." "What is your rank?" "Captain." "Oh! er! That will be all right, sir," and then the wound was dressed and bandaged without more ado, or any further particulars being taken. This story is told to show that sometimes too much discrimination was made between officers and other ranks, but generally in the line at least this was the exception rather than the rule.

But the boys were always well treated by Padre Major Dexter, who every day had a generous issue of rum awaiting the party which had been on burial duty when it returned from its sad and unpleasant job.

The story now returns to Bonneville where the main part of the battalion was completing its organisation and training. The strength of the 11th Battalion, on arrival at Bonneville, was 26 officers and 504 other ranks. Lieut. A. Brooks was left in the rear area in charge of the baggage dump of the 3rd Brigade.

On August 9, a draft of reinforcements arrived from Etaples. This draft only comprised 30 men, and these were divided among the companies. All the troops had to camp in the open as there were not enough tents or billets to go round. This would have been quite all right, as the weather was at its warmest and mildest, but unfortunately it had to rain and this soon made living conditions very uncomfortable.

The intelligence section that had performed such good work since its formation was disbanded on August 10, and the personnel returned to the companies. On this date four men were selected from each company to be trained as rifle grenadiers. This branch of bombing, which was rather erratic and uncertain at first, gradually became more and more important, and with the steady improvement in the grenades and the method of propulsion soon became a useful method of covering the advance in small attacks, and rifle grenades were frequently used against machine gun positions.

Demonstrations in the use of smoke bombs in the offensive were given under divisional arrangements, and there was also a demonstration in air signalling with contact aeroplanes. Several officers attended each practice.

On August 12, 50 reinforcements arrived from Val de Maison, thus bringing the battalion strength up to 25 officers and 588 other ranks. Captain Dixon Hearder and batman reported for duty on August 13.

Bonneville was left on August 14 and the 11th Battalion, less "C" and "D" Companies, which were still in the forward zone, marched to Rubempre, where the troops billeted for the night. Next day the march was resumed to Harponville. Here a party of two officers and 136 other ranks was detailed to act as special carrying party for the ensuing operation, which the 3rd Brigade was about to be plunged into.

At Harponville, that fine soldier, Captain J. S. D. Walker, M.C., rejoined the 11th Battalion from 3rd Australian Machine

Gun Company, and No. 892 Sergeant H. W. Ellemore was promoted 2nd/Lieut., dated August 9, 1916.

The 11th Battalion left Harponville and proceeded to the Brickfields, near Albert, on August 16. The route had been by Warloy, Senlis and Millencourt. It was wet weather and the muddy bivouac at the Brickfields was a foretaste of the trials to come. A few days were spent at this bivouac and the two detached companies, "C" and "D," rejoined the battalion from Becourt Wood and 2nd/Lieut. Ayling reported for duty from England.

August 17 marked the second anniversary of the 11th Battalion's formation.

On the night of August 19 the 11th Battalion received orders to move into brigade reserve at La Boisselle. Working parties of three officers and 133 other ranks were sent to Chalk Pit and to brigade headquarters. These parties, with the 136 men already detailed for special duty, absorbed all the available men of the 11th Battalion.

A rough survey of the position as it presented itself when the 3rd Australian Brigade took over will show the nature of the 11th Battalion's task in the coming battle.

During the time the 1st Australian Division had been out of the line there had been a steady, if slow and costly, advance northward from Pozieres by the 2nd and 4th Australian Divisions, and on August 15, when plans had to be made for the attack by the 1st Division, the salient had reached its maximum. Thiepval was still unconquered. In fact no advance had been made anywhere save the Australian thrust towards Mouquet Farm. This important point, which had been strongly fortified by the Germans, commanded a wide area and was now holding up the attack at the apex of the salient. It was against this fortress, for such it was, that the 1st Australian Division, barely recovered from its 5,285 casualties of only three weeks previously and still hardly two-thirds of its normal strength, was being launched.

The 1st and 2nd Australian Brigades had made their attacks on August 17/19, and had gained a few yards of territory at fearful expense; and then the 3rd Brigade relieved the 1st Brigade on August 19, the 9th Battalion taking over the left of the line, the 12th the centre and the 10th Battalion the right opposite Mouquet Farm and the Fabeck Graben (the Fabeck Trench).

The 11th Battalion was to "carry" for the brigade. This was no light job, as over 100,000 rounds of small arms ammunition, hundreds of tins of water, cases of bombs and other forward line necessaries had to be carried up to the front line by the long detour known as "Tom's Cut."

The above were the dispositions for the attack on Mouquet Farm on the night of August 19 insofar as they affected the 3rd Brigade.

Chapter XXIII

MOUQUET FARM OR SECOND POZIERES

MOUQUET FARM was one of the most unsatisfactory engagements that the 11th Battalion took part in. The chief reasons for this were that in the first place the troops were hardly organised after their recent severe casualties of the previous month, and in the second place the men of the 11th Battalion had been engaged in carrying parties and burial parties right up till the time of the batle, so that there was very little chance of explaining the position to the troops or of giving them any idea of what was expected of them. The whole affair was badly managed from the start, and especially in the case of the 11th Battalion, as this narrative will show, there seems to have been no knowledge of the conditions under which the troops were working, which is putting it mildly, or an utter disregard for anything except the carrying out of a scheduled attack, which previous experience had proved to be an impossible one. Right through from start to finish the engagement was carried out under exceedingly trying circumstances.

The 11th Battalion headquarters was at first in a dug-out at La Boisselle, just to the north of Sausage Valley or Sausage Gully, as the troops generally designated it, and the companies were in trench shelters round about. The long valley below them was still filled with batteries, whose guns mostly pointed to the north, and shells screamed over the reserve positions all day and night.

Brigade headquarters was also in Sausage Gully and liaison officers from all the battalions of the 3rd Brigade were sent there.

All day on August 20 the line battalions of the 3rd Brigade endeavoured to improve their positions by digging or advancing forward, but the Germans had such a splendid site for observation that no movement could take place without being visible to them unless by night or if the weather happened to be foggy or misty. On this account the hostile shelling was very active and well placed, and many casualties were caused.

The 11th Battalion troops were carrying all day on August 20, and the men believed that they were not to be used for the attack; but at the last minute it was determined to use 200 men of the 11th Battalion, under Captain Le Nay and Lieut. W. R. Hallahan, to link up the 10th and 12th Battalions where their flanks met at the old German lines opposite the Fabeck Graben, just before that trench ran into Mouquet Farm. The sector embracing the old German lines had always been a serious difficulty to the advance, as naturally it was full of good dug-outs and prepared positions; and though in this phase of the attack it was approached in enfilade, it did not make the task of the troops any easier, because the enemy could offer a stiff resistance and then retire in comparative immunity along the double line of trenches. There was also a sunken road running parallel with the old German trenches.

Lieut.-Colonel Roberts pointed out that the 11th Battalion would be in no condition to take part in the attack, but his protest was disregarded. The 11th Battalion had been "carrying" all morning on August 21 and the men had done prodigies of work; but, of course, the troops who were to form the attacking parties under Le Nay and Hallahan were still unaware that they were due for a stunt that afternoon.

The 11th Battalion forward headquarters under Lieut.-Colonel Roberts moved up to a dug-out near "The Quarry" in readiness for the assault on the German lines. The other battalions of the 3rd Brigade had been endeavouring to get their troops up to the jump-off positions and had suffered many casualties. The 10th Battalion in particular lost very heavily in moving up, and lost 120 out of 620 men before the attack was launched.

The attack was to be a daylight one, and if the essence of success in an attack is surprise, then the attack was foredoomed to failure from the start, because the Germans could not fail to see the great amount of movement that was going on. The communications were so congested that whole parties of the boys would persist in moving over the top in spite of the heavy shell-fire that sometimes increased to barrage intensity.

While the other battalions were lining up ready for the attack, the parties from the 11th Battalion who had been hastily warned were still a long way back drawing their battle stores at the Chalk Pit dump. They had only returned from carrying fatigue to their lines at La Boisselle at about 3:30 p.m. and were immediately instructed that they were due to participate in a hop-over. A hurried meal was served and the troops were marched to the Chalk Pit, and when they had drawn their supplies were hurried up to the line. This was exceedingly bad staff work.

General MacLagan realised that the troops could never make the jump-off point in time, and instructions were sent from 3rd Brigade headquarters to the 9th Battalion detailing that unit to send one of its companies to take over the 11th Battalion's sector if the latter battalion's party failed to arrive in time.

The Australian barrage was by this time falling on the German trenches and rear as a preliminary to the infantry attack. Meanwhile the two parties of the 11th Battalion under Le Nay and Hallahan were struggling through the German barrage which had been called down in response to the Australian shelling. Lieuts. Hallahan and Clarke were twice buried by exploding shells and had to be dug out, and their party very much disorganised; while Le Nay was only able to reach the starting position with about a score of men after the attack had been launched.

When these few men arrived the 9th Battalion party, hearing that the 11th Battalion troops had arrived, immediately stood fast, and an order was given to the platoons of the former battalion to shelter where they could and await further instructions. This they did in shell holes behind the jumping-off positions. There was now a gap where the 9th Battalion reserve company should have attacked, since the 11th Battalion parties had been delayed through no fault of the officers or troops engaged.

Hallahan and Clarke then arrived a long time after zero hour, and Hallahan was so dazed after having been buried and knocked about that he was really not fit to carry on during the whole tour of duty though, like the splendid soldier that he was, he refused to leave the line. Clarke had also had a rough time. Le Nay was wounded soon after he had reported to Major Rafferty, of the 12th Battalion, who was in charge of the operation in the forward area.

In the meantime the 10th and 12th Battalions had made their attack under a very fine barrage, and the 12th Battalion's advance in particular was carried out steadily and in great style. With the covering fire of the 3rd Machine Gun Company these troops advanced almost to Mouquet Farm, but as they were practically unsupported on both flanks they had to fall back on a line almost on the Mouquet Farm-Courcelette road.

Some parties of the 10th Battalion advanced and reached the Fabeck Graben, which they entered; but owing to lack of support, and also to the frightful mix-up, they were cut off and they ultimately surrendered.

The 11th Battalion parties, with their effective officers all hors de combat, and the men, tired and confused, made a half-hearted attempt to advance along the old German lines about midnight, and they gained a little ground.

The attack by the 3rd Brigade was the first daylight attack in the Somme area by the Australians, and was to have been made under cover of a smoke screen projected by the special brigade of the Royal Engineers; but owing to the fact that these troops were unable to get their trench mortars up to the required position, the attacking troops had to do without this screen and consequently their every more was seen by the enemy.

For a long time after the attack was launched all was uncertainty and confusion at brigade headquarters. Different messages had come through. "The 10th had reached the Fabeck Graben"; "Mouquet Farm was captured"; "The 11th had not arrived"; "There was no smoke barrage." There were long periods of silence, and many conflicting reports tended to make the situation still more obscure.

While this uncertainty prevailed, Lieut. Belford, who, as 11th Battalion liaison officer, was then at 3rd Brigade headquarters in Sausage Valley, walked over to the rear battalion headquarters in La Boisselle to learn what was doing. He was immediately grabbed by Major Denton and instructed to take all the available men and report "at the toot" to forward battalion headquarters.

When the troops, about 80 in number, were ready, they were at once taken forward along the now empty communication trench. It was almost dark and there was considerable shelling, but there were no casualties as far as battalion headquarters. On reporting there nothing could be learned for some time, for all signal communication was gone and could not be maintained, and it was difficult for runners to get through. Lieut. G. C. Ross, the intelligence officer, had already made the trip to the line and had gone forward again, and Colonel Roberts was waiting for his return with the latest news of the position.

The party under Belford was told to stand by, so the boys were sent along an empty trench for shelter and all waited in the chill, drizzling rain for the next development. It became colder and more misty; and after what seemed an eternity, Ross arrived back, having safely negotiated the barrage, which appeared to be slackening.

In a few minutes the party received instructions to accompany Ross over the crater-field to the position in front. The boys were assembled and off they started. It was a strange journey up the long slope that rose ever upward to Mouquet Farm. Luckily it was still misty and the shelling had almost stopped. In the first light of dawn the swirling fog closed down and encircled the troops, and they wandered, a remote band in that shell-torn waste, seemingly shut off from all the rest of the world. Even the shells whining out of the void and falling close by with muffled explosions had a semblance of unreality. No sign of troops or any other life could be seen. After what seemed a considerable time, Ross suddenly said, "Here we are," and the party tumbled out of the mist into a trench. They had arrived in the front line.

But things were just anyhow. By the light of day the troops began to get some idea of how things were, and the nature of their position. Fortunately it was still very misty and the boys were able to move about in comparative safety. The troops were reorganised and pushed forward under a scattered rifle fire, almost on to the objective in some places; some men were sent into shell-holes in front and on the flanks. There were several deep dug-outs, strong and well constructed, but of course their entrance faced the wrong way from the Australians' point of view. Most of these contained German dead in various stages of decomposition. An attempt to move some of these bodies met with disastrous results.

The trenches were full of dead Germans, far more being seen that at Pozieres. There were several machine gun crews dead around their guns, testifying to the excellent discipline and courage of the German gunners. There were few, if any, better troops in the whole of the war zones than the German machine gunners. A good deal of booty in the way of machine guns and trench mortars could have been collected, but it all meant carrying back to the rear, and the 11th troops had no stomach for any more fatigues of that sort. The boys reckoned that they had done enough carrying. The German dead were mostly Bavarians, but there were also some Saxons, mostly young-looking, fair fellows. One of the Diggers asked an officer what the motto on one of the dead German's belt-buckle meant. The motto read, "Gott mit Uns fur Konig und Vaterland." The officer translated, "God with us for king and Fatherland." The Digger looked compassionately at some of the boyish-looking dead and murmured cynically, "Well, God doesn't seem to have done much for these blokes." It was a hard task lifting the corpses in all their heavy leather equipment out of the narrow trenches, as only two men could lift at once. The bodies had to be lifted over the parapet or parados, but it had to be done.

Later in the morning Captain J. S. D. Walker was sent up to take command of the 11th Battalion troops. As he was having a preliminary look at the old German trench that ran into the Australian front line, he failed to notice that the mist was thinning and he was shot and badly wounded outside the trench, just in front of a barricade that had been thrown across the old German trench.

As often happened in misty weather, a puff of wind would blew the vapour away, and visibility would be at once good. This is what happened in the instance above mentioned, and sniping and machine gun fire became general. There was as yet little or no artillery fire in the vicinity of the trenches, owing to the uncertainty on both sides as to the exact position of the opposing troops.

After some trouble, Walker was brought in from the outside of the trench, and though bullets were cracking close no one was hit.

A stretcher party was obtained and Walker placed on the stretcher. The trench was too narrow at that point for the party to move in it, so one of the 'bearers waved a white rag, and then the stretcher was raised to the top of the parapet and the 'bearers climbed out and prepared to lift the stretcher. As they did so the sniper fired again and the bullet hit the frame of the stretcher, making the splinters fly. Walker swore fluently but added that the b—— did not touch him that time, and the gallant bearers soon had him out of sight of the sniper who fired several shots in quick succession at the party behind the barricade, which had been pulled down to permit Walker to be carried into the trench.

It was now impossible to advance in this sector, as all movement in daylight immediately drew well-directed fire. Yet all this day there was a constantly iterated command from brigade that the advance must be made to the objective and the situation cleared up. General White, of Birdwood's staff, had from the first realised that the task was too heavy for the 1st Division and had advised a limited objective that did not embrace Mouquet Farm; but General Walker, commanding the 1st Division, thought that his troops would be able to take Mouquet Farm, and received permission to undertake the bigger task, although it should have been obvious that the troops required conserving as much as possible rather than exploiting to the utmost. The troops in the line knew that there was no earthly chance of carrying out an attack, which not only had been badly arranged from the start and which, in the case of the 11th Battalion, was already spent before the troops had even arrived at the jumping-off position.

Yet by taking advantage of the mist the 11th Battalion had made a considerable advance up the old German lines and the sunken road, and the numbers of German dead testified to the strength of the defence. Naturally the advance up these trenches was slower than on the flanks, for every traverse had to be reported clear before the line could advance, and when the mist lifted there was a small re-entrant in the line. So when further progress over the open was impossible, pick handles were stuck up at each horn of the re-entrant and the boys sapped from one to the other, thus straightening the line. A definite advance had therefore been made by the 11th and 12th Battalions which, if not according to schedule, was more than could reasonably have been expected from the troops engaged when all the difficulties, and the ignorance by the staff of the actual conditions that the troops were fighting under, are taken into consideration.

Thus, on August 22, the day was spent in consolidating the position already gained, and making the line as defensive as possible. As visibility increased and the two sides were able to locate the opposing lines more definitely, the shell-fire correspondingly intensified. The troops had, however, learned something from the Pozieres battle, and they were distributed in dug-outs and shell-holes with a few sentries keeping watch instead of lining the trenches when heavy shelling was directed at them.

After Walker was wounded, Captain R. Hemingway was sent up to take his place. He was accompanied by some more men who had been hastily collected. Among these was Sergeant-Major Shipton, and his voice was soon heard cheering up the troops, and perhaps himself, with his " 'Sall right, boys, 'Shippy's' wiv yer! 'Shippy's' wiv yer!" He was a great old warrior, but he changed his tune when a piece of shell hit him a clout on the posterior, making a nasty gash. Clapping his hand to the spot old "Shippy" told someone to let the Captain know, and then he made off down the trench to the rear, crying, "Gangway! gangway there! 'Shippy's hit! 'Shippy's hit!" and his big voice could be heard rising and falling in diminishing cadence as he made his way down the long slope to the rear until it was lost in the distance. This was always one of the memories associated with Mouquet Farm by those of the 11th Battalion who were in that battle.

There was still great confusion at brigade and divisional headquarters as to the actual points reached by the attacking forces. Both the 10th and the 12th Battalions had given their positions as too far forward, although some of their troops had actually reached these points in the initial attack. Some parties of the 10th Battalion had even occupied the Fabeck Graben, but the main body of the 10th had finished up only a little in advance of their jumping-off position. Hemingway was ordered to verify the 11th Battalion's position and report immediately he had fixed his bearings. This was done with prismatic compass. The contact aeroplane was over at stated times, but it was too misty in the morning and scattered parties gave the required signals from so many different locations that it was doubtful if the observer was able to give much exact information as to front lines.

As the day wore on the German shelling increased in intensity and an attack was expected. The troops were ready for this and had a good field of fire. There were a considerable number of casualties, but owing to the more scattered disposition of the troops the enemy shelling, though well on to the trenches, was less deadly than at Pozieres.

But the troops were by this time very weary and overstrained, especially those who had been employed on the carrying parties; and what with the expectation of attack and the continuous shelling some of the boys were feeling the tension, and messages began to be passed along the line to the effect that the enemy was massing in front. Field-glasses were used, but the officers could see no sign of movement. Reports still kept coming along, and the troops were getting a bit rattled. There was nothing more dangerous-looking than a broken waggon on the Courcelette road just in front. So, to steady the troops, one officer sent along the following message: "Seen, in the middle foreground, a man with a night-cart!" As the message travelled along the line a chuckle of laughter followed it, and the boys were themselves once more.

Even in the line at Mouquet Farm the boys never lost their sardonic humour, although the country and trenches were perhaps as shell torn and desolate looking as any in France at that time; the conditions recalled the lines—

"Where together men and torture lived with foul death, hand in hand.
Horror stricken! God-forsaken! There stretched the war-cursed land."

In this scene of desolation a few of the boys had gathered behind a traverse to have a bite of dinner in a quieter interval. The loathsome corpse-born blowflies were everywhere, and crawling over everything. Periodically a shell would explode and the dust of the explosion would fall over the group. "Have a bit of Fray Bentos, Bill," said a voice. "Right, oh, Jack." Then, disgustedly as his teeth stuck in the tough meat, "Many a b—— man this b—— has chased up a tree." The first voice chimed, "Cripes, Bill! You'll be wantin' flowers on your grave next!"

After a few minutes' silence another voice chipped in, "There's one thing about these bloody stunts, there's none of your six-to-a-loaf. When half the bloody section gets knocked, a man don't need glasses to see his bit o' dodger like he has to in billets."

Out of the sky came a shell which dropped beside the group, far too near to be comfortable. When the dust of the explosion subsided and all found themselves intact, there was a scramble to find another position. As the last man picked up his gear he cried, "Well! they can say what they like. Home was never like this!"

All through the long day the shelling went on, falling mostly in rear on the positions that had been vacated that morning, but sometimes the fire increased to barrage intensity and this made the conditions extremely nerve-racking. The casualties also kept mounting.

Later in the afternoon orders were sent to Lieut. R. A. Clarke to try and bomb forward. He organised his platoon and an advance was made against the Fabeck Graben. The attack had no hope of success, for on the first movement the troops were pinned to the ground by strong rifle and machine gun fire. After several men had been wounded, the troops were ordered to fall back to their own lines. This was the last gesture of this wretched stunt, and that night the 11th Battalion, in company with the rest of the 3rd Brigade, was relieved, and so ended a most depressing tour of the line.

The 3rd Brigade had lost 840 men, of which 79 belonged to the 11th Battalion. This made a total loss of 610 men from the battalion in the last two engagements. Besides this the battalion had suffered two of the most intensive bombardments recorded in France, at Pozieres and at Fleurbaix, although the latter was only of short duration; and if the casualties of the last-named place be added, this brought the losses up to almost 800 men since the battalion's entry into the line only three months before. It will therefore be recognised that the 11th Battalion had undergone what the troops called "a rough spin."

The commanding officer of the 11th, Lieut.-Colonel Roberts, in a long report on the operations at Mouquet Farm again pointed out that insufficient time had been given for the 11th Battalion parties to reach the jumping-off positions in time for the advance, although every effort had been made by the troops to reach their positions before zero hour.

Lieut.-Colonel Roberts finished his report on the battle with these words: "Whilst it was very disappointing that the attacking party was unable to reach its position to attack in time, all ranks spared no effort to convert what looked at one time to be a failure into a pronounced success, and in that regard I wish to bring to notice the good work performed by Captain J. S. D. Walker, Captain R. Hemingway, Lieuts. W. R. Hallahan, R. A Clarke and W. C. Belford.

"The services rendered by 2nd/Lieut. G. C. Ross during the operations are worthy of special mention.

"When runners failed to find their way at night he took important orders to the most advanced lines; was continually passing to and from battalion headquarters and the firing line across open country and in the face of the enemy's barrage, which was at times intense."

On the completion of the relief the 11th Battalion returned to La Boisselle, where the troops rested for the night.

The total casualties that the 3rd Brigade suffered for July and August in the battle of Pozieres amounted to 2,504 all ranks, or considerably over half the brigade strength.

Chapter XXIV

NORTH TO BELGIUM: YPRES

> "I have been exiled for two long years,
> Known many dangers, many pleasant places.
> I have been near to Death just when he rears
> With horrible intent, and gazed upon the faces
> Of stricken comrades after his dread leap.
> In eastern deserts I have worshipped beauty
> Austerely still, where Death and Life do sleep
> And Home is a strange dream and stranger 'Duty.' "
> —From "Songs of the Fighting Men."

RIGHT WELL might many of the 11th Battalion men apply these words to themselves as they lay back in La Boisselle on August, 23, 1916, for home was truly a strange dream in those days; and though the troops were not given to too much introspection, yet the concept of duty was beginning to be rather tangled up in their minds. Most of the boys felt that they had been used in a mere routine attack, and that good lives had been wantonly thrown away in an attack that had absolutely no hope from the first; and though, owing to their too late arrival, for which the staff was entirely responsible, they had not suffered the casualties that the rest of the brigade had in the last battle, that in no way mitigated their resentment at the futility of the whole method of carrying on war at this stage and in this sector. Many of these men were the same who, two years later, under General Monash, attacked so confidently and so gallantly, and who, when they did come up against a temporarily insuperable barrier, accepted their knock in the sure belief that there was sufficient knowledge of military tactics behind them to cause the enemy to be attacked at his weakest point instead of, as in the case of Pozieres, Mouquet Farm or later Bullecourt, throwing division after division of the best troops at the very strongest points of the line and sacrificing hundreds of thousands of men for, apparently, mere obstinacy.

At 9 a.m. on August 23 the 11th Battalion marched to the Brickfields near Albert and camped there till about 3 p.m., when the battalion was paraded and addressed by General Birdwood, who also presented ribbons to recipients of decorations won in the Pozieres fighting. The following were the men so honoured: No. 2482 Private E. Gardner, D.C.M (stretcherbearer), No. 398 L/Sergeant W. Wright, M.M. (A.A.M.C.), No. 1971 Private R. H. Kynaston, M.M. (battalion runner), No. 3146 Private L. W. West, M.M. (battalion runner).

Fifty-five reinforcements arrived from Etaples and reported for duty.

In the cool of the evening the battalion marched off to Warloy. The troops were tired, but every step was towards cleaner and fresher country with its restful and healing effect.

Next day the troops marched to Beauval, where they billeted and rested. All day on August 25 the battalion was allowed to rest by order of brigade. The boys used the time in washing and mending their clothes. Fifty-nine other ranks joined the battalion from hospital, bringing the battalion strength up to 30 officers and 680 other ranks.

On August 26 the 11th Battalion marched to Doullens, where the troops entrained for the north. Much had happened in the six weeks since the troops had arrived in Doullens, and it was not the same care-free battalion that had so gaily made its first acquaintance with the Somme.

The train journey finished at Proven and the battalion marched to Poperinghe, a fair-sized town in Belgium. The troops were billeted in a large school.

Poperinghe was the largest town that the 11th Battalion had been quartered in up to this time. The town lay a few miles over the French border and was about 13 kilometres west of the famous and ill-starred Ypres. The town was in a reasonable state of preservation at this time, although it was frequently shelled by the Germans. During this period of the war it was noteworthy for several things. The chief interest for the troops was that there were still numerous shops, restaurants and cafes. Of the last named, "Skindles" was outstanding. There was also the rest club in the Rue de L'Hospital which later came to be called Talbot House and which was the nucleus of the worldwide movement known as Toc H.

Perhaps the building that was really most appreciated by the troops was the large brewery. Not, alas! on account of its "hops," but because in the immense beer vats there were established divisional baths, where the troops used to be taken to bathe.

Poperinghe, usually affectionately known as "Pop," was always full of bustle and activity.

As already mentioned, the troops were billeted in a school. This building had several floors, and one of the first things to happen was that a man, cleaning his rifle in one of the lower stories, put a bullet through the ceiling and wounded a Digger on the floor above.

The troops were now in a new class of country: the land was flatter and much more fertile, there were splendid crops everywhere and just outside the town there were many fields of hops almost ready to pick. There was no waste land anywhere.

Summer was waning, and cloudy and wet weather was experienced as soon as the troops reached Belgium, and it remained wet nearly all the time the battalion was in this sector. During the time the troops had been in the Somme the weather had been mostly fine, and the boys had been fortunate in that, if in very little else. The dull skies and rainy weather of this northern sector were most depressing.

Still, the amenities of the town and district surrounding helped in no small measure to counteract the effect of the weather. The troops were able to visit a cinema in Poperinghe and to do quite a lot of shopping—at superlative prices—in the many establishments in the town.

One Digger spied some nice-looking peaches (the kind that grow on trees) in a shop and thought that he would buy a few pounds. He entered the "Boutique" and in the absence of knowledge of Flemish or French intimated his requirements by the language of signs. The shop-keeper was charmed and held up two fingers while his face was a question-mark. The Digger pooh-poohed the idea of *two* peaches, and held up both hands with all fingers outspread.

The shop-keeper was staggered, but proceeded to fill up a paper-bag, turning now and then to look to the Digger for confirmation. That worthy kept nodding until the bag was full, and the beaming "boutiquier" handed it over to the Digger with a "trente-cinq francs, Monsieur." "How much?" said the Digger, getting out the equivalent of a shilling. "Tertee-fi' francs, Monsieur." It was the Digger's turn to be astonished. "Thirty-five francs!" he shouted. "Thirty-five bloody 'onks for a few lousy peaches! God strike a light! I've seen tons like them *given* to the pigs at 'ome!" and he threw down the bag of peaches and stalked out of the shop in high dudgeon, leaving the poor shop-keeper feeling as if a shell had landed in the vicinity.

The battalion parades were held in a field just out of town and only light work was given. The boys, who soon learned to know better, were beginning to think that they were going to be fairly comfortable for a week or two, prepared to make the most of their stay. Nearly every one had clothes out being washed at the many "joints" that took in washing, when suddenly on August 29 orders were issued to all companies to be ready to move at once. There was no destination stated. There was an immediate scurry to retrieve the "washing" that was scattered all over the town. There was nearly bloodshed over the business, and if no one was actually killed in the rush there were at least many casualties among the clothing, and not a few garments were posted missing.

The move out of Poperinghe was only a few kilometres away to Victoria Camp, where the troops were quartered in tents. It was a muddy site with ditches full of water all round. The stiff clay and the continued rain made marching and even ordinary walking a heavy task.

As soon as they were settled in their new camp many of the boys hurried back to "Pop" to see if they could find some of their missing "washing," for some of it had been in the copper and several officers had their kit in a nice mess owing to the fact that soaking wet clothes had been hastily crammed into their valises.

Victoria Camp was situated close to a large windmill, and there were fields of beans just being harvested in the adjoining farm. There were several small towns near, among them Reninghelst, Westoutre and Abeele in Belgium, while just over the French border were Boeschepe, Berthen and Godewaersvelde. It was such a rich country that towns were dotted everywhere. To the south could be seen the pleasant range of hills which included Mont de Cats, Mont Rouge, Mont Noir and Scherpenberg, so that the battalion was now only a few miles to the north of the district which it left to go to the Somme in July, and which already seemed aeons of time ago.

Only a few days were spent at Victoria Camp, during which the weather was unceasingly wet and only indoor training and lectures were possible. On September 2 the 11th Battalion moved up to the Busseboom area, about three miles nearer to Ypres. The troops were quartered in huts in an old Canadian camp named "Dominion Lines." The Canadians had been in this sector previously, but they were being transferred to the Somme. They had the battalion's sympathies.

About this time the intelligence platoon was reorganised under Lieut. G. C. Ross.

One of the most important features of the training at Dominion Lines was the equipment and training of the troops with the new gas helmet. The old P.H. type of helmet was withdrawn, and the box respirator type issued. All the troops were put through a course of instruction and every man went through a test in lachrymatory gas in one of the officer's huts. It may have been a good hut for the purpose of gas instruction, but it was certainly not much good to the officers who ate and slept in the hut, for there was always some of the tear-gas liquid spilt, and at certain changes of the weather the gas would rise and there would be the painful spectacle of strong, hard-faced men weeping copiously over their food.

All the men were also put through a course in bombing, each man receiving instruction in live grenade throwing. Lieut. Ray Clarke, the bombing officer, had competitions going among the companies, and brought his own bombing platoon up to a very high state of efficiency. Old Bill Beck was a star performer.

There were hop gardens right alongside the lines, and the hop-pickers were at their annual task. The pickers were mostly old people and young girls, and it was noticeable how many helpers there were when the girls were around. Most of the pickers used to sit on chairs and stools and passed the time pleasantly laughing and talking. What a lot of giggling there used to be when the girls used to try to teach the Diggers to pick hops. "La Mere" used to keep a watchful eye on the girls and speak sharply to them when there was too much carrying on or if she thought that they were wasting their time. It used to be a case of "Allez vite! Coquine!" and a scowl at the attendant Diggers. But no one could be angry too long with the boys.

NOTHING is to be written on this side except the date and signature of the sender. Sentences not required may be erased. <u>If anything else is added the post card will be destroyed.</u>

[Postage must be prepaid on any letter or post card addressed to the sender of this card.]

I am quite well

I have been admitted into hospital

{ sick } and am going on well.
{ wounded } and hope to be discharged soon.

I am being sent down to the base.

I have received your { letter dated _____
{ telegram ,, _____
{ parcel ,, _____

Letter follows at first opportunity.

I have received no letter from you
{ lately
{ for a long time.

Signature }
  only }

Date _____

Wt.W65—P.P.948. 8000m. 6-18. C. & Co., Grange Mills, S.W.

Field Service Postcard as supplied to all troops.

Even if the weather was not of the best, and the climate was getting more wintry-like every day, it was a pleasant time in the first days of September, and the troops were recovering quickly from their experiences in the Somme, at least physically. There were also a number of new troops fresh to the country, and their high spirits helped to bring the battalion back to its usual fun-loving and cheerful state.

While at Poperinghe, a week or so before, one of the officers was censoring a big pile of letters. This was a job that no one liked, but it was part of the necessary routine. One letter written by a newly-joined man was a budget of information and gave many particulars as to the location and movements of the 11th Battalion. The officer asked that the man be paraded, and when he was brought along it was pointed out to him that such a letter could not be passed as it contained too much information likely to be of use to the enemy. After telling the lad just what he could write and what was forbidden, the officer handed him back the letter.

The sequel to this happened at Dominion Lines about a week after. While the same officer was going through the mail, and grinning at some of the Field Service Postcards, whose list of printed sentences was sometimes most humorouly distorted, a common form being: "Dear ———, I am quite well. I hope to be discharged soon," he noticed a letter written by the same soldier whose previous letter he had returned. The franking officer read the first few lines, and then ejaculated, "Well, I'll be damned!" and handed the letter to Wally Hallahan, his company commander. Captain Hallahan read: "Dear ———, I wrote you a letter last week, but it did not go with the rest of the mail, as the officer turned it down. He said that it had a lot of information that it didn't ought to have. *But I have sent it to you by another route.* . . . "

Wally just about hit the roof. The delinquent was paraded once more, but his "lecture" was not so kindly given as on the previous occasion.

While on the subject of censoring letters, it may be interesting to many of the members of the battalion to know that the officers soon got to know their men's letters, and the signature of most was ample proof that their contents need not be perused; but with new men, and some whose pens used to run away with them, it was necessary to read the letters carefully and delete the forbidden matter.

The Field Service Postcards were a convenient and easily franked method of correspondence, and they were very much used by the troops.

The French Army had a similar card.

By this time the first parties of officers and N.C.O.'s were being sent up daily to the lines at Hill 60 to enable them to get some idea of the conditions of the trenches and front line conditions in the new sector. Hill 60 was a commanding position just inside the German lines, and had been the scene of much fierce fighting in the past. There was considerable mining activity there at this period.

On September 4, 86 reinforcements arrived from Etaples. This brought the strength up to 30 officers and 813 other ranks.

The effect of the rest and training at Dominion Lines soon became apparent, and the troops recovered to a great extent from their experiences in the Somme, and those men who had managed to survive both battles had their comradeships cemented by mutual esteem and respect.

In a letter home, one officer wrote on September 9, 1916: "I have a good time with the boys; very rough, it is true, but very merry. The rest of the fellows are most lovable, and when off duty we generally are in each other's arms, or fighting or lighting flares or rockets underneath one another when in the mess, or playing some kind of trick; reading things out of newspapers that aren't there; playing cards—auction or poker or anything that happens to be fancied; generally quarrelling and arguing and making a noise. And then after every stunt there are sure to be some faces missing, and some seats empty, and that is perhaps why we are more gentle with each other than we might otherwise be. I wish I could only give you some idea of them all."

In the above extract, the wonderful comradeship that existed among the boys is clearly shown, as well as the extreme reaction after intense experiences that resulted in an exaggerated boyishness and exuberance of spirits.

Training continued along company and specialist lines until September 11. On that date all the bombing platoons of the 3rd Brigade held a competition at Dominion Lines. There were eight events which were closely contested, and the 11th Battalion bombing platoon won on points. The platoon won four out of the eight events.

Next day the battalion moved up towards the line. The 3rd Australian Infantry Brigade now took over Hill 60 sector of the front held by the 1st Anzac Corps. The 9th and 10th Battalions relieved the 1st and 3rd Battalions on the night of September 12/13, and the 11th Battalion marched to Brandhoek where it entrained for Asylum Siding at Ypres, and then went into support, with headquarters and "D" Company in Railway Dug-outs and the remainder of the companies distributed as follows: "A" Company in Battersea Farm, "B" Company in Strong Point 9 and "C" Company in Fosseway and Sunken Road.

The battalion transport was able to bring rations right up to Railway Dug-outs. These dug-outs were shelters built into the embankment of the railway that ran from Ypres to Courtrai.

On September 12, 2nd/Lieut. Riches returned from a Lewis gun course and he was appointed Lewis gun officer to the battalion.

The 11th Battalion was now in the famous Ypres Salient, a part of the Western Front that was regarded by the High Command as being of the highest important to the Allies, not only from a strategical point of view, but also from the moral effect that the successful defence of Ypres, territorially at least, had upon both sides. The terrible battles that had been fought all round the salient, and the fact that gas had first been used there with such disastrous results to the Canadians and other divisions, gave the sector a sinister name. It was well known that parts of the line, notably at Hill 60, were extensively mined, and the opposing trenches were extremely close in many parts, particularly so, close to Hill 60. All this and the fact that the enemy had splendid observation from the high ground led the troops to believe that they had a particularly nasty time in front of them.

One thing that comforted the troops of the 1st Division was the knowledge that they had an Australian division on either flank, the 2nd Australian Division on the left and the 4th Division on the right. The whole Australian sector, the 1st Anzac Corps sector, stretched from the Menin Road, a name that was to have dreadful significance a year later, to the road a short distance in front of Groote Vierstraat, and which comprised the point and southern curve of the Ypres Salient.

The whole salient was a rough semi-circle whose diameter was about five miles and of which Ypres was the centre, and the trenches were therefore situated about four to five thousand yards from that city. Except on the higher ground, which was mainly in the possession of the enemy, the country was a mass of lakes, streams and ditches, and the Ypres-Commines Canal was the southern boundary of the 1st Division's sector.

As support battalion the 11th was immediately used for fatigues and carrying parties. The trenches at Hill 60 were in a frightful mess and duckboards were urgently wanted, so carrying parties used to be detailed every night to take up quantities of these necessary aids to trench comfort. Every night also the enemy sprayed all the known avenues of approach with machine gun bullets, which could be heard whistling overhead. There were also set rifles, which were trained on certain picked spots, and these were responsible for most of the few casualties that the battalion suffered in this tour of the line. On September 13, No. 3305 Private F. W. Cracknell was sniped, and next day Corporal Sanson was sniped and killed at the corner of Verbrandenmolen and Jackson Streets, presumably by one of these set rifles.

For the first week or so of the battalion's occupation of this sector, although the casualties were extraordinarily few, there seemed to be some "hoodoo" over the place that kept the troops unnaturally subdued. This may have been due to the sinister name that the salient suffered from, but it is more likely that it was caused by the inevitable reaction after their terrible pounding on the Somme, from which the troops had barely recovered.

The Railway Dug-outs where some of the battalion were located were not so much dug-outs as shelters and lean-to's let into the sides of the embankment. They were mostly covered and reinforced with corrugated iron and sand-bags. "D" Company's cookhouse was in one of these shelters with a low iron roof. One day the company "Babbler" was busy at his duties when a Digger came along and started to worry the cook. "Hey! Greasy!" he exclaimed, "Look what I found in the stew last night!" and he displayed some fearful looking objects that he had picked up round the dug-outs. "Get to hell out of this," shouted the "Babbler," and he let drive at the Digger. But the poor cook caught his hand against the sharp edge of the low iron roof and severed two fingers. There was some trouble in the court of inquiry as to whether the wound should be designated "self-inflicted" or not.

The 8th Australian Battery was in position near the 11th Battalion and the artillerymen came over to visit their West Australian friends.

While at Railway Dug-outs, names were called for from those willing to volunteer for a raid. A number of officers stated that they would only take part in a raid if they were detailed for the job, but that they would not volunteer. Asked by Colonel Roberts if he would be willing to conduct a raid, one officer replied that he did not believe in raids on a small scale and that he would not volunteer for the enterprise, but said he would not mind taking part in a real good hop-over with a definite objective, from which the troops did not have to withdraw after making the attack. This pretty well expressed the feelings of most of the troops.

The following is the list of officers of the 11th Battalion in the field on September 14, 1916: Headquarters: Commanding Officer, Lieut.-Colonel S. R. Roberts; Adjutant, Captain K. MacLennan; Medical Officer, Captain E. H. Fisher; Intelligence Officer, Lieut. G. C. Ross; Signalling Officer, Lieut. A. C. Brodie; Machine Gun Officer, Lieut. L. G. Riches; Bombing Officer, Lieut. R. A. Clarke; Transport Officer, Lieut. A. G. Burgess; Quartermaster, Lieut. G. Egg. "A" Company: Captain R. Hemingway, 2nd/Lieuts. W. Dent-Young, P. W. Lyons, D. Hardy and W. W. Graham; "B" Company: Temporary Captain W. Kruger, 2nd/Lieuts. J. L. Barry, C. Prout and W. A. Ayling; "C" Company: Captain Dixon Hearder, Lieut. R. Hall, 2nd/Lieuts. R. Beattie, F. R. Beasley and A. C. Elliott; "D" Company: Temporary Captain W. R. Hallahan, Lieuts. W. C. Belford, J. M. Aitken and 2nd/Lieut. L. C. Cooke.

On September 17 one officer and 64 other ranks from wounded and reinforcements joined the battalion. The actual strength was now 27 officers and 824 other ranks.

On September 19 the 11th Battalion took over the section of trench in front of Hill 60 and including the famous crater. This was the result of a large mine that had been exploded some time previously. It was a huge hole. On the left of the battalion position was "The Gap," a wide, marshy interval between the high ground of the Hill 60 sector and the next rise. There was no trench at this place, and no defensive position for a considerable distance back when the 1st Division took over the line. Even when the 11th Battalion took over, though a good deal had been done in the way of improvement, yet the whole area was in a shocking condition. The trenches were shallow, disconnected, full of mud and water, and generally in a very dilapidated state. General Walker told the troops of his division that they had only two months to prepare for winter. If he did not actually state that the 1st Division was going to winter at Ypres, at least that is the impression that he conveyed to the troops, and so the boys made every effort to make the sector habitable.

No one, not having seen the sector before and after the Australians' occupation, would have believed that such a transformation could have taken place in such a short time. The trenches were drained. "A" frames and duckboards were put in and the walls revetted where necessary, parapets raised and strengthened, dug-outs and shelters made and all surplus water drained into the ditches and ponds behind the lines. For the first few days after the "A" frames were put in, the water flowed continually under the duckboards and this had the effect of drying the area very considerably.

"A" frames were so named on account of their shape, and were made of timber with the cross-piece much nearer the apex than in the letter "A." These frames were inserted in the trench with the apex pointing downward. The duckboards rested on the cross-bars, leaving a drain underneath for the water to flow along the bottom of the trench.

The engineers and pioneers had worked with a will and, of course, the infantry, being convinced that they were there for the winter, did not spare themselves.

During the extensive digging and in making the alterations to the trenches numerous long-dead bodies were dug up. These were French, German, British and Canadian soldiers, who had fought or had been in occupation there. Numbers of these had possibly been killed by the explosion of the big mine on Hill 60.

On September 20 a small mine was fired by the Canadian Tunnelling Company near the crater. This resulted in some damage to the enemy trenches and considerable groaning was heard from the direction of the enemy. A little damage was done to the 11th Battalion lines and one man was injured by a fall of earth.

The wire defences in front of "A" Company's position were in a very poor state, so a wiring party was detailed to put up a belt of wire in front of their sector.

When the battalion had moved up to the line "A" and "B" Companies took over the front line system, while the other two companies were in close support in trenches about 75 yards in rear. After three days the companies changed over. The tour of duty proved to be particularly quiet, and gradually the feeling that there was a "hoodoo" on the sector wore off. The improvement in the living conditions in the trenches had a lot to do with this happier feeling.

There was a slight interchange of artillery fire—that is, slight compared to the awful shelling of the Somme—some sniping and a small "hate" every evening about 4 p.m. This "hate," which was almost as regular as clockwork, mostly consisted of trench mortar bombs and grenades. The trenches were so close together at this point that "Jerry" used to throw over his dreaded "rum-jars," minenwerfer bombs, which burst with such a shattering detonation. The boys soon got to know how to avoid these bombs, which fell mostly on the support line which suffered considerably but in a literal sense, for it was mainly the trenches that were destroyed and the troops had the daily job of repairing the damage after the strafe was over.

A section of the 3rd Light Trench Mortar Battery which was stationed in the support lines used to give Fritz as good as he gave. The Stokes mortars with which these batteries were armed could be fired very rapidly and the bombs had an effective burst.

When the 11th Battalion moved up to the line some of the batmen of "D" Company had souvenired a primus stove, and these lads determined to take it up to the line with them. It was a stove of the "noisy" variety; many other adjectives could also have been applied to it, but "noisy" was its most fitting connotation. It had been carried into the trenches by "Smithy," Captain Hallahan's batman, who was generally cook as well. "Smithy" thought that the primus would be a boon, and so it was, but not in the manner he had first anticipated. This primus stove was undoubtedly the hardest in the world to start, but once going it was quite efficient, though it made a roar like an aeroplane engine starting up.

The batmen soon used up the bottle of methylated spirit that they had brought into the trenches, so one of them suggested trying to start it with whisky, of which the officers had a limited supply—for medicinal purposes. It was simply amazing how much whisky that primus took to start it.

One day while in the support line the batmen managed to get the stove going in order to make some afternoon tea. Admittedly it was a quiet sector. One of "D" Company's officers was passing the dug-out occupied by the trench mortar boys, when suddenly there was an unholy rush and several of the troops became jammed in the door of the dug-out in their eagerness to get inside. There was some cursing and swearing before the congestion was relieved, and then one of the trench mortar lads saw the 11th officer gazing at them in mild surprise. "Quick, sir! Duck in here," he cried. The officer gazed around but could not see or hear anything dangerous. "What's up, anyway?" he asked. "A b—— rum-jar coming," said the Digger. "You listen." Comprehension dawned on the officer, and he started to laugh. "Why, that's only our old primus!"

The relieved troops sidled out of the dug-out looking very sheepish, but they were cheered up a bit when the lieutenant promised them some tea when the billy boiled.

When the companies changed over on September 22, the relieving companies had the wind up because a gallery of one of the mines had been blown in by the Germans on the previous day, and a number of casualties had been caused by the gas generated by the explosion. About 40 cases were treated at the aid-post, but they were not serious. The troops going into the crater at Hill 60 did not quite know what to expect. At this point the trenches were only about 30 yards apart, so it was rather disconcerting to think that hostile troops lived and worked just over the parapet, so to speak.

One day there was a lot of short shooting by the 18-pounders. The artillerymen certainly had not much margin, and there was a great amount of "dud" ammunition being sent forward about this time. But, while allowing for everything, it did not help the poor infantryman any, and no troops like to be shelled by their own artillery. "D" Company was occupying the crater and the 18-pounders were making a target of that unhealthy spot. Sergeant Mick Corin stood it as long as he could, and then dashed back to "D" Company's headquarters, carrying a still warm dud shell in his arms. "God starve the crows!" he cried, "all the new blokes are closer to the ground than a snake's belly! It's bad enough to be shelled by Fritzy, but it's over the b—— fence when our own blokes put in the rough stuff. Look at that, sir!" and he held up the dud shell.

Captain Hallahan immediately got on to battalion headquarters and in due course the expected reply came back from the gunners to the effect that it must have been some other battery firing. However, the short shooting ceased, and that was as much as the front line troops could reasonably hope for.

As the trenches were so near to the enemy all the troops used to exercise the greatest caution, and talked almost in whispers. But, not for long. "D" Company's headquarters was only a few yards away from the crater, and soon after arrival in the front line the batmen started up the primus, and an argument as well. In a few minutes the stove was roaring like a homing bombing 'plane. The boys did not worry about whispering after that.

At nights the German transport could be heard coming up behind the German lines. Harness could be heard jingling and gruff voices talking. Laughing could be heard sometimes. These sounds came over from the other side of a high rise and the actual direction of the sounds was difficult to locate, and the rendezvous of the German ration parties was doubtless changed frequently. Although these nightly evidences of enemy movement were duly reported to battalion headquarters and from there passed on to brigade and division, no artillery action was used against them, possibly because retaliation would have fallen on Australian transport and ration parties which were similarly engaged at the same hours.

On the morning of September 23, while the battalion was at stand-to, the troops were ordered to remain in their positions after the usual hour for stand-down, because the morning was very misty. Suddenly the sentry nearest the gap called the attention of his mate to some movement not far off. As there were patrols covering the gap every night, the men thought it not unlikely to be some of their own troops. As the forms took more definite shape in the thick mist, they were seen to be cautiously moving toward the trench. All the boys had now crowded to the parapet to see what was doing, and it was soon noticed that the men in No Man's Land wore the distinctive "tin lid" of the British forces, so the troops in the trench waved them in.

The patrol, however, who evidently belonged to the battalion on the other side of the gap, appeared completely bushed, as they might well be on such a misty morning, so they hesitated, evidently thinking that they had got to the wrong side; and as the mist settled round them once more they silently withdrew. When the mist lifted again the party could be seen approaching the German wire. Immediately voices could be heard calling "Kommen Sie hier her" and the Germans could be seen waving to them.

The party stopped once more, and as the light was now much better they must have distinguished the coal-scuttle helmets of the Germans, for, with one accord, they turned and made off down the gap, dodging the shell-holes as they ran. Mud or no mud they made excellent time. They were followed by a fusil- ade of shots, but that only encouraged them in their efforts to make the English Channel their first stop.

During the course of the day on September 23, almost at the end of this tour in the line, Sergeant Martin Delbridge met his death in a most unfortunate manner. Sergeant Delbridge was cautioning some new hands about bobbing up and down when observing over the parapet. He explained that quick movements were almost sure to attract the attention of the enemy. After showing the troops how not to observe he then said: "You ought to raise your head slowly, like this." Suiting action to the word, he slowly raised his head above the parapet and was immediately shot through the brain. Delbridge was a splendid type of soldier.

The battalion was relieved on the night of September 24 by the 10th Battalion. The relief passed without incident. There were only six casualties in the 11th Battalion during this tour of duty, three of these casualties being killed. This is sufficient indication of the quietness of the sector. The 12th Battalion had only one casualty.

After relief, the 11th Battalion marched out by way of Ypres to the Asylum Siding, where the troops entrained for Vlamertinghe. It was most eery passing through Ypres by night. Everywhere were the gaunt skeletons of houses and the impressive ruins of the once splendid Salle des Drapeaux (the Cloth Hall) towered over the great empty square. The once busy city was quite silent, the only sounds being the echoing footsteps of the troops in the deserted streets and the low murmur of subdued conversation. Occasionally a shell would whine over, and the crash of the explosion would reverberate

The Ruins of Ypres. (Official Photo.)

among the ruins and add to the already pitiful destruction.

It was with feelings of profound relief that the town was left behind, and many were the backward glances toward that tragic city.

On arrival at Vlamertinghe, the troops marched to Halifax Camp, where the troops were quartered in huts. It is indicative of the close association this whole area had with the Canadians that so many camps, hospitals and other sites were named by the Dominion troops.

Lieuts. W. Belford and A. Brook were detached and sent to 1st Division infantry school near Boeschepe, the former to act as instructor and the latter as quartermaster.

Privates Munro, Mays and Smith reported to division headquarters to undergo examination as candidates for the Royal Flying Corps.

On September 25 the troops had the luxury of a hot bath and a change of underclothing. The baths at this camp were among the best that the troops came into contact with. The "baths" were almost invariably shower baths, that is to say, water was sprinkled on to the troops in varying quantities, and it was often icy cold, and sometimes the pipes refused to run and the troops could hardly get the soap washed off themselves. Still it used to be a wash of sorts, and there was always the welcome change of clothing and socks.

On September 26 Major J. S. Denton, D.S.O., left the 11th Battalion to take temporary command of the 10th Battalion.

The following day Captain G. F. Mason reported for duty from the Australian Provost Corps, with which he had been serving since the 1st Division left Egypt in April, 1916.

On September 28 a party of 24 men, consisting of miners and earth-workers, marched out to join the 1st Pioneer Battalion. In the afternoon the battalion was inspected by Major-General Walker, C.B., D.S.O. The parade strength was 24 officers and 648 other ranks.

Captain G. G. Campbell reported back from wounded and 34 reinforcements joined up on September 29. The total battalion strength was now 32 officers and 935 other ranks. This was almost up to full strength.

A lecture was given to all ranks by Major Nicholas, of the 3rd Field Ambulance, on the subject of "Trench Foot." This was a painful and sometimes fatal disease contracted by troops in muddy and wet sectors of the line. The disease frequently was the cause of excessive loss to the effectual strength of units, and all precautions were taken by those in authority to keep it in check. Whale oil was issued to the troops to rub on their feet in cold, wet or muddy conditions.

Lieut.-Colonel Roberts left for England on September 30. Though it was not realised at the time, this was his last association with the 11th Battalion in the field. Temporary Lieut.-Colonel Denton relinquished the command of the 10th Battalion and assumed command of the 11th Battalion.

The weather had become wetter with the shortening days. The mud had no chance to dry, and conditions were getting wintry. The troops had been having training in the mornings and sports and recreations, when possible, in the afternoons.

At nightfall on October 1, the 11th Battalion moved over to Chateau Belge (Belgian Chateau). The troops were camped in dug-outs among the trees of what had once been a fine park. It was generally stated that Chateau Belge had belonged to an officer of the German High Command. The Chateau was a magnificent building with fine rooms. There were still some valuable pictures in the dining room and the building frequently housed the headquarters of divisions or brigades.

On arrival at Chateau Belge, the troops were immediately sent forward on a trench digging fatigue. The work was in connection with a new defensive line that was being dug southeast of Ypres. This new line was known as the Vierstraat Switch, after the name of a small hamlet, where four roads met.

During the following week the 11th Battalion was used on working parties and fatigues every night. These parties generally consisted of seven officers and about 350 men. The parties used to take tools and gum-boots with them, the latter because of the sloppy conditions. Though the work was hard and unpleasant, it was not dangerous. The troops rested during the day.

On October 3 Lieut.-Colonel Denton left the battalion for three months' leave in England, and Major L. M. Mullen, from the 12th Battalion, assumed temporary command. This was also Lieut.-Colonel Denton's last association with the 11th Battalion on active service.

In accordance with the usual custom, selected parties of officers and N.C.O.'s visited the forward area in order to familiarise themselves with the approaches to the line, so that everything pointed to a further tour of the line in this sector.

On October 8 there was a general clean-up of the line at Chateau Belge. This presaged a move, and accordingly the troops were not surprised to receive the order to march out at dusk that same evening.

The companies moved out with an interval of 15 minutes between companies, but what was most surprising the move was away from the front. After a short journey the 11th Battalion arrived at Devonshire lines, in the Busseboom area.

Next day the troops were started on a programme of instructional work.

Chapter XXV

BACK TO THE SOMME

THERE HAD BEEN a considerable amount of surprise among the troops when they had found themselves moved back almost to Poperinghe, and this turned to uneasiness when rumours began to spread that they were going back to the Somme. For a day or two, however, the troops, relying on the assurance that they were to winter at Ypres, did not take these rumours too seriously; but when the 29th Division, which had come up from the Somme at about the same time as the Australians, was ordered back to the Somme, the troops began to fear the worst. As one Digger put it, "Wherever the 29th Division goes we won't be long in following," and as matters turned out he was a true prophet.

On October 11 all the units of the 3rd Brigade were ordered to be ready to move at short notice, and 100 men of "A" Company of the 11th Battalion were sent ahead to Wisques, near St. Omer, to clean out a big nunnery in order to get it ready for an officers' school. All officers and N.C.O.'s were recalled from divisional and other schools of instruction, and the report was circulated that the 1st Australian Division was to be sent back for training in the St. Omer area (entraining would have been nearer the truth).

Among other officers who rejoined the battalion at this time was Lieut. J. Archibald, who had been invalided home to Australia from Gallipoli and had come out again with reinforcements.

On October 12 the 11th Battalion paraded in full marching order at 9 a.m. and set out on the first stage of its long march westward. The roads were very greasy and muddy at first, and marching was difficult, but things improved as the traffic lessened.

The route lay along the international boundary, with its French and Belgian soldiery at all the cross-roads, through Abeele and then to Steenvorde, where the 3rd Brigade was billeted for the night. Steenvorde was a pleasant little town with a population of about 4,000 inhabitants and there were one or two good restaurants. In the evening many of the officers of the 3rd Brigade attended a dinner in one of the restaurants. This function was enlivened by much singing and good fellowship.

Captain Keighley, of the 11th Battalion, was in great form and sang "The Galloping Major" with great verve. In fact he mounted a chair, which was set on a table, in order to better demonstrate the "bumpitty bump" of the hero of the song. He was cheered to the echo.

The troops also enjoyed themselves as there had been a pay just previous to moving.

Next morning, October 13, the march was resumed. It was misty in the early part of the morning but soon the sun's rays dissipated the fog and the lovely greens and browns of a French autumn were seen on both sides of the road. Mont des Cats, which was the first landmark of note for the 11th Battalion in the war zone, and the adjacent hills were soon left behind, and it was nearly a year before the battalion again returned to the vicinity. The route taken by the troops diverged from the main road, so as to avoid the town of Cassel which, as corps headquarters, was sacro-sanct and not to be desecrated by the feet of ordinary soldiers. The rich district of Oxelaere was traversed and the town of Cassel was seen perched on a hill among its trees and gardens. It was a truly beautiful spot, and many a poor footslogger gazed up at its peaceful roofs and envied the staff the pleasant life it must have led there.

In the late afternoon the battalion arrived at Arneke, a fairly large village and an important railway station. "A" and "B" Companies were billeted in the village, and "C" and "D" Companies were distributed in farms near by.

After some of the men of "D" Company were settled in their billet, which was a big farm with a large dairy furnished with the usual dog-wheel for turning the separator and churn, they started to have a look round. Soon they espied a shed, which, on investigation, was found to be full of rabbit hutches with live inmates, and a few "bunnies" were hopping about on the floor. The careful Madame came round the corner at the moment and was asked in Digger French, "Pourquoi lapin, Madame?" "Pour manger," was the reply. "Combien, Madame?" asked the boys. "Trois francs, Monsieur," said Madame, but added that there was no one to kill the rabbits because all the men folk had gone to "la Guerre."

The lads soon made the arrangement that they would kill the rabbits if Madame would cook them. Immediately there was a mild hunt in progress and a few "bunnies" were captured and slaughtered and Madame cooked a most appetising stew.

In an estaminet of the better sort in the village of Arneke lived a most beautiful girl. She was an accomplished linguist and musician, and had great natural charm and attraction. She had a cultivated voice and sang beautifully. She created great amusement by singing a parody on the "Marseillaise," commencing "Allons! Enfants de la Courtine, Le jour de boire est arrive," of which the following is a rough translation:—

"Come on, lads, of the barrack square,
The day for drinking has arrived.
Listen to the black puddings sizzle
They're cooking them for us.
Listen to the hams and mutton
Roasting in the kitchen.
Faith! we would be dam' foolish
If we turned these good things down,
To the table, citizens! Let us mop up the pots!
Let us keep on drinking while we have good wine
To trickle down our throats."

The parody is interesting, in that it gives an idea of what some of the French troops considered a "good time."

The girl sang other songs, but of a less boisterous nature, and she made an apology for the above and said it was "pour des soldats."

Arneke was, at this time, a huge Army Service Corps depot, and catered for about 250,000 troops. It also lay quite close to Cassel, one of the headquarters of the armies in the north; thousands of troops passed through or near the village weekly. Being such an important centre it was hard to believe that a girl so accomplished and so beautiful, and so obviously of a much superior education than her position would warrant, could be anything but a spy. But it was also hard for youth to believe any harm of one so divinely fair.

Several cases like the above were met with, the girls in question being very good linguists, and these were always in some situation where news would be easily gathered and identifications made of many units. But front line troops like the 11th Battalion rarely stayed long in the rear areas, and any suspicions were soon forgotten in the constant movement.

Next morning the battalion moved off again and marched through country that was definitely Flemish in character. Practically all the place-names were Flemish, such as Roubrouck, Broxeele and Volkerinchove, and the people passed on the way and all the villages all showed signs of Flemish influence. Eperleques was reached in the afternoon, and here the troops were halted and billeted for the night. Eperleques was a peaceful little hamlet situated among woods and orchards and seemed as far removed from war as it was possible to be.

It had been a most interesting march to Eperleques, and though the journey was about 20 kilometres, only one man fell out. The weather was fine and cool enough to make marching pleasant. The route lay through some of the low-lying country north of St. Omer, where deep drains separate the small fields. Each field in some of the low-lying farms was a small rectangular island, with a deep, wide ditch all round, and some of the farmers were getting in their crops by means of wide punts, which were poled along the sides of the fields. For convenience of working these fields were made very narrow.

The battalion marched past the Mont de Watton and the venerable castle of the same name, perched in a strategic position over the valley. It may have been a stronghold once, but as one of the boys said, "One hit with a 'five-nine' and she's a goner." The old town of Watton lay in the valley of the Liette River, alongside of which the troops marched for some time until they reached their destination at Eperleques.

This village seemed very primitive in many ways, and the inhabitants did not seem too used to the ways of troops or of catering for their needs. The boys soon bought out all the available supplies of cigarettes and biscuits and wandered further afield for more. As was the case in all the rest of the villages, the male inhabitants had been all mobilised.

By this time the boys had a shrewd idea that they were to be sent to the Somme once more, in spite of the official intimation that they had been sent to the St. Omer area for a month's training, and the previous admonition to work hard at the trenches in the Ypres sector so that they would be comfortable for the winter. The troops were naturally incensed at being treated worse than little children, and at the pitiful deceptions practised on them.

While at Eperleques the referendum on conscription, which was to be carried out in a few days, was under discussion, and the attitude of the troops was well indicated by their remarks. Many stated that one in the family was enough to be gunfodder, and that if any of the rest wanted to come they could come if they liked, but they (the troops) were not going to vote for compulsion. Naturally the recent experiences of the troops had greatly embittered them, and though Western Australia had sent the greatest number of troops per head of population of all the Australian States, and although that State gave a large vote in favour of conscription, yet the 11th Battalion in speech and manner at least was solidly against the idea.

After a night at Eperleques the battalion moved on to Zouafques on October 15. It was only a short march of three or four miles to the new billets, which were mainly rough barns in the quaint old-fashioned village. There were plenty of good estaminets and, as the weather was getting colder, the troops made good use of them for warmth and refreshment.

Just after arrival the companies paraded to the M.O. for foot inspection. The general report by the medical officer was that the health of the battalion was good. The men were in fine fettle and the numbers had been brought up to strength.

There was also an inspection of clothing and equipment.

The party of four officers and 100 men that had been sent forward to Wisques now rejoined "A" Company.

On October 16, Major E. H. Smith assumed command of the 11th Battalion in place of Major Mullen, who returned to the 12th. A syllabus of training was drawn up and this was immediately put in operation by the companies.

Thirty-three other ranks joined the battalion from wounded and reinforcements.

On October 17 Lieut. Ray Clarke was appointed brigade bombing officer, and his cheerful, ruddy countenance was missed from among his old comrades. Lieut. W. C. Belford was appointed battalion bombing officer.

Next day Lieut. Johnny Long and batman left for the town of Long, near Abbeville, as advance party for the 11th Battalion.

On October 19 the much-discussed referendum on conscription was carried out in the battalion. Voting was done by one platoon at a time, while the remainder of the battalion was engaged in the usual training. Nothing was done by the regimental officers to influence the troops one way or the other, but General Birdwood and Bishop Riley, from Western Australia, visited the battalion. A general parade was not held owing to the very wet weather conditions, but the troops were addressed in the billets.

It was now definitely given out that the 1st Division was returning to the Somme, and preparations were now made for the move. The news was received with mixed feelings, for though it was not unexpected, yet the troops had been hoping against hope that rumour was going to be wrong. Some of the new troops were anxious to see the scenes of the terrible fighting, but not many who had been there before wished to go through the "blood bath," as the Germans called it, again.

Late at night on October 20 the 11th Battalion set out for Audruicq, from which station it was to set out for the Somme. As the troops waited for their train it was noticed that the buildings round about looked rather knocked about, and even in the darkness the trees lining the road near the station looked gaunter than usual. It was learned that Audruicq was famous as the scene of a terrible explosion of a huge dump of shells not long before. This station had been used for a considerable time as the re-filling point for ammunition lorries, and it was successfully bombed by the Germans in the early summer. It was estimated that about £2,000,000 in shells went up in smoke, and every building nearby was razed flat and the trees were so blasted that even in the dark they looked mournful skeletons standing shattered along the roadside.

After a long wait in the icy weather, the troops were given hot tea and then they entrained at 1 a.m. on October 21. It was bitterly cold in the train, and few of the troops slept. The journey was by Boulogne, Etaples and Abbeville, and fortunately was not too long. The troops were nearly frozen when they detrained at Pont Remy. The battalion transport left Zouafques with the remainder of the brigade transport and made the journey by road.

Pont Remy was only eight kilometres from Abbeville and 16 kilometres from Amiens. The houses and other billets in Pont

Remy were in a poor state, and they were not very comfortable in the cold weather. There were plenty of cafes and restaurants which were thronged by the troops, who enjoyed the light and warmth so lacking in their own billets.

The district round Abbeville is famous in history as the scene of many battles in former times. A Roman camp site was quite close to Pont Remy and not far off was the battlefield of Crecy, where such a slaughter of the French took place in 1346; but the troops engaged in war do not worry much about former wars or ancient heroes. The problem of living and of finding creature comforts took up most of their available time when they were out of the line.

The cold, frosty weather continued, and all the roads were frozen hard. On October 23 the battalion left Pont Remy at 8 a.m. and marched to an embussing rendezvous near Mouffliers, about seven miles towards Amiens. On the way there was a halt in a village which boasted a great number of apple trees loaded with ripe fruit. At least the trees were loaded when the troops halted. It is hardly necessary to add that the inhabitants forgot to give the boys the usual hearty send-off. Instead of "au revoir, bon voyage et bonne chance," the most complimentary terms were "Australiens! Beaucoup brigands!" However, the peasants would be amply compensated by applying to the "claims" officer, and as inhabitants of Picardie they would be able to make out a good case for themselves.

When the buses were reached they were found to belong to the French motor transport. The troops clambered into the vehicles allotted, and the boys had what one Digger described as "the best route-march since coming to France." After a joyous journey of about 30 miles the 11th Battalion was deposited at Buire sur Ancre, where the troops went into billets. The battalion transport made the journey by road, and took two days to travel from Pont Remy.

In dull and rainy weather the battalion next day left Buire at 8:30 a.m. and proceeded to Fricourt. There were 200 yards between companies, a precaution taken to prevent congestion on the roads. The roads were in very bad condition owing to the recent thaw. As the troops left the green country and advanced into the war zone, the desolation of the country soon became apparent. The town of Albert did not seem appreciably more battered since the last visit, and the Virgin still hung precariously over the street, causing the troops to glance upwards as they passed underneath. The "Stooping Lady" of Albert was still the outward and visible sign of peaceful fields left behind and indicated the gateway to that wide, war-smashed region known generally as the Somme. The 11th Battalion marched onward until the companies came to an encampment on a high, wind-swept ridge, not far from Fricourt. Here the troops camped in poor accommodation. To make matters worse, rain started to fall shortly after the troops arrived. It was indeed a bleak and desolate spot, with brown, shell-pocked fields stretching for miles and no sign of habitation save the poor, shattered remnants of cottages, now useless as dwellings. The troops prepared for a dismal night, but it took a lot to utterly quench the Australian Digger.

Some of the boys even managed to get to Albert and elsewhere, and several were in a perfectly satisfied condition when they returned to camp. The accommodation in the area was so poor that even the Brigadier was quartered in a tent. This tent was one of the few that still had a light showing when some of the late birds staggered home. Two worthies of the 11th Battalion, carrying rather more than the issue, saw the light in General Sinclair-MacLagan's tent and drifted over, as it was a case of any port in a storm. After they had tripped over a few guy-ropes they started to fumble at the flaps of the tent. The General shouted to them to clear out, but they took no heed, and one of them managed to get half way into the tent. "Get out of here!" the General insisted. " 'Sall right, mate. We're goin' to camp 'ere," said one of the Diggers. "I'm damned if you are," said the General, now thoroughly annoyed, "Get out of here!"

The Digger looked long at the General, and it entered even his befuddled mind that the General was in earnest, so he turned to his cobber and said: "Bill, I reckon we've struck a snag 'ere. Le's go somewhere else." With that the two boys backed out of the tent and floundered off in the darkness. The General retired to his bunk, muttering, "Terrible fellahs! Terrible fellahs!" and later in telling of his experience in the mess he said: "It beats me where they managed to get the drink from."

On October 25, the Commanding Officer, company commanders and intelligence officer visited the front lines in order to get an idea of existing conditions. Their report was far from cheerful.

Second/Lieut. Simmons, from 15/11th, and 2nd/Lieut. P. Patterson, 16/11th reinforcements, reported for duty on the above date.

On October 26 Captain W. Kruger and 2nd/Lieut. D. Hardy and four N.C.O.'s left for England to report to the 3rd Training Battalion. The 3rd Training Battalion was the formation that absorbed all reinforcements for the 3rd Brigade in the depot camp in England. Here the reinforcements received their final training before being sent to France.

During the time the 11th Battalion was at Fricourt the troops were put on road-mending and cleaning and other fatigue work. The road repairing was certainly a very necessary job, but hardly the work a clear-sighted staff would have assigned to storm troops, for so it was intended at this time to use the Australian divisions.

Owing to the continued cold and wet weather the country had no chance of drying, and consequently it was becoming more and more water-logged; and where a month or two previously the troops and even wheeled traffic had been able to travel over the fields by pads and tracks, they were now compelled to keep to the roads. The great volume of traffic thus thrown on the softening roads proved too much for them, and the main arteries quickly disintegrated under the strain.

Speedy measures had to be taken to keep the roads in order and many expedients were adopted. One of the most common in the Somme area was to dig large pits just off the roads, into which all the water and mud was continually drained, and a constant stream of motor lorries brought brushwood, timber, and road metal for the repair of the worst portions. Several roads were entirely rebuilt and deviations had to be made and kept in repair while these portions were out of use.

It was a dirty, wet, muddy job for the troops, and the boys took to the work with bad grace. There were several Tommy labour battalions constantly on the job, but as these practically never did any front line service the boys reckoned that these were only doing the work they had enlisted for, and that consequently they had no grouch. As for themselves, in spite of their grousing, they did good work; but their remarks and their general attitude showed that they resented the work, especially as they knew that they were to be sent into the line almost immediately. In addition, the troops were still sore over what they rightly considered their deception by the staff in the Ypres sector that they had just left.

One day when the boys were disgustedly scraping the mud from a filthy road, along came General Birdwood and staff, all well mounted, and gleaming with red tabs, gold and polished buttons. The General passed along the scattered line of troops, nodding and smiling and speaking as was his wont. Some of the troops acknowledged his greeting and grinned in return, but many only stood and glowered in silence. After the Corps Commander had passed an officer of his staff came up to two fairly recent arrivals in the battalion, who were standing silent and glum, and asked them, "Don't you know who that was?" The two Diggers shook their heads. "Why!" the officer said, "that's General Birdwood, the 'Soul of Anzac.' " "Oh, is 'e?" said one of the Diggers. "Well, I'm Private Smith, the mug of Fricourt." The officer hastily spurred his horse to overtake his party.

Next day, Sunday, October 28, there was a Roman Catholic church parade in the village of Meaulte, which was at no great distance. Archbishop Clune, of Perth, Western Australia, was present at the service and addressed the troops.

For a week the 11th Battalion made daily attacks on the mud, or on the heaps of metal for the construction of a switch road to relieve the traffic between Albert and the area forward of Montauban and Bazentin. All things pass, however, and on October 30 the order to move forward was given.

Before describing the tour of the line that followed, it is necessary to give a short summary of the progress made and of the campaign in the Somme since the 1st Australian Division left the area in late August, just over two months before.

The northward push toward Mouquet Farm had expended itself futilely without achieving anything but a three-to-one slaughter in favour of the Germans, and the loss of the flower of the British and Australian divisions engaged. The hammer-and-tongs policy was nevertheless continued at fearful cost and ultimately by attacking on wider fronts the villages of Flers, Martinpuich and Courcelette were taken on September 15 with the aid of tanks. On September 25 Norval, Lesboeufs, Combles and Gueudecourt were captured. The New Zealanders did great work in this advance. Finally, on September 26, Thiepval and Mouquet Farm were taken and the re-entrant and salient straightened considerably.

By the time the Australians had arrived back in the Somme the weather had broken and winter conditions had definitely set in. It should have been obvious to leaders who had already spent two winters in France that an offensive at that time of the year was impossible and likely to become more so, as greater forces and a heavier weight of artillery were employed; but the commander-in-chief considered that an ordinary winter would not present any obstacle to a great advance, and he was determined to go on with his policy of continual pressure. The fact that his own troops suffered at least twice as heavily as the Germans in this process of attrition or attempt to advance does not seem to have mattered in the least. There have been many apologists for the policy adopted (tactics would be too kind a name), and it is admitted that there were reasons quite apart from the actual military situation that influenced the High Command; yet it must be obvious to even the lay mind that either the commander-in-chief was ignorant of the actual conditions that his armies had to face in this sector, or if he were not ignorant—and it is difficult to imagine that the G.O.C. of the British armies in France could be unaware of the disproportion of the British and German losses—then he was asking his divisions, British as well as Australian, to undergo greater casualties and suffering than the very meagre gains justified.

The casualties had now amounted to hundreds of thousands, but Haig was determined to continue the thrust; and on October 7, 8 and 12 the Fourth Army attacked Bapaume without success, due largely to the inefficacy of the barrages or high-explosive shell in the soft mud. Small advances had been made in other sectors, but it was daily becoming obvious to the ordinary mind that the winter would so slow up the advance as to make it almost stationary.

It was at this juncture that the Australian divisions were thrown into the battle. The 1st, 2nd, 4th and 5th Australians now formed the 1st Anzac Corps, and this corps was allotted to the Fourth Army, then operating in the Somme. This army was commanded by Lord Rawlinson and held the line from Le Sars to just in front of Le Transloy.

The 5th Australian Division, which was the first of the corps to be thrown into line, had not been able to make any progress owing to the impossible conditions.

On October 30 the 1st Australian Division relieved the 29th Division, and the 1st Brigade took over the line at Flers. This brigade had also made an unsuccessful attempt to advance, and was forced back to its own lines. It was on this date that the 3rd Brigade was ordered into the forward area.

The 11th Battalion left Fricourt on the morning of October 30 and marched along the main road to Bernafay Wood. This march, which was done in formation of threes instead of fours, was one of the most tedious of the battalion's long experience. Owing to the impassable state of the country, the whole traffic of the area was concentrated on this one road. There were infantry battalions going both ways; there were transports, artillery, motor lorries loaded with shells and afraid to leave the crown of the road lest they got bogged by sliding into the ditches on the sides of the road. There were also one or two luxurious staff cars, with beautifully dressed "rosellas" inside. Parties of men from labour and other battalions were continually trying to keep the surface of the road free from mud and throwing loads of stones into the worst holes.

All this heterogeneous mass of traffic was interwoven into one slowly-moving body of indistinguishable units. The various components of this slowly-crawling procession would move a few yards, then halt, and then move on again. A lorry-driver would see an opening and make a spurt to gain a few feet, splashing all the poor footsloggers round about with mud till their oil-sheets, which were being worn cape-fashion, on account of the rain, were all bespattered with the clinging, chalky fluid that was so typical of the Somme. The unfortunate transport was stuck most of its time. The limbers were only able to move when the whole column moved, which was only at irregular intervals. The artillery and motor waggons were in like case. Perhaps the best off were the infantry, because they could weave in and out among the other arms of the service; but even they were in a pitiable state and gradually becoming more mud-laden as they caught all the splashes from vehicles, horses and mules. Still, there were compensations.

At one stage of the march, when the congestion was slightly relieved, the authorative blare of a motor-horn was heard behind the troops. Soon a constant hooting was heard behind "A" Company, but the boys were too much occupied about finding their own way ahead to take much notice.

But the hooting was insistent and a "posh" car, bearing a divisional double pennant, came sloshing up and passed the troops amid the curses and vituperation of the Diggers, who received an extra issue of fluid mud from the flying wheels.

But the column ahead had by this time halted again, and the general's car was brought to a standstill in spite of the severe strain on its battery. Immediately an irate Tommy general popped his head out to find out the cause of the stoppage, and then he started to abuse the chauffeur for allowing a lot of miserable infantry to hold *him* up, and he glared at the Diggers, who grinned amiably back at him. The wilder he became the more the Diggers enjoyed his antics. The column by this time was completely jammed, and the chauffeur could do nothing except let his engine idle and hope for the best. The general was furious. "Damn it all!" he cried. "Can't you do something? We must get on!"

The mud was at its best and stickiest, and the chauffeur was loathe to leave his nice comfortable seat. However he had to get out, and he threaded his way forward for some distance. He found the jam so tight that there was no immediate prospect of any forward movement.

His report made the old general more savage than ever (the boys of the 11th felt that they were getting a bit of their own back with interest for the mud that was sloshed over them by the old fellow's car). The general was almost speechless with rage. Just then one of his staff noticed some infantry moving along a track on the higher ground just off the road, and called the general's attention to the fact. The general told him to see if the track was feasible.

After a long, unkind look at the mud, the beautifully-got-up officer stepped gingerly down into the road. As his immaculate spurred boots encountered the mud the nearby troops let out a delighted yell, but it was nothing to the roar that the old general got when he at length ventured forth in all his finery. What a look the old gentleman gave the Diggers. As one of the boys remarked: "It was worse than a b—— gas attack." The sight of that general and his two off-siders climbing the muddy bank and ploughing their way through some real Somme mud was ample compensation for the Diggers, while the chauffeur had also a satisfied smile on his face as he watched their disappearing backs.

Finally, after taking about five hours to travel four miles, the troops arrived at Bernafay Wood and took over the bivouacs of the 4th Battalion Worcestershires. There was very poor accommodation at this camp. The troops had some old tents and what they termed "bivvy-sheets." These were light tarpaulin covers that could be quickly converted into low weatherproof shelters. There were one or two small huts which were used for battalion headquarters and Q.M. stores. Rain fell continuously during the afternoon and night, and conditions were just about as uncomfortable as could be imagined.

The camp was on a hillside pitted with shell-holes. These shell-holes were full of water, and when tents or bivouacs were erected lower down the slopes, the weight of the men sleeping on their ground-sheets used to increase the capillary action of the soil and cause the water to ooze out of the ground in the tents and render them unfit to live in. The position was remedied by draining the shell-holes above the site of the camps, so that the surplus water in the soil could be drawn off. Truly a lovely spot for a camp!

There was a big demand for fuel and the troops scoured the neighbouring countryside for wood. There was a recently made railway not far away, and the troops often used to come back with bags of coal which they purloined from the harassed engine crews. Sometimes they would put an obstruction on the line— the trains always travelled very slowly and the crews kept a sharp look-out for broken rails or bent track—and when the train crew descended to clear the line the Diggers would remove quite a quantity of coal from the tender.

Sometimes some of the boys would start an argument with the crew of a stationary train, and when the argument was at its height, and driver and fireman were trying to make themselves heard in the din, other Diggers would mount the other side of the tender and silently pass down coal to their mates.

The Australian soldier never went short of anything, if there was any reasonable possibility of obtaining it.

Chapter XXVI

FLERS

On november 1, 1916, the 11th Battalion was still camped at Bernafay Wood. The troops were all employed on road work at this date, as were the other battalions of the 3rd Brigade. In the meantime, several officers from each unit were sent up to the line to report on the conditions, and to make a reconnaissance of suitable roads or tracks to the forward area. Captain Hallahan and Lieut. Hall, who were in the 11th Battalion party, reported that the trenches and roads leading to them were in a shocking condition, the trenches in particular being full of liquid mud. This early report laid stress on the fearful ground conditions with which the troops were only too soon to come into contact. The various battles that the 11th Battalion were engaged in had all their own salient characteristics, but in the case of Flers, one word embraced the whole operation, and that word was *mud*.

The conditions were so bad on the whole front that the intended offensive was again postponed, and although numerous small operations were attempted from time to time the weather made it impossible for any major operation to be successfully carried out during the rest of the winter.

The camp at Bernafay was so bad that the Commanding Officer (Lieut.-Colonel Hilmer-Smith) visited the Delville Wood area in search of a more suitable camp site.

All the available men of the 11th Battalion were used during the greater part of the week that followed in working parties of all kinds. The orders for the day on November 2 read:

"Bernafay. The following fatigue parties were furnished by the battalion to-day: two N.C.O.'s and 20 men for telephone line repairing; three officers and 147 other ranks for railway work; five officers and 200 other ranks for road repairs; and at 7:15 p.m. a party of eight officers and 300 other ranks for carrying Royal Engineers' stores to forward dumps."

This gives some idea of the different jobs the men were put to. Besides these there were some particularly heavy tasks, such as carrying 60-pounder shells from railway trucks to a dump, and in sloppy conditions, after heavy rain, this last fatigue was by no means a weakling's job.

The authorities realised that something had to be done to improve the living conditions, and arrangements for dry socks and warmer garments were made. An amusing half hour followed the issue to the troops of sheepskin and goatskin jackets. What a hullabulloo there was; Diggers in goatskins pranced round bleating, and grunting, and butting, and pushing everything and everyone in their way, while mobs of men in sheepskins went maa-ing and baa-ing to their lines. One of the battalion hard-doers had one of his cobbers on the ground and was going through the motion of the "long blow" in the most approved gun-shearer style, the while he bawled lustily for tar.

These woolly coats proved very warm and comfortable, but they had the serious drawback of being unequalled breeding grounds for lice.

After being out on railway or tramway construction the troops would come in soaked to the knees, so a dug-out was fitted up as a drying room, and this was a great boon to the boys.

On the night of November 6/7 the 11th Battalion relieved the 1st Battalion in the support position. Headquarters and details were quartered in dug-outs and cellars in Flers, "C" and "D" Companies in the forward position in Switch Trench and "A" and "B" Companies in dug-outs just south of the notorious Delville Wood. The battalion transport remained in the terrible morass at Pommiers Redoubt and did not shift its lines any further forward.

The relief was carried out without serious incident, but the roads and trenches were in such a terrible condition that the men were absolutely exhausted when they arrived at their several destinations. The only casualty was one of the bombing platoon, No. 5054 Private Blythe, who was wounded by shell-fire.

Lieut.-Colonel E. H. Smith and the company commanders made a tour of inspection of the front line prior to taking over. Rain fell almost the whole day, and every hour the conditions grew worse.

The two companies who were camped near Delville Wood had plenty of opportunity of visiting this famous battlefield that had been the scene of such heroic endeavour. But the actual sight of the Wood made many of the later arrivals realise that the old tag about "The Glory of War" was a pure myth. It was one thing to read in the papers about the gallant attacks of the South Africans, and the fearful sacrifice they were called upon to make; but when the Diggers saw the shattered trees and the poor, mangled remains of the still unburied dead in that nightmare place of twisted branches and pools of slimy mud, and saw the batteries of guns firing unheedingly and unendingly just alongside, these showed them war, shorn of all its glory, in one of its most dreadful shapes. The horror of Delville Wood always remained as one of the terrible memories of France.

On the night of November 7/8 the 11th Battalion relieved the 3rd Battalion in the line. Several diarists report that three Zeppelins, accompanied by bombing 'planes, visited the area and flew over Albert. Many bombs were dropped and an ammunition dump was reported to have been set on fire.

The conditions that prevailed before the battalion took over the line did not inspire any hope that the tour of trench duty was going to be pleasant, but even the greatest pessimist could never' have imagined that troops would be called upon to endure the misery and hardships that were undergone in this sector. Battalion headquarters and some of the details were housed in deplorable shelters dug into the side of a bank of a sunken road in a fairly sheltered position just out of Flers. The officers were no better off than the rest of the Diggers. The headquarters staff and any strays were crowded into a small shelter with never less than three inches of mud on the floor. As soon as this was scooped out, more oozed in from the soggy bank, and made its way through the timber and sand-bags. The occupants had to take their meals sitting on their packs with their feet in the mud; they could not stand up, the roof was too low, neither could they take off their boots on account of the mud.

An attempt to make another dug-out was "kiboshed" by Fritz, and the weather and a landslide settled another attempt. Every fall of rain raised the level of mud in the shelter and continual efforts by all the inmates were required to keep the menace, which was of the consistency of thick cream, at a minimum. This shelter was, with the possible exception of battalion headquarters itself, the best in the front lines.

The following lines were found in the diary of No. 2803 Private G. W. Cotterill, of the 11th Battalion, and they describe the conditions exactly:—

"What is this slimy, dismal hole,
Where oft I'm lurking like a mole,
And cursing Germans heart and soul?
    My Dug-out!

"Where it is—that beneath the floor,
The water's rising more and more,
And where my roof's a broken door?
    My Dug-out!

"Where is it that I try to sleep,
Betwixt alarms, then up I leap
And dash thro' water four feet deep?
    My Dug-out!

"Where is it that I catch a chill,
And lose my only quinine pill
And probably remain until
    I'm dug-out?"

There is generally a little ray of sunshine somewhere, and at this time this was furnished by the Tommy cookers. These were little stoves that burned paraffin wax, and a number were issued to the troops who were thus enabled to heat up cocoa and milk or some other of the tinned goods which were sent up as rations.

There have been many attempts to describe the conditions under which the troops lived in those terrible front line posts and trenches, but no pen could ever adequately describe the misery and privations of the men holding the line. The trenches were ghastly ditches full of water and mud, and the decomposing remains of heroes of already forgotten battles, although these had only happened a few weeks before. The unburied dead lay half covered or almost completely submerged in mud, a pitiful hand and other limbs sticking up here and there. Rain fell nearly every day, there was no drainage, and the weather was too cold for anything to dry. Everything was wet and clammy, and the men shivered and went numb at their posts. When the men were temporarily off duty, sleep was impossible, or nearly so, though it was wonderful to see some of the conditions under which many of the worn-out Diggers could sleep. The removal of mud-laden clothing was impossible. If anything had been taken off it would immediately have been lost in the mud. This is no exaggeration, for mud was the god of this sector. It ruled everything. It even bested the terrible shells. The German 5.9's which, a few months before, had caused such terrific des-

Somewhere in the War Zone. Typical of Front Line Conditions at Flers. (Official Photo.)

truction under summer conditions and hard ground, now came shrieking down and buried themselves harmlessly in the soft earth. Unless a direct hit was made, the only result was a tremor of the earth and a collapse of the neighbouring trenches, and sometimes a high spout of muddy fluid as the shell was detonated. Enemy action was the least of the trials of this sector; the troops in looking back have mostly only one horrible memory of Flers, and that is of the mud. It was as if the whole region had wilted under the terrific strain put upon it, and as if the backbone had gone out of the land, leaving only a soft viscous mass for the troops to struggle and die in.

Movement was only possible with infinite effort; sometimes it took hours for a fit, strong man to traverse a mile. The troops generally moved over the open country whenever possible, and always eschewed the trenches unless enemy machine gun fire compelled them to take shelter.

The awful conditions in the whole sector were beyond description, but these conditions were soon to have serious results which will be narrated in their proper sequence.

The medical report on the 11th Battalion, just before its entry into the trenches, had been very favourable, and the battalion went into the line in good spirits although rather disgusted with the way things had turned out, and not at all confident in the leadership of those "higher up." The men were very fit and able to see the humour of things, and in spite of the depressing conditions there were several very amusing incidents which are still remembered by those who have survived those times.

There is the story of Lieut. J. Archibald, always known as "Archie," who had recently rejoined the battalion from England. In company with C.S.M. George Lamerton, Archie was endeavouring to reach the front line by the long, gluey communication trench. Archie was rather stout and not in the best of condition, and the strenuous journey began to have its effect on him. After floundering through a specially bad bit of the trench, with mud and slop well over his boot tops, he was pretty well exhausted, and during a short spell he informed George Lamerton exactly what he thought of France and the area round about Flers in particular. Lamerton feelingly endorsed his remarks. Then they proceeded on their journey. As they neared the front line the trench got rapidly worse, and Archie put one foot into a place where a shell had burst not long before, and he disappeared in a smother of mud and water. With Lamerton's help he was dragged to his feet and propped against the wall of the trench, where he dripped mud from every part of his clothing and equipment. Gasping and spitting out several unpalatable portions of Picardie, he was a sight to move the gods to tears or laughter. Lamerton gravely scraped him down with a fragment of shell-case, as he would have done a muddy horse.

When Archie found his voice he burst out: "George, I'm ——! I'm absolutely ——! When I left ——, my girl —— told me —— I had —— to win —— a —— medal, but if she —— wants any bloody medals *she'll* —— *have to come out here —— and win them herself!*" Having thus relieved his feelings,

Lieut. Archibald sloshed his way to the forward trench, where he was greeted with unkind remarks.

In the headquarters shelter, where the officers used to wrestle with the mud, Lieut. "Pard" Riches sometimes made rum and milk drinks by using two mugs like a cocktail shaker, and shaking till there was a frothy drink made of Nestle's and the good old S.R.D. The "Pard" used to be kept busy while the supply lasted.

One day while Riches was thus engaged, Captain George Mason looked in under the gas-curtain. Captain Mason had been again seconded to the A.P.M. corps and when the 1st Division had learned definitely that it was bound for the Somme, a few weeks back, the good Captain, who had been watching the division pass as it marched to entrain, jeered at his brother officers as they passed. "Ha, ha!" he scoffed. "They're going to 'Somme,' you poor cows, but they won't 'Somme' me."

So when a weary and muddy George Mason made his appearance, he was received with a delighted "hoy!" from all present, and as he tripped over the mud-stop and then hit his head on the low roof, and finished by flopping on the muddy floor, Riches let out a yell, "By cripes, Mason! they've 'Sommed' you now!"

On one occasion the bombing officer was going up Chalk Lane to visit his forward bomb dumps to see that they had not altogether disappeared into the mud. It was quite a frequent happening for a dump of shells or bombs to gradually sink out of sight in the soft ground. Besides its uses as a reserve of hand grenades, the little island of wooden cases was always occupied by troops in dry weather. The boys used to sit on the dump and this always used to help to push it underneath the mud. There were millions of pounds of ammunition lost in this manner.

As the bombing officer was proceeding up the trench he heard the whine of a 4.2 and he made a dash for the shelter of a traverse just as the shell burst. While waiting for the rest of the salvo (Fritz could always be relied on to send the full issue, as he hardly ever varied his routine) a Digger came splashing round from the other direction and flattened himself against the bank, a split second ahead of the remaining three shells, which landed all too handy. As the lumps of clay and shower of mud started to fall around, a mildly sardonic voice asked the officer, "How would you like to be in Ballidu now, Mr. Belford?" (Ballidu was the officer's home town.)

On reaching the bomb dump, the bombs were found to be half sunk in the mud, and a party had to be sent to shift the the dump and clean those bombs that had been submerged in the mud and water.

The troops in the line were persistently annoyed during this tour of duty by the short shooting of the artillery, particularly by the heavies, and if it had not been for the fact that the shells exploded harmlessly in the muddy ground there would have been a heavy casualty list from this source. Of course the worn condition of the guns had a great deal to do with this, as even new barrels were soon ruined by the grit and mud, and the many "errors" that the artilleryman has to contend with were difficult to counteract or eliminate. Still this did not lessen the infantryman's annoyance or improve his feelings when he saw his painfully constructed shelter sliding in the general welter of mud, owing to the too close detonation somewhere under the ground of a shell that came from the supposedly supporting batteries.

Complaints were frequently sent to the artillery units concerned. These only brought the usual response that, if the troops would send back a piece of one of the shells, or preferably a whole shell—for there were many "duds"—then the matter would be inquired into and steps taken to find out the guns, if any, that were doing the short shooting. Naturally there was a snort of indignation from the front line troops, and one officer savagely remarked: "What the hell do the bastards expect me to do? Catch one of the bloody things before it lobs?" Naturally there was not much chance of finding any shells or fragments in the soft, rain-sodden ground.

The short shooting was fortunately not confined to the Australian side. One day, an order was sent to the front line troops to withdraw from all posts and trenches to a position 250 yards in rear, because the heavies were going to bombard "Fritz's Folly" for an hour and a half that same afternoon. Fritz's Folly was a small sharp salient just to the north of Gueudecourt. The troops were withdrawn, and when the time came the heavies did their worst, and that is no figure of speech, for eye-witnesses who might certainly have been a trifle biassed, stated that not one shell reached the German position and the boys of the 11th

Battalion had the mortification of seeing their own miserable trenches pounded with heavy shells for an hour an a half. If ever any troops were cursed heartily it was the artillery engaged in the operation. The only bright spot in an otherwise depressing afternoon was when the Germans, thinking that they might assist in the demolition of the Australian trenches whilst the going was good, started a return shoot. The first enemy shell fell right in the middle of the Folly and was evidently a bullseye, for duck-boards, sand-bags and other trench furniture flew high in the air, and the Diggers managed a faint cheer. They felt that things had been evened up somewhat.

But the heavies had a bit of luck sometimes. One day, two of headquarters officers were lying on the bank above their shelter, watching the heavies pound Bapaume, which lay directly in front of the sector. They were using the big signallers' telescope. One of the officers had just lowered the spy-glass after gazing at the steeple of the church, and remarked what a fine O.P. it was for the Boche. When Lieut. Brodie, the S.O., put his eye to the glass he was unable to find the steeple; in the short interval of changing over the telescope one of the heavy shells had made a direct hit.

The 11th Battalion official report for November 8/9 reads: "Dug-outs and shelters are being improved with all possible speed. Hot tea was conveyed, both morning and evening, to the boys in the front line trenches from Flers, where it is possible to light fires. Battalion H.Q. was shelled fairly heavily. 'B' Company had three men badly wounded—Private H. J. Smith, W. R. Beckett and C. G. R. Trevor.

"The aircraft were active this morning, both ours and the enemy's. During the night of November 8/9 our front line trenches were heavily shelled by the enemy, and the trenches were damaged to some extent and some men buried. The following casualties took place in 'D' Company: Killed, No. 930 Sergeant W. M. McCallum, No. 2207 Private C. G. S. Wood, No. 3942 Private H. T. Sadler; wounded, 'C' Company, 13 other ranks; number evacuated sick, 56 other ranks.

"Owing to the continuous rains the improvement to the front and support line trenches is rendered most difficult.

"The enemy shelled the front line trenches freely during the afternoon and also in the vicinity of battalion H.Q., but without causing much damage. We had no casualties."

There was an inter-company relief on November 9. The relieved companies were brought back to the support line.

It was at Flers that the boys first saw the land ships or, as they were always known, the "tanks." There was one, which had been put out of action in Grass Valley, quite near to battalion headquarters. It was a source of great interest to the boys, and there were generally some interested spectators round which on clear days was apt to call down some shelling by Fritz.

On November 10 there were 66 men evacuated, only five of these being due to enemy action. The rest were all ill through exposure and trench feet.

A German aeroplane was brought down on the right of the lines, and some reports state that a Zeppelin was brought down near here also.

Next Day, November 11, 46 more men were evacuated sick with influenza and rheumatics. This brought the total of men sent away in three days from sickness alone to 191. The 10th Battalion had 150 men evacuated through sickness in the same period, and the rest of the brigade also suffered proportionately. This is in itself a sufficient indication of the terrible privations that the troops were forced to undergo in this sector.

As already stated, much has been written of the awful conditions prevailing at Flers and Gueudecourt, and no doubt many readers have thought these descriptions greatly exaggerated; but when it is on record that 191 hardy Westralian troops, the large majority of whom were young men at their very best, and who only a short time ago had been pronounced in excellent health, were sent away through exposure and sickness after only 96 hours in the line, and that very many more succumbed after relief, then it must be granted that the conditions were truly appalling.

To make matters worse for the front line troops, there was a gap of over 200 yards between the 9th and 11th Battalions when the 3rd Brigade took over the sector, and this gap had to be constantly patrolled before it was eventually linked up. On November 11 two men were wounded in establishing contact at this point.

During this tour of the line the troops only did garrison duty. There was no attack made by the 11th Battalion.

Instructions were issued that the 11th Battalion was to be relieved by the 12th Brigade, and officers from that brigade were making a tour of inspection of the forward area. Brigadier-General Glasfurd, commanding the 12th Brigade, had been forward to the front line and was returning when he was badly wounded. The 11th Battalion official account of this incident is as follows: "Flers, November 12. Brigadier-General Glasfurd, 12th Brigade, and Lieut. Waterhouse, 1st Infantry Brigated, were rather severely wounded by shell-fire in Chalk Lane early in the morning and had their wounds dressed at the battalion aid-post, and on arrival at battalion H.Q. they were made as comfortable as possible and sent back with all speed to the advanced dressing-station. The Brigadier's dispatches were handed over to the C.O., Lieut.-Colonel E. Hilmer-Smith, for dispatch to Brigadier-General Antill, 2nd Brigade."

Though, as has been stated, the stretcher-bearers used the utmost speed in getting General Glasfurd back to receive proper attention, it took the stretcher parties ten hours to get him to the advanced dressing-station. This, and the fact that the delay in attending to him properly probably caused his death, brought the terrible conditions that the troops had to face to the notice of General White, of Birdwood's staff, and from that time greater efforts were made to render the lot of Diggers more comfortable.

It may not be out of place here to mention the extremely arduous task the stretcher-bearers had to perform in all weathers in the wastes of mud around Flers. The 'bearers worked in relays and camped in miserable shelters beside the track—save the name—at their relay stations. The "carrying" was a fearful business, and the 'bearers would drop exhausted after their carry, which required almost super-human endurance and strength. A measure of relief was experienced when horses and sleds were used to transport the stretchers, but enough horses could not be spared for the purpose, although there were thousands of idle cavalry horses in France at the time with no hope of their ever being used. Men's lives were worth nothing, but animals were valuable. The horses were in many cases much better looked after than the troops, especially the front line troops, who suffered privations that were undreamt of by their more fortunate fellows in other branches of the service.

It was in places like Flers, where everything was so hopeless and desolate that the cameraderie of the Diggers showed at its best in situations where men had to be men in the fullest sense of the word, and the unfailing and generous service of the stretcher-bearers gave them a place in the hearts of the Diggers that will survive while any record of the war lives.

On the night of November 11/12, two fatigue parties under Captain G. Mason were sent out to bury the bodies of the dead which were lying about all over the sector. The dead were all of English regiments, which had taken part in a previous advance. Some of the dead looked pitifully young, and in spite of everything were even boyish in appearance.

The padre of the 3rd Battalion accompanied the parties. Sixty-three bodies were buried and their effects collected and sent to 1st Brigade headquarters. Small crosses were erected over the graves of those who could be identified, and on the others were inscribed the words "Unknown British Soldier." As was always the case, even in the most serious or terrible situations, the dry humour of the Diggers was ever uppermost. On one cross, standing by itself, was this simple epitaph—

"Here lies a Fritzy, his name was Hutzer.
He met an Aussie, and came a gutzer."

Before concluding the description of this tour of the line it is necessary to say something about the battalion transport. Up to the time of this first winter in the Somme, the conditions of life in the battalion transport section had been more of a holiday than anything else. True, the boys had had their busy times, and a spice of danger had been added on occasion when they had to run the gauntlet of shell-fire on some of the roads they traversed or when a bomb or two landed handy to their lines. They generally managed to secure comfortable billets and generally, against all regulations, had managed to carry round on the limbers and other carts extra comforts in the way of equipment and shelter. Their trips to the line generally ended at battalion headquarters, and they had not had the long, wearisome and frightful experiences in the line that their mates had undergone. Even in the Pozieres battles their ordeal had hardly been more than slightly dangerous; and though their lines had occasionally been shelled, the shelling was very desultory and more or less accidental. When the transport lines were at the Brickfields, near Albert, a few heavy calibre shells landed near them, and one big one that dropped close to them hit the ground without exploding and slithered to a stop, leaving a trail of dust and smoke.

Some time afterwards, when most of the boys were having a meal, there was the sound of hammering. The continued "clink, clink" caused some of the boys to gaze in the direction of the sound, but not for long, for immediately there was a yell and a concerted rush in the opposite direction.

The cause of the exodus was "Mulga" Tonkin, who was seated astride the barely cool shell with a hammer in one hand and a cold-chisel in the other, doing his best to get the heavy copper driving band off the shell. The meal was cold by the time the boys returned. In those days life in the transport had been pretty good.

But now all was changed. The horse-lines were knee-deep in mud and they daily became worse. The horses were going sick with exposure and muddy fare. What had been only mild exercise for horses and men became toil and hardship almost incredible. The march up to the forward area, only a few miles from their previous lines, had taken the men nearly all day, and men and horses were exhausted before they started on their real job, that of taking supplies to the men holding the lines.

The use of wheeled vehicles was impossible, and all the rations and other necessities had to be brought forward by pack-horses. In spite of all the disabilities, Captain Alec Burgess and his men never failed the troops in the line, and many were the small comforts that "Burgie" used to bring up to his comrades in the trenches. He used to go far afield to the various canteens, which were often pretty short of supplies in those days, and buy cigarettes and other goods for the boys and perform various other commissions. Sometimes he would even manage to get a case of whisky.

On one occasion Burgess, through no fault of his own, was rather late in going to a certain Y.M.C.A. canteen, and he gave a pretty large order for biscuits and cigarettes for troops in the line. The official in charge of the canteen refused to serve him, because it was *after hours;* and although Burgess pleaded that the comforts were for the poor devils that were up in the mud, misery and horror that constituted the front trenches at Flers, the soft-job holder refused to serve him.

It is on record that that particular Y.M.C.A. man learned quite a lot about his previous history.

As to the actual journeys up to the unloading points, the most vivid descriptions can do no more than give a faint idea of the hardships involved for both horses and men. The pack-horses which had been standing in the rain and mud would be led to the A.S.C. dump and there loaded. Hot food and hot tea in containers and other rations would be picked up from the field kitchens. A start would be made for the line and men and beasts would flounder and struggle through the shelled and broken country. Sometimes a horse would slide into a shell hole full of mud and water; sometimes it was impossible for the poor brute to scramble out, and the animal would only bog himself the more as he struggled. Sometimes other horses or mules would be used to haul him out, but often a horse would sink until only his head and poor imploring eyes would be showing above the morass. A merciful bullet was then the only kindness. Many good horses were ruined beyond recovery through straining themselves in this bottomless country.

Still, the men had to carry on, in soaking rain, splashed with mud from head to foot, their boots sucking in the sticky ground, and their arms nearly useless with dragging their horses forward.

The rations were covered with waterproof sheets, but even so they were sometimes in a very soggy state when they reached the waiting troops; but that was no fault of the drivers. It was lucky that there were hot food containers and jars of rum, which were immune from the elements.

As Pozieres was to the infantryman of the 1st Australian Division, so Flers was the measure by which the first line transport judged all its wartime experiences. "Nearly as bad as Flers" was absolutely the worst a transport-driver could say of any battlefield.

The 11th Battalion was relieved by the 47th Battalion under Lieut.-Colonel Flintoff. The relief was begun at dusk on November 12 and the battalion moved back in small parties to Bernafay Wood. One man was wounded during the relief.

Next day the battalion moved back to Pommiers Redoubt, near Montauban. The roads were still in a very bad state and much congested, and marching was a slow and tedious business. At Pommiers Redoubt, so named because a strong German position had been built in an apple orchard there, there was an inspection of clothing, equipment and weapons. Several of the boys had cut off the skirts of their greatcoats, and it took a lot of persuasion by some of the officers to prevent the quartermaster charging those Diggers for new greatcoats. During the tour in the line the mud had so gathered on the greatcoats that the troops were carrying a fearful load of sticky clay, in addition to eighty or ninety pounds of gear, and naturally the troops had taken the easiest means of ridding themselves of the extra weight.

While at Pommiers Redoubt, Major J. Boyd-Aarons (now Major Julian Boyd) and Captain J. P. O'Neil and 23 reinforcements joined the battalion. It was only seven months before that these two officers were left in Egypt, but ages seemed to have passed since then.

Lieut. F. R. Beasley was evacuated to hospital, sick. The 11th Battalion Transport was only able to move from its lines with the greatest difficulty, as the ground was almost impossible for wheeled traffic.

A big attack had been made by the 5th Army on the left towards Beaumont Hamel, and the 4th Army artillery, which normally covered the Flers and Gueudecourt sector at that time, made a strong diversion and there was heavy artillery fire all night. The 5th Army made an advance, and captured 3,000 prisoners.

From Pommiers Redoubt the battalion moved to a camp nearer Fricourt. The transport moved as a separate body and did not arrive till ten hours later owing to the dreadful condition of the roads. By good judgment, the cookers had been sent on ahead and arrived in time to provide the troops with a hot meal before they lay down for the night.

It was a perishingly cold night under the "bivvy" sheets, which were all the shelter provided. A sleety rain was falling in the early part of the night, and everything was so cold and miserable that there was nothing to do but get in under the shelters. Some of the troops tried to read or write by candlelight, but they soon had to give it up on account of the driving wind.

A party of one officer and 50 other ranks was detailed for fatigue duty at Fricourt Siding immediately after arrival. These troops considered themselves badly treated, as they had to work up till three in the morning.

Next morning, November 16, orders were given to move a short distance to some hutments, but these were still occupied by a British unit, so the men of the 11th Battalion were instructed to pile arms and remove their equipment and stack it.

Then two officers per company and all the available fit men were sent off on road fatigue under the C.R.E. 1st Anzac Corps. Major Boyd-Aarons was in charge of the party. While on this road work 300 German prisoners were observed being marched back. They had been captured in the recent attack, and were very weary and dirty.

On return from this road fatigue the troops occupied the huts, which had been vacated in the interval. The huts were of the type called "Nissen"; they were constructed of iron, and the walls and roof were parts of the same semi-circle. They were lined and floored with timber. They were exceedingly cold in winter time. This was the first time the battalion had been quartered in this type of hut. But these Nissen hut camps were soon to be very common, as they were easy to erect and fairly convenient and comfortable.

All the camp was duck-boarded, and this made for cleanliness and comfort. There was a canteen near, and the boys made full use of it. After the evening meal, singing was heard from several huts. This was rather remarkable in itself, because the natural gaiety of the boys had been much subdued since Pozieres, and song had rarely been heard among the troops since then. But a plaintive melody was rising from some of the huts. These were the words:—

"I want to go home, I want to go home.
I don't want to go to the trenches no more,
Where the whizz-bangs and the Jack Johnsons roar.
Far away over the sea,
Where the Allemand can't get at me.
Oh, my! I don't want to die,
I want to go home."

Then from another hut rose a more rollicking tune—
"We are a ragtime army, no b—— good are we;
We cannot shoot, we will not fight, what —— use are we?
And when we get to Berlin, the Kaiser he will say:
'Ach! Ach! Mein Gott! What a b—— rotten lot
Are the A.N.Z.A.C.'!"

and somewhere in the huts Lieut. Alec Brodie was lifting up his voice in the old classic—

"And when I die, don't bury me at all,
Just pickle my bones in alcohol.

Put a bottle of booze, at my head and feet,
And then I'll know my bones will keep."
All this unaccustomed hilarity was due to the reaction after the nightmare conditions of the past week. If this had been the only reaction the battalion would soon have recovered, but a far more serious effect of the tour of the line was just beginning to manifest itself.

Lieuts. A. Brodie, J. Long and J. M. Aitken.

November 17 still found the 11th Battalion at Fricourt, and no more desolate spot could be imagined than this waste of country in the winter of 1916/17. The whole of the fit men of the battalion were employed under the C.R.E. 1st Anzac on road repairs. The weather had improved, and though cold and frosty the conditions were much more bearable.

Reinforcements were being sent forward in small numbers, and on the above date 2nd/Lieut. A. W. B. Pettit and 20 other ranks joined the battalion. Lieut. W. C. Belford and three other ranks were sent to hospital with influenza.

Next day the 11th Battalion was detailed to proceed to the same work as on the previous day, but at 11 a.m. instructions were received from brigade to recall all parties immediately. This was done, and all the troops were back in their huts at 1:45 p.m. They were ordered to parade with all speed in marching order. The battalion marched out at 3:15 p.m. and, after a journey of about six miles, arrived at Buire sur L'Ancre. Here the troops were billeted in rough sheds and barns.

On November 19 orders were received to move again, and the battalion marched out of Buire and made for an embussing point, where a string of motor vehicles under the direction of the French Mechanical Transport was waiting to receive the troops. Under the instructions of these officers the Diggers filed into the buses, which were of several different types. The junior officers were in the leading vehicles and the officers of field rank were in the cars of the French officers in charge of the convoy.

The fleet of buses arrived at Coisy, near Amiens, about 4 p.m. and the troops went into billets. The houses and barns in which the troops were quartered were most inhospitable and dreary looking, and immediate steps were taken to make them more habitable. It was always wonderful to see the way the boys of the 11th Battalion would "dig up" all sorts of cover and gadgets of all kinds to make themselves comfortable. The only deterrent to their activities was the fact that they never knew the minute that they would be called upon to move, and they did not relish the idea of going to too much trouble for someone else's benefit.

No one ever seemed to take any trouble to improve the billets and camps except themselves, and one of the first jobs on going into a new camp was always to make it ship-shape as far as possible. Possibly the fact that so many of these West Australian troops had been accustomed to make camp for themselves in their own homeland had a great deal to do with the celerity and skill with which they made themselves comfortable.

CHAPTER XXVII

WINTER, 1916: COISY, DERNANCOURT, FLERS

WINTER had now set in, and the troops were experiencing one of the worst winters there had been for many years in France. The late tour of the line had been under extremely wet conditions and the hardships involved were beginning to make themselves felt on the troops. Every means was now being adopted to keep the evacuations down as far as possible, but in spite of this a great number of men were being sent away every day. The battalion was still at Coisy at the end of November, 1916, and the days were mostly occupied with reorganisation and training according to the brigade syllabus. It was recognised that the troops were still suffering from exposure and exhaustion and a battalion hospital ward was established by Major Sawers, who was then medical officer, to cater for the less serious cases of sickness. In this ward the men could receive special treatment and be made comfortable without the necessity of evacuation.

Leave to England was started again, and one man per day from the battalion was about the average at this time. Five per cent. of the men were also allowed leave to Amiens, but the authorities might just as well have made it 100 per cent. for any Digger not on special duty had no trouble in getting to Amiens if he so desired. The trips to Amiens were much appreciated, and the beautiful cathedral greatly admired, as it had just cause to be, because it was and still is one of the finest examples of Gothic architecture in northern France. Amiens at this time was practically untouched by the war. It was full of life and gaiety, and was by far the finest town the boys had the opportunity of visiting near the lines in France.

On November 25 the weather, which had been rather better for some days, changed to heavy rain, and the troops, instead of training in the open, had to be sent back to their billets, where lectures and instruction were given under company arrangements. As the weather was unsuitable for parades, the opportunity was taken to get the troops bathed in the recently established baths.

Next day, which was Sunday, it was still raining, so church parade was cancelled, but the troops of Roman Catholic denomination were taken to the local church at Coisy.

While the battalion was at Coisy, Captain George Campbell was detailed to act as instructor at the Tirancourt School of Instruction, and he was seconded from the above date. Second Lieut. Athol Norrie and his batman joined the battalion from reinforcements.

On November 27 Captain Teague reported for duty and relieved Major Sawers as medical officer. Major Sawers was transferred to the 14th Australian Field Ambulance. The Major had given days of strenuous service to the boys while they were in the mud of Flers. He proved himself a man in every sense of the word and the boys were sorry to see him leave, but luckily his successor was a man of heart and understanding, who quickly endeared himself to everyone with whom he came into contact.

As part of the programme of training, a brigade tactical scheme was carried out on November 28. The weather was cold and foggy.

On the last day of the month, the 11th Battalion marched to Lahoussoye. Here the troops were billeted for the night. The battalion was now preparing to move back to the line and instructions had been given to evacuate all men who, it was considered, were not fit for a long march, and 61 men were evacuated from Coisy before the battalion moved off. The strength of the battalion was now only 24 officers and 578 other ranks. This was close on 400 men below normal strength, and this in spite of several drafts of reinforcements. When it is considered that only a very small proportion of these evacuations were caused by enemy action, it will be realised that the experiences of the last tour in the line were indeed terrible. Nearly all these evacuations, amounting to more than 450 men, had been caused by exposure and exhaustion.

The battalion started on its forward move again on December 1, and left Lahoussoye for Dernancourt, arriving at the latter village early in the afternoon. Inspections of equipment and of the troops' feet occupied the rest of the day.

Next day 400 men were taken to the baths at Viviers Mills, near Meaulte. These baths were in a large shed belonging to the mills, and were exceedingly cold and draughty. The bathing procedure was under strict rules, and only a certain amount of time was given to each batch of men; and woe betide the poor Digger who took too long to soap himself, for when the whistle blew the next batch of shivering men charged into the shed and the poor soap-covered fellow had to get dried as well as he could. But the clean change of underclothing and sox was worth a good deal of inconvenience and discomfort.

On December 3 Brigadier-General E. G. Sinclair-MacLagan, who had commanded the 3rd Australian Brigade since its inception, and who had shared the fortunes of the brigade in Egypt, Gallipoli, Sinai and France, relinquished the command. He visited all the battalions and said farewell before leaving for England.

General Sinclair-MacLagan had always had the welfare of his men foremost in his mind, and under his command the 3rd Brigade achieved a fame and reputation second to none. His successor was Lieut.-Colonel Bennett, C.M.G., of the 6th Battalion, and this officer commanded the 3rd Brigade from this time until the end of its service as part of the A.I.F.

Fricourt was the next stage on the move up to the line. The 11th Battalion reached this bleak spot late in the afternoon. The march had been slow, and it is illustrative of the congestion on the roads to note that the move order stated that there should be 500 yards between battalions and 200 yards between companies, and that there should be a halt of ten minutes every half-hour, and that there should be no mid-day halt. On arrival at Fricourt, there was the usual routine of cleaning up the camp and its surroundings.

From Fricourt the 11th Battalion route-marched to "Melbourne Camp" at Mametz. The Australian influence in camp names began to be noticed from this time. As the battalion drew nearer the line the weather conditions, which had been mostly fine, changed for the worse. It did not take much rain in the cold, wintry conditions that existed to make everything clammy and miserable.

Next day, December 6, was the occasion of another move. This time the battalion marched to "New Carlton Camp" at Bazentin le Grand. The transport, with the exception of the pack-horses, remained at Belleview Farm. (The name might have been appropriate in times of peace, but a more God-forsaken place would have been hard to find in those days of war.) The pack-horses were brigaded at railhead, and from there all supplies were to be brought forward by pack. At New Carlton Camp 44 other ranks joined the battalion from reinforcements, details, sick and wounded.

Several days were spent at New Carlton Camp, and the battalion was used on carrying parties and on work connected with the light railway leading to High Wood.

Padre John Fahey, who had been with the battalion from the early days, and who was liked and admired by all who came into contact wih him, was transferred on December 7. He was relieved by Captain Hayes, who took on the duties of chaplain.

Owing to the adverse weather, the troops had difficulty in getting their clothes dry, so a drying-room was established. The camp and vicinity was shelled by the enemy on the night of December 8 and several men were wounded.

Every day all available men were used on fatigue parties. Looking back it seems strange that the staff failed to recognise that these continual fatigue parties furnished by the troops who were waiting their turn to go into the line so weakened the men's powers of resistance to exposure and disease, and made them unable to stand the abnormal strain which the front line imposed on all the troops, that the wastage through sickness and exhaustion was out of all proportion to the work done previously. In many cases the tasks were allotted as a mere matter of routine, for it is certain that if the staff had any real knowledge of these seemingly ordinary fatigues they would never have ordered their performance by troops due for a tour in the line.

If the infantry battalions had been used for labour battalions and nothing else, the men could have stood all the extremes of weather; but the folly of utilising storm troops, or at least line troops, as labour units before putting them into the line bore its own bitter fruits.

The following officers reported for duty from England: 2nd/Lieut. K. J. Beckwith, 18/11th Reinforcements; 2nd/Lieut. G. F. Priestley, 16/11th Reinforcements, on December 9; and 2nd/Lieut. C. Pope, 18/11th Reinforcements on December 10.

The 11th Battalion official diary has practically the same entry daily for the whole period at Carlton Camp. The troops soon dropped the "New" and the camp was always known as "Carlton Camp." A typical entry is as follows:—

"Carlton Camp, December 15, 1916. Fatigue parties were employed on light railway, roads and carrying parties to the same extent as yesterday, viz., five officers and 291 other ranks; the balance of the fit men were employed on hut-building in this camp. Second/Lieut. B. C. Lehman and 16 other ranks reported for duty. Lieut. P. W. Lyons reported from duty as 'Road Supervisor,' 1st Anzac Corps. Weather conditions: some rain and fog. Situation normal."

Right on to December 21 the same daily routine was carried out. Sometimes there was heavy shell-fire by the enemy, otherwise the chief foe was the all-prevailing mud. Occasionally some of the sand-bagged huts would collapse, and the unfortunate occupants would generally have to get help to repair or rebuild them.

On one occasion the Commanding Officer (Lieut.-Colonel E. Hilmer-Smith, C.B.), "Old C.B.," as the boys generally called him, was wandering round the huts after a particularly dirty night. He espied a Digger sitting dejectedly by a collapsed hut, and asked him why he was looking so forlorn. After a few minutes' conversation with the man, the Colonel hastened to orderly room and ordered the officers' call to be sounded on the bugle. The well-known "There's a land of sunny skies, West Australia!" soon broke the silence, followed by the "Officers, come when you're called! Come! Come! Come!" (There are other versions, of course.) As the officers hastened to orderly room, the Diggers grinned and audibly suggested that someone was "up for it."

When the officers had all assembled, the Colonel addressed them thus: "Gentlemen! There's something wrong somewhere. Just now I was making a tour of inspection of the lines and I came across a poor fellow almost in tears, seated beside the wreck of his dug-out. I asked him why he did not try to get it fixed up, and he said that no one would help him. I asked him why he did not go to his platoon sergeant. He replied: 'Oh! He doesn't care.' Then I suggested that he should go to his platoon commander. He blurted out: 'He doesn't care, either.' Now, gentlemen! There's something wrong somewhere."

After telling the assembled officers their responsibilities towards their men, the Colonel dismissed them.

As a matter of fact, the relations between officers and men in the 11th Battalion were always particularly good, and most of the boys had never any hesitation in approaching their officers and voicing their complaints, if they thought there was the remotest possibility of having them attended to; but, like all independent natures, the boys from Western Australia hated to be "mothered" or interfered with in any little matters that they could adjust themselves.

However, the Colonel's homily bore fruit, as he soon found out, for next day as he was making his usual tour of inspection he came round a corner where two officers were themselves busily engaged in rebuilding their sand-bag hut which had collapsed. The two officers were filling new sand-bags and placing them in position by whacking them with a shovel. The Colonel's thoughts can better be imagined than described, when he heard the following dialogue, interspersed with loud thumps as the bags were placed in their proper positions: "Nobody (thump!) loves me (thump! thump!)," said one voice. "Go to your (thump!) sergeant (thump!), my man," answered another voice. "He doesn't love me (thump!)." "Well, then (thump!), go to your officer, my lad." "He (thump!) doesn't love me, either." With that the first speaker let out a loud wail. "Never mind, my lad, I love you," answered the other. Both officers happened to look up from their work and they noticed the Colonel gravely contemplating them. They both came to attention, and the "Old Man" saluted and passed on without a word.

On December 21 the 11th Battalion was used for carrying parties and for railway construction all day, and in the evening it relieved the 9th Battalion in support. Eleventh Battalion headquarters proceeded to Flers and "A" Company took over "Gap Trench" while "B" Company went to "Switch Trench." The route lay through Longeval and Delville Wood. "C" and "D" Companies took over the new portion of Carlton Camp, which had only lately been completed. The relief was completed without incident.

While in support, the battalion was used on all the work and fatigues incidental to the forward area: carrying parties, reclaiming work, revetting and construction of trenches, hut-building, preparing material for construction of intermediate railway, and many other duties. These all used up the energies of the troops.

There were occasional bouts of heavy shelling and the weather was the usual sample of 1916/17 Somme winter conditions, which is to say, indescribable. Except that the trenches and forward lines had been for some time occupied by Australian troops, and were on that account greatly improved since the last tour of duty, the general conditions were much the same as they had been in November, so a second description is needless. Of course there were some humorous interludes to lighten the burden.

The tales that follow were related by Captain Rex Hall, who was camped with "Pard" Riches in a cellar at Flers.

"On the left of the village towards the front line were what remained of allotment gardens. Fritz at almost regular intervals sent down four coal-boxes on to the gardens. Directly the smoke cleared away the troops, like a lot of rabbits, came tumbling out of their burrows and gathered a harvest of the potatoes that had been unearthed by the shells, and bolted back to their dug-outs on the alarm of another four shells. Les. Riches and I had a good view of it all from the entrance of our cellar, and many a laugh we had."

Just about this time white suits and white overalls had been issued to the troops in the front line. These were to be used on patrol work on account of the snow. Acid drops (yes, the good old lollies) had also been issued to the battalion quarter-masters for distribution to the troops, possibly to keep them from coughing. Somebody must have had a headache to have evolved ideas like those. When Major Boyd-Aarons visited the posts he was delegated to take the supply of acid drops round the lines. It was a sight for the gods to see the good Major enveloped in a suit of white overalls, going round issuing acid drops to the disgusted Diggers.

Captain Hall also tells this one: "During our

Captain Rex Hall, M.C.

turn in the line (I think each company did a week) the only way by which the relief could be made was over the top, as the trenches were half full of water and liquid mud, and once in you stayed put.

"Lieut. Archibald had not long before received a gift of a pair of long *white* stockings to wear under his gum-boots. I was on duty and was to be relieved at daybreak by 'Archie.' We saw him waddling over the mud accompanied by his runner. Suddenly he stumbled and slid into a shell-hole. With great presence of mind he threw himself on his back, pulled his feet out of his gum-boots, which were stuck fast in the mud, and he lay there on his back, waving his white-stockinged legs in the air till his runner had salvaged his gum-boots. What the Hun thought of it all I don't know. He kept very quiet, although it all happened in full view of his front line trenches."

Captain Hall goes on to say: "Sergeant Bill Plunkett made history by refusing to come away from his Lewis gun post at the end of the week. He stayed the full fortnight, helped by an extra issue of rum. Rum saved the lives of three-quarters of the troops.

"We had our greatcoats with us, but the mud clung to the skirts and made them so heavy that the troops could not carry them, so they cut off the skirts. What a row there was when we came out.

"It took two days to evacuate the wounded from the line owing to the mud, although it was fairly peaceful in the trenches. Trench foot was our worst enemy."

The season was now coming round to Christmas once more, but a less Christmassy place could not be imagined. The boys made what preparation they could, which was not much. The ensuing extract from the official diary will give some idea of that Christmas Day, which was for some of the 11th Battalion —though a fast diminishing band—the third Christmas that they had spent away from home:

"Eleventh Battalion, December 25, 1916, Flers. The following fatigue parties were furnished by the battalion for duty to-day: one officer and 50 other ranks for revetting in Hay Reserve ('A' Company) at 6 p.m.; one officer and 50 other ranks as above at 9:15 p.m. ('B' Company); one officer and 30 other ranks for carrying to Hay Avenue (a trench) and Smoke Trench from 6 p.m. ('A' Company); one officer and 30 other ranks at 4 p.m. carrying from brigade headquarters to Tank Dump ('D' Company); one N.C.O. and 24 other ranks at 9 a.m. for reclaiming work in Grove Alley (bombing platoon); one N.C.O. and 24 other ranks for brigade headquarters railway repairs, 5:30 p.m. ('B' Company). The weather conditions are fine with strong south-west wind blowing. The general situation is very quiet, only a few shells falling near the company positions. One man was wounded—No. 3452 L/Corporal W. E. Rowe. Ninety-six other ranks joined the battalion from reinforcements. Captain Hemingway and two other ranks returned from the divisional school at Flixecourt."

Truly a happy Christmas!

The remainder of the tour of duty in support was merely a repetition of the above, and on December 30 the 11th Battalion relieved the 9th Battalion in the front line. The weather, which had been fine and mild, changed to rain with disastrous results to the trenches, as will be seen by reading the official diary for December 31, 1916:

"Eleventh Battalion, Bull's Road. During the night December 30/31, the companies in the front and support trenches were employed in repairing the damage caused to the trenches by the heavy rain. This was continued through the day as far as possible. The amount of damage was considerable, the revetting in many places having given away. Shelters and dug-outs had in many places fallen in, consequently the garrison had to work continually until the trenches had been made habitable. Hot food was cooked in dug-outs in Flers and conveyed in hot food containers to the front line in the early morning and after dusk.

"During the day one of the dug-outs used by 'A' Company as a cookhouse was hit by a shell, and the following men were wounded by the falling debris: No. 3708 Private A. J. Asprey and No. 3407 Private D. MacKay."

That is the final entry for 1916, and it leaves the 11th Battalion well in the mud of the Somme.

A bit of verse which, if not exactly poetry, is at least a good word-picture of the conditions existing at that time is here appended. It was found in the diary of No. 2843 Private G. W. Cotterell, of the 11th Battalion:

"Shattered and shelled by monstrous guns,
Harrassed and harried by wily Huns;

Sniped at by snipers day and night,
Enfiladed from left and right.
Rifles clogged by mud and dirt,
Livestock farms in vest and shirt;
Trenches nearly full of water,
Worried by a big trench mortar.
Parapets blown to smithereens,
Rum-jar broken, awful scenes;
Ration party blown to bits,
Shortage of water, but plenty Fritz.
Matches wet and pipe gone west,
Shelled all night without a rest;
With bully beef and mud-caked bread
(Of course you know how we are fed).
I was just about to have my tea,
When a jolly old sergeant came to me.
He said: 'This seems very much like hell,
But Fritz is having it just as well.'
A pleasant thought—I hope it's true,
May he be battered black and blue;
So I went to sleep, my pillow a bomb,
In a little wet ditch, in the land of the Somme."

ANON.

CHAPTER XXVIII

FLERS, 1917: DERNANCOURT, BRESLE

"To-morrow, and to-morrow, and to-morrow,
Creeps in this petty pace from day to day,
To the last syllable of recorded time;
And all our yesterdays have lighted fools
The way to dusty Death. Out, out, brief candle!
Life's but a walking shadow; a poor player
That struts and frets his hour upon the stage
And then is heard no more. It is a tale
Told by an idiot, full of sound and fury
Signifying nothing."
                                        "Macbeth."

So MIGHT the Digger have greeted the 1st of January, 1917, when hopelessness and disillusion were at their worst, and the days ahead only promised to be uninspiring repetitions of their predecessors. It was at this period that the spirit of the Australian troops was at its lowest point and nothing seemed clear but the absolute uselessness of the operations that they were engaged in. It was not that the Diggers did not adapt themselves to whatever there was of war or work, with the resource that was peculiarly their own, but, owing to the needless shattering of the fine battalions in their first battles on the Somme, and what they considered their deception at Ypres (this was a real source of dissatisfaction and disappointment to the troops, whatever colour has been put upon it by those who should know the facts); and finally the terrible physical strain put upon them in the work and service in the trenches at Flers, and their knowledge of the poor generalship involved, they had been rendered so disgusted and so war-weary that their efficiency naturally suffered. In this state of indifference and hopelessness the 11th Battalion took up the burden of war in January, 1917, in the middle of the French winter.

On New Year's Day, 1917, the 11th Battalion was still in the line at Smoke Trench in front of Flers, and battalion headquarters was situated at Bull's Road. A great deal of work was done on this date in the front line and the approaches. There were carrying parties taking material for revetting and parties cleaning up the trenches and laying down new duckboards.

There was a party of one N.C.O. and six men engaged in wiring the gap between the right and left companies of the sector. This party laid a stretch of wire 50 yards long by five yards wide as a protection at this point. There were altogether 177 all ranks employed on these fatigues, and most of the work was done during the night. The communications were so bad that most of the troops preferred the risk of going over the top rather than walking in the sloppy trenches. Once, a party, under Lieut. J. Aitken, moving overland, missed its way in the dark and stumbled into the German lines. It was a distinct case of "Hail and Farewell," and the boys did not stand on the order of their going. There was a considerable amount of shell-fire in the front area, but there were only six casualties in the battalion. An inter-company relief took place on the night of January 1/2, and "A" and "B" Companies relieved "C" and "D" Companies.

The weather continued to be showery, and muddy conditions increased. The rations were still being brought up to the battalion by pack-animals. While the pack-train was returning on January 2, there was some shelling and No. 1074 Driver H. Wooley was badly wounded.

The transport conditions were somewhat better than in November, but that is not saying much in their favour, as wheeled traffic was still utterly impossible in the forward areas.

Captain G. F. Combs reported for duty on January 22 from the 3rd A.L.T.M. Battery. He was posted to the command of "B" Company.

A draft of reinforcements, comprising 120 men of the 21/11th, was brought forward to Mametz and retained there for roadmaking and improving the camp site.

The front lines remained fairly quiet, but on January 3 the enemy shelled the back areas and Bull's Road during the morning. Ten men of the 4th Battalion were killed by one shell. The 11th Battalion transport also suffered, two horses being killed near the railhead at Montauban, and one man, No. 1333 Driver Dixon, was slightly wounded.

An entry from the battalion diary, dated January 5, is illustrative of the conditions obtaining at this period:

"Eleventh Battalion, Bull's Road, N.31.b.30.15. The night of January 4/5, 1917, passed without any unusual occurrence. Enemy activity about as usual. Lieut. R. Beattie with a working party of 12 other ranks erected 75 yards of wire entanglements in the Gap, working from 7 p.m. till 1 a.m. Improvements to trenches and dug-outs carried out as usual.

"No. 1 Observation Post in our right sector of the front trenches was struck by a 4.2 shell at 11:45 a.m., which killed No. 4449 Private W. Butcher and wounded four others, viz., No. 1855 Corporal H. J. Fowles, No. 407 Private L. W. Blakemore, No. 4895 Private F. M. Steel and No. 5063 Private S. T. Brennan. The last-named died of wounds about five hours later. Privates Butcher and Brennan were buried in the cemetery near the aid-post at N.25.b.8.6. (this is a map location, easily understandable and is a positive identification of locality). Inter-company relief was carried out on night of January 5/6, 1917, without a hitch, the relief being completed by 7 p.m. The weather conditions have been fine and mild, but towards evening it became cold and some snow fell during the night."

For the next three days the conditions of trench life remained much about the same, and the wiring of the Gap was continued without much enemy interruption.

A good deal of trouble and annoyance was caused by the short shooting of the artillery. As before stated, it was always very hard to get the artillery to admit that the short shooting was caused by any of the batteries engaged, although it is a well-known fact that a sudden drop in the temperature would affect the range of guns to a great degree. In very cold weather 18-pounders would lose 500 yards in 2,500, and heavier guns were affected correspondingly. Many troops in the P.B.I. knew these things, and yet all complaints were treated with contumely and disbelief.

A good story is told of some infantry who had been shelled quite a while by their own artillery. At length one of the officers made back to the battery that was doing most of the short shooting and offered to surrender to it if only it would stop firing.

It would have been much better policy if the artillery had admitted the error, for an error that is admitted can always be corrected; but the consistent policy of denial of error destroyed the infantryman's confidence in the batteries at this time, for the troops argued that if the gunners did not know, or at least refused to admit, where their shells went, the next shoot was just as likely to drop on their own front lines as on those of the enemy.

On January 8, officers of the relieving battalion (the 50th) came to take over, and that same evening the 11th Battalion was relieved without incident and marched out of the line in small parties to Coolgardie Camp, where the last details arrived about 9:30 p.m. There had been a few casualties from shell-fire earlier in the day, but none of them were serious.

Next day the battalion set out for Quarry Siding, where the men entrained to Meaulte. On arrival there the battalion marched to Dernancourt, in which town the troops were billeted. Though the 11th Battalion had many rougher and more sanguinary tours of the line than the experiences at Flers, there were none that seemed so utterly useless or so hopeless, or which in any way approached the depth of extreme physical misery than the long period that the troops suffered in the mud which the arrival in Dernancourt terminated. There was no chapter in the 11th Battalion's history to which the boys were so pleased to write "finis."

On January 9, Lieut.-Colonel E. Hilmer-Smith took over the duties of brigadier, during the temporary absence of Colonel Bennett. Lieut. Bickford returned from hospital and reported for duty.

The battalion spent several days at Dernancourt. During this time the usual overhaul after a tour of duty in the line was made. All the troops were fitted with new boots and received new issues of clothing. There were muster parades of all the companies and headquarters details. The batmen and other parade-hoppers were rounded up and ordered to be on parade without fail at a certain hour. Naturally there was a great burnishing up of equipment and rifles. Some of the rifles were disgracefully dirty, and "Scotty's" was in a terrible state. Some one suggested firing a shot through to loosen the fouling. "Scotty" thought the idea sound, so, suiting the action to the advice, he put a cartridge in the breach, pointed the rifle at an apparently empty field, and let fly. A wild scream was the result, and all rushed out to see an old Frenchwoman lying down holding up one of her legs, while the whole neighbourhood resounded with her moans and imprecations. Poor "Scotty" had scored a "magpie," but the old dame was not much hurt; still, "Scotty" was up for court-martial for all that.

On January 12 the troops had a much appreciated bath and change at Vivier's Mills. This was the place where the troops bathed "by numbers," or at least to the blast of a whistle.

Major A. J. Boyd-Aarons was now in temporary command of the battalion, but he and Captain J. P. O'Neil had to go to England on January 13 on a court-martial case, and Major G. F. Combs was in temporary command during Major Boyd-Aaron's absence. Major Combs had been a private at Blackboy Hill, and his appointment as temporary C.O. of the 11th Battalion was at this time held up as an example to the young soldiers to show them what they themselves might hope to rise to if they were fortunate enough to survive so long and if they paid strict attention to their jobs.

Since the battalion's relief from the line the weather had been particularly wet, and large fatigue parties were employed daily in cleaning the town and its surroundings. Dernancourt was at this time a dreary and uninviting village, but a heaven compared to what the troops had come from at Flers and Gueudecourt.

From Dernancourt the battalion moved to Bresle, a village in a deep, narrow valley that led down to the Ancre. The valley looked as if it had been gouged out by glacier action in prehistoric times. It was very sheltered in the valley itself, but up on the high downs it was bitterly cold in these days of winter, for just at this time there was a three-days' snowstorm, and after that there was a frost for about four weeks. The troops were in Bresle at the start of that frost.

On the night of January 14 the men went to a concert staged by an English A.M.C. unit. This, though not so good as some of the concert parties, was much applauded by the Diggers.

During the battalion's stay at Bresle, a series of refresher courses in all branches of training was carried out. The specialist platoons each put in an intensive course. The new hands were also exercised in throwing bombs, and a considerable amount of time was spent in firing rifle grenades which were then made with a short rod that was inserted in the barrel of the rifle. There were a great many coveys of partridges among the stubbles and grasslands, and many a grenade was fired at these birds. The empty bomb boxes, instead of being sent back to ordnance, were retained by the troops and used to warm their huts and tents as firewood. Some of the boys who had a predilection for cheese used to toast big slabs of this not-too-popular delicacy at the fires made from these bomb-boxes. It used to have a most appetising smell, too. Occasionally a bomb-box would be found with the name and address and a message from the girl who had packed the bombs. There were some wonderful letters written in return.

Many of the specialist sections were below strength, and endeavours were made to bring them up to normal. The Intelligence Platoon had lost a good few men, and Lieut. Ross, the I.O., was looking for recruits. He obtained permission to lecture the platoon of partially-trained reinforcements who had joined up after Flers, so that he might impress them with the honour and distinction of being members of the Intelligence Platoon. (The "hobos," as the rest of the battalion generally called them.) After a splendid effort, Lieut. Ross finished his lecture, and waited hopefully. There was no mad rush to join the platoon. Then "Archie," who had charge of the new troops, suggested that some one might like to ask Mr. Ross a question. Private J. Kirkwood immediately inquired why, if the Intelligence was such a fine snap, it was not crowded out with the older hands of the battalion instead of being so much under strength. This stumped Lieut. Ross, but not for long, for he wangled his way out of the difficulty by saying that it was a smart question and the Digger that put it was just the kind of man that the Intelligence Platoon needed. It is almost unnecessary to relate that Kirkwood was the first lad to put his name down.

After the heavy fall of snow, the troops made the most of the occasion and had a great time snowballing each other and also any of the officers that they caught in the open. A great source of amusement was to toboggan down a long slope on a sheet of iron and fly over an eight-foot drop at the bottom. One Digger in the 12th Battalion broke his leg at this game, but others were not deterred from careering down, despite orders forbidding them to do so.

Numbers of German prisoners were employed on the roads round the village. Many of the boys used to give cigarettes and sometimes rations to these poor fellows, but, of course, the guards always stopped anything of the sort if they chanced to see it. The German N.C.O.'s looked very smart and efficient.

On January 18 Lieut. W. C. Belford and 20 other ranks rejoined the battalion from hospital. Captain Purchase relieved Captain Teague as M.O. while the latter was on leave.

An unfortunate accident occurred on January 20 during instruction in the use of the Lewis gun. In demonstrating the stoppages, a live cartridge was accidentally inserted in the breech. This was fired and wounded two men—No. 3329 Private H. A. Flynn and No. 1509 Private Bowring. A board of inquiry to investigate the cause of the accident was appointed, and consisted of Captains R. Hemingway and W. R. Hallahan and Lieut. W. Belford.

The importance of recreation and sports for the troops was beginning to be more fully realised, and football and other games were encouraged. Some willing games of football were played on the wind-swept plateau above the deep ravine in which the village sheltered.

The whole battalion was employed in attack practice during the mornings, and a demonstration was carried out with the new S.O.S. signal on January 20 and the troops were all made familiar with the new rocket. There was often trouble with the S.O.S., as the Germans with their many different flares frequently sent up lights that resembled the British S.O.S. and confusion resulted.

Next day was Sunday, and the battalion paraded for divine service in the Y.M.C.A. hut in the vicinity. The Roman Catholics went to the service in the village church. After church parade 700 other ranks were taken to the divisional baths, as these had been made available to the battalion for the day. This was a clear case of "cleanliness is next to godliness."

In the afternoon the Corps Commander (Lieut.-General W. R. Birdwood, K.C.S.I., K.C.M.G., C.B., C.I.E., D.S.O.) presented medal ribbons to Captain W. R. Hallahan (M.M.) and Sergeant Fred Stahl (D.C.M.).

The weather had now settled into hard frost, and it was bitterly cold on parade. Attack practice was still the chief form of training, and once the troops were on the move and their blood warmed the boys enjoyed the training.

On January 22 the following movements of officers were reported: Lieut.-Colonel Hilmer-Smith left on leave to England, Lieut. Pettit reported from rest camp and 2nd/Lieuts. H. Colvin and F. Dale reported from reinforcements.

Now that the ground was hard and frost-bound, a notable improvement was seen in the spirits and bearing of the men. Though the weather was intensely cold the troops did not seem to suffer much inconvenience, and were often seen without their greatcoats when men of English units would be wearing all the garments they possessed.

With the disappearance of the mud the battalion seemed to be re-born, and never again reached the depth of misery and depression which was experienced in the Flers sector.

CHAPTER XXIX

LAST WEEKS OF THE 1916-1917 WINTER

BAZENTIN LE PETIT, YARRA BANK

ON JANUARY 24, 1917, the 11th Battalion moved out of Bresle. The transport had great difficulty in getting up the steep hill out of the village, as the roadway was covered with a sheet of ice and the horses had not had their shoes fitted with frost-cogs. Nearly all the vehicles had to have leaders to help the teams before they could be pulled up the hill. The weather was bitterly cold and very clear, and many aeroplanes were up. The route lay through Albert, and as the battalion was passing through a German aeroplane dropped three bombs quite close to the column, but there were no casualties. It was so cold that the water froze in the troops' water-bottles. The snow had now covered all the shell-torn country, and a bleak wilderness stretched for miles, intersected by the black arteries bearing the traffic to and from the front lines. The destination of the battalion was Fricourt Farm, and this was reached early in the afternoon. After the troops had been dismissed, the boys had great fun sliding on the frozen shell-holes. Sometimes there would be a connected chain of shell-holes having a long stretch of frozen surface, and on this the troops would have a great game. They carried on just like a lot of big schoolboys, but it was good to see them in high spirits once more.

There was not very much of interest in this desolate camp at Fricourt and the battalion was only waiting orders for a move forward again. On January 25, Lieut. Lehman, who had only been a short time with the battalion, was transferred to the 3rd Machine Gun Company.

Next day Major Boyd-Aarons and Captain O'Neil returned from England and the Major took over the temporary command of the battalion, in the absence of the C.O. The weather was so cold that parades were cancelled and instructional work was carried on inside the huts.

On January 28 the battalion marched to Bazentin le Petit, a camp of Nissen huts beside an important cross-road. On the march up the troops saw several crosses put up by the Germans to British dead. These crosses were neatly constructed and bore the legend, "Hier Ruht Im Gott Der Englischer Soldaten" (here followed name and particulars), or, in the case of an unidentified soldier: "Hier Ruht Im Gott Ein Unbekahnnten Englischer Soldaten," which translated is: "Here rests in God an unknown English soldier."

In spite of many assertions to the contrary, the Germans generally proved themselves worthy foes.

Bazentin was a cold camp, and as soon as the troops were free there were foraging parties all over the country searching for firewood and coal, or indeed anything that would burn. Luckily there was a shattered wood quite close to the camp, and there was an abundance of firewood. It was truly needed, for the nights were bitterly cold. Many a tin of army biscuits was used up on the fires inside the huts. The hard biscuits burned quite well and gave out a lot of heat. Even with the fires in the huts all the men would be covered with rime in the mornings, and boots and damp clothes would be frozen hard. The boots were a great trial, for many of the boys' feet were so swollen and sore with the extreme cold that it was agony to put on these hard boots in the mornings. Many a pair of good boots was ruined in trying to soften them before the fire before putting them on.

About this time there was beginning to be a shortage of several of the staple commodities, and the authorities were sometimes hard put to it to keep up a balanced ration for the troops.

Instead of the standard issue, the battalion was now given dates in lieu of jam and chestnuts in "loo" of potatoes. The latter issue was not much appreciated, although the company cooks used to serve them up in a number of ways, often mincing them and serving them in rissoles and stews; but in these wintry days the chestnuts came into their own, for there would be a group of Diggers round the stoves in the huts roasting the nuts and scrambling for them when they popped.

In the huts the smoke was so thick as to be almost suffocating. There were no chimneys in many of the huts, or if there were they would not draw, and the smoke used to escape out of holes in the walls or roof. It was impossible for anyone to stand up for long. The troops lay or sat on the floors of the huts, where the fresh, cool and heavy air kept the atmosphere bearable, while above their heads the smoke eddied and swayed and slowly escaped from the chinks and crevices. When the orderly officer made his rounds, he would poke his head inside the door of the huts and bark: "Any complaints?" When the answer was in the negative, he would withdraw his head and streaming eyes and pass on to the next hut. Sometimes the boys had trumped-up complaints just to make the O.O. come inside the hut, and they would have a good time while the poor officer coughed and wiped his smarting eyes.

There was a certain amount of training at Bazentin, but so many of the troops were required on various fatigues that there was really no opportunity of progressive training. There was a standing fatigue of one officer and 45 men and two limbered waggons as ammunition dump personnel, and considerable numbers of men were used on road repairs and on the construction of the light railways.

There was considerable movement of troops to and from the various army schools. No. 3690 Temporary Corporal G. W. Murray and No. 4127 Temporary Corporal C. J. Paisley were sent to the 1st Anzac Divisional School as candidates for commissions. On January 29 Lieut. Priestley proceeded to divisional headquarters to take up the duties of intelligence officer. Lieuts. Long, Lyon and Pope, 2nd/Lieut. Campbell and eight other ranks reported back from divisional school.

The official entry for January 30 reads: "Bazentin le Petit. The battalion furnished the following working parties for road repairs: three officers and 150 other ranks. Lieuts. Ross, Simmons and Beckwith with ten other ranks left for the third course at 1st Anzac Divisional School, Tirancourt. The Brigade Commander (Brigadier H. G. Bennett, C.M.G.) visited the camp to-day. Instructional work was carried out by the remainder of the battalion in camp. Lieut. Belford (I.O.) and one N.C.O. visited 1st Brigade headquarters as arranged to reconnoitre the roads, etc. The chaplain (Rev. P. Hayes) and a party of two men from each company visited the battlefield of Pozieres to endeavour to locate some of the graves of members of the battalion who took part in the fight. Twenty-one graves were located, and steps were taken to have them registered and crosses erected."

On the last day of the month, owing to the fact that some of the boys omitted to salute some Brass Hats, the battalion was put through "saluting by numbers." It seems difficult to believe that any officer of sense could have ordered such instruction just behind the firing line, but custom dies hard, and many follow the shadow rather than the substance. Over sixty years before Charles Kingsley, in writing of the same subject, had railed against "that etiquette which is at once the counterfeit and the ruin of true discipline."

The 1st Brigade was in the line at Eaucourt L'Abbaye, near the famous Butte de Warlencourt, a large mound standing like an island in the flatter country surrounding. The Butte was said to be an ancient fort, and it certainly had a commanding position in that countryside. Parties from the 11th Battalion were detailed to visit the divisional sector daily, in order to get an idea of the situation in general and to familiarise themselves with the routes and communications to the front line. The continued hard frost made walking easy, and the trenches were quite practicable compared to the awful nightmares they had been during the last tour of duty in the line.

Some parties visited the 2nd Brigade sector as well, and almost every officer and a good many N.C.O.'s and runners had been up to the line several times before the battalion was ready to take over.

On returning from these visits to the line, the officers had to submit a written report to battalion headquarters on the conditions existing. The officers, like the men, lived in Nissen huts, and there were about a dozen in each of the two huts allotted. Like the men they generally had fires going, and the interiors were filled with smoke and profanity. As can readily be imagined, there was always "something doing" in these huts in the long winter evenings. Sometimes it would be cards, poker and banker being much in favour; sometimes the boys would roast the chestnuts that were issued "in lieu" of potatoes at this time. The most comfortable place, however, was in the valise, for only on the floor or near it was there any respite from the acrid smoke that filled all the upper portion of the hut. At nights, too, the officers who had been detailed to visit the lines had to write their reports in these huts, and a nice job it used to be, among such a wild lot of boys, including "Pard" Riches, "Johnny" Long and "Rag-time" Simmons.

One day, February 6, to be exact, Lieut. J. A. Archibald had been sent up to visit the 2nd Brigade sector, and he arrived back rather late. Most of the boys were in their bunks, but Riches was still afoot, and he had just been treating the occupants of the hut and himself, too, to a tot of whisky. He may have treated himself a few times out of his turn, and he was feeling friendly to the whole world when Archibald blew in. "Archie" was immediately offered a drink, which was just what he needed after his long tramp around the lines. He had a good three fingers, and then proceeded to write out his report so that he could deliver it to battalion headquarters that same night. "Archie" always took his duties very seriously, and he sat down just as he was, with all his equipment on, even to his sheepskin jacket and his "tin hat."

Riches asked him to have another drink, but Archibald waved him away and told Riches not to disturb him while he was writing his report. The good Riches was rather peeved at the cool reception to his hospitable overtures and looked round for something with which to distract Archibald's attention. Nearby was a small hatchet that one of the batman had been using to chop wood for the stove. Riches picked it up and addressed the busy writer in what was meant to be Shakespearian language: "Wilt thou have drink, or hatchet?" he inquired of Archibald's back. "Go to Hell!" was the polite retort. "Drink or hatchet, Archibald?" was again repeated. When no answer was forthcoming, Riches, who was one of the most powerful men in the 11th Battalion, hit Archibald a tap right on the top of his steel helmet, driving the brim nearly down on to the poor fellow's shoulders. It was a very wild Archibald that told the "Pard" exactly what he thought of him and all his forbears, while the rest of the boys in the hut had an appreciated regard for the value of the steel hat as a means of defence for the head.

Before the battalion moved up to the line, the troops treated their feet with a powder advocated by the French Army. It was a great improvement on the whale oil that had been issued prior to this as a preventative to trench foot. The whale oil was not only ill-smelling but it left the feet clammy and cold.

On February 12 the 11th Battalion moved out of Bazentin camp and relieved the 1st Battalion in the right sub-section of the left brigade front. The troops were in scattered posts and trenches, generally described as "Yarra Bank," near Eaucourt

L'Abbaye, and battalion headquarters was in Yarra Reserve. While the relief was in progress, Strombos horns, gongs and rattles were heard all along the line. As this indicated a gas attack, all the troops put on the gas-masks. But there was no gas. The alarm had been given by a man in the 12th Battalion who had been on gas guard near that battalion's headquarters. He had turned the cock of the gas alarm to see how the gadget worked, and then had the wind up and was too flabbergasted to turn the alarm off, and so all the horns within hearing blared out. In spite of the confusion there were no casualties during the relief, although there was a great increase in the number of flares fired by the enemy. These were really beautiful flares, execpt if one was out in front, and they lit up all the surrounding area as they hissed through the darkness, flashing and sparkling in the calm, frosty nights.

The frost was still holding when the battalion took over the line, and the duckboards in the trenches and along the communications were very slippery. The hard, frozen ground increased the effectiveness of the enemy's shells and bombs and several casualties were sustained.

The Germans were also doing a good deal of indirect machine gun fire on the communications, and occasionally fired a number of pineapple bombs. A couple of men were wounded in "B" Company, and they lay all day in the front line, as it was impossible to move them on account of the very slippery conditions.

Captain Teague, the M.O., said that he would go up to the front line himself and attend to the men. The Colonel tried to dissuade him, and said that the wounded would be brought down as soon as it could be arranged. The good Doctor, however, insisted on visiting the boys, so that night a party, consisting of the C.O. the M.O., Captain Hallahan and the I.O. and Sergeant P. Snodgrass (the gas N.C.O.) and several runners, set out for the front line. The I.O. left the party to visit the listening-posts out in front of the trench at Yarra Bank, but the remainder carried on towards "B" Company. Captain Teague then visited the two wounded men, and after attending them the party prepared to return to Yarra Reserve. A German flare burst high in the air, and some of the party must have been seen for a heavy trench mortar bombardment was directed at them. There was an immediate scatter, and the C.O., Captain

Hallahan and others took refuge in a trench nearby. When things had calmed down, it was found that Teague was missing. After a long search his body was found lying just off the duckboard track where he had been hurled by a shell or heavy bomb. He was hardly marked, but he was quite dead. He was a true friend to all the troops and a very gallant gentleman.

Not long after this there was a change in the weather. The long frost that had now lasted for over a month gradually broke, and the trenches that up to this time had been so dry began to be moist and then wet. Soon the conditions were sloppy once more, and sections of the trench began to fall in. It was just then that the divisional commander decided to pay a visit to the trenches.

At the 11th Battalion headquarters dug-out was a guard consisting of two new reinforcements who had recently been drafted to the intelligence section. Their duties were to act as gas guard as well as fulfil all the other jobs required by the intelligence, such as reporting shelling, the location, size and direction of enemy shells, enemy aircraft, enemy movement as far as they could see it, and any unusual circumstances. These two fellows knew their job in a passable sort of a way, but as they had only newly joined the battalion previous to going into the line, they did not know much about their officers or those of brigade or division.

Behold, then, the divisional commander (General "Hookie" Walker) followed by some of his staff approaching these two sentries. The disintegrating trenches and the sticky mud had proved rather a strain on the old General's temper. The sentries had received no instructions about visiting generals, as these were rather rare birds in the trenches at that period, and so the lads took no notice of the members of the party beyond registering the fact that they had no hostile intent.

The General asked the sentries what their duties were. They replied that they did not give information to strangers. The General was peeved. "Who are you fellows?" he barked. "Aussies," was the reply. "Damn it all! What division?" "I dunno," was the laconic answer. "Who's your brigadier?" the General asked one of the boys. The lad shook his head. The furious "Hookie" then roared: "What's the name of your colonel?" The spokesman turned to his cobber for corroboration and inquired, "A bloke named Smith, ain't it?" Just then

Lieut. A. Brodie came along and explained matters, but the General had had enough. "Where's your battalion headquarters?" he snarled. The lad pointed and said, "Downstairs, sir." The General threw aside the slimy blanket that did duty for a gas curtain, and was almost knocked down the steps of the dug-out by the swing back of the heavy weight at the bottom. He stormed into the Colonel's quarters and told him off properly about his battalion and all that pertained to it. Meanwhile, one of the staff remained on top and explained to the unconcerned pair of sentries the enormity of their offence in failing to recognise the General and to give him the respect he was accustomed to. The luckless I.O. also got a good telling-off when he returned to his dug-out.

Lieut.-Colonel E. Hilmer-Smith was never supposed to have much sense of humour, but after this little incident he always used to stop Private Jim Kirkwood, who was one of the sentries mentioned, and ask him if he had had any more conversations with any generals recently.

When the 11th Battalion had taken over the line at Yarra Bank, the ground was frozen so hard that it was impossible to do any work in the direction of improving the trenches, and the hard ground had also the disadvantage of detonating all the explosive missiles that the enemy fired; and this made havoc of the trenches and posts, besides causing quite a few casualties. But now all was changed. Though the trenches were disintegrating they were very easily repaired, and the effect of shells and bombs was much diminished.

The official diary of February 16 reads: "Work on improvement of trenches and dug-outs was continued during the day and night. Four officers and 180 other ranks were employed on this work in addition to the two officers and 136 other ranks employed permanently on the divisional dumps.

"The enemy activity during the day was about normal. During the early part of the night, February 16/17, he became more active, firing bombs and shells over our front line trenches until silenced by our guns. Privates Schultze, Drysdale and Messenger were wounded by shell-fire while on carrying duty. The C.O. and Captain Hallahan visited the right company ('D') of our sector during the early part of the night. A patrol from the intelligence platoon patrolled No Man's Land from 9 p.m. till 11 p.m. and inspected the damage done to and the general state of the enemy's wire entanglements, etc. Weather conditions: Some slight showers of rain fell during the day, otherwise fine with good visibility."

Owing to the fine weather many aeroplanes were up and a British 'plane was brought down in front of the brigade sector. At this stage of the war the British 'planes seemed to be a long way inferior to the graceful and fast German 'planes.

There was a great deal of enemy activity in the "Maze," a small and sharp German salient which lay opposite the 11th Battalion trenches. This unusual movement on the enemy's part called down constant shelling and trench mortar bombing. The enemy's reply was mostly on the communications and rear areas.

A very careful check was kept by the intelligence section on all shell-fire and enemy activity, and this was made into a report which was sent to brigade daily. Also each night the patrol N.C.O. (Corporal Buckingham) used to venture out and examine the enemy wire, and also use a listening-post. When the weather thawed and the muddy conditions returned, he used to come in covered with mud to his eyebrows, through having to "assume the prone" among the muddy shell-holes. One night when he and Private Bob Turner were out on patrol, they ran into a German machine gun post. They could hear gutteral voices talking quietly, so they withdrew a little way and successfully bombed the post. When they crept forward again the post was empty.

Captain L. B. Tollemache, the brigade major, was evacuated sick and died a few days later from pneumonia. "Tolly" had been with the training battalion in Egypt in 1915, and was well known to many of the 11th Battalion troops.

There seemed to be rather more shelling and bombing on the part of the Germans than usual, but it was not sufficiently abnormal to create alarm or arouse suspicion. By day there was intermittent long-range machine gun fire, and high explosive shell was pretty well distributed over the whole area; while at nights showers of pineapple bombs fell on the front lines and indirect machine gun fire played on the back areas and approaches. And all along the whole German line the white flares rose continually, lighting the gloom with their silvery trails.

Before the 3rd Brigade took over the line, an operation order had been drawn up for an attack on the Maze, but owing to several new factors, such as the breaking of the frost and the increased difficulty of movement, the attack had been cancelled and the role of the troops had been to make the lines more habitable and to hold the trenches.

Events, however, were happening that were going to make a vital change in the warfare in the Somme, and the front line troops have sometimes been blamed for not realising earlier that a withdrawal was being contemplated by the Germans. But when it is realised that no troops were more than a few days in the line at a time, and that they therefore had no opportunity of realising that any vital difference was taking place in the enemy's methods of shelling or otherwise carrying on war, it is obviously unfair to blame them for not noticing that things were different. It was surely the function of the divisional or corps intelligence staffs to gather from the mass of intelligence reports that they received over a period, and from a considerable sector of the front, that the enemy was altering his tactics, and to take measures accordingly.

Owing to the increased long-range shelling by the enemy, many men on ration parties and fatigues were killed or wounded.

Another operation order for the attack on the Maze was issued on February 22, but this was again cancelled. On this date the 9th Battalion relieved the 11th, and the latter battalion moved out to huts in Bazentin le Petit.

February 23 was spent in a general overhaul of gear and equipment, and two companies were taken to the baths where the wash and clean change made life worth living again for those who participated.

At night several fatigue parties were supplied. One party had the sad task of burying some of their comrades who were killed on the previous night while on fatigue at the dump at railhead. In the diary of Private N. H. Simpson, of the 11th Battalion, is the following entry:—

"February 24, 1917. To baths, change and clean up; very cold; raided bomb dump for boxes for fire; skating in old wine cellar; party detailed for fatigue; fatigue turned out to be burying a number of our lads killed while working at our dump near railhead. Charlie Hennessey, Arthur Dring and other good lads gone west. *War!*"

The scene here recalls the poignant verse of Lieut. Walter Wilkinson, of the Argyle and Sutherland Highlanders, himself killed in action on April 9, 1917—

"They're bringing their recent dead! No pomp, no show;
A dingy khaki crowd—his friends, his own.
I, too, would like (God, how that wind does moan!)
To be laid down by friends; it's sweetest so
A young life, as I take it; just a lad
(How cold it blows; and that grey sky, how sad!)
And yet, 'For Country'—so a man *should* die;
Comrade unknown, good rest to you! Good-bye!"

CHAPTER XXX

THE GERMAN RETIREMENT—LEBARQUE—
LIGNY-THILLOY

AFTER the terrible fighting that had taken place on the Somme and other fronts, the German High Command determined to shorten the line that was held in the Somme and to withdraw to a selected position a considerable distance in rear from the centre of the salient. The line to which the Germans intended to withdraw ran roughly from Arras to Soissons, and the retirement on such a big front would also have the effect of disorganising and rendering useless at least two great British offensives. The new German position that had been selected was of the highest strategical importance, and became world-famous as the great "Hindenburg Line." The Germans, in withdrawing to this line, not only released a number of divisions for other fronts but also had their new communications intact and had a good terrain to work over, and they were also able to string out the British communications during the wet months of the year so that it made it difficult for any effective attack to be made by the British Command. Thus their preparations had been made in the winter months after the great British attack had so woefully petered out in the water-logged country, and early in the New Year the Germans were ready to withdraw to the selected line, leaving a scene of desolation and wreck behind them.

For a few mornings the weather had been mild and generally foggy or misty, and under cover of this the first preparations for the German withdrawal had been made. So far the troops in the line had not noticed anything except an increased amount of trench mortar and shell-fire. It was afterwards learned that the Germans used to shoot off all their forward ammunition before they retired, but the line troops could hardly have been expected to realise that the increased bombardment was due to the enemy making preparations to retire.

However, on February 24 patrols from the 9th and 10th Battalions reported that the enemy was particularly quiet on the front opposite them. Further patrols were therefore sent out to see if Fritz had vacated his front-line trenches. It was ascertained that he had gone, and reports from the flanking brigade confirmed the tidings and the enemy was observed to be heavily shelling his own late front line as well as the Australian positions.

The 9th and 10th Battalions were ordered to follow the enemy as he retired and to keep contact. The flanking brigades were to act in concert. The newly-relieved 11th Battalion was immediately moved forward in support and occupied these positions: "A" Company, Switch Dump; "B" Company, Yarra Reserve; "C" Company, York Dump and "D" Company, Cough Drop. These were trenches lying in front of Le Barque and Ligny-Thilloy. From these positions the 11th Battalion was used for carrying parties during the first stages of the advance. The weather was still foggy and the parties had a strenuous night, but there were no casualties. The 9th Battalion occupied the Maze in accordance with the instructions previously laid down in the cancelled operation order.

On February 25 the troops rested all day, and at night the 11th Battalion headquarters moved up to Cough Drop. During the night, part of the battalion was used on carrying parties. These were employed in taking rations and ammunition up to the line. When one of the working parties was at Turk's Dump, a shell landed among the troops and killed ten men and wounded 13 others.

Next day the 11th Battalion relieved the 9th Battalion in the line. The official narrative runs as follows: "The front line relief was completed at 9:30 p.m., the whole relief being completed by 11:55 p.m. The dispositions taken over on relief were as follows: One company in Malt Trench-Rye Trench, one company in Oat Lane, one company in Bank Trench and one company in the Maze. Acting under instructions from the G.O.C. 3rd Infantry Brigade, dispositions were at once made to capture and mop up Le Barque. At 10 p.m. two patrols, each of one N.C.O. and three men, were sent out to try to ascertain the positions the enemy were located in, and also the positions of machine guns. The patrols returned at 3 a.m. and reported that they had located enemy machine guns on both our flanks, the right one being in Ligny-Thilloy and the left one in the northern part of Bank Trench. These guns were actively firing across our front throughout the night. While the patrols were out, the enemy sent a number of flares from Le Barque. At 4 a.m. two strong patrols, each of one Lewis machine gun and team, six bombers and six riflemen, were sent out to establish themselves on the right flank of Le Barque. Prior to these patrols being sent out, a bombing team was sent along the trench joining with Rye Trench and running towards Le Barque. This was reported unoccupied. The two posts were reported in position at 4:30 a.m. The remainder of the garrison was reinforced by two platoons from the company in Oat Lane and organised as follows:—

"No. 1, Lieut. Hall and 40 men to move forward along Blue Cut into Le Barque, to mop up and bomb dug-outs.

"No. 2, Sergeant R. Camden and 15 men to move up Yellow Cut to mop up and bomb dug-outs and eventually to link up with Lieut. Hall in the wood north of the village.

"These parties moved out from Malt and Rye Trenches respectively at 5:30 a.m., and no opposition was met with until about 6:15 a.m., when a white flare, bursting into two pink flares, was sent up from the village.

"Immediately the enemy placed artillery barrages on Malt and Rye Trenches, and also on Oat Lane. The barrage consisted of 4.2 H.E. shell and shrapnel. The machine guns, that had been located by our first patrols, swept, with cross fire, the outskirts of the village on either side.

"This fire lasted about 15 minutes, by which time the visibility was good. Our parties observed the enemy rapidly retiring in small groups towards Ligny-Thilloy, and at once pushed forward.

"No opposition was met in the wood north of Le Barque, only one prisoner (a sniper) being captured, and our parties immediately pushed forward into Ligny-Thilloy and proceeded to mop up this village. The enemy had evidently cleared right through to Thilloy (this was another village, just to the north of Ligny-Thilloy) as the first village was found deserted.

"A number of the dug-outs in Le Barque and Ligny-Thilloy were found to have been already destroyed by the enemy.

"By 6:45 a.m. a defensive position had been established about 200 yards north-east of Ligny-Thilloy. A start was immediately made to consolidate the position and a trench four feet deep was dug along this line, while a strong post was consolidated on the right-hand side of Wedding Lane.

"At 7 a.m. a patrol, under Sergeant McKinley, was sent forward from this new position to ascertain the strength of the enemy in Thilloy, as this was our next objective. This patrol went forward about 100 yards when it came under heavy machine gun fire and was held up.

"At 7:30 a.m. communication was established with our left, a company of the 12th Battalion arriving at that time. Our right flank was still in the air, as the battalion on our right was still in Rye Trench. A request was made to the C.O. of the right battalion to push a patrol forward along Black Street.

"Up to 8 a.m. our casualties had amounted to about 30.

"At this time a half company of the 19th Battalion, under Lieut. Allen, which had evidently lost direction, came up through Ligny-Thilloy on our right flank, and our flank was further extended to the east of Wedding Lane, where posts were established. At 10 a.m. Lieut. Allen's party was ordered to obtain communication with the right battalion. This party reported that it had found a patrol of this battalion in Black Street.

"From 8 a.m. till dusk the enemy shelled consistently with salvos of H.E., most of the fire being directed on the villages of Le Barque and Ligny-Thilloy. In addition, our position was subjected to bursts of shrapnel, but this fell about 50 yards short in front of our line. Machine gun fire from the direction of Thilloy was kept continuously on our new position throughout the day, but only slight casualties resulted (20 in all). The strength of the garrison at this time was about 220.

"At 2:30 p.m. a request was sent for artillery retaliation (counter-battery) and also for Thilloy to be shelled. At about 4 p.m. Thilloy was shelled with high explosive and six direct hits were observed, but many shells fell short behind our lines and in the village of Ligny-Thilloy. At about 6 p.m. the shelling ceased.

"The 18-pounders opened fire on Thilloy at 3 p.m., but a number of the shells fell short, several exploding over the left of our own trenches and inflicting casualties (estimated 12).

"At 1 p.m. instructions were received from G.O.C. 3rd Infantry Brigade to advance at dusk, capture Thilloy and establish posts on the further side of the village.

"At 6:30 p.m. two patrols, each consisting of one Lewis machine gun team with six bombers and four riflemen, left our lines and established posts south of Thilloy. No opposition was met with by these patrols. When these posts were established, parties, as follows, were sent forward: Right party, Lieut. Beasley with 20 men and one Lewis machine gun; right centre, Lieut. Pettit and 15 men; left centre, Lieuts. Hall and Long with 30 men and ten bombers; left party, Lieut. Archibald with 30 men and six bombers and one Lewis machine gun.

"These moved through the posts already established, picking up the bombers of the advanced posts as they went.

"On entering the village all dug-outs were systematically bombed; only one dug-out was found inhabited. This was effectually bombed and two Germans who were found at the mouth were captured. These belonged to the Prussian Foot Guards. The parties went right through the village, and by 10:15 p.m. had established five posts about 20 yards apart on the outskirts of the wood near there.

"A patrol was immediately pushed forward and approached Till Trench. Finding it occupied the patrol returned to our line. Patrols were also sent to the right and left to try to establish communication with the battalions to the right and left. On the right flank, about 50 yards from our flank, the right battalion had established a post and our left patrol found a post which had been established by the left battalion about 400 yards from Knotty Point. A start was immediately made to consolidate the new position and posts were established.

"At 8:30 p.m. our line was relieved by a company of the 4th Battalion.

"General.—Telephonic communication was maintained with the front line throughout the operations. North of Thilloy our patrols report that the ground is even, very few shell-holes being seen. There were signs of broad-wheeled transport tracks, quite new, evidently the tracks of guns which had been recently removed from Thilloy. The houses in the village are in a fair state of repair, and the village does not seem to have suffered much from shell-fire.

"I wish to bring under notice the excellent services rendered by Captain John O'Neil, who was in command of the front line, and also Lieuts. Hall, Long, Aitken and Archibald, who showed great initiative and dash throughout."

Lieut. Davidson (11th Batt.), —— Lieut. D. Hardie (11th Batt.), Major J. P. O'Neil, M.C. (11th Batt.), Lieut. J. Long (11th Batt.), Captain Vowles (12th Batt.), Lieut. F. Stahl (11th Batt.).

"My recommendations for award will be forwarded in another despatch. (Sgd.) E. Hilmer-Smith, Lieut.-Colonel, Commanding 11th Battalion (A.I.F.)."

After the advance was made a reconnaissance was at once carried out by the intelligence officer of all the roads and tracks through the newly-occupied territory to find out if there was any possibility of moving guns forward. The country round the Maze was absolutely water-logged and the tracks, roads and trenches were merely gutters of mud and water, and impassable for heavy-wheeled transport. The country beyond Thilloy, however, was practically untouched, and the green fields were a delight to the eye after the brown mud and shell-torn country the troops had been accustomed to for such a long period. But the sunken road that was the main avenue to Ligny-Thilloy,

Yellow Cut by name, was in such a condition that it was astounding to think that the Germans had used it at all. As one of the boys remarked, "No wonder the poor b——s retired."

An interesting account of the foregoing action is given by Captain (then Lieut.) Rex Hall, who was at this time with the 11th Battalion:—

"At midnight on February 26/27, 'C' Company, under Captain J. P. O'Neil, left the dug-outs and trenches in front of the Maze, and after floundering through the mud eventually reached the old German trench called Oat Trench immediately in front of Le Barque. The mud was reminiscent of Flers, and the trench itself was a foot deep in water.

"Scouts had previously been sent out to reconnoitre the outskirts of Le Barque; they reported all clear. Just on dawn the company, under Lieut. Hall, moved out into Rye Trench, and after a few minutes' halt, to get in touch with the right and left flank companies, it then moved forward in line through the left half of Le Barque, Lieut. Hall taking the centre, Lieut. Beasley the right and Sergeant Camden the left. Little direct opposition was met with, but machine gun posts, very well concealed, and snipers were quite active. One of the latter, a mere boy about 16, was captured in tears and he expected to be shot at once. He soon recovered under the kind treatment of the C.S.M. and a packet of fags. Other snipers were more summarily dealt with.

"It was while skirmishing through the village that I saw a most amusing incident. About a dozen fowls, left, no doubt, by some German officer, offered a too tempting opportunity for one Digger who, forgetful of all else, gave chase. I saw him capture two before he passed out of sight.

"Beyond the village we entered a deep, sunken road well furnished with substantial dug-outs. Leaving these for the mopping-up parties, and our objectives having been gained, I decided that it would be safer to move forward off the road some 100 yards and dig in. What a change from our previous stunts! Green fields hardly touched by shell-fire, larks soaring into a cloudless sky, and I even noticed a covey of partridges which were flushed as we went forward.

"It was now about 10 a.m. and the troops, with only their entrenching tools, dug a series of holes in the chalky ground and gradually linked them up into the semblance of a trench.

"The Germans, thinking that we would stop in the sunken road, poured in a few salvos of well-aimed shots right into the road, and kept up an intermittent fire during the morning. Unforunately there were a few casualties, especially among the battalion runners. Captain O'Neil's batman was one of them. It was not possible to get rations to the line, so the troops had to eat their emergency rations. By some good work on the part of the company Q.M.S. a jar of rum hove in sight. I managed to serve out the issue, dodging from hole to hole. There was much cheering over this. We were to have been relieved at dusk, but late in the afternoon Major Boyd-Aarons arrived on the scene with orders for us to go through Ligny-Thilloy and Thilloy. We started at dusk, and meeting little opposition eventually formed some sort of a line in front of Thilloy. One prisoner was captured by Johnny Long who was armed, I think, only with a bottle. The prisoner was very fortunate to escape with his life.

"During the night of February 27/28 we were relieved by the 1st Brigade and made our weary way back again over the mud through the Maze."

A British aeroplane came down just behind battalion headquarters in Yarra Bank, and though a guard was sent out immediately, some of the battalion souvenir-kings had already managed to help themselves to some of the instruments.

Among several amusing incidents the following is told by Major A. J. Boyd-Aarons (now Major Julian Boyd). Some time before going into the line at Ligny-Thilloy the officers had been reading the reports of German atrocities, all propaganda, no doubt, and Lieut. Johnny Long said: "Well! After that I would never take a German prisoner." The Major said: "Nonsense, Long! You could never shoot a German in cold blood." "Couldn't I?" said Johnny.

On the night Le Barque and Ligny-Thilloy were captured, the Major had to visit the front line. He was without revolver and other arms, but had an escort with rifle and bayonet. Just as they got to Le Barque, they saw silhouetted against the moon two tall German soldiers coming towards them. They got behind a tree, the Digger with his rifle ready. When the advancing Fritzies got close enough, it was noticed that they were supporting a wounded Digger between them, and were followed by a little 11th Battalion corporal. The Major asked him who took the prisoners. "Mr. Long, sir," he replied. The Major said that he was glad to see the corporal was making good use of them. "To b—— right, sir. Come along, Fritz, you b——!"

When the Major met Johnny Long next day he asked why he had not shot the prisoners. Long looked a bit sheepish and retorted, "Well! You see, I had only a Very-light pistol or I certainly should have."

The casualties in the brigade in this advance were 59 killed and 213 wounded, of which the 11th Battalion had 14 killed and 36 wounded. So, though the advance is generally described as though it were a mere following up of the retreating Germans, it will be realised from the foregoing that the enemy retired in good order and that they put up a skilful rear action fight.

On February 27/28 the 11th Battalion was relieved by the 3rd Battalion, and on relief moved to Bazentin le Petit, No. 2 camp, where the troops were given a well-deserved rest.

When the muster roll was called, and the names of the killed and wounded were checked, old Bill Beck learned that Private Ernie Sewell, who had been one of his mates in the bombing platoon, had been killed. Bill asked if Sewell's body had been buried. He was told that his mate was still unburied, so he asked for and obtained permission to return to the battle-field and bury Sewell. He set out with Private H. Walker, and the two fine fellows returned through the mud and after a long hunt found their mate's body and gave it decent burial, and a cross was put up to mark the spot. Having accomplished their task they set off after the battalion. This might seem just an ordinary act of mateship, such was common among the troops, but all who knew anything about the awful state of the front at this place, and the very slight chance of finding the body, will appreciate the disinterested and comradely action of the two men in doing this service to their former comrade. "Old" Bill Beck was nearly fifty years old at the time.

For a few days the battalion remained at Bazentin le Petit, doing the usual reorganisation after a battle, and of course supplying fatigues. The divisional baths were handy to the camp and the troops had their customary shiver under a few drops of cold water. But the clean change was always welcome.

On March 2 Captain Alec Burgess, who had been with the regimental transport since Black Hill, in August, 1914, first as transport sergeant and then as transport officer, was sent to the divisional school at Tirancourt, and Lieut. W. C. Belford took over the duties of battalion transport officer. Lieuts. Pettit and Patterson and 13 N.C.O.'s were also sent to the divisional school. Lieut. Jim Aitken left for the 3rd Training Battalion in England on March 3.

A short move back was made by the battalion on March 5 when all ranks, except the parties on various jobs at railhead and Clarke's Dump, route-marched to Scots' Redoubt Camp near Montauban. The fatigue parties were camped at a spot rejoicing in the name of Singer's Circus. The battalion transport remained in a deep valley near Delville Wood. On the above date Lieut. P. E. M. Vowles reported from supernumerary, Lieut. V. B. Daniel, 20/11th Reinforcements and Lieut. P. W. Lyon from hospital.

During the time the 11th Battalion was at Scots' Redoubt it was exercised in the new method of attack that was then being adopted. Great stress was being laid on this method of attacking in waves, and every day's report for about ten days has some reference to the new system. The entry for March 8 is typical:—

"The battalion was instructed in subjects of training as per syllabus attached. The C.O., senior officers and also company commanders attended a lecture given by the G.O.C. 3rd Infantry Brigade (Temporary Colonel H. G. Bennett, C.M.G.) on the new organisation in attack." And the official entry for March 15 reads: "The battalion was exercised in the new form of attack in accordance with the syllabus, and during the afternoon a demonstration was carried out on four objectives. This attack was witnessed by the G.O.C. 3rd Infantry Brigade (Brigadier-General H. G. Bennett, C.M.G.) and Lieut.-Colonel T. H. Blamey (General Staff). The attack was carried out with exceptional ability, officers and men moving to their allotted work like machines."

The troops were beginning to recover from the trying effects of the winter, and the sergeants were so perked up that they had established a mess while at Scots' Redoubt. Corporal "Nigger" Black had been allowed the privileges of the mess, and one night he had done himself rather too well, so he was asked by Harry Vincent, who was in charge of the mess, to get off to bed. But that was no good to "Nigger," for him the night had just begun. However, he was forcibly ejected and he went off vowing vengeance on the whole lot of the sergeants. "Nigger" must have been taking the lessons learned in the new attack organisation to heart, for he soon re-appeared at the door of the sergeants' mess with a live Mill's bomb in his hand. This he immediately threw into the middle of the mess room. The grenade hit Harry Vincent in the middle of the back, and wasn't there a scatter! For the first time on record the sergeants left without finishing their "hops," and the frame of the hut door was nearly wrenched out as they surged through. What a jam there was! Luckily "Nigger" had left the pin in and little damage was done. When the scare was over "Nigger" got such a verbal castigation from the sergeants that he said: "By cripes! I wish I had pulled the bloody pin out!" However, he made a handsome apology next day.

It was with great joy that the troops heard that Bapaume had been occupied by the 5th Australian Division. Bapaume had seemed not very long before to be so well and truly behind the German lines that it was hard to believe that the Australian troops were in possession of the town and the high ridge on which it stood.

On March 17 notification was received that the following troops had been awarded Military Medals by the corps commander for services rendered during the operations on February 27 and 28:—

Nos. 1158 Sergeant McKinley, G. M., 4155 Corporal Black, H. A. ("Nigger"), 1395 Corporal Phillips, F. W., 1776 L/Corporal Buckingham, L. H., 5080 L/Corporal Hill, H. D., 1869 Private Stephenson, C., 2055 Private Ryan, T. P. C., 5684 Private Dick, J. M.

On the above date also the 11th Battalion played the 9th Battalion at football and beat the latter's team.

Lieut. J. M. A. Stewart (20/11th Reinforcements) and 11 other ranks joined up with the battalion.

CHAPTER XXXI

HENENCOURT WOOD, MORCHIES AND
LAGNICOURT

IT WAS NOW nearly the end of March, and the spring equinox had brought the promise of happier days. The returning sun was daily growing stronger and as a result the ground was drying, although in that brown and battered wilderness it took a long time before any appreciable improvement could be noticed. With the lengthening days visibility became much better and in consequence aircraft of both sides were much more active. When the troops were at Scots' Redoubt they had many opportuntities of seeing the then new triplanes, which were attached to an aerodrome not far away. These machines could climb with almost incredible swiftness, but were clumsy in manœuvre, slow in diving and hence unsuitable as fighters. Not many of these 'planes were noticed after this period, so they must have been superseded by more suitable types. Many kite balloons were also "up," and the whole area was showing an animation that had been lacking for many months. There was a balloon crew camped with their "sausage" near Mametz and several of the officers often wandered down to the mess there and swapped yarns or played cards with the balloon men.

March 23 found the 11th Battalion on the move once more, this time back to Henencourt Wood, about four miles west of Albert. At Henencourt the men were allotted to huts. The transport lines were closer to the battalion than they had been for a considerable time, and the horses were stabled in large sheds. Henencourt was a good camp situated among splendid woods, with long rides radiating from Henencourt Chateau, a commodious and handsome building which was at this time General Birdwood's headquarters.

After the battalion reached Henencourt Wood, the C.O. (Lieut.-Colonel E. Hilmer-Smith) was evacuated to the hospital at Edge Hill.

As an earnest that longer and brighter days were ahead, the official time was everywhere advanced one hour on March 24.

Lieut.-Colonel Smith returned from Edge Hill Hospital on March 27, and the following day Major R. A. Rafferty, from the 12th Battalion, visited the 11th Battalion with the view of taking over the command of the battalion. On March 29 Captain K. MacLennan, the adjutant, left for Rouen with orders to look over battalion records and change over orderly-room sergeants. He took with him Sergeant Syd Cousins, a man who had been the mainstay of the orderly room for many months. Cousins was possessed of an amazing memory, and knew the particulars of most of the members of the battalion. It was astounding to listen to him giving the particulars from memory of some Digger who was under discussion with as much ease as if he were ordering his favourite brand of beer.

On March 30 Lieut.-Colonel Smith left for the divisional school at Tirancourt and Major Rafferty took over command of the battalion. This was Lieut.-Colonel Smith's farewell to the 11th Battalion, although the troops did not realise this at the time. He had been in command of the battalion since October 16, 1916, and had proved himself an able, sympathetic and conscientious commander.

The troops were feeling the benefit of the rest and the change from the everlasting mud, and the health of the battalion was much improved. Ever since coming out of the line the battalion had been trained in the new attack formations, first in attacking under barrage conditions, and during the latter portion of the month the training changed to tactical exercises and open warfare, as this latter form of fighting was most likely to be encountered on the return to the line.

The troops liked Henencourt. It was quiet and peaceful there, and the camp was close to the village where there always seemed to be a plentiful supply of the good "oeufs" and the "Pommes de terre frites," and, of course, the "biere" and "vin blanc."

It was pleasant strolling through the woods or over the country near by, where the larks were beginning to sing and where the mad "March hares" gambolled and dashed around. The hares had a pretty short shrift from the Diggers, who did not bother much about their "madness." In the woods the earliest songsters, chiefly thrushes and blackbirds, were filling the air with song. With a strange raptness the troops, big, rough fellows often, would listen to the sweet notes, wondering perhaps how anything could be so beautiful in that land of horror, and wondering, too, how much longer they would be spared to listen. Julian Grenfell, D.S.O., who was himself killed in action, expressed this feeling in the following lines:—

"The blackbird sings to him, brother, brother,
If this be the last song you shall sing
Sing well, for you may not sing another;
Brother, sing."

and the lines of Captain Eric Wilkinson, M.C., who was also killed in action in October, 1917, convey the same idea:—

"O fine, full-throated choir invisible
. . . What wild glee
Has filled your throbbing throats with sound, until
Its strains are poured from every bush and tree,
And sad hearts swell with hope, and fierce eyes fill?
The world is stark with blood and hate—but ye
Sing on! Sing on! in careless ecstacy."

But the troops were always more brusque and rough when they thought they might be suspected of sentiment; and so, with a shrug, some one would say, "C'mon, boys, let's go over to Madame's. Marthe promised to keep us a dozen 'erfs,'" and off they would go to live in the joyous present.

While at Henencourt there was considerable competition among the various company cooks, in which each company endeavoured to have the best turned out field kitchen. Every day a field officer, accompanied by the O.O. and a long tail of sergeants, runners and others, would make the rounds of the cookers. The "Babblers" did their best to remove some of the grease from their tunics and pants, but without much success. They managed, however, to have the cookers looking spick and span. It was always a most amusing inspection, especially if Johnny Long was orderly officer.

The divisional commander visited the lines several times and expressed himself satisfied with his inspection. He also inspected the transport lines and gave the T.O. a wigging because one driver was grazing his horses with their rugs off. The rugs were so constantly on the horses that the animals, like the troops, became very lousy. The driver mentioned, Tom Pearse, one of the many who loved and really looked after his horses, had just taken off the rugs in a sunny, sheltered spot, so that the sun would cause the lice to come out of the horse's skin and so be brushed off. But the General would not allow the irregularity, and the horse-rugs had to go back on again at once. Red tape with a vengeance.

A Field Kitchen, generally called a "Cooker" by the troops. These Kitchens were a very real comfort to troops and served them even in the trenches.

The remarks of the troops required strict censoring after the General's departure.

The same day the veterinary officer, who was accompanying General Walker, was looking round the blacksmith's shop, where Bill Youd and "Mulga" Tonkin were industriously working. "Mulga" had just finished sharpening a pick and had stuck it in the ground to cool when the veterinary officer came along. "I say, my man," said he, "Don't you know that that pick is dangerous sticking up like that." "Mulga" looked at him for a moment and then replied: "Well, you can easily kick the bloody thing over if you don't like it," and suiting the action to the word he kicked the pick over with his foot and calmly went on with his job. The officer passed on without further comment.

One day Lieut. "Ragtime" Simmons went down to the transport lines. The T.O. and veterinary sergeant, "Jock" Vernon, were having a bit of revolver practice, and Simmons drew his gun and joined in. The shooting was far from brilliant, but "Ragtime's" effort was easily the worst. He said: "By God! I hope I never have to depend on my 'squirt' to save my life." It was not very long afterwards that poor Simmons had occasion to put his want of skill to the test, and lost.

On Sunday, April 1, the 11th Battalion had the opportunity of seeing the 5th Army Commander in the flesh. General Gough, who held that command, attended the church parade at Henencourt Wood camp, and he was the cynosure of all eyes. Not a few of the boys remembered that he was in command of operations in the terrible battles of Pozieres, Mouquet Farm and Flers.

Sergeant Tommy Hetherington left the battalion to take a commission in the new 70th Battalion, which with other battalions of the new 6th Division was being formed at this time.

April in the northern hemisphere is always noted for unsettled weather, and a heavy snowstorm came to indicate that winter was not quite gone. This made conditions very muddy again. There was a general inspection parade of the 3rd Brigade held on April 2. The troops marched to Bresle and were inspected by the divisional commander. In the afternoon a lecture was given to officers of the 3rd Brigade by Colonel T. Blamey. The subject was "Tanks."

On April 4 the battalion turned its face to the line once more, and the first camp on the way up was at Montauban. Snow fell in the morning on the march up, but it was fine again in the afternoon. The roads, however, and the camp site were in a fearful mess. Even a light fall of snow was able to make the country a quagmire in a very short time.

Next day the weather was sunny and fine, and the troops were in great spirits as they marched forward past Bapaume to their next camp at Haplincourt, about four miles east of Bapaume. On the march the troops were able to see the terrible havoc and destruction that the retiring Germans had caused in this beautiful part of France. A Frenchman, a member of the Gardes-Champetre, in speaking of this part of the country, said: "Now that you have been here you can say, when you get back to Australia, that you have been in the Garden of France."

The country was still fresh and green, with the first signs of spring showing; there was little evidence of shell-fire, but all the important road junctions had been mined and there were many gaping holes in the roads. Great numbers of trees, that are the glory of the roadsides in France, had been chopped down so that they had fallen and interlaced their branches on the roads, preventing any traffic. Orchards were destroyed, wells were poisoned and booby-traps left everywhere. Whole villages were laid in ruins and lovely chateaux gutted. Factories were smashed to pieces, and much valuable machinery ruined. The stock had all been driven back behind the German lines, and nothing of value had been left. Even the countryside was rendered unsafe for horse traffic on account of "crows' feet" having been left everywhere. These were four-pointed iron stakes, a few inches across, which when dropped had always one sharp point sticking upwards, and any horse treading on them was liable to get his feet badly wounded.

This wholesale destruction, which was no doubt quite good tactics on the part of the enemy, seemed to the troops much more terrible than that caused by the chances of war. The deliberate laying waste of the fertile country seemed more in keeping with the name of "Hun" than any other of the "outrages" for which the Germans were blamed.

Even the churches had not been left unscathed; some had undoubtedly been hit by shell-fire, but there were many that had been wantonly destroyed. Of course it must always be admitted that the spires made splendid observation posts, and there is very little sentiment in war, at least on the actual battle-fields.

Great numbers of Allied aeroplanes were lying wrecked in the evacuated area. This seemed to give the lie to the daily statement in the Press that the Allies were everywhere victorious in the air. As a matter of observation at this time, the Allied 'planes seemed to be much inferior in speed and manœuvre to the German 'planes.

Everywhere on either side of the roads and surrounding villages could be seen great belts of barbed wire entanglements. These stretched in brown irregular lines as far as the eye could see. Owing to the impassibility of the roads, the wire had to be cut and a passage made through the fields. The pads thus formed were very serviceable as long as no wheeled traffic was allowed to use them. They were comfortable to march on and were ideal for the movement of infantry.

It was a great experience for the troops, who had long been accustomed to the muddy, shell-torn country, to be once more operating in practically unbroken country, and country, moreover, that had but lately been in the hands of the enemy. A sense of adventure pervaded all ranks, such as had not been in the battalion since before Pozieres, when the troops had been promised open warfare as a result of the great offensive.

The troops were again eager and curious, and when they had been dismissed to their billets in Haplincourt it was not long before they were spread all over the countryside souveniring, examining everything and discovering all sorts of things. They behaved like a lot of schoolboys on holiday, and everywhere could be heard the explosions of the German "potato-masher" bombs, which the Diggers always delighted to throw. It was great fun to pull the string and to heave the bomb on to a heap of rubbish and watch the tin cans and the old boots go sailing through the air after the explosion. To those who loved the battalion it was most heartening to find the boys recovering their former high spirits and love of fun.

The battalion did not stay long in Haplincourt. A sudden move order came and the buglers were ordered to sound the "fall-in." Through a mistake, "A" Company's bugler (Private E. Brickhill) sounded the ever-welcome "cook-house," and the troops came joyously out of their billets anticipating some special feed. Captain Hallahan, who had ordered the "fall-in," looked at Brickhill in disgust and said: "Good, God! Bugler! I want these men to *fight* not *feed*." The boys were rather a chagrined lot when the correct call was blown and to fall-in at the double, and the companies soon moved up to Morchies, where the troops were mostly camped in a sunken road just south-east of the village. While here there was a draft of 20 men sent to the

Brigade Mining Company, and Lieut. W. Graham, who had reported back from a Lewis gun school on April 6, was sent in charge of the party.

A heavy battery was emplaced in the sunken road, close to where the battalion was located, and this position was discovered by the enemy. He shelled the position with heavy stuff just after sundown, and the gunners got for their lives. One shell fell among the 11th Battalion headquarters details and killed nine of the boys and wounded eight more, including R.S.M. Norman Pittersen. Pittersen was so severely wounded that he died shortly after. Norman Pittersen was a member of the original "D" Company. Bob Jennoe, a runner, who had been pre-eminent for gallant work in many stunts, was also killed. Among the wounded was Sergeant Harry Naylor, who was lying down without his tunic when the shell burst. He was evacuated without it, and it was found that he had left about £30 in notes in one of his pockets. His mate, Charlie Irons, collected the money and forwarded it to him, on hearing which Jim Kirkwood, one of the intelligence platoon, remarked, "Some blokes are lucky, alright."

R.S.M. Norman Pittersen
(Killed at Morchies)

After Pittersen's death, No. 694 C.S.M. W. Jelfs took over the duties of regimental sergeant-major.

The 3rd Australian Brigade had now received orders to capture the village of Boursies and the neighbouring ground, in conjunction with the 1st Brigade, which was instructed to attack the village of Hermies.

The 10th and 12th Battalions were to make the attack, with the 11th Battalion in support of the 12th. The attack was to be without artillery support, but arrangements had been made with the artillery to shell certain areas, and S.O.S. lines to protect the existing front lines had also been arranged.

To ensure speedy information of the troops' advance, the usual dawn aeroplane was to sound its klaxon horn over the position and the troops were to light ground flares in the posts they had reached.

For some reason the intended attack was postponed, but on April 9 "D" Company of the 11th Battalion moved up in support of the 12th. The weather was misty, with some snow and sleet, and there was a good deal of intermittent shelling by the enemy, but only one casualty in the 11th. In spite of heavy rifle and machine gun fire, the 12th Battalion advanced to the high ground, but its position was for some time insecure on account of the failure of the 1st Brigade to advance, and because the 10th Battalion met unexpected opposition near the centre of its advance. Later the 1st Brigade advanced on the right and the 12th Battalion was able, with the assistance of the supporting company of the 11th, to establish a post on the right of Boursies and to send a mopping-up party into the village. At 4 p.m. orders were sent to the 12th Battalion to consolidate Boursies, and for the 10th to occupy the high ground in front of its sector, while the 9th Battalion was to advance in co-operation. For this purpose, "B" Company of the 11th was sent to the 12th Battalion and "C" Company of the 11th to the 10th Battalion.

The 12th Battalion official diary for Monday, April 9, 1917, states, *inter alia*: "Portions of 'B,' 'C' and 'D' and two platoons of 'B' Company 11th Battalion attacked the Sunken Road. On the left 'C' Company and the 11th Battalion attacked from the Cemetery Road. This attack was again held up by machine gun fire from the left flank, but the 11th Battalion was able to push on and join up the left with 'B' Company on the right."

The 11th Battalion had three men killed, one of these being No. 1051 Private Bill Leahy, and 11 wounded, among whom were Lieut. Beckwith and No. 694 acting-R.S.M. Jelfs. Next morning the 10th, 11th and 12th Battalions advanced about 1,500 yards without much opposition and then dug in and consolidated.

The 10th Battalion diary states: "With the assistance of 'C' Company 11th Battalion, the line was pushed well forward of Boursies. Practically no opposition and no casualties."

The official report of the 11th Battalion for the same operation runs thus: "The whole of the battalion is now in the line. Two companies in support of the 12th Battalion and two companies in support of 10th Battalion. Casualties in 'B' Company: 2nd/Lieut. B. Bunny and 2nd/Lieut. G. Campbell. Battalion headquarters changed over with 12th Battalion. Captain MacLennan (adjutant) left for Scotland on ten days' leave. Lieut. H. Colvin took over the duties of adjutant temporarily. Lieut. A. Brodie left for the 3rd Training Battalion, England."

As will be seen from the above reports, the 11th Battalion only played a subsidiary part in a minor operation, but this was only a prelude to a battle, the brunt of which was to be largely borne by the West Australian troops.

On April 11 the 11th Battalion relieved the 10th

Private W. Leahy (killed at Morchies)

in the line in front of Louverval. The weather was cold and there was a fall of snow. The 9th Battalion was on the right and the 1st Battalion was on the left flank.

The Commanding Officer (Major R. A. Rafferty) and the I.O. (Lieut. C. G. Ross) visited the lines on the morning of April 12, and after a second visit some time later it was decided to alter the dispositions and advance the line as soon as the positions then held were consolidated. This consolidation was completed that night without much interruption save intermittent shell-fire. The same night another heavy fall of snow occurred, making everything cold and miserable again.

The posts that the troops were now holding were considerably scattered, and there were several different points for the battalion transport to deliver rations to. There were many delays, and it was a long time before the transport officer managed to collect all his scattered limbers. When the drivers reached their lines, after their long ride in the snow and sleet, many of the men were so numb that they could hardly unharness their horses and feed up for the night.

At this time the 3rd Brigade was holding a series of parallel and gently undulating spurs running north-east from the main Hermies Ridge on the north of the main Bapaume-Cambrai Road, and roughly about a thousand yards from the famous Hindenburg Line. The 3rd Brigade line ran across the forward slopes of these ridges. The country was not much wooded here, and was everywhere very open, but a number of shallow valleys and sunken roads made movement possible and also afforded ideal positions for defence by well concealed machine gun posts. There was a very fine field of view from most of the brigades' forward positions. In the brigade forward area were the villages of Louverval, Morchies and Lagnicourt, and as these positions were of great value to the Germans instructions were issued that they were to be defended at all costs.

By this time it was realised that the enemy withdrawal was not altogether undertaken because of a shortage of men in the Central Powers, but more because the Germans wished to free a number of divisions in order to strike a great blow at the Allies. The British Intelligence Staff had not then found out where this blow was intended to be made, and consequently it was necessary to safeguard all the doubtful parts of the line.

So, while the troops were instructed to keep up a continual steady pressure on the enemy, they were also impressed with the necessity of consolidating their position so as to be ready to drive back a possible counter-attack.

The orders given to the troops were specific. First, to advance the line until they were in a position to attack the Hindenburg Line; and second, to arrange their dispositions so that any German counter-offensive on any large scale would meet with defeat.

The role of the 3rd Brigade was therefore to consolidate its position thoroughly. In addition it was intended to advance the front gradually and systematically by means of posts, which were to be well supported, until the divisional line was within striking distance of the great Hindenburg Line.

As the brigade front had been greatly extended, it meant that careful co-operation and careful siting of posts were necessary, and positions were to be selected where they could best assist one another with covering fire and so prevent isolation of any of the posts.

The defence of the brigade was to be in depth rather than by the old system of a continuous line. There were to be three defence systems: first, a line of outposts, then the brigade reserve line and thirdly the corps main line.

The advanced line of resistance of the 3rd Brigade, which was held by two battalions, was about 6,000 yards wide. Each battalion held one outpost sector. The 11th Battalion was on the right and the 9th Battalion on the left, and the outpost lines were held first by a line of sentry-groups then by a picket line with supports. The orders were to defend the picket line at all costs.

This was the first occasion in which the 11th Battalion employed this system of defence.

On April 13 orders were sent to the line companies to again advance. This was done, and the battalion front was now extended still further and comprised a sector over 3,500 yards wide. The line held by the 11th Battalion was divided into four sub-sectors, each held by one company and distributed as follows from left to right: "D," "B," "C" and "A." Machine gun posts manned by the 3rd Machine Gun Company were also established in suitable sites.

The 3rd Brigade position was now close up to the Hindenburg Line, with the 11th Battalion holding the most advanced sector.

To troops who had been accustomed to the heavily defended lines that had been the accepted form of warfare in France up to this time, the system of defence employed seemed most inadequate. Not only was the front to be defended of abnormal width, but the weight of supporting artillery was very much below what was usually employed. To those who were privileged to be in the lines of communication it seemed as if the

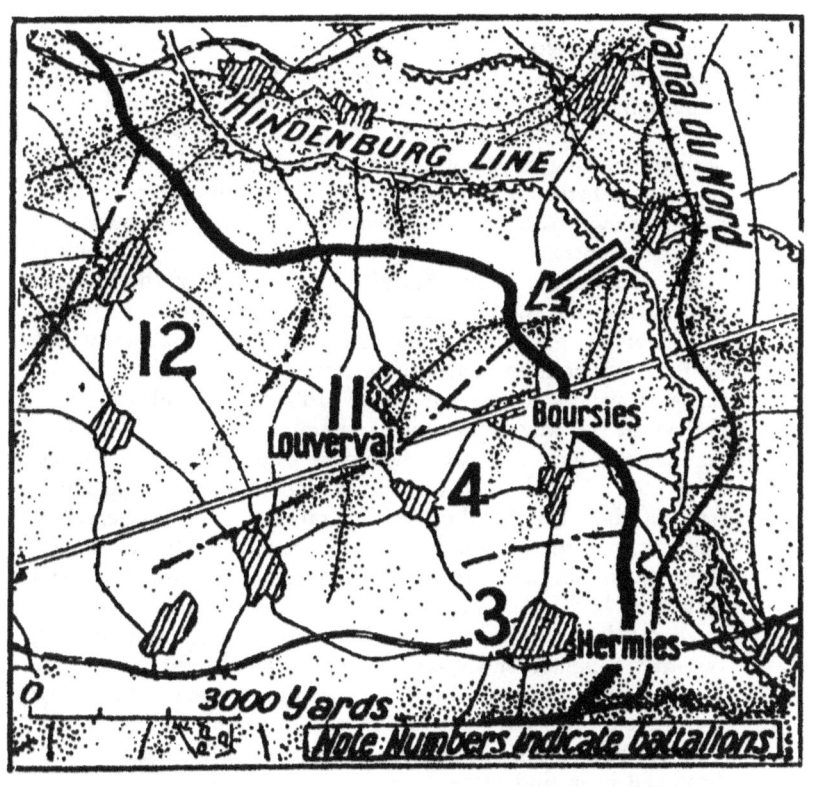

The position at the Battle of Lagnicourt. (Official Map.)

front was held only by the slenderest force, both in width and depth, and that there was a singular lack of obstructions of any kind for miles behind the lines, save the old German wire, and this was very scarce and broken after Haplincourt and Fremicourt were passed. As a matter of fact, the writer, who was then battalion transport officer, had ridden many times across country in the dark and in the snowstorms that occurred about this time, from Louverval Chateau as far back as Fremicourt, without meeting any worse obstructions than the signal wires running to batteries and unit headquarters. It was possible to canter or even gallop for miles without striking any trouble.

The country was so open, save for the gullies and sunken roads already mentioned, that visibility was one of the features of this area, and the Germans from their high points at Queant and elsewhere on the Hindenburg Line generally had an almost perfect view of all movement that occurred by daylight. Motor-lorries travelling down the Cambrai-Bapaume road would be shelled all the way to Beugny, and transport and artillery limbers, even a long way back, would be sniped at with 4.2's and even 5.9's. One day, Drivers Heast, "Scotty" Gauld and Dumbrill, of the 11th Battalion, taking rations up to Louverval in daylight, had to run the gauntlet of accurate shell-fire, and on their return journey they broke all existing records for speed in getting back after they had delivered their loads.

Some days previously Major Boyd-Aarons had been pointing out that a lighter and speedier type of horse would be better for first-line transport, as in the event of open fighting the transport could gallop into action with ammunition and bombs. This remark of the Major's did not get an enthusiastic hearing from the boys, and after the above experience "Scotty" Gauld said: "I don't know about galloping *into* action, but galloping *out* will always do me!"

The description of the new defensive system adopted is not intended as an adverse criticism of the tactics employed, for after events proved that the system fulfilled both functions that were required of it; but it was such a departure from the usual that a good deal of wonder and doubt as to its efficacy was current at the time, and there was no doubt that the system would sacrifice any front-line troops who were stout enough to resist should a strong and determined enemy attack be made on them. So, when on April 14 the report came back that the

Germans had broken through the outpost line and captured many prisoners, the doubters felt that they were justified in saying, "I told you so."

The 11th Battalion official diary for the date is: "Louverval, April 14. Two posts of 'C' Company were attacked and captured by the enemy. These posts were re-established by 'C' Company during the afternoon." There is a long story of fighting, suffering and heroism summed up in these few words.

As the main attack was borne by the outpost line, the following account by Private J. Kirkwood, of "A" Company, who was in one of the sentry groups, is an excellent first-hand description of the engagement:—

"On April 13 I was out with a patrol under Lieut. Patterson. We found no sign of the Germans, and that night we advanced our positions several hundreds yards. In the afternoon 'C' Company advanced its position. Captains Hemingway and Hallahan were with 'A' Company at this time. 'A' Company had the 4th Battalion on its right flank. The line was held by outposts about 150 yards apart; our post was the second from the 4th Battalion. Each post (sentry-group) consisted of five men. Our instructions were to hang on at all costs, and though the enemy was believed to be retiring, anything was likely to happen. Hemingway and Hallahan each visited the outposts twice during the night. Hemingway came round about midnight and said that look-outs must not be kept by reliefs but that every man had to stand-to all night.

"Early on the morning of April 14 we had a good deal of shell-fire, but nowhere exceptionally heavy. Before daylight we knew there was something doing, though the disturbance seemed to be away to our left. As day dawned we saw the fighting across to our left where the other companies were. Then the Germans advanced on our front. Corporal Ron Arundel, in charge of our post, said: 'Gee! The only b—— time I've seen any use for a machine gun,' but there was not any gun with our post. We were sending rifle fire to our front when we heard the shouts from the outpost on our right; we turned to find the enemy behind us. They had broken through the 4th Battalion and were coming back, evidently to keep their advancing line in touch. The post on our right was surrounded and occupied by the German troops, who were using their rifles against us. One bright lad asked the Corporal what we were going to do. 'Fight to a finish, or sling it in if we can't do anything else,' was the reply. We had made the mistake of paying all our attention to our right, and as things were quietening down we were unable to say what had happened on our left. We knew that the posts a few hundred yards away had gone, but were not aware of the fate of those closer to us. It was now bright day.

"We had just decided to open fire on a party of Germans when we discovered that they were dressing our wounded. Some of our troops could still be seen being taken back by the enemy. 'Well,' said one lad in the post, 'is it better to die for the Motherland or to make roads for the Fatherland?' The firing from the post on our right ceased. I am certain they had run out of ammunition. We had very little left ourselves. We then decided to go quiet and wait events. I tore up my diary and buried it in the bottom of the trench. Ron Arundel and the others gave any of their possessions that might have been of use to the enemy a decent burial also. We ate our emergency rations—against the wish of the Corporal.

"Nothing happened during the day. In the post on the right were now about a dozen Germans, and they and we were very interested in each other all that day. We were ready for anything. At night we held a consultation and decided to visit the post on the left. The Corp. and I went across very cautiously. As we approached the post and were not challenged we were not very comfortable, so we held a whispered conversation and then went on. We decided that the post was empty and entered it. One of our dead troops lay in the bottom. War! Hell! I have only one man to thank that I was able to pull myself together. Before I had ever been in the line at all I heard an officer lecturing his platoon on conduct in the line, and his words came back to me: 'Of course we are frightened, we all are; but we have to be men enough to put fear aside and *get on with the job.*'

"So we got on, but we hardly knew what to do. Ron said: 'Wonder if we can get back?' but I suggested trying the next post, as it seemed safe enough and was not far. When we got close to it we saw three Germans enter it, so we made tracks to our own post. As there seemed nothing to be gained by remaining, it was decided to get back, and after a bit of trouble we got back to 'A' Company's headquarters, where we received a warm reception.

" 'Old Shippy' (C.S.M. Shipton) and Lieut. Archibald always reckoned that 'A' Company held the Hun at Lagnicourt. Captains Hemingway and Hallahan were the only officers left with the company; Pope was killed and Patterson wounded before the stunt. Ron Arundel received a D.C.M. for his good work."

The above fine account of the actual happenings in a post during the break-through of the enemy is supplemented by an abridged version of the official report by Major R. A. Rafferty, C.O. 11th Battalion:—

"At 4 a.m. on the morning of April 14, 1917, an intense enemy artillery barrage was opened on the picket line held by the 11th Battalion, and this shelling was gradually carried back to Louverval and beyond battalion headquarters.

"This barrage lasted 15 minutes and 'D' Company (Captain J. P. O'Neil) on the left flank reported that the enemy was attacking. Captain R. Hemingway, 'A' Company, reported from the right flank that he thought that the Germans meant to attack, and this report was confirmed shortly afterwards.

"Almost immediately afterwards 'A' Company reported that the enemy had broken through the company on his left ('C' Company) and taken up a position in an old trench threatening 'A' Company's positions and that the enemy was still advancing from the direction of Noreuil."

Major Rafferty then sent another half company of his reserve to Captain Hemingway, who organised a local counter-attack and dislodged the enemy from some of his positions in the old trench.

Meantime the picket posts on the right were being hard pressed and ammunition was running short. Their right flank was in the air as the right battalion had fallen back, so they also gradually fell back until their right flank conformed to the 4th Battalion's position. Here they held on.

But "A" Company's posts were in a desperate position, and no firing was now coming from them as they had used up all their ammunition. As the enemy converged on the posts, the remainder of the garrison was seen to rush out of the position and charge the enemy with fixed bayonets. Lieut. Pope was in charge of this section and a later patrol reported having found his dead body.

The left picket of "A" Company, under the command of Lieut. P. Lyon, held out after the company on the left had been broken, thus gaining time for the company commander to make his rear line of resistance secure in the support line. This effort resulted in the complete loss of Lieut. Lyon and his platoon.

There was now a gap on the left of "A" Company, and this was covered by a company and a half from the 10th Battalion and two Vickers guns.

The position held by "B" Company, which had not moved forward with the rest of the battalion, was now in prolongation of the gap held by "A" Company, the gap being covered as above mentioned. The attack made on "B" Company was very light as compared with that on the rest of the battalion and was held off without great difficulty.

"D" Company, which was holding the line on the left of the battalion, was successful in holding its position, although for a time its position was very precarious owing to the battalion on its left having to withdraw for a short period. Wire in front of this position prevented the enemy from rushing this position. After a vigorous defence by this garrison the enemy was forced to retire and withdrew to a ridge about 200 yards distant.

All day long the left flank position was shelled. At dusk on the evening of April 15, Major Rafferty sent half a company from its position into a sunken road to support "D" Company. This was a well-justified precaution, because the enemy again attacked and succeeded in overwhelming the right picket of the left company. A company of the 2nd Battalion, which had reported during the day, was put into the gap between "A" and "B" Companies. This connected up the whole line, which was then consolidated.

After this the situation became normal, and an inter-battalion relief was carried out in the evening.

Major Rafferty concludes his report by stating: "Although our outpost line was forced back to a line previously decided upon and prepared in case of such events as had happened, we were, in spite of heavy losses, able to prevent the enemy (on whom heavy casualties had been inflicted) from breaking through the line held by the 11th Battalion."

Two prisoners were sent back to brigade headquarters. Two more companies of the 2nd Battalion arrived as supports, and the 10th Battalion took over half the battalion frontage.

As usually happens in any battle, it is difficult for any one report to adequately describe the whole of the battle, as often an engagement is broken up into a great number of smaller fights and struggles. In the case of the Battle of Lagnicourt, the operation was pre-eminent among all the battles that the 11th Battalion took part in in France as being one which consisted of small individual actions. When it is remembered that the battalion had to defend a line about two miles in length by means of small posts a long way apart, and by the supporting pickets and reserves in depth, and even these a long way back, it is obvious that the action must have been a series of small engagements.

Short accounts of some of these small actions are interesting in relation to the ultimate result of the whole battle.

Lieut.-Colonel R. A. Rafferty.
Assumed Command March, 1917.

In the interests of truth it is here necessary to state that there was an almost culpable weakness and indecision on the part of certain officers who were largely responsible for the wont of support given to their front-line posts, and whose conduct might have led to a serious disaster; but no praise is too high for the tough West Australian boys who held the isolated little posts against overwhelming odds (the odds were more than four to one) until they were either killed or entirely cut off from their fellows.

After the Germans had made their first attack, and the pickets under Lieut. Hall and Sergeant Cartwright behind their wire were able to hold their position, it was at once reported that two picket posts on the right were lost; but though one had been immediately overwhelmed, the other, under Lieut. Stuart and Sergeant Reg. Camden, the latter a splendid soldier, held on in its hopeless position all day, repulsing attack after attack. Runners were sent back for assistance, but failed to get through. The post was completely surrounded, all the ammunition was expended and with a third of the defenders gone the post could only surrender. But it had put up a strong resistance and checked the attack.

The German thrust fell most heavily on the posts held by Lieuts. Beattie, Lyon and Pope, who, with the other troops of the 11th Battalion, were holding a position well out on a protruding spur in the centre of the Australian sector. A most gallant resistance was offered by these posts, and when the number of German dead lying round them was noted afterwards it was realised that the Germans must have pressed the attack with determination and courage. Lieut. Bob Beattie and his picket fought hard to keep back the foe, and Beattie and many of his boys were wounded, but they still carried on. There were scores of German dead lying in front of this post. At length ammunition ran out, and with the officer wounded and many of the defenders killed, and their retreat cut off by the enemy, the post was captured. The Germans were so annoyed at the stout resistance put up and the number of casualties that they had suffered, that they were very rough with the prisoners they took, and Beattie was forcibly hastened along to the rear, for being wounded he was unable to keep up with the rest. Some of the troops who were taken prisoner with Beattie stated on their return from Germany that, if any man deserved a V.C. for good work it was Bob Beattie for his defence of this post.

Lieut. Peter Lyon also put up a fine defence, and by skilful handling of his men and ammunition he inflicted great slaughter on the enemy and held the Germans until weight of numbers and want of ammunition and support forced him to surrender. After his Lewis guns had become useless for want of ammunition he managed to destroy them before he surrendered.

The next picket, under Pope, was in the same desperate situation as the other two above mentioned. Surrounded and cut off from assistance on all sides he, too, hung on until the last. When all hope was gone he still ordered his men to hang on at all costs, and was himself killed in front of his post. For his conduct in this action Lieut. Pope was awarded a posthumous Victoria Cross. Lieut. Pope's runner, No. 3797 Private A. G. C. Gledhill, had made a gallant effort to bring help to Pope's position. He managed to get back to the rear and led a party of troops with ammunition and bombs forward, but a strong detachment of the enemy had meanwhile thrust in between Pope's post and the main line, and the reinforcements were not able to get through.

Lieut. Simmons, the same who, only a few days before had stated that his revolver would not be of much use to him if he had to depend on it to defend his life, was also cut off and surrounded and then shot dead at very close quarters. Sergeant Bill Plunkett, one of the battalion's best front-line soldiers, was in the next post, which was also overwhelmed by sheer weight of numbers, and Plunkett was killed.

Though the posts had been sited to afford the most protection to each other, the fact that the attack had been made in the semi-darkness discounted this factor, and few of the sentry-groups could make out what was happening at even the next posts, so far apart were they. The country was also broken into gullies down which the attacking troops advanced until they were behind the posts in the front line. Owing to the great distance from one another, it was a simple matter for the attackers to mop up a sentry-group or two, and then push along the dead ground until they were in rear of the posts.

But in spite of everything the German attack was not able to penetrate the main line. The dogged defence of the picket line gave the battalion commanders plenty of time to concentrate their reserves where they were most wanted and so prevent a break-through.

The 11th Battalion had borne the brunt of the attack and had suffered 245 casualties, of which 180 were missing. Not only was the 11th Battalion right in the centre of the attack, but it held a position far in advance of any of the other battalions holding the line. (See map.)

It was afterwards learned that the Germans had attacked this sector on account of the speedy advance that had been made there, and because the line was so thinly held. The German High Command was also desirous that a severe check should be given to the advancing troops so that their offensive spirit might be crushed before they came up against the Hindenburg Line.

There were four German divisions employed against the 1st Australian Division, and extra batteries had been brought into action by the Germans; there were also trench mortars and flammenwerfer employed. The 1st Australian Division's casualties were 1,010 and the German casualties 2,313, mostly from rifle and machine gun fire.

It was stated at the time, and since proved to be entirely without foundation, that this attack was the result of information having been furnished to the Germans by a non-commissioned officer of the 11th Battalion, who had been captured previous to the battle. Numbers of rumours were spread, but the general view of the majority was that it would have been impossible for any man of the 11th Battalion to have acquired the vast amount of detailed knowledge of the various units and gun positions which were reported to have been betrayed to the enemy, even if he had been trying to do so, as the battalion had only been in the vicinity for a few days and during that time was constantly on the move and engaged in actual warfare. The whole affair was speedily regarded as a "furphy" and as quickly forgotten.

Though the German attack had so signally failed, yet the foremost troops had reached several forward batteries and about half a dozen guns were destroyed. The batteries had been caught napping as regards their own particular defence, their personnel having scarcely a rifle amongst them, nor were there any other means of keeping off hostile infantry; so when the German fighting patrols approached, the artillerymen were helpess to defend their own guns. The artillery was so accustomed to rely on the protection of the infantry, and this had been so effective up to date, that the Australian artillery had become a little slack in the matter of its own defence. Immediate steps were taken to ensure that this mistake would not be repeated and thus the slow and painful school of experience was educating the Australian troops, and gradually efficiency and confidence grew out of the errors of the earlier battles.

On April 16 the two companies of the 2nd Battalion, which had been sent to support the 11th, were withdrawn. A prisoner was brought to 11th Battalion headquarters at midnight and from there sent to brigade headquarters. In the early morning Major Rafferty visited the front line and made arrangements for the further securing of the position. Patrols were sent out with the intention of gaining touch with the enemy. These patrols came under light rifle fire. During the afternoon other patrols were sent out to search for any wounded and dead, and for the collection of enemy identifications.

On the morning of April 17, the 11th Battalion was relieved by the 6th Battalion. The 11th moved back to billets in the village of Velu, where the troops rested for the remainder of the day. Next day a working party of two officers and 118 men was supplied for road-mending near Lebucquiere.

The 11th Battalion quartermaster's store had been established in one of the more or less intact buildings in Velu. The R.Q.M. (Captain Geoff. Egg) had just left the building a minute or so earlier when the whole store blew up through the explosion of a mine that had been left by the Germans during their retirement. There were no casualties, but one of the boys in looking at the wrecked building, and hearing that the Q.M. had only escaped by a few minutes, remarked, sourly: "Pity the old b——'s watch hadn't been ten minutes slow." Quartermasters were seldom popular with the troops.

This is no reflection on Captain Egg, who was well liked by his associates and was a conscientious officer who did splendid work in his long association with the 11th Battalion; but the troops in general regarded all Q.M.'s as species of ogres, whose speedy removal would have considerably brightened military life.

The blowing-up of this building put the wind up the troops and they were only too glad to make use of a number of tents that were drawn from ordnance. These were pitched in inconspicuous places, in the shelter of buildings and in among the trees, and as the weather had taken a turn for the better the boys were fairly comfortable.

The 3rd Brigade was now in the role of reserve brigade of the 1st Division. The line of defence was the Beaumetz-Morchies Line. The battalions of the 3rd Brigade were to be ready to move in twenty minutes if notice to that effect was given. For the purpose of rapid communication, two signal orderlies of the 11th Battalion were to be kept day and night at 10th Battalion headquarters.

On April 21, while the 11th Battalion was still at Velu, the Army Corps Commander (Lieut.-General W. Birdwood, K.C.S.I.) visited the troops.

On April 22, "C" Company left for Beaumetz to act as an escort for guns.

Spring was now well on the way, and the natural life of the country was much in evidence. There was an abundance of small game, and partridges were common and were just beginning to pair off. Of course the troops could not let such splendid opportunities go begging, and partridge shooting was one of the pastimes in this area.

One day Captain Alec Burgess and Lieut. "Pard" Riches were out trying to shoot some of these delectable birds. The two officers were clad only in issue flannels and strides, and looked pretty rough. They were using ordinary .303 rifles. A pair of partridges flew up from a slight rise just in front, and both blazed away "ten rounds rapid" with no apparent result. But not for long; for on the cessation of the fusilade, a purple face appeared on the other side of the rise and a most furious voice was heard yelling: "Stop! How dare you! Do you know that you nearly hit *me*?" Soon a Tommy colonel and his staff dashed up on horseback and the colonel glared at the two grinning Australians.

"Where are your officers?" barked the outraged old gentleman. "Well," drawled the "Pard," "I'm a bit of an officer." The colonel took an eyeful, then nearly exploded with rage. "You! How dare you! This is preposterous!" he roared. But Riches merely nodded towards Alec Burgess and said, adressing the colonel: "Better talk to him, colonel, *he's a captain*."

The whole party of English officers was horrified and their eyes goggled, but the two hard-cases merely came to attention, then laughed and wandered off to pastures new. When the colonel at last was able to find his tongue, all that was heard by the departing pair was, "Well I'm demned!"

Captain K. MacLennan returned from leave on April 23 and resumed the duties of adjutant, and Lieut. W. Graham reported back from Brigade Mining Company with 20 other ranks.

Next day the 11th Battalion was relieved by the 5th Dorsets at Velu, and the 11th took over from the 6th Lincolns at Haplincourt. Two companies, "B" and "D," of the 11th Battalion were placed as garrison in the Beaugny-Ytres Line, which was the corps main line of defence, and "C" and "A" were in support in the village of Haplincourt.

The duties in this defence line were chiefly patrolling the length of the sector, both by day and night, placing standing patrols at all the breaks of the wire, establishing anti-aircraft posts and consolidating and improving the line generally.

On April 24, 70 reinforcements from the base joined the battalion and the divisional guard of one sergeant and 29 other ranks reported back from Henencourt Chateau, where they had been stationed since March 28. Second/Lieut. George Lamerton, who had previously been C.S.M. of "D" Company, reported for duty from 1st Divisional School on April 25.

Battalion headquarters was in Haplincourt, in one of the least shattered of the houses. The chateau in this village was in a terrible state of ruin. One day the owner came along to revisit his home. The chateau had been a lovely place situated in pleasant wooded grounds in a charming corner of Picardy. What the feelings of this man must have been can hardly even be imagined when he saw his trees felled, his orchards ruined and his home with its lovely possessions broken and scattered around. When some of the troops expressed their sympathy, the Frenchman gave a Gallic and gallant shrug and said: "C'est terrible! mais, c'est la guerre."

The battalion was chiefly occupied, when not on actual defence, in supplying fatigue parties for the railway construction work at Fremicourt, in salvage work and in fumigating their blankets. There were occasional bathing parades and these were rather humorous, as the only baths the troops could get hold of were those out of the ruined houses, and as there was only a limited number, and all of different shapes and sizes, these parades were quite a change from the orthodox.

On April 27 Lieut. C. W. Mathews, 21/11th Reinforcements, reported for duty.

The Australian Commonwealth elections were being contested about this time, and on April 29 "A" Company men polled their votes. Australia was a far land in those days, and the elections meant nothing to the troops. Next day the remaining companies registered their votes, a total of 502 being recorded for the 11th Battalion.

The total casualties for the month of April were as follows: Officers: killed, 2; wounded, 5; missing, 4. Total 11. Other ranks: killed, 34; wounded, 103; missing, 176; sick, 3. Total 316. Grand total, 327.

The battalion strength on April 30 was 24 officers and 643 other ranks.

As before mentioned the battalion transport lines were at Fremicourt. From there the rations and ammunition and other material for the front line had been carried up by limber, and it was a long journey for the horses; but, of course, the drivers worked according to roster and it was seldom that the same team would have two strenuous days in succession. The horses, though well looked after, still showed signs of the hard winter they had come through, and several had to be evacuated to remount lines. Horses were very valuable at this time, and it is no exaggeration to say that a man's life was counted as nothing to a horse's or mule's. Some one had well said that the ratio of the value of a man's life to that of a horse was as 5d. is to 5/-.

Most of the drivers were passionately attached to their teams and would steal forage or anything else that would add to the comfort and well-being of their charges.

When off duty in this locality the transport section was digging a deep hole in order to try to locate water. A divisional order had been circulated to the effect that every unit was to make every endeavour to locate new water supplies, as, owing to so many of the wells having been poisoned by the Germans, the available supply in the forward area was limited. It was easy digging in the beautiful loamy soil, and soon a deep excavation was made, but there was no sign of water.

Driver Stenton had a nice pair of horses, named "Georgina" and "Sport." The latter was very sick, and the divisional veterinary surgeon worked a long time on him without avail. At last he said there was only one more thing that he could do and that was to give the animal a hypodermic injection. The officer said: "It's a shame to see a £120 horse die without trying everything. But this will be kill or cure." This incident is described to show the value that was placed on horses in those days, and the care and attention with which they were treated.

Stenton was naturally worried about his horse, and when it died, which it did almost immediately after treatment, he was much cut up. Horses were real friends during the war.

As no water was showing in the deep hole the boys had dug, the horse was dragged over and dropped in and buried there. Stenton had a cross made and erected over the grave with these words: "Here lies 'Sport.' A true Australian, who did his bit."

CHAPTER XXXII

NOREUIL AND BULLECOURT

THE TROOPS had been expecting to get the order to move further back, but May found the 11th Battalion still doing garrison duty on the Beugny-Ytres line. This was the corps defence line, and the sector held by the battalion lay due west of Bapaume and to the right and touching the main Bapaume-Cambrai Road. On May 1 General Walker, the divisional commander, visited the sector and made several suggestions for the improvement of the position. Troops that could be spared were used on fatigues and on railway construction work at Fremicourt.

The following officers and other ranks reported for duty on May 1, 1917: Major A. H. Darnell and Lieut McKean, from base details; 2nd/Lieut. E. M. (Dick) Clarke, from Cadet Training Battalion, England; 2nd/Lieuts. D. A. James and L. L. Summers, from reinforcements and 35 other ranks.

On May 3 an order was received from 1st Australian Division, stating that the 11th and 12th Battalions must be ready to move at short notice to the 2nd divisional area, which lay to the north of the Bapaume-Cambrai Road. The order came through at 2:45 p.m. and, although "C" Company was engaged on railway construction work near Velu, which was some distance away, the 11th Battalion reported "Battalion assembled" before 5 p.m. At 7 p.m. the troops were ordered to resume normal conditions, but to be ready for an immediate move. The order to move came through at 10:15 p.m. and by 11 p.m. the battalion had reported "Battalion moved out," and that all first-line transport was in readiness to move.

The 11th Battalion changed over to the 2nd divisional sector and took up a position on the Beugny-Ytres line east of Vaulx. At 4 a.m., on May 4, Lieut.-Colonel Rafferty reported to Brigadier-General Wisdom, of the 7th Brigade, 2nd Australian Division, and he was instructed to move the 11th Battalion to a sunken road near Noreuil. The move was completed by noon and the cookers and rations were brought up under cover of darkness, and after the troops had supper the cookers were withdrawn to a position in rear. The enemy shelling during this move was steady and well directed. The sunken road was especially subjected to fire.

Orders were received to relieve the 4th Battalion in the line that night. The 4th Battalion was holding a recently captured part of the Hindenburg Line. The relief was carried out successfully and was completed in the early hours of the morning of May 5.

The 11th Battalion was ordered to change over with the 12th Battalion at 4:30 p.m., in order to be in a position to carry out a bombing attack on the morning of May 6. The attack was to be on the two German trenches opposite the position, and the objective was to be a communication trench leading into these trenches. The attack was to be supported by a rolling barrage from west to east, which would pause on the objective for three minutes and then move eastwards at the rate of 50 yards every three minutes. Major Darnell was in charge of "A" and "B" Companies, and Captain Jack O'Neil in charge of "C" and "D" Companies. The attack was to be supported by trench mortars and the Vickers guns of the 3rd Machine Gun Company.

The whole line held by the 11th Battalion was heavily shelled during the early part of the morning of May 5, and among others Lieut. W. Dent-Young was killed. After 9 a.m. there was a lull in the bombardment, and the troops made use of this period to repair the damage done to their trenches and in consolidating the position generally. After sunset the enemy was noticed massing in the sunken road (the Moulin Sans Souci Road) and the artillery was notified. A very prompt and successful response was obtained. At 10 p.m. a wonderful display of multi-coloured flares was sent up by the Germans opposite, who had been engaged in digging a jumping-off trench about 75 yards in front of the 11th Battalion's position. On seeing the flares the supporting artillery again put down a barrage on the Germans, just as they were moving to attack, and completely shattered the attempt. There was a terrific amount of shell-fire on both sides, and the troops were unable to put out any wire in front of their position and the intended change-over with the 12th Battalion was not carried out.

The rations (hot and cold) and water and hot tea were again carried well forward by the first-line transport, so that the ration parties were spared as much as possible in view of the proposed attack on the following morning.

On the morning that the bombing attack was to have been carried out, the Germans disorganised the whole affair by getting in first, for soon after midnight on April 6 they started to make a number of raids on the 11th Battalion lines. At about 3:30 these raids developed into a strong attack and a S.O.S. barrage was called for. This was immediately put down, and the shelling drove the enemy back to his dug-outs. Severe artillery retaliation followed the failure of the German attack and very heavy casualties were inflicted on the 11th Battalion, and many of the troops who were in both battles reckoned that the shelling was almost as bad as at Pozieres. As a matter of fact the shelling on this occasion was the most intensive that had been recorded on the front, but fortunately it was not of long duration. While it lasted it was heavier than the worst of the Pozieres shelling, but owing to the relatively short bombardment it had not the same terrible effect as in the earlier battle.

After this heavy bombardment and the German attacks on the 11th and 12th Battalions, the troops were in no condition to make the attack that had been scheduled. The Commanding Officer of the 11th insisted that the attack must be made, but Major Darnell, the senior officer in the line, who knew the state of affairs and the small numerical strength of the available troops, refused to give the order for the attack to be carried out and the troops hung on in the position they were holding.

The enemy attacked again about 5:15 a.m. This attack was successfully pushed back, although it had been strongly pressed by the Germans. The supporting artillery barrage was so well laid down, however, that the Germans had very little hope and the remnants of the attackers were easily driven back by the 11th Battalion troops, although the battalion on the left had its right flank pushed back along the O.G. 1 (Old German Trench) and consequently the 11th Battalion troops were forced to conform and they withdrew to the sunken road.

A counter-attack was immediately organised, the enemy was driven back and the original position restored. During this counter-attack the supports in the O.G. 2 manned the parados of their trench and by rifle and machine gun fire helped greatly in driving back the enemy. The artillery fire was again very effective, although there were many complaints of short shooting. This, however, was hardly avoidable, as the trenches were so close to the enemy, and even with the best of artillery fire something like four per cent. of the shells fired must fall on troops 75 yards from the barrage line, and the percentage greatly increases as the distance lessens.

In this battle the Germans used flammenwerfer against the 11th Battalion troops. At first the effect of the flame-thrower was most demoralising, but it was soon discovered that the bearer of this weapon was very vulnerable as he was such a conspicuous target.

There were heavy casualties during this long day of fighting and among others the following officers were hit: Lieut. V. H. Daniels (killed) and Captains R. Hemingway, J. P. O'Neil and Alec Burgess and 2nd/Lieuts. H. Colvin and L. L. Summers (wounded). In the diary of No. 5686 Private R. Duncanson is this entry for April 6: "Terrible shelling all day and continuous stream of stretchers going back."

Bullecourt was one of those ding-dong battles which seemed to be all shell-fire and counter-attacks, and there was no phase of the 11th Battalion's tour of the line that was particularly outstanding. In all the attacks there were so many units mixed up, and the individual actions were so small, though desperately and fiercely contested, that it is hard to pick out any events of special significance.

Sergeant Veitch's defence of Ostrich Avenue was of inestimable service in holding up the German attack in that sector, and the bombing attacks by Captain W. Hallahan and "Chook" Fowles were gallant sorties up the German trenches which culminated in the driving out of the enemy.

Hallahan had told Fowles to attack from the left while he led a bombing party round by the right. Hallahan had only two men with him—Privates Kirkwood and Gillard—and as they pushed up the trench they were met by a party of Germans with a flammenwerfer. This weapon was not working too well and only a few feet of flame issued from the thrower. Hallahan and Kirkwood each threw a bomb and these forced the enemy out of the trench, but young Gillard was killed and the two survivors hardly knew what to do. However, they went forward and ran slap into a party of the 12th Battalion who had been bombing from the other direction. The N.C.O. in charge said to Hallahan: "By Cripes, Skipper, you are lucky you did not stop one of ours!" Having seen that everything was satisfactory in the recaptured trench, Captain Hallahan went in search of "Chook" Fowles and was relieved to see him coming up the trench, but with a sadly depleted party.

The German troops engaged in this battle were Wurtemburgers, and were fine stamps of men and mostly big fellows.

The German shelling increased in intensity and many of the boys were killed, wounded or buried. Mates spent a lot of time digging out their cobbers after the frightful shell-bursts. The casualties were very heavy.

If the conditions in the line were bad, the state of affairs in the communications was also very severe on carrying parties and stretcher-bearers. Further back the artillery and transport had difficult conditions to work under. The sunken road at Noreuil, through which most of the traffic for the battalion lay, was almost continually under shell-fire and many casualties occurred here.

The stretcher-bearers, as was usual in a big stunt, were overworked and in this sector they had specially bad conditions to work under, but they nobly carried out their job. There was a constant stream of wounded passing through the aid-post, and though the 'bearers were at their last gasp yet all the wounded were dressed and evacuated with the least possible delay. The excellent work performed by "Doc Robbie" (Captain G. S. Robinson, the M.O.) and his staff was much appreciated by the troops, and "Robbie" endeared himself to all the boys by his kindness and considerate treatment of them. He was a very capable M.O. and a man in every sense of the word.

There were a good many dug-outs in the sunken road at Noreuil and they were of great use to the troops camped there, but the boys could not always be in these shelters. One day the writer rode up to Noreuil with Major Boyd-Aarons, who had been summoned from Fremicourt, where the transport lines were still situated. The Major was required to take over the command of the battalion, as Lieut.-Colonel Rafferty had been wounded. While waiting for the Major, who had gone to battalion headquarters, the writer was sitting on his horse in the sunken road at Noreuil. As he was having a yarn with one of the boys a shell burst on the bank above the road and a splinter passed over the horse's neck, causing the "troop" to duck. As the writer turned to follow the sound of the flying metal, a man's head and shoulders appeared coming out of a dug-out. The splinter took the man fairly between the eyes and he died immediately. A man, standing by, remarked: "His name must have been written on that piece."

The Germans also shelled many of the cross-roads and important corners, and as they had not long been driven from the area it was only natural that they should know all the spots likely to be most used.

On May 7, as the 11th Battalion was so exhausted and weakened by the continual enemy action, the troops were relieved by the 12th Battalion and they moved back to close supports. The relief was completed at 11:20 p.m. There had not been any enemy action except artillery bombardment on this last day, and the battalion Lewis gunners had an "open go" at parties of Germans moving to and from one of the strong points opposite the sector. It was estimated that from 30 to 40 casualties were inflicted on these parties.

The 11th Battalion casualties were as follows: Officers, killed, 2; wounded, 6; missing, nil. Other ranks: killed, 44; wounded, 146; missing, 78. Total: 276. Third Brigade total: 949.

While in support in the sunken roads the following officers reported to the battalion: Lieuts. Archibald and Beasley and 2nd/Lieuts. Dale and F. Stahl, from division and army schools. C.S.M. D. Walker also reported back from 5th Army School and eleven N.C.O.'s left for 3rd Training Battalion in England and seven N.C.O.'s went to 5th Army Musketry Camp, Warloy. It will be realised from the above movements that the great organisation of the Australian Army in France was now carrying on with machine-like efficiency and regularity, and that the vicissitudes of battalions or even brigades in no away affected the general routine.

The Bullecourt "stunt" was one of these unsatisfactory engagements in which a great many casualties were suffered by the battalion without much to show for the suffering and slaughter. The battle could never have been anything else but futile, as it was only part of a glorified demonstration to relieve other fronts and specially to help the French who were feeling the strain. If the casualties were lighter than those of Pozieres it was because the troops were not so long in the front lines, and also in a less degree to the much improved artillery support and the co-operation of other arms. In the case of the 11th Battalion, the artillery support was particularly good at Bullecourt, while the courageous handling of trench mortars, particularly by Lieut. McNeil, of the 3rd A.L.T.M. Battery, and the siting and support of the brigade machine gunners gave confidence to the troops in the line. The men could not fail to perceive that the staff work had improved out of all knowledge. While realising all this, the troops felt that they had been given an impossible and useless task and that the battalion had been sacrificed needlessly, and for a long time the Second Battle of Bullecourt left a nasty taste in the mouths of many.

On May 9 the 11th Battalion was relieved by the 53rd Battalion and moved out from the sunken roads at 2:30 a.m. The troops moved independently to Vaulx, where they were collected at 5 a.m.

There were some heavy guns in position near Vaulx and these were continually shelled by the German batteries. One big gun mounted on a railway truck used sometimes to fire from the field hospital near by. The detonation of this gun was so powerful that all the lights in the vicinity would go out when the gun was fired at nights. Not only was the great explosion a terrible trial to the patients in the hospital, but the extinguishing of the lights was both inconvenient and dangerous. The German reply to this gun also caused a lot of shelling in the neighbourhood of the hospital. There was a distinct lack of co-ordination somewhere.

From Vaulx the troops marched to Beugnatre, where they bivouaced for a few hours. Here the troops rested and breakfasted and then held that saddest of all parades, the "roll call," after battle. The answer to a name "killed in action" or "missing" meant that one more good fellow had gone, and when this reply was called out more than a hundred times it cast a gloom over the battalion. Even in coming out of the line after being relieved there were four casualties, two men being killed, one missing and one man wounded. "Missing" generally meant killed in battles of heavy artillery fire.

At 8 o'clock the battalion moved off to Bapaume, which was reached at 10 a.m. The men were billeted in the shattered houses and cellars. They were allowed to rest for the day.

The battalion strength was 24 officers and 402 other ranks. The brigade total was 2,480. In the last two actions the 11th Battalion had lost 521 men.

There was an interesting brigade memo. issued on May 13, 1917, entitled "Lessons learned in recent operations," from which a few extracts are given.

"The outstanding feature was the great success of the power buzzer and amplifier for keeping communication with the actual front line."

"One communication trench is not enough. Numbers of lives were lost owing to so many reliefs going in at once down the same trench."

"Closer co-operation is necessary between the brigade machine gun company and battalions. Also much closer co-operation is required between pioneers and engineers and the battalions in the line."

"The great value of the rifle-grenade was fully demonstrated. By the use of these one company was enabled to keep the enemy bombers at such a range that it made the enemy's bombing attacks futile."

(Compiler's note.—The Germans at this time used a small oval grenade called by the troops "egg bombs." These bombs could be thrown much further than the Mill's grenade, and consequently in a bombing fight the Australian troops were at a disadvantage. Adaptations had been made to the Mill's grenade and the ordinary rifle, so that the standard bomb could be used as a rifle-grenade if required. This overcame the disability the British troops had been labouring under.)

CHAPTER XXXIII

BAPAUME AND RIBEMONT

LIEUT.-COLONEL RAFFERTY, who had been wounded in the hand but had remained on duty, was granted leave of absence to England on May 10 and Major J. Boyd-Aarons took over the command of the battalion. The troops were instructed to have a general overhaul of clothing and equipment and were given the rest of the day off. The boys took advantage of the occasion to explore Bapaume and neighbourhood. There was much of interest and many were the tales of the town and its surroundings. There was, of course, the church, by this time completely shattered and with the beautiful organ in matchwood. There was a heap of skulls lying exposed in the broken vaults, which created a lot of controversy. The boys had many weird stories as to how they had got there. Some believed that they were relics from the days of the French Revolution and the guillotine. The most generally accepted story was that when the church was built the skulls of the faithful were gathered from the vaults of the surrounding churches in the diocese, and these were placed under the new church so that the edifice would be representative of the whole district.

Many of the boys took the opportunity of visiting the old German positions on the Bapaume Ridge and looking back over the country they had so painfully fought over, and where they marched and bivouaced during the summer and winter of the previous year. Looking down from this vantage point the troops could see the whole panorama of the battlefields The landmarks of the fighting in the Somme, insofar as it had affected the Australian divisions concerned, were clear and distinct in the lovely bright days of the early summer. Just before them the boys saw Thilloy and Ligny-Thilloy, where they had been fighting not so long before. The butte of Warlencourt raised its bulk on the right, and further back Le Barque and Flers had their memories. Gueudecourt was an outstanding target more to the left, and it was remembered how this village used to be shelled unceasingly day and night. Back in the distance was Pozieres and far off Albert could be seen, with its buildings showing faintly through the haze. The troops looked long at all this country and sad and bitter were their thoughts, no less so because generally unexpressed. The general remark passed by most of the boys was that it was a marvel that the German was ever forced back at all, seeing that he had every advantage of position and observation. Traffic could be seen moving on

This was a village.

the roads almost as far back as Albert. The position was truly one of great strategical importance.

During May 11 and 12 the battalion was still resting after the Bullecourt Battle. The necessary reorganisation was being carried out and the customary fatigue parties were supplied. Second/Lieut. Gemmell and 104 other ranks reported from reinforcements and 2nd/Lieuts. McKinley and Inman from divisional school.

On May 15 there were large working parties supplied to the railway transport officer at Bapaume, and next day the same number of troops was asked for. This so depleted the battalion that there were not sufficient men to parade and the training, which was scheduled to start on May 16, had to be carried out with skeleton companies.

Owing to the fact that the divisional commander had been granted leave of absence, Brigadier-General Bennett, commanding the 3rd Australian Brigade, took over the temporary command of the 1st Division.

On May 21 the enemy shelled Bapaume rather heavily. Many buildings collapsed under the bombardment, but there were no casualties in the 11th Battalion. The troops were still mostly absorbed in fatigue parties and the remainder of the battalion was occupied in refresher and instructional work.

The 11th Battalion was relieved by troops of the 5th Australian Division on May 22, after which it marched to Bazentin le Petit, where the troops went into huts. This was the last time the battalion camped in this one-time village, which was now far behind the firing line, but still a long way into the empty lands that lay beyond Albert. This great space was now covered with lush grass and the horses of the transports were now revelling in the plentiful feed. When the battalion was camped at Bazentin on this occasion, the transport drivers were grazing their horses near an old trench when they came upon a whole line of unburied British dead. The poor lads had been caught by machine gun fire just as they had hopped out of the trench, and they lay there exactly as they had fallen. The advance had passed on, and in the furious tide of war these heroes were forgotten. The troops reported the location and the particulars were sent to the proper authorities.

While in this camp at Bazentin, it was noticed that one hut had its interior adorned with all sorts of verses and near verses. From the subjects of some of these effusions it was obvious that the hut in question must have served at one time as a "boob" or guardroom.

Some of the verses were witty, and the following one is worthy of mention:

"Apres la guerre finit,
Australia will always do me.
You can do your own stunts
On any old fronts
Apres la guerre, fini!"

Of course any Digger could supply a better line than the fourth one.

Lieuts. J. Long and F. Rooke, Private C. Sebo and Lieut. C. Prout. Out of the Line having a "Spot."

Next day the battalion marched to Ribemont. The whole 3rd Brigade was on this march, with the necessary intervals between units, and there were special instructions about letting faster-moving units through should the necessity arise. The battalion reached Ribemont in the afternoon after a long march.

Ribemont was a fair-sized place on the River Ancre, a tributary of the Somme. Here the battalion went into good billets, mostly in the barns and out-houses of the many farms of which the village was composed. The battalion transport was camped in an apple orchard where the trees were in full bloom when the troops arrived. It was a lovely shady spot near the river. Brigade headquarters was in a large mansion in the main street, and the other units of the brigade were also billeted in the village.

The winter was now quite over and the sun was daily increasing in strength, drying up the lately water-logged country and making living conditions as pleasant as the battalion had ever experienced in France.

An intensive course of company and battalion training was adopted, and every effort was made to smarten up the troops. Courses of instruction were held in all the specialist sections, the personnel was brought up to strength and equipment and weapons were overhauled and renewed.

Ribemont was situated on a slight rise above the River Ancre, which at this place meandered through the middle of a wide valley bordered by steep hills. The portions of the valley nearest the river were thickly wooded, giving a cosy and sylvan look to the countryside. Further off the bare hills of Picardy rose abruptly from the flat plain and stretched in rolling downs as far as the eye could see, mostly treeless and bare of settlement.

The villagers were mostly engaged in agricultural pursuits, but there was a large woollen mill which at this period was only working part-time. The village of Mericourt, which was adjoining but on the other side of the river and out of bounds to the troops of the 3rd Brigade, also had a fair population, so that there was a considerable amount of life and movement about the area. The main Albert-Amiens Road ran past Ribemont about a mile to the north, and this artery was always moving with traffic.

The rest at Ribemont was one of the bright memories of the 11th Battalion's service in France, and as it lasted for several weeks more than a passing reference to this period must be given.

In the first place the fresh green of the fields and the trees was a tonic in itself and the friendly village life was balm to the war-weary troops who were pleased and amused at the simple, homely scenes around them. The boys used to be interested in the local blacksmith, and the way in which he tied up the horses' feet to a steel rail while he shod them. Some of the bushmen used to wonder how some of the station outlaws would have finished up had their legs been tied to the rail.

Then the communal shepherd and his big dog used to intrigue the troops. The shepherd was a grizzled old man and his dog was something after the style of the old English bob-tail sheepdog. Each morning the shepherd would start at one end of the village with his dog. The wise animal would hop in through the wicket gate leading into a farmyard, and out would come half a dozen or more sheep; then the dog would visit a farm on the other side of the road and appear driving a few more "moutons." (The usual custom in this part of Picardy was for a number of farms to have their buildings grouped in villages while the farms themselves might be quite a considerable distance away, and every morning if circumstances demanded it the farm workers would set out for their fields. This huddling together of the farmhouses in communities was said to be a survival from ancient times, when the inhabitants of the country had to gather together for protection. At any rate Ribemont was no exception to the general rule, and farm steadings were in close proximity all along the several streets of the village.)

To return to the sheep. As the shepherd and his dog progressed along the street, the flock would be continually augmented until the full quota had been gathered. The shepherd would then take his charges out among the unfenced fields and only allow them to feed on certain areas.

The dog would keep the sheep off any fields that had crops in them, and woe betide any sheep that trespassed over the often invisible boundary. How the dog knew was a mystery, unless the shepherd made signs to him; but he seemed to be aware exactly where the sheep ought and ought not to go. After letting the sheep graze all day the shepherd drove them home and the reverse process to the morning's operations was carried out. It was amusing to see a few sheep leave the gradually diminishing flock and hop through a little gate to the right, and then some more run to the left and so on, the while the old dog kept a watchful eye on them to see that there was no silly business. When the last sheep were disposed of, the shepherd and his dog returned to their own domicile.

Before going on to the stories of the Diggers themselves, the story of the 11th Battalion's stay at Ribemont would be incomplete without reference to the kindly relations that existed between the troops and the villagers. Officers and men immediately adapted themselves to the conditions of life as they found them, and were received into the family circles of the people they dwelt among. The battalion M.O. even officiated at a local maternity case, while Lieut. Riches shared a case of lovely West Australian Cleopatra apples, which he had sent out from home, with the admiring and appreciative French folk.

The Diggers helped Madame and her family with their daily tasks, and even the Brass Hats took an interest in the life of the residents to the extent of allowing their veterinary staff to assist the inhabitants in any way they could, and they also put the battalion transports on to cleaning up the town by carting away a great deal of accumulated rubbish.

The following extract is from a letter to the compiler from Sergeant "Jock" Vernon, the 3rd Brigade veterinary N.C.O., who was attached to the 11th Battalion and was with the unit throughout its whole period of service:

"The times at Ribemont were good. I still have a pass issued to me by the town major to allow myself and one other rank to proceed to Mericourt (which was out of bounds) to attend a Frenchman's horse and dog which were sick. Since coming back to Australia I've received a letter of thanks from these same people. Where they got to during the fighting of 1918 I do not know, but their home was blown to bits. Then the cow you mention belonged to the village postman. He was so delighted when I doctored it that he raced around, and when I refused to take anything in payment he tried to cram a pair of live squabs in my tunic pockets. I was later called out to the baker's horse, and on the Sunday following its recovery the baker's boy arrived with a huge raspberry pie. I'm sure you remember that!

"There are two other outstanding memories of Ribemont (no, not Incinerator Kate!). The fishing you and I attempted to do there and the cricket we played, the latter made possible by your own good wife sending us equipment from Scotland."

There were many incidents at Ribemont that will always be remembered by the troops. It is hard to choose among so many humorous episodes, but the following will serve:

While on this long rest every attempt was made to make the 3rd Brigade as efficient as possible. Saluting was insisted on and guards and other ceremonial parades were turned out as from the "book." There was keen competition among the various battalions as to which unit should turn out the smartest brigade guards.

Brigade headquarters, as already mentioned, was in a large mansion in the main street of the village. There was a circular drive in front of the building and there the changing of the guard took place with all due ceremony. The old guard would be drawn up to receive the new guard, which was played up the street by the battalion band. On reaching brigade headquarters the band would march round the circular drive and await the relief of the old guard, which it would play off the brigade ground and so down the street to battalion headquarters for dismissal.

On one occasion, Lieut. Archibald was in charge of the 11th Battalion guard. "Archie" generally took himself and his duties very seriously, and on this occasion he had surpassed himself in the matter of attire. He shone and glittered like the resplendent officers seen mostly on the films. He was also particularly careful over the appearance and equipment of his command. When all was ready, Lieut. Archibald gave the order, "Guard! T'shun! Slo—pup! Fo-o-rm fo-s! Right! By the right, qui-ck march!" and the band struck up and off the guard went up the village street with all the Diggers and civilians and children and dogs lining the paths to watch the boys go by. And it was indeed a brave show that they made, for the troops were exceptionally well turned out and they would have been conspicuous in any company for appearance and smartness.

On this occasion the band was at its best, playing the troops forward to "Only one more bloody route-march. Only one more church parade," and behind the band was the stout Lieut. Archibald in all his glory. He seemed to be determined to uphold the prestige of the 11th Battalion against all comers. The troops lining the road were delighted with the turnout any many of them followed the band down to brigade, and there was a greater crowd than usual to watch the changing of the guard.

As was the custom, the band turned in at the gate leading into the circular drive in front of the brigade headquarters, and all the brigade staff had appeared at the windows to watch the proceedings.

The old guard was drawn up in position, and on came the band in great style, with "Archie," with his chest out and stepping like a Guardsman, following immediately behind. He was the cynosure of all eyes. The band passed the old guard, but the new guard, in accordance with instructions, paused and marked time in front of the old guard. Not so Lieut. Archibald; he kept on right behind the band and was played right round the circle, marching by himself. His face, when he came round and met the amused gaze of the entire brigade staff and the assembled crowd, was red as a turkey-cock's, but he still kept time to the band and marched on, doing his "pas seul," until he came up to his guard which was still marking time, when he then took charge.

Everything went without a hitch thereafter, which says a lot for Lieut. Archibald. But the sight of his dapper form strutting round the circular drive on its own will always be one of the memories of Ribemont to those of the 11th Battalion who were there. The sequel to this tale was a request signed by all the junior members of the 3rd Brigade Staff to the effect that the next time the 11th Battalion was detailed to supply the brigade guard "Would the adjutant please detail Mr. Archibald as officer of the guard?"

Then there is the recollection of the billet where the battalion guard was situated. It was the usual Picardy farmhouse, with entrance by a high, covered gate, the usual manure-pit and the walk round the two sides with the dwelling-house facing the gate.

But in that yard was a long cask of wine; a tunne or pipe, or some wonderful name like that. Perhaps the guard was there to look after that cask. However that might have been, it is evident that those responsible had forgotten the well-known Latin tag, which translated freely runs "Who keeps an eye on the guard?"

At any rate it was not long before the precincts of the guardroom used to be the most popular place in the village. All went well until the guard made a fearful exhibition of one of its turnouts, and several members were noticed to be obviously "under the influence."

A visit of inspection was made; everything seemed correct except the unlucky guard, who got it "in the neck."

Not long afterwards the owner of the billet had his suspicions aroused by the constant throng of visitors, who always seemed to be playing cards or sitting on or near the big cask. So he pounded on the barrel and the hollow sound startled him. Closer investigation showed a neat augur hole and a length of rubber tubing. Then the beans were spilled with a vengeance, and there was a nice bill to foot.

While on the subject of guards, this story cannot be left out. It happened that "Jock" Ferguson was in charge of the guard, and as he had but newly put up his third stripe he was determined that everything should be ship-shape. Unfortunately one of the boys detailed for guard was about the most casual soldier in the whole Australian army, and his presence in the guard worried "Fergie" so much that he took him aside and gave him a lot of private instructions as to what he should do if he saw the Commanding Officer or a field officer approaching. The Digger promised to do his best.

When his turn came for sentry-go, it seemed as if the Fates had heard Sergeant Ferguson's prayer, for hardly a leaf stirred in the village. But "Jock's" coaching was not to be wasted, for Major Boyd-Aarons, who was then temporarily in command of the 11th Battalion, appeared at a considerable distance away. The sentry immediately came to the slope and then gave the Major a smart "present" (i.e., he presented arms). There was no response, as the Major had not noticed him.

But the casual one was not to be baulked in this manner. He lowered his rifle, put his fingers in his mouth and emitted a piercing whistle. The C.O. stopped dead in his tracks and gazed in the direction of the sound. The sentry waved his hand, pointed to himself and then in his best style presented arms. The Major, who was always a real sport, appreciated the situation and returned the salute.

The weather towards the end of May was pleasantly warm, and there was much bathing in the Ancre and in the backwaters that ran everywhere among the wooded flats of the river valley. There were many eels and some perch and pike in the pools, and some of the boys did a little fishing with lines. The bombers were more successful. At nights the peace of the evening would be shattered by a gramophone situated somewhere in the direction of the 12th Battalion billets. It was surely the loudest gramophone in the whole world, and nightly it disturbed the echoes with

"Everyone on the beach could see
Ten little fingers, ten little toes,
Two little eyes and one little nose." Etc.

On May 28 there were brigade sports, in which the 10th Battalion came out top with a good margin of points. The 11th Battalion made a poor showing as far as points were concerned, but as the battalion was at this period numerically by far the weakest in the brigade, it naturally was at some disadvantage.

The battalion strength as at May 31, 1917, was as follows: Officers, 29; other ranks, 596; total, 625. Brigade total, 3,035.

The battalion was now enjoying quiet, peaceful days after the stress of war. The troops were gradually becoming fitter and being much smartened up by their training. Drafts of reinforcements and details from hospital were helping to bring the battalion up to strength. A fair amount of leave was being granted, but occasionally local leave would be stopped for one reason or another.

During one of these temporary cessations of leave, the C.O. (Colonel Rafferty this time) informed the adjutant that he was going to attend a conference at division, and that he would not be back that night. He and the M.O. mounted their horses and moved off in the direction of Henencourt.

No sooner were they gone than long Joe Barry sauntered into the orderly room and, addressing the adjutant, said: "I say, Jerry. Where's the Old Man gone?" He was told that the Colonel and the Doctor had gone off to division and would not be back till next day. After a few casual remarks Lieut. Barry walked out, but as soon as he was round the corner he made use of his legs to some purpose and soon reached his billet, where he told a friend the good news. In a short time the two bright lads were on a motor-lorry bound for Amiens.

They negotiated the barriere safely (the barriere was for the purpose of checking all troops, vehicles or civilians entering the city of Amiens). Then they proceeded to enjoy themselves after the manner of those who visit towns after a long sojourn in dry desert places. The city was without lights at night, and it was difficult for visitors to find their way about in the darkened streets. The cafes and shops were still gay at this period, and Amiens was just like a little Paris. The two gay sparks managed to visit quite a number of places of amusement and refreshment before they considered it time to be thinking of wending their way homeward.

Reluctantly leaving the gaiety and comforts of their restaurant, they stumbled out into the intensified darkness of the night, and now the puzzle was to find the way back to the barriere so that they could catch an east-going motor-lorry. But all directions were the same to the revellers, and so they decided to find someone to direct them to the barriere. Just then the silhouettes of two officers were seen in the dim light of a doorway.

"There you are, Joe. Ask one of these chaps," said the other delinquent.

Joe immediately bowled up to the two officers and then stopped dead in his tracks. He was a bit short-sighted, but even with that disability he was able to recognise Lieut.-Colonel Rafferty and the M.O. It was too late to retire with honour, so Joe saluted and gazed down from his high altitude on the short and dapper Colonel and waited to be officially slain. The verdict was short and to the point: "Will you please return to your billet immediately, Mr. Barry, and consider yourself under arrest. I will deal with you to-morrow."

Poor Joe said "Yessir," clicked his heels together and saluted and marched off. The two worthies continued their search for the barriere, which they eventually found, but unfortunately they were unable to find any lorries going towards Albert, and the revellers had to walk all the long way home. It is on record that "Long" Joe's remarks on this occasion would have been a liberal education for any young soldier.

Mention has been made of "Incinerator Kate." This was a poor half-wit that used to hang around the camps and billets. From her habit of collecting old garments and boots around the incinerators, she gained her sobriquet. She was a grotesque, uncouth figure with her stocky form clad in a Digger tunic and her feet stuck into boots several sizes too large. She does not come into the story any more than that she was a part of the scenery that all the troops who were at Ribemont remember. She was a dingy figure, whose recollection only made the rest of the stay brighter by contrast.

The official battalion records for this period are very meagre, and there are only a few details given for the month of June. During the first week the battalion competitions took place and the troops took a keen interest in them. The competitions were all of a military nature and were all really a part of the test to decide which was the best company in the division. In the 3rd Brigade heats, the 11th Battalion was at the bottom of the list in both company and battalion competitions, but as mentioned previously the 11th was numerically by far the weakest battalion in the brigade. The battalion transport made a better showing, and Driver Harry Dumbrill, of the 11th Battalion, was first in the limber competitions.

On June 12 the battalion marched to Henencourt Wood to take part in the divisional sports. An unfortunate accident happened at this meeting. During one of the bombing competitions Lieut. Ray Clarke, the divisional bombing officer, and formerly of the 11th Battalion, was dangerously wounded by the premature burst of a bomb. He was evacuated to Edgehill Hospital and for several days his condition was precarious. This news evoked the deepest sympathy in the battalion. Lieut. Clarke was terribly torn by the bomb, but a strong constitution pulled him through. The effects of the wounds were such that after evacuation he never returned to France.

After two days at Henencourt Wood the battalion returned to Ribemont on June 15.

Bomb accidents seemed to have been associated with this period, for on June 23 Lieut. Fred Stahl and two other ranks were slightly wounded while throwing bombs. They were all three evacuated.

After a month of rest and training at Ribemont the 11th Battalion in conjunction with the rest of the 3rd Brigade left on June 24 and proceeded by route-march to Mailly-Maillet, passing through the villages of Lavieville, Millencourt, Senlis and Headeauville. The route lay through pleasant country, lying under a summer sun, and the fields were carrying crops almost ready to harvest.

The purpose of this move was for the purpose of carrying out manœuvres near Beaumont-Hamel, where the initial attack on the Somme in 1916 had started. Included in the area allotted to the 3rd Brigade were the villages of Engelbelmer, Martinsart, Mesnil, Auchonvillers, Serre and Beaumont-Hamel and a part of Aveluy Wood, all names that were famous in the war.

The village of Mailly-Maillet was a fairly large place, with a fine wide square. The houses had been considerably knocked about, but many were habitable and the troops were billeted in the best of them. The transport lines were in a large grassy park and later in a sheltered glade among the trees, and the horses had an abundance of feed.

The day following the march the troops were warned that there would be night operations, so that there were no parades for that day. The boys took the opportunity to visit the surrounding country and to have a look at the trenches from which the original "hop-over" took place in the first Battle of the Somme in the July of the preceeding year. What especially struck the troops was the comparatively unshelled state of the ground compared to some of the battlefields of horrible memory that they had only been too familiar with.

The June return showed that the 11th Battalion was still greatly under strength, only an increase of 90 being shown over the previous month's return. The figures were on June 30: officers, 28; other ranks, 690. Total, 718, out of a brigade total of 3,569.

The night operations that were to have been carried out on June 25 were put off owing to heavy rain, for though the troops had commenced operations they were forced to discontinue them, and the order was given to return to billets.

Next day the 11th Battalion took up a position on the ridge on which Auchonvillers was situated. An attack was launched by the 12th Battalion. There were no casualties.

On June 27 a night attack practice was carried out, but the rain again fell before the battalion returned to Mailly-Maillet and the troops were soaked to the skin. The next day was spent in resting and furbishing up equipment and drying clothes, as an early start was to be made on the following day. Accordingly the battalion was on the move before 6 a.m. on June 29 and the day was spent in attack practice and battle formation. More rain fell at the end of the week, and once again the proceedings had to be cancelled.

A big stunt was done under divisional arrangements on July 2, and great satisfaction was expressed at the way all the details of the attack were carried out.

The battalion transport and all other sections were engaged in this "battle," and while the transport was waiting for the next move Lieut.-Colonel Rafferty came along. The T.O. was standing by his horse over which the Colonel ran an appraising eye, and his glance rested on the nicely-polished saddle. "By heavens! Belford," he said, "That saddle looks like the one I lost when the brigade came to France." "Well, it can't be," said the T.O., "for this is the sadde I took over from Captain Burgess." "Funny," said the Colonel. "It's the dead spit of mine and my name was stamped on the underside of the stirrup-irons." The transport officer said: "Have a look for yourself, sir," and he turned up the stirrup-iron next the Colonel. It was a good thing that the Colonel's attention was diverted by something else at the time for, held up to the Colonel's inspection were these particulars, deeply stamped into the metal on the underside of the stirrup-iron: "Captain R. A. Rafferty, 'D' Company, 12th Battalion (A.I.F.)." At that moment the C.O. was called away by a runner and the matter dropped; so was the stirrup-iron.

The T.O. was in a bit of a quandary over the saddle, but the sergeant, Tom Allsop, explained that there had been a bit of a mix-up of equipment when the division left Egypt for France, and gear had been issued to various units that was quite different to that which had been handed in; and that though the stirrup-irons no doubt originally belonged to Colonel Rafferty, the saddle belonged to the 11th Battalion.

The transport officer let it go at that, but Rafferty never knew how he just missed seeing his own stirrup-irons.

More training on the lines that the troops had been undergoing was carried out until July 3, when the battalion again turned its face towards Ribemont. Mailly-Maillet was left at 6 p.m. and the battalion marched in the cool of the evening reaching Ribemont before dark. The people of Ribemont were unfeignedly pleased to see the boys back again, for the troops had won their way to the villagers' hearts.

On July 5 Major J. Boyd-Aarons left for the 3rd Training Battalion in England to act as second-in-command.

On July 6, in addition to the usual and inevitable route-march, there was a flammenwerfer demonstration. Major Steele reported for duty as second-in-command and Major J. Newman reported from England.

On July 8 orders were received for one officer and 40 other ranks from every battalion in the 1st Division to attend the unveiling of a memorial to all those troops of the 1st Australian Division who were killed near Pozieres during the offensives there in July and August, 1916. Captain W. R. Hallahan was in charge of the 11th Battalion party.

The memorial was erected at Pozieres. There was an impressive parade, for in addition to selected men from all the units of the 1st Division, there were representatives from corps headquarters, the 1st, 2nd and 3rd brigade staffs and many senior officers. There was a simple service conducted by the padres of the Church of England, the Presbyterian, the Salvation Army and the Roman Catholic denominations, after which General Birdwood gave a short speech in which he paid a special tribute to the boys who had given up their lives in those terrible battles that were fought round Pozieres. He then unveiled the memorial. The troops presented arms, and then in the pregnant silence that followed the sad and beautiful strains of the Last Post stirred all hearts with their haunting cadences, while far in the distance the great guns still muttered and rumbled out their messages of hate and destruction.

And the thoughts of the troops may be best summed up in the verse of Private J. Peterson, of the Seaforth Highlanders:

"And upon the stretches barren
Far I saw the thousands lie
That the winds of war had blasted,
Sweeping on without a sigh.
In the hollows, huddled hundreds
Who were not afraid to die."

On July 12 orders came for the 3rd Brigade to march to the Albert-Amiens Road in order that the troops might be inspected by His Majesty King George V. It was a wet, drizzly day, and the lads were not too enthusiastic about the long march in the rain. However, orders are orders, and the troops were led off. The selected site having been reached, the troops were arranged on both sides of the road and instructed to cheer when the King appeared.

After a long and uncomfortable wait a commotion was seen on the road, and then a motor-car swept quickly past. No one realised that the King was in the car and by the time the officers had given the signal to cheer the royal car was almost out of sight; but the cheers were not wasted, for several cars containing staff officers followed, and as the status of the occupants decreased in importance so the cheering swelled. Some mounted military police brought up the rear, and as these passed the assembled troops the cheering swelled into such a roar of derision, and the yells of "Pretty Joey" were so loud and so oft repeated that the "heads" must have been amply satisfied with the troops' acclamation.

After what was afterwards recognised as the best spell the 11th Battalion enjoyed in France, a move was made from Ribemont on July 17, much to the regret of both the troops and the French villagers, who had come to know and appreciate each other.

The new destination was Bronfray Farm, which was reached after passing through Treux, Ville sous Corbie and Meaulte. The camp lay mid-way between Bray and Carnoy, and not far from Fricourt and Mametz of unpleasant memory. The winding valley of the Somme lay just to the south and the lush growth of a bounteous summer had covered up many of the scars of war.

Bronfray Farm had been a French camp and the huts were very large and quite different from the Nissen huts to which the troops had been accustomed in the latter portion of the Somme struggle.

There was a picture theatre which was run by the Y.M.C.A. close to Bronfray Farm, and the troops had the opportunity of seeing some good films while camped at this place.

Third Brigade headquarters was at Bray, and here General Birdwood presented medals and ribbons to the personnel of the 1st Division on July 24.

The battalion changed over to Grovesown Camp on July 25, and there was an alteration in the routine of training; the programme was cancelled and the men put on to cleaning and overhauling their gear and equipment.

During the next few days the 3rd Brigade was transferred to the 2nd Army area behind Ypres. The brigade was moved in sections and by eight different trains. One company of each battalion was detailed to assist in loading transport, and the move was carried out without any unusual occurrence.

Chapter XXXIV

STAPLE, BAYENGHEM; NORTH TO 2ND ARMY;

DOULIEU AND LE VERRIER

THE MOVE that was undertaken by the 1st Division in the last days of July, 1917, marks the commencement of one of the most strenuous of the campaigns in France and Belgium. The troops had been expecting that they would be thrown into the line after their long rest and almost looked forward to the change. On July 27 an early start was made and the battalion marched to Albert to entrain for the north. The battalion and transport were loaded without incident and the boys were all excited to be on the move once again. The journey lay through the old rest-billet areas which the troops knew so well—Dernancourt, Buire and Merricourt, with Ribemont beyond. Greetings were passed between the troops and those of the village folks that the boys remembered. It was a daylight journey and the route followed the Somme valley to Abbeville and then turned to the north. It was nearly night when the battalion arrived at Steenbecque in the Hazebrouck area. This was the detraining point and the troops stretched their cramped limbs and dragged their equipment off the train. That very efficient organisation, the Australian Comforts Fund, had hot cocoa waiting for the troops on arrival, and this was greatly appreciated by the boys.

After the refreshment the battalion marched past Sercus and Wallon-Cappel to the neighbourhood of Staple. Here the troops went into billets, chiefly in the barns and outbuildings of the large farm of La Schotterie and towards Longue Croix. The country and farms were a contrast after the poorer farms of Picardy, as this district was in the rich Flanders country with heavy red clay instead of the grey, chalky soil to which the troops had been so long accustomed.

As usual, the boys were soon at home with the peasants, and were to be seen calling in the cows and helping Celie and Mignonne with the milking, and there was much laughter in putting the milk through the big separators and then helping to feed the pigs or doing the hundred and one jobs that are always to be found on farms. Most of the farm houses were large and well built and often hundreds of troops would be billeted at one farm.

Saturday, July 28, was pay-day, and was rather an unfortunate one for three of the officers on headquarters staff. Captain Keighley, who was I.O. at the time, was in charge of headquarters details which included the regimental transport, A.M.C. section, signallers, runners and orderly room staff. Captain Keighley drew and signed for the pay for headquarters and then asked Lieut. L. C. (Elsie) Cooke to pay the troops.

Headquarters officers were all billeted in a large farmhouse and "Elsie" Cooke, who was then signal officer, proceeded to pay the men. When he had nearly finished the job a message was sent to him to report to headquarters "at the toot." It was then late on Saturday afternoon, and as all work for the day was finished the transport officer was reading a magazine near by, so Cooke asked him if he would carry on until he returned. Cooke added that if there was not enough money on the table there was a bundle of notes in the drawer.

Cooke then hurried off and the T.O. paid two or three men. The former then came back and took over again and paid the remainder of the troops. The balance of the money was handed back to headquarters. Not long afterwards division rang up and inquired if the 11th Battalion money was correct, as there was a discrepancy of some thousands of francs. The battalion sent round to the various companies, but all reported that everything was correct. The sequel to this somewhat irrelevant interpolation occurred several days later.

On Sunday, July 29, it was so wet that there was no church parade. In the evening Major-General E. Sinclair-MacLagan, who was now in command of the 4th Australian Division, visited the battalions of his old command (the 3rd Brigade) and greeted those whom he remembered. He visited the 11th Battalion at Le Schotterie and called at headquarters mess where he wished all assembled the best of luck. General Sinclair-MacLagan's visit was much appreciated, for he always was affectionately termed "Old Mac" in the 3rd Brigade.

Early next morning a movement order was received, and the battalion was instructed to get ready to march out immediately. The brigade transport had already started off and the battalions marched to an embussing point near Wallon Cappel, where they were picked up by motor buses and borne, not eastwards, as all the troops had been expecting, but westwards through the villages of Eblinghem, Renescure, Arques, Blendeques, Wizernes, Hallines, Serques, Lumbres and Bayenghem to Lettinghem, a small village of primitive accommodation and customs.

The brigade transports moved together under the command of the 11th Battalion transport officer (Lieut. Belford). The transports had left two hours before the battalion, whose column passed them at Wismes, and the horses had a very long and heavy trek before they arrived at their destination. Even then their troubles were not over, because the troops to be relieved had not evacuated the billets and the battalion had been diverted to another village at the last minute, so it was very late before the field kitchens reached the hungry troops.

There had been a noticeable increase of traffic on the roads due to the great offensive that was just being started east of Ypres.

Lettinghem was one of the most old-fashioned villages that the boys had struck up to this time, but the village folks were kind and endeavoured to do all they could for the boys. The houses were very primitive and the cooking arrangements unbelievably simple. There was generally a large, open fireplace, without any sort of grate or stove; the fuel was simply a small faggot of twigs, and it was quite a work of art to cook even the universal omelette on the blaze formed by the quickly-burning faggot. Madame had to bend almost double as she cooked over the open flame, and it looked a most uncomfortable business. But it is wonderful how custom inures people to almost everything.

The village was so small that many of the troops were camped in the school, and the troops soon bought out all the available supplies of eggs and other comestibles.

The weather had turned wet and misty, and the old village folks attributed the continual rain to the fierce and prolonged bombardments that were taking place beyond Ypres at this time. These bombardments could be heard even from this village, remote as it was from the front.

In the morning the battalion moved again, this time to Bayenghem, only a few miles distant. The country looked very fresh and green after the rain, and though the roads were still muddy they dried up rapidly in that hilly country. The troops enjoyed the short march among the pleasantly wooded slopes, with little rivulets everywhere. It was a lovely, peaceful-looking countryside, remote from war. After a couple of hours marching the battalion arrived at Bayenghem, where a stay of several days was made. Bayenghem was a pretty village, with a beautifully clear trout stream running through the village. In some of the quiet stretches some nice trout could be seen rising. The river was also very convenient for the watering of horses and the cleaning of vehicles.

The move to Bayenghem had been unexpected, so much so that when the "fall-in" was sounded a number of the Diggers who had been sampling the "Cafe-et-Cognac" at a nearby village were late for parade. Consequently they were "up for orderly room" upon arrival at Bayenghem. Bugler Brickhill was one of the delinquents, and for some days afterwards he had to suffer the barracking of his mates, for not only had he himself to sound the "Angel's Whisper" (the call for defaulters) but he had also to act as "right-marker" for the parade.

The battalion strength at the end of July, 1917, was: Officers, 45; other ranks, 838. Total, 883. Brigade total, 4,205.

It will be noticed that the battalion was rapidly increasing in strength and that the officers were over strength.

The next few days were spent in attack practice in a wild and hilly area some miles north of the village and close to the Boulogne-St. Omer Road. Here trenches were dug on the face of one of the hills on July 31. These were to be used in the attack practices.

The great offensive that had been so laboriously planned had been launched on the morning of July 31, and news began to trickle through. As usual the successes were very much magnified, and although a considerable amount of material and several thousand prisoners had been captured, the advance was badly held up by the nature of the country which was rendered almost impassable by the wet conditions.

On August 1 rain fell all day, and the battalion was forced to do its training in billets. August 2 was a repetition of the previous day as far as weather was concerned, and the attack practice was again put off. It had been originally intended to move back to Staple on the following day, but Generals Birdwood and Walker arrived at brigade headquarters at Lumbres and they decided that the 3rd Brigade should remain a further three days in the area.

Route-marches were held on August 3 and 4, although the weather was still very wet. The continued rainy weather, and the feeling that the offensive would be disastrously held up, had a most depressing effect on the troops and Jeremiads were well to the fore.

The next day, August. 5, was a Sunday, and by a miracle it dawned clear and fine, so all church parades were cancelled and the troops were ordered to parade in fighting order and the training programme was carried out. This included attacks on the trenches and machine gun and Lewis gun work and a demonstration by the Stokes' gunners. All the operations were carried out satisfactorily.

The sequel to the pay-day at Staple occurred while the battalion was at Bayenghem. A "For your information and necessary action, please" came from the divisional pay-office to the effect that the 11th Battalion returns for the last pay were 2,000 francs short (about £70), and the deficiency being traced to the headquarters company pay-sheet the three officers involved in the payment of the troops and the 11th Battalion pay-sergeant (Sergeant Orr) were sent for and came before a court of inquiry. Captain Keighley had handed over the money in the presence of the pay-sergeant and Cooke and Belford explained what had taken place at the farm at Staple. Lieut. Cooke suggested that the missing money might have been left in the drawer of the table where the boys had been paid. So he received permission to cycle back to Staple in order to have a look and to make inquiries. He returned next day and reported that he had been unsuccessful. The result of the court of inquiry was that the three officers concerned were debited with 666 francs each but the finding stated that there was no reflection on any of the officers. For a long time the disappearance of the 2,000 francs baffled the officers concerned. A solution was offered some time later. It was noticed that the new 10-franc notes which had been lately issued were very similar to the old 20-franc notes that had been current for some time, and it was suggested that three bundles of 1,000 ten-franc notes had been issued to division (for division was also 1,000 francs short) instead of three bundles of 20-franc notes, and that the 11th Battalion had signed for 2,000 francs too much and likewise the officer concerned.

Whatever the reason, the three officers who were debited with one-third of the loss each had their paybooks "slugged" to the extent of nearly £23 each, but the finding of the court also stated that if this amount caused their paybooks to be overdrawn it would not interfere with the drawing of a reasonable amount of pay. All three officers appreciated the treatment that they had received, because the members of the court could easily have been excused if they had taken a very much

Hazebrouck. (Official Photo.)

harsher view of the case. There is a further and pleasant sequel which will be related when the incident falls due.

The 14th Brigade relieved the 3rd Brigade on August 6, and the 11th Battalion moved back to Staple. The battalion transport in conjunction with the rest of the brigade made an early start, as the journey on the crowded roads always required a good margin of time to allow for unforeseen contingencies. The transports moved off in good order and they looked very efficient and capable, and as after events turned out it was well that horses and men were in such fine condition.

The companies of the battalion followed several hours later and travelled to Arques by bus and from thence back to their old billets at Staple. Only one night was spent there, and then the battalion moved on to the Doulieu-Le Verrier area. This was a definite move towards the line and the route lay past Hazebrouck, which was then being heavily shelled by the Germans as the battalion passed. It was pitiable to see all the townspeople hastening away from their houses with all the gear they could wheel away on perambulators, hand-carts and, where procurable, drays and waggons. In some cases heaps of furniture and bedding were piled on to army motor-lorries, and the distressed refugees were given a lift by the sympathetic drivers.

But it was a mournful procession. There was not one of the boys that did not realise what a horrible thing war was. What happened on the field of battle seemed to be all part of the game, but this shelling defenceless towns and the sight of weeping women and terrified children placed the whole business in an entirely different light. Of course the troops had known that such things happened, and were more or less happening all the time, but it was quite a different thing to see the actual desolation and misery caused by this side of the war.

After passing Hazebrouck the route lay through the Foret de Nieppe. This was a forest of great extent, and there were several towns and villages in close proximity, and the Canal de Nieppe and the Bourre Canal ran through the forest and met at La Motte, through which village the troops passed.

It was very pleasant and tranquil in the forest, and when a halt was made and the cookers drew up for lunch it was with the greatest contentment that the boys threw themselves under the shade of the trees and so passed a restful hour. After the troops had resumed their march they reached a part of the forest where much of the timber had been chopped down, mostly for war purposes.

The march lay through Vieux Berquin, and then the battalion went into very scattered billets at Doulieu and Le Verrier. The farm houses were large, with big, spacious but not too comfortable barns of the same variety as those which the troops first lived in when they came to France over fifteen months before, and indeed the troops soon learned that they were billeted just half-way between Fletre and Caestre to the north-west and Sailly sur la Lys (of pleasant memory) on the south-east and at no great distance from either area. The boys, or at least those sadly diminished numbers that had come with the 11th Battalion to France, felt that they were in a district where they would be sure to meet many old friends.

As the battalion remained about six weeks in this area, owing to the fact that the terribly wet weather had held up the projected offensive, it is only natural that the time spent at Doulieu and Le Verrier should be full of remembered incidents in the life of the 11th Battalion.

Owing to the scant population and the scattered nature of the billets, the 3rd Brigade was scattered over a very wide area. Brigade headquarters was at Vieux Berquin, about three miles away from the 11th Battalion billets, and the 12th Battalion troops were at least five miles from brigade. Nearly all the land was under crop and mostly ready for harvesting when the battalion arrived, and there was hardly sufficient room for battalion training in the small fields available. Most of the drill was under company arrangements.

The most vivid recollection of the battalion's stay at Doulieu was the nightly bombing by German 'planes. The situation of these billets was not very far from the lines at Armentieres, and in view of the great effort by the British troops at Ypres, the Germans tried to harass the fresh troops behind the lines so that they would have their nerves shaken before entering the line. It is safe to say that many troops would rather face anything than continual or even occasional bombing in the quiet and darkness of night; and truly it was a nerve-shattering business, during the next four months, to lie and wait for the "eggs" to fall, not knowing when or where they would drop. The troops were subjected frequently to this unpleasant and trying experience and it proved too much for many poor fellows.

There was anti-aircraft Lewis guns mounted by all the companies to meet this menace, and nightly the boys would wait for the hum of the twin-engined German 'planes. All lights would be put out or screened and those who had glasses would scan the dark heavens and frequently pick up the fast flying night-birds. Searchlights would flash from all directions and anti-aircraft guns would open fire; machine guns would disclose their positions by streams of tracer bullets, but to no purpose. The raiders would drop their bombs and fires and destruction would follow in the wake of aircraft, which would then disappear into the clouds that formed such an easy avenue of escape.

On August 15 a brigade officers' school was formed at Vieux Berquin. This was to be a school of five weeks' duration and 17 junior officers were detailed to attend.

A feature of the battalion's stay at Doulieu was the number of route-marches that the troops were made to do. This was partly due to the lack of suitable training grounds, but it was generally recognised that these marches, though hated by many of the older men, were of great service in keeping the men in hard physical condition.

On one of these route-marches there was a bit of concertina-ing (not the musical kind) as there were occasional short halts to allow other traffic to get along. "C" Company was well in rear of the column with Lieut. Archibald in charge of No. 11 platoon and Lieut. "Oxo" Piesse in charge of No. 12. Archibald's platoon changed step twice in a very short distance of marching and Piesse's men had to follow suit. When a third change was made almost immediately afterwards, "Oxo" got exasperated and shouted to "Archie," telling him to make his men keep the proper step. "Archie," like the good soldier he was, instead of giving the usual Australian answer, marked time till "Oxo" drew level, and then they had a long and heated argument, which finished up with "Archie" telling Piesse to mind his own b—— business. Piesse was one of the mildest of men, and one of those rare birds who had never been known to swear; but this was too much. He grew purple in the face and roared out at the top of his voice, "Your bally platoon is up to mud."

"Archie's" remarks would have been worth repeating, but unfortunately they were drowned in the roar of laughter that followed Piesse's indignant criticism.

August 17, 1917, was the third anniversary of the formation of the 11th Battalion. There were no celebrations, but the Germans made a bombing raid on the billets at night and two men were wounded.

Besides the route-marching, another means of keeping the men fit was by encouraging all kinds of sport. Battalion sports meetings were held on August 18 and the 3rd Brigade held sports on August 22. Just before this event, General Birdwood inspected a battalion composed of four companies, one from each battalion of the 3rd Brigade. This composite battalion made an impressive show. In the brigade sports the 9th Battalion was first with the 11th Battalion only one point behind in second place.

At Doulieu a number of the old hands returned; some of them had been on "cushy" jobs for some time, but as reinforcements were getting scarce a round-up was made and all fit men were sent back to the line battalion. Route-marching did not agree with some of the resurrected birds.

Taken as a whole, the sojourn at Doulieu was a very pleasant memory, for not only did the boys often go over to Fletre or Sailly to visit their old friends and to drink a cup of "cafe," but they soon found new friends among the villagers and farmers. There were several good estaminets and the light "Bock" was pleasant to drink. Fruits, including plums and walnuts, were ripe and the good folks were often generous.

Mention had been made of the old friends of the first billets in Fletre and Sailly. It is no exaggeration to say that the boys returning after over a year's absence were greeted like long-lost sons or brothers, and the welcome was obviously sincere for all sorts of questions would be asked about how the boys had fared since they had left. Inquiries would be made about "Snowy" or "Darky" or "Blue," and tears would fill the good folks' eyes when they heard that they had gone west. Madame would say of someone or other, "Helas! le pauvre gar! Comment il etait drole!" (Ah! the poor lad! And what a wag he used to be!).

It was always heartening to come back to such a pleasant reception and to think that even with the many thousands of troops continually living and moving among these people and then passing on that the boys from the other side of the world held such a firm place in their affections.

The brimming eyes of Madame or Maman, and the surreptitious tear of the valiant old grandpere sitting in the corner by the stove were unmistakable evidences of their feelings, while the bright cheeks and the glowing eyes of Jeanne or Marthe or Julie are unforgettable even after the lapse of so many years.

The Brigadier and staff visited the 11th Battalion on August 27. They made a thorough inspection and the report was satisfactory, as all clothing and equipment were up to the necessary standard.

Of course there were some good stories associated with Doulieu. One day Major Steele told this yarn against himself in the officers' mess. He said that he had that day had "Combo" Smith up before him at orderly room. Looking at "Combo's" regimental history sheet, to give it a more euphemistic designation, the Major said, "Do you know, Smith, that you are the worst soldier in the battalion?" (the Major meant by this that "Combo" was the worst offender against the regulations that were such a sore trial to bushmen like Smith, and there was no reflection on "Combo's" qualities as a front-line soldier).

"Combo" looked the Major up and down and his eye was caught by the crown on the Major's shoulder-strap, so he said: "Well, Major, that may be. Perhaps I am the worst soldier, but if you were half as good a soldier as you think you are you would have had crossed swords under that crown long ago."

The second sequel to the "lost pay" incident happened on the occasion of the first pay in the Doulieu area. When the officers had been paid, and just after mess, Lieut.-Colonel Rafferty handed Captain Keighley an envelope, and said that the officers had had a muster and had collected a few francs, which he hoped that he and the other two officers concerned in the loss of pay would accept as a token of goodwill and sympathy from the rest of the officers of the 11th Battalion, and he also said that he hoped that the sum would in some way help to cancel the deficit in each of the three officers' paybooks.

The envelope contained about 1,400 francs, and the action was a striking testimony of the spirit of camaraderie that existed among all ranks of the Australian Army, and not least among the West Australian boys. Lieut. "Elsie" Cooke was killed not long afterwards and Captain Keighley was discharged in England, so that the relation of the above is ample testimony that one officer at least has never forgotten the kindly spirit that existed among his comrades of the 11th battalion.

While there was a splendid relationship between the French folks of the Doulieu area and the troops, it is to be regretted that the boys were not always so honest as they might have been.

In the first line transport there was always a shortage of fodder. The further back the troops and horses the better deal they always got in the matter of rations and equipment. If there was any shortage of anything it was never the base wallahs or the troops on the lines of communications that suffered; it was always the troops that bore the brunt of the battle.

To men that loved their horses the shortage of fodder was always a source of grief, but hard-doers like Corporal Mick Roche or Sergeant Tom Allsop did not go short if there was any reasonable way of supplementing the light "issue." There were fields ready to harvest all round them. But they were no tyros at the game. They did not cut the crops where the farmer would notice the loss. They waited till nightfall, then sneaked into the middle of the fields with a reap hook and cut all they required. The companies, too, supplemented their rations from the potato crops, the peas and the turnips. Some of the old farmers must have got an unpleasant surprise when, during harvesting operations, they reached the depleted middle portions of their fields. But the depredations of the troops were not so bad as the telling of them seems to indicate, for the farmers had only to lay a claim for damages, "reclamations," as they were called, and they frequently received far more than the damage inflicted.

The constant return of men from hospital and details, and the arrival of reinforcements had greatly augmented the strength of the battalion since the last strength state. The figures at the end of August, 1917, were 44 officers, 1,002 other ranks. Total, 1,046. The brigade total was 4,874. The number of officers was much in excess of strength, but low compared to the other three battalions of the 3rd Brigade, each of which had more than 52 officers.

On September 1 two men of the 11th Battalion were detailed to help some of the farmers to harvest potatoes and corn. While on the subject of harvesting, the writer noticed a binder working in a field close to headquarters. The fields in this part of the country were generally surrounded by ditches, more or less full of water. As the binder progressed cutting a crop of corn, it was noticed that the depression left by the main wheel was immediately filled with water which oozed out of the ground. This is related to give some idea of the state of the ground in these parts in the very driest time of the year, that is after the long warm days of summer. But the weather had recently been phenomenally wet for some time before the battalion's arrival in that area, and if this was the state of the country under ordinary conditions of life, then the area under prolonged bombardment must have truly been in an awful state, and it was no wonder that the advance was held up for it is easy to realise that the country must have been well nigh impassable.

Every effort was being made at this time to make the 11th Battalion as efficient as possible, and there was constant inspection of guards and billets. A good story of one of these inspections is told by Private Jim Kirkwood. While the 11th Battalion was billeted at Doulieu in September, 1917, "A" Company took its turn to supply headquarters guard. When the guard was mounted and everything quiet the sergeant in charge drifted down to his favourite coffee and rum-joint, where he met several pals, and he drank more than was good for a decent sergeant, so his cobbers took him home to his billet. The corporal of the guard got him next morning, but the sergeant was still "under the weather."

The corporal went down to the R.S.M. to get him to send another sergeant along. But time was going on, and the Commanding Officer was due to make his rounds of inspection. But that did not worry the troops, for one full rear-rank private rose to the job like the good Westralian that he was. He took off the sergeant's tunic, slipped his own off and made the change.

When the Colonel appeared, he turned out the guard and put them through their stuff in a way that quite satisfied the "Old Man."

"A smart turn-out, sergeant," beamed the Colonel. "What company?" " 'A' Company, No. 2 Platoon, sir."

Then we thought the game was up, for the "Old Man's" face wrinkled as no other face could, and he said: "I don't remember you, Sergeant." But the quasi sergeant never turned a hair. "No sir. Been away, sir. Wounded at Flers; Colonel Smith Commanding Officer at that time." Colonel Rafferty smiled all over his face. "Good, Sergeant! Keep the boys in trim. We will be doing big things shortly," and he passed on

There was hardly any difficulty in camp or field of battle that was not adequately met by the boys of the 11th Battalion.

It was only natural that after such a long and pleasant rest the health of the battalion should have been excellent. A further helping feature was the frequency of the trips to the baths at Oultersteene, near Merris, where the men received a change of underclothing. There was also a Foden engine, which was used to fumigate the blankets, and this in conjunction with the bathing and the clean change was greatly appreciated by the men, as it gave them at least a temporary relief from the soldier's most persistent enemy.

A route-march of 15 miles was carried out by the 11th Battalion on September 5. The men were in great heart and marched well. There were no stragglers. On the same date the office system and records of the battalion were inspected, and the report stated that the system was very satisfactory and the records in good order.

On September 6 there was a battalion competition in which the drill of the four battalions of the brigade was judged by the Brigadier. All the units looked well. They were dressed in drill order and most of the drilling reached a high standard. A silver trophy was presented by General Bennett and was gained by the 10th Battalion, the scores being as follows: 10th Battalion, 83 points; 11th Battalion, 68 points; 9th Battalion, 58 points and 12th Battalion, 51 points.

Rumours were now circulating that the 1st Division was to be used shortly to attack Polygon Wood, a key position on the line of advance in the great Third Battle of Ypres. Polygon Wood was just east of the famous Westhoek Ridge. On September 7 the Brigadier called together the battalion commanders of the 3rd Brigade and outlined the position.

A few days later most of the officers and many of the N.C.O.'s of the 11th Battalion had the opportunity of visiting a well-constructed large-scale model of the area to be attacked. This model was at Devonshire lines near Bussebom and was an exact replica of the country that the troops were to operate in, with trenches, roads, railways, lakes, ditches, hills in contour, barbed wire entanglements and even forests, woods and single trees all clearly marked and beautifully constructed. It was a most instructive model, and was of great assistance to all who had the privilege of studying it in enabling them to locate the various points, as all the salient features had been marked with small notice boards.

A brigade attack practice was held on ground allotted on the west side of Vieux Berquin. General Sir Herbert Plumer, general officer commanding the 2nd Army, was present. The attack practice was a great success and all the specialist sections and the regimental transport were employed. After the attack practice was completed General Plumer gave a short lecture on the modern method of attack.

CHAPTER XXXV

THIRD BATTLE OF YPRES. GLENCORSE WOOD

THE SUMMER was now over, and the Third Battle of Ypres had been going since the beginning of August without much definite result except the shattering of new divisions. The rains presaging the winter had started to fall and early August had been exceptionally wet, thus holding up the projected advance considerably, and now the Australian divisions were to plunge into another of the frightful campaigns of the war. A close study of the reasons that decided Haig to enter into this battle at this especial time is not possible here, and many of his apologists have found justification enough for his policy; but the fact remains that it seems strange and even culpable that, with the experience already gained from the winter of 1916/17 in the Somme, that the attack should have been commenced and carried out so late in the season in an area that was so much wetter, and which even in ordinary conditions was a maze of ditches and rivers. Not only were few major lessons seemingly learned from the campaigns of the Somme, but it appears also hard to believe that the British High Command had forgotten how, in the first months of the war, the tired and shattered troops of the original British armies in France, ill-led, badly-equipped, hopelessly outnumbered by the enemy in battalions, machine guns and, above all, in powerful and modern artillery, had successfully defended that same country beyond Ypres against the pride of the German Army at the height of its splendour and when elated by victories everywhere. How, in the First Battle of Ypres, the names that were to be again on everyone's lips, "Polygon Wood," "Nonne Bosschen," "Inverness Copse," "Glencorse Wood" and many more, were the scenes of German disaster, due chiefly to the nature of the country rather than to the defence, heroically splendid though it was, which the spent troops opposed to the enemy.

And now the conditions were to be reversed, and the rested and reconstructed divisions of the Australian Army were to be thrown against the strongholds of the Germans.

It must have been obvious to the higher command that the attacking side must always have thrice-shelled country to traverse while the other force could withdraw, if need be, to new country, where operations were not hindered in any way by the state of the country. With the terrific weight of artillery used by both sides any wet ground soon became an impassable quagmire and the unfortunate start to this battle created this condition right away.

It may be of interest to learn that in nineteen days of preliminary bombardment in this offensive there were 120,000 gunners engaged on the British side, and these fired four and a half million shells of a total weight of 128,000 tons against the German positions, and this alone was sufficient to render the country impassable without the return strafe of the Germans.

While an advance in this class of country might have been possible by a surprise attack in the summer time, it is hardly creditable that anyone could believe it possible in winter time, or at least in winter conditions against strong and well-organised opposition. Ludendorf has truly said: "Sir Douglas Haig bled his new armies white at Passchendaele."

But the determination had been made and the battle was on. The turn of the 1st Australian Division to go into the line was fast approaching, and "Their's not to reason why; their's but to do or die." It was not good for line troops to think too much over projected offensives. Besides, as in the case of the 11th Battalion, the troops were very fit after their long spell and more or less eager for a "go" at the enemy. The gigantic preparations behind the lines and the terrible weight of artillery all impressed the boys, and all felt that Fritz was going to "get a bit of his own back."

On September 13 a new feature was introduced into battalion routine. As soon as it was known that the battalion was due to go into the line, a selected body of officers, N.C.O.'s and men were detached from the battalion and sent back to reinforcement camp or other quarters. This detachment was called the "Nucleus Battalion" and its function was to preserve a skeleton battalion formation on which to build a new battalion should the casualties in any action be so severe as to necessitate the formation of a practically new battalion. It was also useful as a rest for those troops who had had a pretty rough spin in the line. This "Nucleus," as it soon came to be called, was changed every time the battalion did a tour of the line and soon became a recognised part of battalion life.

The first nucleus from the 11th Battalion consisted of 85 other ranks under the command of Major Steele, D.S.O., and was sent to the 3rd Brigade wing of the 1st Divisional Reinforcement Camp at Rouge Croix, near Fletre. Major Steele was in temporary command of the 3rd Brigade wing.

On the same date, September 13, the 11th Battalion made its move forward, starting at 9 a.m. and passing through the village of Oultersteene, Merris, Strazeele and Caestre, reached the Thieushouck area about 2 p.m., where the men went into billets. Maps and plans of the position to be attacked were distributed, and a large-scale map was explained in detail to all companies.

Next day the battalion marched forward to the Wippenhoek area. The route followed lay over the uplands of Mont des Cats and adjoining hills. It was always pleasant among these hills; the wooded slopes, with little villages nestling in the folds and valleys, had a charm all of their own, possibly because they were a change from those of the flat country surrounding. Lieut. Fordham, a newly-joined officer who was killed only a few days later, expressed surprise that war was so close to scenes of such tranquil beauty.

When it was definitely learned that the 1st Australian Division was to go into action at Polygon Wood, every battalion in the division was exhorted to do its utmost in the coming battle. The following address was promulgated to all ranks:—

"First Australian Division.

"After a lengthy period of rest and training we are being called upon to participate in an operation, the success of which will have the most important results, not only for the British armies, but for all the Allies.

"The part this division has to play is the most important of all. The position we have to attack is the keystone of the whole. If we fail the tasks of the divisions on our right and left will be rendered extremely difficult. I am full of confidence that the 1st Australian Division will achieve success and add to its already enviable record and that, having carried our objectives, we shall hold them against all counter-attacks, living up to our division motto—'*What we gain we hold.*'

"Last year we took Pozieres under much more difficult circumstances and with little preliminary preparation or reconnaissance. In the impending operations we shall have the best of artillery support and everything is in our favour. Each Australian soldier is equal to any two Germans. Let every officer and man know where he starts from, the direction of the attack, what everyone has to do, and all be determined to succeed in spite of difficulties.

"H. B. Walker, Major-General."

At Wippenhoek instructions for the forthcoming "stunt" were promulgated to all the troops, and another visit was made to the relief map of the Polygon Wood area and further particulars noted. The weather was dull, misty and wet.

As the officers were discussing the approaching operations in one of the huts, Lieut. "Joe" Dale came in and said: "I say, you fellows, I've been put in charge of one of the dumps." Dale was immediately gravely informed that he had better make his will, as dumps were notoriously dangerous places when there were any wars around. Nearly everyone had something tragic to tell about dumps and the woeful tales made Joe rather worried, so he said: "You chaps are only saying all this to put the wind up me; but I don't care. It's better than the line, anyway."

One officer laughed (the times were hard) and said that he had a premonition that the dump would go up and Dale with it. After a bit of ragging the incident was forgotten, but there was a sequel.

On September 15 Majors Newman and Darnell, Captain Keighley and Lieuts. "Elsie" Cooke and G. C. Ross visited the line. Lieut. Ross was wounded. Next day while other officers were visiting the line Captain J. P. O'Neil and Lieut. H. Colvin were wounded. The same day the 11th Battalion moved forward by Reninghelst, Outerdom and Dickebusch to Chateau Segard. The roads were now beginning to be very congested with all kinds of traffic, and the muddy conditions made marching extremely tiring.

On September 17 the order came to take over the reserve position at Half-way House. The relief was completely successful, but there were 13 casualties from shell-fire, including two men killed. One of the killed was Corporal Tom Cleverly, a fine soldier.

After nightfall on the following day the 11th Battalion relieved the 1st Battalion in the line and the great attack was to be carried out on September 20. The disposition of the companies of the 11th Battalion at this time were "A" and "D" Companies in the line, "B" Company in supports and "C" Company in reserve.

It is necessary here to revert a little, in order to describe the country and the various objectives and the relation and position of the various units of the 1st Division and the divisions on the flanks.

After the salient at Messines had been more or less straightened out, Haig turned his attention to the sector north-east of Ypres. This sector held the three famous ridges, the Westhoek, the Broodseinde and the Passchendaele ridges, which afforded the Germans such a complete and easily held field of observation, and consequently the command of the whole Ypres salient as well as the territory further north.

The attacks by the British were to be pushed forward on these ridges on a. 15-mile front, and while the main object was to drive the enemy from this favourable position, yet General Haig was always hoping for a break-through so that he could roll up the German flank from the coast and thus overwhelm the German armies. There were many circumstances that militated against this plan which cannot be gone into here, but as has already been stated, the weather and the condition of the ground were not the least of them.

In spite of everything, and probably because many of the assisting factors had gradually to be discarded, Haig was determined to push on the offensive.

The 2nd Army sector, in which the 1st Australian Division was operating, stretched from opposite Warneton to Steenstraate, south-east of Dickebusch and the 1st Division's sector was roughly opposite Glencorse Wood and the Nonne Bosschen and Polygon Wood and Racecourse. (Polygon Wood was so named from its conformation.) The 2nd Australian Division was on the left and the 23rd British Division on the right. There had been several attempts to take this sector and the position was regarded as one of great tactical importance.

Nonne Bosschen (Nun's Wood) consisted mostly of marshy country, almost impassable in its present condition, and Polygon Wood presented the obstacle that all dense timber provided.

Nonne Bosschen (Nun's Wood), Ypres. (Official Photo.)

The mind had only to go back to Delville Wood, to High Wood, to Trones Wood, or indeed to any of the scenes of desperate encounter associated with the direct attack on woods to know that Polygon Wood was a difficult objective to carry. Hence it was regarded as the key position in this sector.

The Australians were at this time fresh troops, and as they were noted for their elan and dash they were placed at the apex of the attack.

To come to the 3rd Brigade sector. In the official diary it is stated: "The 3rd Australian Infantry Brigade, in conjunction with the 2nd Infantry Brigade on the right, and the 7th Australian Infantry Brigade on the left, will capture the enemy-defended area of Nonne-Bosschen/Polygoneveld (Polygon Wood) on a day to be notified. The 1st Australian Infantry Brigade in divisional reserve will be holding the present front line."

(Here follow the brigade boundaries, which were roughly through Clapham Junction and the middle of Glencorse Wood on the right, and from Hooge Chateau to the north edge of Polygon Wood on the left. Map p. 763 Official History.)

The objectives were allotted as follows:—1st objective, 11th Battalion (line marked red); 2nd objective, 12th Battalion (line marked blue); 3rd objective (line marked green). This line to be captured by two battalions, the 10th Battalion on the right and the 9th Battalion on the left.

The attack was to be delivered in three stages on the leap-frog principle, each battalion deploying two companies in the front line and two in support.

It will be noticed that in this attack, as in all important battles in which they were engaged, the 3rd Brigade had the place of honour, and that the 11th Battalion was chosen to make the first attack on the enemy.

The barrage for this battle was to be put down 150 yards in front of the leading troops, and the 11th Battalion was instructed to press on close up to the barrage. The barrage was to move on at the rate of 100 yards in four minutes for a start, and then after a stated interval it was to slacken its forward movement to 100 yards in six minutes and then the barrage was to halt in front of the red line (i.e., on the German side) for 45 minutes, during which time the 11th Battalion was to capture all strong points in the area and consolidate the line of objective.

The troops were to be in fighting order and all officers to be dressed the same as the men. The troops were to carry 120 rounds S.A.A., two sandbags, two bombs, 1 ground flare, 48 hours' rations. In addition the bombers were to carry six extra bombs; rifle grenadiers, six grenades, and officers and No. 1's of Lewis gun sections were to carry two S.O.S. rifle grenades.

Before the attack the front and flanks of each battalion were to be pegged out by brigade and battalion intelligence staffs, and a tape line had to be laid in front on the "hop-off" line by the same details. In order that the various attacking troops should be easily distinguishable, the battalions attacking the various named lines were instructed to paint colour patches on their helmets. Thus the 11th Battalion had a red patch, the 12th had blue and the 9th and 10th Battalions had green patches.

These orders having been promulgated, the troops were then ready for the attack.

Lieut. Oxley (Oxo) Piesse was detailed to act as liaison officer between the 1st and 2nd Divisions. Private L. D. Warner, who accompanied him, writes of this duty: "His runner, Eric Graham, and I went with him. We had thousands of instructions and a cage of pigeons. The German barrage opened before ours that morning and Lieut. Piesse was wounded. This officer would not leave the line, although he was advised to, but stayed on the job until he was duly relieved."

Lieut. Piesse died of wounds in Rouen Hospital some time later.

This incident is mentioned not only as a tribute to a gallant soldier but also to call attention to the fact that the 1st and 2nd Australian Divisions were fighting side by side. This was the first occasion that Australian divisions had fought side by side in a major operation.

It was now the evening of September 19, and the 11th Battalion was in line in front of Clapham Junction with "C" Company in reserve at Half-way House. All day the battalion had been resting as much as possible. This was not very much, for Fritz kept up a considerable fire all day. As it was afterwards found out, the enemy had received information of the impending attack and was at this time consistently shelling all battery positions and trenches and posts.

The following extracts from the diary of Private J. A. Sanders describe the situation and the ensuing attack: "Wednesday, September 19. We lay 'doggo' all day. Fritz gave us little peace. We suffered three bombardments. Our objective was Glencorse Wood. We were told that it had been fought for two or three times already.

"We went out on patrol at 11:30 p.m. Our job was to find two tape lines with about 50 yards separating the two lines. The first we found was for the 12th Battalion; the second we searched for in vain. Later we learned that the plan had been altered. Only one tape line was put down and the two battalions were to assemble on it. The 11th Battalion first and the 12th later and leap-frog.

"Some time after midnight we were returning to our trench and met the battalion coming out to take up their position. Hardly had we got into position than the enemy opened up with his barrage. Some of our men were hit.

"Thursday, September 20. Some little time before daybreak our barrage opened with a tremendous roar. It was said to be one of the most intense bombardments of the war. I don't think it was possible to find a square foot of ground that was not disturbed. We met with little resistance and reached our objective with a minimum of fighting. The principal work was mopping up. This was done carefully and methodically. Twice that day the enemy counter-attacked, but was beaten back. We dug ourselves in and consolidated our position."

The battalion official diary for this engagement was very brief, but unusually exuberant. It runs as follows:—

"Eleventh Battalion, Clapham Junction, September 20, 1917. The day of days. Our boys got out on the forming-up position like the disciplined soldiers they are and formed up without a hitch. At a few minutes before zero Fritz noticed them and put down a barrage, but our barrage came right down on the tick and our boys did their job.

"Considering the operation our losses were remarkably light. Officers wounded: Captain G. F. Mason, Lieuts. J. Barry, Brown, Clarke, Archibald, Joe Dale, O. Piesse and Lieut. Fordham killed.

"Trophies: one field gun, three machine guns and 150 prisoners.

"About dusk the enemy massed for a counter-attack, but this was dispersed by artillery before it could deploy."

And that is all. It has been truly said of the 11th Battalion that its motto was "Deeds, not words."

Besides those reported casualties in the above record, Lieut. C. W. (Dad) Mathews was also wounded, and the total casualty list was as follows: Killed, 17; wounded, 103; missing, 40; officers abovementioned, 9. Total all ranks, 169.

So much for the individual and official reports. As in all battles of any magnitude only a broad, general description can be given, and the following is the story of Polygon Wood and Glencorse Wood as far as it affected the 11th Battalion.

The troops had been very fortunate in having fine weather before and up to the date of their entry into the line, but on the evening of the attack it commenced to rain, and all began to think that they were in for a bad time, especially as the region of Nonne Bosschen in particular was extremely low lying and boggy. There was even some talk of postponing the attack. But the corps commander decided to carry on. So the troops made their way to their positions, over the muddy ground in the rain and darkness. The attacking waves of the 11th Battalion were lucky to get on to their jumping-off positions without much trouble, though Fritz was shelling heavily. Most of this shell-fire was passing over to the rear area, but it was noticed that a considerable proportion of gas shell was being used. The gas was largely the new "Yellow Cross" or "Mustard Gas." One fortunate feature of the sodden ground was that the effect of the high explosive shells was much neutralised, as many exploded deep in the soft mud.

Before the hour for attack the rain eased off and soon it was fine again. It was a wonderful scene: the shadowy figures of the men cautiously and silently moving forward in the fitful glare of all kinds of flares and lights; the bright, dazzling light of an exploding incendiary shell throwing up the dark figures into sharp relief, and then the welcome darkness once again; the feeling of keyed-up excitement as the men slipped and squelched through the mud, and the determination to get on at all costs. All this made a memory of outstanding clarity for all those who survived. Nearly half of the battalion was composed of men who were going into the line for the first time, and their discipline could never have been surpassed. It was in such situations that the real discipline of the West Australian troops became apparent.

The troops had got out to their hopping-off line when some occurrence alarmed the enemy, for instantly German S.O.S. flares were sent up and a heavy barrage descended on the front. The 11th Battalion was fortunate in being well forward, and thus they escaped most of the barrage; but there were a good many casualties, though the battalion did not suffer so severely in this respect as the rest of the brigade in rear. These battalions had a trying time until the Australian and British barrage for the hop-over fell with frightful results on the enemy lines at 5:40 a.m.

The Westralian Diggers then got up and lit the usual cigarettes and moved forward with the barrage just as they had been instructed to do, and pushed on up to the German pill-boxes and posts, closely followed and even accompanied by the troops of the 12th and other battalions who had pressed forward to escape the German barrage.

When the barrage halted, this mixed forced bombed and machine-gunned the pill-boxes and rushed any parties of the enemy that appeared. There was a deep sunken road at the north end of Glencorse Wood and there was some delay in mopping up this portion of the objective. Some gallant German machine gunners had managed to drag a machine gun on to the top of a pill-box, and from there they were doing considerable damage. One of the 10th Battalion officers, Lieut. Weaver, while doing good work was shot here, and then Corporal "Darkie" Hodge, of the 11th Battalion, dashed forward and shot the gunner and put the gun out of action. (Hodge was awarded the D.C.M. for this action.) The rest of the troops charged the sunken road, and after bombing heavily and killing many of the enemy they captured about 40 prisoners.

Poor young Lieut. Fordham was killed not far from this road as he was trying to rush a German post. It was his first and last time in.

The mopping-up of the posts was thoroughly carried out and the red line was captured exactly according to time-table. It was a most successful attack.

Private Jim Kirkwood relates this incident: "It was in this stunt that 'Bandy' Turner went west. 'Bandy' was an old original battalioner who had been invalided to Australia from

Gallipoli and had returned with the 20th Reinforcements of the 11th Battalion. He was badly knocked about. The M.O., the good 'Doc Robbie' (Captain Robinson) went up to the line and amputated 'Bandy's' arm in the front trench. As the arm was thrown aside 'Bandy' remarked: 'That's the best part of old 'Bandy' gone.' A brother of 'Bandy's' was in another part of the trench and was sent for, and he went back to the aid-post assisting the stretcher-bearers with 'Bandy.' This brother, 'Stormy,' by nickname, was missed from his section and later placed under arrest for leaving the line. Lieut. P. E. M. Vowles took the matter up and after a bit of trouble 'Stormy' was cleared. 'Bandy' died at the aid-post."

Mention was made some paragraphs back of Lieut. Joe Dale and the joking remark about his being blown up with his dump. The dump was indeed hit by a shell and Dale wounded. In the attack on the green line by the 28th Battalion, Lieut. Archie Tye, a former member of the 11th Battalion bombing platoon, and a very fine lad, was killed. Tye had done good work at Pozieres and Mouquet Farm and had been recommended for a commission. He had been appointed to the 28th Battalion.

The above described action was one of the best managed that the Westralian troops had been engaged in, and all ranks were elated at the success of the operation and the efficiency of all branches of the forces. The organisation of all units and the co-ordination of all arms reached a pitch that had not been experienced before, and though the division was to work under still better staff-work in a later phase of the war, the improvement was so marked that it could not fail to impress those troops who had been through the earlier battles, and naturally this raised their spirits and they felt that the war had some meaning at last.

Of course a great deal of the success of the operation was due to the fact that the ground was in fair condition after the long, dry period just before the 3rd Brigade entered the line, but the Somme weather of the previous year had been good up till September yet no one could fail to notice the difference in the troops after this last battle compared to the dejection after the Somme battles. Even the wounded going back were full of spirit and telling of the wonderful attack. There was also a great preponderance of artillery on the British side on this occasion which quite reversed the experiences in the Somme.

The barrages in the Somme had also often been very ragged, but the British and Australian barrage of September 20 was always held up as the paragon of bombardments. It was indeed a wall of shell-fire.

After the troops had settled down for the night, Lieut.-Colonel Rafferty visited the line and he told this yarn against himself. He had lost his bearings and was wandering somewhere in front of the posts when he was challenged by a sentry. He disclosed his identity and Sergeant W. Beck ("Old" Bill Beck) immediately strode out and said: "Oh! It's you, is it? Cripes! You take more lookin' after than a kid. Don't you be goin' out here again without tellin' me," and he guided his Colonel back to the rear. All men were the same to "Old" Bill.

On September 21 the enemy appeared to have been so hammered and shattered that hardly any serious shelling took place on the 11th Battalion's line, and so the troops passed a quiet day and were relieved by the 1st Battalion at 9:30 p.m. The battalion moved back to Dickebusch without a casualty. The code-word sent to brigade on completion of relief was "Right-oh!"

The day of September 22 was mostly spent in checking equipment and making up losses. The battalion had a general clean-up and the men were pleased to be able to have a bathing parade.

At 2 p.m. on the following day the battalion lined up along the Dickebusch road in parties of 25 under an officer or senior N.C.O., and each party was detailed to a motor-bus. The column then moved off to the Steenvoorde area and arrived about 4:30 p.m., thus giving the troops plenty of time to have a look around before settling down in their billets for the night. The battalion transport had proceeded independently and had a slow journey owing to the congestion of the traffic on the roads.

About a week was spent in the Steenvoorde area, with the battalion going through the usual routine of reorganisation and training. A number of reinforcements joined up and the nucleus returned from the 1st Division camp at Caestre.

The Steenvoorde area was in a rich country with large, prosperous-looking farmhouses. Many of the troops had pleasant recollections of previous visits, and as the village of Steenvoorde was larger than most of the centres that the troops were usually associated with, there were more shops and other attractions than were generally found near their billets. The country, too, was quiet and peaceful, with the trees showing their autumn tints, and the stay was a pleasant rest after the excitement of the previous week. The peace was destroyed one night by a big German bombing raid, but fortunately no bombs dropped near enough to do any harm.

On the last day of the month the battalion returned to the forward area and the troops went into shelters in the "Canal Dug-outs" in the Chateau Segard area.

A strong flight of German bombing planes came over the area in the evening, and the Gothas dropped many bombs. There were a number of casualties in the 12th Battalion lines, but the 11th Battalion was again fortunate in being in good shelters and bomb-proof "possies."

CHAPTER XXXVI

BROODSEINDE RIDGE

"So here, while the mad guns curse overhead,
And tired men sigh, with mud for couch and floor,
Know that we fools, now with the foolish dead,
Died not for flag, nor king, nor emperor,
But for a dream . . ."

IT WAS now October, 1917, and the winter was setting in in earnest. The conditions of the front lines and neighbouring positions were fast approaching to those of the Somme winter of 1916/1917. Except that the British and French had now an overwhelming superiority in artillery, there was nothing that warranted the hope that a successful break-through could be made, and a hope based on artillery alone was vain. There was nothing that could be put forward to justify the fearful sacrifice that the line troops were called upon to make, nor to compensate for the shattering of the fine divisions; yet the Third Battle of Ypres continued. Up to date there had been some little gain, glorified to a great extent by the Press and used as a means of stimulating and encouraging the Allies, who were at this time at the bottom of the curve of despair and disappointment at the unsatisfactory results of the war so far. But the gains were inconsiderable and out of all proportion to the terrible cost in men and material.

In spite of everything Sir Douglas Haig kept up his plan for capturing the three ridges, and by the time the 11th Battalion moved up to the line again on October 1 the battle was for the possession of the second or Broodseinde Ridge.

The battalion moved into reserves at Westhoek Ridge and relieved the 42nd Battalion. There were no casualties during the relief, but it was a trying march up past the hated "Shrapnel Corner" and along the corduroy tracks with the big German shells screaming over and often bursting on the roads. After the relief the troops were immediately put on fatigues and working parties. There were parties detailed for burying cable and there were the usual carrying parties up to the line. There were two Diggers wounded and three gassed.

It was here that the effect of the new mustard gas began to show. When a shell burst in a trench it impregnated the walls or sides with the yellow liquid it contained. Then perhaps some poor Digger would lean against the side of the trench and his clothing would be saturated. In a short time the man's skin would begin to itch and soon great blisters would form, which were exceedingly painful and in many cases fatal.

On October 2 the ridge was shelled intermittently all day, but owing to the good shelters at Westhoek there were no casualties. At 10 p.m. the 11th Battalion moved out of the reserve position at Westhoek Ridge to allow the troops of the 2nd Brigade to take up position there. The 1st and 2nd Australian Brigades were making an attack and had moved up to Westhoek Ridge as a preliminary to the hop-over. The 11th Battalion moved back to Canal Dug-outs for the night, and on October 3 went back to the reserve positions at Westhoek Ridge. Next day the battalion lay in reserve all day. The forward routes were reconnoitred by officers and N.C.O.'s. The troops were used for carrying parties for the other brigades of the division. There were five men wounded.

Officers of the battalion made a reconnaissance of the newly-won ground on Broodseinde Ridge. The attack by the other brigades had been successful, and at 8 p.m. the 11th Battalion advanced to the line held by the 6th and 7th Battalions and relieved them. The 12th Battalion was on the right, then "A," "B," "C," and "D" Companies of the 11th Battalion in that order, with the 18th Battalion on the left flank. The shelling was intense; five men were killed and four reported missing.

Opposite the 11th Battalion was Celtic Wood, or what was left of it. There were a number of dug-outs in this wood and the remains of many huts. It was not known if the wood was held in strength or not. The wood was mostly in a valley, at the bottom of which ran a ditch, and the ground was extremely boggy.

A raiding party was detailed from the 11th and 12th Battalions to find out if Celtic Wood was held in any strength and also to secure enemy identifications. The officers in charge of the parties were Lieut. P. E. M. Vowles (11th Battalion) and Lieut. A. L. S. Davey (12th Battalion).

The official report on Celtic Wood raid is appended.

"Eleventh Battalion Headquarters, October 7, 1917, Broodseinde Ridge. Orders to raid Celtic Wood in conjunction with the 12th Battalion were received at 3:43 on October 6, 1917. I at once consulted with Major Darnell, 'A' Company, and arranged for a party consisting of Lieut. Vowles and Lieut. Gudgeon and 30 other ranks to be held in readiness.

"Immediately after making these preparations I went to 12th Battalion headquarters and saw the C.O. (Lieut.-Colonel Elliot, D.S.O.) and he kindly consented to allow me to issue the orders and to be responsible for the raid.

"Composition of the raiding party was as attached order: 'Brigade's message requiring zero hour to be delayed until midnight was not received by 11th Battalion until 11:7 p.m.'

"At 12:2 a.m., what seemed to me to be only one battery of 18-pounders, commenced a desultory fire on the arranged lines. Their effect was so feeble that the 2nd Machine Gun Company's gunners which were to assist in the box barrage did not think it was time to commence, and we thus lost valuable support.

"Although in doubt whether or no the barrage was down, Lieut. Vowles (11th Battalion, O.C. raid) led the party forward with such vigour that the enemy was completely surprised. The Germans were mostly caught in their funk-holes and were either killed or captured quite easily.

"At 12:10 a.m. the return signal was fired, and by 12:25 a.m. the O.C. raid reported that he had been successful.

"By 12:40 a.m. raid had reported to 11th Battalion headquarters, and all the 11th Battalion portion of the raid had reported through 'A' Company headquarters. Contrary to the orders I had issued, the 12th Battalion portion of the raid did not report back through the 11th Battalion headquarters, nor have I had any report from Lieut. Davey (12th Battalion). C.O. 12th Battalion reported that his portion of the raid had taken ten prisoners and one machine gun. Casualties: 12th Battalion, one other rank wounded.

"Results: Prisoners of 449th Regiment, 12 other ranks; prisoners afterwards secured by 11th Battalion in raid, three other ranks; machine guns, one; estimated enemy killed, 11th Battalion portion only, 20; enemy wounded, approximately, 30; our casualties: killed, nil; wounded, 11th Battalion, one: 12th Battalion, one."

In a summary on the raid, Major Steele stated that he was of opinion that the artillery had ample time to arrange their barrage for the original zero hour of 11 p.m., and that the delay of one hour might have easily meant the failure for the party, and it also meant that the party had to lie out in No Man's Land for a whole hour.

Major Steele also pointed out that the barrage was almost useless, but that good work had been done by the Stokes mortars of the 3rd A.L.T.M. Battery under Lieut. Miles.

Major Steele also pointed out that had the barrage been put where he asked, many of the enemy who escaped would have been killed or taken prisoner. The prisoners who were taken stated that there were two lieutenants and 150 men in Celtic Wood, and they had been so surprised at the vigour of the attack that they had made little resistance.

The summary concludes with the following paragraphs:—

"I would like to sum up by saying that the success of the raid seems to be due to the skill and energy of the officers (particularly Lieut. Vowles), to the good arrangements and accurate fire of the 3rd A.L.T.M. Battery and to the fine spirit of the men.

"I desire to bring to your notice the excellent work done in the above raid by Lieut. P. E. M. Vowles and Lieut. A. H. Miles, 3rd A.L.T.M. Battery.

"Signed A. Steele, Major, Commanding 11th Battalion."

Besides the official account there are two interesting extracts from diaries relating to the Celtic Wood raid. The first is Private Jim Kirkwood's account: "'A' Company sent out a raiding party on the night of October 6. Lieuts. Vowles and Gudgeon were in charge. It was a rotten affair, but ended well. The Hun position was supposed to have been ascertained, but if it had they had shifted back probably 150 yards during the previous 24 hours. The raid was in conjunction with the 12th Battalion. We got a good few prisoners, but only had one casualty. One Fritz was 'stiff' on this occasion. When we were cleaning out a bit of a post, this Fritz, who was bare-headed, was patting his head and pointing to a small dug-out. One of the troops waved him toward the dug-out and the Hun made a mad dive for it and was shot by another Digger. The first troop (i.e. Digger) said, 'Poor cow! He only wanted his tin hat,' but the second replied, 'The bastard might have been after a machine gun.'

"When we were returning with the prisoners two troops who were bringing up the rear heard some movement behind them, and on looking round saw a Fritz calmly following behind. This man was put ahead and seemed to be mighty satisfied to be with his pals."

The other account is from the diary of Private J. A. Sanders, and is also interesting: "Thursday, October 4. The 1st and 2nd Divisions went into action in the early morning and made a notable advance. According to report they achieved a complete success. The casualties appeared to be heavy from what we saw of the battle-ground that morning as we passed through carrying all manner of material up to the line. We also saw many prisoners.

"October 5. Moved into the front line. Quiet, and little shelling. The country in front of us is green and not greatly broken. It is a contrast to that behind us, which is a veritable quagmire.

"October 6. A raid. Thirty men from the 12th and 30 from the 11th Battalion. Zero hour was to be 11 a.m. Everything seemed to go wrong. Lieut. Vowles in charge. . . . The time was wrong and we had to lie on the wet ground an hour longer than was intended. The barrage failed us. In the end only one battery firing. At the appointed hour the officer leapt to his feet, and in a loud voice cried: 'Come on!' We followed, quaking in our boots. Our men mistook the enemy position and were running round some skeleton pill-boxes crying, 'Come out, you b——s!'

"The enemy trenches were some 60 yards away. However in the end we got there and took some 20 prisoners and had only one man wounded. I myself took two prisoners. Unfortunately on our way back I and others gave our prisoners to the 12th Battalion troops in mistake. I discovered it and asked for my prisoners, but was told it was all the same. Our battalion captured the prisoners, but the 12th Battalion got the credit."

From these three accounts a pretty accurate idea of the raid is obtained. This raid reflected very great credit on the 11th Battalion troops engaged, for they succeeded when everything possible seemed to be against them. The long wait in the mud owing to the error at the start was a severe test for the best of troops.

The day following the raid on Celtic Wood was very wet. Heavy rain fell and flooded the posts and trenches. The supports and battalion headquarters were very heavily shelled, and Major Steele and Lieut. L. C. (Elsie) Cooke were killed. Lieut. L. C. Cooke was one of the original battalion and a very fine officer. There was also one Digger killed and eight others wounded. A shell had landed near the pill-box where Major Steele had his headquarters, and this caught many of the troops. Nothing remained of Major Steele save his tunic.

One report states that the Major had fired off some German flares, whether by accident or design is not known, and the resultant German barrage was due to this. Second Lieut. Harry Hartill was also wounded on this date.

Several more prisoners were taken by patrols during the day. These belonged to the 450th I.R. of the 253rd German Division, and these gave valuable information. The 11th Battalion claimed 21 prisoners. One of these was captured under amusing circumstances.

On the morning after the raid one of the machine gun outposts saw, just at daybreak, a forlorn Fritz roaming around. He was coming towards the post, so the garrison kept low. When the German was close up they saw that he was unarmed, so they attracted his attention, beckoned to him and in he came. Not a word could be got from him, however. He ate their rations, smoked their cigarettes and had a good sleep, but he never uttered a word. After dark that night he was sent to company headquarters. Poor Fritz was making a slow passage along the slushy front line, so one of the boys said: "I wish the clumsy cow would get a move on," and another answered, "He can't; he's too fat." The troops were then greatly surprised to hear Fritz answer in good Australian, "No bloody fear! There's not enough food in Germany to fatten a flea."

After dark the 9th Battalion relieved the 11th Battalion and the troops moved to the support line. Major J. Newman took over temporary command of the battalion.

Following a moderately quiet day on October 8, the 11th Battalion was relieved by the 7th Battalion and the companies moved out to reserve position on Anzac Ridge. Owing to the continuous rain the track out was nearly impassable, and in consequence the troops were greatly fatigued with the journey back. To make matters worse, the trenches were flooded and the tired troops had to spend the night in the open. From this time onward the Third Battle of Ypres began to be a replica of the later stages of the Somme battle, but the forward drive was insisted on for a considerable time after this, even after it was apparent to every one, except perhaps the leaders, in their comfortable quarters many miles behind the lines, that the impossible was being asked of the infantry.

But it was not only the infantry that suffered. This story would not be complete if the indescribably fine work of all the assisting arms was not mentioned. The artillery, the engineers and pioneers had a fearful time; the first-named in shifting their guns and preparing new positions and the others in making and constantly repairing roads and in siting new trenches and communications.

The conduct of the divisional ammunition columns, in bringing up their daily quota of shells along the few and accurately shelled roads and tracks, was such that every one had to admire them. Sometimes there would be a jam on the roads, and these arteries woud be packed for miles with all descriptions of traffic. Motor lorries laden with ammunition, guns going forward, limbers and waggons and pack-horses with rations and ammunition, troops coming or going, engineers with loads of brushwood for filling up shell-holes in the road, and every short distance strings of horses or oftener mules loaded up with shells for the guns. Often when a jam was on, the road would be subjected to frightful shelling, and after the bursts, horses and mules would be rolling on the ground in death agonies, their drivers killed or wounded, and the survivors unable to do anything but stand to their horses' heads until the shelling would slacken. The sights on these roads, the Hooge Road and Hellfire Corner and the Menin Road beggar description.

The waste of material, as exemplified by the shattered heaps of all kinds of vehicles and guns, the carcases of horses and mules, and the heaps of shells slowly settling into the mud, must have been seen to be adequately realised, and each day that the attack continued the wastage increased. It was not possible to move off the roads, except in a few places, and then only by lightly-armed troops or with lightly-loaded pack-horses. The wounded were carried along duck-boarded tracks and very often German prisoners were made to act as 'bearers, and it must be admitted that they worked well. But only too often these men were cursed, because carrying wounded they had the right of way, and the passing troops had to flounder in the mud at the side of the duckboards until the stretchers had passed.

The battalion transports had to take up rations and supplies through all this, and there is no question that they performed their jobs nobly.

To come back to the march out of the line of the 11th Battalion on October 8. The official diary states that the number of casualties on this occasion was five other ranks killed and eight missing, while one officer and 12 other ranks were wounded. It would not be too much to state that several of the missing were simply swallowed up in the mud.

There was a disastrous raid by the 10th Battalion on October 9. This is mentioned here to illustrate the conditions existing. The raid consisted of five officers and 80 other ranks, and the objective was Celtic Copse. Things did not go too well, and out of the 80 odd men who went out there were only 14 unwounded members of the party who returned. Two officers were killed, two were wounded and one was missing. Of the remainder there were many that simply disappeared for ever. No trace was ever discovered concerning them. They must have been lost in the darkness and swallowed up in the mud. This may seem a strong statement to make, but the writer has seen horses and mules sink up to the neck in these morasses, and the more they struggled the more they sank, and the only kindness that could be given was a bullet in the forehead. Truly it was a frightful place.

A summary of the operations for this period appears in the official diary of October 9, and the last few paragraphs are illuminating.

"On the evening of October 8 the battalion was relieved by the 7th Battalion and moved back under order independently by companies to reserve line on Anzac Ridge, and this was a severe trial to the men who were already very fatigued. The country crossed was pitted with shell-craters full of water and mud, forming an almost impassable bog. The night was pitch dark, tracks almost obliterated and impossible to find. In spite of these difficulties the battalion reached its position on Anzac

Ridge, where there was little accommodation. Owing to the heavy rain which was falling the trenches were full of mud. What few pill-boxes were available were filled and the remainder of the battalion had to distribute itself amidst shell-holes and bits of trench under most trying conditions.

"On October 9 the men remained on Anzac Ridge soaked to the skin with mud and rain until relieved by the 59th Battalion at 3 p.m. The battalion then withdrew under orders to Belgian Chateau without incident.

"During the whole of the operation the highest credit is due to all ranks for the cheerful and gallant manner in which they carried out their duties under these exceptionally trying conditions. Special praise is due to the carrying parties who supplied troops in the forward area with necessaries; also to the runners and guides who were called upon at all times and cheerfully carried out their duties under heavy shell-fire. Praise is also due to the transport who, under most trying circumstances, never failed to keep the forward dumps supplied, enabling the battalion to carry on throughout the period."

The casualties during this tour of the line were: Killed, officers, 3; other ranks, 6. Wounded: officers, 1; other ranks, 36. Missing, 17. Total, 63.

Before passing on to the next phase of the 11th Battalion's story, a short personal experience which may throw a little light on the state of the country east of Ypres and the terribly exhausted condition of the men may not be amiss.

The writer at this time held the position of transport officer in the 11th Battalion and was in a position to note the fearful conditions in rear and up to the lines. It was a firmly fixed principle of all first line transport, no matter what happened, that it must not let the front line troops down, and the 11th Battalion transport, right through its career, carried out this principle in a manner worthy of the best traditions. A finer body of men it would have been hard to find.

On the night when the battalion was relieved and came back to Anzac Ridge, word came back through brigade that the rations had not been received by the battalion. (It later transpired that the rations had been correctly delivered, but owing to the rain and mud, everything was ruined except jars of rum and the fatigue party detailed was too tired to bother with mud-laden food and only took the rum.)

Immediately a fresh supply of rations was got ready and sent up to the line, the writer leading up one pack-horse himself, as it was his "pigeon" if anything was wrong. The conditions after the drenching rain were appalling, and it was with difficulty that the mare bearing the rations could be led over the shell-torn country. Several times she was almost lost, but by dint of hard work and encouragement the poor creature was dragged up to the battalion position.

The mare was taken to all company headquarters, but the men were too exhausted to come and get their rations. The men were absolutely done up. Some of the N.C.O.'s came and took charge of the rum and after it had been issued the men began to brighten perceptibly and gradually they were fit to eat their rations. And yet there are some people who will insist that rum can never do any good. Many troops who do not touch alcohol still state that the rum issues saved many lives.

When returning from this trip the mare was so tired that she could hardly be dragged along, but eventually she was led back to the transport lines. This mare had been one of the best animals in the battalion transport, but she never recovered from this terrible trip and had to be destroyed. She had strained herself beyond recovery. The conditions that the men had to put up with can therefore be imagined.

The battalion spent a night at Chateau Belge and then moved off to Devonshire lines on October 10. The details from nucleus joined up with the battalion before leaving the huts and the battalion transport accompanied the troops to the new area. The congestion on the roads was so great that 800-yards interval had to be kept between battalions, 200 yards between companies and 400 yards between transports of units and companies. The battalion reached Devonshire lines at mid-day.

The next few days were devoted to bathing and cleaning up generally. The men were allowed to rest on October 12 as they were much wearied by the effort they had made in the previous tour of the line. Second Lieut. Keeley was evacuated to hospital on the above date. The following day was spent in reorganising the companies and making up the various sections.

October 14 was a Sunday. After a church parade the 3rd Brigade marched past General Walker, G.O.C. 1st Australian Division. Lieut.-Colonel Rafferty assumed temporary command of the 3rd Brigade during the absence of Brigadier-General Bennett who was on leave. Major John Newman was temporarily in command of the battalion.

Training and instructional work were recommenced on October 15, and the various specialist sections were brought up to strength and work started in these sections. The 11th Battalion lost the services of a fine officer on this date. Major "Doc" Robinson, M.C., left the battalion for Abbeville. The Major was a true friend to the boys and all the troops were sorry that he had to leave. He was a real man, and all ranks were the same to him.

A good story was told by himself, which is characteristic of the man. One day while on leave in London, he met "Old" Bill Beck, well known to all 11th Battalion men who served in France. The "Doc" was pleased to see Bill, who was then a sergeant, and he invited him to come with him to a show that evening and to have dinner with him before the event.

They met as arranged, and the Doctor took Bill to the Piccadilly restaurant and did him well. The dinner ran to many courses and the wines were carefully selected. After dinner the show was duly appreciated. On parting for the night Bill thanked Major Robinson for the entertainment and added that everything had been "tres bon," but he told the Major confidentially that if he really would like a good feed, he (Bill) would take him to a "dinkum" place on the following day. The Doctor said that he accepted Bill's invitation, and added that Bill had done him really well, but he would never divulge where Bill had taken him.

Some chapters previously mention had been made that several members of the battalion had reported to England to join the new 6th Division. Owing to insufficient reinforcements, this division had to be disbanded and many officers and other ranks were returned to the older divisions. Among these, Captain Tulloch and 93 other ranks reported to the 11th Battalion from England.

During the time the 11th Battalion was at Devonshire camp, there were frequent bombing raids by the Germans. These were carried out with great daring and were frequently made in broad daylight.

On October 19, before the officers sat down to mess, Major Darnell, who was senior officer at the time, said he had a rather distressing announcement to make, and he then informed the assembled officers (all the mess orderlies and stewards having been sent out of the hut) that he had the promulgation of a court-martial to read. This order was to the effect that Lieut. Dave Hardy was to lose six months' seniority on account of over-staying his leave when ordered to proceed from England to France. (The offence was purely technical and was only due to a mistake in the time of departure of a train, but the authorities chose to take a serious view of the matter, with the abovementioned result.) All the officers were full of sympathy for Hardy, who was a fine soldier. Hardy, however, was deeply chagrined, and took the matter very much to heart.

Just after lunch German bombing 'planes were heard overhead and "eggs" began to fall around. Most of the officers quickly evacuated the hut and old Con. O'Brien and the rest of the orderlies cleared out.

Dave Hardy still sat moodily in his chair, so the writer went up to him and said: "Come on, Dave, let's clear out of this or Fritz will be dropping one of his 'eggs' on top of us." But Hardy would not move. "I don't give a damn," he said, "if the bastards drop one right on top of my head."

That afternoon there was a practice in live bomb throwing and Lieuts. Hardy and Summer were in charge of the party. During the practice there was the premature burst of a bomb and both Hardy and Summers were very seriously wounded and Sergeant Bill Beck and Private R. F. Bell, of the bombing platoon, were also wounded. All were immediately rushed to hospital, but Hardy and Summers both died a day or two later.

The strength of the battalion was increased on October 20 by 42 details and reinforcements from England, and on October 23, 13 details reported from the base.

CHAPTER XXXVII

ZONNEBEKE

THE BATTALION had now been resting for a fortnight, so it was no surprise for the troops to receive the order to return to the line. On October 24 the battalion embussed at 9 a.m. and was transported to a camp a little distance outside the famous Menin Gate at Ypres. The site was in a little natural basin behind a rise. The camp was in a deplorable condition, and the men were immediately set to work cleaning up the dug-outs and the area generally. This job of cleaning up seemed to be the 11th Battalion's prime duty everywhere it went, and the boys used to wonder if anyone else in the whole of the war zone ever did any cleaning up besides themselves. The same report as to dirty conditions was made by all the units of the 3rd Brigade. The brigade official diary for October 26 states: "All units proceeding with training of specialists and improvement of billets which *were in a very filthy condition.*" On the same date "B" Company, of the 11th Battalion, moved to a more suitable position in Ypres as the camp they had been in was in such a very bad state.

Up to October 28 the battalion was busily engaged in training its specialists for the coming tour of the line; luckily there were facilities for bathing near the camps and the boys were all paraded for this purpose.

During the few days spent at Menin Gate the troops had ample opportunities to have a look round. In spite of the constant shelling and bombing, the swans still lived in the moat round the gate. There were also coots and water-hens. It was wonderful how little notice these birds took of the shells that sometimes fell in the water. The town was much more destroyed than when the battalion was there a year before, and hardly any buildings had any kind of a roof. The town major permitted the transports of the various units to take stones and bricks from the more shattered buildings in order to make solid stances for the horses and waggons in the transport lines. Much material was also used for the repair of tracks and roads. Ypres itself lives in memory as the epitome of desolation and destruction.

On October 30 the battalion moved out from the dug-outs at Menin Gate at 9 a.m. and marched to Sexton House, Westhoek Ridge. From there the troops moved up to relieve the 7th Battalion in the line near Zonnebeke. "A" and "C" Companies were in the front line, and "B" and "D" Companies in supports. There were only three casualties reported during the relief. The weather was fine but cold and windy, and the ground was still soft and boggy. There was a considerable amount of shelling on both sides.

Duckboard Track near Zonnebeke. (Official Photo.)

Lieut.-Colonel Rafferty had resumed command of the battalion from Acting-Brigadier, 3rd Australian Brigade.

The 1st Australian Division had been detailed to take over the line near Decline Copse and to act as a protection for the right flank of the 4th Canadian Division, which was making an attack on Passchendaele. The 2nd Australian Brigade had been holding this position and the 3rd Brigade had now relieved its sister unit.

On the last day of the month of October the 11th Battalion headquarters and other details were in dug-outs at Zonnebeke, while the companies were in the line in terrible trenches and posts. The shelling was severe all that day, and the troops were busy making shelters and "possies" in the most suitable locations. There was not much choice in the matter of positions, but the boys did their best. It was wonderful what the Diggers could do in the way of making themselves comfortable, even under the most appalling circumstances.

It is hardly possible to describe the conditions under which the men existed. The gun-fire was so intense that there was no area of ground left untouched, and the troops lived in a welter of mud and broken trenches.

If one looked back from the front line, for miles behind there was an almost unrelieved morass in which derelict waggons and guns lay shattered here and there; where low mists rolled and eddied; and where the falling shells sent up geysers of mud and water. Ever and anon the crescendo of the guns would increase until the drum-fire reached barrage intensity, which immediately brought retaliation, and the air would be full of screaming shells and flying fragments and lumps of wet mud.

Through this terrible bog ran the few straight roads that fed the front lines, and it seemed as if they were never entirely free from shelling and it was a marvel that supplies were maintained. The engineers and pioneers had a nightmare time keeping the communications open, and the former were continually carting up loads of brushwood and blue metal to fill up the huge shell-holes that constantly and continually appeared on all the roads. Along the roads could be seen sickly-looking pools of yellowish liquid; and though this was by no means confined to the roads, but was splashed about the trenches as well, for it was the hated mustard gas, yet it always seemed most noticeable near the main arteries; and it gave rise to painful headaches even to breathe the emanations from the pools, while the splashes from the liquid caused terrible burns.

On a clear day—and these were few—if one looked over the German lines a vision of green and almost untouched country met the eye. It was a strange and beautiful contrast to the awful scenery in rear of the British and Australian positions, and many an envious look was cast at the fair terrain the Germans occupied, and it was difficult to imagine that those who held the much better positions in every way were being really driven back.

Site of Zonnebeke Railway Station, Ypres Sector, October, 1917. (Official Photo.)

But fine days had their drawbacks, for the German airmen were active then, and they used to machine-gun the trenches and avenues of approach. British 'planes seemed to be outclassed at this period.

Besides the ordinary shelling and mustard gas shells, the Germans put over a great deal of blue cross gas, but there were no casualties from this source. The battalion suffered considerably from high-explosive shell. There were 13 men killed and 15 wounded. Among those killed was Sergeant H. A. (Nigger) Black, D.C.M., M.M., a very fine soldier, and one who had been the life of "C" Company. "Nigger" was killed on patrol duty by H.E. shell.

The Canadian troops who had been on the battalion's left flank were relieved on this same date, October 31.

The official diary for November 1 states: "Zonnebeke. Weather fine. Our lines heavily shelled by the enemy during the day, but his luck was out. 'D' and 'B' Companies relieved 'A' and 'C' in the front line. Relief carried out without incident. Strong patrols went out but failed to locate the enemy. Ground very boggy.

"Casualties: four other ranks killed, 11 other ranks wounded. Captain Le Nay evacuated owing to eyes being affected by mustard gas."

On November 2 one of the 11th Battalion posts, which was situated in Decoy Wood, was hit by a shell just after midnight and blown in. Second Lieut. Irving and four men were killed, while five others were wounded. The post was re-established immediately.

The official diary goes on to say: "Our transport was heavily shelled near Zonnebeke but finished their job. Five other ranks wounded; two horses killed and three horses wounded.

"The 9th and 12th Battalions took over our front line and supports. Relief carried out without incident.

"Casualties for the 24 hours: six killed, 10 wounded."

The reference to the heavy shelling that the 11th Battalion transport underwent was also mentioned in the 12th Battalion official diary. This was the 11th Battalion transport's heaviest casualty list in all its service, and the incidents of that day indicated the awful conditions existing on the roads leading up to the front.

At this period the orders for the day would generally state that trial barrages would be put down at various times during the 24 hours, and as the trip to the line from the transport lines was about seven miles each way, and the British barrage invariably called down an answering barrage from the Germans, it was often a problem for the transport officer to know just when to make the trip that would land his boys in the least trouble. On the date mentioned above, there were barrages listed at intervals over the whole day and there was no hope of altogether escaping the retaliation that would most surely follow.

But the line troops had to be fed, and supplies had to go up. On this occasion there were several limbers, but there was also the usual pack-train. The drivers drove or led their charges forward, an N.C.O. in front (Corporal Harry Harn on this occasion) and the T.O. brought up the rear. When the party had passed Potijze and had reached the crest of the Frezenberg Road that lead on to Zonnebeke, there was a noticeable slowing up of the column in front and soon the boys were winding in and out of the crowded mass of waggons and ammunition columns that had halted on the road. Soon Harry Harn cantered back with the news that an officer was stationed on the crest of the ridge, and that he would not allow any one to pass as the Germans were putting down a most terrific barrage all over the valley in front and through which the road lead. The transport officer galloped to the head of the column and had a long look, and though the prospect was none too pleasing it seemed as though the shelling was easing, so he told the officer that his men were going on. Harn then led off with the limbers and the pack-horses followed. As the little party moved slowly down into the valley the shelling died away altogether, but not before a few strays had landed near and wounded some of the party. With the T.O., whose duty it was to bring up the rear, was Corporal Jacky Lee, a splendid lad, and as there was a pack-horse that had lost its driver, Lee was told to bring the horse along as rations were precious. A shell lobbed in the mud a long way off, and the T.O. turned his head to see Lee fall out of his saddle. He was badly wounded. Luckily there was an aid-post near and stretcher-bearers soon had him inside. The T.O. took the horses—they were more precious than men in these terrible days—and hurried forward after his men, the remainder of whom had got through the valley safely and were then climbing the slope toward Zonnebeke church, or what was left of it. Looking back over the route just traversed, the party could now see the whole road filled with moving horsemen and vehicles of all descriptions, and then Fritz's barrage fell once more. The 11th Battalion party were beyond the area shelled but the sight of that awful carnage will never be forgotten. Men, horses, guns, waggons and lorries were blown clean off the road. Wheels were sent spinning into the air and men and horseflesh strewn over the countryside. No more need be told. The rations were safely delivered to the battalion at Zonnebeke.

The shelling was still intermittent on the return trip and a few more men and horses were hit, but there was no terrible barrage as on the trip up. It was learned that Corporal Lee had been evacuated, and it was later ascertained that he had died soon after. Lee was a good man if ever there was one. On the journey back the most pitiful sights were witnessed, but these were too awful to be described. It was different from a battlefield, where the carnage is spread over a large area and therefore not so noticeable; but there on the Frezenberg Road it was just one shambles that day. The transport officer had to use his pistol many times to put poor brutes out of their misery.

The official entry for November 3 runs: "Zonnebeke. At 4:50 a.m. the enemy attacked along the Ypres-Roulers railway on the 9th Battalion front. The 11th Battalion was ready to move to the assistance of the 9th, but our aid was not required.

"The enemy shelled the railway very heavily during the day, not quietening until 6 p.m.

"Casualties: one other rank killed; 14 other ranks wounded; three other ranks sick."

After another day in supports the battalion was relieved by the 3rd Battalion on November 5. This relief was completed by noon. The battalion reached its new position by 3 p.m. and the relief was carried out without a casualty. When the battalion arrived at the Canal Dug-outs, No. 8 Lock, on the Ypres-Commines Canal, some amusement was caused by the sending to brigade headquarters of the code message signifying that the relief was complete. The message on this occasion was: "What about the rum ration?" Doubtless there were a few who would have liked to hear a favourable answer to that query.

Some of the passwords and code messages were rather funny but these would need a chapter to themselves. But to give an example, one in use only a short time before this was "Moon Shining Bright." As it was as dark as hell and pouring rain when the message came through, some wonder was expressed as to what b—— fool sent the message.

The tour of duty just completed was the last time that the 11th Battalion participated in the disastrous Third Battle of Ypres. But indeed the battle had already run its course. Like the winter battles in the Somme the weather conditions and especially the mud had been effectual in slowing up and eventually stopping altogether what appeared to be a bold attempt to advance under superiority of artillery. With the wet weather that persisted almost all the time the result could not have been otherwise, and it was felt by the troops that the attack had been prolonged far beyond the time that gave any hope of success; and it was also felt that the line troops and artillery had suffered needlessly in the last phases of the operations.

The 1st Australian Division had lost over 6,500 men in casualties. Of this number the 3rd Brigade had lost 1,464 in its three tours of the line.

Lest it may be thought that the writer has exaggerated the conditions pertaining in the Third Battle of Ypres, and that the criticisms offered have been biassed or too severe, the following extracts from a British heavy gunner's account of the four years of war are appended.

"From the military point of view the tragedy of Passchendaele was that the common soldiers who fought in that bloody and futile enterprise—and I speak as a common soldier—ceased to believe in the High Command. They understood the realities too well to suffer any further illusions."

The same writer states: "The Somme destroyed the very flower of young British manhood who had volunteered adventurously and without misgiving at the first impulse. Passchendaele destroyed the best of the later recruits and NEARLY BROKE THE STRONG BACK OF OUR BRITISH MORALE." (Compiler's capitals.)

Chapter XXXVIII

RESTING AT COURSET

UNTIL NOVEMBER 9 the 11th Battalion rested and reorganised at the Canal Dug-outs at Number 8 Lock. The divisional baths were situated close to the Lille Gate on the south side of Ypres and here the men were sent to bathe. The effect of the yellow cross gas was noticed on many of the men, and numbers had great blisters where the gas had come into contact with their skins. Some of the troops were very badly blistered and the new medical officer (Captain Leonard May) treated them at the aid-post he had established at Number 8 Lock.

The next move took place on November 9 when the battalion marched to Vancouver Camp, not far from Outerdom. As the brigade passed along the Outerdom-Poperinghe Road, General Sir Herbert Plumer, the 2nd Army commander, watched the troops go by. The camp was reached at 2 p.m. and the troops utilised the rest of the day in straightening camp, which was a muddy and unprepossessing place. A little ray of sunshine was the presence of the corps concert party near by This party, the "Anzac Coves," gave a good show which was much appreciated by the troops.

There was a big Chinese labour corps camp situated not far away from Vancouver Camp, and during one of the nightly visitations of the German bombers the Boche dropped a few bombs close to this compound. One of the boys had ventured the remark a little earlier in the day that the "Chows" did not seem to be very speedy "birds," but he had good cause to change his opinion because when the bombs exploded there was a mad stampede of terrified Chinese in all directions, and it was reported that a good many of them were not collected for many days afterwards.

At Vancouver Camp Sergeants Naylor, Jim George, H. Holley and Murray were given commissioned rank.

On November 11 the Battalion moved by motor omnibus to Campagne, near St. Omer. Here the troops went into billets.

The battalion transport with the rest of the brigade transports under the command of the 11th Battalion transport officer left by road, and had a long march to Ecke. The steep hills over the ridge of the Mont de Cats and the slippery and muddy roads were a severe trial to the horses, which had been through a rough time in the last "stunt." Rain started to fall and the column had almost reached its destination at a farm called Hagedorn (in English, Hawthorn) when a railway train halted right across a level-crossing in front of the leading waggons and held up the column. In desperation, after vainly trying to get the driver to pull up his train a little, the troops were ordered to pull round in front of the train and over the rails. It was a rough passage, but all the waggons managed to make the crossing.

In the dark the whole brigade transport pulled into a large, muddy field and somehow or other the boys managed to get their horses out and under cover; and soon all were well catered for in the way of straw for bedding.

It was a very large farm, with great buildings and outhouses. All the menfolk were "a la guerre" and Madame and her three fine daughters ran the big farm. Many of the troops were allowed to dry their soaking wet clothes and all received the greatest kindness and consideration.

In the morning Madame and the girls waved the troops farewell as they passed on. It was a bright sunny morning after the rain, and troops were cheerful after their comfortable night. The remembrance of the cheery "Bon voyage et bonne chance" was retained for long afterwards.

Another long trek in fine weather brought the transport to the Renescure area, each battalion transport going to its own unit, the 11th going to Campagne.

The troops had an easy day on November 12 and in the afternoon the battalion band, which had lately been reformed, played for the troops in the village square.

Next day a route-march of 17 miles took the battalion to Wismes. Only one man fell out on the march. Though the men were not carrying packs, this was a very creditable march.

Wismes was a quaint out-of-the-way sort of place, but as usual in such places the peasants were extremely good-hearted and endeavoured to make the troops comfortable. There were plenty of omelettes and the wine was good. All the water for drinking purposes was drawn from one well in the centre of the village. The well looked to be hundreds of years old. Horses and stock were watered in the village pond.

The kitchens of the houses, which were of course the main living rooms, had great cupboards in which were hung all the crockery and brassware used in the house. All these utensils were highly polished and these high cupboards gave a bright and cheerful appearance to the rooms. The stoves were, as is usual in northern France, in the middle of the kitchens, and here the coffee-pots used to give out their delicious aroma. Sometimes Madame would bring out a bottle of Malaga and invite the troops to have a glass. "Bon pour les vieux," Madame would say, and when the troops pointed that they were not yet old, Madame would reply, "Bon pour les jeunes aussi" (good for young people, too).

It was dull weather while the battalion was at Wismes and very often it was wet. The village pond in a hollow of the area was overflowing and the streets were muddy. Most of the battalion training was carried out under shelter. Occasionally there was a route-march. Major J. Newman assumed command of the battalion during the temporary absence of Lieut.-Colonel R. A. Rafferty, D.S.O., who went to England on leave.

After a pleasant week spent at Wismes the 11th Battalion left at 8:30 a.m. on November 18 for the Samer "C" area and arrived at Courset at 3 p.m. after a good march, during which no one fell out. Courset was a rather large village with a fine chateau. It was situated not very far from Boulogne. Never before was the battalion in rest billets so far away from the line, and as the duration of the stay here was rather longer than usual there was naturally a crop of anecdotes connected with the sojourn.

When the battalion arrived after a muddy journey and the companies were allotted to their billets, the transport was billeted in the stables and outbuildings of the Chateau de Courset. As the vehicles pulled into the fine yard the lady of the chateau cast rather a contemptuous eye over the travel-stained vehicles and men. "How dirty and untidy your men look," she said to the transport officer. "Why, we had the —— British cavalry here for about eighteen months and they were always so smart looking and their buttons and badges used to shine." This remark rather annoyed the T.O., so he turned to the lady and said very quietly: "That may be so, Madame, but then you see *these men are soldiers.*" The innuendo may have been lost on the lady, but it was so unfair to compare these boys with their war-worn kit and their travel-stained horses and waggons with the "spit-and-polish" troopers of a crack cavalry regiment that had been resting 18 months that the T.O. may well have been excused for being a bit short in his reply.

Immediately after this slight passage of arms the C.O., accompanied by the adjutant and the M.O., came along to the chateau which had been allotted to them as their billet. On learning their purpose, the lady invited them to follow and led the way along a fine terrace to the door of the mansion. The T.O. followed. There was a halt at the big door of the chateau, where the lady pointed out that the boots of the party were dirty and that the hall inside had been lately polished and that "a cause de la guerre" there was only a small staff to keep the house clean, and would all the officers please remove their boots before entering. The T.O. stood fast, but the other three sat down and removed the offending footwear; and the T.O. had the sight of his life to see the C.O., followed by the M.O. and Jerry Campbell (the adjutant) mount the steps and enter the portal with their leggings and boots carefully held in their hands, while Madame La Baronne had a good eyeful of the holes in their socks. The T.O. and later the M.O. found more congenial billets, but the other two lived at the chateau.

As they were going along the hall for the first time, one of the officers gazed around at the lofty walls and at the spacious rooms and remarked: "Doesn't this remind one of *home.*"

The following day, November 19, was devoted to a much needed overhaul and clean-up of equipment and arms, and of course the inevitable clean-up of billets.

Training was recommenced on November 20 and rifle ranges, bombing grounds and bayonet-fighting courses were established. The afternoons were devoted to recreational training and sports of all kinds were encouraged. Leave was granted daily to two men per platoon to visit Boulogne, which was at no great distance, and the troops were conveyed thither by motor lorry and brought back by the same means of conveyance. The route lay through the extensive Bois de Boulogne, in which deer and wild boar were said to roam.

The troops were soon at home among the villagers, and of course there was always someone ready to help Marie and Marthe with the cows and pigs. One Digger in "C" Company was so enamoured of a little French maid that he used to rise at four o'clock and milk the cows for her. In spite of this gallant work the damsel proved cold, so the Digger decided that after all bed was a much better place at that early hour, so in future he waited for the bugle to wake him up.

On November 30 "A" Company was picked to represent the battalion at brigade sports. There is no official record as to how the troops acquitted themselves.

The 11th Battalion strength on this date was 32 officers and 756 other ranks. The 12th Battalion was over 300 men stronger, having 58 officers and 1,065 other ranks.

Two companies, "A" and "C," of the 11th Battalion, were moved to the adjoining village of Sacriquier and remained there for the remainder of the rest period.

At this time an order came out requesting that a list of all the troops' occupations in civil life be taken. Lieut. D. James, of "C" Company, was going down his list, and he came to Oscar Edburg. James put the usual question: "What was your calling in civil life?" Oscar replied with dignity: "Man of independent means, sir." Then Corporal Jack Pearce's turn came. (Jacky was a window-dresser by profession; he was also noted for a high-pitched, squeaky voice.) "What's yours, Jacky?" said the officer. "Window-dresser, Mr. James," piped Jacky. "Put him down as a window-cleaner," barked James.

On December 3 brigade military competitions commenced, and "D" Company was chosen to represent the battalion. The rest of the battalion went on with the programme of training.

It was very pleasant country in this out-of-the-way spot, and though the trees had lost their leaves and the fields were bare the apples still hung on many of the trees in the orchards.

Madame La Baronne was very much afraid that the troops would help themselves to her apples, and she was very anxious to know if the boys were good, honest soldiers. She solved the vexed question by getting all the apples in her orchards picked and stored in sheds.

There was a complete cider-making plant at the chateau and the old Baron seemed to be the chief executive. There was a large shed of apples ready to be pressed and vats and containers of all descriptions; and one day the boys had the opportunity of seeing the press in full working order and, needless to say, the Baron had plenty of willing helpers on that occasion. The horses got a lot of apples that day.

The official entries for this period are: "Courset, December 4. In view of the fact that brigade competitions are being held in the afternoon, morning was devoted to practising battalion drill."

"At 1 p.m. the battalion was judged by Brigadier-General Bennett, C.M.G., and in this part of the competition we got second place."

"December 5, 1917. Brigade competitions continued. Shooting event taking place on 9th Battalion range. 'D' Company represented this battalion. Other companies carried on under company arrangements; 'C' Company carrying out range practice on our own range. During the day polling took place in regard to the referendum question."

This refers to the vote on conscription, the second referendum taken by the Australian Government, in order to test the feeling of the country on the question of meeting the great demands that were required in the way of reinforcements to the five Australian divisions.

The Australian divisions had suffered an enormous number of casualties, but nothing like so many as some of the Imperial divisions, notably the famous 29th British Division or the 12th British Division, whose casualties were really appalling; but there were so many evacuations that there was some fear that the reinforcements then coming forward would not be sufficient to meet requirements, so this second referendum was authorised. The troops seemed to treat the matter with apathy.

The reinforcements sent along at this period were very different in appearance from the earlier drafts, but they were equally sound in spirit and ably filled the places of the fine men who had fallen or had become incapacitated. As examples of the types of reinforcements at this time were the Winters (father and son) who came with the 25/11th Reinforcements. The elder Winter was 51 and the son, No. 7467 Private J. A. Winter, was 16 when he joined up. The father had tried three times to enlist before he was at last accepted, and he was stout enough to see the remainder of the war through and was still hale and hearty at 72 in 1937.

So though the splendid physical types of the earlier drafts were now replaced by all sorts and ages, the same old spirit animated the newcomers.

On December 6 there was a field exercise that lasted all day. The 9th Battalion attacked the 11th Battalion, which had taken up a position on a ridge. There were no stretcher cases.

The troops had several opportunities of attending the baths at Desvres, a neighbouring town of considerable size. Here there were potteries of some importance (not to be confused with Sevres) and some fine examples of the potter's art were on display in some of the shop windows.

The battalion's stay in the Samer "C" area came to an end on December 13 when the 3rd Brigade turned its face to the line once again. The battalion transport set off on a three-days' trek eastward through Elnes, Staple and Bleu to Neuve Eglise, but the battalion only proceeded as far as Ledinghem where it billeted for the night.

Next morning the battalion set off eastwards again and after a long march reached Avroult. Though the march was long the boys were in great heart after the pleasant spell, and the journey among the hills and woods of that countryside was always interesting. There was little traffic on the roads here, so that the march was carried out without congestion or the continual stops that were so trying to the troops on the roads in the forward zones.

The next stage of the journey was to Wizernes on December 15, and from there the troops moved by train to Kennebak siding, near Mont Kemmel in the Wytshaete area. From De Kennebak siding the troops were marched to Lindenhoek camp, where they camped for the night in huts and tents.

CHAPTER XXXIX

MESSINES RIDGE; NEUVE EGLISE

As MOUNT KEMMEL was to be a familiar landmark for the troops during the next three months, and as it was a position of some importance in the eyes of the British High Command, a few words are needed to describe this hill. Mount Kemmel was the highest and most easterly of the well-known group of hills which included Mont des Cats, Mont Noir, Scherpenberg and other lesser eminences. These hills always made an agreeable break in otherwise rather flat country, and the fact that Mont Kemmel was the highest and somewhat isolated from the others made it of great strategic importance, especially as it was much nearer the German lines than the rest of the group. The British High Command was rather worried at this time about the very significant quietness of the Germans, and feared that they were planning to break through on one or more of the vulnerable sectors. Kemmel was of such great importance that a strong defensive line was in course of preparation in front of it, and the 1st Australian Division was accordingly sent for to take part in the defence of this sector and to help in carrying out the necessary work in the construction of defensive positions throughout the area.

During the afternoon of December 16 the battalion moved into the brigade reserve position at Gable Farm, close to Wulverghem, and relieved the 9th Battalion. Next day the nucleus moved back to divisional camp at Caestre while the remainder of the battalion was mostly engaged on fatigues and carrying parties. Works officers were appointed in every battalion and their duties were to supervise all the operations in connection with the defences of the sectors in which their battalions were operating. The intelligence officers of each battalion were also ordered to keep a "wire map" showing all the wire that was put out as defences. The wire put out was to be entered daily, so that an accurate map of the wire on the brigade front could be made.

On December 18 all company commanders visited the front line and they studied the nature of the terrain and the conditions that existed in this new area. The trenches looked over Warneton, whose church spire was a conspicuous landmark. The famous Messines Ridge was only a mile or so in front of the dug-outs in which the troops were camped at Gable Farm, and the front line was just over the ridge. There was a considerable area of marshy ground behind Messines Ridge and the Douve River ran on the extreme right of the brigade position. This was deep and swollen by the winter rains, but according to the map it had hardly any water in the summer time. One thing puzzled the troops very much, especially those men who had been in several of the big battles of the war, and that was the comparatively unshelled state of the country. In a battlefield such as Messines the troops had expected to find the ground pulverised like that of the Somme or at Broodseinde Ridge or any of the Ypres battles, but the ground on the Messines Ridge and round about showed very few signs of a fierce battle compared to those upon which the 1st Division had achieved its successes.

The ground had been very muddy and the trenches had been quagmires when the 3rd Brigade took over, but fortunately the weather grew frosty and everything was soon frozen hard and conditions, though cold, were very much better.

The 11th Battalion was mainly engaged on carrying and working parties until December 24 (Christmas Eve), as there was a lot of material to be taken up to the line where the engineers and the brigade mining company were assisting in a scheme of trench improvement for, as usual, the 3rd Brigade was unfortunate enough to take over trenches that seemed to have been absolutely neglected in every way. This, too, in one of the quietest sectors that the battalion was ever in in its long career in France. One redeeming feature for the working parties was the presence of an excellent Australian Comforts Fund stall, where hot cocoa and biscuits were always provided for the troops both going to and coming from the lines. The Australian Comforts Fund organisation was always definitely a help to the troops and was correspondingly appreciated.

On December 24 "C" and "D" Companies of the 11th Battalion relieved companies of the 9th Battalion in the support and reserve positions, and at 6:30 a.m. on December 25 "A" and "B" Companies relieved two companies of the 9th Battalion in the front line. A Merry Christmas indeed!

This was the fourth Christmas that the 11th Battalion had spent away from Australia, and this time it was in the frosty trenches in front of Messines Ridge. The ration dump had been blown up and there was only bread at the rate of one loaf to seven men, but there were extra comforts sent up to all the troops to help them to realise that this was the great holiday, when peace and goodwill ruled throughout the Christian countries. The thoughts of the troops are best left unrecorded.

There was not much shelling by the enemy, but his machine guns were active. There was also a "furphy" going the rounds that Fritz intended to make a big raid on this sector as a Christmas celebration; but this may have been circulated as propaganda to prevent fraternisation on the "Day of Peace and Goodwill on Earth" rather than from any real information on the subject. At any rate there is no mention of any such intelligence in the battalion or brigade official diary of the period.

In one way it was a real old-fashioned Christmas, for it snowed frequently throughout the day. The G.O.C. toured the front line and visited all units of the brigade.

Boxing Day was a quiet day. There was no race meeting but there was a little mild excitement on December 27. After "C" and "D" Companies had relieved "A" and "B" Companies in the line, a small German patrol was heard in front of the posts that constituted the outpost line. This patrol was attacked by "C" Company, which dispersed the patrol and killed two of the enemy and captured one, thus securing identifications of the 102nd German Infantry Regiment. There was one Digger of the 11th Battalion wounded.

An inter-company relief again took place on December 29 without incident, and the front remained exceptionally quiet.

On December 30 Lieut.-Colonel Rafferty left for England and Major Newman assumed command, but next day he also left for England and Major Phillips assumed temporary command of the 11th Battalion. The strength of the battalion on this, the last day of 1917, was 32 officers and 687 other ranks.

The year's fighting had developed a new type of soldier and the troops of the 3rd Brigade had learned many lessons from the war, lessons that this brigade was to put to brilliant use before another year had passed.

New Year's Day, 1918, found the 11th Battalion still in the line at Messines. The day was ushered in by a few desultory shells and an occasional burst of machine gun fire. There was a white mantle of snow over the land and the pools and ditches were frozen. It was cold and cheerless in the line, but the country had not the absolutely lost look of the Flers country of a year before. There were trees and hedges here and there, leafless it is true, but still giving some kind of comfort to the countryside. The surface of the country was also intact, and even in wet weather it was a long way better than the hopeless morass of the Somme country. The organisation of the administrative units was a great deal more efficient, though added experience and a change of command brought this to an exceedingly high peak before the year was out.

The greatest improvement was, however, in the troops themselves. From being inexperienced and reckless soldiers, the events of the war had forged them into a wary, cunning adversary, wise to the wiles of the enemy and more than able to meet him in any branch of front-line warfare. Though cautious the troops had always the outstanding Australian characteristic of being willing to take a risk, but not as heretofore on any and every occasion, but only when there was a definite end to be gained. The specialist branches had reached a very high state of efficiency and the troops were confident, alert, ready for anything, having due appreciation for a gallant, capable and determined enemy, yet holding themselves equal to or better than any troops in the field. The Australian Army had come through the terrible years of the war and had emerged from the ordeal infused with a new spirit. The war had become something that was a part of themselves. It seemed at this time to be something that had no end in sight, and the troops accepted the fact with a fatalism that was peculiarly their own. Most of the boys entered the line, believing that it was most likely to be the last time in, not for the battalion but for themselves. When Diggers had seen their dearest cobbers killed alongside them they could not hope that they would always escape themselves, so they accepted the situation with a certain amount of stoicism that in no way interfered with their efficiency.

The 11th Battalion was at this time composed of such troops and the word that could describe them best is the single word of their own battalion motto, "Vigilans," which translated in its broadest sense means wide-awake, alert and capable.

With the development of efficiency among the fighting troops there was also a corresponding improvement of the conditions under which the reinforcements were trained, and huge camps were formed in England where the new arrivals from Australia were given instruction. The 11th Battalion reinforcements were sent to the 3rd Training Battalion, which with other Australian units had its headquarters at successive camps near Salisbury, on the plains or on the downs surrounding that centre.

Various experienced officers and N.C.O.'s were sent from all the battalions of the brigade in France, both as a change and a rest for the personnel and to ensure that the new troops were instructed by men who had actually seen and been engaged in the fighting of modern battles.

Though this is not exactly 11th Battalion history, yet, as it was a part of all the training of the later reinforcements and also a phase in the life of many of the original officers and N.C.O.'s of the 11th Battalion, a few features of these Australian base camps in England inasmuch as they affect the 11th Battalion are given.

After its transfer from Egypt the 3rd Training Battalion was first established at Durrington Downs, but the base was eventually shifted to Sutton-Veny in the Wylie Valley. This training battalion absorbed all the reinforcements for the 3rd Brigade. The young troops were put through a thorough course of training before being sent to France. Besides the training battalion there was also the depot at Perham Downs, where the convalescents from the hospitals passed through. Major Croly, of whom frequent mention has been made in the early pages of this story, and who since his wound at Anzac was unfit for active service, was second-in-command at Perham Downs, and it follows that there were many amusing stories about that great officer. There was rather a witty piece of verse dedicated to him, which ran as follows:—

> "He is known as O.C. Cripples, and you'll find, so help me bob,
> He has what you'd term a mild appraising eye.
> If you're fit at all for yacker, he'll put you on a job.
> I suppose he'll place me somewhere by-an-by.

If you're feeling somewhat rocky,
Been in civil life a jockey,
And you think you'd like a billet in the band,
Just go to Major Croly
And you'll find, by all that's holy,
You'll be made a blooming blacksmith by the Second-in-Command."

This verse alludes to the fact that all convalescents were given more or less light jobs, until they were fit again, when they were sent over to France or to one of the training camps.

The time spent in these training camps or, as they were generally called, depots, was generally far from strenuous. There were many amusements and a good deal of leave. As was to be expected, there were more applications for leave than could reasonably be granted, and many and wonderful were the tales of the troops as to why their particular applications for leave should be considered. The adjutants of these camps soon got wise to the wiles of the troops, as the following verses will show. These verses came from Major Croly's scrap-book:

"The adjutant; my 'art is nearly broke.
Romance is worse than wasted on that bloke.
I do believe it fills him with delight
Upon our application forms to write
'Not Approved.'

"How often have I pitched a lovely tale,
One that I'd bet a dollar couldn't fail;
Yet e'er the night t'would wander back again
And on it I would read with pain—
'Not Approved.'"

In spite of these little tales of woe, and other little peccadilloes, the troops really did good work at the training depots, and when they were sufficiently trained they were sent in drafts to the front accompanied by either reinforcement officers or those officers whose duty on "cadre" was finished. Cadre was the term applied to the permanent establishment of the nucleus brigade in England, otherwise the 3rd Training Battalion. When the writer was on cadre in early 1918 those fine officers, Wally Hallahan and George Lamerton, of the 11th Battalion, and the equally splendid Billy McCann and Roy Hurcombe, of the 10th Battalion, and many other good fellows of the 3rd Brigade were on duty at the depot, so that a very representative lot of experienced soldiers were at the base to train the new troops. An additional advantage of this system was that the reinforcements got to know some of the battalion officers, who often accompanied them over to France, and this made things much easier for the new troops as they had someone they could approach with confidence in any difficulties in their new life.

All these circumstances of training and experience helped to make the battalion more efficient and more confident, and so at the dawn of 1918 the troops were able to face the coming year, and all it had to offer, either good or bad, in the dark and uncertain days of this period of the war, with the casualness and humour that were such dominant characteristics of the Australian troops.

New Year's Day, January 1, 1918, passed without incident. The battalion was relieved by the 9th Battalion and took up position at Wulverghem as brigade reserve. The relief was completed at 11:20 p.m. and there were two casualties. Concerning this relief, No. 6580 Private Harold Spragg, "D" Company writes: "This night was very frosty and the ground very slippery. It was pitch dark and falls were numerous. Corporal Jackson broke his wrist and two other men their legs. I myself slipped down over the side of a railway embankment head first, and being weighed down with the Lewis gun and other gear I found it impossible to get up till assisted."

The official report was written from Ramilies Camp, but the troops were quartered at Gable Farm on relief. They remained there several days. Next day the inevitable working parties were in full swing, and the 11th Battalion sent its quota of six officers and 290 men to help in building the defensive system. Several small batches of reinforcements joined up with the battalion during the stay at Gable Farm. Working parties were supplied every day; the ground was so hard that sparks used to fly off the ground from the picks of the troops as they were trying to widen existing trenches.

On January 6 Captain L. L. Le Nay reported back from hospital.

On January 9 the battalion relieved the 9th Battalion in the line. The front was very quiet, but things were made unpleasant on January 10 when a thaw set in and made all the trenches muddy and unpleasant to live in. It had snowed all day on January 9, and what with slush and melting snow and mud the conditions can be better imagined than described. Lieut. F. R. Beasley was evacuated to hospital.

It was abnormally quiet on this sector and one day passed after another without incident until January 13, when the Germans located the battalion No. 5 post. This post was blown out early in the morning. The occupants were all casualties, five being killed and four wounded. There was an inter-company relief the same night, "C" and "D" Companies taking over the line.

The 11th Battalion was relieved by the 7th Battalion on January 15. Owing to the extreme softness of the ground and the muddy trenches the relief took a long time, and it was a very weary battalion that went into huts at Ramilies Camp at Kemmel. Some of the troops did not arrive till after midnight.

Some idea of the conditions existing can be had from the account in the diary of Private Harold Spragg: "It had been very quiet in the line but the trenches were very wet. There were duckboards in the trenches and as the water rose so another duckboard was added, until there were often three or four piled on top of each other. It snowed on January 14 and rained all day on January 15 and the trenches were in an awful state when we were relieved by the 7th Battalion. We were nearly up to our waists in water and mud during the journey out. The communication trench had three feet of water in it. It was one of the worst reliefs we had, but luckily there was no shelling.

"When coming out, the chap in front of me went down into a mud-hole up to his shoulders and I stepped on him without noticing him in the darkness. He yelled out in time and, by cripes, he did take some pulling out!"

The whole of the next day was spent in cleaning and drying clothes and equipment.

On January 17 working parties were again sent forward. The 3rd Brigade was at this time divisional reserve and was drawn on for all duties. One battalion was working nightly on corps line and one battalion on reserve line. Besides this, one company was used on burying cable and one company was detailed for road repairs. The mining company of the brigade had been for some time on pill-box reclamation and in reclaiming dug-outs in the forward areas.

Up till January 22 the same routine was continued. On this date 56 reinforcements arrived under Lieut. Warrington and Lieut. M. E. Clarke reported back from hospital.

On January 23 the 3rd Brigade relieved the 2nd Brigade in the Messines-Wytshaete sector, the 11th Battalion taking over from the 7th Battalion. Fortunately it was fine weather and an agreeable change from the last relief. The sector was still extremely quiet and was voted the quietest part of the line that the 11th Battalion had ever been in. The only unpleasant interlude was when the headquarters bombing platoon came up to the line and sent over rifle grenades, and Fritz rather overdid the return of the compliment by sending over minenwerfers.

This unusual quietude on the part of the enemy was still causing the High Command great anxiety, but in spite of everything no definite information could be obtained of the German intentions. The troops were kept very busy on the formidable defensive line in this area, and in this work the 3rd Brigade carried out what must have been a record achievement and the total of work was almost staggering, as will be recorded in due course. The battalion works officer at this time was Lieut. Toby Evans.

All the available official and private records of this period stress the fact that the front line in this sector was notably quiet. An extract from Private Jim Kirkwood's notes runs: "Very quiet in the line. Snow-covered fields and bright moonlight nights. There were no stunts. We were just holding the line. There were patrols and wiring parties out every second night; we reckoned that this was to allow Fritz and Co. to use the other nights. One morning a Fritz came over from their lines with full pack up. No shots were fired at him and he jumped joyfully into our trench."

General Birdwood visited battalion headquarters on January 26. On the same date the official diary states that enemy aeroplanes were brought down just within the German lines. The machines were in flames and soon were completely burned up. It is not stated whether the aeroplanes were brought down as a result of a "dog-fight" or whether they were shot down by machine gunners or anti-aircraft guns. The official diary is often very vague.

There were six casualties on this date, three men being killed. Nothing of further interest occurred during the rest of the month and the troops were relieved by the 32nd Battalion (A.I.F.) on January 31. The relief was carried out without a hitch and the battalion moved off to Neuve Eglise of happy memory.

Lieut. F. R. Beasley and four other ranks left for the 2nd Training Battalion in England.

The battalion strength on the last day of January was 39 officers and 754 other ranks.

Neuve Eglise.

After the battalion came out of the line there was the usual routine, but a new departure was inaugurated by the establishment of a brigade sports committee. This committee immediately drew up a programme which catered for all branches of sport and recreation. The brigade concert party also opened at the hall in Neuve Eglise and there was a divisional cinema at Aldershot Lines. This organised effort to amuse and interest the troops was much appreciated by them, and it helped to make the stay at Neuve Eglise one of the pleasantest rests in the history of the 11th Battalion. The weather was remarkably fine during the whole period of the stay at Neuve Eglise and this was not the least factor in making the rest enjoyable.

On February 4 parties from the 11th Battalion were engaged in the construction of a miniature rifle range, and others

11th Battalion Band, Neuve Eglise, 1918. (Official Photo.)

A German Postcard of the "Lubeck" Infantry Regiment with the motto: "We Germans fear God, but nothing else in the world."

were engaged in building protective earth walls against the attack of bombs or shells dropped near the billets where the troops were quartered.

A party of seven officers and 150 other ranks left Neuve Eglise on February 5 and proceeded to the musketry school at Tilques. The remainder of the battalion started on its training programme.

For the next fortnight the routine consisted of training in the mornings and sports and recreational training in the afternoons except for those troops, generally upwards of 150 men who were employed on the defensive or other works.

Football, under Australian, rugby and and association rules, was started. On February 14 the troops who had been at the musketry school at Tilques returned, and in the afternoon the 9th Battalion won the rugby series, beating the 11th Battalion and brigade headquarters respectively.

February 18 was held as a general holiday for the 11th Battalion in place of the Christmas Day spent in the line at Messines. Extra food and comforts were purchased and sports were held in the morning and afternoon. In the evening "The Boomerangs," one of the Australian concert parties, gave an entertainment solely for the benefit of the 11th Battalion troops in the large hall in the village.

One afternoon when there was a sports meeting in progress, Lieut. Riches appeared in a fancy dress costume which he described as that of a "prehistoric cupid." It was mostly birthday suit. Several Sisters from a neighbouring hospital were present and were duly impressed when he made his bow.

During this period of rest and training a divisional rifle competition was carried out under the rules of the Army Rifle Association (England). Medals were to be presented to each member of the winning platoon. The 11th Battalion competitors were a long way behind those of the 12th Battalion, whose platoons put up some really excellent scores and whose No. 2 platoon ultimately won the divisional shoot.

On February 23 there was a short route-march in the morning and in the afternoon the corps official photographer took several photographs of the 11th Battalion. These were all officers, all N.C.O.'s and the regimental band.

It was wet on February 25 and training was somewhat hampered, but whenever it was possible field firing was carried out.

11th Battalion Officers at Neuve Eglise.

The brigade had received orders to move to the Hollebeke area, somewhat to the north of the last sector, and five officers from the 11th Battalion reconnoitred the new positions. A practice alarm was held at 6 p.m. and all the battalions were in position and ready to move at 7:5 p.m. This was a very satisfactory effort, and spoke well of the efficiency and discipline of the troops.

On February 26 the intelligence officer with a reconnaissance party left by bus for the forward area. The I.O. remained with the battalion which was to be relieved.

The period of training and recreation at Neuve Eglise was now fast drawing to a close, and the battalion was preparing to move once more. The finals of the brigade cups were played on February 27 and the 11th Battalion was defeated at soccer by the 9th Battalion. On the last day of the month practice with live grenades and bombs was carried out, and this completed the training.

CHAPTER XL

THE HOLLEBEKE SECTOR

THE 3RD BRIGADE was now in the process of relieving the 4th Australian Brigade and already the 9th and 10th Battalions had taken over the line in the Hollebeke area, but the 11th Battalion was still at Neuve Eglise on March 1 and 2. The time was spent in preparing for the move, and on March 3 the battalion moved off at 9:30 a.m. and proceeded by route-march to Tournai Camp, at Confusion Corner, near Lock Number 8, on the Ypres-Comines Canal, where it took up position as brigade reserve, in which situation it relieved the 13th Australian Battalion. As brigade reserve, the 11th Battalion was immediately utilised for working parties, and as there was a very great deal of reconstruction of the defensive system to be done as well as the formation of new positions, the troops were worked very hard on this front. It might seem from this story that no other troops ever did any work, and the boys frequently thought the same thing; but it must be remembered that due to constant enemy action and the effect of the weather on trenches and earthworks that there was a never-ending job to keep defensive systems in order.

On March 4 all the company commanders visited the front lines and acquired a knowledge of the various dispositions. The battalion was more or less familiar with this portion of the line, as it had been in this sector several times previously, and only a few months previously had been camped at Number 8 Lock. Brigade headquarters was situated at this lock.

This was a much less quiet front than the last sector the troops had occupied. The enemy artillery was fairly active and the Germans were much more aggressive in spirit. In fact the 10th Battalion was raided on its first night in the line just as the troops were taking over.

The system of defence in this sector was the standard one of outposts with a support and a reserve line. When the 3rd Brigade took over the line the whole defensive system was considered inadequate, and prompt measures were taken to strengthen the wire in front of the outposts and a systematic policy of wiring was immediately put in force with parties that were more or less permanent on the job. These permanent parties always made for more efficiency.

The support and reserve lines were mostly continuous trenches, and were in some places full of water and the wiring was poor. Dug-outs and cupolas had to be built. The line battalions were responsible for the outpost system, while the support and reserve battalions had to attend to the maintenance and improvement of their respective positions, helped by the brigade mining company. This company was then fairly strong and was composed from troops of the four battalions of the 3rd Brigade. Lieut. Wally Graham, of the 11th Battalion, was O.C. of the company for a considerable time.

The great amount of material necessary to carry out this extensive scheme of improvement was drawn from dumps, situated near the railway line and tram tracks, and the stores were frequently pushed along the lines in special trucks for a considerable distance. This helped to speed up the work. The closest co-operation was maintained with the engineers and other specialists, and this also made for greater efficiency.

The Germans were shelling a great deal more than in the past weeks. They were also using trench mortars and machine guns with great persistency and their patrol activities had increased in marked degree.

On March 6, in addition to a heavy bombardment of H.E. shell, an intensive barrage of gas shell (mustard, phosgene and lachrymatory) was put down in the vicinity of the 9th Battalion headquarters with the result that nine officers and 150 men of that battalion became casualties. The 11th Battalion headquarters staff, under Lieut.-Colonel Rafferty and Lieuts. C. Gostelow, R. W. Blair and Sadler, was ordered to take over the position, and "D" Company (11th Battalion) relieved "D" Company (9th Battalion). As the area had been drenched with gas, which still lingered in the hollows and trenches, this section was evacuated and battalion headquarters moved to a new dug-out on the railway and the gassed area placed out of bounds to all troops.

There were a few gas casualties among the 11th Battalion troops, including Lieut. G. C. Porter.

The remainder of the 11th Battalion took over the front line on March 8, "B" Company taking over the right sector and "A" Company the left sector. The relief was normal.

The companies in the line were relieved every 48 hours, a change-over being made with the support and reserve companies. The enemy was becoming increasingly active and his shelling was much heavier. Patrolling by the battalion was active, and on account of the elastic nature of the German outpost system, in which he altered the location of his posts quite frequently, the patrols were liable to run into trouble occasionally, especially in places like Hessian Wood and other broken country.

Much the same procedure was carried out by the Australian troops and the outposts were sometimes vacated during the day or only very lightly held, the balance of the troops going back to dug-outs or other shelter to sleep, and then manning the posts immediately after dark. Sometimes the garrisons were spotted by Fritz, and the troops had to do a belly-crawl in or out of the posts.

On one occasion a patrol was out and one of the Diggers, Billy Hobbins by name, became separated from his companions and was roaming in No Man's Land near his own lines. When challenged he made off in the darkness. The troops challenged again and he dropped to the ground without answering. When he got up he was shot. The boys brought him in thinking he was a Fritz, but found that he was their own man. The Brigadier was at "A" Company headquarters that night and Major Darnell reported the matter. But there was no blame attachable to anyone, for the troops had merely done as they were instructed. It was just a sad accident of the war.

The Germans had some well-sited machine guns in this sector and during the time "D" Company was in the line one of the outposts was in a wood and the front of the post was built behind a big log. This log the German gunner opposite had ranged to a hair, and he used to send his bullets skimming just over the top. The boys in the post had great respect for this gunner's skill, but at the same time they were ready for a return of the compliment.

The metal of the Diggers is well portrayed in this little story told by Private L. D. (Plum) Warner, of No. 11 Platoon, "C" Company:

"When I returned from leave the battalion was in the line at Spoil Bank. I had palled up with Tommy Lake. He stuttered badly. We were together on listening-post about 20 yards in front of the little outpost held by Corporal Jacky Pearce and four others. Figures were seen moving in front. (We had agreed, against orders, that listening-post meant that one of us was to have a sleep.) Tommy gave me a kick then grabbed half a dozen bombs and his rifle and stuttered out, 'Y-y-you h-h-halt the b-b-b-b——s, "Plum," an' I-I-I'll sh-shoot the whole bl-bl-bloody lot of them,' but they turned out to be our own men and so the war went on."

On March 10 the Germans shelled the outposts just before dusk and killed one man and wounded five others. Though the casualties were not particularly heavy there was a steady evacuation of men all the time the battalion was in the Hollebeke area, always referred to by the Diggers as "Spoil Bank," and 46 all ranks were sent away during the 14 days spent in and out of the line. As an instance of how some of these casualties came about, the following account from Private Jim Kirkwood is interesting in its realism:

"When in the line in front of Spoil Bank we were occupying an old pill-box. It was here that young Jack Brabner was killed. During one of the frequent Hun bombardments young Jack was watching through a small opening and he was killed outright by a minute fragment of shell that penetrated the opening. A new officer, Lieut. O'Mahony, had just joined the battalion and this was his first time in the line. He was very upset, and said: 'Christ! A clean young life like that wiped out! Surely somebody will pay for this bloody war.' Sergeant Jock Ferguson called for volunteers to carry Jack Brabner back. The whole platoon would have gone, but Jock detailed eight and they carried Brabner in parties of four and buried him in the cemetery behind the lines."

But there were some humorous episodes, too. One day "Plum" Warner was detailed to take a "hundred-gallon tank" (a hot food container) on his back up to the lines to the forward troops. Unfortunately this container leaked, and poor Warner dropped back behind his companions, as he could not keep up with them without being nearly scalded with boiling tea. Luckily big Bill Armstrong, of the battalion signallers, noticed him and came to his rescue. He solved the problem by plugging up the leak *with mud*. Warner then made off up the line and went round each outpost, while the armed guards served out the tea to the seven or eight troops in the posts, and no one complained that the tea had a muddy flavour.

There is an unusual and interesting entry in the 3rd Brigade official diary for March 11, which runs thus: "Situation normal. Both artilleries active and outposts very alert. Pushing on hard with defensive works. *The Boche sent over a number of our own H.E. 9.2 shells, presumably brought from Russia!*"

Gas was beginning to affect the troops and Captain E. Tulloch and Lieut. Wally Graham were evacuated sick. The effect of this form of warfare can be judged from the following note by Private Harold Spragg: "We were in here for about a fortnight and used to go back to the chateau dug-outs when the other companies relieved us. One night we had a lively time when out with a wiring party. Fritz spotted us and had us down on our bellies most of the time. While at chateau dug-outs we were given a great doing with gas of all sorts, including mustard gas, and I had my first sniff of tear gas. A lot of us lost the use of our voices and the effect of the mustard gas was very painful."

There had been several preliminary reconnaissances with a view to making a raid on Game Copse, an enemy strong point. Lieut. Davison, of the 11th Battalion, and 50 other ranks were then training as a raiding party at Tournai Camp, and the carrying out of this minor operation was to be assigned to these troops.

On March 17 there was very heavy shelling at "The Clusters," the headquarters of "A" Company, and one huge shell, probably a captured British 9.2, landed almost on the dug-out. Major Darnell described the concussion as "terrific." Next day the whole of the brigade sector was shelled heavily with gas, even the outposts and tracks being shelled with gas from light minenwerfers. There were few casualties, but the experience was very trying as the small box respirator was found to be extremely uncomfortable when worn for any length of time. When used at night the eye-pieces became so dim that vision was restricted to a few feet, and the troops mostly took off their masks and only used the nose-clip and breathing-tube.

Besides this attention to the front lines the Boche was strafing the rear areas with high velocity guns and doing a great deal of counter-battery work. It seemed as if a great attack was impending.

An interesting account of this sector is found in a letter from Lieut. Frank Goundrey: "The battalion headquarters was situated in the railway embankment and the Hun had been shelling us with gas for several days, and most of the time we were wearing our gas masks. One night Lieut. 'Pard' Riches turned in with his gas-mask on. He was found some time later with the rubber tube stretched out as far as it would go, and the box container somewhere between his legs. Why he was not gassed was a mystery; some of the boys reckoned that he was saved by taking a drink out of a petrol tin that was lying near. The 'Pard' thought it was water, but it turned out to be kerosene."

But the "Pard" was a hard man to kill. It was shortly afterwards that he and Jim Aitken took to practising cutting the spots out of a pack of playing cards with their revolvers in the small dug-out in which four officers were camped. As Lieut. Goundrey says: "What the noise was like in that confined space may only be guessed at, to say nothing of the lead that used to spatter in all directions from the walls."

Frank Goundrey goes on to say: " 'B' Company was holding the front line of outposts in front of Spoil Bank. Game Copse was immediately opposite. Our company headquarters was in a pill-box behind us. All the tracks led up to this pill-box and this was naturally observed by Fritz. He put over some of the biggest stuff that I had ever seen. The pill-box fairly jumped out of the ground and the vicinity was torn up for yards around. There was one direct hit, and this set alight a lot of Mills bombs. This was where Q.M.S. Walker went west. Lieut. Joe Barry was in that pill-box in charge of the company. . .

"Game Copse was to be raided by the battalion, and every night some party was sent to examine the wire and to note if there were any changes in the enemy's dispositions. Lieut. Paul McInerny took a party out and struck one of Fritz's patrols. There was an interchange of bombs and one Fritz was left behind in front of my post. He could speak English and kept calling for some one to help him. He also called out in German, 'Mutter! Mutter!' (Mother! Mother!). Later some of his own friends crawled out and got him."

The weather was often foggy at this time and the gas fumes hung about for long periods so that the troops suffered considerably; so much so that Major May, the M.O. of the 11th Battalion, sent in a strong report in which he stated that the men of the 11th Battalion were suffering from the effects of gas, and that though, thanks to good gas discipline, there had only been one definite case of pure gassing, a large majority of the men were unfit for continued service under the strenuous conditions of trench warfare and heavy fatigue work on relief. The medical officer finished his report as follows: "I ascribe this condition to a combination of gas, lack of sleep, military strain and hard fatigues, and consider that the men have too long a tour of duty in the line and that spells of four or at the most six days should be given in the line under circumstances such as these...

"I think it my duty to lay these facts before you and to state that in my opinion the battalion should not be left in until the men are seriously affected and require a long rest to recover."

An inter-company relief was carried out on the night of March 20, "A" and "B" Companies taking over the front line. The situation was normal at the time of relief, but towards midnight the enemy shelling increased in intensity until there was a regular bombardment at 4:30 a.m. on March 21. At 5:20 a.m. the S.O.S. was fired by a unit on the left flank of the 1st Division sector. All working parties were cancelled by the 1st Division. At 5:55 a.m. the 1st (the left) Brigade asked for S.O.S. artillery support. The enemy then increased his bombardment on the 11th Battalion (on the left of the brigade sector) and a report of enemy movement was made by the 1st Brigade about 6:20 a.m. The 12th Battalion on the right of the 3rd Brigade sector then sent up an S.O.S. The 1st Brigade then reported that the call for S.O.S. was a mistake and that the enemy movement was on its right. There was some difficulty in getting the protective barrage stopped. After a bit of confusion things were straightened up, and the official brigade report goes on to state: "At about 6:30 a.m. the listening-post in front of post 11.0.6 (manned by Private Branche) saw about eight Germans approaching the group and fired. The Lewis gun post 11.0.6, in charge of Corporal Chambers, opened fire on the Boche, who immediately took cover in shell-holes. Corporal

Chambers then led a party out under cover of the Lewis gun to investigate. He found four Germans, three of whom were wounded. (One died while being carried down the communication trench on a stretcher.) The remainder of the enemy patrol could not be located.

". . . The enemy patrol seemed to come from the direction of Game Copse. The outpost was not shelled nor barraged."

The prisoners belonged to the 153rd Regiment.

On the same day 2nd/Lieut. L. Green, who had been for a long time R.Q.M.S., was killed and there were also three other ranks killed and four wounded. Major A. Darnell was evacuated to Rest House, Le Touquet.

The following wire was received from 2nd Army on the same date: "Intense bombardment started at 4:30 a.m. against whole of 3rd and 5th Army fronts and against French, leaving out Rheims sector. It has since slackened in places, but is still intense between Senset and Moy against French. No attack yet."

The 3rd Brigade comment is as follows: "The news does not worry anyone much; it's a relief to know after expecting it so long."

So at last the great German attack of March, 1918, was in the process of being launched between the Scarfe and the Oise and the full power of the Hun armies was about to fall on a wide battle front. The swiftness and success of this attack, which was not going to "worry anyone much," was about to alter the whole complexion of the war and to make important and far-reaching changes in the whole conduct of the operations, changes in which the Australian troops were to play a distinguished and unique part.

The intensive bombardment on the 1st Divisional and other neighbouring fronts on March 21 was obviously staged more as a demonstration to keep the local reserves in the northern area rather than as the preliminary to an attack.

The sector had become relatively quiet on March 22, and the 11th Battalion anticipated relief as the 9th Battalion advance parties had arrived during the day. While on patrol Lieut. A. R. Retchford was wounded by enemy machine gun fire. There were also five other men wounded during the course of the day.

An extract from the brigade diary has rather an amusing tale attached to it. The extract is as follows: "The raiding party, known as 'X' Company, are progressing in their training and becoming fit. Body armour has been issued to them and is very popular, after testing it with a revolver bullet at short range."

This is the tale: Lieut. "Blowfish" Davison, who was in charge of the raid, which, by the way, never came off, had donned one of the bombproof jackets or vests, and was expatiating on its virtues as body armour and especially on its ability to stop a revolver bullet even at close range. Lieut. Freddy Stahl, who was always a bit of a dare-devil, was standing by taking it all in.

When Davison paused for breath Freddy asked him casually if he meant all he said. The answer being in the affirmative, Freddy then said: "Would you let me have a shot at you, 'Blowfish,' dressed as you are now?" Incautiously Davison replied: "Too right I would!"

Like a flash Stahl whipped out his revolver and fired at the middle of Davison's breastplate and the bullet knocked him clean over. Davison got up, groaning and vowing all sorts of vengeance on Stahl. The armour had successfully stopped the bullet, but Davison had a lump as big as a good-sized pudding bowl where the bullet had hit. He was a very wild man.

On March 23 the 11th Battalion, less "B" Company, was relieved by the 9th Battalion. The relief was completed by 11:30 p.m. without any undue trouble, and the battalion moved back to "Beggar's Rest Farm."

CHAPTER XLI

BEGGARS' REST FARM; THE RUSH TO AMIENS
AND BACK AGAIN

IN THE MEANTIME the great German Offensive had started and the disquieting news of the success of the enemy attack began to filter through. At first it was reported that the line had not been broken save at a few points, and even at these points the penetration had not exceeded a thousand yards; but the later reports were not so encouraging, for it was officially stated that Bullecourt, Lagnicourt and Louverval and all the territory that the Australians had gained in the hard-fought campaigns of the previous year had been lost, and that the Germans had captured over 200 guns and an estimate of over 16,000 men. This was bitter news, but the full extent of the German victory was yet to be learned.

The 3rd Brigade official diary for March 24 gives some indication of the dislocation caused by the Germans' successful break-through. The report states: "There have been a good many orders and counter-orders during the day and consequent confusion. (The withdrawal of several divisions from the northern area is indicated by these conflicting orders.)

"The front of the 1st Australian Division is being extended southwards as far as the Wambeek. (The Wambeek was a small stream flowing eastwards and lying mid-way between Hollebeke and Messines.)

"The 2nd Australian Infantry Brigade is relieving two battalions of the 14th Brigade in the line on the night of March 24/25, and one battalion of the 8th Brigade in the line on March 25/26.

"The reserve battalion (the 11th) and one battalion of the 1st Australian Infantry Brigade will become the divisional reserve. They will not be drawn upon without authority from divisional headquarters."

It will be seen that changes were being rapidly made in the dispositions of the various divisions in order to cope with the

German advance, which was by this time assuming alarming features; and well it might, for now reports had come through that over 40,000 prisoners had been taken by the Germans and that Bapaume had fallen. It was learned that two Australian divisions had been despatched to help stem the tide of the German advance. Many other rumours had come through, and it was not known what to believe; but the chief feeling engendered among the troops was one of mortification and disgust to think that the Huns had been able to advance so far in such a short time. As one man in "D" Company put it: "Strike me b——y pink! The cows have captured in one blanky day what it took us blokes two flamin' years to get!" and everyone thought that there must have been something far wrong somewhere.

However, the ups and downs of war had become a part of the life of the troops, and they soon ceased to worry about the great battle raging further south. Their worries were mostly confined to the area round Beggars' Rest Camp, and their tours of duty as reserve to the 9th Battalion, which duty was filled by each company of the 11th Battalion in rotation, as the 9th Battalion was still numerically weak after its severe gas casualties of a short time previously.

Besides this duty, the 11th Battalion was supplying working parties on the defensive scheme, and the men were also undergoing training and occasionally the balance of the battalion would be sent for a route-march to keep the men fit.

On March 27 Lieut. Wally Blair, who had been assistant adjutant, relinquished his appointment at his own request and was posted to "C" Company. On the same date "A" Company relieved "C" Company as reserve to the 9th Battalion. On March 28 Lieut. C. Gostelow was appointed battalion intelligence officer in place of Lieut. W. W. Gudgeon, M.C., who was posted to regimental duties.

On March 29 modifications were made in the dispositions of the 1st Divisional Reserve, and the 11th Battalion was detailed to provide nucleus garrisons for the 2nd zone defences. These were allotted as follows: One platoon south of the canal, two platoons between the canal and the railway and one platoon at Hill 60. There were special instructions sent to the 11th Battalion, which stated that the posts were to be handed over to the 11th Battalion on March 29, and further instructions were as follows:—

"These nucleus garrisons will be allotted to definite posts in the firing line system. They will be detailed to carry out warden duties under their definite written instructions, and they will not be withdrawn from their posts to take part in any action in the forward zone.

"The commander of the nucleus garrison of each post will receive written orders before moving forward to occupy the post. The orders will state the number of the post, details of the nucleus garrison, number, bearing and distance of each post next on the flanks, and to the front and rear. They will also lay down that the post is to be held at all costs and that the post commander is to take under his command (as part of the garrison) any stragglers moving towards the rear, past the vicinity of the post during an action."

It will be seen from these instructions what importance was placed on the defence of these posts, and the responsible position the 11th Battalion occupied in the event of a major attack by the enemy.

A lecture was given by Captain A. S. Keighley to all ranks on "Sea Power and the War." The lecture was much appreciated, as Captain Keighley was a good speaker and had the ability to make the subject interesting.

Captain L. L. Le Nay reported from duties as brigade R.T.O. as owing to changed conditions there was no longer any need of the services of such an officer.

A route-march and recreational training on March 30 occupied those of the battalion not on garrison duty or the inevitable working parties. In the afternoon several high-velocity shells were fired at Beggars' Rest and one shell landed near battalion headquarters, severely wounding the adjutant, Lieut. Gerry Campbell. Gerry was immediately taken to hospital and was pronounced to be in a critical condition. Lieut. E. C. O'Mahoney was appointed assistant adjutant. Major A. H. Darnell returned from the rest camp at Le Touquet.

On March 31 there was a lecture by the Brigadier to the officers and N.C.O.'s of the 11th Battalion on the subject "Open Warfare in Defence." After the successful break-through by the Germans towards Amiens there was a justifiable amount of "windiness" among the "heads" and everything was being done to prepare the troops for any eventualities.

Major J. Newman, who had been on duty in the United Kingdom, returned to the 11th Battalion on this date.

The strength of the battalion at the end of March was 42 officers and 722 other ranks.

There is an interesting resume of the work done by the 3rd Brigade while in the Hollebeke area, which came out in brigade orders for March 31.

"Report on work done for period March 1 to 31, 1918:—

"On taking over the Hollebeke sector on March 1 the brigade commenced to improve the three defensive systems of the forward zone.

"For the first three weeks the brigade supplied approximately 1,200 men daily on works throughout the sector. These, with the exception of the special wiring parties of the two front-line battalions and the brigade mining company, worked under the supervision of the 2nd and 3rd Field Companies north and south of the Ypres-Comines Canal respectively.

"The difficulties to face were mainly the long carry for R.E. material, which in many cases was carried over rough ground throughout pitch-black nights (for the first ten nights). Gas shelling also interfered with these working parties.

"During the last ten days the working parties were reduced to approximately 600 men per day, which was due to the taking over of a larger sector and also the condition of the men. On three days the working parties were cancelled in order to give the men a rest. Wet days were taken advantage of for these rests, which were ordered by the divisional commander.

"The following is a summary of the work done and the material used by the brigade for the period, the mining company statistics being shown separately:—

Work done and material used by the four battalions—
(a) Work—
    9,930 yards barb wire entanglements, being mostly double apron, about 700 yards being over French wire.
    1,107 yards parapet, sandbag revetted.
      740 ,, parapet, thickened by banking with earth.
      505 ,, trench revetted.
      291 ,, trench and drains lower revetted.
      500 ,, drains dug.
      347 ,, trench dug.
      650 ,, cable trench dug 6 feet and electric cable laid.

              583 „   track cleared for duckboarding.
              606 „   duckboard laid.
               57 cupola dug-outs erected to accommodate 3 men each.
                3 footbridges constructed across the canal.
    (b) Material used on above work—
            2,176 coils barb wire.
              111 coils French wire.
            9,822 corkscrew pickets.
           26,940 sandbags.
              279 cupolas, large and medium.
              698 sheets corrugated iron.
              656 "A" frames.
            1,153 duckboards.
              539 panels (revetting).
              886 angle-iron pickets.
              124 windles (stay wires).
               96 yards expanded metal (duckboards).
                5 rolls camouflage.

There was a correspondingly large amount of work done by the brigade mining company, such as 7,260 yards of double apron wire entanglements erected, 1,100 yards of sandbag parapet erected, 1,057 coils of barb wire used and 14,160 sandbags filled, to select just a few items. It will be readily seen from this report that the work done independently of the service in the front line by the 3rd Australian Brigade, under the conditions related in the day to day reports, in a gas-drenched area, was nothing short of marvellous, and was a fitting testimony to the splendid fellows that comprised that famous brigade.

The actual strength of the brigade at the end of March was 202 officers and 3,417 other ranks.

April 1 found the battalion doing the usual routine of working parties and garrison duties. The garrisons of the special posts had to provision and water their posts in readiness of a prolonged defence. Rations and numbers of petrol tins full of water were stored in the posts. On this date, word was sent from Godewaersvelde casualty clearing-station that Lieut. Gerry Campbell had died of wounds lately received. When Lieut. Campbell was wounded, someone said: "You've got a nice Blighty, Gerry." But Gerry shook his head and answered: "This is no Blighty, boys." Big, jovial, Gerry's passing was keenly felt by all his friends and orderly room and mess seemed strange without his cheery voice.

Lieut. C. Gostelow was evacuated gassed, and many of the troops were still suffering from their recent tour in the trenches, which were still reeking with the deadly fumes of gas.

On April 3 the battalion received a sudden summons to move, and at 5 p.m., after having been relieved by troops of the Scottish 9th Division, the battalion moved off to Curragh Camp and arrived at 8 p.m. Curragh Camp was situated near Locre. While the battalion was there, Major Newman was posted to the 10th Battalion as Temporary Lieut.-Colonel and to command.

From Curragh Camp the battalion was transported by bus to Caestre. The brigade moved in two sections, each part filling 78 motor lorries. After debussing, the battalion marched to La Brearde, where it camped for the night, and next day marched back to Caestre where the troops entrained for Amiens.

The reason for this sudden and hurried move was that the situation was exceedingly serious in the south. There had been heavy fighting everywhere and much ground had been lost, but the New Zealanders had recaptured Beaumont Hamel and the 4th Australian Division had been successful in breaking up two powerful German counter-attacks. The 3rd Australian Division was also doing good work near Morlancourt. But the Germans were now beyond the positions from which they had been driven back in 1916, and all their troops were full of confidence and fight, as had been shown by the increased morale of the troops opposite the 1st Division in the sector just left.

Before the 1st Division left Caestre, there were many expressions of concern by the French people over the departure of the Australian troops from their district. Though the statement may seem a bit exaggerated, yet it was the simple fact that there were many prophecies by the villagers that as soon as the "Australiens" went the "Allemands" would attack on this sector and drive them from their homes. How true these predictions were, the next few days' happenings only too faithfully revealed.

The journey down to Amiens was made in trucks that had been recently used for horses, and the accommodation was very limited both for officers and men. The route lay through Calais and Abbeville, and from thence to the siding at St. Roch, on the outskirts of Amiens. From there the 11th Battalion marched to billets in Bertangles, where corps and divisional headquarters were situated at that time. Brigade headquarters was in the chateau of the Marquis de St. Sauveur.

After their uncomfortable night in the train the troops were in no fettle for marching, and next day was devoted to an overhaul of gear and a general clean up.

A few days were spent at Bertangles. These were filled in with the customary training interspersed with C.O.'s parades, and there were tactical exercises on April 10. On this date the following officers reported for duty: Captain J. S. D. Walker, M.C., Lieuts. H. Colvin and H. Dale and 2nd/Lieut. C. Ross.

After a day's range practice, where the troops were exercised in rapid fire, the battalion was again rushed off to Amiens to entrain for the north. The prophecies of the French peasants had been fulfilled and the Hun had broken through immediately the Australian troops had gone. The break-through had been on the front that the Portugese were holding, and the well-known villages of Sailly sur la Lys, Estaires and Bac-St.-Maur were captured. It is not intended to suggest that the Boche was waiting for the departure of the 1st Australian Division from the vicinity before he made his attack, but it was a peculiar coincidence that the attack should have been made almost immediately that division had gone, with the doleful forebodings of the French villagers ringing in their ears.

It was on that date, April 11, 1918, that Sir Douglas Haig sent out his much-criticised "Backs to the Wall" message. The following is the complete text:—

"To all ranks of the British forces in France: Three weeks ago to-day the enemy began his terrific attacks against us on a 50-mile front. His objects are to separate us from the French, to take the Channel ports and to destroy the British Army.

"In spite of throwing 106 divisions into the battle and enduring the most reckless sacrifice of human life, he has as yet made little progress towards his goal.

"We owe this to the determined fighting and self-sacrifice of our troops. Words fail me to express the admiration which I feel for the splendid resistance offered by all ranks of our army under the most trying circumstances.

"Many amongst us now are tired. To those I would say that victory will belong to the side that holds out the longest. The French army is moving rapidly and in great force to our support. . .

"There is no other course open to us but to fight it out! Every position must be held to the last man; there must be no retirement. With our *backs to the wall* and believing in the justice of our cause each one of us must fight on to the end. The safety of our homes and freedom of mankind alike depend upon the conduct of each one of us at this critical moment.

"D. Haig, F.M., Thursday, April 11, 1918."

To revert to Amiens and the 11th Battalion. The battalion, in conjunction with the rest of the 3rd Brigade, had marched to bivouac positions north of the Citadelle of Amiens and was in place by 4 p.m. While waiting for the troop-trains to take them north, the troops were heavily bombed for three hours. Lieut.-Colonel Rafferty moved the troops into a tree-lined boulevard where they were well hidden. The 11th Battalion suffered several casualties; one man was killed. Among the wounded were Lieut. Archibald and 2nd/Lieut. Sharp. Some of the bombs dropped were aerial torpedoes. One that dropped near the 11th Battalion made a hole in the ground about fourteen feet deep and thirty feet in diameter. The hole was so huge that a great number of the troops took shelter in the crater, partly on the principle that bombs or shells very seldom seemed to land in already-made craters and partly because the hole seemed to offer complete protection from further bombing. The troops had received orders to fire at a low-flying aeroplane just prior to this, and the pilot or observer may have noticed the flashes of the rifles and so paid his unwelcome attentions. The bombing raids so disorganised the railway traffic that the battalion was held up till daylight. Then the air raiders came over again and unloaded a fresh supply of "eggs." Some fell quite close to the 11th Battalion troop-train, but fortunately no damage was done.

This bombing raid, which was easily the worst that the 11th Battalion was ever subjected to, always remained a very vivid picture in the minds of all the troops who were with the battalion on this occasion. The bombing was carried on hour after hour by successive squadrons, and all night the crash of the missiles could be heard far and near. Many fires were started in the town and ruin and destruction followed the raiders' visits. In the midst of the turmoil several parachute flares were dropped from the enemy 'planes. These only glowed faintly at first, but gradually brightened until they burned with fiercely brilliant lights, which illuminated the whole country for miles around, rendering all objects as clearly defined as if in daylight.

There was nothing to do but stand fast. The scene was unforgettable. There were thousands of troops in the process of entraining or waiting their turn to entrain. In the fierce lights of the flares could be seen the burning town, with columns of smoke rising, and here and there the multi-coloured flashes and terrific explosions of the bombs and the reverberations of crashing buildings. Overhead the great bombers droned, circling nearer and nearer. There was not a man but believed his last hour had come, and when finally the bombs dropped all round the battalion, and one even within 30 yards of "C" Company but luckily in very soft ground, though all the nearby troops were knocked over by the concussion when it exploded, it was with feelings of relief and astonishment that the troops realised that the battalion had escaped annihilation.

Some of the other battalions of the 1st Division were not so fortunate. There were about 80 casualties in the 2nd Brigade, which was in the railway yards at St. Roch siding when the 'planes came over.

While the bombing was at its worst, Colonel Rafferty signed to one of the Diggers standing near and handed him a paper bag, saying: "Hold this for a minute, will you?" It was a parcel of eggs in the shell, and history is silent as to where the Colonel obtained them. In the dark and in the confusion of the bombing, this Digger soon got "lost" and when he was allotted to his truck bearing the well-known legend, "Vingt Hommes, Huit Chevaux en long" (twenty men, eight horses) he was still holding the eggs.

It was only natural that the parcel should be divided among the always-hungry warriors, and this soon happened and then only one, and that an obviously "high," egg was left. The occupants of the truck decided that it was only fair that the Colonel should have the last egg, but no one was game enough to hand it back.

After this hectic night the 11th Battalion, less "B" Company, managed to entrain in safety, and after a twelve-hours' journey arrived at Hondeghem at 4:30 on April 13, just eight days after leaving the sector. From Hondeghem the troops were marched to billets in Morbecque; "B" Company followed five hours later.

CHAPTER XLII

HOLDING THE HUN AT HAZEBROUCK

THE 3RD AUSTRALIAN BRIGADE was ordered to take up a position defending Hazebrouck from the east, and each battalion was given its instructions as it detrained. Hazebrouck was an important railway junction, at least seven different lines meeting in that town. It was a town of Flemish character: clean and with a fine large square. The countryside round about was typically Flanders farmland, rich and heavily cultivated. It was important as a railway junction, and the fact that it lay on a slight ridge that rendered the town so valuable to the Allies, and which made its defence imperative. Besides it was only 33 miles from the English Channel. The fact that an Australian division—and in this case the 1st Australian Division—was chosen to defend this, the apex and immediate objective of the northern German attack, was sufficient testimony to the morale and fighting qualities of this great division and to the confidence which the Higher Command had in the Australian troops in general.

The 3rd Brigade report for April 13 stated that the situation was still obscure, but that the Boche was attacking from Vieux Berquin and Merville, and also from the north of the former village. The 4th Guards Brigade was holding on between Neuf Berquin and Vieux Berquin, with the 29th Division and the 92nd Division on the flanks (the 29th British Division was sure to be in it if there was any serious fighting). The enemy was in Oultersteen, but Merris had been recently occupied by the British troops. The 1st and 2nd Australian Brigades had pushed in behind the abovementioned British troops and were preparing to take over the line from them, while the 3rd Brigade was divisional reserve.

In General Haig's despatch relating to this action, a summary of the events of the northern break-through by the Germans is given, and the various attempts to hold up the German advance. Haig concludes by saying that the 1st Australian

Division took over the line and the German advance was definitely stopped.

It was a woefully different country from that left only a short time before that the 11th Battalion returned to. Where there had been prosperous farms there were only deserted houses, with stock running all over the fields. The villages and shops lay open to the first comers, and already showed signs of having been looted, for the inhabitants had nearly all cleared off at the first approach of the Germans.

Brigade headquarters staff were shelled out of their billet and had to seek another. While the 11th Battalion was in Morbecque the troops had the time of their lives. There was food and wine for the taking. The troops had no compunction in helping themselves, for the fortune of war made the stuff available and if they had not helped themselves the food would only have gone bad or someone else would have taken advantage of the absence of the owners. Troops about to go into the uncertainties of action are never sticklers for convention.

On April 14 the battalion, less transport, nucleus and "B" Company, moved up by route-march to reserve position in billets in the Sec Bois sector. The nucleus at this time consisted of 10 per cent. of the battalion strength, and they were left at Morbecque along with the transport.

The battalion was immediately given battle positions: "A" Company, line right; "C" Company, line left; "D" Company, support and "B" Company, reserve. "B" Company, immediately on detraining, moved up to the line left position, which was close to detraining point, and was relieved by "C" Company at 8 a.m. when it then took up its allotted position in reserve.

On the march to Sec Bois numbers of civilians were seen hurrying from Hazebrouck with as many of their household effects as they could pile on wheelbarrows, perambulators and handcarts. These refugees were mostly old people, women and children, and the troops were again much moved by the sight. This was always a horrible aspect of war.

Sec Bois was completely deserted and the boys made the best of things and had the pick of the houses in the village to camp in. There were also plenty of eggs, poultry and pigs. At one billet the boys had four young porkers killed and nicely dressed when the rightful owner braved the shell-fire and returned to her home. Private Dave Jolly, who prided himself on his French, was deputed to pacify Madame for the slaughter of her best porkers. "Madame," said Dave, "You comprez Allemand?" The lady replied that she knew all about the "Sals Boches." "Well!" floundered Dave, "We thought the cow was coming so we killed them. Compree?" Madame looked moderately pleased, and said "Oui, oui," but it is hardly possible that she understood.

In some of the estaminets there was beer and wine a-plenty, and all for the taking. It was necessary to picket the shops to prevent drunkenness.

Meantime the brigade had been working on a defensive line and the work was well forward. Platoon posts had been dug and camouflaged. The general situation was quiet, but the staffs were taking no risks and all men had to be in their billets when not on duty, and the roll call was held three times every day. On April 15 "A," "B" and "C" Companies were at work digging trenches and strongpoints. There was only slight shelling.

Next day, in addition to their usual work, the boys had the job of rounding up all the stray cattle in the area. These were driven into a fenced enclosure and handed over to the military police under instructions from the A.P.M. Over 80 cattle were rounded up.

But all the cattle were not handed over. It was quite the fashion in these days for brigades, battalions and even companies to have their own milking cows. The following humorous anecdote from Major Jack O'Neil illustrates this:

"There was an old cow picked up by my company ('C' Company). This cow accompanied us on our wanderings and used to give a nice supply of milk. Suddenly she went dry, and then I discovered that several of the boys used to sneak along at night to her stall and milk her into their mess-tins, and she went on strike at this treatment and refused to give another drop. She was then slaughtered and turned into steak and rounds of beef.

"The executioners, who were full of rum and vin blanc, tried to murder her with an axe, but they missed her every time they had a swipe at her, so she ended her days with a bullet."

On April 16 Lieut. E. C. F. O'Mahoney was evacuated sick and Lieut. J. M. Aitken took over the duties of acting adjutant. The battalion strength on this date was 47 officers and 783 other ranks.

On April 17 the Germans bombarded Hazebrouck during the night with gas and high-explosive shell. The 11th Battalion moved up to Courte Croix and took over the reserve position from a battalion of the 29th Division. The battalion was observed moving up and was shelled, and was fortunate in only receiving one casualty, one other rank wounded.

It was expected that the enemy would make an attack somewhere in the vicinity of Strazeele and Caestre, and the probable line was given as the Meteren Becque, a stream flowing southeast and then south in that sector. The 11th Battalion was immediately ordered to dig a special line of defensive works from Strazeele to the old army line which ran east of Fletre.

On April 18 the whole area was heavily shelled, the German gunners paying special attention to all roads and cross-roads. Numbers of dead horses were seen on the roads after the strafe, which testified to the German gunners' accuracy. Most of the farmhouses had also been hit by shells, and they were generally in a frightful mess of bricks and rubble and household effects, all scattered about. The Germans were using the new instantaneous fuses on the shells. These shells were named by the boys "Daisy-cutters," as they had a very flat burst. They were very effective missiles, and even small stock and wild birds were often killed by the flying splinters.

The 11th Battalion transport moved from Morbecque to Rouge Croix. This was the same village that the transport was camped at on its first arrival in France, when the 11th Battalion had gone into billets in Fletre and the farms nearby. The rest of the battalion was quartered in the vicinity and naturally the whole district was well known to many of the older members of the battalion who had their first impressions of France and the rear areas in this locality. It was with something of sadness that the Diggers gazed at the dilapidated farms and villages and they wondered what had become of Yvonne and Marie, and what poor old Madame was doing after having been driven out of her home and her nice little business of selling "Pommes de terre frits" and "oeufs," which had been so tragically destroyed.

It was a strange experience for the boys to visit the well-known villages of Caestre, Fletre, Strazeele, Moolenacker and

Caestre, 1918. (Official Photo.)

Rouge Croix, where they had so often drunk the "plink plonk" (vin blanc) and the sour "vin rouge" and quaffed so many cups of coffee, and to find all the old cheerful life gone and nothing but shattered houses and a few khaki-clad figures lounging about. This was indeed war, but sentiment had little place in the soldier's life.

On the night of April 19/20, the 3rd Brigade took over the front line at Meteren, with the 11th Battalion on the left, just to the north-east of the town. The battalion relieved two companies of a French unit (the 116th Chasseurs) and some elements of British troops (the 93rd Brigade) on the French left flank. The whole of the line to be relieved was under the command of the G.O.C. 133rd French Division, and the services of interpreters had to be utilised to effect the necessary transmission of standing orders and other details of the change-over. There were also two international posts formed as liaison posts; one of these was manned by a platoon of the 11th Battalion.

The relief was completed satisfactorily and with much amusement on both sides. One little Frenchman wished to convey the fact that a machine gun was very dangerous at a particular corner. He went through a lot of motions and made a lot of noises, to all of which the Diggers solemnly said, "Oui, oui"; but there was a roar of laughter when the Froggie gave a realistic exhibition of what to do when the gun fired. The Frenchman was somewhat disconcerted, but he soon shrugged his shoulders and grinned in return.

The 11th Battalion held important positions covering crossroads and, if attacked, the battalion was to be supported by the 3rd T.M.B.

The great German attack in the south was now definitely held up, not only because there were resolute troops opposed to the Germans, but also because the advance had so extended the German front in making the great salient with its apex opposite Amiens that nearly all the reserve divisions had been used up. However, there was still the possibility that the enemy would persevere in his attempt to break through on the Hazebrouck front, and General De Lisle, the corps commander, had issued an order that the Fontaine Houck Ridge, lately taken over by the 3rd Australian Brigade, must be held at all costs.

The brigade was engaged in digging a defensive system of front and support lines in the forward zone, and in preparing the defended localities of Courte Croix, Phincboom, La Besage Farm, Fontaine Houck and Les 4 Fils Aymon. While on this work the troops were subject to a great many attacks from German aeroplanes. These 'planes came over and bombed the roads and billets and even dropped "pineapple" and "egg" bombs on single individuals walking along the roads. All this used to make the troops wonder at the reiterated boast of the Allied air supremacy. During the early Somme battles of 1916 the Allies appeared to own the sky, but since then the German Albatrosses and Halberstadts had made a fair bid for supremacy. The Germans were the first to use twin guns firing through the propellor. Even the 3rd Brigade diary for April 22 makes reference to the paucity of British 'planes over the sector. Here is the extract:—

"An enemy aeroplane was brought down . . . at 9 a.m. . . . the pilot was wounded. R.A.F.C. report that the enemy is not using our aeroplane markings, but this is very doubtful. Very few of our 'planes have been over the sector. One or two artillery machines only having been seen."

With reference to the enemy 'planes bearing Allied markings the following extract from No. 2803 Private G. W. Cotterill, 11th Battalion, is interesting: "About mid-day a Fritz 'plane came over to see exactly what we had been up to, and it was the first 'plane we saw with the new identification marks on it; their colours in circles and one on the tail similar to the Allied 'planes. When we went back leaflets were distributed drawing attention to the new markings on the German 'planes."

It was evident that if the German aeroplanes were not using Allied markings, they were so nearly the same as to cause a lot of confusion and trouble.

The 3rd Brigade was ordered to capture Meteren. This operation was to be carried out by gradually advancing the line on the flanks with the idea of squeezing the enemy out and then mopping up the town itself. The operation was to be assisted by the discharge of 200 gas projectors, but only if the wind was suitable.

Meantime, on April 22, the battalion area had been heavily shelled during the afternoon and evening and battalion headquarters was forced to evacuate its quarters and move to another billet. There were three other ranks killed and four wounded by this shelling.

In the attack on Meteren all battalions had to make their own artillery arrangements; four light trench mortars were allocated to each battalion for use as required.

The troops had been expecting a fight for some time, and everything was in readiness for the "hop-over." On April 22/23, the night of the attack, the gas projectors could not be used on account of the unfavourable wind, and so the brigade moved out under Lewis and machine gun covering fire, while an artillery barrage was laid down on Meteren and beyond. The objectives were named the "blue," "green" and "red" lines respectively to avoid confusion.

On the right the 12th Battalion met with some opposition, but soon pushed forward and captured machine guns and prisoners.

The 11th Battalion met with little opposition, and with its characteristic dash was soon in position on the blue line. There were only a few casualties in this operation, one being Lieut. D. A. James, who was wounded. The 11th Battalion official diary records: "At 2:30 a.m. the whole line advanced with very little opposition and a new defensive line was dug. Battalion less 'C' Company relieved the 10th Battalion and became reserve battalion. Relief completed without incident."

It will be noted that this report on a successful operation by the 11th Battalion runs true to form. "Deeds, not Words" are again strikingly exemplified. The whole report takes up nearly *six lines* of typescript, while that of the 12th Battalion on exactly the same engagement takes up more than three *pages* of foolscap.

The instructions received by the 3rd Brigade were to exploit the success gained on April 23, and in pursuance of this order a second phase of the attack was arranged for April 24. The 9th and 10th Battalions were detailed to make this advance, and "C" Company of the 11th Battalion was allotted the task, in conjunction with one company of the 12th Battalion, of mopping up the village of Meteren.

Naturally the enemy had been stirred up by the successful attack the previous night, and he was prepared for a repetition of the attempt, so that the attacking battalions had a much harder task than the 11th and 12th Battalions on the previous day. Also there was too much over-confidence and too little regard for an intelligent foe, in certain quarters, and this brought its due punishment.

The general idea of this second phase of the attack on Meteren was for the two attacking battalions to make an encircling movement round each flank of the village and to leave the village itself to be mopped up by the companies detailed for that purpose. To do this without adequate artillery support was asking too much of the troops engaged, as the element of surprise was lacking.

The 10th Battalion, in spite of a determined assault, was unable to make much headway. The right company met with very strong opposition and was unable to advance, while the left company, after advancing, was forced to withdraw owing to heavy enfilade fire from both flanks. "C" Company of the 11th Battalion was naturally unable to do its job of mopping up as the right attacking battalion had not advanced. In trying to rush the village, Lieut. S. M. Wood, Sergeant J. A. Ferguson and two men were killed, and Lieut. Fred Stahl, D.C.M., and ten other ranks were wounded. Lieut. Wood was an original member of the battalion and had only recently received his commission.

Owing to the fact that the two horns of the attack were in the air, with intact enemy machine gun posts commanding all the approaches and also enfilading the advanced 3rd Brigade positions, the attack was abandoned. Meteren was in flames, whether through artillery fire or set alight by the Germans was not known, and considerable enemy casualties were reported.

The following interesting account from Private Richard J. Bastian describes the stunt from the Diggers' point of view: "I made one of a mopping-up party in the attack on the village of Meteren. It was supposed to be a surprise attack, but there was a full moon and we were observed and came under heavy machine gun fire. Some of us hopped into a small trench for protection. Some dead Tommies were lying in the trench, having been shot some time previously while digging the trench. Some of us had to stand on their bodies. We lay there three hours and then had to bolt back in twos to safety, as the machine gun fire and shelling were very heavy. It was a marvel how many escaped. Lieut. Stahl stalked a machine gun and silenced it with a bomb. It was a very brave act. Lieut. Woods, two sergeants and a number of men were killed. My diary says:

'A poorly-arranged affair; quite idiotic,' and that we advertised our intention by the digging of jumping-off trenches the previous night. It was a needless waste of valuable lives in a stupidly arranged affair."

The above letter is specially interesting as it is a typical example of the intelligent criticism which the average Digger brought to bear on the operations he was engaged in.

And Dr. Bean states in the Official History, volume V, pages 497/498: "The second phase at Meteren cost the 3rd Brigade 160 casualties and the whole minor operation about 200. The sharp repulse was undoubtedly a shock to the division, and although the spirit of the troops was much too high to be perceptibly affected—as their actions . . . most brilliantly showed— it was evident that the Germans . . . had been treated too lightly. . . .

"The consequent burning of fingers was a useful lesson to the division (i.e., the 1st Australian Division) even in the ensuing months, when the audacity of its exploits was *setting a new standard for the army*."

Thus the above operation, though not wholly successful, marks the turning point of the war in the north, just as the action of the other Australian divisions in front of Amiens brought the German advance to a halt in the southern sphere of operations and wrested the initiative from the enemy. The 1st Australian Division, which had been rushed north to save Hazebrouck, not only definitely stopped the German advance but in a few days effectually turned the tables on the enemy; and though its operations had not been brilliantly successful so far, the division was soon to show the wonderful metal of which its troops were composed.

On April 25 "C" Company, 11th Battalion, was relieved by a company of the 10th Battalion and moved back to reserve position with the remainder of the battalion. Captain J. P. O'Neil, M.C., reported from the United Kingdom for duty with the battalion.

Greetings were sent from division to all members of the battalion who had served on the Gallipoli Peninsula, the date being the third anniversary of the Landing.

From a German prisoner a report was received that the Germans were going to attack on April 25 at 5 p.m. after a heavy bombardment. All ranks were warned to be in readiness;

and the nucleus battalion was ordered to be prepared to man the line in the vicinity of Thieushouck. The French division to the right was also expecting to be attacked, and the 11th Battalion was ordered to be ready to support these troops, if necessary.

There was no attack that day, but early next morning an enemy 'plane bombed Fletre and later the same village was subjected to a heavy bombardment of mustard gas shell. The whole place was drenched with gas, so much so that the village was declared out of bounds to all troops. There was also a considerable bombardment along the support line as far as the brigade right boundary.

At 9:30 p.m. 160 gas projectors were fired from the 1st Division area as there was a gentle five-mile-an-hour breeze blowing from the north-west.

Two companies of the 11th Battalion were detailed to dig trenches in the support line. This line extended from Fletre Mill, north to Coc de Paille, a small village on the slopes near Mont des Cats. In spite of all these preparations and rumours no German attack eventuated. But there was still a feeling of uneasiness among the staff, and it was felt that a big German attack was imminent and orders were sent to all units to be in readiness to conform to a general withdrawal should the occasion arise. The regimental transports were under the command of Captain Alec Burgess, of the 11th Battalion, who was brigade transport officer. The transports were divided into two echelons, and Captain Burgess received detailed instructions how to move the 1st and 2nd echelons should the necessity arise. The locations of the various stages were given, and the times of movement and the full particulars of roads to be used.

The peasants were gradually coming back to their homes, and it was a terrible sight that met their gaze. The 3rd Brigade official diary of April 27 states: "There are still a number of cattle and pigs about, though feathers only remain of most of the fowls. The farms have been smashed by shell-fire in most cases—the debris in the rooms is pitiful, most of the inhabitants having left at very short notice."

On April 28 the 11th Battalion was relieved by the 1st Battalion (A.I.F.) and moved back to reserve area at Thieushouck. Before the battalion was relieved there were four men killed and four wounded by shell-fire. Among those killed was

No. 584 Private C. S. Philbey, an original member of the battalion. During the month's operations the battalion lost 12 killed and 38 wounded.

On April 29 the usual day's rest, after relief from the line, was given, during which time the reorganisation of companies was taken in hand. Cleaning and overhaul of equipment was also the order of the day.

In the evening "A" Company provided an entertainment for the amusement of the company and the battalion headquarters staff in Fletre brewery. Colonel Rafferty was very pleased with the concert and all the boys declared that they had had a good time. The songs sung may have been some indication of the Diggers' reaction to the war. Sergeant Harry Vincent sang "When I Leave the World Behind" and Frank Fenton sang "A Nice Quiet Spot." Private Humphries was billed to tell some of his famous yarns, but when he saw the "Heads" he wanted to pull out, but the troops would not let him. The chief hit of the evening was the famous song having an unlimited numbers of verses entitled "The Best Battalion." It was sung on various important occasions after this date. Lieut. Jim Aitken was adjutant at this time, and he looked very disgusted when the Diggers sang—

"If you want to find the Adjutant,
We know where he is, we know where he is;
If you want to find the Adjutant,
We know where he is—
Down in the deep dug-out."

and the Colonel grinned when the boys shouted—

"If you want to find the Colonel

. . . . .

Look where they buy the fights."

The verse that took the Diggers fancy, however, was the one which ran—

"If you want to find the best battalion,
We know where it is, we know where it is;
If you want to find the best battalion,
We know where it is—
'Tis the first from W.A."

This brought the house down, and the verse has since been frequently sung where 11th Battalion ex-members meet.

On the last day of the month musketry practice was started again in the battalion. The brigade diary states: "Our own front is quiet. Schools are beginning again (i.e., military schools) so the situation must be causing the high authority less anxiety."

The 11th Battalion strength on April 30 was 29 officers and 630 other ranks.

On May 1 Lieut. J. A. Archibald returned from hospital and resumed the duties of adjutant. The battalion held rifle inspection and musketry practice by platoons in billets.

Endeavours were made to have the whole battalion bathed and issued with clean clothing. In a report by the 3rd Brigade diarist, he states: "Some men have salved ladies' underclothing for wear, and they say the cotton fabric is not favoured by lice." There must have been something doing when the troops went to hand in their underclothing for a clean army change.

The routine on May 2 was the same as on the previous day except that 100 men were sent to work on the divisional defence line switch from Coq de Paille to Fletre. Captain A. S. Keighley, the intelligence officer, visited the forward zone prior to the battalion taking over. There was scattered enemy shelling over the whole of the reserve area and some of the billets were struck by shells. The 11th Battalion had no casualties, but a shell landed on the ridge of a billet occupied by some of the 12th Battalion. Ten men were killed and 14 were wounded as a result.

The 3rd Brigade was due to relieve the 2nd Brigade and the following dispositions were to be adopted: There were to be two battalions in the line, one battalion in support and one in reserve.

On May 3 there was an inspection of all arms in the battalion during the morning. All the company commanders went forward to reconnoitre the forward area and to find out the positions their companies would be taking over.

There was a great deal of aerial activity over the sector, which was rather a change to what had been noticed for some time previously. Many large formations of British and Allied 'planes were in the air. There had been several strongly-pressed attacks on the French troops just north of the Australian sector but these had all been repulsed, and the great aerial activity was to prevent the possibility of a big surprise attack such as fell upon the luckless Portugese six weeks before.

A number of civilians had returned to Thieushouck and other villages. These poor people had braved the dangers of frequent and accurate shell-fire to be near their homes. However, as their presence was an embarrassment to the military authorities, in cases of gas-shelling and other eventualities, these people were evacuated by ambulance to Caestre by order of brigade.

On May 4 the 11th Battalion relieved the 7th Battalion in the front line. The battalion occupied the left sector of the brigade frontage, with "C," "D" and "B" Companies in the line in that order and "A" Company in support. Each company in the line had five posts out in front with a Lewis gun in each, and the flank companies had each one platoon in support. The support company was in trenches. There was no wire out except in front of the support company.

As soon as the battalion had settled down, an attempt was made to link up the front line system where necessary, and to put out wire in defence of the posts. Many of the troops felt that the wire showed the position of the post, and was the cause of many of these being blown out; but there is no doubt that the presence of wire to the front and flanks gave the troops greater confidence and, as at Lagnicourt, the wired posts were generally found to be able to stand a sudden attack, whereas the unwired posts were liable to be suddenly overwhelmed by a determined enemy raiding party.

In carrying out this work of wiring, the parties were shelled and three men were wounded, and on May 6 a shell landed on the regimental aid-post. Although it was a direct hit, there were fortunately no casualties to the medical personnel, but there was some excitement for a while.

About 260 gas projectors had been fired in the direction of Merris on the previous night. There was no record as to their effect. The German reply was to shell the rear areas and billets and also the roads, evidently in the hope of disorganising troops moving up to the line.

At this time the 11th Battalion headquarters was in the cellar of a burnt-out farm. The ruins were still smouldering and the cellar was uncomfortably hot.

Things livened up somewhat in the sector on May 7. In the evening the enemy strafed the 11th Battalion very heavily with 5.9, 4.2 and .77 mm. shells. Some of the posts were also bombed with minenwerfers. At 10 p.m. the Germans fired two red and two green flares. These were taken to be S.O.S. signals fired by the 12th Battalion, but that unit disclaimed firing any S.O.S.

In the counter-shelling by supporting artillery, a number of 18-pounder shells fell short and considerably annoyed the Diggers in the front line posts. But there were luckily no casualties from this source.

When the German shelling had eased down, Sergeant Dave O'Neil and six men from "B" Company left No. 2 listening-post and patrolled to a point just north-west of Merris, where they found a lately-killed soldier of the 62nd Prussian Regiment. There was no enemy attack after the shelling, which had evidently only been harassing fire, possibly in retaliation for the gas sent over on the previous night.

For some time Captain A. S. Keighley, the battalion intelligence officer, had been airing his views on the subject of daylight raids. He declared that the daylight raid would be so utterly unsuspected by the enemy that there would be a good chance of making the project successful, and that also, being in daytime, there would be no possibility of confusion as was the case when raids were made in the darkness, and it would give the raiders a much better chance.

On May 8 the good Captain visited his scouts and observers. He was accompanied by his corporal ("Long" Dick Wearmouth). The intelligence platoon had been living up to its name, and on this afternoon was enjoying the contents of some bottles of wine that had been "salvaged." The Captain was offered a drink. The wine was good so he had a few, and he then set out with Wearmouth down the leafy lanes that led him to the enemy lines. It was a lovely May afternoon and the drowsiness of the early summer lay over everything. As the two warriors approached the Germans lines, Captain Keighley, who was leading, suddenly recollected that he had no arms with him, so he asked Wearmouth for his Webley (the scouts were privileged to carry revolvers). The "squirt" was handed over and the pair moved on, but Wearmouth was now unarmed save for a bayonet.

Nothing stirred on either side, and the German posts that the twain visited were empty, evidently being occupied only at nights. Finally the two wandered to the old Meteren baths, beside the Meteren Becque, where the battalion had so often bathed in the days before Fritz had made his advance. Here they found a somnolent German, who was so utterly astounded that he offered not the faintest resistance. Keighley poked him with the revolver and forced the man to accompany him back to the 11th Battalion lines. It was a strange little party that came triumphantly back in broad daylight. The short, dapper Captain in front, then the German prisoner and lastly the tall, lanky Wearmouth trying to make his great height as inconspicuous as possible bringing up the rear. Many eyes popped as the trio passed between the posts on their way in. The good Captain was mighty pleased that he had proved his point about daylight raids. The Captain received a Military Cross and the Corporal a Military Medal for this little piece of work.

Later on the same night a patrol of one N.C.O. and six men from "C" Company bombed an enemy outpost in the same vicinity from which the prisoner had been taken. They inflicted casualties on the enemy, but had one man killed.

The 11th Battalion was relieved by the 9th Battalion on May 9. The weather was clear and fine and the troops could not leave their area until 9 p.m. owing to the great visibility. The relief was extremely late on this account, but it was probably just as well, as most of the enemy shelling was over by the time the troops started to move out, and thus there were no casualties.

After the relief the division was allotted a revised area, which had a one-brigade front instead of a two-brigade front as heretofore in the Meteren sector. The brigade front was now 5,000 yards long, and though thinly held the new dispositions of the troops would give them considerably more rest, at least from front line service, though the immediate effect was to make it harder on the brigade in the line.

It was rather a surprise to the troops, however, when they heard they were to return to the line on the night of May 10. The boys were allowed to rest all day and then they moved up again to the line and relieved the Worcester Regiment and the 10th Australian Battalion. Patrols and sentry-groups were at once established, and the harassing of the Germans was started again. This was so much a routine during this time that very few references are made to this form of warfare in the official diaries.

There was always a good deal of patrol work and frequent encounters were held with the Germans, generally to the latter troops' disadvantage. In fact, from this time onwards, there was absolutely no question as to the superiority of the 1st Australian Division over all the German divisions that were brought against it, as the records of the next three months plainly show.

A feature of the war in the Meteren area was the accurate shelling by the German artillery. Billets and huts were frequently struck and the shelling of Pradelles or Strazeele or other villages was far too accurate to be pleasant. On May 11 the support billets were severely shelled and Lieut. Phil. Vowles, M.C., and two other ranks were killed and Lieut. G. C. Murray wounded. Vowles and Murray were supervising the issue of rations to "A" Company when the shell landed. Captain W. R. Hallahan, who had just returned from cadre in England, was sent up from nucleus to take Vowles' place. Wally was much affected by Vowles' death, for they had both received their commissions on the same date and had been friends before the war.

The enemy generally had several kite-balloons up in this sector (this was a sure sign that the Allies had no air superiority at this time, in this sector at least), and these "sausages" were the eyes of the German artillery, as there was splendid visibility in the mornings and this accounted for a great deal of the accurate shooting.

In the line the 11th Battalion patrols were very aggressive, and while out that night they captured three infantrymen belonging to the 62nd German Regiment.

Nothing very startling occurred during the remainder of the battalion's tour of duty, and the troops were relieved on the night of May 14/15 by the 8th Battalion. The relief was completed without incident and the battalion moved back to a camp near the Borre Becque (a becque is a small stream and corresponds to the English "Beck") north-west of Hazebrouck and not far from Hondeghem.

Lieut.-Colonel R. A. Rafferty was evacuated to hospital (sick) and relinquished the command of the battalion on May 14, and Major Newman was appointed to command temporarily. Major Newman had been O.C. of the 9th Battalion before being transferred back to the 11th.

Lieut.-Colonel Rafferty was always regarded as a great front-line soldier, and the troops appreciated his constant visits to the front line trenches as it made them feel that they were in close touch with battalion headquarters, and that the "Old Man" knew the conditions they were living under and the obstacles they were up against. It was wonderful how this personal touch made for popularity.

For the next few days the usual procedure of a resting battalion was carried out. There was little to report save the movement of troops from hospital or depots. There were muster parades and the usual commanding officer's inspections. The baths at Borre were available to the battalion. Among the movements of officers, the following were reported: Major Newman, to the 10th Battalion and to command, vice Major Shaw (sick); 2nd/Lieut. Archie Ross, from Cadet Battalion; Captain Alec Burgess and Lieut. Dale, to hospital (sick). At nights there was considerable bombing by enemy 'planes, but this was regarded so much as part of the ordinary routine of war at this time that it was hardly ever referred to in the diaries except when casualties occurred.

On May 18 the 11th Battalion was relieved in the support area by the 4th Battalion. On relief, the battalion marched to Sercus and went into bell-tents among the trees in that locality.

Next day was Sunday, and a brigade church parade was held at 10:20 a.m. General Walker was in attendance and after the parade the 3rd Brigade marched past the General in column of platoons. It was a splendid sight. In the afternoon the troops received orders to camouflage their tents with mud and green branches so as to make them as inconspicuous as possible from the air. This indicates the ever prevalent enemy bombers. A guard of one sergeant and three other ranks was supplied for brigade headquarters by the 11th Battalion. Schools for musketry and Lewis gun instruction were again established, and special training for patrol men was commenced. On May 20 the G.O.C.'s guard was again supplied by the 11th Battalion. The rifle range at La Belle Hotesse was made available on May 21 and all the companies exercised their personnel in musketry. In the afternoon, battalion sports were held and in the evening a concert and a cinema were arranged for the battalion at Sercus. Half the battalion went to one amusement and half to the other. It was a pleasant change for the troops, as there was very little distraction for the boys now that most of the civilian population had fled from the area. Lieuts. J. L. Barry, H. V. Howe and M. A. McGuire reported from the Army School of Instruction.

On May 22 a ceremonial parade of the whole 3rd Brigade was held in a field near Sercus. The divisionnal commander, Sir H. B. Walker, K.C.B., D.S.O., inspected the troops, who were marched past in column of half-companies. Battalion sports were held in the afternoon.

On May 23 the whole battalion was detailed to act as a working party for cable laying for the XV. Corps Signallers. In the afternoon bathing parades were held, but the newly-started schools for Lewis gun and musketry instruction were cancelled owing to the large fatigue party supplied in the morning.

When the brigade guard returned to battalion a complimentary letter was sent by brigade expressing the G.O.C.'s appreciation of the 11th Battalion guard supplied.

Chapter XLIII

MONT DE MERRIS

About this time the 1st Australian Division was asked to submit a plan for an attack in the vicinity of Merris, and the general officer commanding the 3rd Australian Brigade received an order from the divisional commander, stating that he had been asked to submit preliminary plans for an attack on a frontage of 4,500 yards and on a depth of up to 1,000 yards. It was further stated that the attack would probably be carried out by the 3rd Brigade during its next tour in the line, and General Bennett was asked to submit his proposals to divisional headquarters by May 24. These were to include the general plan of attack to be adopted, the number of troops to be employed, the artillery support required and the suggested zero hour. This was rather an easy way for division to obtain a well-thought plan of action, which would naturally be eagerly carried out by the originator, if division should have thought fit to adopt it.

Brigadier-General Bennett's reply was to the effect that the plan was too ambitious and that it could not be safely attempted with less than a brigade, especially as the available artillery support was limited.

The Brigadier suggested that, as an alternative scheme, the operation should be limited to the capture of the Mont de Merris and the ridge adjoining, and he stated that this scheme could safely be attempted by two battalions, and he outlined a plan that was at once simple and at the same time comprehensive. This preliminary outline of the projected attack is given at some length, as the 11th Battalion was destined to play the most important role in the battle of Mont de Merris, which will be narrated in its proper sequence.

On May 24 there was to have been a demonstration by No. 4 Squadron R.A.F., but owing to inclement weather it had to be cancelled. The demonstration was to have included the use of the new "T" (Popham) panel for signalling to the contact aeroplane in the case of an infantry advance.

The last few days of the stay at Sercus were very wet and training was interrupted. Brigade sports were definitely cancelled. The battalion diary reports a considerable movement of officers. Lieut. R. Retchford, M.C., returned from hospital, Lieut. J. A. Archibald was evacuated (sick) and Captain J. S. D. Walker assumed the duties of adjutant. Lieuts. W. D. Brown and H. A. Holley left for the XV. Corps School and Lewis Gun School respectively. Lieut.-Colonel Rafferty was seconded for duty with the No. 1 Training Battalion at Sutton Veny (England) and Major J. Newman was appointed to command the 11th Battalion with the rank of Temporary Lieut.-Colonel. Lieut. W. A. Keeley left the battalion for the Indian Army Training College in England. With regard to the last-named officer, when his friends learned that he was going to join the Indian Army, they gave him a farewell evening and the toasts were many and thoroughly dealt with. Keeley was presented with many bogus letters of introduction to imaginary Indian potentates, such as the "Nizam of Buk" and the "Khan of Creem." He was so overcome with the expressions of good-will and kindness that he was almost tearful, and in reply to the toast to himself said that if he had known how much he was appreciated he would never have put in an application to join the Indian Army.

On May 26 the battalion was relieved by the 5th Battalion (A.I.F.) in the divisional reserve area, and in conjunction with the rest of the 3rd Brigade moved by route-march to the reserve area at Hondeghem. As the head of the brigade column was approaching Hazebrouck, and just after it had passed the division and brigade commander, two heavy shells almost fell on the 9th Battalion, and as the shelling continued the rest of the brigade had to make a deviation to avoid the town.

On May 27 the 11th Battalion relieved the 4th Battalion in the reserve position of the front line system. Battalion head-quarters was in Pradelles, which had been subjected to a drench-ing by gas shell during the two previous nights. Just before the 1st Brigade was relieved by the 3rd Brigade, three German prisoners were captured by the former troops. These prisoners stated that the Germans were going to attack the 29th British Division, which was holding the sector to the south of the 3rd Brigade. This news put the wind up the staff and hasty dis-positions were made in case the enemy was successful in penetrating the lines. "D" Company was disposed as a garrison in Strazeele, which was a strongly fortified point.

As usual, when everyone and everything were prepared for an attack, nothing out of the ordinary occurred, and the night passed off quietly. During the next two nights the 11th Battalion had large working parties out digging trenches in the support line, and they were also engaged in draining and improving other trenches. On May 28 they dug over 600 yards of trench 5 feet 6 inches deep, and on May 29 over 500 yards were dug. "D" Company in Strazeele was heavily shelled while on garrison duty, but there were no casualties.

The 10th Battalion had made a small advance of about 200 yards, and owing to casualties sustained they rang up the 11th Battalion for three squads of stretcher-bearers. These were supplied.

The enemy shelling had materially increased since the battalion's last tour of duty. This was due chiefly to the vigorous policy of the 1st Division patrols which kept up a constant pressure on the enemy and annoyed him considerably by continually capturing his advanced posts. Strazeele always received more than its share of heavy shelling and was bombarded with 5.9 shells. These made very large craters in the soft ground.

In view of the approaching attack on the Mont de Merris, two officers from each company were sent forward to reconnoitre the front and to study the lie of the land. On May 30 "A," "B" and "C" Companies were again working on the support defences and completed 450 yards of trenches round Strazeele. These trenches were drained, deepened and otherwise improved. "D" Company remained on garrison duty in the village.

Two men from each company joined the 10th Battalion patrols to gain knowledge of the ground to be fought over in the impending attack on Mont de Merris, as it was now definitely arranged that the 11th Battalion was to make the attack. The Commanding Officer (Lieut.-Colonel John Newman) called a meeting of company commanders at battalion headquarters to discuss the necessary preliminaries.

On the last day of the month the battalion was going through the same routine of trench digging and improving. One new feature of the defence was the digging of a tank-trap. Runners and signallers were sent forward to reconnoitre lines for the approaching stunt and to lay signal wires. Colonel Newman had received the brigade orders for the attack on the Mont de Merris, so he visited the front line and made the necessary adjustments for his plan of attack. The battalion order was then compiled and "D" Company officers were informed of the dispositions, for having been confined to Strazeele they had not been able to attend the other conferences.

Battalion headquarters was situated in a very dilapidated farmhouse which offered little protection from artillery fire, so the walls were reinforced with barrels full of bricks and sandbags were built against the most vulnerable portions of the walls.

The sector held by the 1st Australian Division was dominated by a low hill and ridge which were in the German hands. This eminence gave the enemy good observation over all the country to the north-west and west, and consequently its capture was of the greatest importance for future operations against the enemy. This eminence was the Mont de Merris, and arrangements for its capture by the 11th Battalion were now well on the way towards completion. The date of the attack was fixed for the night of June 2/3, and the objective was roughly a diagonal from south-west to north-east embracing the hill and ridge.

The 11th Battalion was to attack in two waves on a two-company frontage, and the second wave was to pass through the first after the first objective had been gained. Special mopping-up parties were to be with each attacking wave. The 10th Battalion was to co-operate by having companies on the flanks and advancing in conformity with the main attack, and each flank company had to establish a post to right and to left of the 11th Battalion's objective.

The 10th Battalion intelligence platoon had to lay tapes on the jumping-off position and were to guide the 11th Battalion companies into position on the night of the attack. This was not done as ordered. Lieut. Gostelow, of the 11th Battalion, saw to this business, and but for him there would have been a mess-up.

The attack was to be supported by light and medium trench mortar batteries, by rifle grenades and by batteries of 18-pounder guns. The 1st Australian Machine Gun Battalion was also to give flanking fire in order to neutralise any enemy machine gun fire.

When the first objective was captured, a special rifle grenade rocket was to be fired. This rocket would show a white over green light. In the same way a green over red over green light was to denote that the second objective was taken. All the troops of the 11th Battalion were to wear a white patch on each arm and the flanking companies were to wear a white patch on one arm only. The right flank company was to wear the patch on the right arm and the left flank company on the left arm.

The usual other details necessary for an attack were laid down, but a novel feature and one that turned out successfully was that from three minutes after the attack was launched an incendiary shell was to be fired by one of the 18-pounders every minute to seven minutes to mark the centre point of the attack.

A contact aeroplane was to fly over the lines at dawn.

On June 1 one of the enemy's 'planes came down in flames at 6 a.m. It appeared to be on the Hun side of the line. Later in the day two officers and 80 men were sent, as a carrying party, to assist the 10th Battalion in view of the forthcoming attack. This party carried up engineering material and ammunition.

Lieut.-Colonel Newman was very careful that there should be no hitch, and after nightfall "A" and "C" Companies and afterwards "B" and "D" Companies were led on to a tape line to practice for the lining up on the following night. The rehearsal went off very satisfactorily and all the troops were keen for the real thing on the next night.

June 2 passed very quietly and the final preparations were made for the attack that evening. The troops were instructed to note all prominent objects in the line of advance, three houses being particularly pointed out. The responsibility for maintaining direction was allotted to Captain W. R. Hallahan, M.C., M.M. All prisoners captured in the attack were to be passed back through the 10th Battalion, and the 10th Battalion headquarters at Tiflis House was to be used by the 11th Battalion, which was to be responsible for the sector during the attack. Zero hour was to be 1 a.m.

After a hot meal at 10 p.m. the companies of the 11th Battalion left independently for the jumping-off position. The front wave companies left first, at 10:45 p.m., and the second wave followed after a short interval. "C" Company lost two men (wounded) by a 4.2 shell in moving up, and "D" Company had 14 men gassed on the way in. There was no further trouble. It was a perfect night for the undertaking, and the troops were met by the guides and led to the tape line, where they formed up and were in position in good time before zero hour.

All the lads were now keyed up to that pitch that made them burn with eagerness for the barrage to start, and when the suspense-breaking roar of the guns and trench mortars fell on their ears it brought a wonderful feeling of relief to know that the attack was on at last.

The barrage started at 1 a.m. and the lads were soon pressing forward as close as it was safe, and many a good deal closer than that. The 18-pounder barrage was very effective and quite impressive, but after the battle all ranks were enthusiastic over the efficiency of the trench mortars and the No. 36 rifle grenades. Many Diggers were heard to say that the T.M. barrage would "always do them." The retaliatory barrage of the enemy fell at 1:5 a.m. but, owing to the speed of the advance, it was rendered comparatively ineffective. The direction of the attack was well maintained, and the first wave soon overwhelmed the weak resistance of the Boche. It happened that an enemy relief was in progress, and the Germans were confused and only too glad to surrender. The Diggers would capture a few of the enemy and immediately point back over their shoulders, giving some of the dopey prisoners a kick on the posterior to help them in the right direction. The middle of a battle is no time for politeness. On reaching the first objective the success signal could not be displayed, as all the rockets were "duds," but soon numbers of German prisoners, belonging to the 13th Reserve Infantry Regiment, began to arrive back at battalion headquarters, testifying to the success of the first phase. "A" Company captured about 85 prisoners in a few minutes and "C" Company sent about as many back. "B" and "D" Companies then passed through the first wave with great dash and mopped up trenches and machine-gun posts as they charged through. In their eagerness they had moved up with the front wave. Lieut. Roy Retchford was killed while gallantly leading his men forward, and Lieut. H. Davison and 2nd/Lieut. A. C. Ross were severely wounded.

A tougher resistance was put up by the Germans on the second objective, but the hardy Westralians soon captured this position also and sent up the success rocket, green over red over green, thus relieving the anxiety and strain of the watchers in rear. Meantime the 10th Battalion troops on the flanks had been successful in advancing their line and in capturing their allotted objectives and in sending back a number of prisoners. The 11th Battalion lost no time in consolidating its position and patrols were immediately sent out in front to act as a screen. Numbers of enemy dead were seen lying all around, and at least 80 German dead were in the captured area. The 11th Battalion casualties were 92 in all, of whom 13 were killed. Captain W. R. Hallahan and Lieut. J. M. Aitken were both wounded, but remained on duty.

A total of five German officers and 253 other ranks were captured, nearly all by the 11th Battalion. A considerable amount of war material was also taken, including 26 light machine guns, one heavy machine gun, 13 light minenwerfers, five grenade-throwers and one 77 mm. Q.F. field gun and a large number of rifles and equipment. (The field gun mentioned here is now mounted in Subiaco Municipal Gardens, Western Australia.)

The prisoners captured belonged to the following regiments: the 13th Field Artillery Regiment, the 13th Reserve Infantry Regiment, the 39th R.I.R. and the 57th R.I.R.

The attack was voted a great success by all the boys, and they were at last satisfied that the Allies were winning the war, because, on making the prisoners give up their rations before they were sent back, the troops found the bread that the German soldiers were given was of the black variety and very mouldy, and ill-smelling at that. The Diggers all reckoned that the Germans could not possibly be winning the war when they supplied their soldiers with such vile rations.

In this operation 2,050 Stokes mortar shells were fired. This was not only a tribute to the mortars but also to the efficiency of the personnel.

After the attack there was a good deal of harassing fire from the enemy machine guns, but two of these guns were silenced by grenades fired by the Diggers from captured granaten-werfer. There was no artillery retaliation on the captured position. It appeared as if the attack had so confused the Germans that they had no idea of the extent of the advance.

At 5 a.m. on June 3 the contact aeroplane, flying over the line at that time, was able to pick up the new positions and a message was dropped at brigade headquarters with the necessary co-ordinations.

The 12th Battalion took advantage of the 11th Battalion's attack to advance their posts, but their flank was found to be 80 yards in rear of the 11th Battalion's line, so a further forward movement had to be made by the first-named battalion, which also captured some prisoners in the operation.

As usual, the 11th Battalion official diary is practically silent on the results of the Mont de Merris attack, and though there were a considerable number of decorations awarded there is no mention of these in either battalion or brigade reports.

Fortunately there is a good account of this battle in Lieut. Peter Snodgrass's diary, from which the following extracts are taken:—

"The battalion came up by easy stages from a long way back and bivouaced one night and most of the day before the attack about three miles back from the line in a small field surrounded by hedges—a real beauty spot.

" . . . By about 12:50 a.m. we were all lying along our tape which had been laid previously by our guides. We were to follow a trench mortar (Stokes, mainly) barrage, and zero was to be marked by a heavy gun firing a shell directly over our portion from a long way back. The filing out on to the tape had been carried out without a hitch and without a sound. Everyone was alert and ready. The word was passed along the line, 'Three minutes to go.' Presently, 'One minute to go' whispered its way quickly along the line; everyone tense and eager, with a 'fag' in his mouth and a box of matches in his hand. 'Boom!' echoed over our heads. Instantly our Stokes mortars opened their barrage, their shells bursting with lurid flashes only 30 yards in front of our line of men. In less time than it takes to write it, the cloud of dust and smoke was dense enough only to show a blurred flash where the bombs exploded, and in that time about 90 per cent. of the troops had a smoke of some sort alight.

"As soon as the barrage started to 'creep,' we picked up the white patches which the guides wore on their backs and followed the general direction as well as possible. 'A' and 'C'

Companies were to take the first trench and 'B' and 'D' Companies were to leap-frog 'A' and 'C' and take the second and final trench."

Here follows an account of the capture of the first prisoner:

"The first trench offered no resistance and was quickly captured with many prisoners. (It was here that 'Chook' Fowles got the bar to his D.C.M.) We passed on (there was no leap-frog, because I think the four companies took the first trench) and took the second trench, also without resistance except for one machine gun which, fought by one man, remained in action until our men were on three sides. Private Roper threw a bomb which burst quite close to the gunner, and he then stood up and raised his arms in surrender. Our men were loath to shoot for fear of hitting a comrade. Roper rushed forward and shouted: 'Don't shoot! This man is too brave to be shot down in cold blood.' He took the prisoner back and personally delivered him to battalion headquarters and then returned to the line."

Here follows an account of the capture of trophies. Lieut. Snodgrass goes on to say:

"We were in an excellent position, overlooking a vast stretch of flat country, and we could see for miles. We were told we were to hold the line for 24 hours, but we did 48 hours.

"We were informed that the stunt had been the most successful for its size during the war, up to that time."

After the capture of the lines Lieut. Snodgrass goes on to say: "During the hours of daylight, a sniper was causing annoyance, but no casualties, from a sort of 'bush-shed.' Some one had a brainwave and sent over a red phosphorus bomb which immediately set fire to the shed. Fritz chose risking the 50 to 60 yards sprint to the cover of a brick wall to burning alive. He was pursued by about 20 bullets, but apparently arrived safely and unhurt."

With reference to the field gun mentioned in the official report, Lieut. Snodgrass states: "Lieut. Riches hauled the field gun from No Man's Land with volunteers from battalion headquarters."

A good deal of the success of the operation was due to the thorough preparation beforehand, and the instruction of the company commanders and others in their respective parts and by the C.O. (Lieut.-Colonel J. Newman).

The report for June 4 states that prisoners were still coming in to battalion headquarters. These were Germans who had been overlooked in small posts and dug-outs, and who either surrendered or were rounded up as the area was better examined. In the style of warfare adopted at this time, a much greater area was allotted to units and the posts were scattered both in width and depth, so that it was quite possible for a few of the enemy to be overlooked for a short time. On the other hand, the aggressiveness of the Australian troops was never higher than at this period and frequently a small party consisting of an officer or N.C.O. and a few men, or sometimes several of the Diggers on their own initiative, would take it into their heads to investigate a German post, or go out to silence some machine gun, and there was always a trickle of prisoners coming back. The boys used to call it "peaceful penetration," but the Germans regarded the whole business very seriously. Owing to these small stunts, there was a surprising number of prisoners captured during the time the 1st Australian Division was in the Merris sector.

The 11th Battalion took over the 10th Battalion sector on June 4. It will be remembered that battalion headquarters was already in position, having taken over before the attack on Mont de Merris. "B" and "D" Companies remained in the newly-captured front line, "C" Company was in close support and "A" Company was in reserve. There was a considerable amount of shelling while the relief was in progress, but there were no casualties.

On the night of June 5/6 the 11th Battalion was relieved in the line by the 6th Battalion. As on the relief of the previous night there was a fair amount of enemy shelling, and though the 11th got out without casualties, the 6th Battalion had four men killed and several wounded at Estaminet Corner, on the Strazeele-Vieux Berquin road, as the companies were marching up to the line.

The 11th Battalion moved out to La Brearde, a small hamlet about two miles north of Hazebrouck. The troops were mostly billeted in farms round about.

CHAPTER XLIV

MERRIS

ALL DAY on June 6 the men rested at La Brearde after their strenuous duty in the line. The weather was the lovely French summer at its best and the troops enjoyed the peace and tranquility of the beautiful day. Though their tour of duty had been short the excitement and danger and hard going of a battle are very exhausting, and the reaction generally left the troops very limp and played out. The thing most appreciated was a bath, and wherever possible the men endeavoured to avail themselves of this real luxury. Fortunately, on June 7, the divisional baths were made available to the 11th Battalion and all ranks bathed and were issued with clean underclothing.

While at La Brearde the troops noticed a German aeroplane getting a rough spin from several British 'planes. The German pilot dived for safety and was forced to make a landing about 50 yards from the 12th Battalion lines, less than a mile away, at La Kreule. In reference to this incident, Private H. Spragg writes the following: "The battalion had just come out of the line and some of the lads were kicking a football about in a field near La Brearde. Soon they noticed a couple of our 'planes having a go at a Fritz 'plane. All of a sudden he dived straight down towards the field where the lads were. I was on the Lewis anti-aircraft guard, so opened fire. He did not land, but skimmed along over some trees that lined a road on the edge of the field. I shot a full magazine at him, and the lads said he put up both hands while I was firing (the range was about 100 yards). He crashed about half a mile away and the troops could be seen running in all directions towards the 'plane. I was unable to leave my post, but still have a piece of ply-wood from the 'plane that was souvenired by a cobber. The pilot was wounded and his 'plane riddled with bullets. This 'plane was one of the Scarlet Circus. I do not claim to have brought the 'plane down, but the lads reckoned that I must have hit him when he put his hands up. Anyway, I could hardly have missed him at 100 yards."

June 8 was devoted to a thorough clean up of billets in view of the arrival of the 3rd Battalion, which took over the camp. The 11th Battalion moved to Sercus, arriving about 4:30 p.m., and occupied the same camp to which it had been allotted on its last visit to this area. On the last occasion the weather had been mostly inclement, but this time the weather was almost perfect, and under such conditions Sercus was a splendid camp, situated as it was among shady trees in beautifully grassed parks. The trees offered good cover against enemy aircraft, which were still very active, and the welcome shade was much appreciated by the troops, for bell-tents are extremely hot in the summer time.

Though some of the inhabitants had returned to their farms and houses by the time the troops revisited the district, yet there was little civilian life, and that so completely disorganised that the troops had to find their own recreation and additional comforts in the way of food and drink. Canteens were established and canteen officers were appointed who scoured the back country for tobacco, biscuits, chocolate and beer, and any other commodities that the troops might be expected to buy. These were retailed at the battalion canteen at a reasonable rate. Lieut. Johnny Long officiated in the capacity of canteen officer for the 11th Battalion, and his excursions into the hinterland produced wonderful results.

Training and sports were indulged in for the next few days and there were brigade sports on June 12. It was a great occasion, and the Diggers enjoyed themselves to the full. Not only were there well-contested events, but there were many and amusing impersonations of all sorts of different characters, some world-famous and some well known to the troops. The impersonations were rendered much easier for the troops on account of the easily-procured garments of all kinds from the abandoned farmhouses.

"Charlie Chaplin" was there, and caused great fun with his antics. There were beautiful girls dressed in the latest fashion and they tripped mincingly backwards and forwards, ogling the lads and casting the "glad-eye" hither and yon. They were charming girls until spoken to. A strict censorship is necessary on the remarks of the other Diggers.

The feature of the meeting was the appearance of a splendidly mounted and red-tabbed personage with an orderly, bearing a pennant, following in rear. On all sides could be heard the expression "The Corps Commander." Guards turned out and presented arms, all ranks came to the salute, and the recipient rode up to Brigadier-General Bennett, who raised his hand to salute; but something caught his eye, and he burst out laughing instead. It transpired that the "Corps Commander" was a groom at brigade headquarters and he had made up for the occasion. His impersonation was extremely good and he had all the troops deceived. Unfortunately for the "General" his success made him too popular, and he succumbed to the frequent libations that were pressed upon him in honour of his achievement and he had to be assisted home to his billet. "How are the mighty fallen!"

The whole battalion was engaged in cable-laying on June 14 for five hours—7 a.m. to noon. In the afternoon preparations were made for an early move on the following day. The battalion official report for that move is naive and interesting, suggesting that Lieut. Archibald had returned from hospital and had again assumed the duties of adjutant.

"June 15, 1918. Reveille at 4 a.m. (mon Dieu!). By 6:30 a.m. everything for the move was complete, and we marched out passing the starting point at 7 a.m. and reached our destination near La Kreule, where we bivouaced in a field for the day and night. The simple life indeed, but the lovely weather made the affair a picnic. Advance parties went forward to the line from each company. To-morrow night we move in and take over from the 8th Battalion, holding the Mont de Merris, the very valuable ridge our battalion so recently wrested from the Hun with such *eclat*."

The Higher Command was still very apprehensive over a threatened German attack. Reports from prisoners had all gone to show that this attack was pending. A precautionary stage was therefore adopted by all units near the line. Though the "heads" were windy, this feeling did not affect the troops in any way, and next night the battalion relieved the 8th Battalion on the left sector of the brigade front.

The report of this relief is again reminiscent of "Archie": "June 17, 1918. An excellent relief complete at 1 a.m. without incident. The Hun has been quiet. The weather good to us. 'A' and 'B' Companies are holding the line, 'C' Company in support and 'D' in reserve.

"Precautionary dispositions. Every effort is being made to improve our trenches. The brigade on our right let off cloud gas over Fritz. A new stunt. Fritz got very 'windy' and put down a barrage on our right. He shelled us a little between 10 and 10:30 p.m. We have been very busy since we came in, cutting down crops that impede our view and field of fire—an unavoidable waste. The intelligence officer established a fine O.P. in Strazeele—the one drawback being a dead horse in the doorway! (C'est la guerre.)"

June 18 was a quiet day, and in the fine bright weather numbers of German aeroplanes were doing all kinds of evolutions among the fleecy puffs of bursting shells that the "archies" (anti-aircraft guns) were throwing all around them.

Several very heavy shells were dropped near Botha Farm, where "C" Company's headquarters was situated. After the shelling, Captain Keighley (the I.O.) came over to inspect and report. Botha Farm was pretty decrepit by this time and there were many heaps of fallen brickwork, among which the rats often disported themselves. There were also a few fowls which had managed to elude the troops. After finding out what he wanted, Keighley asked Lieut. Belford (who was O.C. "C" Company) how the commissariat was. "Not so good," was the reply. The dapper Captain immediately said: "I noticed a rooster near the pond, so I'll see what I can do," and drawing his revolver out he went. In a minute there was a fusilade of shots, and back came the Captain and his runner, the latter carrying the mangled remains of a large white rooster, which was handed over to the tender mercies of "C" Company officers' batmen.

It was a welcome addition to the mess. The strange part about the business was how the bird could have survived so long, as the Australians had been over two months in the area and everything was fish that came into the troops' net. It was supposed that the recent shelling must have released it from some place where it had been concealed from the troops.

At this time the battalion was suffering from a plague of boils and, what was worse, a very severe kind of trench fever broke out among the troops. Various names were given to this complaint, Spanish Influenza, La Grippe, or, in the vernacular of the troops, "Dog's Disease." Evacuations soon grew in number and many of the boys carried on with aching heads, painful limbs and high temperatures.

On June 19 the "wind up" of the Higher Command was somewhat alleviated, and the orders to assume normal conditions was once again issued. As far as the troops were concerned this order meant nothing, for there was no noticeable change in the routine.

The following day, which was wet and unpleasant, the 9th Battalion on the right flank and the 3rd Battalion on the left flank both carried out minor operations against the enemy in order to wipe out machine gun posts that had been causing some trouble, and also in pursuance of the policy of continually harassing the enemy. The 9th Battalion advanced its outpost system and the 11th Battalion pushed forward two posts in conformity. The 3rd Battalion was heavily counter-attacked, but managed to repulse the enemy. The 11th Battalion lines suffered a retaliatory barrage. There were six casualties among the troops who formed the patrols and three wounded through shell-fire.

An inter-company relief took place on this date, "C" Company taking over the right sector and "D" Company the left sector of the battalion frontage.

Captain A. S. Keighley, M.C., was transferred to brigade as intelligence officer and Lieut. Walter C. Belford was detailed to act as 11th Battalion Intelligence Officer, Captain J. P. O'Neil, M.C., taking over "C" Company.

The long delayed entry of the American army into the arena of the Great War had at last taken place and details from various units were sent to gain experience in actual line conditions with seasoned battalions in the front trenches. A detail of American troops was attached to the 11th Battalion. These troops were fine specimens physically, but, naturally, were green and fresh to everything. They did not compare very favourably as soldiers with the hard-bitten West Australians, as they were simple and unsophisticated, and it was estimated by the boys that they would be easy marks for the wily Hun when they came to play the game of war with that past master of the art, a conjecture that was only too well borne out by future events.

The American details with the 11th Battalion consisted of an officer, a top-sergeant and several N.C.O.'s. The officer remained at battalion headquarters and the sergeants were allotted to the companies in the line. Most of the Yanks seemed to be good fellows and eager to see a bit of the real thing.

The official diary for June 21 reads: "To-day is very unsettled. The enemy put down a severe barrage on front-line companies in the morning. 'Minnies' (minenwerfer) were chiefly used." And next day this report was entered: "A local enterprise was carried out this (at 2:30 a.m.) morning by Lieut. R. S. Inman and 18 other ranks of 'D' Company against a farm situated opposite our line. Barrage and commencement were carried out as planned. On arrival at farm, as there was no enemy resistance, Lieut. Inman, Sergeant Reed and L/Corporal Emery went forward to a sunken road, on east of farm. A search under Corporal Cross was made for machine gun positions in farmhouse, but none were found. A machine gun post was located about 60 yards east of sunken road. Lieut. Inman, with great gallantry, set out to capture it, when he encountered three of the enemy. One of these was killed by Lieut. Inman and another was wounded. The wounded man and the third man were taken prisoners. The wood-heap near the farm was kerosened and four phosphorus bombs inserted, and it is still burning feebly at time of writing. Owing to the machine gun position abovementioned being in Stokes barrage area, Lieut. Inman was not able to reach it, whereupon he got his party and two prisoners back to our trench 17 minutes after zero. Enemy put up S.O.S. flares and called for destructive fire, which came down at 22 minutes after zero. A very heavy barrage ensued, which resulted in the death of three of the raiding party, three wounded and three buried by shell-fire. Lieut. Inman was severely wounded after reporting the operation concluded. He was evacuated to hospital."

Next day the enemy attempted a raid on "D" Company's posts as a reprisal for the previous day's attack. Under a trench mortar barrage several parties of the enemy attempted to advance, but there was no real spirit behind the attack and the attempts soon petered out under the warm reception the 11th Battalion troops gave the enemy.

Later in the day a very stiff barrage was put down on "D" Company's front and several casualties were incurred, including Acting-C.S.M. Jorgenson and others of "D" Company. In an entry in his diary on this date, No. 5686 Private R. Duncanson writes: "June 23, 1918. We were on a fatigue just before daylight carrying in two dead when a shell dropped on us, killing five out of the stretcher party of six." Duncanson was the only survivor of this party and his diary has a gap of over two months from this date, so that his own wound was no light one.

This barrage happened while the American N.C.O.'s were in the front trenches, and these "Doughboys" received a liberal education during the short time they were in the line. Just before the barrage fell the Germans had their usual pyrotechnic display, and the visitors were duly thrilled. "Say! you guys!" said one of the Yanks, "I guess that beats the 4th of July to a frazzle." But the ensuing bombardment put a different aspect on things. When the shelling and bombing got bad, one Yankee sergeant gave a good exhibition of the snake act, and as the bottom of the trench was of the usual muddy consistency after the late rains, the Yank's efforts to make himself as inconspicuous as possible caused no little amusement among the boys. But it was as nothing to the yell of delight from the Diggers when, after the show was over, the Yank rose triumphantly from the mud and cried: "Waal! you boys, I reckon I didn't show th' white! I didn't show th' white!"

The American officer at battalion headquarters was a very fine fellow, as indeed there were many amongst the Yankees as in every army. He was interested in everything pertaining to the war, and also in the 11th Battalion's methods of running things. He was also impressed with the effect of the German shelling, for which he was wise enough to have a wholesome respect. The headquarters officers, in quiet spells, used to stroll down to Strazeele station, which was about five or six hundred yards to the south, and there gather strawberries from a nice patch they had discovered there. The only fly in the ointment was that Fritz had a habit of shelling the vicinity at any odd hour. This was such a departure from his usual regular habits in this respect that it was most disconcerting to the troops. But the strawberries were worth the risk, and many a visit was paid to the field. On one occasion the American officer was induced to accompany a small party. But this time the boys were unlucky, for the shelling started just as they got to the railway and one or two shells fell uncomfortably close. To one new to the game, like the Yankee officer, it must have seemed that he was the target. The party withdrew and waited, and the Yankee, a little breathless, caused some amusement by saying: "Say! you guys. Do I look as big as the side of a house! Because I sure feel like one." As Fritz kept up his fire it was resolved to return to headquarters, and it was considered a good opportunity to "have a spot."

The whisky bottle was produced and the Yank asked to have a glass, but he muttered something about regulations and politely declined.

Not long afterwards he was sauntering round the ruined farm buildings in which battalion headquarters staff and details were camped. The Germans occasionally used to drop a few heavies round the billet and these shells could be heard coming from a long way off, and when they fell they exploded with a terrific detonation and the countryside was spattered with huge lumps of soil out of the very large craters they formed.

The American officer had a camera and was taking a few snapshots of the buildings and of the Diggers. He asked if one of the boys would take a picture of himself, with a background of ruined barns as local colour. After he had struck a satisfactory attitude, and the camera was being focussed, the well known and dreaded whine of the big German shell could be heard coming closer. All the troops stood fast: there was really nothing else to do; everybody had the feeling that this one was going to land very close, and *close* was right, for with the terrific shriek of its last rush it buried itself just behind the wall where the American was waiting for Kingdom Come. There was a terrific detonation and the wall, the officer and a considerable portion of the landscape were temporarily obliterated from sight.

When the dust and the falling debris began to settle a bit, a white-faced and dusty figure emerged from where the wall used to be, and a husky voice, in which many emotions were mingled, managed to croak: "Say! you guys! I guess I'll hev thet whisky *now*."

He got it, and a long drought was broken.

On June 24 the 1st Australian Division reported that prisoners captured on the previous night stated that an attack was to be made by the Germans on the Mont Des Cats after a heavy bombardment. On receipt of this news new dispositions for a precautionary stage were issued to all battalions.

The enemy also seemed to be in daily fear of an attack and was very nervy, and on the slightest provocation he would send up all kinds of flares and light signals. The American N.C.O. was not far out when he reckoned that the firework display was better than the national celebrations on the 4th of July. On one occasion after the S.O.S. had been sent up by Jerry, his artillery replied promptly, but unfortunately for him the barrage fell short. In reference to this, Private H. Spragg writes: "In the late afternoon Fritz put a heavy barrage down on his own line, and kept it up for some time, too, despite a lot of signals sent up by the troops occupying the trenches. The shells were right on the spot and we could hear the Fritzies screaming, and judging by the numbers we saw they were evidently massed in the trenches for a raid against us. Our artillery pelted shrapnel at them for a while, so the poor blighters had a lively time of it and their casualties must have been heavy."

The official diary for June 25 runs thus: "We have established a record for this tour of duty. To-night the 10th Battalion is to relieve us and we go back to support in Pradelles. Lieut. W. D. Brown and one man were wounded by a 'minnie' to-day. Last night our patrols reported an enemy relief." What the "record" was the compiler has not been able to determine, but the above is typical of the battalion entries.

The relief passed off satisfactorily and the battalion moved back to Pradelles on the night of June 25/26. The support position was a fairly comfortable one. Some of the men were billeted in the ruined village and some were in trenches. Battalion headquarters was situated in the cellar of a one-time brewery, or local "brasserie." This brewery cellar was quite a luxurious place, completely furnished with beds, sheets, blankets, rugs, easy chairs and furniture of all kinds which had been taken from the handsome chateau near by. There was even a complete acetylene lighting plant installed by one of the batmen. This was excellent up to a point, but had this disadvantage that all the lights would be snuffed out every time a shell landed in the vicinity, which was too often to be pleasant, as the inhabitants of the cellar were nearly suffocated by the abominable odour of the escaping gas and they had to take shelter outside until the air inside had cleared sufficiently to be breathable. Still, this was only a minor disadvantage compared with the real comforts that the cellar afforded.

After June 27, eight officers and over 200 men were detailed nightly on engineers' fatigues, and in addition two parties of 20 men each from "C" Company, under Lieuts. Simpson and Elliot, were sent up to the assistance of the 10th Battalion on June 28 to act as carrying-parties during a minor operation that the 10th was carrying out to keep the opposing artillery busy, what time the 31st British Division carried out an attack of some importance on the right. The 10th Battalion made a successful advance at the expense of comparatively few casualties. In the 10th Battalion official report it states, *inter alia*: "During the day of the 28th inst. (i.e., June) very valuable work was done by carrying-parties from the 11th Battalion."

When this attack was on there was a good deal of enemy shelling directed at Pradelles and the support lines generally. There was a battery position a few hundred yards south of 11th Battalion headquarters, and this position was well and truly strafed by Fritz. The shooting was very accurate and the watching infantrymen were full of admiration for the gunners who stuck to their guns among that hail of shells. One of the guns was knocked out, and the watchers could not see the others for smoke, shell bursts and dust. Still the remaining guns kept on firing. It was a very heartening sight for the boys to see these fine fellows and to know that when they themselves were in the line that they had such troops to back them up.

On June 30 the strength of the battalion was 28 officers and 548 other ranks. The total casualties for the month were: officers, killed, 1; wounded, 5; sick, 1. Other ranks: killed, 19; wounded, 196; missing, 10; sick, 125. Total, 355.

The artillery suffered another barrage while the 11th Battalion was in Pradelles, but this one had its humorous side and the footsloggers felt that they had got a little bit of their own back for the short-shooting on some of their comrades by the artillery, although the whole affair was quite accidental on their part.

Pradelles church had been rather knocked about by enemy shell-fire, though the church steeple was mostly intact. The rooster that did duty for a weather-cock had been knocked sideways and looked in imminent danger of falling down at any time, so some of the members of the battalion staff thought that they might indulge in a little rifle practice as well as perform a service to the community, so they spent a couple of hours trying to knock down that battered old bird. At last it toppled down among the loose slates of the church roof just as a pair of breathless artillery officers dashed up, waving their arms and trying to voice their indignation at the outrage that the infantrymen were perpetrating. The party tried to explain that the bird would have fallen at any time, but when the gunners had found their breath properly they said they were not worrying about the damned weathercock, but they complained that there had been a well-directed fire falling on their battery position for the last two hours and none of their men had been game to leave their dug-outs. It was some time before the gunner officers could see the joke, but the footsloggers were much tickled with the idea of an infantry barrage on the artillery. At any rate peace was soon established in the old-accepted manner, to the sound of those wonderful words, "Here's how!"

At the beginning of July, 1918, the 11th Battalion was garrisoning the outer defences of Strazeele. These defences were of great strategical importance, as they commanded a wide area of country and also the ridge on which they were situated formed an effective screen for the country behind and the important railway junction of Hazebrouck. The Brigadier complimented the battalion on the fine siting of the trenches and their general arrangement and cleanliness. The troops were in fine fettle and the weather was now beautifully warm and pleasant.

Lieut. R. W. Blair, who had been signal officer to the 11th Battalion, left at this time to join the air force, and Lieut. Frank Goundrey was appointed in his place.

Major-General Sir H. B. Walker, the divisional commander, who had been in command of the 1st Division since its arrival in France over two years before, was transferred to a command on the Italian front, and Major-General Glasgow was appointed in his place and took over the command of the 1st Division at this time.

For the first few days of July the troops were employed on fatigue parties assisting the engineers in the construction of defensive works. The Germans were very nervous and frequently indulged in violent bursts of shelling. After a very severe bout of shelling on July 4 the enemy attempted to raid the 10th Battalion, but he was repulsed with much slaughter.

The 11th Battalion was ordered to "stand to," but its services were not required. During this barrage all the signal wires were cut and communication could only be made by runner. A fine run was made by No. 5134 Private Ramsay, who took a message to Strazeele garrison and back in record time, although he was badly gassed in passing through the barrage. There were several casualties due to shelling and gas.

On July 5 the battalion salvage party, under Lieut. L. Riches, sent back over two tons of sheet copper which had been salvaged mostly from the brewery. As copper was then in the vicinity of £210 per ton, the day's work must have been regarded as profitable.

Naturally, as the civilian population had left so hurriedly, there was a great deal of useful material in the district, which was only being gradually destroyed, so the higher authorities ordered all intact articles to be collected and sent to the various battalion quartermasters, who forwarded the salvaged articles to central depots with the map locations of the places at which the articles were salvaged marked on each article, so that the civilian population could claim their property "Apres la guerre."

Many and weird were the articles salvaged, and many of the articles found new owners. There were pieces of furniture, curios, shot guns, copper and brassware, bedsteads, crockery and carpets and other things too numerous to mention. The writer saw a pair of venerable cross-bows complete with steel quarrels, and some of the Diggers were heard to remark that they wouldn't mind the risk of a daylight raid if Fritzy used these weapons instead of their machine guns. Truly war had assumed a deadliness unknown in the old days.

The quartermaster (Captain Geoff. Egg) had occasion to complain to Riches that he was not particular enough about putting on the correct map locations on the articles that his men had salvaged, and that division was kicking up a fuss. Riches grinned, and said he would attend to the matter, so that day he salvaged a rather intimate article of furniture on which he affixed a very large placard bearing the legend, "This was found at W.C. Central" and left division to make the best of it.

The 2nd Battalion relieved the 11th Battalion on July 6 and the 11th moved back to bivouacs at La Kreule, in a field less than a mile from Hazebrouck. The next day was Sunday, and a special parade was held before General Sir William Birdwood on the parade ground of the 10th Battalion. Each battalion of the brigade was represented by 200 men and "Birdie" presented medals and ribbons to officers, N.C.O.'s and men of the 3rd Brigade.

For the next week there was the customary programme of training, sports and fatigues, with inoculation to add a spice of variety. Hazebrouck was strictly out of bounds to all troops, but that only made the place more desirable and many of the boys visited the deserted town and some came back with all sorts of things, including a lot of wearing apparel. It was also strange under the circumstances where many articles of furniture came from, for messes and offices were well supplied in this respect.

It was while the 11th Battalion was at this camp that Colonel Brennan, the famous "Doc" Brennan of Gallipoli days, visited his old friends in the battalion. The officers made it a festive occasion and a special dinner was put on at mess that evening with all the frills. The battalion band was detailed to attend and furnish sweet music while the dinner was in progress. Unfortunately, that afternoon there had been sports, and the band had been in attendance. The players had been thirsty and the heat of the afternoon had been mitigated by copious ambrosial draughts from which the musicians had barely recovered when their services were requisitioned again.

However, they did their best, and painstakingly massacred some well-known tunes. Some more liquid refreshment was sent out in the hope of improving matters, but it was no good. One by one the bandsmen deserted their posts, and finally there were only three players left—the bandmaster, the big drummer and the trombonist. The others had vanished. Bandmaster Balling was doing his best with a cornet and was waving his baton frantically as he played, but he could not do much on his own for by this time the drummer had frankly given up the unequal contest and all the trombonist could do was to dribble into his instrument. Everyone was in fits of laughter over the band, but the residue had to remain on duty until the King was "drunk." A veil must be drawn over that, and then the adjutant came out and dismissed the three survivors. It was a great night.

Padre O'Donnell joined the 11th Battalion at this time and, being a newcomer, it was some time before he found a niche. Consequently for the first day or two he used to wander about alone. On one occasion he had strolled down to a pond in the middle of the field where the battalion lines were situated. Here he stood with his hands behind his back, contemplating the little ripples on the water and the dragonflies and the reflections of the trees mirrored in the water. Unknown to him, Lieut. George Lamerton tip-toed up behind him with a Very-light pistol, and while the padre was pondering over his Sunday's discourse Lamerton fired a flare between the chaplain's legs into the water. What with the "pop" of the shot, the hiss of the flare and the subsequent splash and disturbance in the pond the poor padre got the shock of his life, and only saved himself falling in the pond by hanging on to Lamerton, who had rushed to his side. This episode broke the ice, and the padre soon became one of the battalion.

At this period of the battalion's history the Powers-that-Were tried to encourage baseball among the troops, possibly because of the arrival of the Americans in France and the desire to promote "L'entent cordiale." At any rate a set of baseball gear was purchased and several attempts made to get the lads to play.

On the night of July 13/14 the 11th Battalion relieved the 6th Battalion in the line. The relief was carried out successfully, battalion taking over a farmhouse near "The Brickfields" and the companies were disposed as follows: "C" and "B" Companies in the line, right and left respectively, "D" Company in support and "A" in reserve.

As the country in this area had not had any very heavy fighting over it, a great many of the gardens were practically untouched, and now in the height of summer many of these gardens were glowing with flowers, some of them being beautiful roses. It was always sad to see these evidences of human care lying neglected beside the empty houses that only a few months back were happy homes where the industrious Madame and her fair daughters lived. The beauty of the flowers in this battle area recalled the quatrain of Omar Khayam—

"I sometimes think that never blows so red
  The rose, as where some buried Cæsar bled;
  That every hyacinth the garden wears
  Dropt in its lap from some once lovely head."

It was in such a farm that the 11th Battalion headquarters was situated, just alongside the old rifle range that the troops used soon after their arrival in France over two years before, when they were billeted at Fletre and when they used to visit all the pleasant farms and villages that were now lying around in ruins. What a lot had happened in those two years of the battalion's history!

Now began a series of minor operations, almost unique in the history of the war. The 1st Australian Division had shown such a marked superiority over the Boche that the troops were once more the audacious, casual soldiers that were the envy of all unit commanders who saw them in action, and the glory and pride of all who had the good fortune to command them. This description may seem somewhat bombastic, but the reader is asked to suspend his judgment for a short time until the opinion of the British divisions and their commanders, with whom the 1st Australian Division was associated, is set forth. The boys themselves tempered their recklessness with the skill acquired in the years of fighting, and during the month of July the line troops carried out daylight raids and patrols nearly every day, harassing the troops opposite them and making their lives an intolerable burden. A little advance would be made here, and a farm snatched there, or a few posts would be mopped up with very few casualties on the Australian side but with heavy casualties for such small operations on the German side. A typical entry is on July 17: "Enemy shelling has been livelier to-day. The employment of mules for carrying rations has worked very well indeed, and undoubtedly it has saved us a number of casualties. Patrol work is very active.

"The O.C. 'D' Company (Captain Tulloch) this morning did some very useful daylight patrol work in the outskirts of Merris, and discovered a couple of enemy posts that he (the enemy) occupied at night only. Captain Tulloch attempted to get into Merris, but he was observed by the enemy and driven back by machine gun fire after gaining a lot of very useful information and locating three enemy machine gun posts that had been giving us trouble."

The use of the mules for carrying rations had been ordered by the C.O. (Lieut.-Colonel J. Newman) several days before. Colonel Newman had always the welfare of the boys at heart, so much so that he often made himself unpopular with brigade and division rather than let his men down or be imposed on. One day about this time, when the 11th Battalion received a severe strafing, because the battalion had the lowest return of *fat* in the division for a certain week (this fat was supposed to be sent back for the purpose of making munitions) Lieut.- Colonel Newman sent a strong letter saying that he would never be a party to the mulcting of the men's rations for the honour and glory of sending the highest fat return to division. He stated that the rations were quite slender enough, and that all the fat was required to make energy-giving meals to the troops. Not only did Newman try to get a good spin for the boys but he personally saw to it that hot meals and other comforts went to the line all the time that he was in command.

Owing to the constant moving forward and the construction of strong points in conjunction with the advances made, there was a great amount of war material lying about, and consequently in addition to their other duties the troops had a great deal of salvaging to do and much material was sent back to the dumps. The troops also did a good bit of salvaging on their own. In the support lines in the trench not far from Strazeele, most of the troops had their trench shelters lined with sheets taken from the cottages, "to keep away the chats" one of the lads volunteered with a grin.

The country in which the battalion was operating was covered with crops of all kinds—wheat, roots and an occasional field of hops. Summer was at its height and the growth was at its maximum, and it was easy for runners and visiting officers to get from post to post by crawling in daylight along the hedges or through the crops. The Germans had many snipers posted in cunningly-concealed places, and occasionally these marksmen took toll of some of the more adventurous or careless troops. On one occasion Lieut. McGuire, of "C" Company, rallied one of the boys for crawling between his post and the next one, stating that he himself often *walked* across. That same evening McGuire was found lying dead between the two posts. The pitcher had gone to the well once too often.

On July 18 the divisional boundary was extended to the south and as the 11th Battalion was the right flank battalion of the 3rd Brigade sector, "C" Company took over a company frontage from the 1st Border Regiment. The battalion's front was now the widest that had been held up to this date in the brigade since Lagnicourt. The posts were in some cases 150 yards apart, and most of them lay on an exposed knuckle of country under complete command by the enemy machine gunners from Merris and Meteren.

During the day there was a fair amount of shelling with "whizz-bangs" and 5.9's. As the enemy was now using the instantaneous fuses on nearly all his shells the air was filled with flying splinters, and casualties were hardly avoidable during even light shelling.

Captain J. S. D. Walker, M.C. (with shovel), and Lieuts. Elliot and Riches near Merris. (Official Photo.)

On July 19 a fine daylight raid and advance was made by the 9th Battalion, in which the Queenslanders captured 98 prisoners and a quantity of machine guns and other war material. The 11th Battalion had to conform to this advance, but owing to the exposed position of the line companies there was a good deal of delay and difficulty before this operation could be accomplished. The 9th (Scottish) Division on the left attacked Meteren on the above date, and consequently the Germans were stirred up and very vigilant. Intercepted wireless messages pointed to a projected counter-attack by the enemy, so second-Lieutenant J. Moss was sent up with a platoon to reinforce "A"

Company. During the heavy shelling which followed, Moss and five others were killed and thirteen men were wounded.

After two days of unsatisfactory attempts to get forward, during which projector gas was used against the enemy, a definite move forward was made on July 21 against Gerbedoen Farm, an enemy strong point. During the preliminary stages, that fine soldier, Captain J. S. D. Walker, M.C., was shot dead while attempting to get forward in daylight. There was to have been a supporting artillery barrage, but it was weak and ill-directed and many shells fell on the outposts. The divisional artillery had been ordered to support the Scotties on the left and possibly the batteries had not switched back to the targets on their own divisional front. Lieut. L. Riches was sent up to take charge of "A" Company, and before nightfall Gerbedoen Farm was captured, along with some prisoners and two minenwerfers. The enemy shelling and machine gun fire was well directed and concentrated throughout, but good work was done by Lieut. W. Gudgeon, M.C., and his platoon, and the outpost line was advanced generally and the new line handed over to the 10th Battalion that same night, and the 11th Battalion moved back to the support position with battalion headquarters in the small chateau at Pradelles.

On July 22, the following complimentary message to the 1st Division was received from the 9th (Scottish) Division, one of the most distinguished divisions in the British Army, and one that had a record second to none:—

"I wish to thank you for the effective support given by your field artillery and light trench mortar batteries in our operations yesterday, as well as for the energetic action of your infantry on our right flank, which I am glad to see resulted in the capture of a large number of prisoners.

"In April we owed much to the admirable defences of the Hollebeke sector, which we took over from your division a few days before the battle (the Battle of the Lys, when the Germans broke through at Armentieres) commenced, and during the last two months *we have admired the successful activity of your troops in defence.*

"Permit me to say on behalf of my division that we sincerely hope *that the 1st Australian Division may be on our flank when active operations are resumed.*"

Even the most unbiassed reader must confess that a higher compliment was hardly possible from one division to another, and the whole of the above message showed the remarkable appreciation that the "Jocks" always had for the "Aussies," a feeling that was wholly reciprocated.

For a week the 11th Battalion lay in support and suffered a fair amount of shelling, especially "D" Company, which occupied the Strazeele defences. "D" Company was so worn out with the constant shell-fire that "B" Company was sent to relieve the former company.

A large proportion of the battalion was being used nightly on fatigues.

The house where battalion headquarters was billeted was surrounded by a large moat. The house had been considerably knocked about by enemy shelling, but it was in a fair state of repair on the side away from the trenches. Besides the battalion staff, most of the headquarters details were quartered in the building or outhouses attached thereto. Strange to relate, there were still some large pike remaining in the shallow water of the moat, and the boys used to kill these by stunning them with a rifle bullet fired into the water alongside. On one occasion "Darkie" Smith, of the intelligence section, was wandering round the moat with his rifle at the ready. As soon as he disappeared round the angle of the house one of the intelligence boys dashed out and placed a stuffed heron, that had been found among a collection of birds in one of the rooms, in a most realistic attitude among some rushes at the end of the moat. When "Darkie" got round to the other side of the house his quick eye immediately spotted the the bird, and he fired point blank.

The heron was still there after the first shot, so "Darkie" took careful aim and knocked its head clean off and was surprised to see the bird still standing upright in the same position. A roar of laughter burst from a lot of his cobbers who had been watching, and "Darkie" had to grin at his own discomfiture as he reckoned he ought to have known it was a plant when the bird did not fly away at the first shot.

On July 28 the 11th Battalion supplied over 200 men on working parties as well as 100 men to assist the 10th Battalion, which was preparing for an attack on Merris. This attack was entirely successful, the more so that the enemy was evidently preparing to evacuate a position that had been rendered almost untenable by the constant attacks and raids made on it by the 3rd Brigade during the previous fighting. A good haul of prisoners was made, 120 unwounded Germans being counted on the night of the stunt and more were expected to come through in the morning. A party of the 11th Battalion was sent up before the position was consolidated to assist in getting back the prisoners and "C" Company moved up to a position in support of the 10th Battalion.

This attack and capture of Merris has been described as the "greatest one-battalion stunt in the war," and Colonel Wilder-Neligan, of the 10th Battalion, received congratulations for his brilliant strategy from Army Headquarters downwards. It is only fair to state here that the plans for this attack were drawn up by Colonel John Newman, of the 11th Battalion, who had been given instructions from General Glasgow to draw up a scheme for capturing the village. This he did, and the attack by the 10th Battalion was based on his plan. This in no way lessens the brilliant action of the 10th Battalion nor the skill with which the operation was carried out, but it is only just to give credit to the originator of the sound strategy of the plan of attack who was, as stated above, Colonel Newman, of the 11th Battalion.

Lieut.-Colonel John Newman, D.S.O.

An advance party from the 6th Battalion arrived and went forward to the trenches, and next day the 11th Battalion relieved the 7th Battalion in the second zone between Borre and Rouge Croix. During the relief "D" Company had the misfortune to have one of its platoons hit by a shell and two men were killed and eight men wounded. The trenches in the reserve area that the battalion took over were in good order and were clean and dry. It will be observed that these trenches were taken over from an Australian battalion.

The last day of July, 1918, was spent in overhauling kit and weapons and in resting after a hard month's work.

On August 1 the battalion moved from Borre siding by route-march and bivouaced at La Kreule. The second zone area was handed over to the 29th British Division.

The battalion transport left by road for the Heuringhem area. This was the XV Corps reserve area.

The 1st Australian Division was still in the XV Corps under General de Lisle, while all the other Australian divisions were under General Monash, in the Somme area, near Amiens.

Chapter XLV

THE GREAT PUSH: LIHON'S RIDGE AND
CREPY WOOD

ON THE MORNING of August 2 the 11th Battalion paraded early and marched to an embussing point from which the troops had a bus ride to Campagne, a moderately large village situated near St. Omer and the XVth Corps reserve area. This was the battalion's good-bye to the fighting in the northern sector, where it had been engaged in so many battles and had so distinguished itself. A pleasant few days were spent in the vicinity of St. Omer, which was the most important town in the neighbourhood and was situated on the canal running from the Lys to the coast at Calais. It was a very ancient town and noted for many things in connection with the war. It was for a long time the headquarters of the British Army in France, the famous G.H.Q., which was subsequently transferred to Montreuil. It was at St. Omer that Lord Roberts died in the early days of the war, and it was the headquarters of the Inland Water Transport that fed the front by means of the network of canals. The barges that the boys used to unload at Sailly and Bac St. Maur were controlled from St. Omer. The town was a fairly good shopping centre and much more French than Flemish in all its ways, thus being quite a change from the towns further east. There was a very large aerodrome near Longueness, only a mile or two distant, and the presence of the gallant young airmen did much to keep the town lively.

Campagne was a clean-looking village in hilly country southwest of St. Omer. Here the 11th Battalion was reorganised and deficiencies were made up. The battalion was mainly resting and the boys had a good opportunity of looking round the country. There were several "Archie" batteries round about with powerful searchlights to defend the big aerodrome not far off. About a mile or two away from Campagne in a big natural basin-shaped depression a large camp was noticed, and here, tucked away out of sight of all the world, were the tents of our good allies, the Portuguese.

It was now learned that the 1st Australian Division was to be transferred to the Somme, and was to be combined with the other four Australian divisions under General Monash; and in view of this the following letter from XV Corps headquarters was ordered to be promulgated to all troops of the 1st Division:

> XV Corps Headquarters,
> August 4, 1918.
>
> Major-General T. W. Glasgow, C.B., C.M.G., D.S.O., Commanding 1st Australian Division.
>
> "Before your magnificent division leaves my corps, I wish to thank you and all ranks under your command for the exceptional services rendered during the past four months.
>
> "Joining this corps on April 26, during the Battle of the Lys, the division selected and prepared a position to defend the Hazebrouck front, and a few days later repulsed two heavy attacks with severe losses to the enemy. *This action brought the enemy's advance to a standstill.*
>
> "Since then, the division has held the *most important sector* of this front continuously, and by skilful raiding and minor operations has advanced the line over a mile, on a front of 5,000 yards, *capturing just short of* 1,000 *prisoners,* and causing such damage to the troops of the enemy that *nine divisions have been replaced.*
>
> "The complete success of all minor operations, the skill displayed by the patrols by day as well as by night, the gallantry and determination of the troops and their *high state of training and discipline* have excited the admiration and emulation of all, and I desire that you will convey to all ranks my appreciation of their fine work and my regret that the division is leaving my command.
>
> "(Sgd.) Beauvoir De Lisle,
> Lieut.-General Commanding XV Corps."

Such a generous statement made by an officer of such wide experience as General De Lisle, on the top of the complimentary message from the 9th (Scottish) Division on July 22, is convincing proof of the efficiency of the 1st Australian Division as a fighting force, and the fact that the 11th Battalion had headed the list with the number of prisoners captured in the division and that the 3rd Brigade had captured considerably more than half of the above total should make any man proud to have belonged to such a division, such a brigade and, above all, to such a battalion as the 11th.

The whole encomium must be gratifying to any Australian, and is a sufficient refutation to all those who have decried Australian troops as lacking in training and discipline.

On August 6 the battalion marched to St. Omer, where the troops bivouaced in the old barrack square for a few hours and then entrained and travelled by Abbeville to Longpre. The entraining was carried out in the record time of five minutes. "B" Company was detailed as a loading party for brigade and travelled separately, entraining at Wizernes. On arrival at Longpre, hot cocoa was served and then the battalion marched to Long on August 7. The same day the 1st Division moved up to the war zone, the 11th Battalion travelling by motor bus from Longpre to Coisy, which was reached at the ghastly hour of 1:30 a.m. on August 8. From there the battalion marched to Cardonette, where it was billeted in dreary houses and barns for the rest of the night. At 2 p.m. the troops were on the march again. It was misty at first and there was a drizzling rain, and the last salvoes of a heavy bombardment could be heard over to the east.

As visibility increased great numbers of aeroplanes could be seen all over the sky; there were big squadrons of bombing 'planes making for the German rear areas. Reports began to filter through of a successful advance on a wide front and the appearance of droves of prisoners coming from the direction of the front lines lent colour to the rumours. The battalion marched through Allonville, Querrieu, Pont Noyelles and over the rivers Ancre and Somme at La Neuville and Fouilloy, finally finishing up near Hamel about 9 p.m., where the troops bivouaced for the night. There were now plenty of evidences that a successful advance had taken place and word came through that the Australian divisions engaged had been well to the fore and had advanced seven or eight miles with very light casualties. This sounded something like an advance, and was a great improvement on the usual miserable and dearly-bought advances of a hundred or two yards that were all the gains in the previous piecemeal policies. In the confusion of the big advance there was a lot of gear left about, and Lieut. Riches managed to secure a motor bike, which soon elicited a "please explain." It was noticed with a considerable amount of surprise that the terrain round the jump-off lines, that is, the country in which the other Australians had been fighting for some time, had been shelled only lightly compared to the trenches the 1st Australian Division had lately come from. The troops had expected to see a much more battered country.

Early next morning Lieut. Jerry McKenna (the works officer) and the I.O. were sent ahead to spy out the land. These officers were instructed to take bicycles, but having had experience of the heavy military bikes on previous occasions they

Infantry of 1st Australian Division moving up to attack near Harbonnieres, August, 1918. (Official Photo.)

determined to walk and trust to getting a lift. They set out for Rozieres. It was a wonderful experience to wander all over the newly-captured ground and see all the wreck that the swift tide of war had left in its wake. There were tanks which had been blown up by land mines, and occasionally one that had suffered from a direct hit. Here there was a captured German battery and there a bunch of trench mortars. Newly-wrecked aeroplanes of both sides lay shattered here and there, while enemy material of all kinds was lying around. On the roads were the corpses of horses and mules and, occasional, still, grotesquely-lying figures in field grey were encountered. Newly-constructed works and some in process of construction had been abandoned everywhere. All the billets and dug-outs smelt of Fritz, and this is no mere figure of speech, because any confined space lately occupied by the enemy had a peculiar and never-to-be-forgotten smell, a musty odour savouring something of garlic and new leather and frowsy humanity.

The journey was continued through Warfusee-Abancourt and Lamotte and on to Bayonvillers. Everywhere were the signs of a swift retreat, though signs of attempts at hasty demolition by the German engineers were also apparent. At a field kitchen a drink of tea and some breakfast was offered and gladly accepted, and the Diggers told of the great advance of the day before. Everyone was elated, and the constant passing back of prisoners to the "cages" showed that the good work was still going on. Not far from Harbonnieres a gunner officer hailed the two 11th fellows. It was Oscar Zehnder, of the 8th Battery (A.I.F.). He told great tales of the artilleryman's dream; that of galloping into action, and on the command "Action front!" wheeling to find a living target, at which shooting could be done over open sights. It was a great experience for the artillery after years of dug-in positions and "blind" firing.

At Harbonnieres was a scene of bustle, but an activity without confusion. Everything pointed to an efficient organisation behind the Great Push. All ranks were confident in the new leadership that had so ably co-ordinated all arms and was utilising the whole resources of the army as an inter-dependent unity instead of heretofore as a conglomeration of individual arms.

Harbonnieres church had been used by the Germans as an O.P. and there was a well-equipped signal station in the sanctuary, with wires running in all directions. Some of the treasures of the church were lying scattered about, and there was a complete set of model animals possibly from some Noah's Ark set littered about the floor. The church had been shelled a good deal.

At the railway line, where it crossed the road just east of Harbonnieres, it was noticed that the Germans had tried to blow up the permanent way in several places, but already preparations were being made to repair the damage.

Further forward the 2nd Australian Division and the 2nd Brigade were making an attack in the direction of Crepy Wood and Lihons. After finding out these particulars, the two officers returned to Hamel to find the 11th Battalion already on the move. Colonel Newman gave the reconnoitring party a severe wigging for not taking bicycles as ordered, and after he had received the report he ordered the officers to follow on as quickly as they could. All kits and gear had been packed for the transport, but the tender hearts of the company cooks made them produce a nice snack from the travelling cooker, and the two tired warriors sat down by the wayside and refreshed themselves. The remaining companies passed at recognised intervals and many were the sarcastic remarks directed at the pair as to whether they had definitely retired from the war or were only malingering. The battalion was soon overhauled, as owing to many halts it was only making slow progress, owing to the great congestion of traffic moving up to the front line. The battalion made for Harbonnieres and passed that village about 4:30 p.m. Fritz was shelling Harbonnieres with heavy stuff and the buildings were going up in the air. The troops were halted in the open not far from Vauvillers alongside some old brickworks. When the 11th Battalion transport pulled in, the men made their lines close to the deep trenches where the clay for the bricks had been excavated. The 9th Battalion transport men had got in first and all their horses were snugly ensconsed in the deep trenches with only their heads above the level of the ground. The 11th boys were so weary that they did not even throw up the prescribed earth wall to protect their horses from the effects of bombs and shells.

As the battalion was having its evening meal a 'plane swooped down and dropped several bombs on the transport lines. None of the 11th Battalion horses was injured, although several had minor scratches, but the carefully-housed 9th Battalion horses suffered considerably, many of them being killed outright. The "daisy-cutters" dropped by the 'plane had burst flatly along the ground, and while the pieces flew harmlessly under the legs of the horses standing in the open, the horses, in what were regarded as ideal shelters, suffered. Fate is surely a blind goddess.

The same 'plane that bombed the transports made off towards Framerville and immediately set fire to several kite balloons, one of which had been following up the advance and had only been newly elevated. The observers could be seen floating earthwards on their parachutes, swinging to and fro in long arcs.

Several reliable observers have stated that the aeroplane mentioned above was a British or at least Allied 'plane which had mistaken its targets, but it was so low that this is hardly credible, and as before mentioned there had been some difficulty in distinguishing the markings on some of the newer German 'planes from those of Allied 'planes.

The men had just settled down for the night when orders were given for a further advance closer up to the line. This was done in the darkness over more or less open country. When the troops halted in front of Vauvillers, instructions were issued for the attack which was to be made at dawn the following morning. The attack was to be made by the 9th and 11th Battalions, and the 12th Battalion was to support the 11th. It was a difficult kind of an attack to make, for the 11th Battalion as left battalion was to pivot on its left flank and take Crepy Wood in its advance. The objectives were marked as brown and blue lines, but as these convey nothing to the average reader it is better to state that the ground to be attacked consisted of a ridge of high ground in the neighbourhood of the village of Lihons. There were several small woods on the ridge, named respectively Crepy Wood, Auger Wood and Cressaire Wood, which offered considerable difficulty, and there was an elaborate system of old and new trenches running all through the sector which added to the defensibility from the enemy point of view.

The troops were very weary, having had several broken nights in succession and days of long marches, but otherwise they were in goood heart and keen to have a go at the open warfare that they had heard so much about.

The morning dawned very mistily and the battalion moved forward in artillery formation—"A," "B" and "C" Companies in attack and "D" Company in support. The mist soon cleared away and the attacking columns of the 9th Battalion could be seen converging on the 11th Battalion's objective. At the same time a German aeroplane sailed over, and when the pilot or observer saw the advancing troops he fired several white flares. Immediately a heavy rifle and machine gun fire burst on the advancing troops, who at once charged and went through the

7th Battalion troops who were holding the line. The German 'plane came sailing back and sprayed the attackers with lead. A scattered artillery fire also fell on the attacking waves. The supporting fire was almost useless, as far as the attack was concerned, being far too far forward. Back came the German 'plane with the observer leaning well out. He was fired at by every Australian within range, but he only waved his hand in a gesture of derision and farewell and skimmed on at a great speed. Most of the troops fired directly at the 'plane instead of aiming a good way in front, and consequently most of the bullets passed harmlessly behind.

The jumping-off line was not as far ahead as the operation order indicated, or rather the troops holding the line were not so far forward as supposed, and long before they reached their jumping-off mark the 11th Battalion boys were met by a deadly and well sustained machine gun fire. On they dashed and into the maze of trenches, and an almost hand-to-hand battle took place. Many on both sides were shot through the head at close range. A battery of German 4.2 guns that had been firing at close quarters was rushed and captured by "D" Company. Several prisoners were taken belonging to the 19th Bavarian Regiment. The troops pressed on. Officers and men went down, but the advance was one of the finest in the history of the battalion. Rifle and machine gun fire from the flanks and from the front could not stop the charge. Captain Le Nay fell and with him the gallant Lieut. Jim Aitken, who had been at the Landing at Anzac and in most of the big stunts since that day. Lieut. George Lamerton was killed, and Lieuts. Gemmell, Black and Sharp and many good N.C.O.'s and men gave their lives in this attack. Lieut. Harry Naylor was killed early in the action and five more officers were wounded, including Lieut. M. E. (Dick) Clarke, who was shot through both eyes and had a frightful wound. The machine gun fire was intense. The 12th Battalion following 1,000 yards behind suffered many casualties, including their C.O. (Lieut.-Colonel Elliot).

After a stiff resistance the enemy was eventually pushed off the ridge at Auger Wood, and the troops under Captain Jack O'Neil followed up and penetrated to the further side of the wood where they took up a strong defensive position. There was a big gap on the left of the 11th Battalion which remained open during most of the tour in the line, but which was patrolled from time to time. There was also a gap on the right between the 9th and later the 10th Battalion, but this was to a large extent covered by Lieut. C. Gostelow with his two platoons of "D" Company, and also to a less extent by the men of "C" Company under Captain O'Neil, who were a long way ahead

Newly-captured trench at Lihons, August 10, 1918.

of the rest of the troops and had a fine field of fire to their front and to their left. The rest of the companies took up positions in the old French trenches, as there was still a good deal of stubborn resistance by the Germans among the maze of trenches. The Germans were using a good deal of gas shell and the fumes hung about, chiefly in the wooded country on the right of the sector.

There was considerable enfilade sniping along the road in which battalion headquarters was occupying a shallow dug-out, and several men were killed in the vicinity. Battalion headquarters was later shifted to a deep dug-out with a face-cut shelter built into the trench above it.

The following is part of the 3rd Brigade report for August 10: "In the morning the battalions moved forward—11th on the left, 9th on the right, 12th left support, 10th right support. The advance was across open flat ground, cut by a few roads bordered by trees, to the high ground above Bois Crepy (Crepy Wood) and Lihons. There is a low, bare hill on the left of the 11th. The remains of the old French defences of 1916 are just being met with. The 2nd Brigade had not reached the red line, and consequently our troops, even before reaching the front line, met with terrific machine gun fire and moderate hostile barrage. Our barrage was wretched—skimpy and without sting; what is worse the start line was 700 yards short of the red line. This allowed room for most of the Boche machine guns to be on our side of the start line."

In spite of such an unfavourable start, and against well-organised enemy resistance, the battalion had managed to make headway.

The 12th Battalion had been detailed to support the 11th Battalion and Lieut.-Colonel Newman was depending on using these troops, if occasion should arise. As the existing frontage was now too wide for his numerically weak battalion, Newman sent to the 12th Battalion for a company to fill the gaps, but the 12th Battalion had been drawn into the fighting on the right, by the orders of Lieut.-Colonel Neligan, and neither he nor 3rd Brigade headquarters had advised Newman of the fact. This left Newman in an awkward position, and orders had to be given for the left flank to be sent back to gain touch with the brigade on the left, which had not moved forward. This seriously hampered the advance of the battalion, but with the help of the 3rd L.T.M. Battery the situation was relieved and later satisfactorily adjusted in spite of all the difficulties and setbacks. The 10th Battalion, which had gone to the assistance of the 9th, was particularly hard pressed in Crepy Wood and for a long time there was a strenuous battle there in which Captain Billy McCann, of the 10th Battalion, particularly distinguished himself.

The action of Lieut.-Colonel Wilder-Neligan in taking the support battalion of the 11th was high-handed in the extreme. Neligan was a soldier of outstanding personality, who had great influence at brigade and division. This influence he did not hesitate to use for his own advantage when occasion offered without consideration of the needs of his fellow battalion commanders in the brigade.

The 11th Battalion official diary of August 10, 11 and 12 thus describes the engagement after the opening stages: "At midday two platoons of the support company ('D' Company) were sent forward to assist—one to the centre company and the other under Lieut. H. L. Evans—to hold the gap between the centre and left company.

"The remnant of 'D' Company was sent forward at noon to the right flank, the O.C. (Lieut. C. A. P. Gostelow) taking over the command of 'B' Company, as the enemy was reported by our patrols to be massing on our right front. The enemy then counter-attacked the right and centre companies but was driven back with heavy losses, the two Vickers guns that had been sent forward materially assisting.

"As the four companies were now committed to the attack a company of the 12th Battalion was sent forward to help us, one platoon of which carried forward. This company was not, however, used in the actual fighting on our front and was later withdrawn to assist the battalion on our right.

"Sixteen men under Corporal Grubnau were then sent to us for carrying duty by the 3rd Brigade Mining Company, and rendered yeoman service. At nightfall everything possible was done to reorganise and gain the blue line, but the almost continuous enemy machine gun fire prevented any material advance. At 4 a.m. on August 11, in conjunction with the operations of the 10th and 12th Battalions on our right and the 7th Brigade on our left, our whole line was advanced considerably.

"A further effort was made to dislodge the enemy on our left but without success.

"Under cover of fog at 6 a.m. on the same morning the enemy struck a blow at our weakest point—the gap between our left and centre companies which was held by Lieut. Evans and a platoon 17 strong. With rifle and Lewis gun fire and 36 grenades this officer drove off two determined enemy counter-attacks. The enemy came on a third time, but owing to the gallant resistance shown by our post he broke and fled in disorder, suffering severe casualties.

"At 9 a.m. the enemy attacked our right, but was driven back. Later, in conjunction with the 10th Battalion on our

Men of the 11th Battalion in Battle of Lihons, August, 1918.

right, assisted by a section of the 3rd Light Trench Mortar Battery, our right and centre companies advanced against serious opposition to the blue line, suffering many casualties.

"These companies consolidated in the old French line astride Salamander and Du Bois Alleys, the centre company extending its left flank to join up with the left company.

"As the left company was still meeting with great opposition a platoon was organised from headquarters details, under Lieut. L. G. Riches, and was sent at 3 p.m. on August 11 to the assistance of this company. That night, under cover of darkness and assisted by trench mortar fire, the enemy trenches on our left were captured and liaison was established with the left battalion.

"After this things were much quieter, and it was reported that the enemy was withdrawing."

In the above fighting, Sergeants Wally Goodlet and Craig did great work on the left when things were at their worst.

Prisoners from the 19th Bavarian Regiment were sent back to brigade. Some of them were interrogated at battalion headquarters, and they were offered tea, cocoa and even rum. One read-headed Boche thought that these beverages might contain poison and would only drink "wasser," even though several officers drank of the "brew" to allay his suspicions.

There was a good deal of both direct and indirect machine gun fire in the earlier stages of the battle, and during a burst that spattered round battalion headquarters one bullet passed through the thin planking of the shelter and pierced every one of a pile of maps that the I.O. was marking for the various companies.

There were many signs that the Germans had done themselves well as regards food supplies. There were many fowls about and some cattle, and several bottles of wine were found. One rooster was challenging the world, undismayed by the turmoil of battle around him. He was in plain sight on the top of a heap of stable manure. There were some German snipers operating over beyond where the bird was, but in the same line. One of the boys said: "That rooster is my meat," and levelled his rifle and fired but missed. Several shots were then fired and the bird fell over, dead. Though a few shots had come from the snipers before the bird was shot, no more were fired after that. Next day when the I.O. and his runner were coming back from a tour of inspection of the line they happened to visit several posts which might possibly have been snipers' "possies," and in the "possy" nearest the battalion headquarters they found two Germans not long dead with heaps and heaps and empty cartridges lying alongside them. They were lying directly in a line with the shooting of the rooster of the day before.

Further up the trenches was a hive of bees. It was a fine, strong hive and the bees were working well. It was strange to hear that pleasant hum so suggestive of rural peace among the trenches and noises of war. Lieuts. C. Gostelow and J. George were poking round some abandoned stables and huts and they found a milking cow in one of the sheds. She had a broken leg. The officers endeavoured to put her out of her misery and fired half a dozen shots into different parts of her anatomy without effect. Hearing the fusilade, another officer and his runner dashed up to see what was doing, whereupon the newcomer put his revolver to the forehead of the poor brute and killed her.

There was a considerable group of wooden buildings at this place, which was a well-protected hollow. Among these buildings was an excellently appointed German field hospital, which yielded a large quantity of valuable drugs much of which was sent to Captain May, the M.O., who used the drugs to good effect. There were several British dead lying beside the hospital, including a corporal of the Tank Corps. Their wounds had been carefully dressed and bandaged.

It has been stated that there was a maze of old trenches in the sector that the 11th Battalion was holding; many of these trenches were parallel to one another, and locations were sometimes a bit confusing, even with good trench maps. The I.O. had been issued with an excellent aerial photo. map which was almost a picture in miniature of the area in question, and with it he was verifying all the company positions. While in "B" Company's trench and having a look around, one of the Diggers said: "You'd better keep the old head down just there, for Fritzy's sniping with a '77.' " The officer took the hint, and sure enough when he had passed a little way down the trench a whizz-bang shaved the top of the parapet and burst in the parados, sending splinters everywhere. Some way behind Captain Wally Hallahan had his company headquarters, and a comparison with the air photo. showed that the location of his position was given about 200 yards ahead of where the trenches actually were. As the front seemed pretty quiet, it was resolved to advance to the position that had been sent back to brigade. The boys were ordered to move forward and immediately a red flare was fired by the Germans, but fortunately no enemy action took place, and in a few minutes the troops were in the location given and everything adjusted without a hitch.

The 11th Battalion official diary goes on to state: "During the whole of August 12 the enemy was singularly quiet and appeared to have vacated the position on our front. Daylight patrols were sent on the afternoon of August 12 and definitely located the enemy in strength at Madame Wood."

As previously mentioned, the brigade on the left had not at first moved forward with the 11th Battalion, and consequently the left company of the 11th Battalion had an uncomfortable and dangerous position for the first two days of this advance; and though patrols were periodically sent out, there was a considerable amount of enfilade fire by the enemy and casualties kept occurring. As an example of the enemy's accurate fire the following incident is mentioned: There was a gap in the trench on the way up to the front line and the enemy had this ranged to a hair. An ammunition party was moving up to the front and an officer jokingly told one of the Diggers to tilt his steel hat sideways as he passed this gap. About an hour after-

Captured German Gun Position, Cressaire Wood, Lihons.
(Official Photo.)

wards this same Digger sought out the officer who had joked with him, and pointing to his "tin lid" said: "Look! Mr. ———, what the bastard did to my tin hat," and sure enough there was a bullet hole clean through the brim.

The battalion was relieved by the 9th and 12th Battalions on August 12/13 and went into supports. The official report by Lieut.-Colonel Newman sums up the battle in these words: "On the night of August 12/13 the battalion was relieved —without incident. Booty captured: four field guns (4.2 hows.), four trench mortars and 50 machine guns. Our casualties for the operation were: officers, seven killed and five wounded. Other ranks: 35 killed, 137 wounded and seven missing.

"In conclusion I would like to express my appreciation of the loyalty and wholehearted co-operation of all ranks in assisting to bring to a successful conclusion a most difficult operation. In spite of the fatigued condition of the troops, caused through the long marches and lack of sleep prior to the operation, all ranks showed throughout the utmost fortitude and tenacity and a fighting spirit worthy of the battalion's past traditions. I would like to express my thanks to the officers and men of the 3rd Machine Gun Company, the 3rd Trench Mortar Battery and also the carrying parties supplied by the 12th Battalion and the 3rd Brigade Mining Company for the wholehearted co-operation they rendered the battalion throughout. Their initiative and willingness were at all times a valuable assistance.

"The battalion fought magnificently over most difficult country, gaining almost impregnable positions at the bayonet point. Our losses, however, have been severe, some of our most valued officers going under, men whom neither the A.I.F. nor Australia can afford to lose."

This is a fine tribute from Colonel Newman, and showed the high esteem in which he held his command and his men. The heavy losses of his already depleted battalion affected him most strongly.

The 11th Battalion spent the day of August in the support trenches. Enemy aeroplanes were very active and dropped bombs close to the neighbouring batteries, which were also subjected to constant shell-fire. During this shelling a dump of Stokes' trench mortar bombs was set alight by a bursting shell, the wooden cases were soon burning briskly and creating a great deal of smoke. As it was thought that the smoke and explosion of the dump would attract further shell-fire, volunteers were called to put out the fire. Immediately Corporal Harry Paine and Private Frank Sims and others of the intelligence platoon rushed over with shovels and, by carrying off the blazing bomb-boxes and depositing them in shell-holes and throwing earth over them, the fire was subdued without casualties, although one of the boxes of bombs blew up after it had been placed in the shell-hole.

After dusk the battalion relieved the 12th Battalion in the line. Next day advance parties from the 4th Brigade arrived in the forward area. Their presence was welcome, as it indicated the approach of the relieving battalions. The dispositions of the battalion were altered just before relief, the battalion being distributed in depth with "A" Company in the front line, "B" in support, "C" in close support and "D" in reserve.

The battalion was relieved at dusk on August 16. Just before the relieving troops arrived, their movement was seen by enemy aeroplanes and the 16th Battalion was heavily shelled in moving up to the lines and they suffered several casualties.

On moving out of the line the 11th Battalion marched to a bivouac near Harbonnieres. A good hot meal and a rest put new life in the boys. Numbers of enemy bombing 'planes were active during the whole night. Next day the battalion marched about seven miles to Vaire-sous-Corbie, close to Corbie, on the Somme. While on the march the sight of American troops moving up to the line was the subject of much dry comment by the Diggers.

At Vaire, on August 14, the battalion went into camp under shady trees, close to the river, and for the next few days a restful time was passed. Bathing and swimming were appreciated by all the troops, and the men were re-equipped and the companies reorganised. Very few of the troops who had joined up on August 14, 1914, were now with the battalion.

The boys had a pleasant time at Vaire and had leisure to visit the many villages round about and note the destruction that the Germans had effected during their retirement. The work of restoration was already in full swing, but in spite of the engineers' endeavours there was a great deal of congestion on the roads near the river and canal.

Lieut. Athol Norrie was at this time appointed aide-de-camp to General Glasgow, and he was the subject of much cheerful abuse from his old comrades of the 11th Battalion when he came to visit them. Lieut. Bill Gudgeon used to reckon that Norrie's chief function as aide-de-camp was to test the temperature of the Somme water, in the chilly mornings, before the General had his morning plunge.

Although the troops had had a hard time in the last battle, their mood was vastly different from that of two years before after Pozieres and Mouquet Farm. In place of the bitterness and sense of futility the Diggers felt that they were at last getting somewhere, and though the casualties of the stunt just completed were very severe compared to the strength of the battalion, the battle had not left the troops dazed and dispirited. It is true that they were physically tired for a few days, but mentally they were alert and cheerful. A large map of the complete front line from Dunkirk on the English Channel to Belfort on the Swiss border used to be kept posted up outside battalion headquarters, and every day the latest developments used to be marked in different coloured pencils. This map was continually surrounded by Diggers of all ranks, and a most intelligent interest was shown in all the movements of the front line.

On August 20 there was a brigade swimming carnival. During the swim under water one competitor of another battalion failed to reappear and immediate steps were made to locate him. When found the unfortunate Digger was discovered to have died through heart failure.

Corbie was not far off, and here there were great P.O.W. cages alongside the lock on the canal. Many of the boys used to wander down and view the great droves of prisoners that were continually pouring in. In the deep water above the lock the boys used to bathe and many would converse with the Germans in the hope of picking up a few souvenirs, though most of them realised that they had not much hope in that respect.

On one occasion a rather short and naked Australian emerged from the water on the cage side of the canal and, after looking hard at a tall and stately-looking German officer, who was pacing up and down by himself, he ventured to approach him and ask: "I say, Mister! Could you tell me the time?" The German looked at the Digger, then broke into a smile and said in excellent English: "Ah! my boy! You are too late. One of your friends asked me that question about an hour ago."

The weather kept fine all the time the troops were at Vaire and the nights were perfect. When darkness fell the nightingales and sedge warblers would sing in the bushes and reeds alongside the river, while the rumble of guns was heard faint and far off. Australian leave was just starting in the battalion, and in the quiet of these lovely nights the wonderful thought that home was no longer an impossible dream came to cheer many of the boys.

CHAPTER XLVI

THE BATTLE OF CHUIGNOLLES

ORDERS were once more given for a move forward, and on August 21 the 11th Battalion, less nucleus, marched up to the Cerisy area. The nucleus, under the command of Lieut.-Colonel J. Newman, moved back to Corbie. The day was very hot and great parties of German prisoners were being marched along the roads back to the cages. The poor devils looked very thirsty and likely to drop from weariness. Major Phillips was in temporary command of the battalion which, with the rest of the 3rd Brigade, was in divisional reserve and liable to be called upon at any time. All day on August 22 the battalion rested at Morcourt, south of the Somme. Battle equipment was completed and all made ready for the operation which was expected on the following day.

Captain W. R. Hallahan, M.C., M.M., received orders to march out to go on transport duty to Australia. All ranks joined in wishing him good luck, for if ever a man deserved respite from the war it was Wally Hallahan. He was inundated with messages to friends and relatives at home, and he almost broke down at having to leave his many friends in the battalion.

At 9 p.m. on August 22 it was learned that the battalion would be attacking on the left of the divisional frontage in the morning. The line to be attacked stretched from just west of Chuignolles to immediately north of Rainecourt. The 11th Battalion's frontage was opposite Chuignolles and north-west of Proyart, a village lying south of the Somme. The battalion's role in the first attack was primarily to support the 12th Battalion and exploit any success that might be gained by the 1st Brigade.

After instructions had been given to the company commanders the battalion moved off from its bivouacs at 2:30 a.m. on August 23 and took up positions in St. Germain Wood without incident. At 4:30 a.m. the 11th Battalion was in its battle position on the right rear of the 12th Battalion, with battalion headquarters in a sunken road on the east edge of St. Germain Wood.

At 4:45 a.m. the barrage opened, whereupon the enemy promptly retaliated with a severe and accurate counter-barrage. Almost immediately Lieut. W. A. W. Gudgeon, M.C., and 2nd/Lieut. Archie Ross were wounded and five Diggers were killed, while 26 others were wounded before 5 a.m. The 12th Battalion also suffered heavily during its advance.

At 12:45 p.m. "D" Company, under Captain Tulloch, and "B" Company, under Lieut. A. Norrie, were instructed to go forward to follow up the advance of the 12th Battalion. These companies formed up in front of Long Wood and at 2 p.m., under cover of a barrage, the attack on the blue line, from just north of Chuignies, through to Cappy, a village on the River Somme, was commenced. The 9th Battalion, which was attacking in line with the 12th, had a difficult sector to deal with, so the 11th Battalion companies, under Captain Tulloch, were detailed to assist the former battalion in a frontal attack and then change direction to the left and so engage the enemy in flank. This they did by taking advantage of a ravine, but they suffered many casualties from enemy artillery fire in taking up their position. Under cover of a protecting barrage, "B" and "D" Companies advanced, but came under heavy cross machine gun and rifle fire, which kept the men pinned to the ground for some time. Through some fine individual efforts these machine guns were silenced and several prisoners were captured.

There was a high steep ridge named Froissy Beacon, the sides of which were so precipitous as to be almost cliffs. Here there was a very strong enemy resistance, especially from machine gun fire. A certain amount of shelter was given to "D" Company by buildings and an old timber stack, but the 9th Battalion was unable to advance until the machine guns on Froissy Beacon and in the railway embankment nearby were driven out by the 11th Battalion troops. "D" Company by this time was very much exhausted by the rapid advance and the rugged country that the men had been operating in, and so after driving out the machine guns on Froissy Beacon Captain Tulloch took up a position to support the 9th Battalion, which then went through his position.

"B" Company, which had been acting as a defensive flank to the 9th Battalion, encountered the enemy in strength in front of Froissy Beacon. By a gallant and spirited attack, and by the skilful handling of its Lewis guns, it drove the enemy from this position and captured 35 prisoners and two machine guns. This company also dug a defensive position on the hill as support for the 9th Battalion. "A" Company, under Lieut. F. Charles, was sent forward at 6:20 p.m. to assist the 12th Battalion and dug in on a line north of Garenne Wood.

At nightfall the battalion was withdrawn to a position in St. Germain Wood, where the boys had a much-needed rest.

The 3rd Australian Division was now pushing along the north bank of the Somme and was in the bend at Cappy, so instructions were issued on August 25 for the 3rd Brigade to again advance on the south side of the river in conjunction with the attack on the north bank. Accordingly the 3rd Brigade was to attack on a front roughly from the River Somme to an east and west line running just south of Chuignies.

The official battalion record is the following: "Report of operations carried out by the 11th Battalion (A.I.F.) on August 25/26, 1918: At 2:50 p.m. on August 25 a telephone message was received from brigade stating that 12th and 9th Battalions were to continue the advance under cover of a barrage at 4 p.m. and that the 11th Battalion was to support the 12th Battalion and to render any assistance that the 12th Battalion might require.

"All companies were then warned to hold themselves in readiness. 'D' Company, under Captain Tulloch, being detailed to support the left company of the 12th Battalion, and 'C' Company, under Lieut. W. W. Graham, M.C., to support the right company of the 12th Battalion.

"Eleventh Battalion headquarters was moved forward to the left of Chuignolles (a village near Chuignies). The company commanders of the supporting companies were then given instructions (1) to assist the 12th Battalion in every possible way; (2) to exploit the situation to the utmost.

"At 4 p.m. the barrage opened and the 12th Battalion advanced. As their left flank immediately met with difficulties, 'D' Company of the 11th Battalion was quickly involved. . . . This company which had been advancing in a due easterly direction, in artillery formation, came under well-directed machine gun fire from both flanks, though no enemy posts were visible. The ground was devoid of cover and advances were made in short rushes.

"As a gap existed between the 9th and 12th Battalions an endeavour was made to advance and link up this gap. One platoon was therefore sent along a trench running eastwards with instructions to get as far forward as possible to cover the advance of the remainder of the company. By this means, and with the assistance of the Stokes mortar co-operation, the company reached the embankment on the north of Olympia Wood Liaison was maintained with the 12th Battalion.

"Efforts were made, but without success, to bring Lewis gun fire to bear on enemy machine gun positions. These, however, could not be located and the enemy maintained superiority of fire. Earl's Wood and Olympia Wood were searched by patrols but no enemy could be located in either position. Touch was gained with the 9th Battalion whose right still remained in the shelter of a road embankment. The enemy was then shelling this position with 77 mm. and 5.9 guns. At 7 p.m. the enemy put down a smoke and gas barrage, under cover of which he withdrew from his most advanced positions. At this time, on receipt of orders from brigade, 'D' Company was instructed to remain in its present position where it would be relieved by the 9th Battalion to enable it to assist in the advance which the 9th Battalion was to make at 10 p.m.

"In the meantime the right flank of the 12th Battalion had met with difficulties, the company commander being killed and the company suffering many casualties by machine gun fire from Canard Wood and from a determined bombing attack on the part of the enemy.

" 'C' Company, 11th Battalion, led by Lieut. W. W. Graham, M.C., with great energy and initiative went to the assistance of the 12th Battalion's right flank and moved through the 12th Battalion and bombed down the old communication trench running east through the German lines. There was determined opposition to our advance, but, keeping up a barrage about 100 yards distant with rifle grenades, enemy opposition was steadily overcome and an advance of over 1,000 yards was made to a position that not only outflanked Canard Wood but commanded the valley due north of Lapin Wood. Mopping-up parties were sent out which routed out isolated enemy posts, many of the enemy being killed and six prisoners taken. Posts were then put out on either flank, covering a frontage of about 500 yards in front of the north-east corner of Canard Wood, which was mopped up by one platoon of the 12th Battalion under Lieut. Muir, who followed up our advance and who was placed by Lieut. Graham on the extreme right flank. Orders were then issued for companies to assemble for a general advance in conjunction with the 10th Battalion on our left at 10 p.m., but these orders were subsequently cancelled by brigade."

The report goes on to state that the 11th Battalion was instructed to take over the 12th Battalion's lines, but the latter battalion's positions were found to be so irregular that it was deemed better for the 11th to take up a new position in front of the 12th Battalion. This was carried out, and at dawn the 11th Battalion had formed a new line with its right flank linking up with the 3rd Battalion of the right brigade and it held the most advanced position gained during the attack.

At 6 a.m. the whole 3rd Brigade line was advanced, pivoting on the right flank until the 11th Battalion's left was resting at a point 300 yards south-west of Yakka Wood, a very small copse on the wide, bare, flattish summit of the hill that the brigade was attacking. Touch was gained with the 10th Battalion and the whole line was ordered to advance at 10:30 a.m. on August 26.

The official diary goes on to say: "'A' Company, under Lieut. G. F. Charles, was sent forward to cover the advance of 'C' and 'B' Companies, and by 2 p.m., on August 26, we had advanced and consolidated on a line running practically north and south about 800 yards from the sugar factory. Here liaison was established with the 3rd Battalion. At 2 p.m. a telephone message was received from O.C. 'C' Company stating that further advance was held up by machine gun fire. Locations were asked for and handed to artillery liaison officer and effective fire was brought to bear on the sugar factory and neighbouring positions, allowing our patrols to get forward. Touch was then gained with the enemy along our whole front. Our line was then slightly advanced. At 6 p.m., under mutual arrangement with the C.O. 10th Battalion, we took over 300 yards of his line, and then in conjunction with the 10th again pushed forward our line finally extending in conjunction with the 3rd Battalion."

In all this second day's fighting the 11th Battalion, by skilful use of ground and cover, only lost three men killed and 12 wounded, although the number of enemy killed was considerable. Though the enemy was fighting a rearguard action, he had the advantage of constructed positions and carefully selected ground. This battle shows the pitch of efficiency to which the 11th Battalion troops had attained. A study of the battle arrangements and the liaison and co-operation between all units is also helpful in understanding the distance the Australian troops had travelled since their arrival in France over two years before.

If a map of the terrain be examined, over which this strenuous battle was fought, it will be noticed what a difficult country

Artillery going into action between Proyart and Chuignolles passing men of 11th Battalion. (Official Photo.)

it was to fight over. There were bare hills and deep valleys, and woods and small copses dotted here and there, all offering good positions for enemy machine guns. Every time the troops breasted a new rise they were met by intense machine gun and rifle fire and often by accurately placed artillery fire as well.

An amusing story is told of Lieut. Johnny Long in this connection. Long had been on leave and had just arrived back at nucleus battalion in Corbie. Owing to officer casualties, Long had been sent for and he proceeded up to the line clad in his "glad rags" just as he had come in from leave. And

Johnny's clothes were glad. On arrival at brigade headquarters he was given a guide to take him forward. The brigade major, also a very smartly-dressed officer, determined to go forward with Long. The guide took a long distasteful look at the pretty pair, in their brass-work, their gleaming Sam-Brownes and their light-coloured uniforms. What he thought is another matter. The party set off and as the crest of the first hill was reached on the journey up to battalion headquarters a few bullets zipped round. Next time the three appeared on the skyline the firing was more concentrated, and the guide did not like it at all. These symptoms increased the nearer the party got to the firing line, until at last the guide in desperation stopped dead and pointed to a small wood. "Look," he said, "11th Battalion headquarters is over there, an' if youse two blokes think I'm goin' any further with a coupler pretty joeys like you, an' draw all the bloody crabs in the area, well! you've got another thought comin'. So long!" and off he dashed back the way he had come

It was in this battle that the troops of the 11th Battalion were stirred by the sight of the Australian field artillery galloping into action. The guns were rushed into position and wheeled, and the gunners laid and fired the 18-pounders just as if they had been on the training ground, while the unlimbered teams galloped hell-for-leather for cover.

On the night of August 27 the battalion was relieved by the 22nd and 24th Australian Battalions, and the 11th Battalion moved off to bivouac positions in Proyart Valley. While in this bivouac the battalion was visited by General Bennett, the Brigadier. He rode round all the companies and personally thanked them for their work, and complimented the troops on their gallantry in the last operations.

It was not often that General Bennett gave the troops any praise, and it must indeed have been superlative work on the part of the 11th Battalion to have called forth such encomium.

The battalion moved out on August 27 and marched back along the Somme to Hazel Wood near Cerisy. Here nucleus joined up and all the battalion went into tents and bivouacs. The weather had been generally excellent and it continued fine, so the "bivvies" were no hardship.

At Hazel Wood, in addition to the usual reorganisation after a battle, an innovation was introduced that marked the first step in the dissolution of the fine battalion which had now been in existence for over four years. On August 29, as there was now no longer any hope of an adequate number of reinforcements to keep the battalion up to strength, and as the existing four companies found it hard to fill all duties with their reduced personnel, the number of companies in the battalion was reduced to three, and as "B" Company was weakest numerically, it was decided to break it up and distribute its members among the other companies. This was done, and so a fine company ceased to exist save as a glorious memory.

The River Somme was only a short distance to the north and every opportunity was taken to let the troops have a swim. These swimming parades were greatly enjoyed. Every opportunity was also taken to encourage sports, and there were many keenly contested musketry and Lewis gun competitions while at Hazel Wood.

The machinery for repatriation had now begun to move and General (Bishop) Long addressed the brigade commanders and senior officers of the 1st Division at the Y.M.C.A., Cerisy, on the subject of training the troops for vocations after the war. In the battalion a list of all the men was taken, and their prewar occupations were noted and an inquiry was made as to the occupations that the men wished to follow on demobilisation. Not many of the boys took this interrogation seriously, and some even resented it, considering firstly that it was a bit out of place to ask a man what he intended to be when he was discharged from the army, when it was more than probable, as things were then, that he would never live to be discharged; and secondly, many independent spirits felt that they were quite able to look after themselves when and if they got back to Australia, and they felt that it did not concern anyone but themselves.

There was a great deal of German war material lying around the area that the battalion occupied: piles of howitzer charges and cartridges, rifles and bombs and machine gun belts in great number. Near the lines was a great gun with its muzzle blown off, and this legend painted in white on a board attached to the breach: "Found, fired and —— by the 14th Battalion." The boys used to amuse themselves lighting heaps of the howitzer explosive in the little numbered bags, and they also used up much German ammunition firing at petrol tins and bottles. Some of the officers tried out their Webleys on the German steel hats. This helmet would stop a revolver bullet even if fired at the concave side, but the British helmet would only turn a bullet on its convex side. Of course the German helmet was much heavier.

There was not much of very outstanding interest at Hazel Wood, but there were always a few incidents that broke the monotony of camp life. A lad named Wilson used to look after the battalion gramophone and a small cinematograph plant, that was more or less a "dud." Wilson had been A.W.L. for a couple of days and was toeing the line before Lieut.-Colonel Newman. The C.O. asked him where he had been. Wilson said that he had been hunting round for somewhere to get some *gramophone needles sharpened*, as he was unable to purchase any new ones. The C.O. was so astounded at the excuse given that he let the man off with a caution.

One day Lieut. "Snowy" Howe was walking near Cerisy and a party of German prisoners was being marched back to the cage. On seeing Howe, a tall German officer stepped up to him and said, in good English: "Sir! I demand a motor car to convey me to the prisoner-of-war camp. It is not fitting that I, an oberst (a colonel), should be herded along with the common soldiers." "Snowy" looked him up and down, and then pointing to a fellow officer who was walking past he said: "Do you see that officer, and do you see me! Well, a fat chance there is of *you* having a ride, if *we* have to walk," and left him to carry on.

On September 1 it was Sunday, and a brigade church parade was held in the gully near Hazel Wood (Hazel Wood lay between Lamotte and Cerisy). This was the first church parade that had been held since June at Sercus.

Captain Priestly, of the 1st Division Intelligence Staff, and formerly of the 11th Battalion, gave a most interesting lecture on enemy identifications and showed how the intelligence department had all the movements of the German divisions analysed and the deductions that they were able to make concerning the enemy's strength from these movements. He stressed the importance of immediately sending back any information about prisoners or enemy dead. Captain Priestly also showed the troops some of the methods by which information was extracted from the prisoners in the "cages."

After a restful ten days spent at La Motte, the battalion was warned on September 6 to be ready to move forward early next day.

CHAPTER XLVII

FAREWELL TO ARMS

IN THE DARKNESS of early morning on September 7 the silence was disturbed by the old familiar bugle call, "There's a land of sunny skies, West Austral-i-a," followed by Reveille at 4 a.m. After breakfast the tents and bivouacs were struck and returned to store. The battalion transport, under Lieut Paul McInerney, moved off at 8 a.m. and the battalion marched out at 9 a.m. and moved to Cerisy, where the troops embussed at 11 a.m. and set off towards Mont St. Quentin. The route lay through Chuignolles and Chuignies, the villages that had figured so prominently in the fighting of a fortnight previously. These villages were now far behind the line, for the tide of war had rolled swiftly forward. The long column of vehicles raised a thick cloud of white dust that hung in the air and settled over everything. All the troops were dust-coated and glad when they reached their journey's end, in front of the great bulk of Mont St. Quentin. Here the troops descended from the buses and went into quarters in old German trenches early in the afternoon.

The battalion was now in the vicinity of Peronne, and the famous Mont St. Quentin rose right up in front of the bivouac. It seemed incredible that the Germans had been dislodged from such a position in such a short time, and much admiration was expressed by the 11th boys at the feat of the 28th Battalion and the rest of the 7th Brigade in accomplishing such a fine piece of work and driving the enemy from such seemingly impregnable positions. Looking at the long slopes of the Mont, with position after position, each with a perfect field of fire, it seemed impossible that any troops could have taken such a strong system of defences, and one 11th man was heard to say, that if he were asked to state what he considered the most brilliant feat in the Somme battle he should unhesitatingly say: "The assault and capture of Mont St. Quentin."

There were still numbers of German dead lying about all over the area and parties were sent out to bury these bodies. On one of the graves was placed a cross with these words: "Here lie two unknown German soldiers. They met an Aussie."

From the Peronne area the 11th Battalion moved up to Marquaix, near Tincourt, and soon afterwards shifted up to a hutted camp further north but still in the Tincourt area. While here, officers were sent up to the forward area, first of all to the north opposite Templeux. Here the advance had only lately passed over and several teams of small horses, possibly of Hungarian breed, were lying where they had been killed near some captured German guns. The horses had been shot down as the crews vainly tried to save the guns, and the drivers and gunners were lying dead not far away.

The weather had been really wonderful for a long time, but now a period of stormy and unsettled conditions set in and a good deal of rain fell. The official diary for September 12 states: "The weather is still rough and stormy. During the night and early morning Fritz's bombing 'planes were busy, but though he dropped some near by no damage was done. In the morning Lieut. W. C. Belford, the battalion intelligence officer, went forward to gather information from the line battalion (which attacked this morning but appears to have made little progress). Instructions were received this morning to dig posts to join up a defensive line, and the C.O. and the adjutant went forward to reconnoitre the ground. The men spent the night digging these posts."

During the time the battalion was in this hutted camp, a long-range high-velocity gun used to shell the area, and many of the shells landed only too close. One night, when all the troops were in their bunks, the rush and roar of a big shell was heard, but there was no explosion. "That was a dud," someone needlessly remarked, and all dropped off to sleep again. All, that is, except one. That one was Private Phil. Sims, Major May's batman. The shell that had landed so close had passed through his hut and under his bunk, where the upheavel of earth had partially buried him, and either the force of the shell hitting the ground or the wind of its passing had rendered him unconscious. At any rate he lay there for a long time and was only released in the morning when the M.O. sent someone to see why his batman had not turned up. Sims was quite all right except for some bruises and a strained back.

On September 14, 1918, Lieut.-Colonel Newman, D.S.O., and the first batch of leave men for Australia left the battalion. There were many who envied them, but all joined in wishing them good luck. The battalion had carried out many successful attacks under Colonel Newman's command. The Colonel had been one of the original officers and had a long service with the battalion. Major Aubrey Darnell now assumed command of the battalion.

At nights German 'planes used to visit the back areas and, as the Huns knew all the suitable places for dumps, camps, bridges and the like, these nightly bombing excursions cost the Allies dearly. But the Germans did not always have it their own way. On the night of September 13 the usual nightly bombing squadrons were heard passing over, and immediately every searchlight and anti-aircraft gun in the area was in operation. The long beams of the searchlights stabbed the darkness and

Major Aubrey Darnell, C.O. 11th Battalion. Killed in action September, 1918.

the roar and rattle of the "archies" shattered the stillness when a searchlight managed to locate and hold a 'plane in its beam. In the fierce glare of a nearby searchlight all the troops could see a large Gotha, and gradually searchlight after searchlight picked it up until there was no escape for the Gotha, twist and turn as she tried, and every gun was turned on to her. It was a great spectacle, but not for the Gotha.

Suddenly in a lull in the shooting the rat-a-tat of a machine gun high up in the air could be heard, and the thin lines of tracer bullets were noticed coming from above the German plane; and then caught in the beams of the searchlights was seen a tiny little plane, seeming just like a gnat compared to the great moth-like form of the giant Gotha.

Instantly all the searchlights were shut off and the roar of the "archies" ceased, although the flashes of their bursting shells showed vividly in the now intense darkness for some time after. Soon the bursts stopped and there was silence for a while save for the drone of engines far up in the darkness. Not a sound came from the troops. It was as if the whole world were stationary waiting for the inevitable. There must have been thousands upon thousands of troops all gazing expectantly up into the darkness. Suddenly things began to happen. There was a burst of tracer bullets quite distinctly seen and then the faint staccato bark of machine gun fire. Then a slight explosion high up in the Stygian darkness, which was followed by a 'plane bursting into flames.

A searchlight pierced the night and was soon focussed on the falling 'plane. What a yell of joy burst simultaneously from thousands of throats when the big Gotha was seen falling wing over wing. The light followed the burning 'plane down, and a wonderful display of fireworks was witnessed as the various coloured flares carried by the bomber burst into flame and left trails of vivid colour. The 'plane crashed not far off, lighting up the ground for a minute or two before the flames died away, to leave only a smoking ruin. It was a sight never to be forgotten.

Later on in the same night another bomber was shot down. Some records state that four 'planes were shot down that night.

Next day everyone in the battalion was astonished to see Captain Hallahan back again. It was thought that he would have been already well on the way to Australia, and it was rather a shock to see him in the flesh. He grinned in his usual cheery way, but there was a great deal of bitterness in his voice when he said: "The b——'s can do as they like with me now. I don't care a damn! One of us will get home, anyway." (He was referring to the fact that of the four brothers Hallahan, though two were killed, a third was a P.O.W. in Germany.) Later he told his friends that he had fixed up to get married to a nurse in England on the Thursday before he sailed, and he had suddenly been given orders to return to France on the Wednesday (the day before his intended marriage) and therefore he was back with the battalion once more. He had indeed cause for disappointment, and he received the wholehearted sympathy of every officer, N.C.O. and man in the battalion.

Maps of the new area were issued and the I.O. was instructed to proceed to Hervilly and Hesbecourt to gain what information he could. On September 16 instructions for a hopover in the direction of Villeret were issued, and the I.O. was again ordered to visit the front lines to make arrangements for the laying of a tape on the evening of September 17. Accordingly, very early on the morning of September 17, a visit was made to the lines near Villeret. There were numbers of officers and N.C.O.'s of all arms visiting the front, and it was strange that Fritz did not find out that a big advance was contemplated there was so much movement in the front lines and posts. A slight mist may have made visibility bad from the German side. However, the position of the tape line was fixed without accident and that night after dark the I.O. accompanied by Sergeant R. Wearmouth, M.M., and party successfully laid a fine wide tape about 80 yards from the enemy's trenches.

Meanwhile the battalion was making preparations for the attack. Maps showing the position of the tape line and the various objectives had been issued and all the usual battle gear, and the troops were instructed concerning barrages and other pertinent matters. Major Darnell, the C.O., had detailed Captain Hallahan to be O C. moppers-up, in order that he should be exposed to as little risk as possible in the coming attack, and as his party was to be the last to go over the top his job was expected to be more or less a routine one.

The whole attack was to be on a very wide frontage. The 4th Army in conjunction with the 1st French Army on the right and the 3rd British Army on the left were to attack the enemy's defensive positions in front of the Hindenburg Line. The Australian Corps, under General Monash, had the place of honour in the centre of the 4th Army, the IX Corps was on the right and the III Corps on the left.

The 1st Australian Division was on the left of the Australian Corps, with the 4th Australian Division on the right and the 74th Division on the 1st Australian Division's left. The 1st Australian Division was to attack on a two-brigade front, with the 3rd Brigade on the right and the 1st Australian Brigade on the left. Two tanks were allotted to the 3rd Brigade and also a troop of the 13th Australian Light Horse Regiment was also attached in case of a break-through. This was the first occasion on which the light horse had been attached to the 3rd Brigade in an attack in France.

The first objective on the 3rd Brigade sector was allotted to the 11th and 12th Battalions. This objective was a ridge of ground about 3,000 yards from the jumping-off tape, which ran just in front of Hesbecourt and Jeancourt. This ridge was defended by an intricate system of trenches and wire, with

Villeret, France. This was the scene of the 11th Battalion's last battle in the War. (Official Photo.)

Fervaque Farm on the left and a large area of cut-down timber in Grand Priel Woods on the right. There was a steady rise from the tape line to Fervaque Farm and the village of Villeret lay in the hollow beyond.

In the brigade order for the attack one clause laid down that "Men will be forbidden to neglect their duty for souveniring," and another was, "Troops will be warned against booby traps." In regard to "booby traps," there were very few of these encountered in this last phase of the war, as possibly the Germans had not had the time to instal them; but numbers of tanks had been scuttled by land mines at cross-roads and other likely places for the passage of these moving forts.

As for souveniring, all that need be stated is that "Troops will always be troops!"

In the early morning of September 18 the troops for the attack began to march up to their battle positions. The route was over the dry weather overland tracks through Hamelet and Hervilly. Officers were posted at Marquaix and on the neighbouring railway line to prevent the battalion from being mixed up in the dark with the troops of the 1st Brigade who were crossing the battalion's line of approach.

On reaching the vicinity of the jumping-off line, battalion headquarters and details remained in the sunken road leading up to Jeancourt, and the three companies filed over the bank and made for the tape that had not long been laid. Here the troops lay down. "C" Company was led by Lieut. W. W. Graham and "D" Company by Captain E. Tulloch. The last of the troops to go over were the moppers-up under Captain Wally Hallahan. Lieut. Frank Goundrey, the signal officer, and the intelligence officer were standing in the sunken road, and as Hallahan came up he stopped to talk. He and the I.O. had been very intimate since the far-off days of Habieta, in the Sinai Desert. When his boys had filed over his two friends wished him good luck, and as he followed he waved and murmured, "Cheerio, you old b——!" It was his last farewell.

The hour for the attack was fast approaching, and all the gunners near and in the sunken road were making their final preparations. A tenseness began to be felt. Zero hour was at 5:20 a.m. This gave the attackers time to get into position in the dark and yet it was near enough to the dawn to let the troops have some light by which to see their objectives once they had got a move on. The attack was to be on a 50-mile front, so that daylight was necessary even in the initial stages of the operations.

At 5:15 a.m. everything was ready, and now time seemed to stand still. The seconds ticked off loudly on the watches, each second dropping off into eternity as if reluctant to leave the present. A few feeble jokes were passed. "Fritz will never hear Reveille *this* morning," and "How do you like your eggs cooked, Fritzy?" and a few such; but a nervous excitement held most of the boys quiet. Then only ten seconds to go, and as the last ones ticked off the fearful blast of a 50-mile barrage hit the air and the battle was on.

A thick mist came down and gradually enveloped everything. The troops on the tape line waited the prescribed time, then slowly moved forward at 50 paces a minute. The barrage was nearly perfect. As one of the boys afterwards remarked, "All you had to do was to lean on it."

The 3rd Brigade report on the 11th Battalion's action is as follows: "From the moment the barrage moved forward the advance maintained until the objective was won. The two line companies adhered throughout with marked success to the principle of advancing along the high ground and avoiding the valley which ran through the centre of the sector. In addition, gaps were left in the line of advance, thrusts being made into the enemy positions, the gaps thus becoming outflanked were mopped up. By this means prisoners and machine guns were captured with a minimum of loss. This method of advance proved an unqualified success, giving both flexibility and room for manœuvre. For the first 500 yards the enemy was not encountered, but from there onward stiff opposition was frequently encountered, particularly in the old trench system and copses in the line of advance. The right company first engaged the enemy on the brow of the ridge, and the left company in Carpeza Copse. In front of the right company the enemy repeatedly made a resolute stand, his machine gun nests being distributed along the trenches and switches in the neighbourhood of Fervaque Farm. In each case the enemy positions were out-flanked and captured without seriously hindering the advance, while the mopping-up platoon, under Lieut. McKinley, M.M., closely co-operated and did excellent work. At Fervaque west and in Grand Priel Wood the platoon also assisted in outflanking and mopping up machine gun nests and enemy posts. In Grand Priel Wood over 40 prisoners and eight machine guns were captured, while by the time the brown line (the 11th Battalion's objective) was captured the right company in conjunction with the mopping-up platoon had captured over 80 prisoners, 40 machine guns, three field guns and two anti-tank guns. The company had very few casualties.

"Meanwhile, the left company, under Captain Tulloch, had met with some opposition at Carpeza Copse. This was quickly dealt with by the mopping-up platoon and a section of the trench mortar battery, and the company continued its advance along the high ground. The company then advanced to the trench system, where difficulty arose as to direction owing to the density of the fog and smoke. Captain Tulloch, C.S.M. Shipton and Private G. Moore going forward to reconnoitre suddenly came upon two heavy machine guns and their crews. A brisk revolver and bomb fight ensued, in which all three showed great coolness and pluck. The gun teams were killed or wounded and the guns captured. The company then completed the advance to the brown line, having throughout kept touch with the battalion on the left.

"Both companies reached the brown line simultaneously and were soon hotly engaged, the enemy being established in Caution Dug-out and the trenches and sunken roads nearby. The enemy's machine guns in the trench system east of Villeret also opened fire, but this was greatly minimised by the prompt action of the Vickers' guns who engaged them. The enemy's guns on the left were put out of action after a brisk fight. This was largely due to the gallantry and skilful leadership of Corporal Grubnau, of 'D' Company. On the right the situation was promptly cleared up by the action of the mopping-up platoons which, assisted by the trench mortars, made an attack on Caution Dug-out and the strong point adjacent. The attack succeeded, eight machine guns, two heavy minenwerfers and 30 prisoners being captured. The tank allotted, which had not been able to keep pace with the advance, now came up and rendered most useful help by pushing forward through the barrage and silencing machine guns on the front. It then rolled down the wire entanglements to assist the 9th Battalion to pass through."

There were not many casualties in the actual attack, but Lieut. D. Elliot, who had enlisted in 1914, and had been sent home as under age and who had rejoined with a commission, was killed along with several more original members of the battalion. The 11th Battalion advanced over 3,000 yards, and then the 9th Battalion took over the attack and advanced another 2,000 yards, finishing up on a ridge overlooking the famous Hindenburg Line at Bellicourt, near the tunnel of that name, on the Canal Du Nord. A great many prisoners were passed back. Most of them were a poor type. There were a good many Saxons and they were a very friendly lot. After capture, one of the prisoners stated that he had been a barber in Manchester (England) before the war.

As the signal section and other details were following the advance laying telephone wire as they progressed, a daisy-cutter landed close and one of the intelligence platoon was seen lying in the shallow shell-hole after the shell exploded. Besides shock his only injury was a bad wound in the hand. While Lieut. Goundrey and the I.O. were tying up the wound, word was brought that Captain Hallahan had been killed. The statement was received with incredulity, but Private Frank Sims, who used to be batman to Hallahan, offered to go over and find out for certain. In a few minutes he was back. "Wally Hallahan is killed alright," he said sadly. "He doesn't seem to have any wounds, and he still has the same old smile on his face." This was a terrible blow. It just did not seem possible that he could have been killed after coming through so many battles. But war is war and the troops had to advance. The boys carried his body out of the line and also young Elliot's, and the two officers were buried in Tincourt Cemetery. Lieut. J. J. Simmons, of the 12th Battalion, who had been acting as liaison officer to the 11th for his battalion, was also badly wounded and died next day.

A telephone wire had now been run out as far as the brown line by Lieut. Goundrey and Sergeant Armstrong. A position was chosen for battalion headquarters and Major Darnell informed of its location by 'phone. Later the 11th Battalion took up positions in an old German trench about four or five hundred yards behind the 9th Battalion, to which it was now acting as support. The enemy could be seen blowing up bridges and roads a long way back.

The following is a list of material captured in this the last battle of the 3rd Brigade: 13 77 mm. field guns, two Austrian howitzers, two 6-inch minenwerfers, seven trench howitzers, 58 light machine guns, 21 heavy machine guns, and a great deal of other war material too great to be detailed.

The 3rd Brigade casualty list was: Officers killed, 8; wounded 16; missing, nil; other ranks: killed, 51; wounded, 242; missing, 12.

It will be noticed from the above account that the 11th Battalion in conjunction with the rest of the 3rd Brigade had reached a pitch of excellency as a fighting machine that could hardly have been surpassed. This was not only due to the fine courage and military skill of the boys themselves, and these qualities were certainly pre-eminent, but a great deal of the success was also due to the fact that the troops were at last backed by efficient staff work and given tasks that were well within their power of accomplishment. Not only all this, but the co-ordination of aeroplanes, tanks, machine gun companies and trench mortar batteries, backed by artillery that the troops had confidence in, rendered a great deal of the work of attack mere routine, where heretofore there had been a great deal of blundering and a sacrifice of splendid men in efforts that seemed to lead nowhere.

It must not be forgotten that the enemy morale was not of the high standard of the earlier times, but anyone who was up against the Germans in this last phase of the war could not but admire the splendid way in which they conducted their withdrawal, fighting back step by step and only retiring when all hope was gone, mostly leaving numbers of casualties on both sides as witnesses of their stout defence, and the German machine gunners maintained the traditions of a fine force.

One has only to remember the awful carnage that was inflicted on the inexperienced Americans by the Germans in this last phase of the war to realise that the Germans' defeat, as an army, was caused not so much by any deterioration among their own troops as by the increased efficiency of the opposing forces.

While in support, behind the 9th Battalion, the troops did a good deal of souveniring in spite of orders, and some valuable maps and documents were found at a German signal station. Trophies of war were seen everywhere, and besides the official list given above there were all sorts of weapons that intrigued the interest of the troops. Two lads had found a tank rifle and were examining it. One wagered the other he was not game to fire it. The Digger with the rifle laid the huge affair on the parapet of a trench, put his shoulder to the butt and then decided that he had better remove some of the charge out of the big cartridge, as the recoil promised to be considerable. It was not until he had emptied quite a lot of the explosive that he was game to fire, and it took the bullet all its time to push its way out of the long barrel.

On September 19 the troops had a splendid view of a big French attack away on the right towards the town of St. Quentin. It was a most inspiring sight to witness this battle.

It was just like viewing a moving picture, only that an immense area was visible and the noise was so far off as to be just a confused roar. The dense cloud of smoke rolling onwards, with the sparkle and flash of the bursting shells; the lines of tiny blue-clad figures moving so steadily behind the crawling walls of exploding missiles and flying fragments; the aeroplanes circling and diving above the troops as they made their successful advance left a lasting impression on the minds of all. But the boys were entirely agreed on the subject that war was more interesting viewed from a distance.

The enemy did not shell the position in which the 11th Battalion was in support, but the long valley leading down to Hervilly and Roisel was shelled consistently. At the head of the valley nearest the German lines was a fine deep dug-out, and the area round about used to be well strafed, but there were few casualties.

The weather, which had been fine for some time, now broke, and with the rain the trenches soon became muddy and the ground soft. The soft ground had the effect of neutralising the shell bursts to a great extent.

The 11th Battalion relieved the 9th Battalion in the line on September 21 and occupied an old German trench with posts out in front, looking on to the Hindenburg Line. Headquarters was in the deep dug-out already mentioned. Fritz used a good deal of gas-shell round the battalion headquarters, but the fumes used to drift down the valley and dissipate themselves harmlessly.

The battalion at this time numbered barely 200 men, and consequently nearly all the troops were used to man the sector.

The troops were still finding a good deal of booty, and among other loot Lieut. Wally Graham found a large sack filled with bottles of German wine. Lieut. "Pard" Riches had gone to visit his machine gun posts and he was so long away that Major Darnell wanted to know where he was. The I.O. rang up the companies in the line and Wally Graham replied that the "Pard" had just left the front line with as much wine as he could comfortably carry. As the "Pard's" habits were well known, an unauthorised search party was sent out, which soon found a tuneful "Pard" loaded both inside and out with "the good brew." It was a feat requiring some careful navigation to get him safely down the long stairway into the dug-out, and he would persist in laughing. What the C.O. and the adjutant thought of it all will never be recorded, for both were killed that same night.

Meanwhile the advance parties of the 118th American Regiment were arriving and were being shown "over the ropes." They were keen but woefully ignorant and inefficient. On the night of September 23 the 11th Battalion was relieved by a company of the above American regiment. The "doughboys" came into the line with all their gear up and looking like Christmas trees. They were led to their "possies" in the lines and they made a great deal of noise, calling out to one another and generally acting like raw and over-confident troops. Lieut. Wally Graham admonished them and told them not to make such a row, for, as he explained, Fritz was pretty good with his machine guns and the trenches and posts were hardly any protection against shell-fire. One of the Yanks replied: "Don't yu worry about us, Lootenant, we'll be okay." They were! So much so that when Lieut. Belford (the I.O., who was later attached to the Americans in an advisory capacity) took some American officers to visit the same position only a few days later it was all he could do to find the site of the trenches. The whole place had been blown to bits and the posts wiped out. All the officers had been killed or wounded and the troops were badly shaken. Experience is always a costly thing to buy, as the 11th Battalion had found, but it is a commodity that is difficult to pass on to other people.

To get back to the doings of the 11th Battalion it is necessary to regress a little. The relief took a considerable time, as the American troops were new to all the conditions, but eventually all the line troops were relieved and Lieut. W. W. Graham reported all clear. The change over at battalion heaquarters was necessarily slow, as everything had to be explained in detail, and maps and plans, which the relieving troops had a poor working knowledge of, had to be handed over and discussed. As the Americans did not bring any signalling gear, the battalion 'phones were handed over one after another and the American signallers were connected up and their duties explained. Sergeant Armstrong was detailed to remain until the whole brigade relief was complete, so that he could satisfy himself that the new signallers were through to their own brigade headquarters and everything was in working order.

When all the battalion staff were satisfied that the Americans had a working knowledge of their duties, Major Darnell gave the order to move out. Lieut. Goundrey was sent off with the headquarters details except Armstrong and another signaller. The remaining officers moved off to the other side of the valley where Lieut. Paul McInerney (the T.O.) had horses waiting, so that the headquarters officers could ride back to Tincourt. The party of officers consisted of Major A. Darnell, Lieut. Archibald, Major May, Lieuts. Belford, W. Graham and McInerney. As the party left the dug-out the enemy started shelling heavily, no doubt having been alarmed by the noise the Yanks were making. The party ran the gauntlet without incident and then the M.O. and I.O. stopped to wait to see if the two signallers would get through safely, as they had been getting their gear together in preparation to leave. At length the two signallers could be seen running from shell-hole to shell-hole. Sergeant Armstrong, a big, strong fellow, was helping his mate along. The two forms would be lost in the darkness and then the next second the light of a bursting shell would show them running forward until obscured by the smoke and explosion of other shells. It was with feelings of relief that the two officers at last saw the two Diggers emerge scatheless and to hear them answer that they were quite all right.

When the horses were reached Private Sugars was waiting with three animals, the remainder of the party having ridden on ahead. When the rest were overhauled, "Archie" dropped back beside the I.O. and said: "Jock, I feel so happy to-night. We have done a great stunt and the battalion has excelled itself The only thing that spoils everything is that poor old Wally Hallahan and young 'Dud' Elliot were killed and the other lads. But for that I've never been so happy in my life. The 'good oil' is that we are going out for a long spell." After some more general conversation Lieut. Archibald rode forward and joined Major Darnell at the head of the party. The above conversation is recorded to show that not every one had a premonition of his coming end.

The I.O. dropped back and rode along with Tom Sugars, who used to be his groom when he was T.O. It was now well after midnight on September 23, and the party had just passed Roisel when a tremendous explosion in the latter village attracted their attention. It was later learned that a large bomb dropped by a 'plane had killed and wounded a great number of the 9th Battalion as they were passing through the village after they had been relieved.

A minute later the I.O. heard the drone of a German 'plane coming up behind. Immediately he and Sugars cleared off the road they were following and almost cannoned into a couple of bombs that exploded just beside them. They made all haste back to the road. At that instant the German airman let go four small daisy-cutter bombs which fell right among the party of horsemen causing several horses to bolt. When the animals were quietened and controlled it was found that Wally Graham's horse had cleared off with him and two riderless horses had followed him. The remaining officers rode slowly back and found the C.O. and the adjutant lying on the ground.

Lieut. J. A. Archibald.

On dismounting it was seen that Major Darnell was quite dead, but that Lieut Archibald was still moaning. A splinter of bomb had gone clean through his steel helmet, piercing his head. He never recovered consciousness again. Sugars was sent off at the gallop for an ambulance and the four remaining officers (Wally Graham had by this time returned; he had a slight wound in his leg and his horse was badly hit) got a stretcher from nearby and carried Lieut. Archibald until they met the approaching ambulance, which took him at once to hospital. He died shortly afterwards. The M.O. examined Major Darnell and the latter's only wound was a tiny aperture over his heart where a piece of bomb had struck him.

Lieut. Goundrey, who was just in front of the party at the time, on hearing the 'plane coming had moved his men off the road, but only in time, and his party was fortunate in suffering no casualties.

Thus, in the last battle that the 11th Battalion was engaged in, for so it happened that this was the "Glorious" 11th Battalion's "Farewell to Arms," the four officers who were killed were all original members of the battalion, as were most of the Diggers who were killed. The total casualties were: four officers killed and there were 10 other ranks killed, 51 wounded and three missing.

Nothing could have been more truly "stiff" than the case of Wally Hallahan, and the fact that Major Darnell and Lieut. Archibald were killed within a few minutes' ride from their

Tincourt. Major A. Darnell, Captain W. R. Hallahan, M.C., M.M., Lieuts. J. Archibald and D. Elliot buried here. (Official Photo.)

camp and just when the battalion had left the line for the *last* time only proved what most of the troops had long realised: that a man can never escape his fate, be what it may.

There was a most impressive funeral service next day when Major Darnell and Lieut. Archibald were buried alongside Hallahan and Elliot in Tincourt Cemetery. The feelings of the troops can best be expressed by the beautiful lines of Omar Khayyam:

"Lo! Some we loved, the loveliest and the best
That Time and Fate of all their vintage prest,
Have drunk their cup a round or two before,
And one by one crept silently to rest."

And though all these officers were respected and loved, yet Wally Hallahan stood out as typical of the best of the 11th Battalion. He was idolised by all the Diggers and loved by all who knew him. His war service was a record of gay courage and all-round efficiency, and his presence in the line and among the troops was a continual encouragement. His death was felt by the troops more than that of any other officer or man, and one of the finest tributes that any battalion could have given to one of its officers was made in the case of Captain Hallahan. The battalion pioneers of their own accord constructed a most beautiful cross for his grave, and on its plinth were the words: "Loved by all." What finer epitaph could any man have?

On the same day Lieut. W. C. Belford and four N.C.O.'s were detailed to go on what was known as "The American Mission." The duties consisted in acting in an advisory capacity to the American troops during their projected advance on the Hindenburg Line. While on this detached work Sergeant Badger received an American decoration for conspicuous gallantry in the line.

On September 25 the troops rested all day among the trees at Tincourt, and between whiles swapped souvenirs and articles of kit with the American troops who were everywhere round the area. An overhaul of equipment was made and a general clean up was ordered in preparation for the move back to a rest area on the following day.

An early start was made and the troops entrained at Tincourt for Longpre on September 26. Longpre was the village from which the battalion had started on the Great Push, just over six weeks before. A most interesting journey was made through all the recaptured country and the villages the troops knew so well. From Longpre the troops marched to L'Etoile, a pleasant village on the banks of the lower Somme, about 11 miles from Abbeville.

Comfortable billets were found for the very small battalion and the troops looked forward to the long-promised rest, but the first day was spent in the old traditional way, that of cleaning up quarters and smartening of personnel.

Chapter XLVIII

THE ARMISTICE

L'ETOILE was a village nestling under a steep hill, on which there was an old Roman camp (Camp de Cesar). The country to the north was hilly, but the wide, flat valley of the Somme lay to the south and a long bridge leading to the village of Conde spanned the river between the two villages. L'Etoile was one of the villages that remained a vivid memory to the battalion because of the long period spent there.

Battalion rear area routine commenced on September 28, when battalion guards and company guards were mounted with all due ceremony. The men looked smart and soldierly. Captain E. W. Tulloch was appointed to the command of the 12th Battalion temporarily.

Next day was Sunday and there was a combined brigade church parade. The official battalion diary for September 30 states: "The past month has been one of considerable event. The attack on Villeret attended with such magnificent success may be regarded as one of the most successful operations under taken by the battalion.

"When it is considered that the battalion undertook the operation with its strength reduced to three companies, of an average strength of 70, advanced 3,000 yards and remained in the support and front lines under adverse weather conditions, something of the fine spirit and tenacity of the men may be gathered. Their rest in the present comfortable billets is well earned and comes as a pleasant respite from the bareness, discomfort and danger of the battle zone."

For nearly six weeks the battalion lay at L'Etoile and the weather was the usual French October, with its dull, shortening days and its mists and rain. Still, the boys were able to appreciate their conditions compared to the previous two years.

Parades had frequently to be cancelled, and the sports which formed such a considerable part of the training were seriously interfered with. In early October the I.O. and other details who had been with the American Army reported back to the battalion, and many were the tales that circulated in the mess that night about the doings of the troops of that splendid but *very* inexperienced army.

One story will serve to show these troops' reactions to the "shootin' gallery," as the "doughboys" contemptuously referred to the war; that is, before they had had a taste of it.

The American troops to whom the 11th Battalion details had been assigned came chiefly from Tennessee and North and South Carolina. They were in general simple and unsophisticated. When the details reported to the American divisional headquarters only a hazy idea could be obtained from that source as to where its brigades were likely to be, and when after some trouble the brigade sought for was found (map locations and such-like aids to topography being apparently unknown) it was almost dark before the 11th Battalion details discovered the American battalion to which they were to be attached, at Bois de la Croix.

There were no shelters of any kind save the "half-sheets," with which all the American troops were issued, and the writer (who was one of the party) retired for the night with a Yankee officer as camp-mate in a little "bivvy" made of these half-sheets.

The night was foggy and bitterly cold, and the enemy started dropping high-velocity shells all round the camp site. Some of these shells landed very close, and the Yankee troops could be heard running in all directions. The American officer was a bit "windy" and he asked the writer if it would not be better to change their quarters, and received for answer that it was no safer elsewhere and certainly no warmer.

Just then a shell landed almost alongside, and the occupants of the neighbouring bivouacs could be heard gathering all their impedimenta together and dashing off to destinations unknown. One "doughboy" passing close by was heard to shout: "Nossir! I wouldn't give ten cents an acre fer this land!" and he sped off into the night.

Lieut. Belford was appointed education officer and was sent for a month's training at Cambridge, England. A comprehensive course was given to fit officers and N.C.O.'s for the task of preparing the troops for demobilisation and return to civilian life.

The battalion came again under the command of Colonel Rafferty, who was determined to keep the troops up to the mark. On one occasion during a practice attack the "Old Man" was quite dissatisfied with the performance of the troops. This story is told in the words of Private Jim Kirkwood: "It was the 'Old Man's' practice to plan out a stunt, detail same to the battalion, line up the band to represent the barrage and then let her go. 'Keep up to your barrage, men,' he would shout.

"One day in the fields behind L'Etoile, 'A' Company heeded not his advice, and after the stunt the men were severely rated for their short-comings. 'Do you know, men, I have followed *eighteen* yards behind a barrage,' the "Old Man" roared. 'Eighteen yards! What do you think of that?' He paused, waiting for the words to sink in, but the silence was broken by 'A' Company's runner who squeaked in a high treble: 'Eighteen yards *behind!* Hell! That's nothing! Up in Merris Major Darnell and I went *right through* the whole b—— thing!'

"The Colonel glared. The company waited. The silence seemed long. Then the 'Old Man' smiled. His good humour overcame his ire, and turning to Captain Alec Burgess, who was temporarily in charge of the company, he said, in his own inimitable way: 'Captain, this battalion will never go down, even if arms and ammunition fail us. 'We'll always have "A" Company to *talk* us out of trouble.'"

On November 2 an interesting event was held at the neighbouring village of Long. It was a Requiem Mass organised by the Roman Catholic chaplains of the 1st Australian Division to commemorate all those who had died in the war. Troops were brought in various motor vehicles from all over the scattered divisional area. About 2,000 troops attended and the Bishop of Amiens was present. Padre O'Donnell, of the 11th Battalion, preached the sermon, after which the Bishop of Amiens, in a fine address, stressed the gratitude of the French people for the great sacrifices the Australian people had made in the war, and he spoke highly of the achievements of the Australian Imperial Forces.

Lieut. Jerry McKenna, of the 11th Battalion, was in charge of the guard of honour, and after the Requiem Mass, Last Post was played and the guard presented arms.

After the education officer had returned from Cambridge efforts were made to start classes in as many subjects as teachers could be found for, and which the boys would take an interest in; but hardly had the classes started than the battalion received orders to move up towards the line. Reports were circulated everywhere that there was to be one big final advance, which was to push the Hun back over the Rhine.

On November 9, in icy cold weather, the battalion entrained at Pont Remy and after a long and tedious journey arrived at St. Quentin. The original destination had been Roisel, but it was ascertained that the Germans had bombed or shelled the railway line near Rozieres, between that village and Peronne, and so the troop-train was sent round by the loop passing through St. Quentin. By the time the troops had reached St. Quentin they were famished, as they had missed their issue of rations through the alteration to their route. Arrangements were therefore made to issue the troops with a French ration at St. Quentin. Soon the ration parties were en route for the French commissariat. They returned with some very hard biscuits and gallons of thin, red wine. Some of the batmen were a bit more enterprising, for a bit of a commotion was heard at the French Q.M. store over in the town, and a short time later the "Dingbats" arrived with some pretty good bread. When asked if they purchased it, they replied that they had seen the bread and had said: "Pour officier," and in spite of the protests of the indignant French quartermaster they had helped themselves. There were few better foragers than Australian batmen, who always deemed it a point of honour to see that their officers never went short of anything that was reasonably procurable.

It was now afternoon on November 11, 1918, and considerable excitement began to prevail among the French soldiery with which the town was thronged. There were also parties of British Tommies, a few Americans and several French military police. Numbers of Poilus from different French regiments were at the battered station, and all these took a great interest in the celebrated Australians. Suddenly a French soldier rushed up and cried: "L'Armistice est signee! La guerre est finie." Instantly there was a babel of noise on the platform and many of the French troops dashed off for confirmation. Back they came, all jubilant and reiterated the cry "The Armistice is signed! The war is finished!" But the 11th Battalion Diggers met the outburst of joy and enthusiasm with the usual Australian response, which if the words were not understood by the French the meaning certainly was. The Poilus waved and shouted, but their raptures left the Diggers cold.

After the troops had had their meal and vented their opinion of the sour French wine that they had been issued with, the 11th Battalion band took up position on the platform of the station and played a selection of tunes to an appreciative audience. The Froggies went mad when the "Marseillaise" was played. They waved their arms and shouted, "Vive La France! Vive L'Australie! La guerre est finie!"

In spite of all this, as there was no official confirmation of the tidings about the armistice being signed, the troops were not impressed with the general joy and refused to take the report seriously.

The troop-train remained in St. Quentin till nearly dusk, and then started on its journey again, this time taking a northerly direction. It grew bitterly cold as the train rumbled and jolted over the patched railway. There were many stops and starts, but all those who have travelled on a troop-train in France know all the painful symptoms of such a journey, so a veil is best drawn over this special variety of misery. It got to be so cold that the resourceful batmen again came to the fore, Frank Sims and the others bringing round a dixie full of hot sugared wine, as there was nothing else to drink. That hot drink tasted like nectar and helped to put new life into those who were lucky enough to participate.

The troops were at length ordered to detrain at a station named Epehy. It was dark as ink and the cold was intense. From the station the boys struggled over to some huts, being greatly heartened on the way by a drink of hot cocoa at one of the Comforts Funds' booths. The Comforts Fund was always to be depended upon in the worst of conditions, and the booth and the good fellows that ran them were indeed "life-savers."

The Diggers flopped into their huts, and in spite of everything were soon asleep. They had been about 48 hours in the train.

Reveille was pretty late next morning, but after breakfast the battalion was paraded and the C.O. announced that the Germans had signed an armistice on November 11. This is the text of the original message: "Hostilities will cease at 11:00 to-day, November 11. Troops will stand fast on the line reached at that hour which will be reported by wire to Adv. G.H.G. Defensive precautions will be maintained. There will be no intercourse of any description with the enemy until the receipt of instructions follow. Acknowledge. Advised all armies, cavalry corps and advanced operations, R.A.F. Reported all concerned. Adv. G.H.Q.0650. The troops received the announcement *in dead silence,* and almost with incredulity. It seemed impossible that the war should be over at last. One man was heard to mutter: "Another bloody furphy, I suppose." There was no excitement, and no cheering, contrary to what might have been expected, and from the quiet way in which the announcement was received it might have been thought that the troops were sorry that the war was ended. The truth of the matter was that the boys had become so used to the fact of war that they could hardly realise that the thing that they had so earnestly longed for had really happened.

When the troops were dismissed there was some discussion over the news, but almost immediately the battalion was ordered to fall-in again and it was then marched off to an embussing point and carried through towns and villages full of excited Tommies, who yelled and sang and called to the boys "Hey, Choom! You're goin' t'wrong way. T'war's over." But even then it seemed as if there must be some mistake, for the motor buses were hastening onward and bearing the 11th Battalion up to the front. Near Le Catelet the battalion debussed and the troops marched to billets in an adjoining village. There was some trouble over the quarters, so the troops were moved to the neighbouring village of Mazinghem, where a day or two was spent.

From Mazinghem the battalion marched to Bohain, which was a pretty large town, and one that was obviously suffering from the late German occupation. Pitiful tales were told by the local residents. The whole town looked badly in need of a clean up, and, of course, the battalion had more than its share of this work to do. The 11th Battalion stayed at Bohain for a week and there was at that time some talk of the 1st Division marching into Germany as part of the Army of Occupation, but there was never any further mention of the matter. On November 22 the battalion marched to Beugnies, a village just east of Avesnes.

Attempts were made to get the education classes going again and Lieuts. Colvin and Charles did a lot of good work in this direction. The classes suffered a good deal of interruption and the instructors did not get the support that they were entitled to from headquarters. Still, it was a very difficult business to keep all the necessary duties going with such a small and dwindling battalion, and it was only natural that the daily fatigues and other services should receive first consideration.

An incident occurred at Beugnies which had a semi-humorous side, although the main result was a distinct minor tragedy. Some of the French inhabitants who had fled before the Germans in 1914 arrived back in the village while the 11th Battalion was there.

Immediately on arrival at her home, one good lady hastened down to the garden, and reaching a certain tree in the orchard she dug up a heavy iron box. This was taken into the house with much rejoicing, and when it was opened a bundle of paper money was extracted and placed on the table. Unfortunately the damp of four and a half years had softened the notes and made them stick together, so that they could not be separated without tearing.

The poor woman was now in a terrible fix, but cheered up at the suggestion of a Digger that she should dry the bundle of notes in the oven. This was accordingly done, but when the unfortunate woman took the bundle out some time later she found that the whole bundle had gone as hard as a brick and that the notes were now fast glued together and it was impossible to prise one apart from the other.

The stay at Beugnies was diversified by a good deal of sport. Every afternoon was devoted to games of various kinds and inter-battalion matches were arranged. On December 3 the 11th Battalion played the 10th Battalion at foobtall. The game was well contested and the result was in favour of the 10th Battalion.

Bishop Long lectured the troops at Beugnies on demobilisation and education facilities, and there were many other lectures given by competent officers on subjects of interest to the troops.

On December 17 the battalion moved up to the Belgian border and passed over the international boundary in the vicinity of Beaumont, near which the troops rested for the night. Next day the troops marched to Tarciennes, and on December

19, 1918, the 11th Battalion made its last move as a battalion to a new area. The destination on this eventful occasion was Chatelet, a town in the mining and manufacturing district of Charleroi, the latter town famous as having given its name to several celebrated battles.

Chapter XLIX

CHATELET

AFTER the long journey to Chatelet the troops were distributed among the townspeople, who gave them a warm welcome and received them right into the bosom of their families. The boys were very pleasantly surprised when they found that they were to have real beds to sleep in. This was something like a war at last!

Though the 11th Battalion was still a distinct unit, it was from this time—December 20, 1918—that the purely military side of the battalion's life began to have less and less importance, and the remaining story, though interesting, may be justly considered as the initial stages of demobilisation.

The story of the very pleasant stay at Chatelet is most fittingly commenced by the address of welcome, which was read by the burgomaster to the Australian troops on arrival at the town.

This is the address: "In the name of the town of Chatelet, represented by members of its administration, officials, heads of industry and its leading citizens, I extend a welcome to you, sir, who represents the Australian Army.

"You have come from afar; your country is on the opposite side of the world to ours. You have crossed the seas and their thousand dangers to place your sword at the service of a noble cause—the defence of the oppressed. You have been drawn by chivalrous feelings, as the knights of old, of whom you are the symbolic incarnation. Your conduct is all the more noble seeing that you were not compelled to take up arms. You are not a military nation, although we know that the Australian divisions form part of the flower of the British Armies. You have pledged yourselves willingly to come to our assistance.

"This noble sentiment gives us a lofty idea of the spirit of your people. Belgium will remember for ever how the Australian Army has rendered its generous assistance to defend Right and Justice, despised by perfidious Germany; and so it is without whole hearts that we welcome you and your gallant troops.

Place de Perron, Chatelet.

"We are happy to receive you as our guests and will strive to make your stay amongst us as pleasant as possible.

"The whole population welcomes you, and they will know how to prove their sympathy and gratitude for the immense service you have rendered to Belgium. May you retain a pleasant memory of your reception which we should have liked to have made more solemn (impressive) still.

"When our country fades gradually into the shadow of darkness at the same time as Australia becomes clearer under the warm rays of the sun, and as your thoughts remind you of the events that brought you to Europe, may you have a pleasant recollection of the little town of Chatelet, which has shown itself happy and proud to receive you within its walls."

This address, although a little ornate and flowery, was soon discovered to be absolutely sincere in its representations of friendship and welcome, for almost without exception the towns-folk endeavoured to make the troops at home. The memory of the real kindness of the people and the happy time spent at Chatelet will always remain with the troops who were privileged to be billeted there.

To show that the happy relations that existed between the inhabitants and the troops were real and lasting, an extract from a letter written on January 20, 1938, by a lady in Chatelet is given here:

"Ne pense pas que les Australiens du 11 Battalion sont oublie. Non, on a cause bien souvenir et les gens de Chatelet ne regrette qu' une chose. C'est que l' Australie soit si loin de nous.

"Vous oublier serait de l' egoisime, 'n' avez vous pas quittes tout ce que vous aviez de plus cher pour venir combattre pour notre liberte? Ce que l' on a fait pour vos soldats est bien minime a cote de ce que vous avez fait pour nous.

"Pour notre part personelle nous avons fait notre possible pour vous rendre un peu la vie de famille avant de retrouver votre vrai famille.

"Vous pouvez dire bien sincerement a tous vos soldats du 11 Battalion qu' ils ne sont pas oublie a Chatelet, et que le nom Australie est grave dans leurs coeurs pour toujours."

The translation is as follows: "Do not think that the Australians of the 11th Battalion are forgotten. No! We have cause to remember, and the people of Chatelet have only one cause for regret and that is because Australia is so far away.

"For our own part we tried our best to give you a little home life before you returned to your own families.

"You can, with all sincerity, assure all the soldiers of the 11th Battalion that they are not forgotten in Chatelet, and that the name 'Australia' is engraved on the hearts of our people."

Among such a community of good-hearted people it was only natural that the Diggers should be quite at home. The boys had a natural faculty of adaptation to conditions that was unsurpassed anywhere, and as the people really liked the boys they came to be treated as part of the family. After parades the troops would visit their special friends and of course the coffee-pot would be produced. On one occasion there was no milk in the house. "Ca ne fait rien," said the guest. But Madame told him just wait an instant and she would go and milk the "brebis." "Sheep!" exclaimed the guest. "Oh yes! Of course. Would you like to come and see it milked?" On going with Madame to the little yard at the back of the

Members of the 11th Battalion Drum Band with a Belgian soldier friend, Chatelet, Christmas, 1918.

house there was discovered a little shed, and in it was what must have been the biggest sheep in the world. Without more ado Madame sat down and milked it, and there was the milk for the coffee.

While on the subject of milk, there was also an old woman who used to lead a flock of goats around the town, and when a customer wanted any milk a vessel was brought out of the house and the old woman milked one of the goats into the receptacle provided. There could be no complaints as to the freshness of the milk.

The dog-carts were always a source of wonder. It was astonishing what loads the "chiens" could pull. Sometimes there were teams of three or four big dogs harnessed abreast, pulling a cart with a stout farmer and his sonsy wife aboard. The dogs also pulled loads of coal, firewood, milk and other farm produce. Often a woman, a boy and a dog would be all pushing at or pulling the same cart.

Most of the vehicles of larger size were pulled by cattle, cows were just as common as bullocks in ploughs or carts and

Battalion Signal Section, December, 1918.

sometimes a horse and a cow would be seen yoked to the same vehicle.

Chatelet was a busy mining town situated on the River Sambre, about five miles from the historically and commercially notable city of Charleroi. The Sambre, like most of the Belgian rivers, was canalised and a great traffic of barges was continually passing through or being unloaded at stagings in the town and along the banks. Chatelet was situated in the famous old province of Hainault, which is now one of the greatest industrial regions of Belgium. Charleroi, the chief city of the district, was a busy town, and at this period was continually thronged with troops. There were fine restaurants and shops in the city and tramlines ran to all the many outlying towns in the vicinity.

The town was notable in the war, as nearby were fought the two battles of Charleroi, the first of which was fought just out of Chatelet, and a well-kept cemetery full of French and German graves bore witness to the fierceness of the fighting.

In addition to the comfortable billets the troops were well looked after by the military authorities in the way of canteens and amusements, and bathing was held often in the well-equipped baths belonging to one of the up-to-date coalmines nearby.

Christmas came round once again, the fifth Christmas away from home for some of the boys; but this one at least was spent under happy circumstances. Nearly every family in Chatelet had one or more Diggers to dinner, or otherwise entertained them in some way. Some of the troops had two or three dinners and some did not remember how many they went to. Some of the officers dined with the boys, dined at some private family and then dined at the mess. It was a terrible ordeal and the troops suffered much in a good cause. The Christmas dinner at some of the wealthier homes was a four- or five-hours' feast, with all the proper drinks and other frills. For days afterwards the good folk would always produce "galettes" (a sweet cake something like a crumpet) and "gateaux" (small cakes) and a bottle of the very fine wine that the Belgians drank, and they insisted that these be partaken of by those who called. It is said that the best wines of France and Germany find their way to Belgium, and there is no doubt that there were fine wines in Chatelet.

While at Chatelet a definite effort was made by Captain W. Belford to get the education classes going and an education staff was formed. Sergeants Fisher and McCarthy were prominet among the N.C.O.'s of the education service.

A school was started in a large mansion near the battalion parade ground, but the whole system was foredoomed to failure from the start, at least as applied to the battalions still in Belgium, because of the continually disintegrating units. No sooner were lecturers or instructors obtained and classes started than the latter were broken up by the lecturers being sent back to Australia, or because half the class would be put on fatigues. When rooms had been fixed up for the troops to have classes in, the owner returned from "abroad" and then new quarters had to be found. After several attempts had been made and half started, a building was secured for the school and after long arguments with the C.O. and the Brigadier, the E.O. arranged that the men taking the classes were to be exempted from parades and fatigues. But the battalion was getting smaller and smaller every day and the classes, though enjoyed by the men, could never be called a success.

Interesting tours were made to the more important of the great industrial concerns in the surrounding districts, notably to the great rolling mills and foundries of the Usines Metallurgiques de Hainaut. This was a huge industry that employed over 7,000 men. Here the boys saw locomotives made, and great wheels cast, and the manufacture of rails and angle and channel iron.

One good feature of the education service was the installation of an education library at divisional headquarters at the Chateau de Presles. Here books on all subjects could be purchased at a very reasonable cost and several of the troops benefitted greatly from this library.

Demobilisation was the chief theme at this time and the education officer used to be continually asked by the boys to recommend them to some non-military employment, and R.S.M. Shipton—the incomparable "Shippy"—was busy studying a map of the London streets with a view to becoming a taxi-driver in that city. The boys used to be sorry, long in advance, for any fares that "Shippy" might deposit at the wrong address. Whenever the E.O. appeared in sight "Shippy" used to ask when he was going to be "demobbed," so that he could take up his taxi-driving.

As was natural, all things military began to have less and less interest, and when the troops were not expecting immediate transfer to England for transport to Australia they used to avail themselves of generous leave granted to places such as Charleroi, Namur, Mons and even to Paris, Brussels, and as far as Cologne in Germany. Many of the boys visited Brussels, passing the field of Waterloo en route. The lion on the statue in the field was reputed to have been turned round by the Germans and made to face towards France. It was strange to think that just over a hundred years before the British and Germans had been fighting side by side and had ultimately crushed France on that field.

Brussels was very gay and full of life in these days. Troops of all the Allied forces were to be seen there. On one occasion some Australian officers were standing on the dummy of a car, in close proximity to some charming Belgian girls. These girls were having an animated conversation about the big hats of the officers, and the girls were under the impression that the Aussies were Americans. Such is fame! Brussels was hardly touched by the Germans. It was said that the citizens paid a heavy indemnity to save the city.

Other places of interest visited by the troops were Dinant and Namur, the latter famous for its citadel.

It was indeed a good time at Chatelet, but at the same time a peculiarly unsatisfying and rather unhappy period, for the

Headquarters Staff, Chatelet.

reason that all the old friends were going and the fine old battalion was dwindling and dwindling. Friends that had been through everything together, who had shared the good and the bad, and who had been all in all to one another were now severed, and many never beheld their comrades again. The battalion that had been the father and mother and the only real home that the boys had known for years was now losing all its big family, and this left a feeling of unreality and unrest.

Home, and Australia, that had seemed so far off and not to be thought of save as an impossible dream now took shape again, and all were eager to see the land of their birth or adoption, and the time hung heavy for those who were waiting.

It was a peculiar dissolution for a great battalion; one that had fought in Gallipoli, France and Belgium; one that had over 9,000 men pass through its ranks, many to rest for ever in foreign soil. The total casualties of the 11th Battalion were 3,539 all ranks, of which number 1,115 gave their lives. When it is realised that two out of every five men who enlisted in the 11th Battalion were casualties, and that one man out of every eight was killed, then it will be understood what a sacrifice this West Australian battalion made in the war, and that any reputation or honour that it may have gained was indeed paid for in blood, and that of the flower of the battalion and of Australia.

Of the gallant fellows that lost their lives in the war, Rupert Brooke, who himself died at Gallipoli, has written these splendid lines—

"These laid the world away; poured out the red
Sweet wine of youth; gave up the years to be
Of work and joy, and that unhoped serene
That men call age; and those who would have been
Their sons, they gave, their immortality."

But the final stages are yet to be told, and the following events that happened after January 1, 1919, may be taken as the last phases in the battalion's history.

CHAPTER L

THE END

The constant withdrawal of drafts for demobilisation reduced the battalion very quickly, although there were a certain number of arrivals from hospital and base camps. Major J. P. O'Neil, M.C., was now in command, and it was becoming a hard job to find enough troops for the necessary duties. It was therefore resolved to unite the 11th and the 12th Battalions to form one unit, to be known as the 11/12th Battalion. This was done on February 5, 1919, and the new unit existed for several weeks and was then combined with the rest of the 3rd Brigade and so lost its identity.

February 5, 1919, therefore, may be taken as the last day of the 11th Battalion's existence as an independent unit, and so is the most fitting date on which to conclude the history of the 11th Battalion. The remainder of the time spent by the members of the battalion on service is chiefly concerned with demobilisation and the sending of drafts to England, thence to be allotted to troopships and returned to Australia, not as individual units as the battalions originally left Australia, but as composite drafts from all units as available for return to Australia.

On the above date, then, ended the active service of the 11th Battalion, one of the finest associations of men that the world has ever seen. The motto of the 11th Battalion was always "deeds, not words," and this record is almost the only departure from that rule; but if it has in any way shown the comradeship, the loyalty, the essential humour and the unfailing cheerfulness of the boys of Western Australia, then it will have served its end. If small mention has been made of decorations or honours, it is not because the heroic deeds that won these distinctions were not outstanding, but simply because there were just as many heroes whose exploits were unrecorded, and many of these gallant lads still lie "over there," and also because decorations were not so often given for outstanding services as for the way in which they were written up. This is not to say that those who won decorations were in any way compensated for their valour or efforts, for their services were above reward, but simply to point out that the number of decorations and honours that any battalion may lay claim to is no criterion of its worth.

As Dr. Axel Munthe writes in "The Story of San Michele": "Do you know why the V.C. is so rare in the British Army? Because bravery in its highest form, Napoleon's 'courage de la nuit,' seldom gets the V.C., and because courage, unassisted by luck, bleeds to death unrewarded."

The 11th Battalion may justly and proudly stand on the encomium in the foreword by Major-General E. G. Sinclair-McLagan: "This battalion took its full share of all the fighting and hardships which fell to the lot of the 3rd Infantry Brigade (A.I.F.) in Gallipoli, France and Flanders, and *never failed its commanders in any operations in which it took part.*" There is nothing that can be added to these simple words.

This book has been written for those of the 11th Battalion who remain, and also as a tribute, however poor and inadequate, to all those gallant comrades who once lived and loved and laughed and fought alongside them with "the eyes o' men, that ha' read wi' men, in the open books of death"; and so the story may be fittingly concluded with the beautiful words of Lieut. Walter L. Wilkinson, of the 8th Argyle and Sutherland Highlanders, himself killed in action:

AT LAST POST

"Come home! Come home!
The winds are at rest in the restful trees.
At rest are the waves of the sundown seas;
And home—they're home—
The wearied hearts and the broken lives—
At home! At ease!"

www.ingramcontent.com/pod-product-compliance
Lightning Source LLC
Chambersburg PA
CBHW022004300426
44117CB00005B/30